SCRIMSHAW

The Whaler's Legacy

Text and Photography by

Martha Lawrence

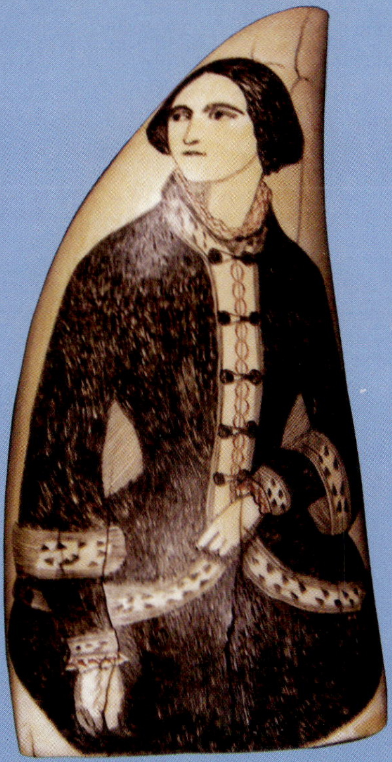

Schiffer Publishing Ltd

77 Lower Valley Road, Atglen, PA 19310

Dedication

In memory of my mother, Ruth Campbell Crichton, courageous woman, gentle lady, and my grandfather, William Livie Crichton, marine artist and craftsman.

Cover photo: *Courtesy of Mystic Seaport Museum.*

Library of Congress Catalog Number: 93-85225.

Book design by Ellen J. (Sue) Taylor

Printed in the United States of America.
ISBN: 0-88740-455-3

Published by Schiffer Publishing, Ltd.
77 Lower Valley Road
Atglen, PA 19310
Please write for a free catalog.
This book may be purchased from the publisher.
Please include $2.95 postage.
Try your bookstore first.

We are interested in hearing from authors with book ideas on related subjects.

Acknowledgements

It never fails to touch and amaze me how kind and generous people can be with their time, talent and ideas. Once more, I have been the fortunate recipient of such help, indeed right from the beginning of this project. After the completion of *Lightship Baskets of Nantucket*, both Paul Madden, an antiques dealer and well-respected scrimshaw expert from Sandwich, Mass., and Mimi Beman, knowledgeable proprietor of Mitchell's Book Corner in Nantucket, each suggested in separate conversations the possibility of a book on scrimshaw—richly illustrated with color photos that might introduce new readers to the fascinating story of scrimshaw while also providing those more familiar with the craft opportunity to examine photos of pieces that had never been previously published.

Before long, Paul Madden's boundless and infectious enthusiasm for scrimshaw was channeled into educating me in the fine points of the subject. With his help, I secured the opportunity to photograph examples from the extensive collection of the Nantucket Historical Association, which was being recataloged at the time.

Concerned that my existing photographic equipment and expertise might not be up to the challenge of the highly polished pieces of scrimshaw I would encounter, I sought advice from Bob Williams and Carrie Gardiner of The Camera Place in Wellesley, Mass. They offered solid suggestions and patiently answered my many questions. Next, neighbor Jeanne Kitz generously allowed me to "practice" photographing her wonderful collection of contemporary scrimshaw so that I was able to head to Nantucket with some feelings of confidence.

There, Michael Jehle, Curator of Collections, and Maureen Dwyer, Assistant Curator of Collections, were not only helpful and supportive, but also admirably tolerant as I invaded their tiny recataloging area with lights, camera, and snaking electrical cords. In addition, they kindly allowed me to shoot some of the wonderful pieces "at home" in the NHA's 1800 House so that we might give a sense of the integral role such items played in daily lives of the last century.

From that point, all that remained was to supplement the NHA photographs with those of a few choice private collections. I began at the home of the ever-gracious Maddens. There, just as she had done at the Nantucket 1800 house with scrimshaw from the NHA collection, Diane Madden proceeded with her unerring eye to beautifully arrange the pieces so that the resulting photographs are truly more than the sum of their parts. I was then fortunate enough to proceed to the wonderful collections of Ray and Elizabeth De Lucia, Curt Nyquist, good friend Charlie Manghis, and others who prefer not to be named. Each of these people shared not only their objects of incredible beauty, but also the knowledge gleaned from years of collecting and study. It was a privilege for me to see, touch and photograph these unique mementos of a bygone era. Each collector gave me new insights into the craft and increased appreciation for it.

Adamant in my intent to give a feeling for the men who created these wonders, I headed to the Mystic Seaport Museum in Mystic, Conn., where I boarded the *Charles W. Morgan*. The November morning was brisk and windy—I was the only visitor on the ship. It was thrilling to walk the decks and visit the off-shore home of the whaler/scrimshanders who had sailed that vessel in her eighty years of service. Similar emotions were evoked in a subsequent visit to the Seaman's Bethel in New Bedford, Mass. In that quiet chapel, I was in awe of the bravery of those who go to sea. I thank both the Mystic

Seaport Museum and the New Bedford Port Society for the opportunity to photograph their wonderful exhibits.

Between photography sessions, I was of course, reading all I could obtain on the subject of whaling and scrimshaw. From prior experience, I knew the librarians at the Peabody Museum of Salem would be welcoming and would generously share their materials and knowledge. I was not disappointed. To conduct any research remotely touching on whaling, the library of the New Bedford Whaling Museum is a necessary visit. There, Judith Lund, Acting Curator, and Judith Downey, Manuscript Librarian, were extremely helpful. They searched out appropriate logs, and even provided a corset to photograph so that readers might understand the mysteries of busk placement! Finally, I headed "home" to the library of the Nantucket Historical Association, where the very capable and always gracious Jacqueline Haring, Curator of Research Materials, directed me to previously untapped sources and produced treasures such as the example of Frederick Myrick's penmanship. Also at the NHA, Peter MacGlashan, Audio-Visuals Librarian, was encouraging in my ultimately fruitless search to find the portrait of a scrimshander whose work I had already photographed.

Fortunately, Florence Fitts of the Falmouth Historical Society was able to fulfill that wish by providing me with photos of both Samuel and Mary Lawrence. Also, Claudia Bourne of Richard A. Bourne Co., Inc., of Hyannisport, Mass. and Rod Cardoza of the West Sea Company of San Diego kindly lent me wonderful transparencies of well-known pieces of scrimshaw which had previously been illustrated in their auction catalogs.

In the project's final weeks, I received a visit from Bruce Averill of San Francisco, who was anticipating a relaxing New England vacation. Instead, he was coerced into proofreading my manuscript. I thank him, but note that any errors that follow are solely his responsibility!

Some people were involved for the duration of the venture. Among them are Phil Juliani and Beverly Collari of Wellesley's Photo Wizard, who spent the last two and a half years developing and redeveloping hundreds of rolls of film, trying to get just the right shade of this tooth or that bodkin—and managing to keep me laughing all the while. Also in for the long haul were Nancy Schiffer and Jay Press—thanks for being there.

I must also mention my husband Geoff Lawrence, who sees me through these often disruptive projects with the best grace he can manage; and doesn't seem to mind that I never get around to securing that much-threatened "real" job. Thanks to him and also to my sons, Matthew and Doug, for the great joy they each bring me.

My hope for this project is not only that it will accurately convey in both words and photos the fascinating story and incredible range of 19th century scrimshaw, but also that these beautiful pieces will be appreciated not merely as the museum treasures they are, but as the amazing work of ordinary human beings—dirty, lonely, work-hardened men, engaged in gestures of creativity and love. Any success this book achieves in communicating these ideas is due largely to the help of the many good people mentioned above.

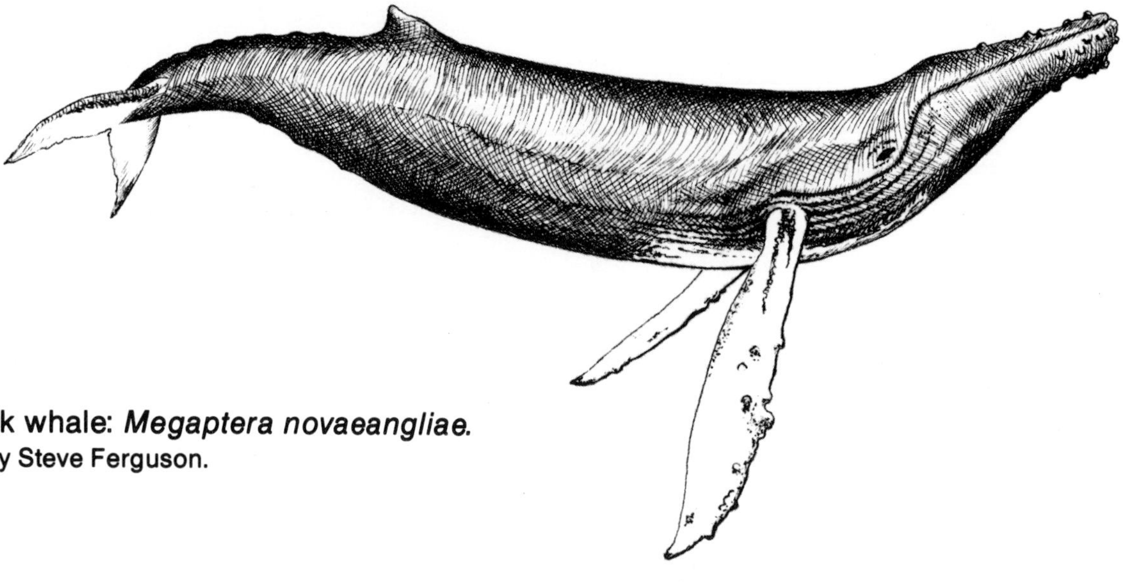

Humpback whale: *Megaptera novaeangliae.*
Illustrated by Steve Ferguson.

Contents

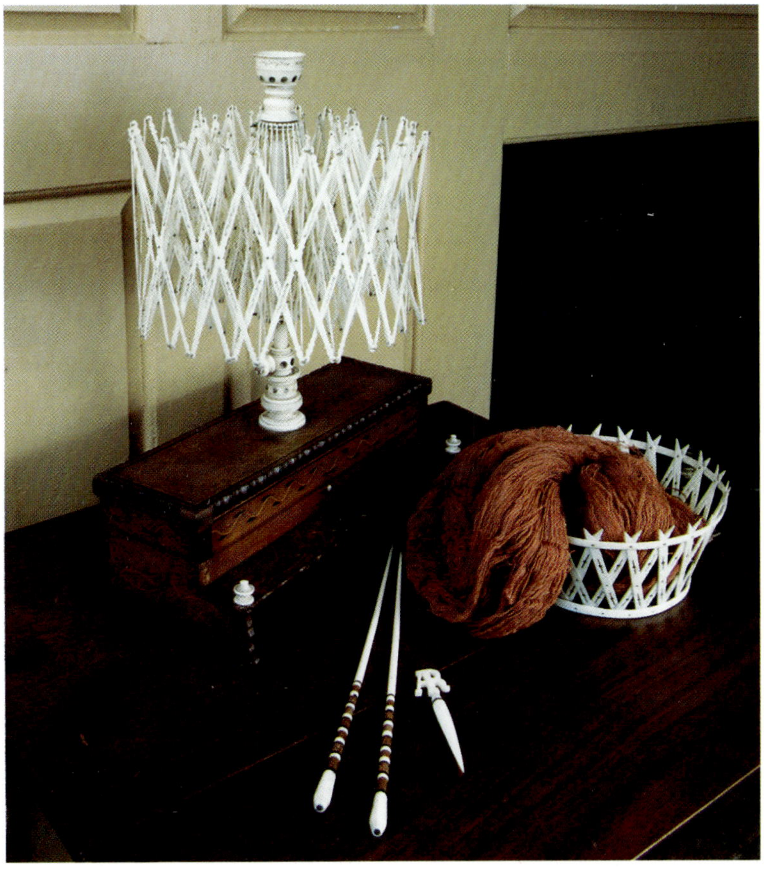

Courtesy of the Nantucket Historical Association.

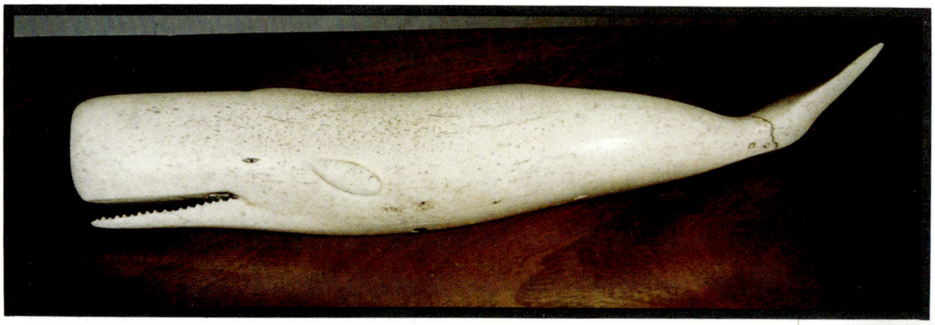

Carved whalebone sperm whale. *Courtesy of the Nantucket Historical Association*

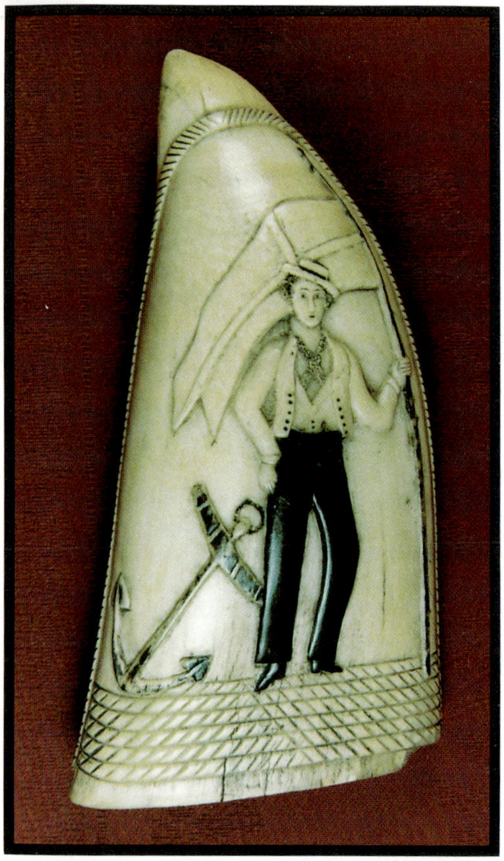

A proud British sailor is pictured within a ropework border in this unusual sculptured tooth. *Madden Collection*

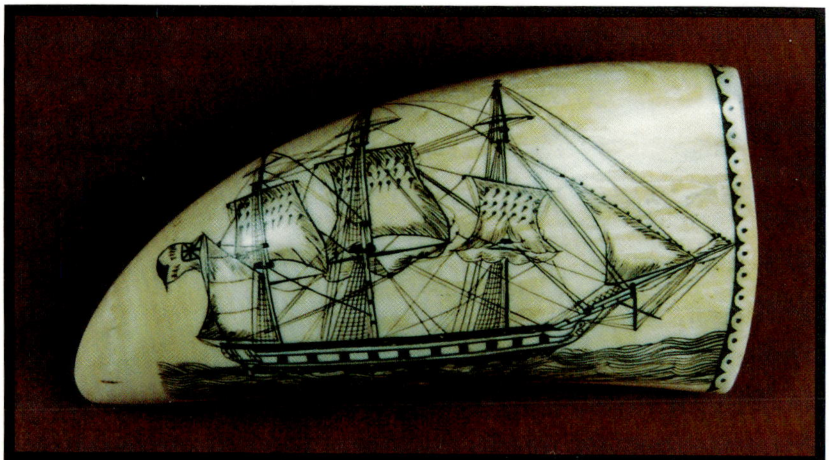

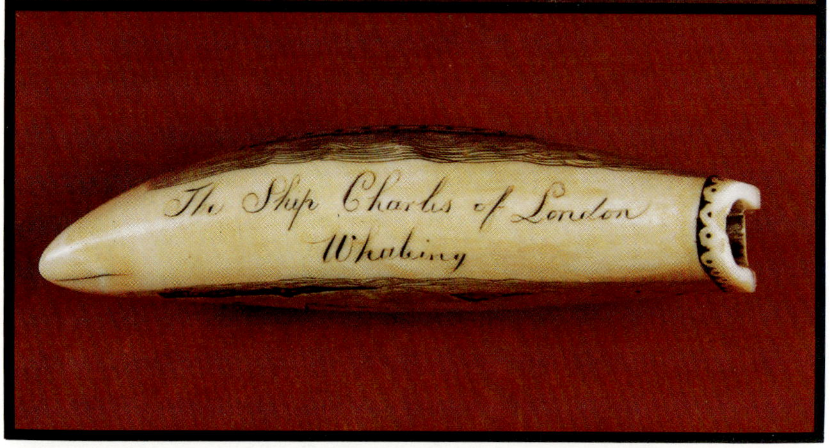

Although the ship pictured is the *Charles* of London, the tooth is attributed to an American, Edward Burdett, the earliest documented engraver of sperm whale teeth. *Madden Collection.*

Introduction

Scrimshaw...This unusual word is shrouded in romance, mystique, and, unfortunately, often confusion as to its proper meaning. In fact, George Blanchard, keeper of the log of the ship *America*, fully realized the dilemma the term might create when he wrote on June 28, 1840, "All hands *'skrimshoning'. (Theres a puzzler for a landsman.)" For we shore bound illiterates, however, he kindly went on to explain the asterisked term: "*Skrimshoning. Working White and Black Bone into Canes, Corset Boards, Paste Cutters, Knitting Sheathes, Thimbles ect ect ect."[1]

The origin of the word, which was spelled in a variety of ways including "scrimshoring, sckrimshorning, scrimshanting, and skrimshonting", has intrigued etymologists for years. The fullest analysis of the term is found in E. Norman Flayderman's *Scrimshaw and Scrimshanders, Whales and Whalemen*. The most current and widely accepted definition of "scrimshaw" is that employed by Stuart M. Frank in his *Dictionary of Scrimshaw Artists*: "Scrimshaw is the indigenous occupational handicraft of the whale-hunters, a creative and often ingenious art form employing byproducts of the fishery to pass the idle hours on shipboard and fill time ashore between voyages."[2]

In the following discussion, "scrimshaw" will refer to either the practice of the craft or the finished product; and "scrimshander" will denote the artist. Unlike some purists, I will also refer to current craftsmen, albeit far removed from whaleships, as "scrimshanders" but emphasize the difference between them and their nineteenth century predecessors by referring to their work as "contemporary scrimshaw."

Despite the inextricable evolution of scrimshaw within the context of whaling, occasionally other seamen in both the naval and merchant services were also practitioners. Furthermore, although scrimshaw is most often associated with American whaling, and references in the following chapters will often be to "Yankee whalers," it must be emphasized that scrimshaw was by no means limited to ships flying the flag of the United States. The practice also flourished aboard vessels of British, Australian and Portuguese registry.

Scrimshaw was not limited by political or ethnic boundaries, but rather belonged to the international band of mariners roaming the unexplored oceans of the world. In fact, the crew of a mid-nineteenth century American whaler represented a wide range of nationalities; and because of their dominance in the sperm whale fishery, American whalemen were often hired as officers for foreign whalers. As voyages ended and officers and crews regrouped aboard different ships, scrimshaw techniques, styles and ideas were exchanged and disseminated.

In addition, not all Yankee scrimshanders were whale *men*. Occasionally, fascinating journals and letters of the brave band of women who accompanied their whaling captain-husbands to sea document their own attempts at the craft. Elizabeth H. Morey, Annie Holmes Ricketson and Sallie G. Smith are a few of the women who tried their hands at scrimshaw.

Thus, the frequent references to Yankee whalemen/scrimshanders in subsequent pages are intended generically, assuming that the reader is aware that artists of other nationalities, genders and maritime occupations also made important contributions to the craft.

01 George Blanchard, "Logbook of the Ship *America*" (New Bedford, Mass.: Old Dartmouth Historical Society).

02 Stuart M. Frank, *Dictionary of Scrimshaw Artists* (Mystic, Conn.: Mystic Seaport Museum, 1991), xix.

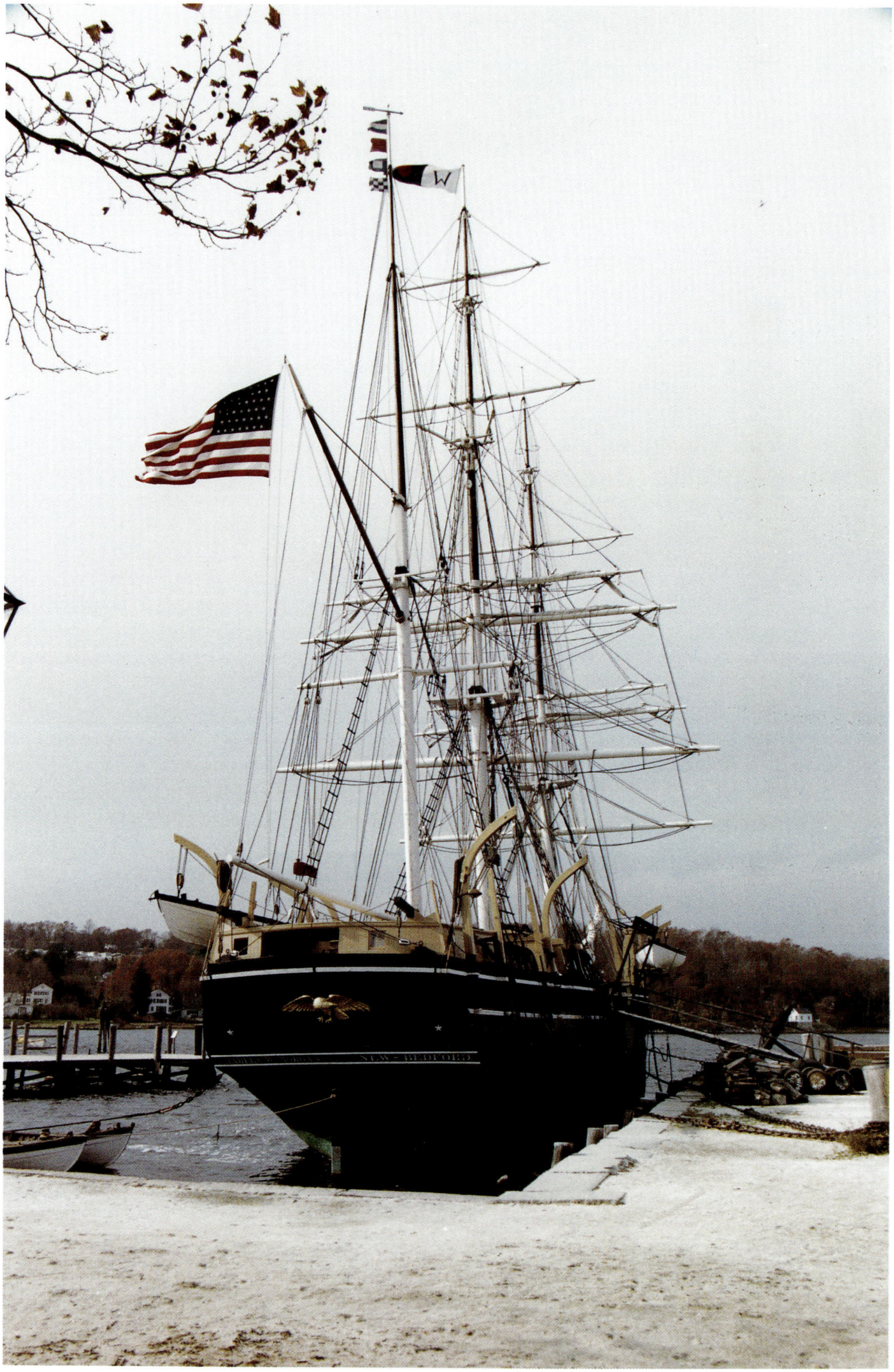

Courtesy of the Mystic Seaport Museum.

1. Dawn of an Industry

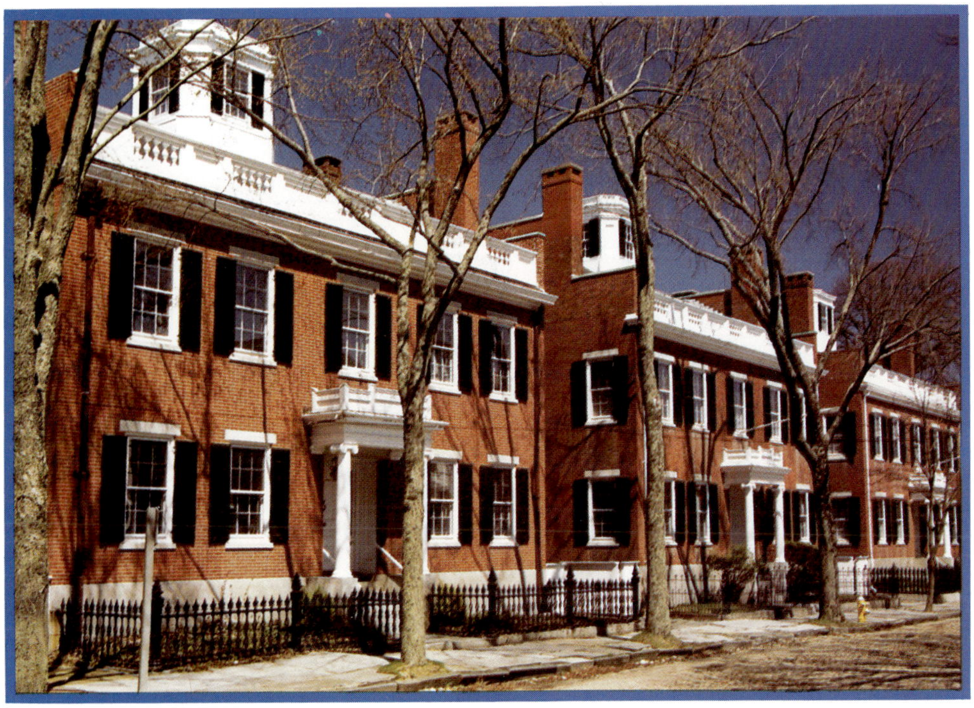

The enormous wealth realized from the whaling industry is symbolized by Nantucket's "Three Bricks" which were built in the 1830s by whaling merchant Joseph Starbuck for his three sons.

Mention of America's whaling era can evoke visions of adventure, romance, loneliness, or gory drudgery. In reality, for New England ports and the fledgling nation as a whole, the whaling industry was an economic miracle. Whaling profits were invested in financial ventures across the country—agriculture, railroads, shipping, and real estate. In his early nineteenth century *History of Nantucket,* Obed Macy repeats a prophetic anecdote first related to him as a child: "In the year 1690...some persons were on a high hill...observing the whales spouting and sporting with each other, when one observed, 'there,' pointing to the sea, 'is a green pasture where our children's grand-children will go for bread."[1] In the ensuing two hundred years, the words of the anonymous soothsayer were proven true as numerous grandchildren's children went forth to find not only bread but wealth on the deck of a whaler.

Inherent in this primarily economic pursuit were the nurturing elements necessary to produce the art of scrimshaw. The wonderful examples of scrimshaw that remain today can stand on their own as remarkable creations. Yet, fuller appreciation of their themes is enhanced by awareness of the context in which they were created and the motivation of their makers.

The roots of nineteenth century Yankee whaling are found in the earliest days of settlement. Colonists to the New England shores, familiar with the existing whale fisheries of Europe, were quick to appreciate the bounty abundant in the surrounding waters. In 1620, the choice of Plymouth as a home for Pilgrims aboard the *Mayflower* was influenced by the fact that "It was a place of profitable fishing, for large whales of the best kind for oil and bone came daily alongside and played about the ship."[2] Like the native Algonkian Indians, the colonists took advantage of any drift whales—those whales either washed ashore or stranded in shallow waters—harvesting them for their thick layer of fat which could be rendered into oils for lighting and other purposes.

The settlers of Long Island were the first group to organize whale hunting as a community activity and industry. By 1650, men from Easthampton and Southampton no longer waited for whales to become stranded, but actively watched for spouting whales and launched boats to pursue them.

The methods of the Long Islanders were soon adopted by inhabitants of Cape Cod and the islands. Residents of the island of Nantucket, situated within easy reach of rich whaling grounds, embraced this more aggressive pursuit eagerly and successfully. Once the whale was beached, its blanket of blubber was cut and removed in strips. To render the oil, pieces of blubber were boiled in large iron pots, or tryworks, situated on the beach.

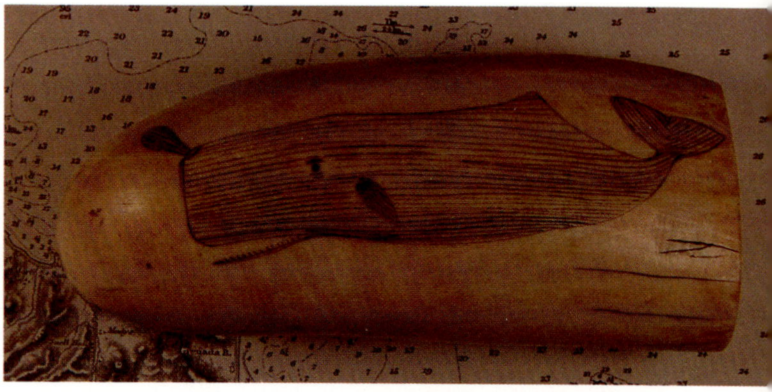

Although the technique employed by the engraver of this sperm whale appears somewhat primitive, his knowledge of his subject matter is evidenced by the correct positioning of the whale's spout. Whalemen could identify species of whales at a great distance solely by the differing appearances of their spouts. *Private Collection*

In addition to "saving" the oil, thrifty Nantucketers also made use of the bone. Resistant to rot, whalebone was considered a desirable construction material on the sparsely wooded island. Before the evolution of the decorative pieces now deemed "scrimshaw," skeletal bone was being transformed into functional items such as chopping blocks, fenceposts, survey markers, and milk stools.[3]

By the turn of the century, "along-shore" whaling was being supplanted by "off-shore" whaling in which islanders undertook voyages lasting four to six weeks. The object of the hunt was the right whale, *Balaena glacialis*. This whale, which can reach sixty feet in length, was named by whalemen who considered it indeed the "right" whale to catch. Whalers did not have

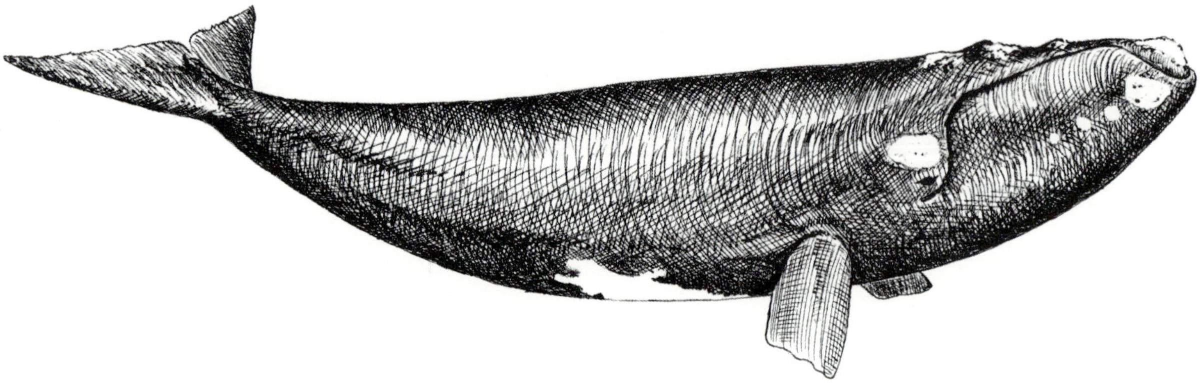

Right whale: *Balaena glacialis. Illustrated by Steve Ferguson.*

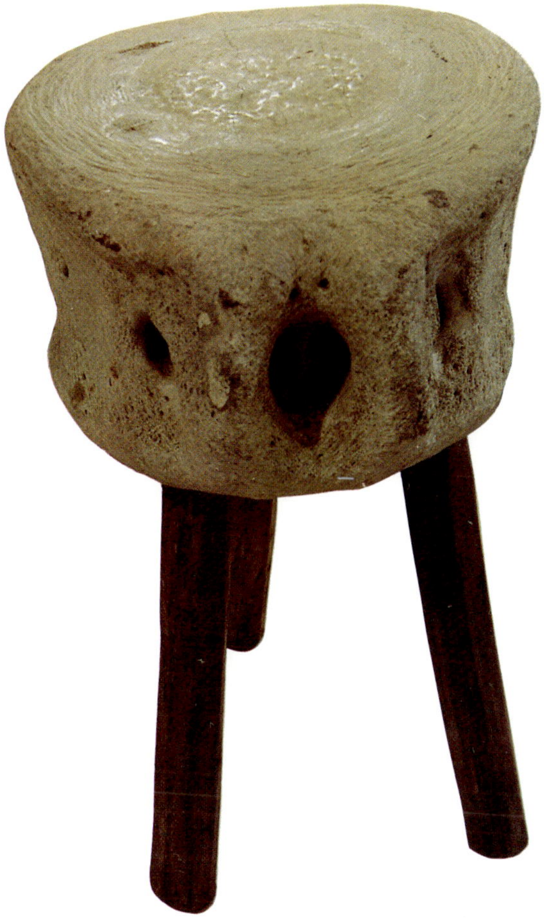

This early nineteenth century stool constructed from a whale vertebra exemplifies the many uses to which skeletons of drift whales were put. *Courtesy of the Nantucket Historical Association*

to venture too far from land to find the right whale as it feeds in relatively shallow waters. In addition, its speed is leisurely enough to allow capture, its blubber is very thick and oily, and it does not sink when killed. Blessed with a rather docile nature, the right is not inclined to attack; however, significant damage could be done to a small whaleboat by the sideways swipe of the eighty ton mammal's flukes.

The most distinctive feature of right whales is the three to five hundred rows of keratinous baleen which hang in ten foot lengths from the roof of its mouth. After the whale ingests a mouthful of sea water, the fringed baleen plates enable it to expel the water while straining out nourishing organisms. Baleen, a pliable, plastic-like material, would become as important an item of trade in the nineteenth century as the whale oil itself.

Occasionally a sperm whale, *Physeter macrocephalus*, was stranded or washed ashore; but tradition holds that it was not until about 1712 that a Nantucket whaler, blown off-course in a storm, found himself in a herd of sperm whales, seized the moment and inadvertantly directed Nantucket's fledgling industry on an unimaginably profitable course.

A toothed whale, the sperm can reach sixty feet in length and sixty tons in weight. The oil rendered from its twelve inch blubber was of finer quality than that of the right and considered a superior choice for both illumination and lubrication. In addition, spermaceti, found in the large head cavity, or case, of the whale, was cleaner burning, and thus more precious than

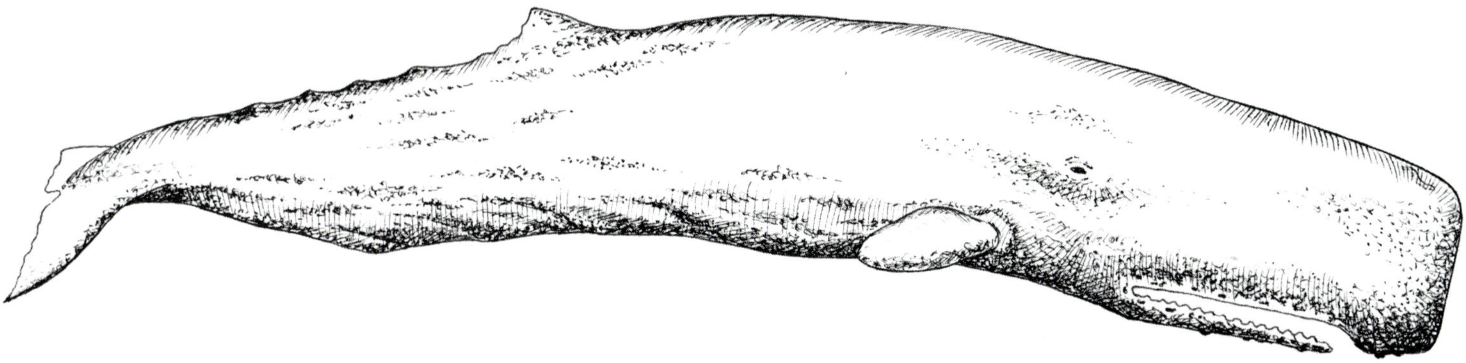

Sperm whale: *Physeter macrocephalus. Illustrated by Steve Ferguson.*

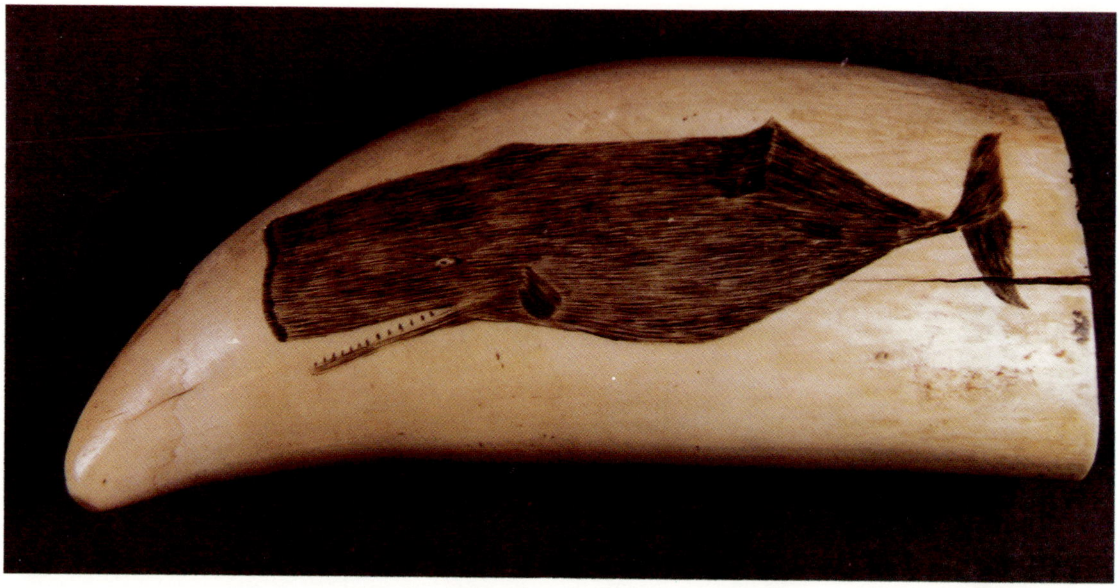

A scrimshander's depiction of *Physeter macrocephalus*
Courtesy of the Nantucket Historical Association

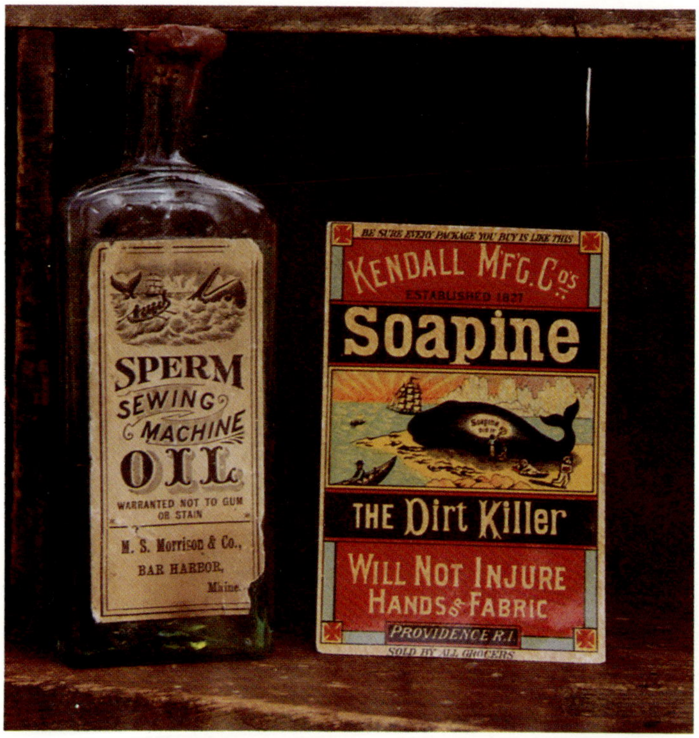

These nineteenth century products were some of the many for which high quality sperm oil was required.
Collection of Charles A. Manghis

the body oil. Because the sperm whale actively hunts for squid and other prey, it feeds in deeper waters than the right whale, and its pursuit necessitated voyages further from shore.

No oil burned more cleanly or brightly than that of the sperm whale and the demand for this product increased markedly as the eighteenth century unfolded. Whether for public or household lighting, soaps, paints, varnishes, or fine machine lubrication, sperm oil was the most highly prized. In 1749, a process for the manufacture of candles from spermaceti was discovered. Virtually smoke and odor free, spermaceti candles were a marked improvement over tallow. Candle factories sprang up across New England, insuring an increased and constant demand for the sperm whale's products.

As with any economic success, the flourishing whaling industry did not exist in a vacuum; its profits and requirements spilled over to affect other businesses. On Nantucket, for example, new wharves, warehouses and tryworks were needed to handle the increased commerce. Carpenters, shipbuilders, coopers, riggers, shipwrights, and sailmakers were all busy supplying the industry's needs.

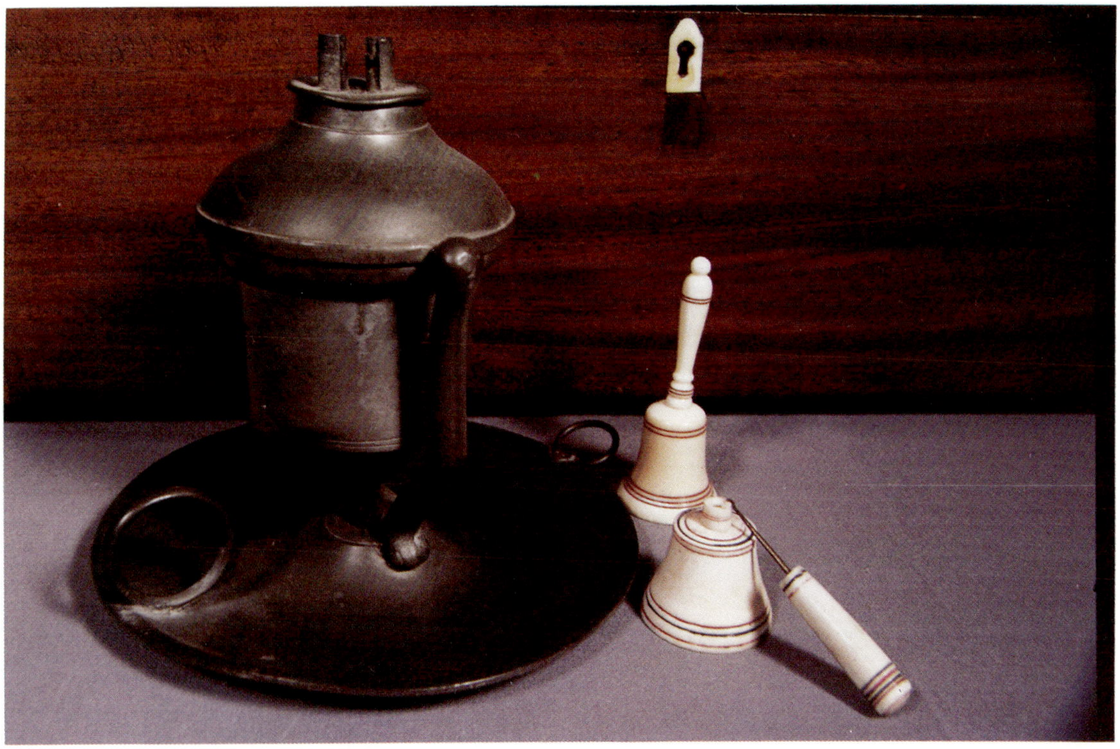

Sperm whales yielded both the oil to light this lamp as well as the ivory from which this practical pick-wick was turned. The pick was used to raise the lamp's wick when it had burned out of reach. *Courtesy of the Nantucket Historical Association*

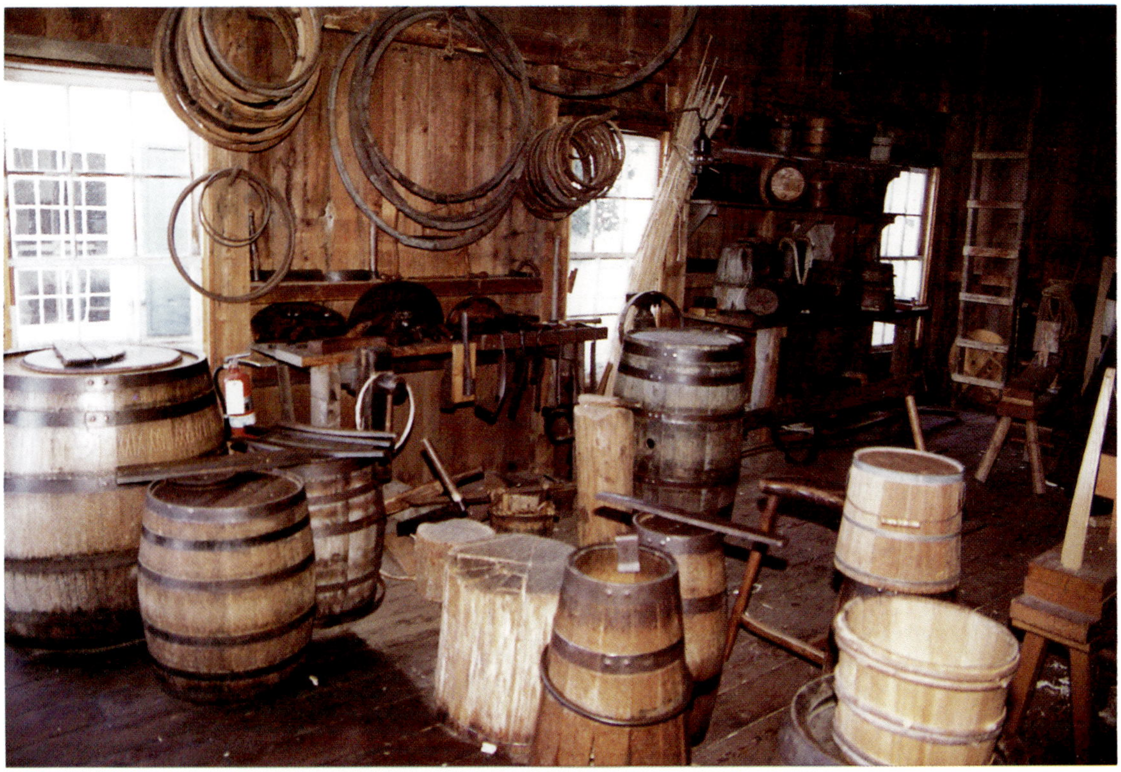

The cooperage at Mystic Seaport recreates the site of one of the whaling industry's most important ancillary trades. *Courtesy of the Mystic Seaport Museum*

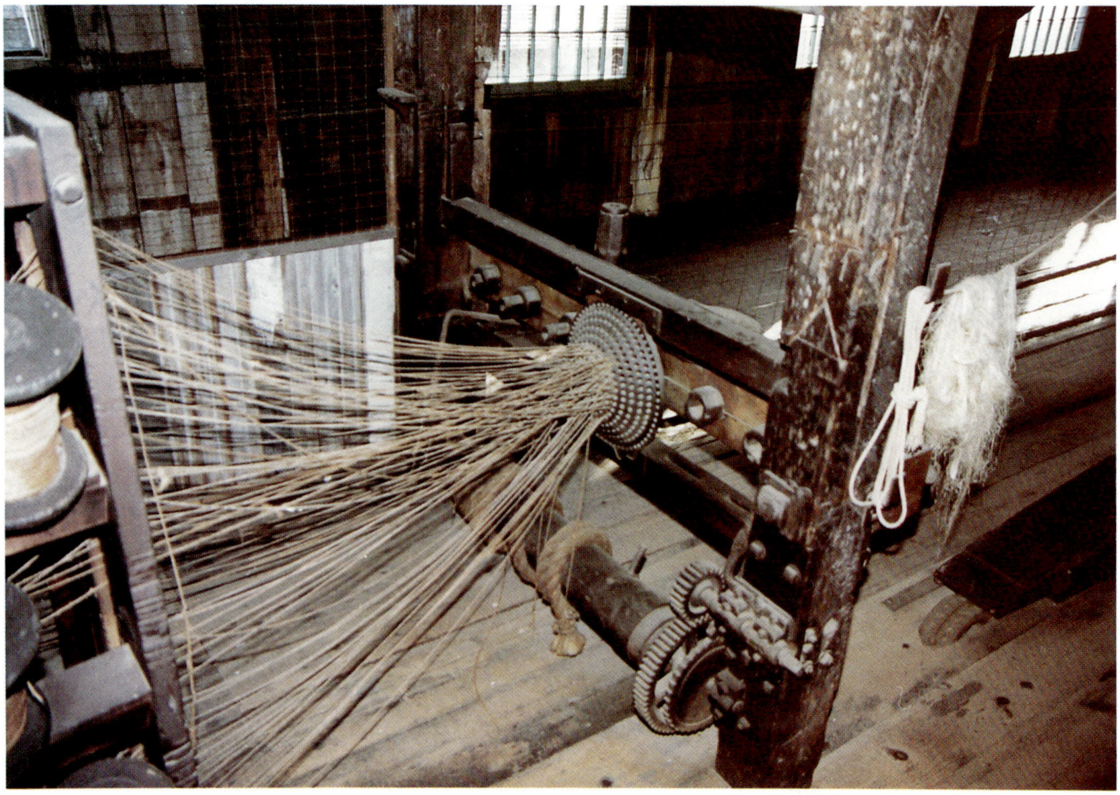

Hemp or manila fibers were twisted into various gauges of line in the ropewalk. *Courtesy of the Mystic Seaport Museum.*

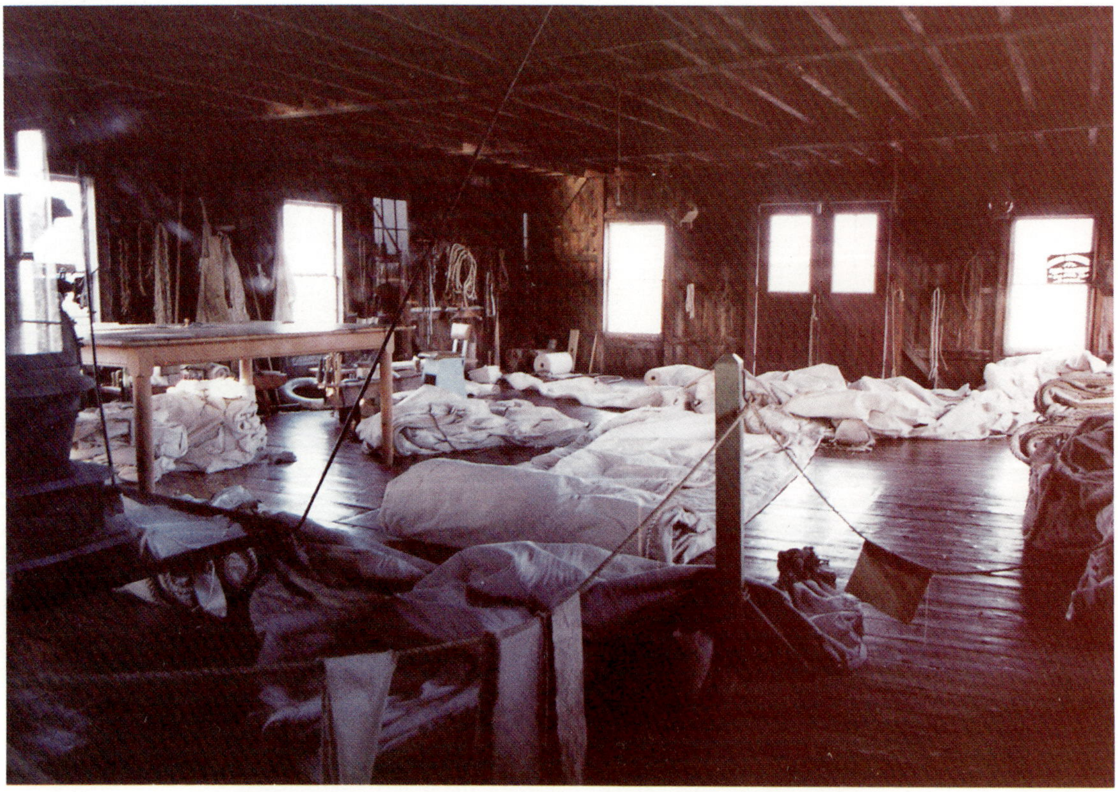

The sail loft at Mystic Seaport. *Courtesy of the Mystic Seaport Museum*

An eighteenth century visitor to the island confirmed the extent of whaling's economic influence:

> At my first landing, I was much surprised at the disagreeable smell which struck me in many parts of the town; it is caused by the whale oil and is unavoidable; the neatness peculiar to these people can neither remove or prevent it. There are near the wharfs a great many storehouses, where their staple commodity is deposited, as well as the innumerable materials which are always wanted to repair and fit out so many whalemen. They have three docks....and there is room around these...for 300 sail of vessels. When their fleets have been successful, the bustle and hurry of business on this spot for some days after their arrival would make you imagine that (this) is the capital of a very opulent and large province.[4]

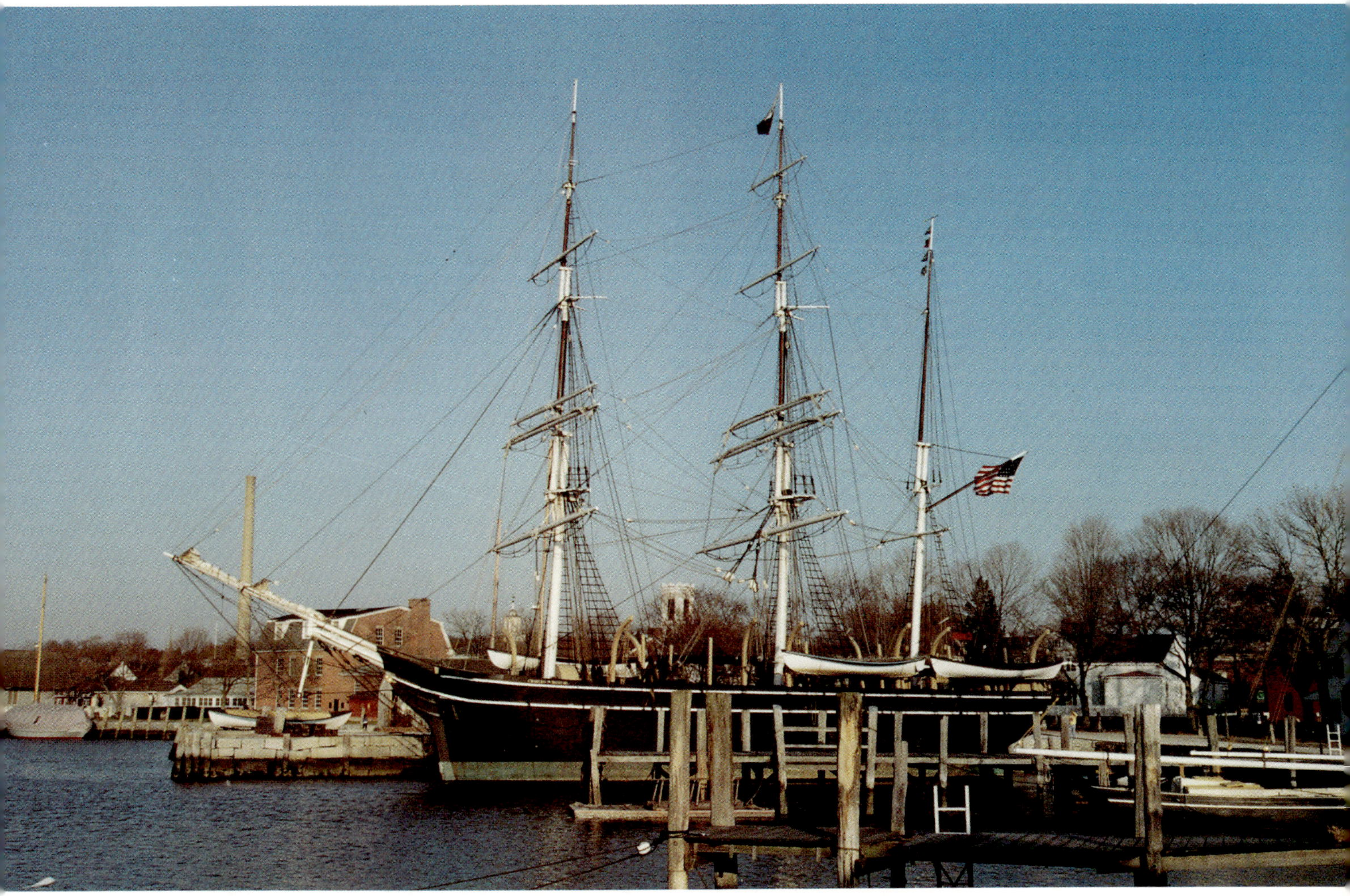

The one hundred and five foot *Charles W. Morgan* was launched in New Bedford in 1841 and typifies whaling vessels of its day. At first rigged as a ship, she was converted to a bark in 1867 and served as a whaler for eighty years. *Courtesy of the Mystic Seaport Museum*

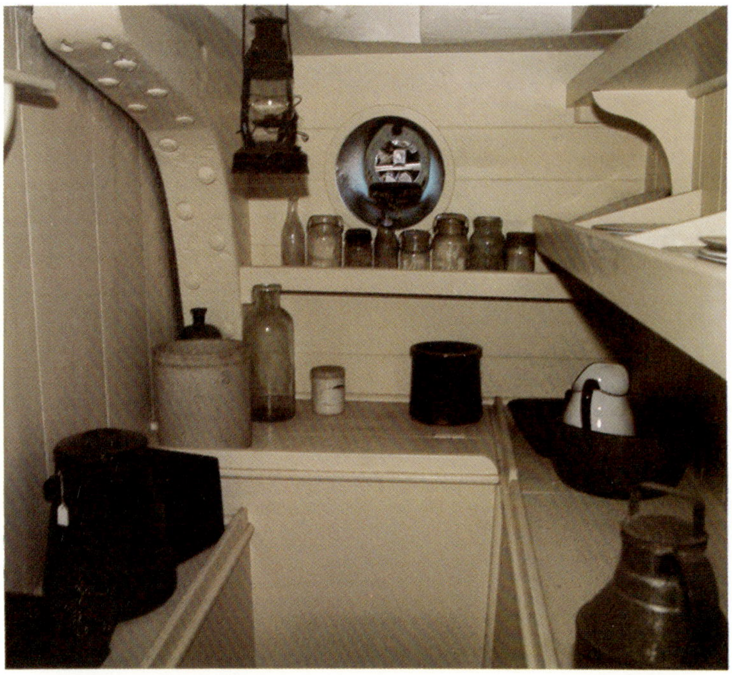

Pantry of the *Charles W. Morgan. Courtesy of the Mystic Seaport Museum.*

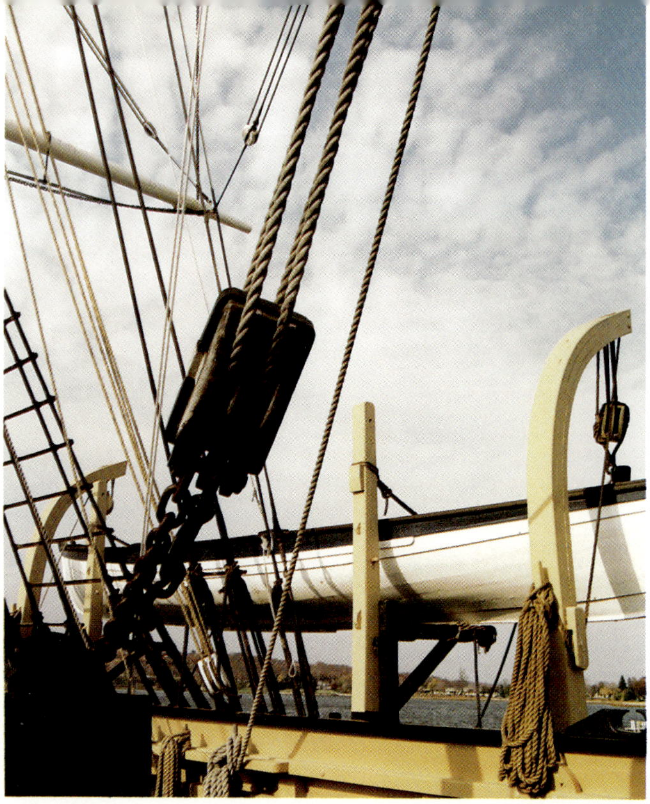

A graceful whaleboat hangs from its davits aboard the *Charles W. Morgan. Courtesy of the Mystic Seaport Museum.*

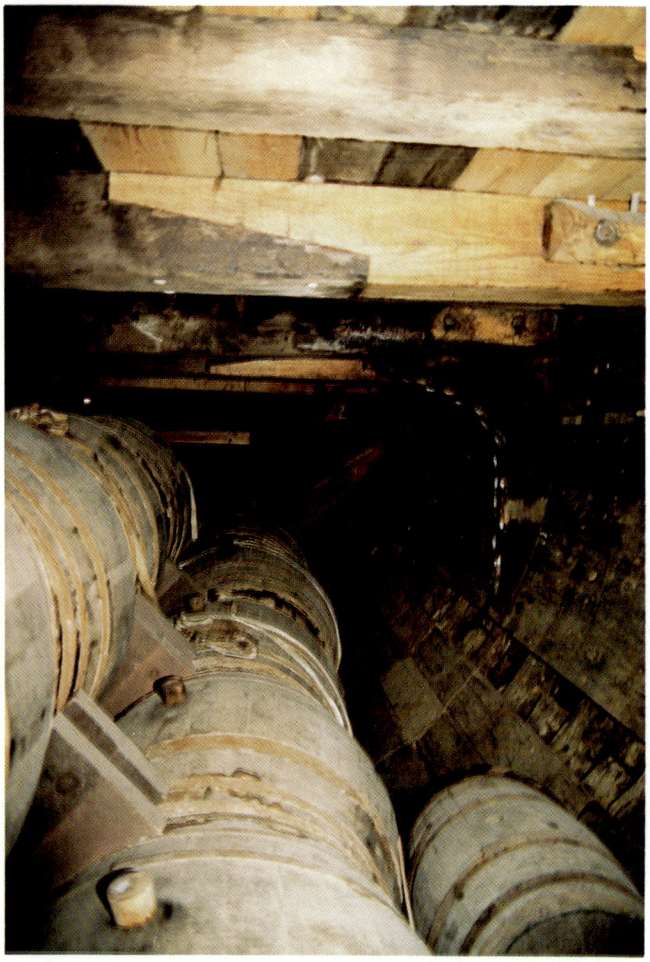

Casks of oil were stowed below decks in the hold. *Courtesy of the Mystic Seaport Museum.*

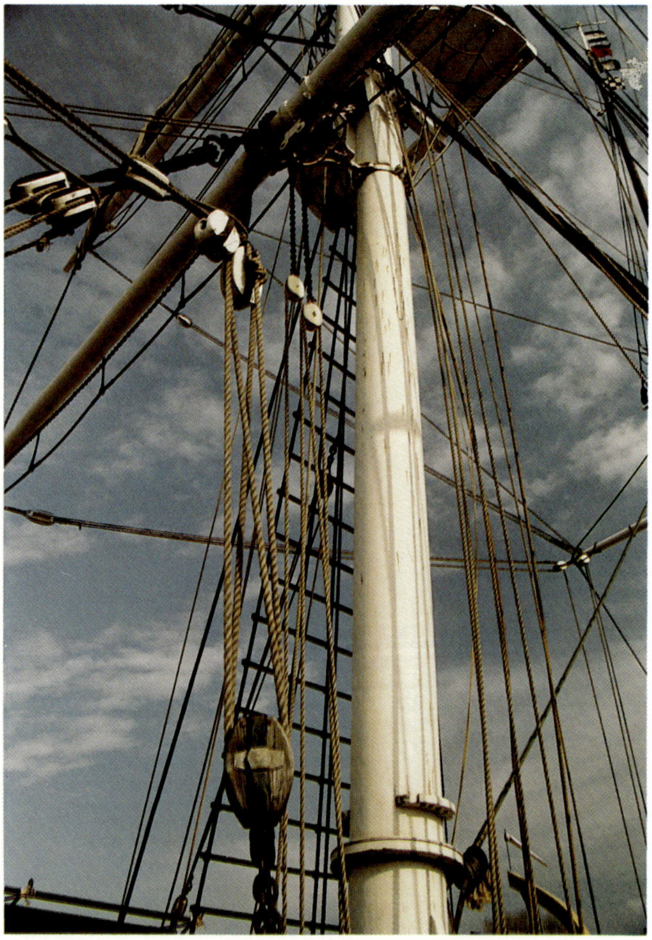

Mainmast of the *Charles W. Morgan* pierces the sky. *Courtesy of the Mystic Seaport Museum.*

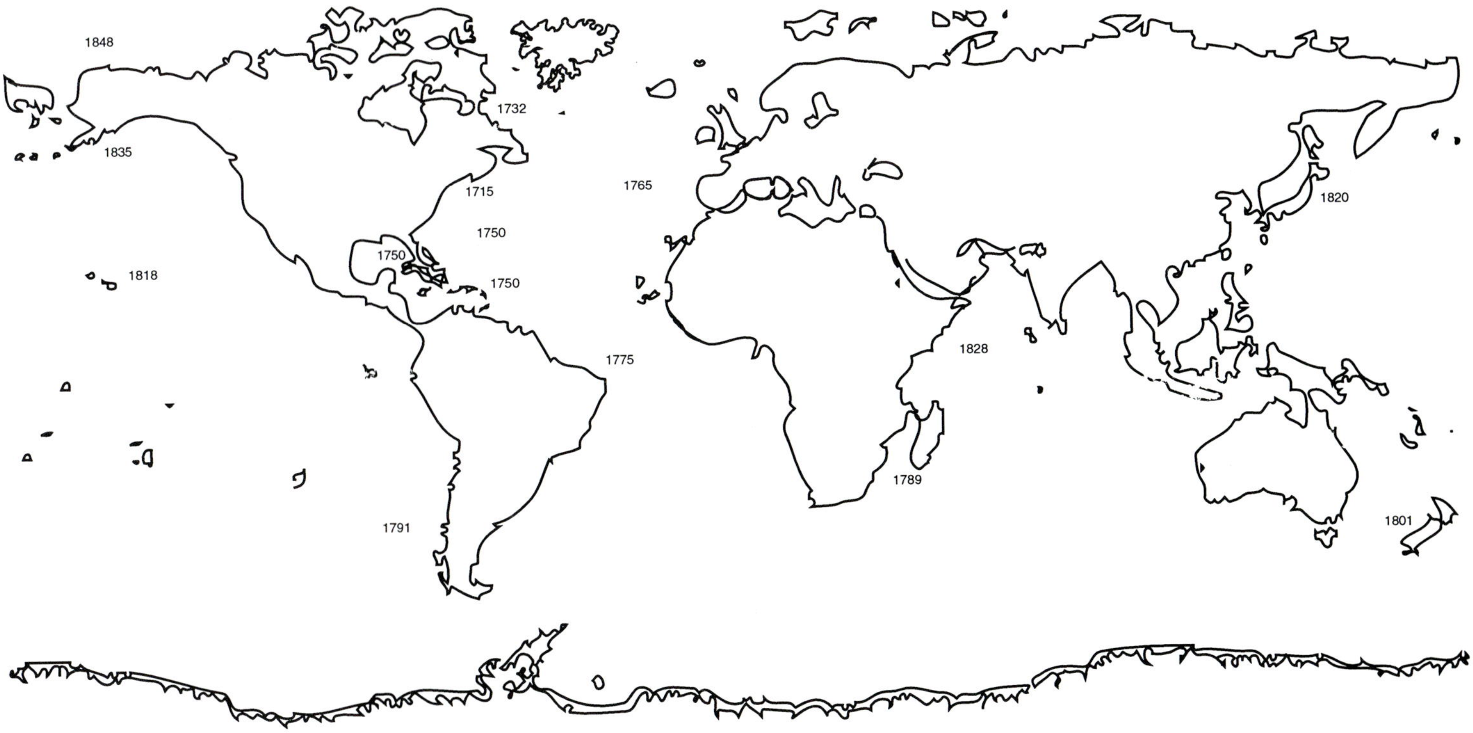

By 1715, six Nantucket sloops were whaling "in the deep." After these first ventures, Yankee whalers began to sail farther and farther from their Northeast ports in search of sperm, and later bowhead whales. Dates included on the map above indicate the year in which newly discovered whaling grounds began to be fished.

Although Nantucket was home to the greatest number of whaling ships (one hundred and twenty-five by 1770), and considered whaling's leading port, Dartmouth, Fairhaven, New Bedford, Wellfleet, Martha's Vinyard, Boston, New London, and ports in Long Island and Rhode Island participated actively in the sperm whale fishery as well. In fact, the promised revenues prompted ship owners to launch larger vessels and venture farther from their home ports. By the 1730s, Yankee whalers were sailing along the Gulf Stream to Nova Scotia, the Grand Banks, Labrador, Newfoundland, the Davis Straits and the Greenland Grounds. Within the next twenty years they were off to Bermuda, the West Indies and the Gulf of Mexico; by 1765, the Azores; and by the 1770s, the west coast of Africa, the Falklands, and the Brazil banks; and by the 1780s they had rounded the Cape of Good Hope, sailing onto the Delagoa grounds of the Indian Ocean.

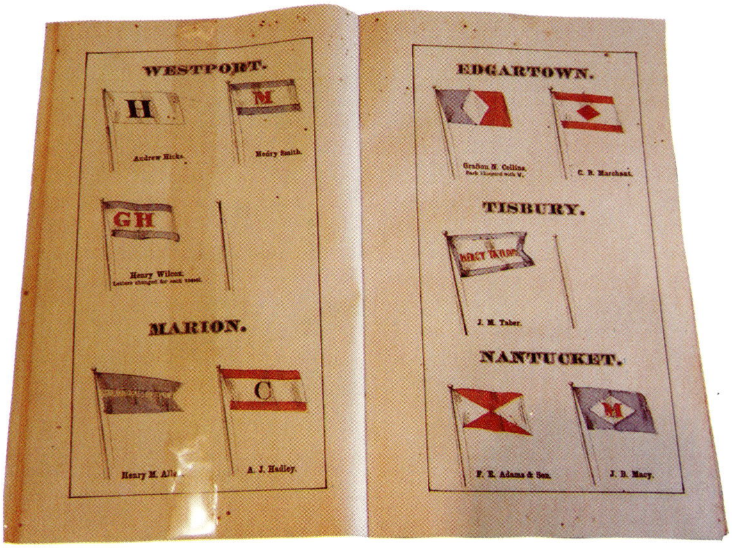

A *Whaling Directory of the United States* dated 1869 illustrates the various flags which identified a vessel's owner and home port. *Courtesy of the Nantucket Historical Association*

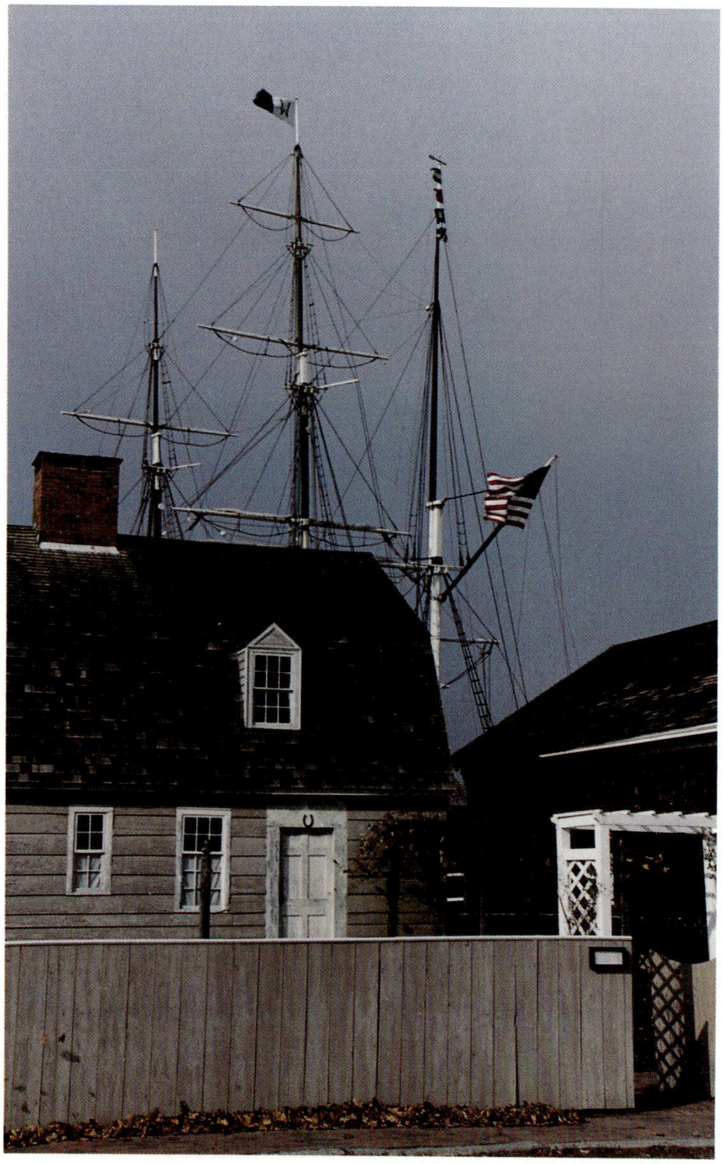

The demand for sperm oil remained strong and American whalers were determined to fill it. Yet, by the end of the century, previously rich grounds had been sorely depleted and locating whales in abundance necessitated finding new habitats. In response, shipbuilders began constructing vessels which carried their own tryworks, allowing oil to be extracted and stored during the voyage. In 1791, the *Beaver* of Nantucket was the first United States whaler to round Cape Horn and enter the Pacific Ocean. The age of deep-sea whaling had arrived, as had the proper setting, amount of leisure time, and availability of materials for the art of scrimshaw to flourish.

[01] Obed Macy, *The History of Nantucket* (Mansfield, Mass.: Macy and Pratt, 1880), 45.

[02] Alexander Starbuck, *History of the American Whale Fishery* (Secaucus, N.J.: Castle Books, 1989), 4-5.

[03] Charles H. Carpenter, Jr. and Mary Carpenter, *The Decorative Arts and Crafts of Nantucket* (New York: Dodd, Mead and Company, 1987), 164.

[04] J. Hector St. John de Crèvecoeur, *Letters from an American Farmer* (New York: Fox, Duffield and Company, 1904) p. 111-112.

Mystic Seaport Museum includes a restoration of a working nineteenth century seaport, at which is berthed the whaling vessel, *Charles W. Morgan. Courtesy of the Mystic Seaport Museum*

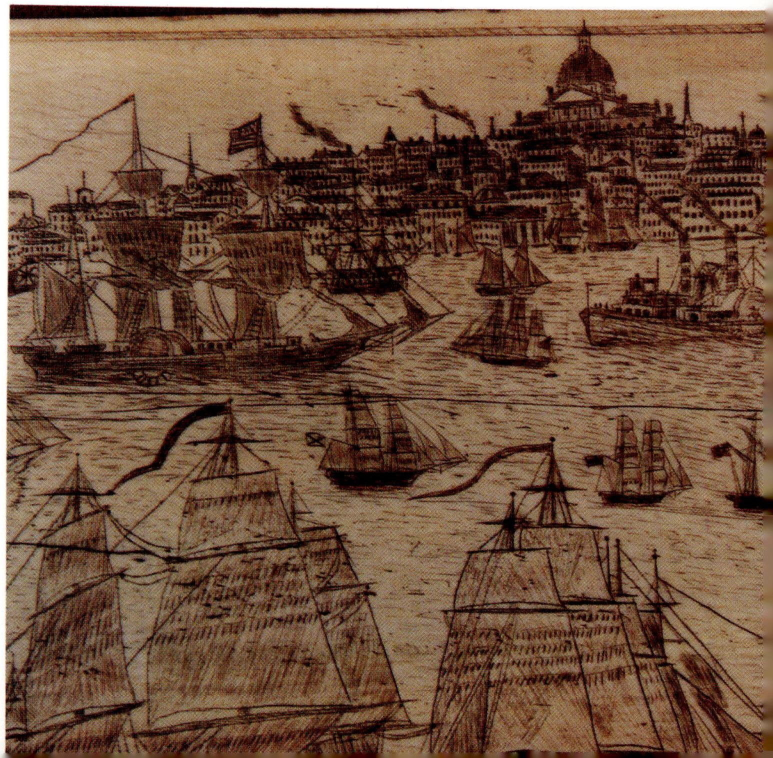

This highly detailed panbone engraving pictures a bustling Boston Harbor crowned by Beacon Hill. The names of the twenty-four vessels depicted are engraved on the bottom of the piece. *Private Collection*

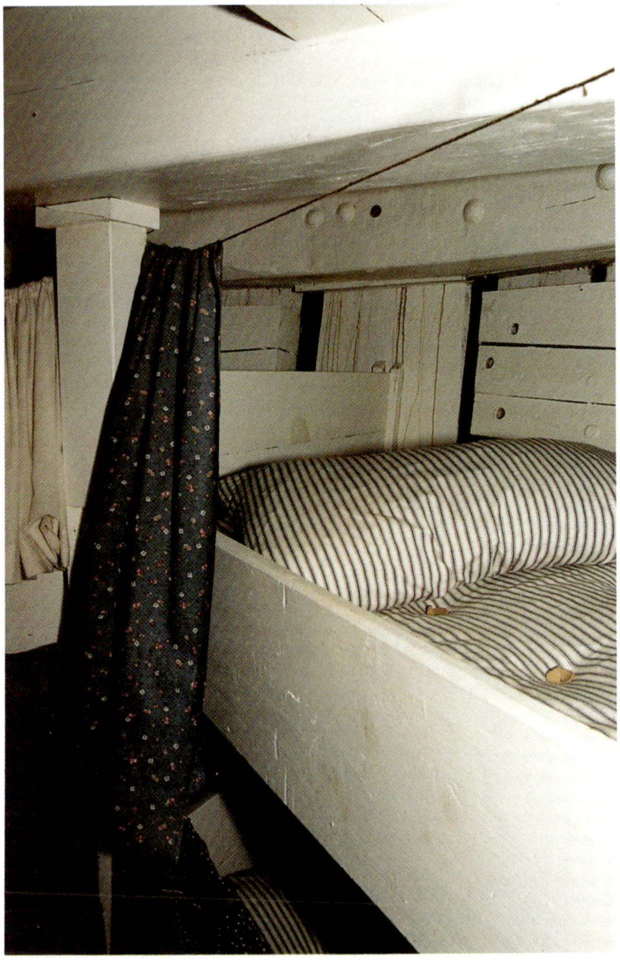

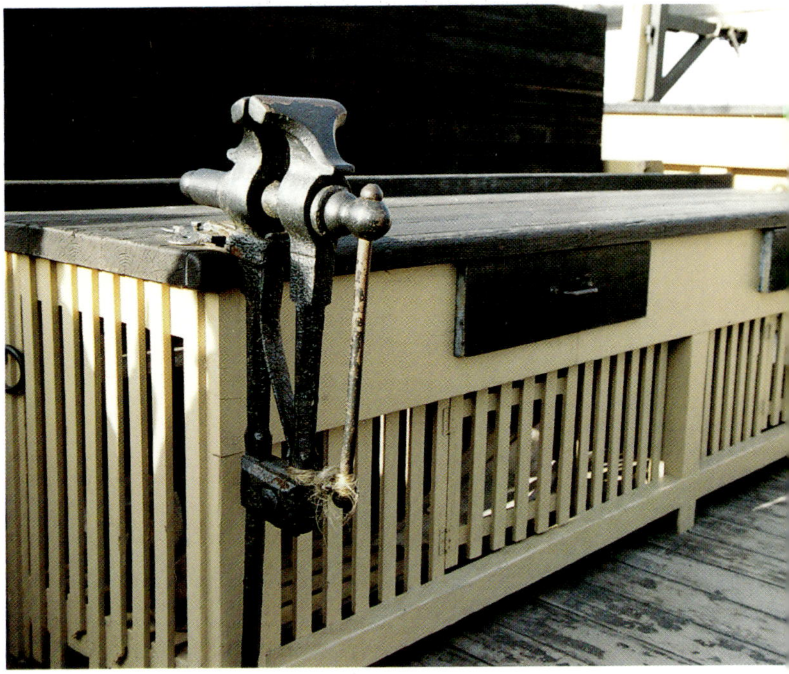

A chicken coop fits snugly below the carpenter's bench on the *Charles W. Morgan's* deck. *Courtesy of the Mystic Seaport Museum.*

Foc'sle berths aboard the *Charles W. Morgan* were wedged below decks directly in the bow. *Courtesy of the Mystic Seaport Museum.*

The fires in the *Morgan*'s tryworks were fueled with scraps of blubber. A reservoir of water under the works protected the deck below from the intense heat of the fires. *Courtesy of the Mystic Seaport Museum*

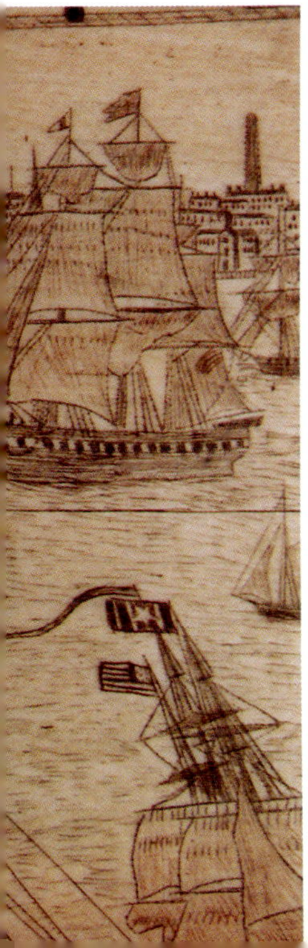

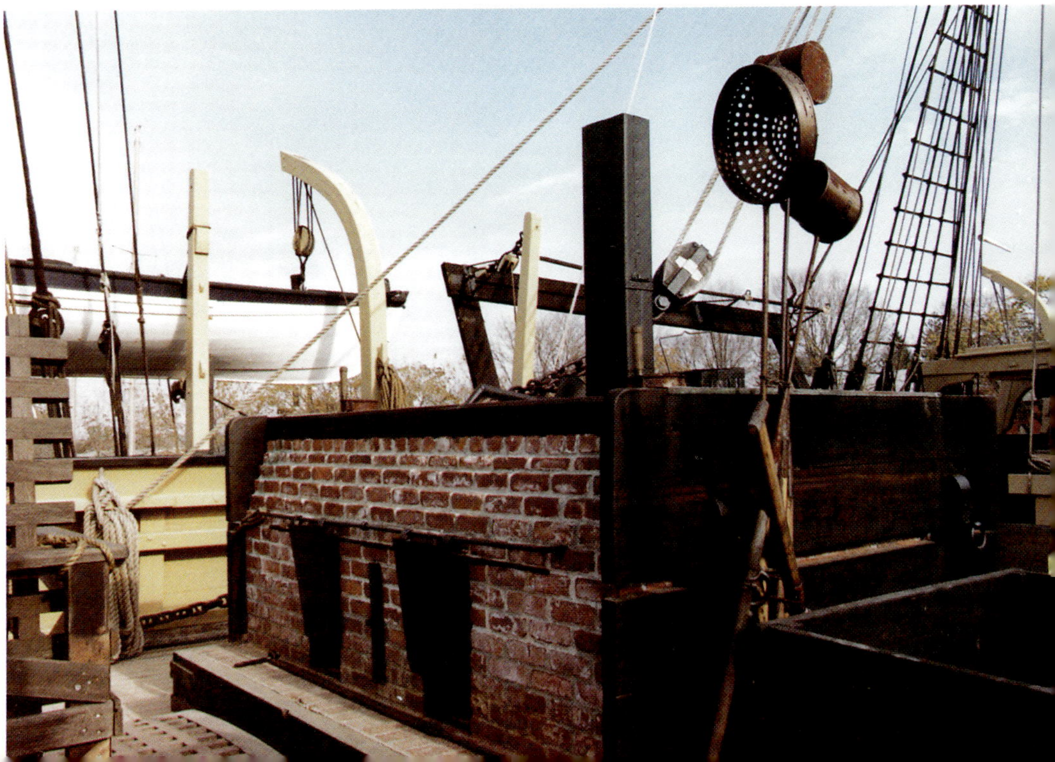

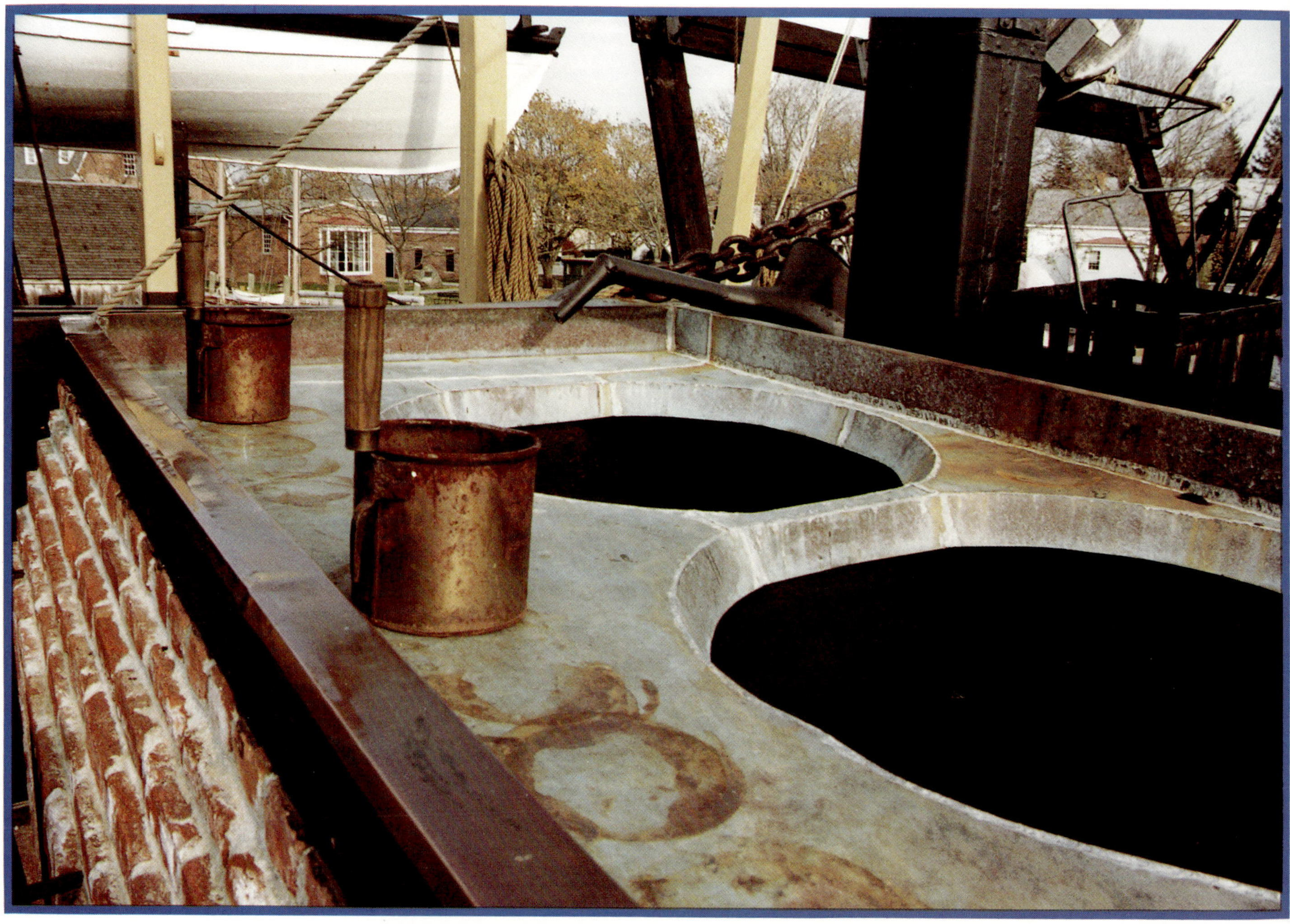

The ability to render oil aboard ship in cast iron try pots allowed vessels to stay out from port for years at a time. *Courtesy of the Mystic Seaport Museum*

Throughout the book, stanzas of poetry are taken from "A Journal of a Whaling Voyage on Board Ship *Dauphin* of Nantucket" by Charles Murphy, 3rd mate.

Voyage began Sept. 4, 1820

Sept fourth, on Monday morn,
The weather fine and clear,
We weighed our ancor to the bow,
And eastward we did steer...

-

Unto the girls we bid adieu,
Left on our native shore,
And likewise unto all our friends
For two long years or more

'Twas one-and-twenty men we had
This voyage to pursue
And a-sperm-whaling we were bound
On Chile, and Peru.

2. The Golden Age

By the early nineteenth century the average whaling voyage had increased to two and a half years, and by 1818 whalers had ventured as far as the Hawaiian Islands. Within two years, ships were fishing new grounds off the coast of Japan. Further and further they sailed, exploring unknown waters of the South Pacific.

Navigational charts available at the time were incomplete and imprecise. Whaling chronicler Alexander Starbuck noted, "The first intimation that many a vessel had that she was sailing on dangerous ground was the splash of the breakers close at hand, or the grinding of her keel upon the treacherous rocks."[1]

The series of *Susan*'s teeth engraved by Nantucket's Frederick Myrick coincided with the end of the first decade of Pacific whaling. This tooth is dated February 6th, 1829 and shows the *Susan* both "whaling on the coast of Japan" as well as "homeward bound". The inscription "Death to the living(.) long life to the killers(.) Success to sailors wives and greasy luck to whalers" appears on other Myrick teeth. *Courtesy of the Nantucket Historical Association*

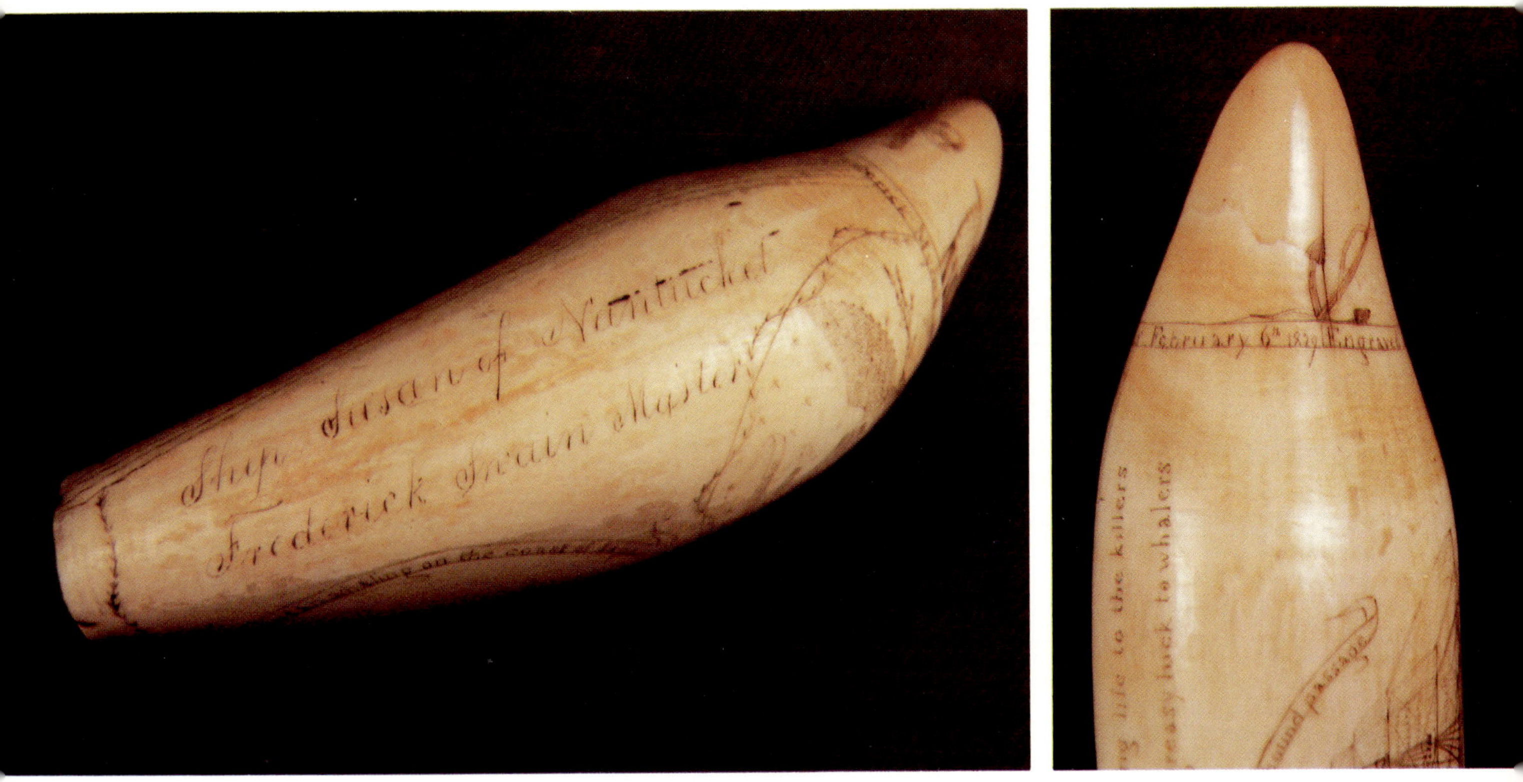

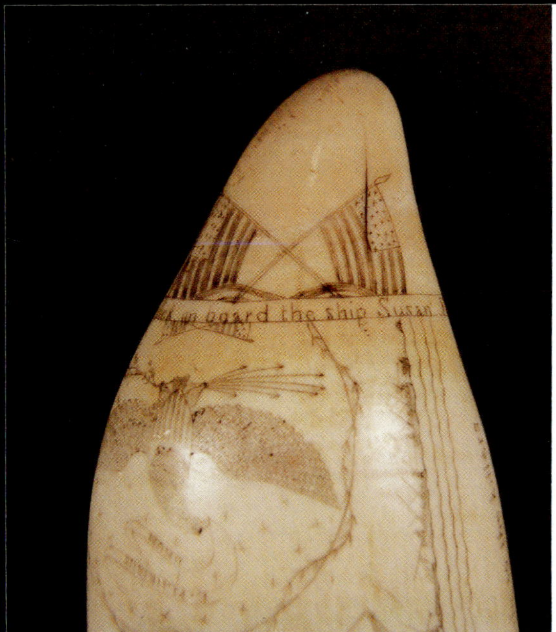
on board the ship Susan

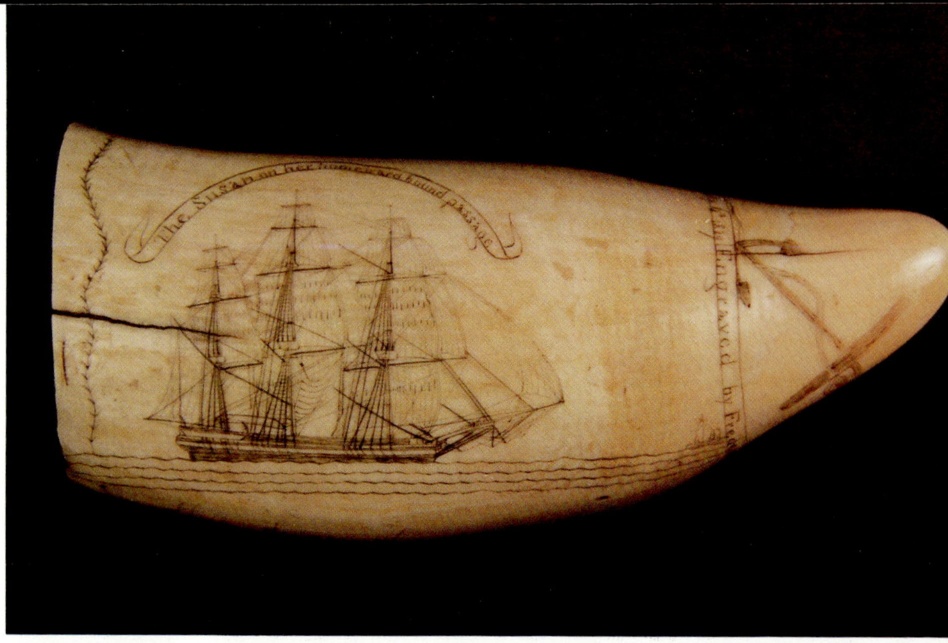
The Susan on her homeward bound passage

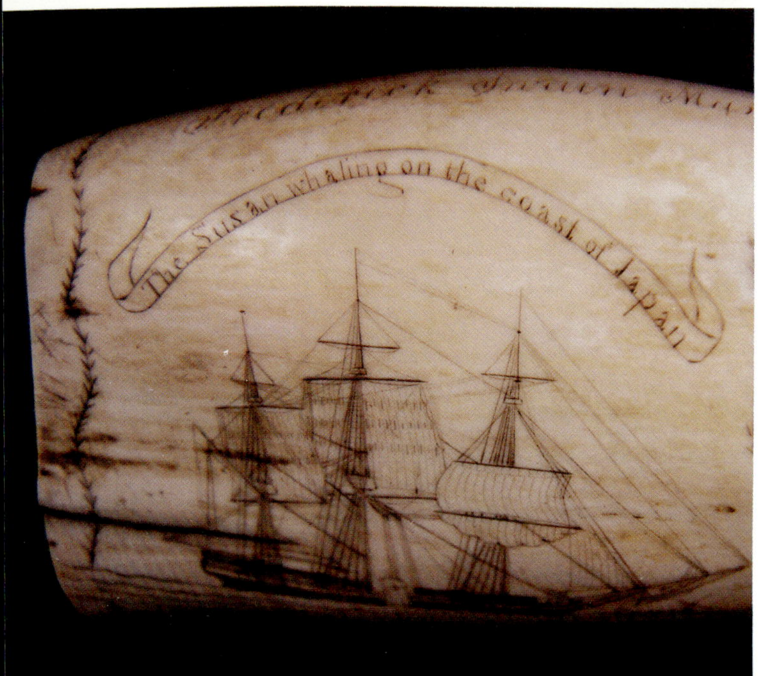
The Susan whaling on the coast of Japan

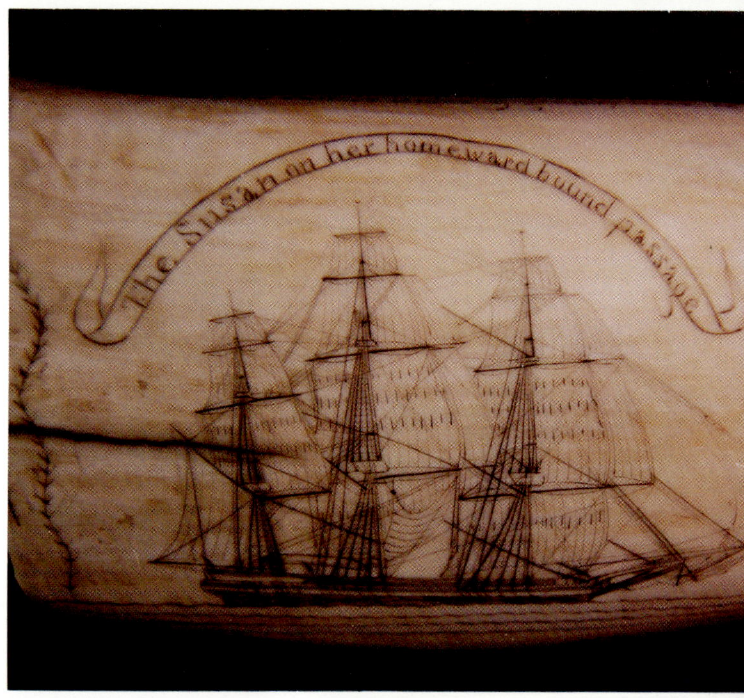
The Susan on her homeward bound passage

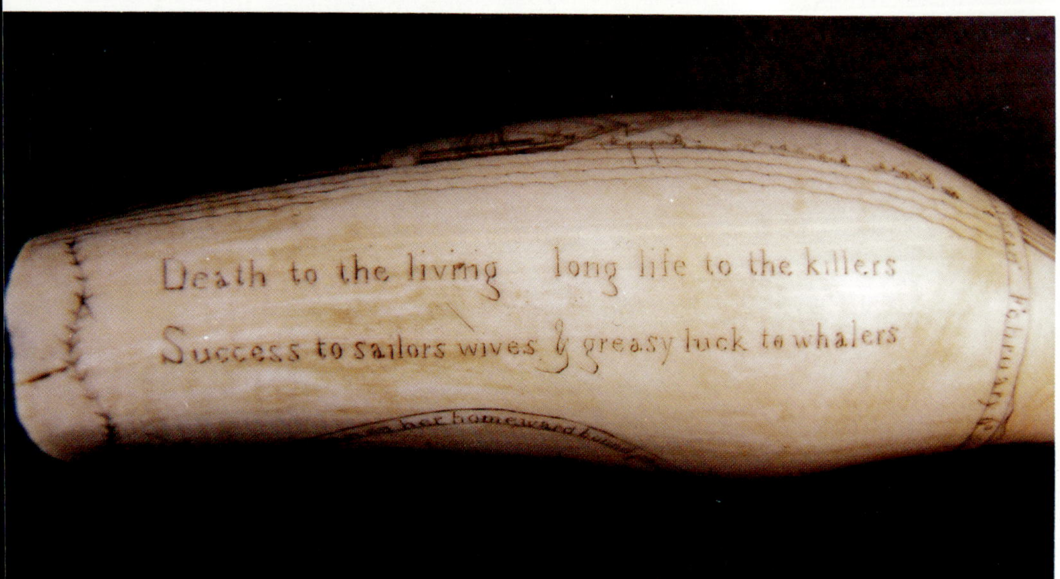
Death to the living long life to the killers
Success to sailors wives & greasy luck to whalers

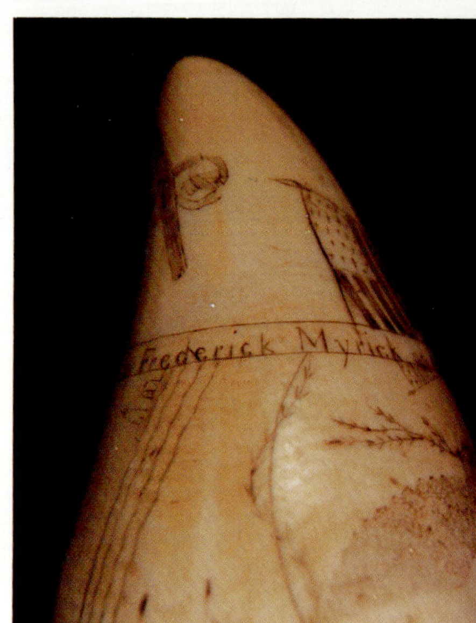
Frederick Myrick

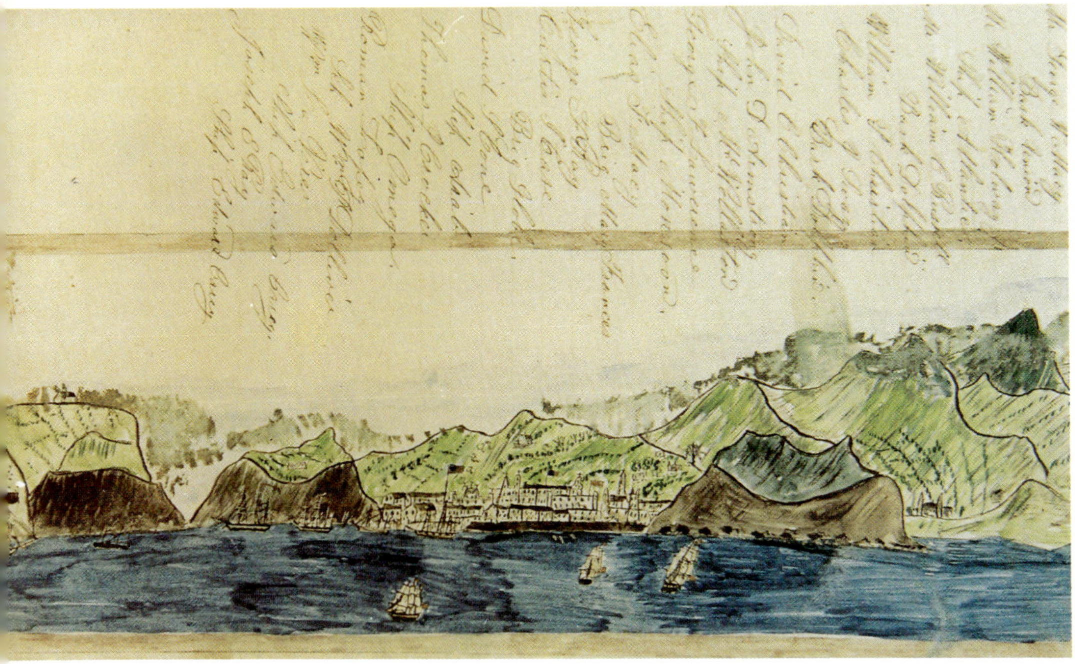

The beautifully illustrated log of the ship *Edward Cary* kept by boatsteerer Joseph E. Ray shows a group of whalers in port at Fayal in the Azores, July 1854. *Courtesy of the Nantucket Historical Association*

We cruised the coast of Chile o'er,
And cruised it round about,
And cruised it up and cruised it down,
And cruised the season out.

-

And all the time that we were there
Upon the rugged coast,
Ten tuns of oil or thereabouts
Was all that we could boast.

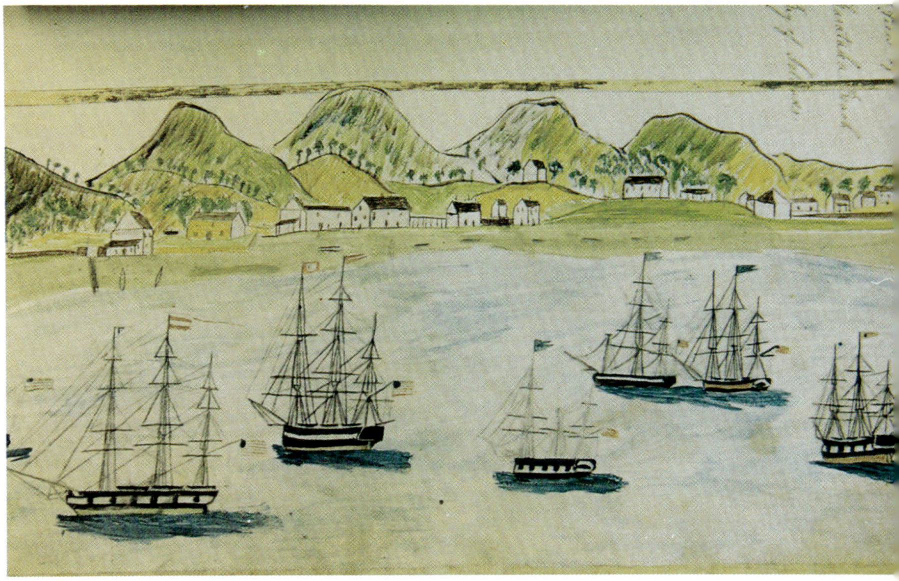

The *Edward Cary* at "Bay of Islands" in the Pacific, February, 1855. *Courtesy of the Nantucket Historical Association*

As whalemen explored new waters, they inadvertantly bequeathed one of their greatest maritime legacies—the observation and charting of tides, currents and weather patterns. In fact, during World War II, the U.S. Navy relied on information compiled by nineteenth century whalers to detail the countless islands and reefs scattered across the Pacific.[2] The scope of the whalers' endeavor is aptly reflected by the many atolls, reefs and islands that still bear the names of Yankee whaling captains.

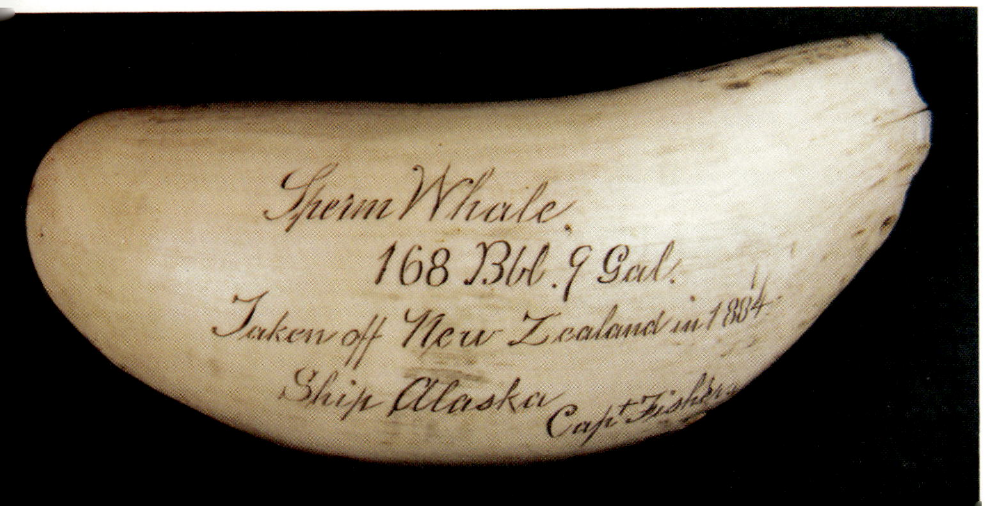

Inscriptions such as this one engraved in 1884 by Captain Charles Fisher, Master of the ship *Alaska* of New Bedford, have left a record of the many locations visited by the world's whaling vessels. *Courtesy of the Nantucket Historical Association*

At home, ports were not only bustling, but booming. As the Industrial Revolution exploded, its machines craved the lubricating effects of whale oil. Newly erected lighthouses dramatically increased demand for the clear burning sperm oil. And, prosperous American households, no longer satisfied with inferior tallow candles, called for the spermaceti candles previously reserved for wealthier European markets. The 1820s launched the dawn of the "Golden Age" of whaling. By the 1830s, New Bedford had outstripped Nantucket as the leading port in the industry. For the merchants, ship owners, and ancillary businesses, this was a period of great prosperity.

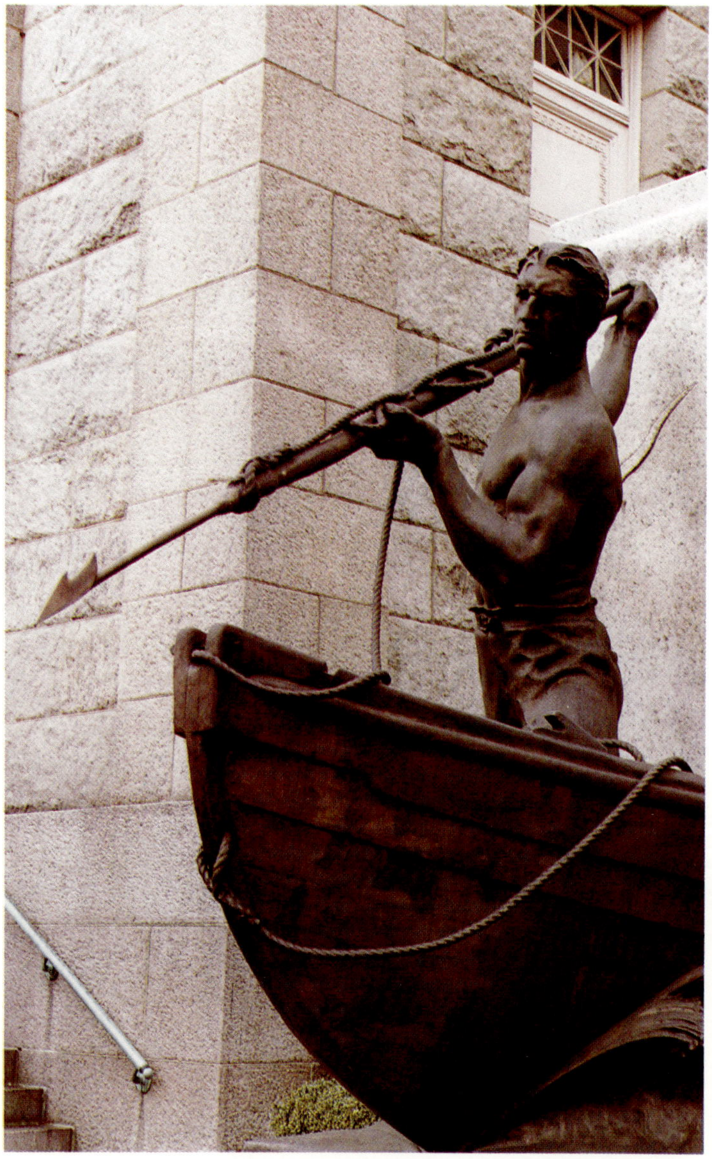

Harpoon at the ready, a New Bedford whaleman stands immortalized in front of the city's public library.

New Bedford's Seamen's Bethel was built in 1832 to serve the spiritual needs of the many mariners passing through this busy port. God's word was fittingly preached from the bow of a ship. *Courtesy of the New Bedford Port Society*

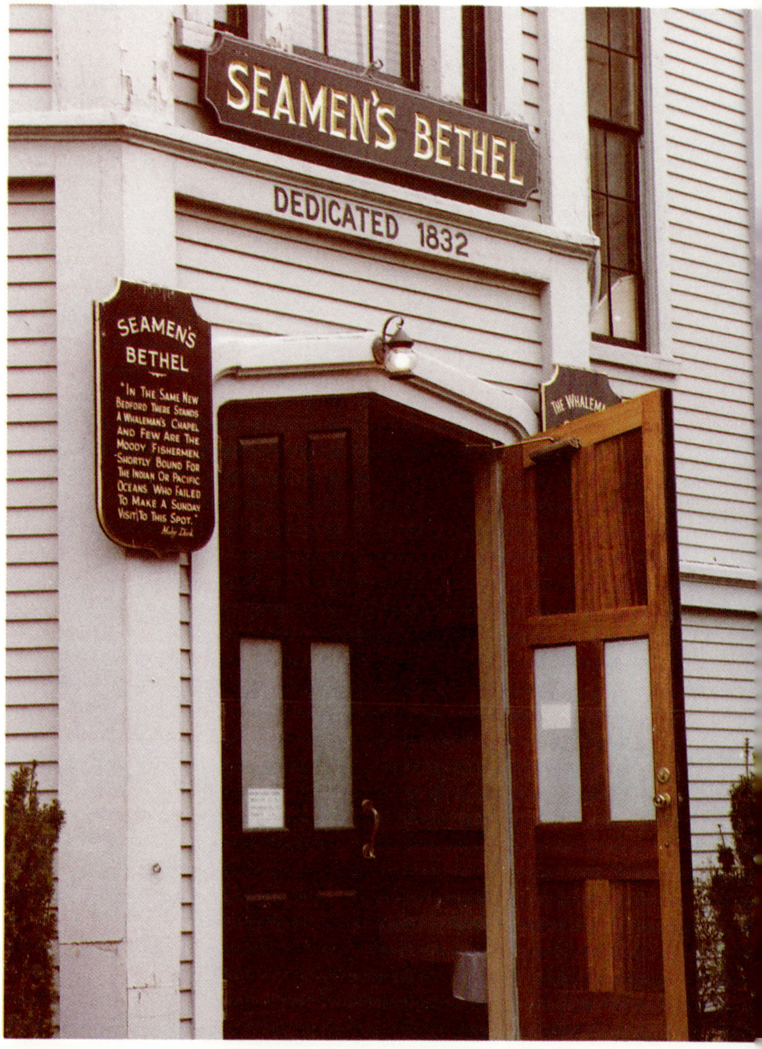

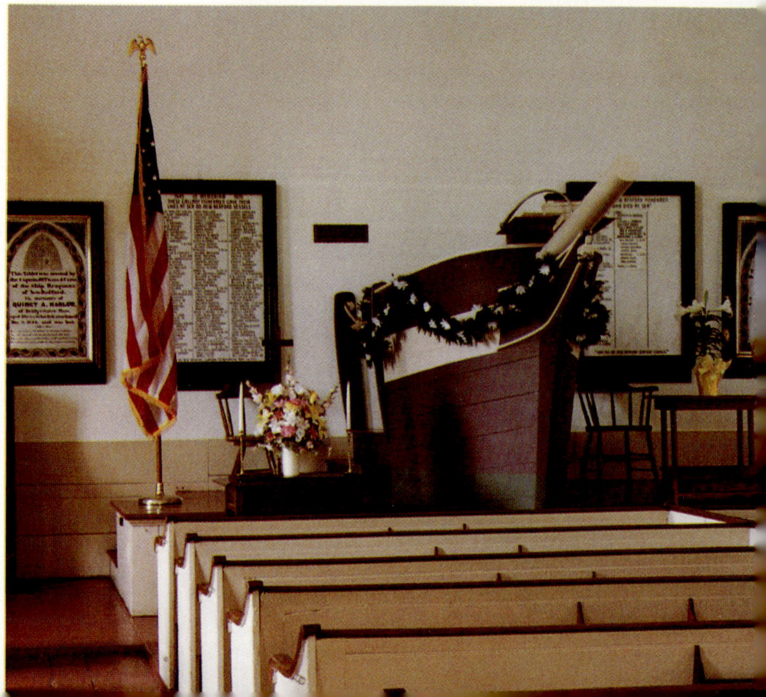

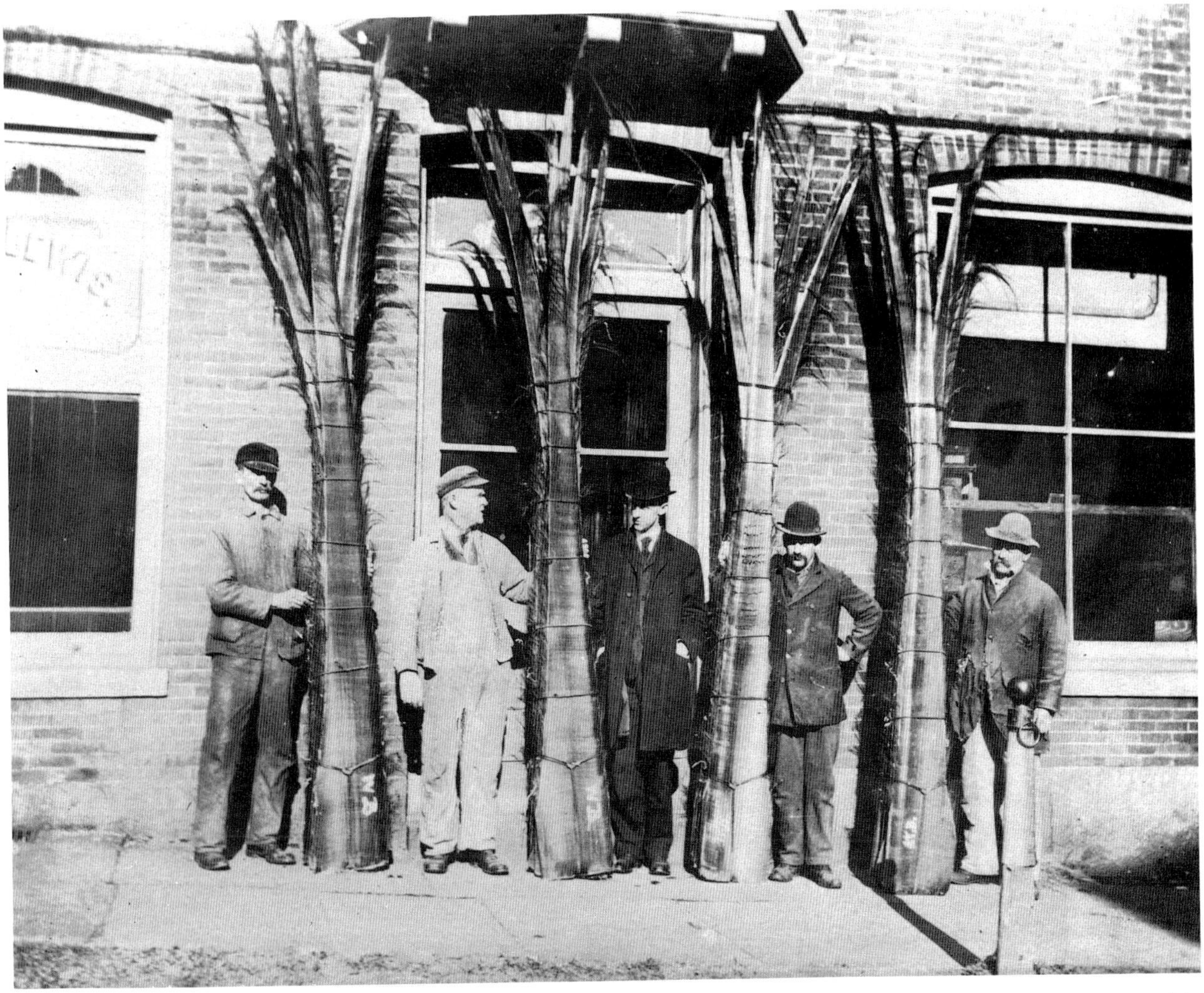

The neatly wrapped bundles of baleen photographed in San Francisco in 1905 hint at the size of the whale from which they were taken. *Courtesy of the New Bedford Whaling Museum*

As the nineteenth century unfolded, the plastic-propertied baleen of right whales was being utilized for everything from corset stays to fishing rods. Reports of heavy baleen consumption was welcome news to Mary Lawrence, wife of the master of the whaleship *Addison* sailing in the Pacific in January of 1858:

> Captain Curry told us of the still further rise of whalebone, which is a matter of rejoicing to us. An unheard of event...for whalebone to be $1.50 per pound. The ladies are to be thanked for that, and I presume all interested in right whaling are truly thankful for this skirt movement. May the fashion long continue.[3]

Both right and bowhead whales were discovered to be abundant in the North Pacific. In 1835, the *Ganges* of Nantucket took the first right whale on the Kodiak hunting grounds and eight years later the *Hercules* and *Janus*, both of New Bedford, captured the first bowheads off Russia's Kamchatka Peninsula.

And on the ninth day of July (1821)
'Twas blowing mackerel gales.
Another shoal we then did raise
Of spermaceti whales.

-

And on the purlieus of the shoal,
We plainly did espy,
A noble seventy barrel whale
Spouting there did lie...

-

At three o'clock we had her dead;
To tow we did begin;
At five we had her safe longside,
Next day we cut her in.

Arctic cousin of the right whale, the bowhead, *Balaena mysticetus*, yielded more oil and baleen than any other. Although only slightly longer than the right, the bowhead was half again as heavy. Sheathed in a twenty inch blanket of blubber—necessary insulation in the frigid northern waters—a large bowhead might yield a few hundred barrels of oil. (The average sperm whale yield was seventy-five to ninety barrels.) In addition, three thousand pounds of baleen could be extracted from its hundreds of fourteen foot plates.

In July, 1848, the *Superior* of Sag Harbor was the first American whaler to pass through the Bering Strait and into the Arctic Ocean. During the following summer, the *Ocmulgee* of Martha's Vineyard took so many bowheads that her crew could not process the whales as fast as they were captured. Unboiled blubber filled the decks and more was rafted behind the ship. On July 25, 1849, the log records "Plenty of whales in sight, but all hands to busy to even look at them."[4]

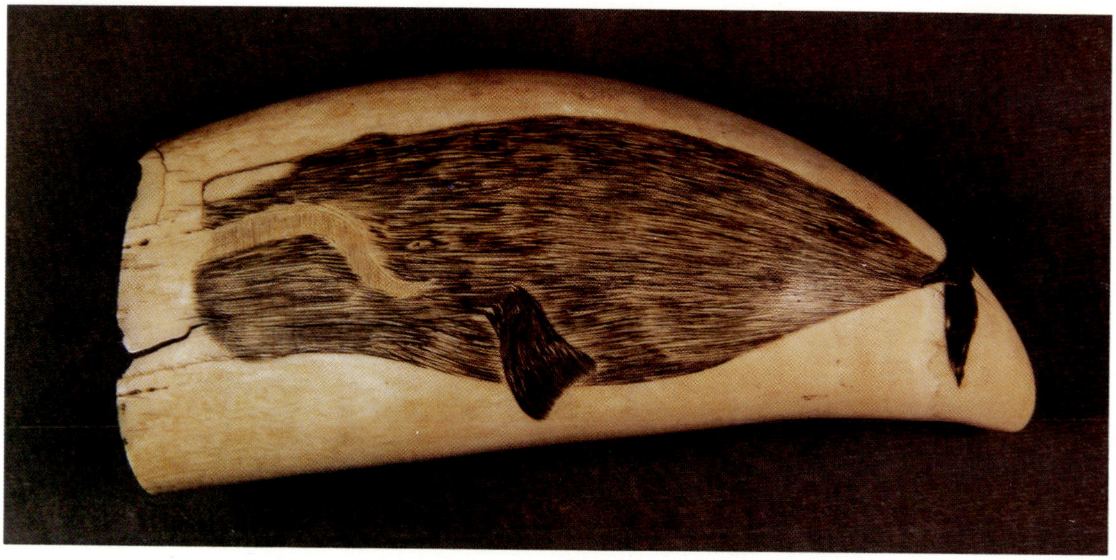

The hefty right whale boldly engraved on this tooth is a subject with which the average scrimshander would be most familiar. The engraved sperm whale illustrated on page 12 is found on the reverse of this tooth. *Courtesy of the Nantucket Historical Association*

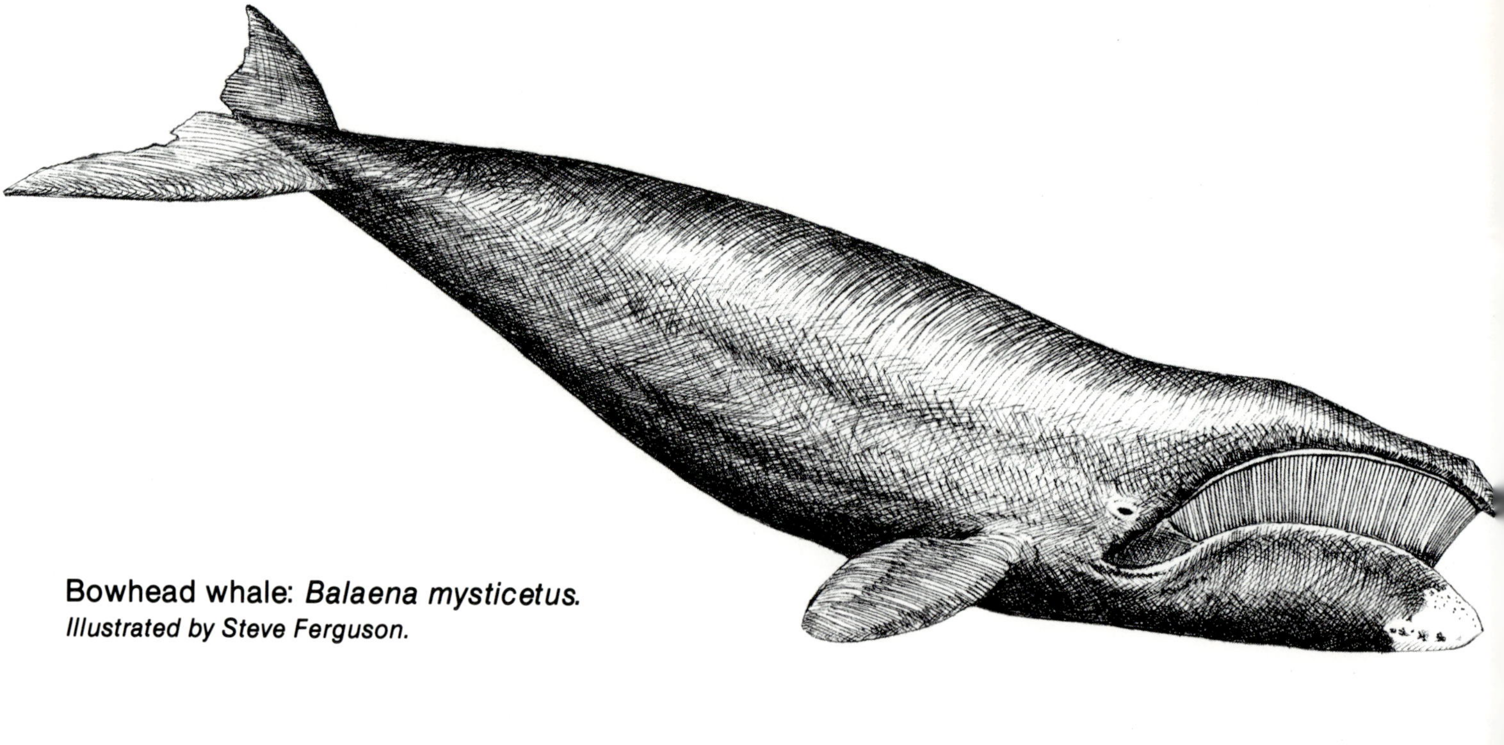

Bowhead whale: *Balaena mysticetus.*
Illustrated by Steve Ferguson.

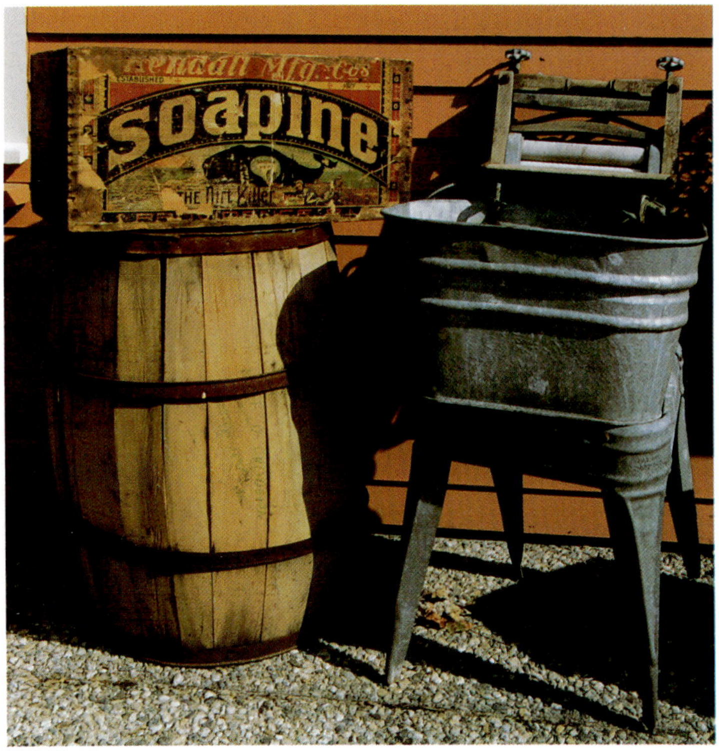

Demand for whale oil products such as the Kendall Company's "Soapine" insured work for the hundreds of whalers around the world.

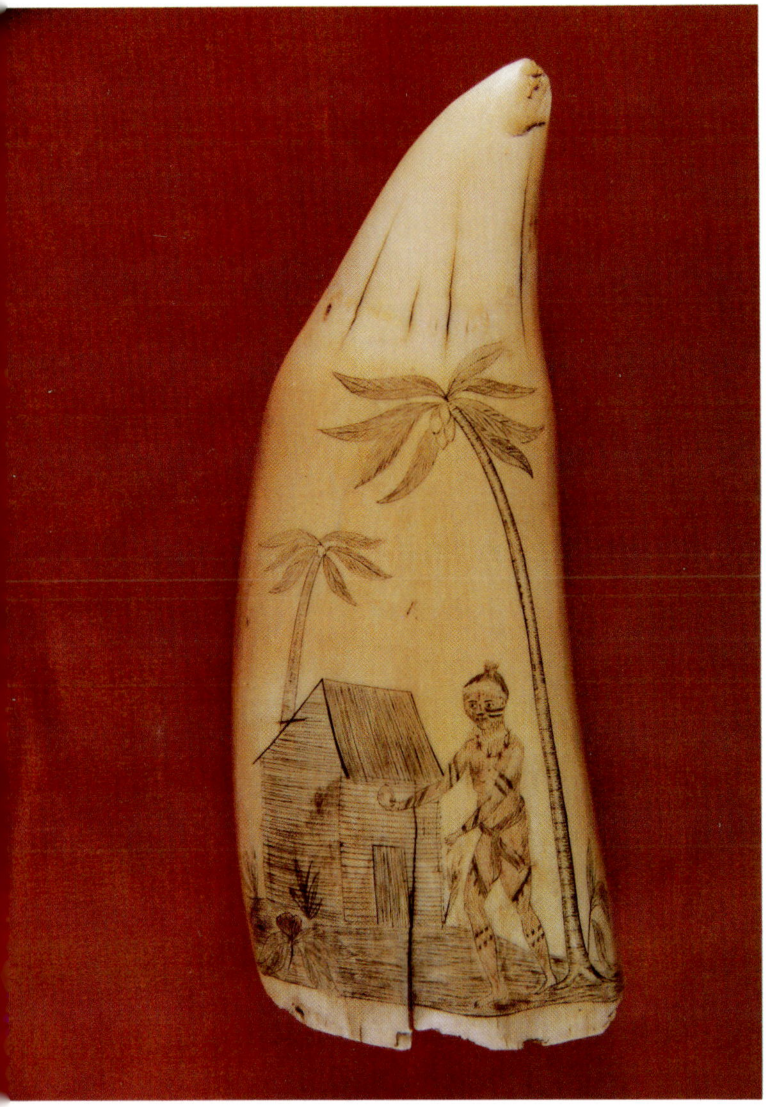

Longer voyages gave artistic seamen the opportunity to record exotic sights such as this gourd-bearing native of a tropical island. *Private Collection*

Voyages commonly lasted from three to over four years as whalers travelled to the Bering Sea and Arctic Ocean in summer and the South Pacific and Indian Oceans in winter. The size of the United States whaling fleet peaked in 1846 with seven hundred and thirty-five vessels. At a given moment twenty thousand men could be found engaged in the business of hunting whales. Each year millions of dollars of sperm oil, spermaceti, whale oil, and baleen were brought back to New England by Yankee whalers. While deploring the slaughter of countless thousands of whales during these years, *Men and Whales* author Richard Ellis gives a sense of the powerful economic motivation for nineteenth century whaling by likening it to the prominence of the petroleum and plastics industries today.[5]

The decline of whaling was more precipitous than its growth. During the Civil War, many Yankee whalers fell prey to Confederate war ships; and, although whaling continued after the war, the number of vessels engaged was greatly reduced. The rising production of relatively inexpensive petroleum, or "earth oil," lessened the demand for sperm oil. Although the market for baleen remained strong, the Arctic fleet was decimated in 1871 when thirty-four vessels were trapped and crushed by ice off Point Belcher.

In the last quarter of the nineteenth century, whales had become scarce and the average whaler required more months to fill its hold. Longer voyages involved greater outfitting costs for ship owners, produced fewer profits and foretold the death of New England whaling. By the 1880s, New Bedford had been replaced by San Francisco as whaling's busiest port due to its easy access to the Arctic whaling grounds. Although the last square-rigged whaler did not leave New Bedford until 1924, the economic miracle which had sustained northeast ports for over a century had come to an end.

After Nantucket's last whaler, the *Eunice Adams* returned to port, Obed Macy's grandson William painted a haunting portrait of an industry's demise: "In l870, Nantucket had not a ship, bark, (or) brig...suggestive of the vast amount of business done in the past. In place of the busy click of the caulker's hammer, as it sent its echo from one wharf to another, naught could be heard but the lick of the wave, as it washed, and washed again, the ruins of piers which once groaned beneath the weight of millions of wealth."[6]

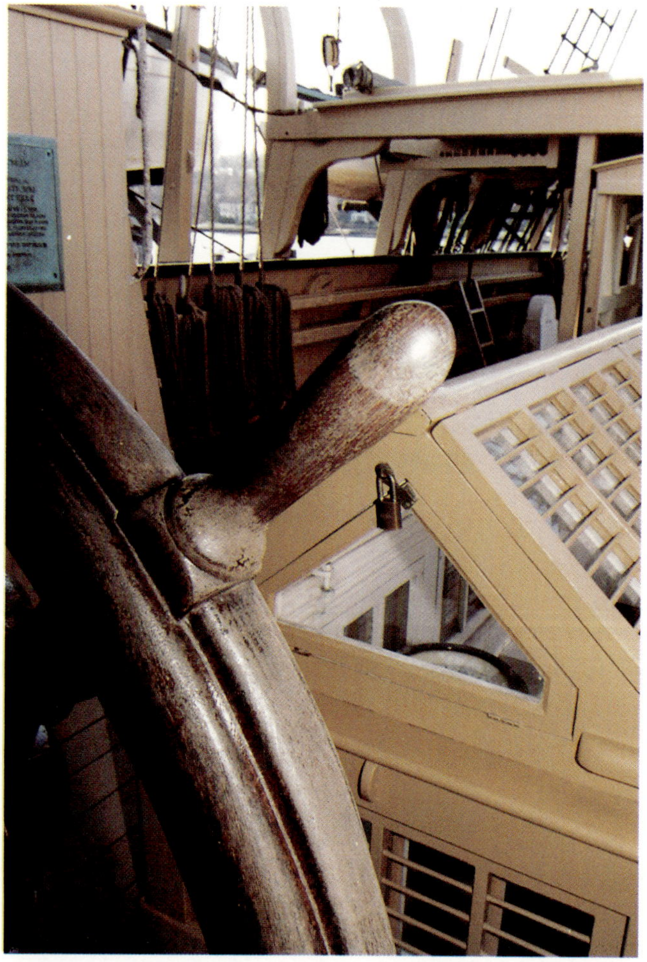

View from the helm of the *Charles W. Morgan. Courtesy of the Mystic Seaport Museum.*

01 Alexander Starbuck, *History of the American Whale Fishery* (Secaucus, N.J.: Castle Books, 1989), 97.

02 Clare Barnes, Jr., *John F. Kennedy, Scrimshaw Collector* (Boston: Little Brown and Company, 1964), 50.

03 Mary C. Lawrence, *The Captain's Best Mate* (Providence, R.I.: Brown University Press, 1966), 67.

04 Arthur C. Watson, *The Long Harpoon* (New Bedford: George H. Reynolds, 1929), 49.

05 Richard Ellis, *Men and Whales* (New York: Alfred A. Knopf, 1991), 55.

06 Obed Macy, *The History of Nantucket* (Mansfield, Mass.: Macy and Pratt, 1880), 301.

In eighteen hundred twenty-two
'Twas on the New Year's day,
A large sperm whale we did espy
To the leeward of us lay...

-

That served to cheer our spirits up,
In hopes that through the year
Good luck would still continue on
And better days appear.

3. The Men who Hunted Whales

The whalemen who ventured into uncharted waters of the world faced incredible danger, back-breaking work, aching loneliness and often killing boredom as they built this nineteenth century industry of international importance and repute. The large whaling community, thousands of miles from home for years at a time formed a unique and closed society that provided not only the conditions necessary for the birth of scrimshaw, but also the setting in which it could develop and flourish in isolation. This strange assortment of men, representing a wide variety of national and social backgrounds, shared a common occupational language, rigorous working and living conditions, a surplus of free time and the desire for a creative manner in which to fill it. All these elements contributed to and were incorporated into the art of scrimshaw.

Home for whalemen was a sturdy, bluff, often unattractively styled vessel ranging between one hundred and one hundred and fifty feet in length. Usually square-rigged as either a ship or bark, she was not designed to comfortably house human beings but soley to hunt whales, boil blubber and store as much oil as possible. Built with the strength and endurance necessary to weather Pacific gales or Arctic ice, the whaler was in fact a floating factory and warehouse.

'Twas on the thirteenth day of March,
Quite early in the morn,
The island of Maui ahead
We plainly did discern...

-

And now our decks with girls were filled
Of every sort and kind,
And every man bought shells and beads,
The best that he could fine.

-

Our sails were furled, our good ship moored,
And everything put to rights.
Two weeks we here at anchor lay,
And cruised on shore of nights.

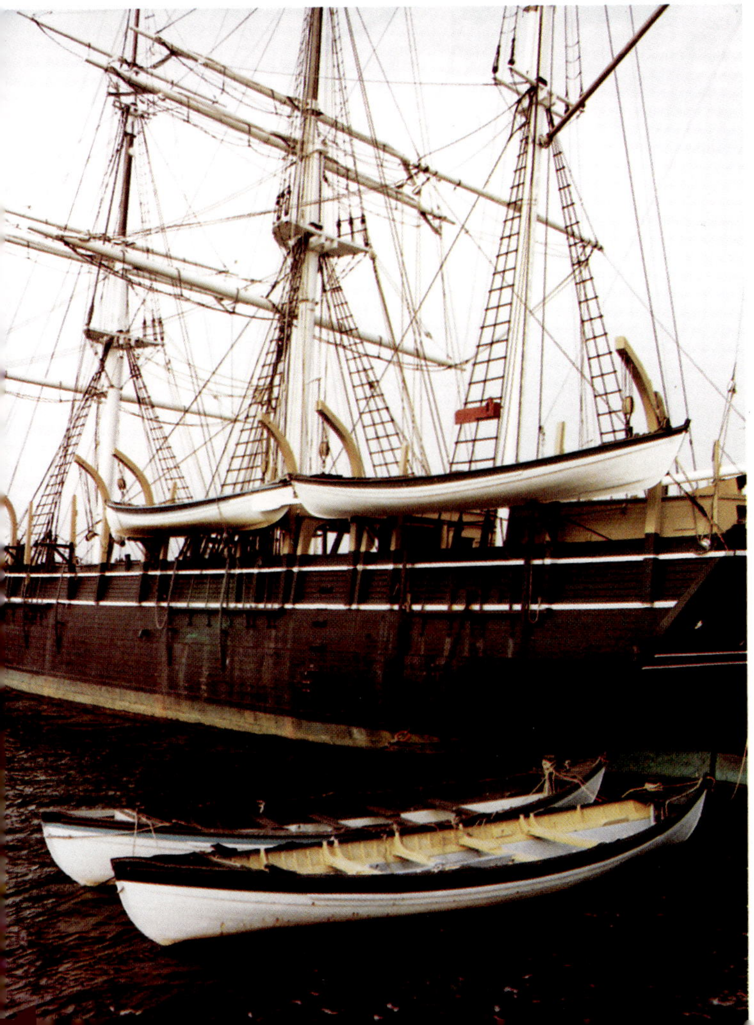

Whalers such as the *Charles W. Morgan* were home to seamen for voyages lasting three to five years. The actual whale hunt was conducted from the double-ended whaleboats carried by each ship. *Courtesy of the Mystic Seaport Museum*

The life of a common sailor aboard a whaler was not one aspired to by many seamen. In Frank Bullen's *Cruise of the "Cachalot"*, he related how he signed his seaman's articles in New Bedford, unaware of the type of ship in which he was sailing. He described his unhappy surprise the following morning. "As we passed under her stern, I read the name *Cachalot*, of New Bedford; but as soon as we ranged alongside, I realized that I was booked for the sailor's horror—a cruise in a whaler."[1]

Rather than the wages common to the merchant service, each man was assigned a "lay," a percentage of the voyage's eventual profit. Although the portion of the lay diminished with rank, the system theoretically served to increase the spirit of joint endeavor. In reality however, by the end of a long whaling voyage, the per diem remuneration was negligible at best; and in some instances the men owed money for purchases such as clothing or tobacco from the ship's "slop chest."

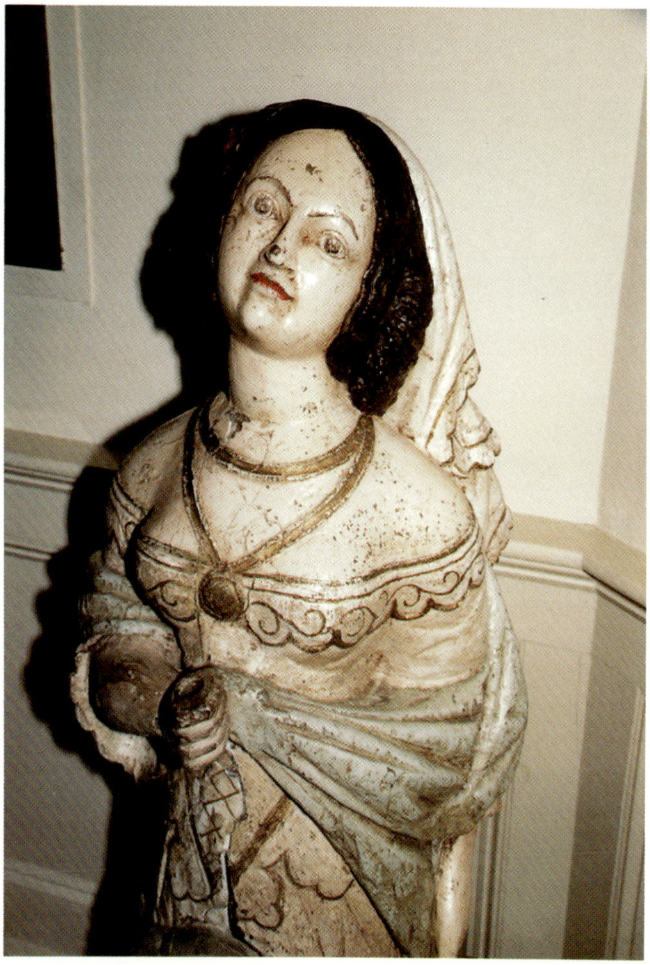

Simple, scrolled billetheads or small, discreet busts of wives and daughters were more common aboard whaling vessels than full-sized figureheads, perhaps because of Quaker ship-owners' disdain for excessive ornamentation. An exception to that generality is this lovely figurehead from the whaler *Lydia* which sailed from Nantucket in 1840 under the command of Captain George Cathcart. Presently exhibited at the Nantucket Whaling Museum, *Lydia* is on loan from the Mystic Seaport Museum. *Courtesy of the Nantucket Historical Association*

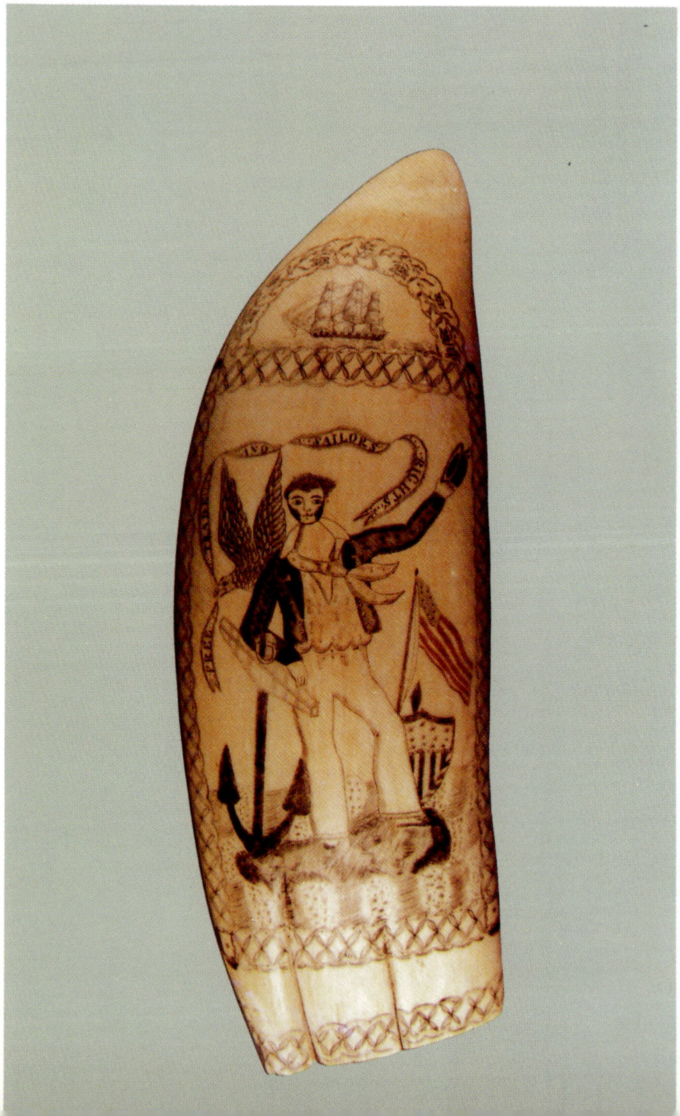

The young sailor on this tooth was created by the *Ceres* artisan, a scrimshander to whom a body of work has been ascribed based on stylistic similarities. The work of this anonymous artist is believed to have been executed on the *Ceres* of Wilmington, Delaware in the mid-1830s. Patriotic symbols, as well as references to free trade and sailors' rights, were common themes of pictorial scrimshaw. *Courtesy of the Nantucket Historical Association.*

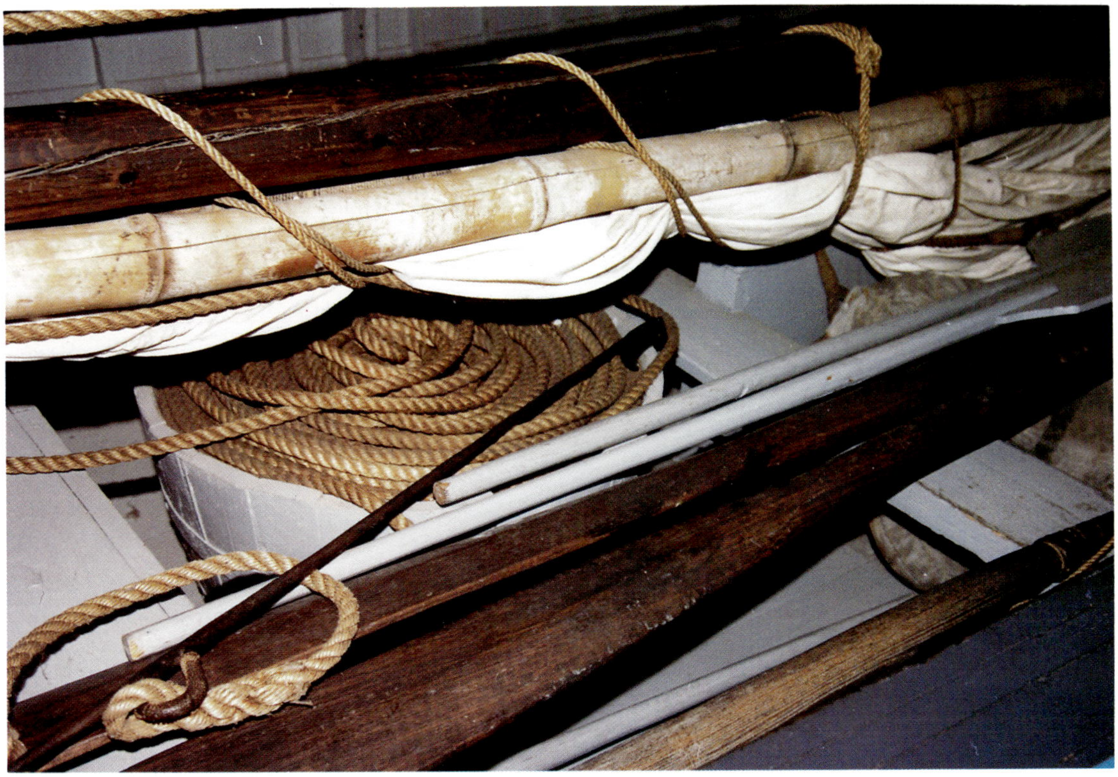

Thousands of feet of line coiled in tubs would pay out in seconds once the whale was harpooned. *Courtesy of the Nantucket Historical Association*

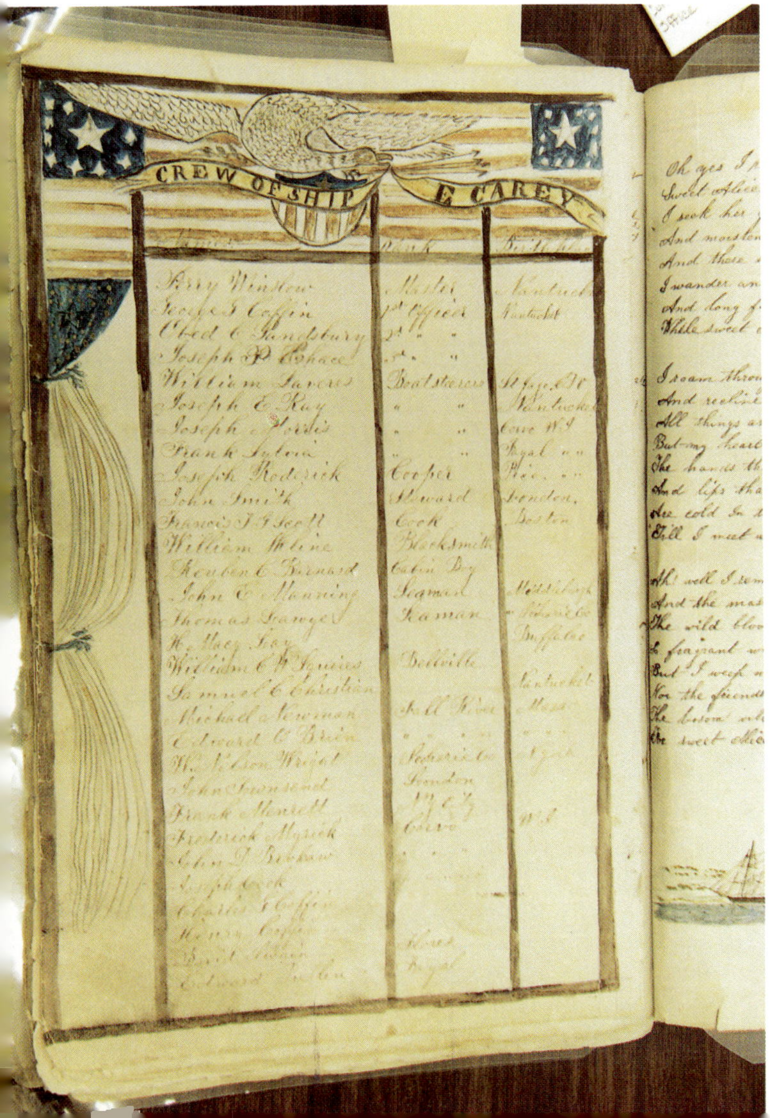

And for the Japan coast we steered
Expecting there to find
The bosom of the briny deep
With spermacetis lined...

-

Same day while running before the wind,
About the hour of two,
We plain discovered, right, ahead,
The island of Oahu...

In his illustrated log, Joseph Ray listed the names of the men who sailed aboard the *Edward Cary* in May, 1854. *Courtesy of the Nantucket Historical Association*

In the narrative of his voyage as harpooner aboard the *Charles W. Morgan*, Nelson Cole Haley described three harrowing days engaged in the capture and cutting-in of a whale in unusually heavy winds and seas. After the extraordinarily difficult and dangerous task was completed, he wryly commented:

> The whale, when tried out, made about thirty-five barrels. The share of each green hand out of that would be about five dollars; a rather slow way to get rich. Still, when we take into consideration the Glory attached to a whaleman's life, one perhaps ought to be happy. One should not want the whole world.[2]

However, as promotion could be relatively rapid aboard a whaler, many young men who shipped as greenhands did so planning to eventually attain the rank of mate or even master. Illnesses and accidents often created unforseen openings for new harpooners or boatsteerers. Opportunity and advancement were predicated on skill and perseverance rather than background or color, and the whaler provided a place of opportunity not found as easily on other ships or in society at large. Thus, a smart and dedicated young greenhand who chose to make a life for himself aboard a whaler could anticipate progress through the ranks. Captain Edmund Gardner, who was master of his own ship at age 22, wrote of this sort of purpose:

> I...was born and lived at Nantucket until sixteen years. It was a Commercial place and most of the young men looked towards a seafaring life. I had imbibed the idea of commanding a ship, it was on my mind a polar star for direction, during my early voyages, (I) did all in my power to gain preferment.[3]

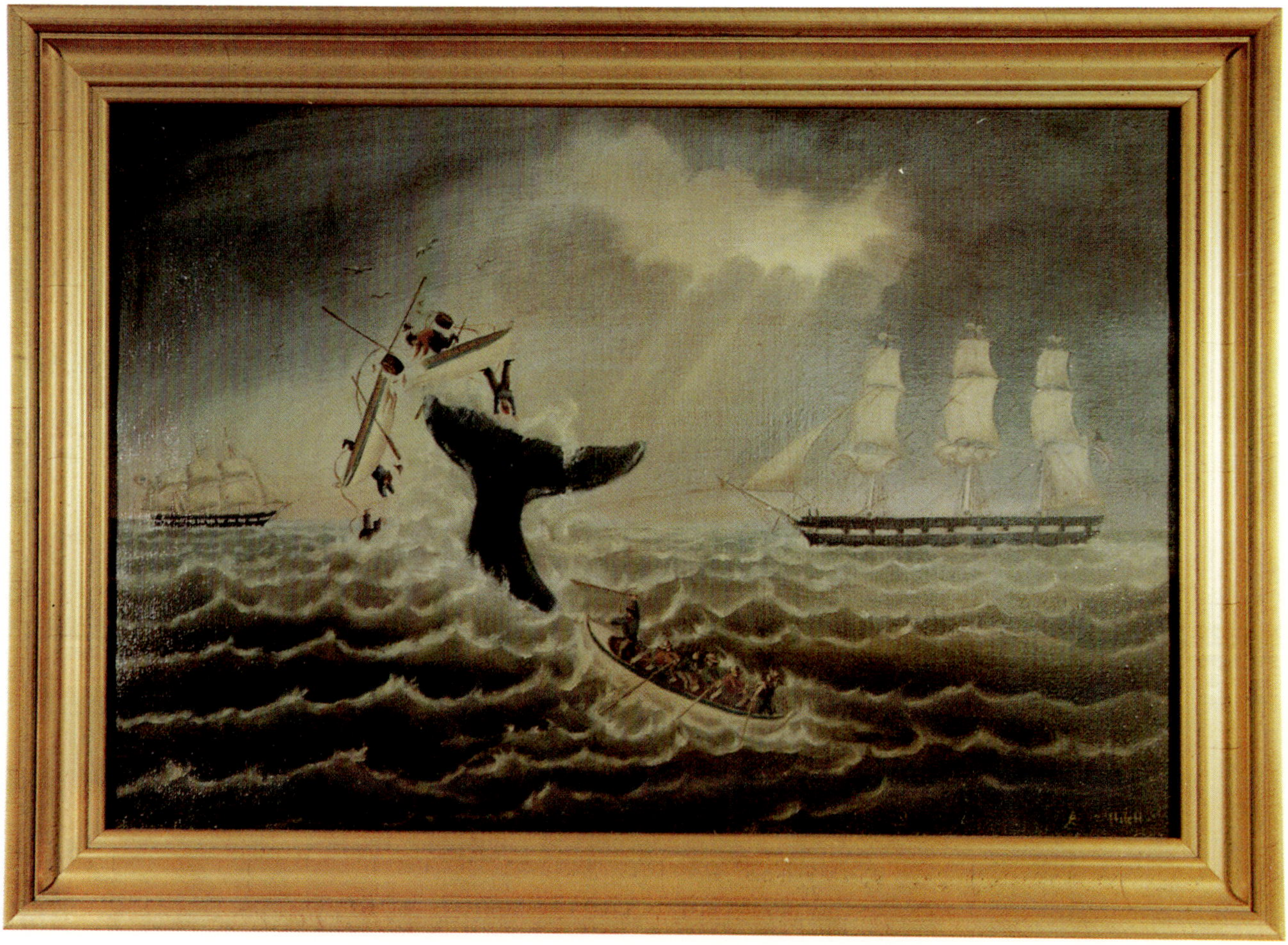

The lash of a sperm whale's tail could create tragedy for some and job opportunity for others. *Private Collection*

Responsible for his crew, the ship and the ship owners' profits, the captain's mission was to be daring enough to secure a profitable cargo of oil while simultaneously protecting crew and ship. The locations where he performed these duties—frigid waters studded with ice floes or tropical islands surrounded by jagged reefs—made his job a challenge. Captain Samuel Lawrence's wife, Mary, commented in her journal entry of April 4, 1858, "This trouble with the absence of whales wears upon Samuel. He grows thin and has lost his appetite, but it may be that all will turn out right in the end."[4]

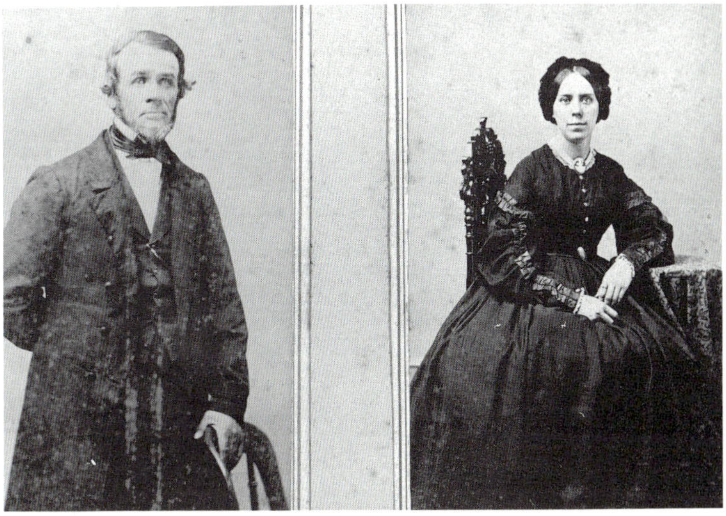

Captain Samuel Lawrence and his wife Mary. *Courtesy of the Falmouth Historical Society.*

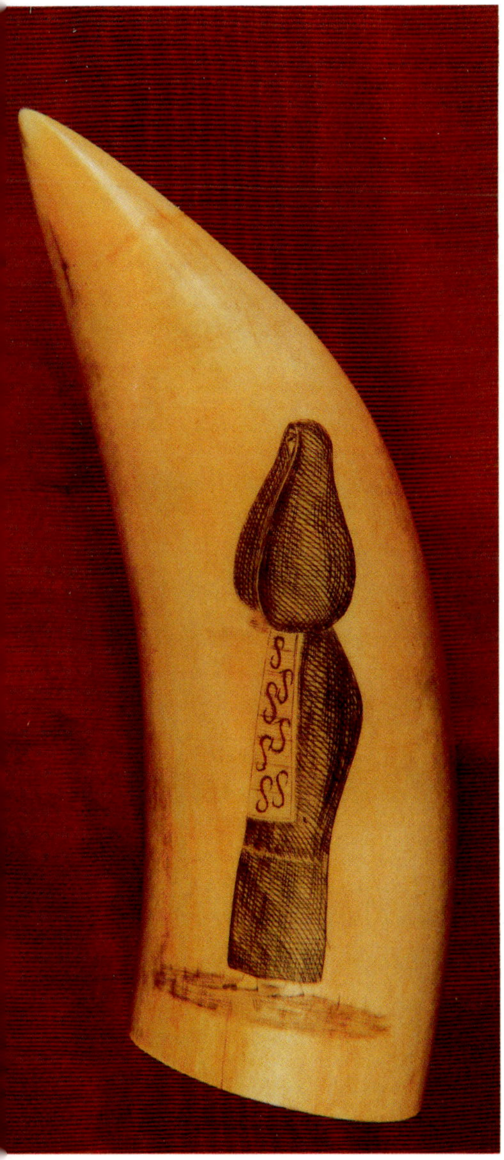

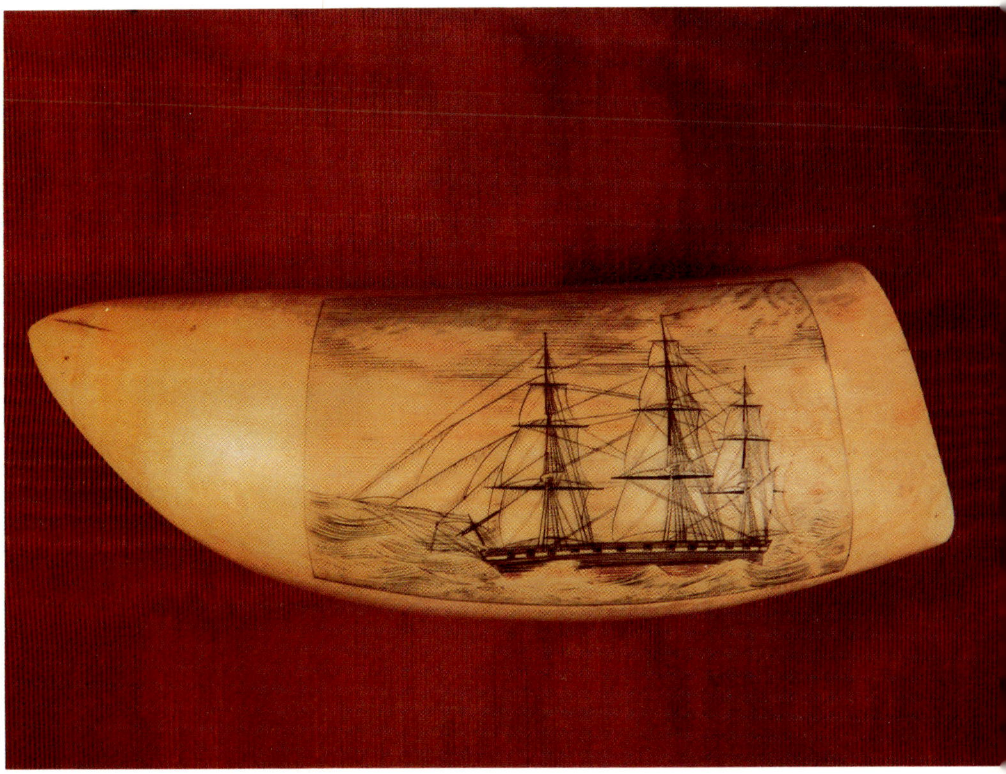

Before sailing on the *Addison*, Samuel Lawrence was master of the *Lafayette* of New Bedford. On this voyage, which began in 1847, he engraved this sperm whale's tooth with renderings of both the *Lafayette* and a woman in native Azorian dress. Unfortunately, the *Lafayette* was wrecked on the Galapagos Islands in 1850 and Captain Lawrence did not secure another position as master until the *Addison* sailed in 1856. *Collection of Raymond and Elizabeth De Lucia*

Directly below the captain in rank were three mates who each commanded one of the whaleboats during the hunt and three to five boatsteerers. (During the hunt, the boatsteerer actually stood in the bow and harpooned the whale but later took the helm of the whaleboat from the ranking officer, thus receiving his confusing name.) Other specialized personnel were the cooper, carpenter, cook and steward.

Below decks, situated around the mizzen mast, were the officers' dining quarters. Opening onto this area were the cabins of the mates and captain. The first mate shared his cabin with only a small writing desk where he was responsible for keeping the ship's log. Forward of the mates' cabins was steerage, in which the boatsteerers and craftsmen were berthed three or four to a cabin. Officers' cabins and steerage occasionally boasted small portholes, but more commonly the only light was that which weakly filtered through glass prisms mounted on the deck above.

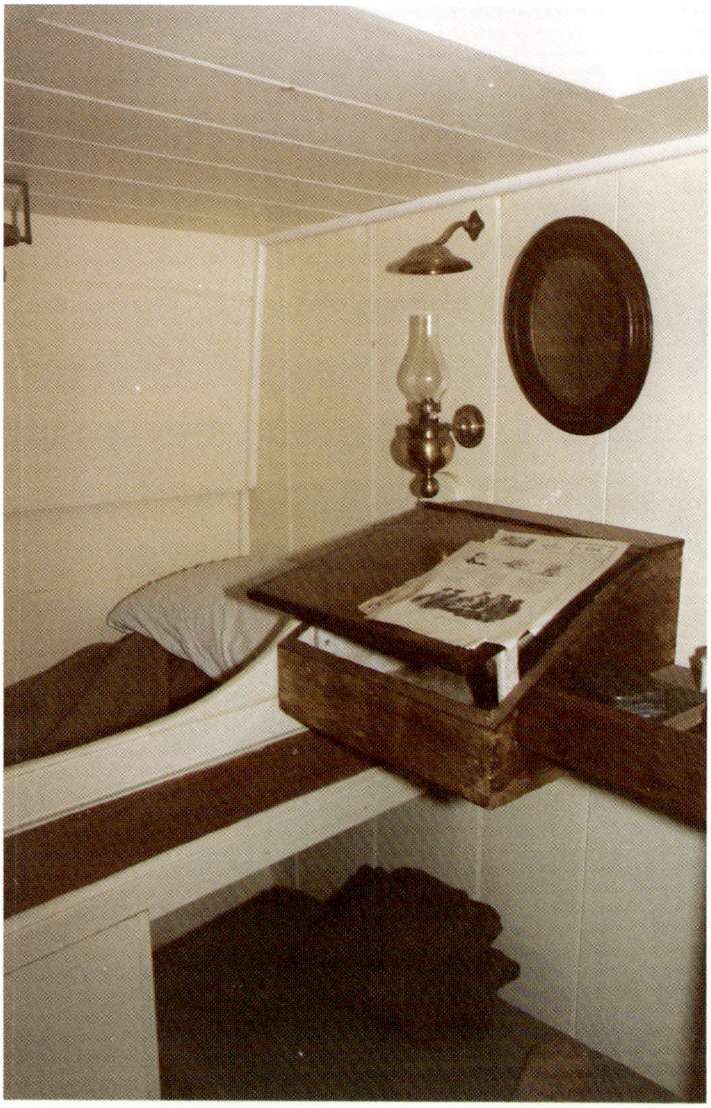

The first mate's cabin aboard the *Charles W. Morgan* included a desk where he could record daily information in the ship's log. *Courtesy of the Mystic Seaport Museum*

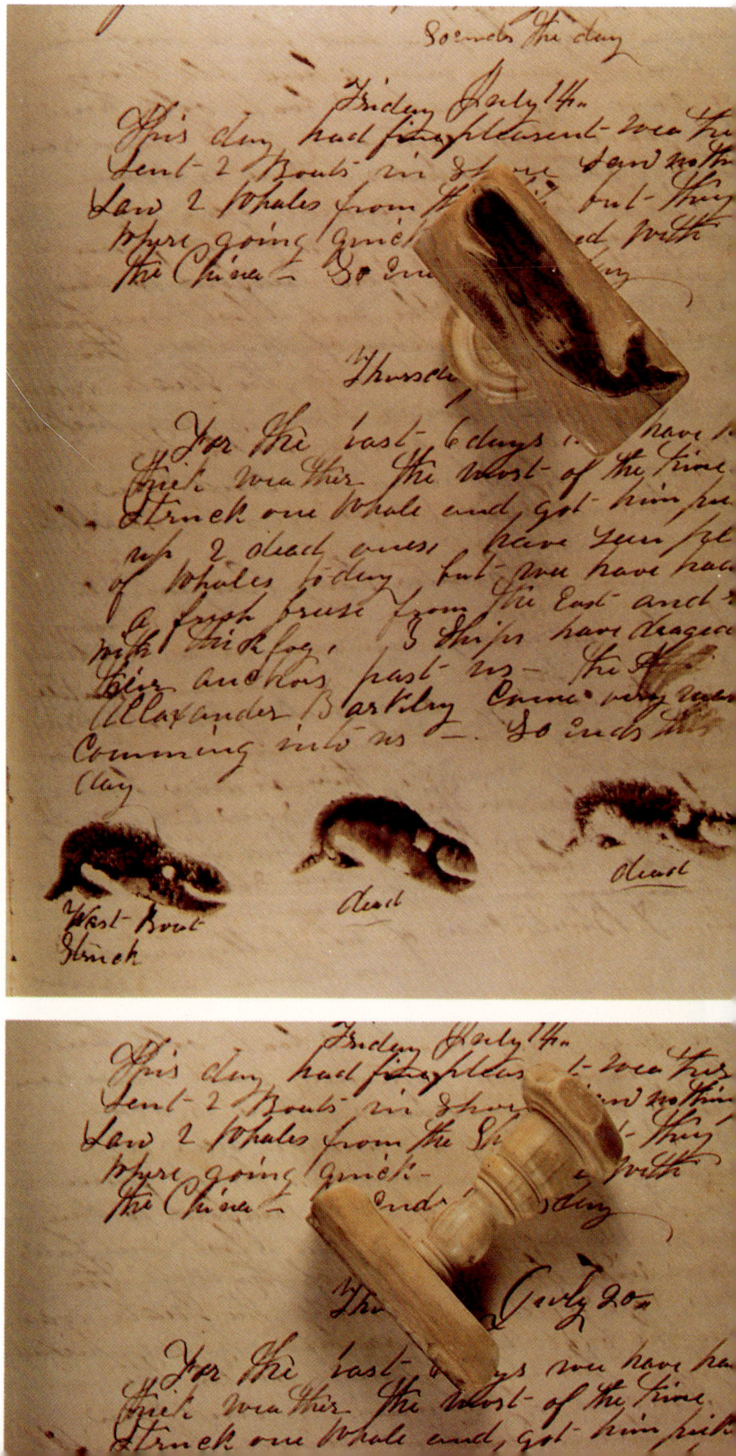

The log recorded not only location and weather conditions, but also any sightings or captures of whales. Stamps such as this whalebone example were used to indicate the presence of whales. *Collection of Raymond and Elizabeth De Lucia.*

A whaler required approximately twice as many men as a comparably sized merchant ship. Twenty-five to thirty men were needed not only to man the three to five whaleboats carried by each ship, but also to perform the many hours of labor necessary to transform the captured whales into hundreds of barrels of oil. The crew of a merchant vessel were constantly scrambling up and down the rigging to ensure that sails were set for the greatest possible speed. Once the whaling grounds were reached by a whaleship, however, she cruised about slowly, scanning the area for whales, the men unconcerned with the fine points of sail management so important to their brothers in the merchant service.

Yet the first weeks of a voyage were busy ones for the "greenhands" who were adjusting to the reality of the long separation from families; seasickness; bad food; the cramped, malodorous foc'sle that was now home and the sadistic manner in which they were often introduced to their new tasks. They were expected to master these new skills quickly. "Learning the ropes" involved activities such as climbing a hundred feet to the swaying royal yard to adjust a sail or act as lookout. In addition, it was imperative to develop the abilities necessary to handle the whaleboats and equipment with which the crew would be expected to successfully capture the whale. Shortly after leaving port, drills were conducted in the whaleboats to simulate the chase and capture of a whale.

All this preparation was geared toward one main purpose—the hunt. When the cry "Thar Blows" was heard from the mainmast, every man aboard must know his duties and execute them with utmost skill. Otherwise, failure in the hunt or death of a crew member could be the result.

The procedure for pursuit and capture was well established. After the sighting, the sloop-rigged whaleboats were quickly lowered. They carried oars, paddles, harpoons, lances, sails and a half mile of manila line carefully coiled in tubs. The boat's mast could be quickly dismantled when the whales were neared, leaving the six man crew to row or more quietly paddle the remaining distance.

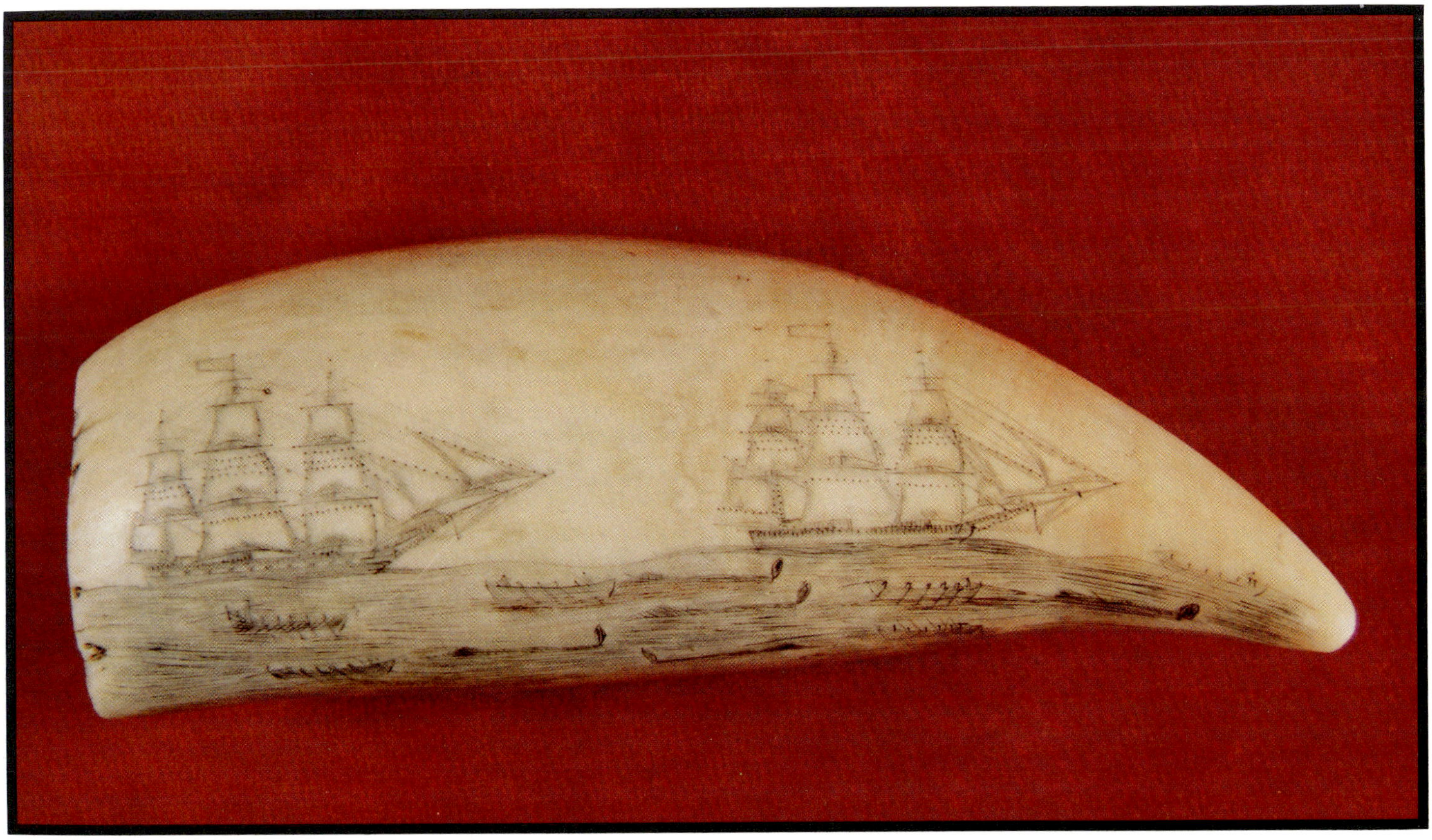

A scrimshander's depiction of a classic hunt scene.
Private Collection

The whales did not make it easy for their hunters to reach them, however. They often took off to windward precluding the use of sail and necessitating hours of rowing. In *The Yankee Whaler,* Clifford Ashley described one such afternoon:

> For four hours or more we tugged at the oars....our throats were parched our hands were bleeding.....Suddenly from somewhere back of us came a faint sonorous whistle. I twisted my neck, and caught a glimpse of a dark mass cleaving the water a hundred fathoms ahead. Our oars bent like reeds, the boat leaped ahead like an animal under the lash....Again the whale spouted...that long-drawn whistling exhaust; and the humid vapor escaping from the pent-up lungs drifted like a mist over the boat, and we felt on our necks its dampness. The rankness of it was still in our nostrils, when there was a swirl and a rush, and the huge monster breached clear of the sea, and with mighty flukes tossed high, for an instant was silhouetted against the yellow of the afternoon sky; then with a deafening roar of displaced waters, disappeared beneath the surface.[5]

Perhaps because his crew was already engaged in cutting in, boatsteerer Joseph Ray, unlike Ashley, was able to avoid a lengthy row to windward when whales were sighted from the *Edward Cary:*

> First Part Employed cutting in and clearing decks. Latter Part started fires. Saw whales again but did not lower. Whales going quickly to windward.[6]

After reaching the whale, the boat approached quietly from the rear, out of the whale's lateral line of vision. A swift throw by the harpooner made the whale fast to the boat. At the cry "stern all," the men hastily manuevered the double-ended boat backwards to escape the fury of the whale's lashing tail. It was not uncommon for a wounded sperm whale to turn on his attackers, dashing a whaleboat to pieces with his powerful flukes or rising from the depths to lift the boat out of the water, capsizing it and leaving the men to the mercies of the waves:

> Rolling over on his back, with head out of the water, he lashes out with his jaw, snapping and chewing to splinters everything within his reach.[7]

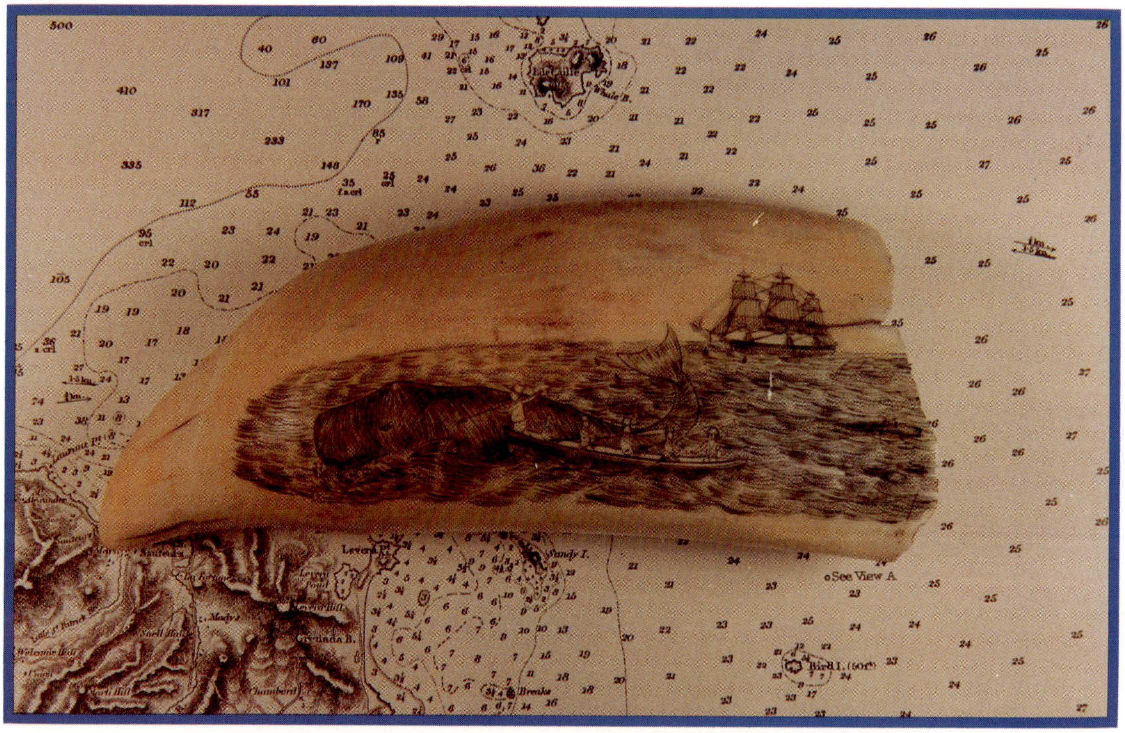

Approaching from the rear of the whale, the boatsteerer, knee braced in the whaleboat's clumsy cleat, prepares to harpoon his prey. (The reverse of this tooth is illustrated on page 27.) *Private Collection.*

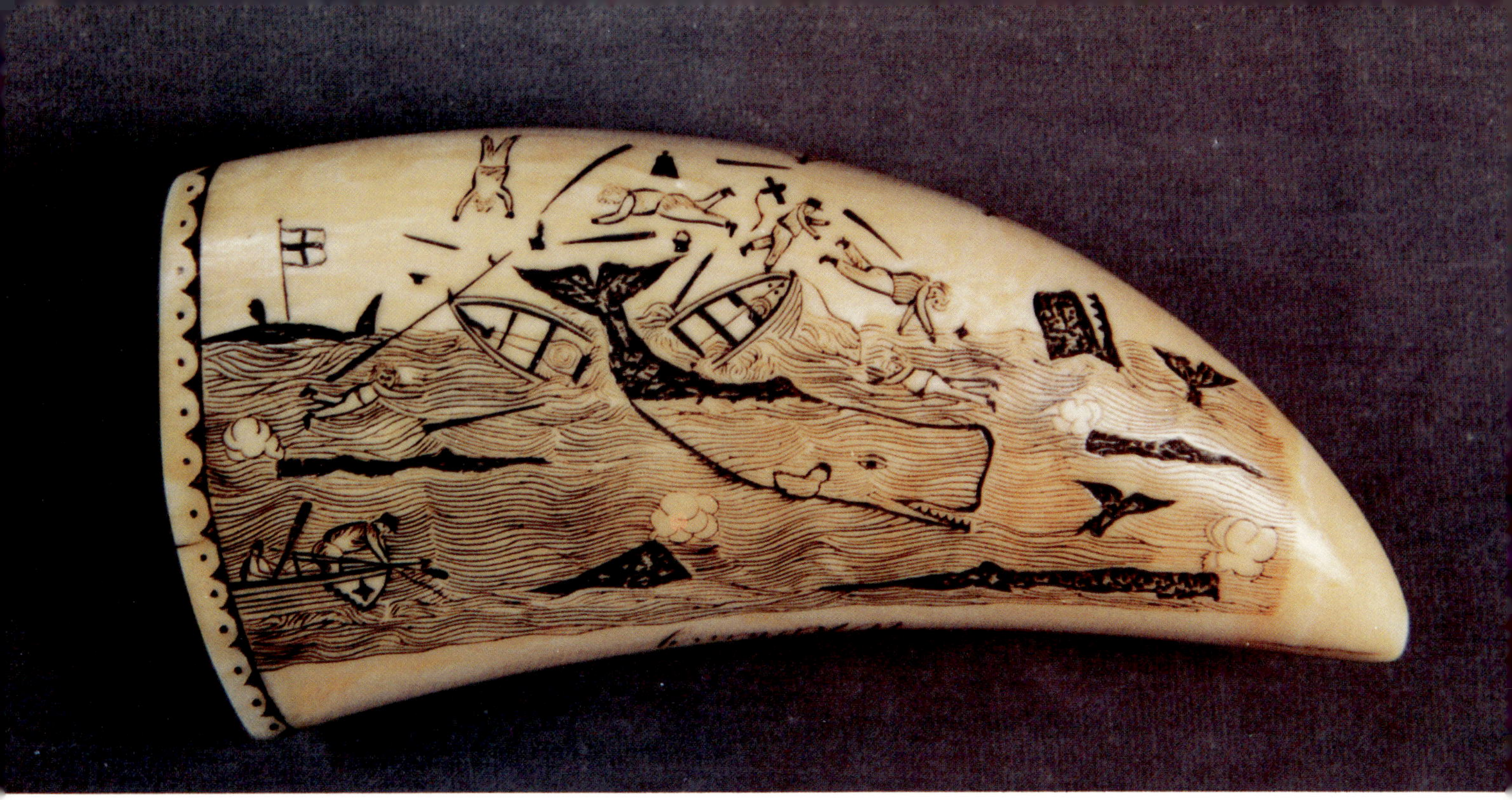

The action-filled scene engraved on this tooth attributed to Edward Burdett is wonderfully rendered and accurately detailed. The whale floating in the upper left of the scene, marked by a flag, was said to be "waifed." The flag marked his location so that he might be recovered when the hunt was ended. If other whaling ships were engaged in the same location, the ship's flag provided proof of ownership. (The reverse of this tooth portrays the *Charles* of London and is illustrated in the Introduction.) It is especially ironic that Burdett who could so expertly render the danger inherent in the chase was himself killed in 1833 on a voyage as first mate aboard the ship *Montano* of Nantucket. During a hunt, the twenty-eight year old whaleman/artist was caught in the harpoon line, dragged from the boat and drowned. *Madden Collection*

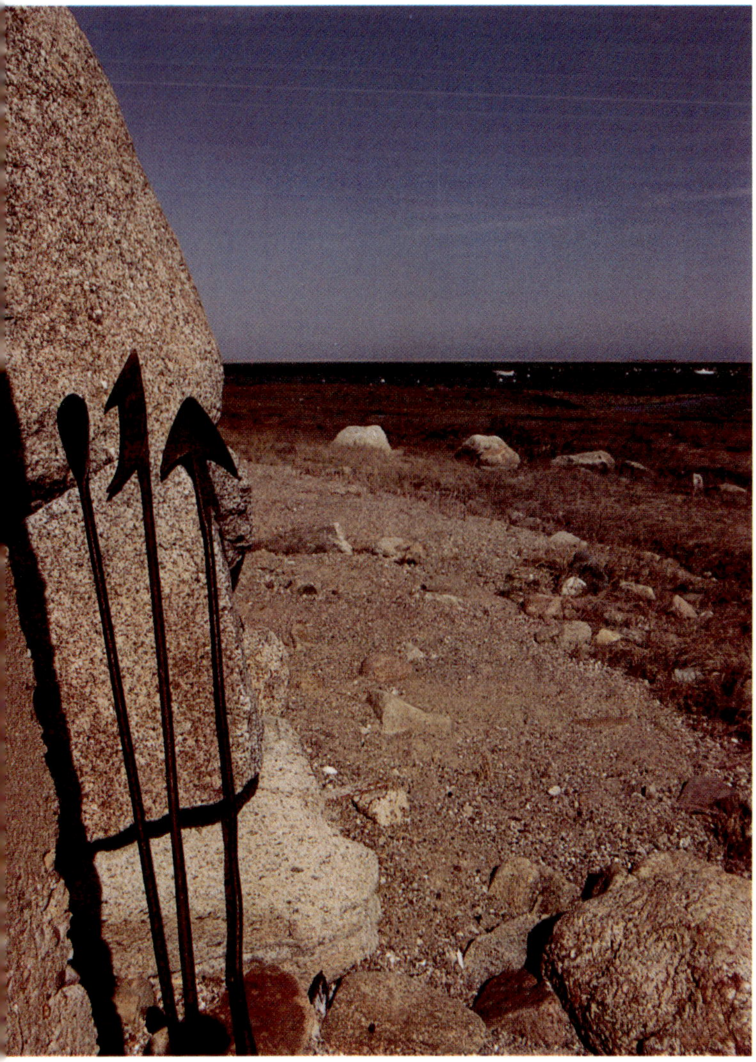

The graceful damsels from the shore,
As soon as we were moored,
Came paddling off in their canoes,
While others swam aboard.

-

For here 'tis the same as at Maui,
The women are all for trade;
Calicoes, rings and scrimshaun work
Are sought by every maid.

Their working days long past, a lance, toggle harpoon and two-flued harpoon rest on an Atlantic shore. *Private Collection*

On rare occasions, the whaleship itself was attacked by an angry whale. In the Pacific on the morning of August 21, 1851, the *Ann Alexander* of New Bedford lowered three boats to pursue a large sperm whale. One of the boats successfully harpooned the whale, however the injured animal turned, crushed one whaleboat in its jaws, then rammed and sank a second. The two boat crews were rescued from the water by the third whaleboat, and all eighteen slowly made their way back to the mother ship.

Angered by the loss of two boats and the injuries to his men, Captain John Deblois decided to pursue the whale in the *Ann Alexander* herself. When the ship reached her prey, the captain unsuccessfully tried to lance the whale which proceeded to furiously turn and ram the ship, opening a huge hole in her side. Within minutes the crew abandoned the sinking *Ann Alexander* in the two remaining whale boats. Very fortunately, all were picked up the next day by another whaler cruising, by chance, in the same area.

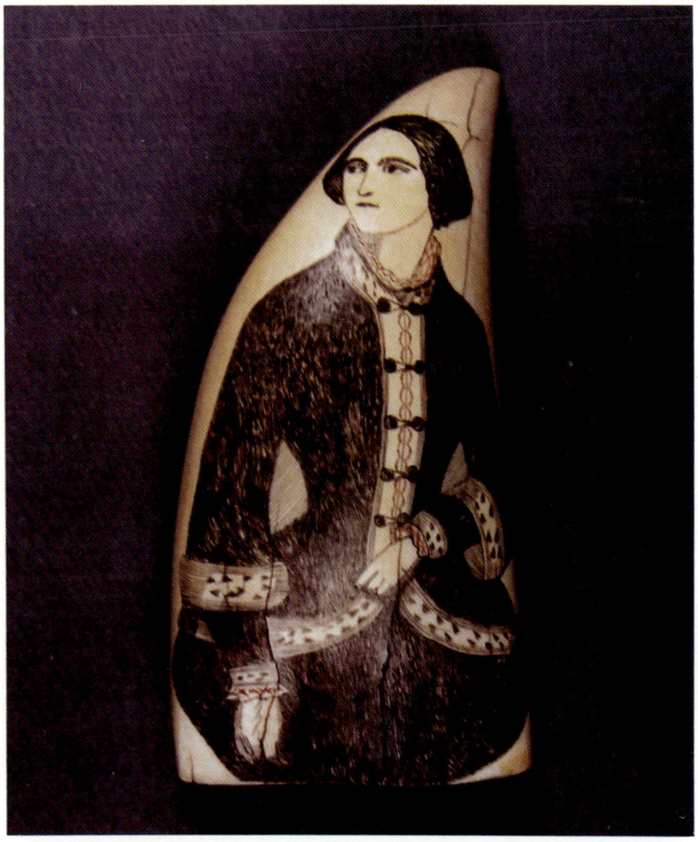

One of the three teeth from the *Ann Alexander* whale presented to Captain John DeBlois. *Courtesy of the Nantucket Historical Association*

For Captain Deblois, however, the story was not ended. Five months later the *Rebecca Simms* captured a large bull sperm whale a few miles from the site of the *Ann Alexander* sinking. The ship's captain, William Jernegan, found timbers embedded in the whale's broad head as well as a harpoon in its body marked "*Ann Alexander*." Captain Jernegan had three of the whale's teeth engraved with portraits of Victorian women and later gave them to Captain Deblois as a memento of his encounter. The teeth today are in the Nantucket Whaling Museum, a testimony to the unhappy fate of the *Ann Alexander*.[8]

More often than attacking either the ship or the whaleboats, however, the frightened whale tried to escape, ensuring a wild "Nantucket sleigh-ride" for the whaleboat's crew, often towing them out of sight of the mother ship:

> A jerk pitched those unprepared in a heap to the bottom....Then we were off with the speed of an express train, with the water pouring in a sheet over our bows...till the last of us was drenched to the skin. Writhing and squirming from (the) tub...the line whistled and tore, sometimes with a rumble like the roll of drums, sometimes with the wailing shriek of a siren....We tore in an arrow-like flight due westward, till the ship disappeared in the distance.[9]

When the whale finally tired, it was reached by arduously pulling in and coiling the thousands of feet of released line. The boat cautiously pulled up to the wounded animal, so close that its sides brushed the barnacled skin. The ranking officer, who had taken the place of the harpooner, now boatsteerer, in the bow, would then deliver the fatal blow with a long lance.

Successful though they were, work for the six men had only begun. If the whaleboat was in sight of and downwind from the mother ship, the ship could make her way toward the boat. More often, however, the rendevous involved another long hard row, retracing the miles they had been towed, perhaps in the dark of night or the impenetrable mist of an Arctic fog. In addition to the fifteen hundred pounds of boat and equipment, the oarsmen had the dead weight of their huge prize to manage. Sperm whales averaged one ton of weight for each foot of length. Bowheads and rights were

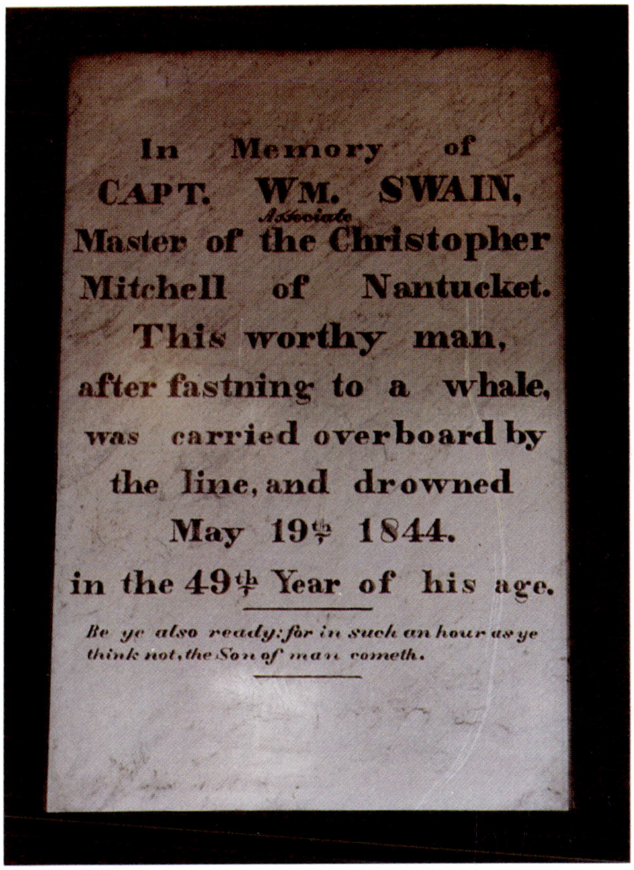

A cenotaph in New Bedford's Seamen's Bethel marks the all-too-common fate of many a whaleman. In *Moby Dick*, Herman Melville wrote of the chapel, "It needs scarcely to be told with what feelings, on the eve of a Nantucket voyage, I regard those marble tablets, and by the murky light of that darkened, doleful day read the fate of whalemen who had gone before me." *Courtesy of the New Bedford Port Society*

heavier.[10] Not surprisingly, whalemen had a low opinion of this duty:

> I have often felt so desirous of obtaining a whale, that I have pulled at the oar until I could not see; and yet the moment after the whale was dead, I would have rejoiced to see him sink, that I might not be obliged to perform the labor of taking care of him.[11]

> Of all the clumsy things to tow with boats, a sperm whale is about the worst....To dip your oar about three times in the same hole from whence you withdrew it, to tug at it with all your might, apparently making as much progress as though you were fast to a dock wall, and to continue this fun for four or five hours at a stretch, is to wonder indeed whether you have not mistaken your vocation.[12]

After the hunt, the crew could look forward to more days of arduous, dirty work. The job of harvesting the oil began as crewmembers, precariously perched on the narrow, "cutting-in" stage, cut and stripped the thick blubber from the carcass, which floated alongside the ship. In *Incidents of a Whaling Voyage*, Francis Olmstead observed:

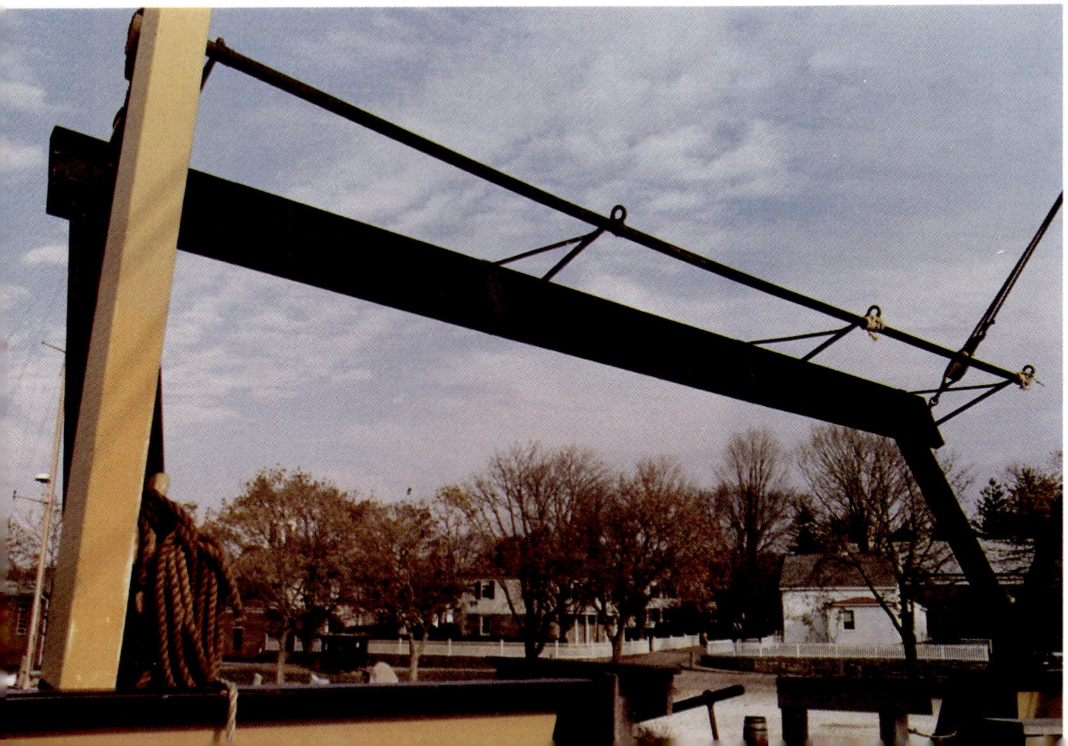

When not in use, the cutting stage of the *Charles W. Morgan* remained lashed to the side of the ship. The narrow planking did not provide much protection for crew coping with both a rolling vessel and the massive weight of the shackled whale. *Courtesy of the Mystic Seaport Museum*

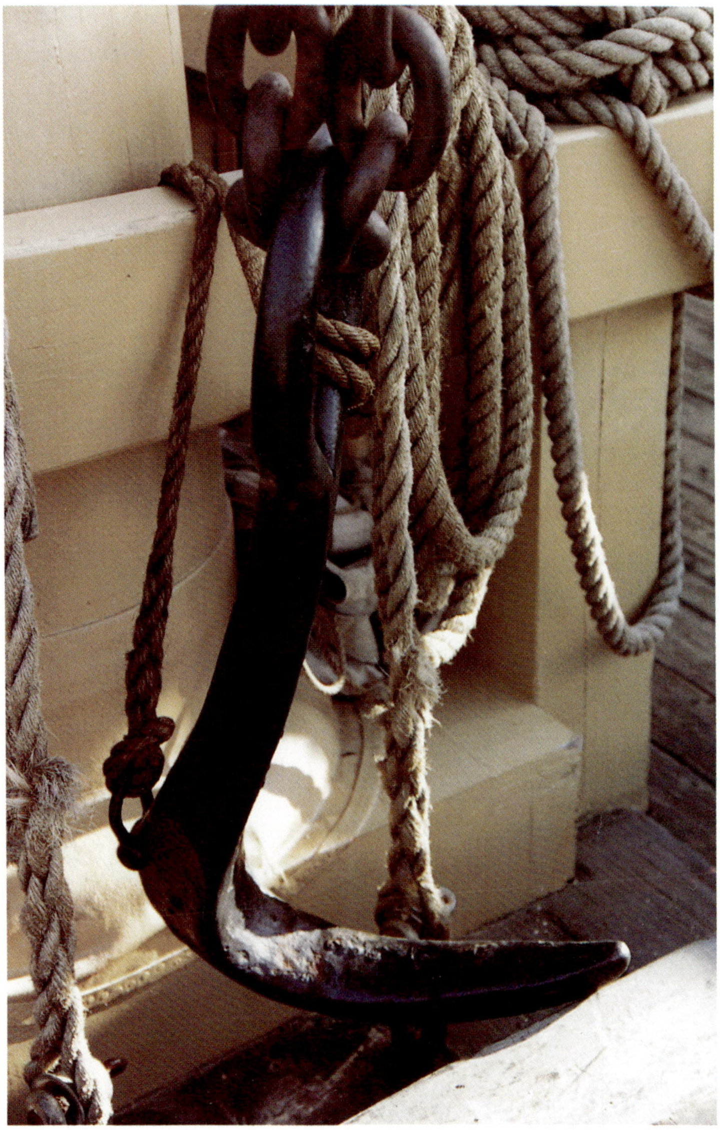

Blubber hook aboard the *Charles W. Morgan*. *Courtesy of the Mystic Seaport Museum*

> It is no very easy matter to introduce the (blubber) hook into the proper place, while the sea is dashing the whale against the ship...so that a man runs the risk of being strangled...The danger of being horribly mutilated by the sharks that assemble in great numbers during the 'cutting in', attracted by the scent of blood, is by no means inconsiderable.[13]

Meanwhile, employing blubber hook, blocks, tackle and windlass, the crew hoisted the massive "blanket pieces" of blubber onto the deck, cut them into smaller "horse-pieces", boiled them until the intense heat of the tryworks rendered them oil, and finally stowed the cooled treasure into huge casks that were painstakingly lowered into the ship's hold below.

Eliza Williams described cutting-in aboard the *Florida*, "The ship is the dirtiest place that I ever saw when they are cutting in and trying out whales."[14] According to Bullen, the men in the blubber room were "perfectly saturated with oil...for as the vessel rolled it was impossible to obtain a footing and every fall was upon blubber running with oil."[15] And, another captain's wife, Annie Holmes Ricketson, added, "It smells so it makes me sick, but we can get along with all this for it will be clean money."[16]

The whaleman's work not only involved processing the oil, but also included hours engaged in extracting, cleaning and preparing the thousands of pounds of baleen harvested from each whale. "There was almost always something being done with the wretched stuff—drying, scraping, etc."[17]

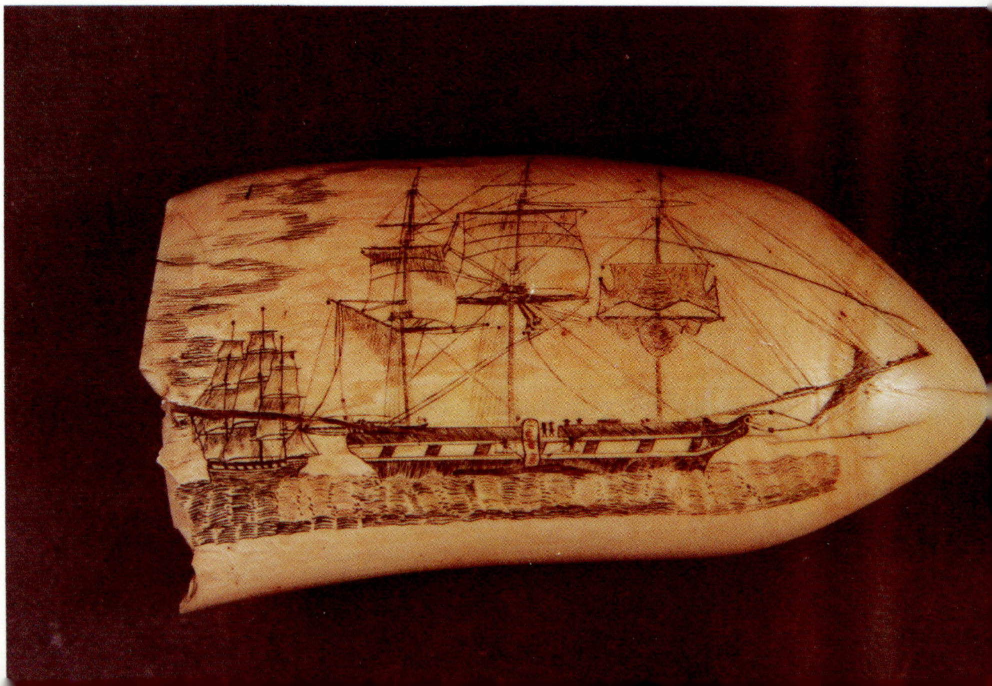

In this realistic rendering, the crew is busily engaged in cutting-in. As the whale lies alongside, the blanket piece is hauled aboard by men perched on the cutting stage above. *Courtesy of the Nantucket Historical Association*

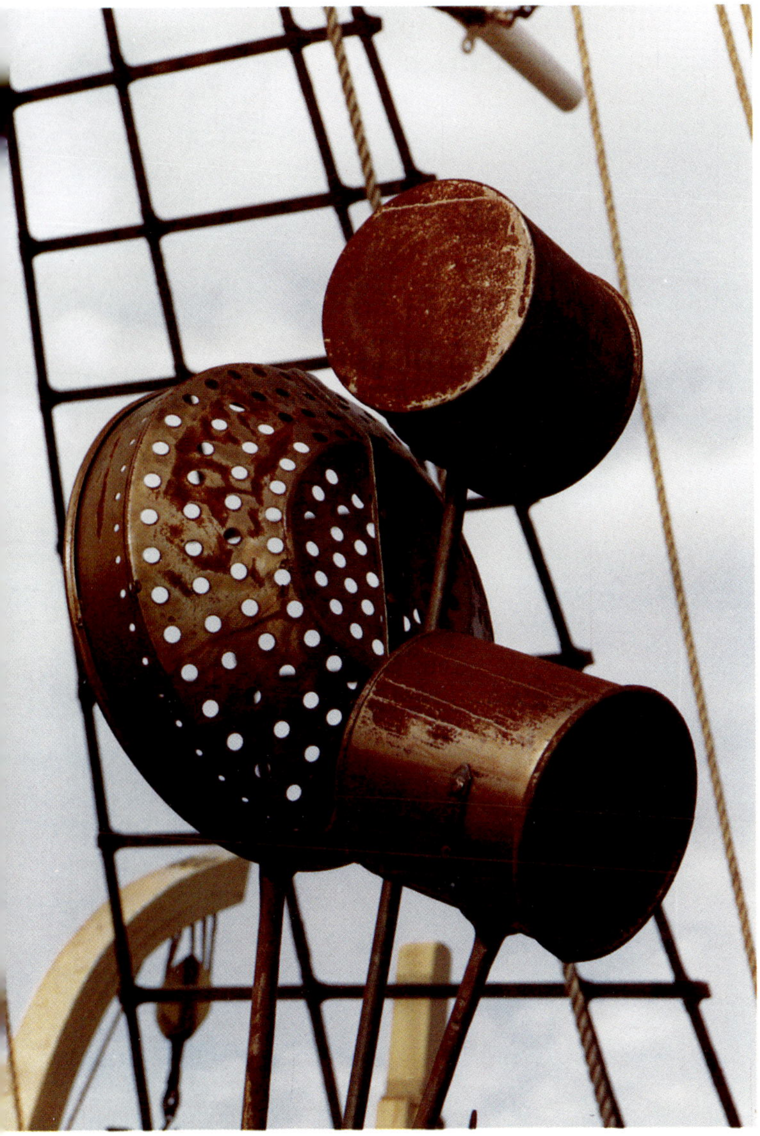

These long-handled bailers and a skimmer aided the crew manning the trypots. *Courtesy of the Mystic Seaport Museum*

When not actively engaged in either the pursuit or trying-out of the whale, the men occupied themselves repairing and maintaining the ship, the whaleboats and their equipment:

> In common with most people, I once had the impression that whaling was a lazy, aimless sort of life...I soon had this idea shaken out of me. I have never seen men toil more unremittingly...[18]
>
> The next day after stowing down the oil, the whole day was devoted to scrubbing the rails, paintwork and decks...[19]
>
> Crew employed in repairing fore royal and foot ropes....Carpenter making a bit. Cooper making buckets....Crew employed in setting and twining in the main topmast back stays....Cooper and carpenter repairing tryworks cover.[20]
>
> With the regard to the mending of old clothes, the crew are indefatigable....Coats and pantaloons...they work upon, and cover over with patches of various colors, until not a vestige of the original is left.[21]

Yet, when all the tasks were completed, and no whales were in sight, there were many idle hours to fill on the overmanned vessel. Sometimes weeks might pass without sight of a whale. Aboard the bark *Globe* on January 2, 1871, John S. Coquin lamented that they had "not seen a whale for ten months."[22]

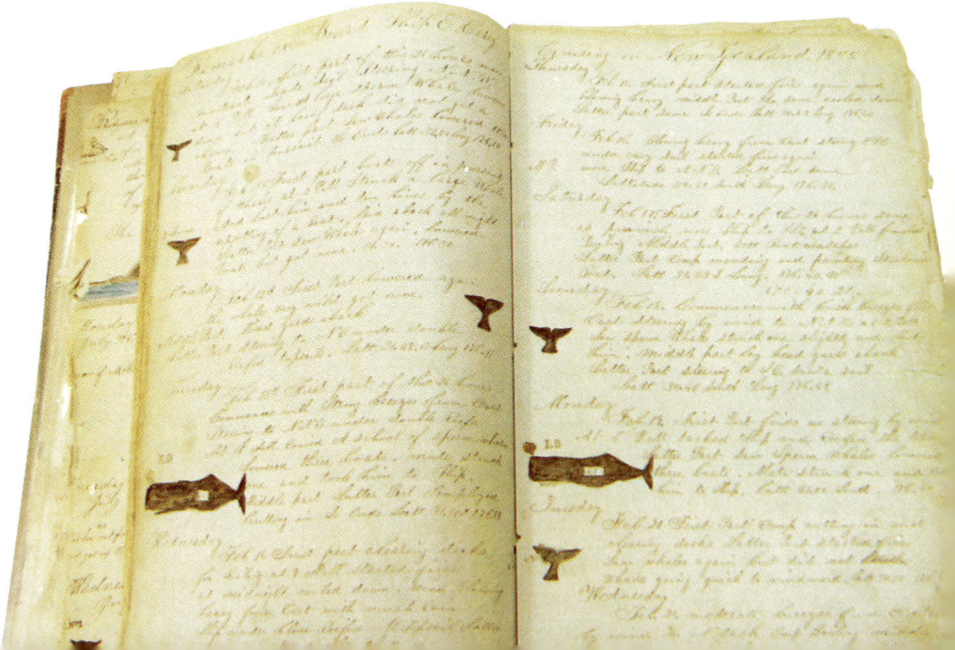

Entries in the log of the *Edward Cary* describe the busy shipboard routine when on the whaling grounds. *Courtesy of the Nantucket Historical Association*

The empty hours were monotonous and seemingly endless. They prompted complaints, sarcasm and even, in the mind of the *Arab*'s Captain Samuel Braley, a secret desire for a man overboard whose rescue might relieve the boredom:

> I hope that there will be something soon, if it is nothing but the cry so shocking to sailors (as) 'man overboard' if we can save him.[23]

Michael Cumiskey, aboard the New Bedford bark *Abigail*, worried to his journal:

> I am unsettled in mind for the want of work. Saw nothin, and work all dun. An idle head is a workshop for the devil. Employed scrimshan.[24]

Likewise, William Davis was concerned with the effects of idleness on the personality:

> The sky is clear, with fresh winds. We are now regularly cruising, with not enough to do to keep a man off a growl. As this habit only cankers the soul, I prefer to scrimshone.[25]

Joseph Hersey, third mate of the schooner *Esquimaux* attested to the spirit scrimshaw could bring to the crew who would otherwise be in the doldrums:

> In the morning we divided our share of teeth from the last whale....Our officers and crew appear to have received new animation (of late) for they have once more bent their minds to haberdashing.[26]

On October lst, 1871, nine hundred and fifty days at sea, John Coquin busied his hands with scrimshaw, but his heart was elsewhere:

> I strapped several blocks, scrimshawing, Over the seas tonight I roam, my mind still will wander homewards.

And, eleven days later he added:

> May God bring the voyage to a speedy termination.[27]

These were the hours in which scrimshaw was worked. Although its emergence is often credited solely to the abundance of idle time, scrimshaw can also be understood as an extension of the building, repairing, and recycling necessary aboard ship and common to an era when things were hand-made by artisans proud of their work. Scrimshaw was a natural outgrowth of the sailor's need to keep busy, the availability of materials that might otherwise be wasted, and perhaps, most importantly, a need to create something of beauty.

For some practitioners, scrimshaw was a pastime, for others a passion. William Manchester, the 2nd mate of the bark *Palmetto* wrote in the log entry of September 15, 1881:

> Nothing in sight and no signs of any spirm whales around here. The old man and the mate devote there time a Sckrimshorning. That is all they think of.

Giving clear evidence that his own mind was occupied by weightier matters, Manchester added, "Killed a Pig."[28]

Without regard for station, scrimshaw emanated from the captain's cabin to the foc'sle. Located in the stern of the ship, the captain's quarters included a sitting room as well as bed chamber. Larger and more elaborate pieces of scrimshaw were often the product of the captain as he had not only the first choice of materials, but also the most space in which to work. Swifts, for example, could not be folded up while under construction, thus a work area greater than that available in the foc'sle was required.

Opposite page:
The captain's cabin allowed sufficient room to work on a piece as complicated and large as this beautiful swift.
Madden Collection

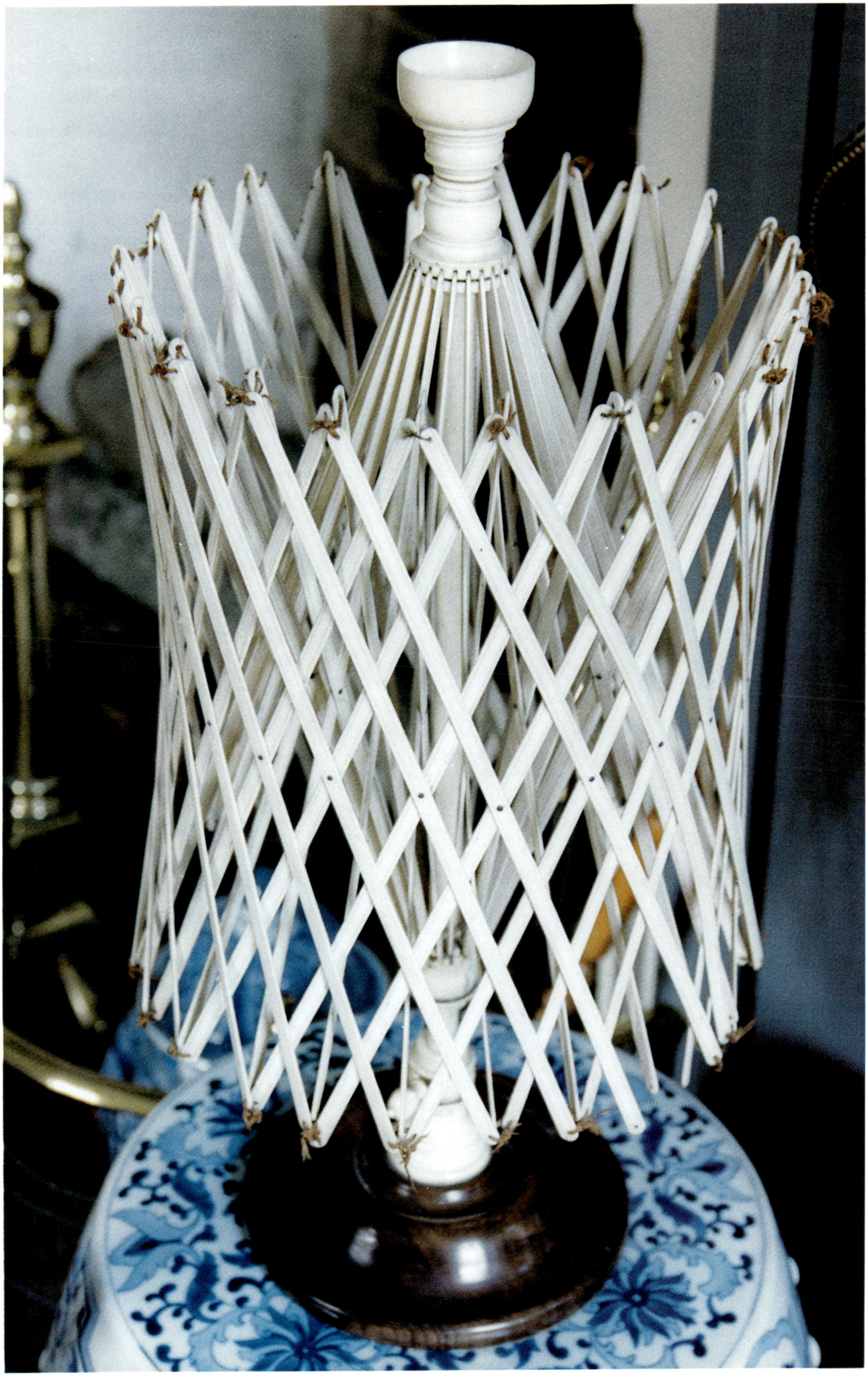

On Christmas Day, 1859, Mary Lawrence reports:

Minnie awoke bright and early this morning to examine the contents of her stocking....Her father made her a pair of ivory candlesticks with little candles of the same material, which were very cunning.[29]

On May 4, 1860, Captain Lawrence was again busy:

Fine weather as usual. Samuel commenced scrimshawing again for the first time after having a lame side. His work today was turning a bedstead for Minnie.[30]

In an anonymously written journal from the voyage of the bark *Messenger*, Captain John Gifford is reported to have been an ardent practitioner of scrimshaw:

Capt. scrimshoning nearly every day....the Capt. is making canes & it always takes 3 or 4 to help him when he is doing anything.[31]

And obviously no whales were being hunted on New Year's Day of 1838 when the log of the bark *Benjamin Cummings* records:

Captain Jennings and wife and all hands scrimshoring.[32]

Not all whaling masters were enamored of the pastime and some even forbade the crew to engage in what certainly appears to have been a productive and psychologically healthy method of filling time:

The captain would not allow any work of this kind performed by the crew, he claiming that it distracted from doing their regular ship's duties....The captains of many whalers gave their sailors teeth to make fancy articles but our skipper took them and kept them in the cabin. The same old story.[33]

Commonly, the most highly skilled scrimshanders aboard the ship were the cooper or carpenter, men already skilled in woodworking and with tools readily available to them. According to Ashley, "About the most important single article of equipment aboard a whaler was the cask, and one of the most important men on shipboard and one who always commanded a good lay was the cooper."[34] Given their skills and position aboard ship, it is not surprising to find many intricate and fine pieces of scrimshaw attributed to these craftsmen.

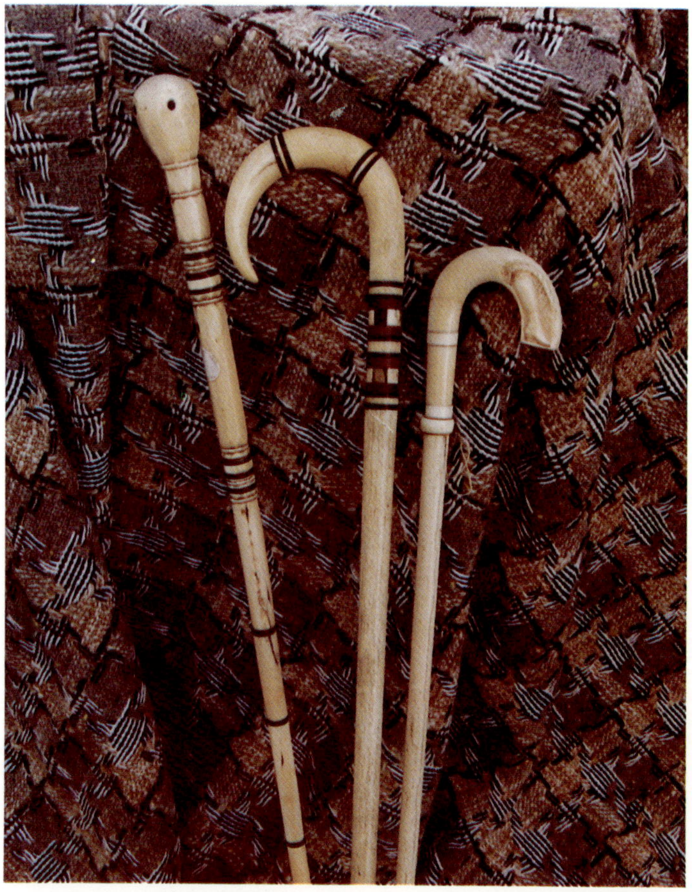

"Handsome canes are made of the white bone from the broad pan of the jaw of younger sperm-whales, also from plates of black whalebone, heated and twisted." (William Davis, *Nimrod of the Sea*, page 265) *Collection of Charles A. Manghis*

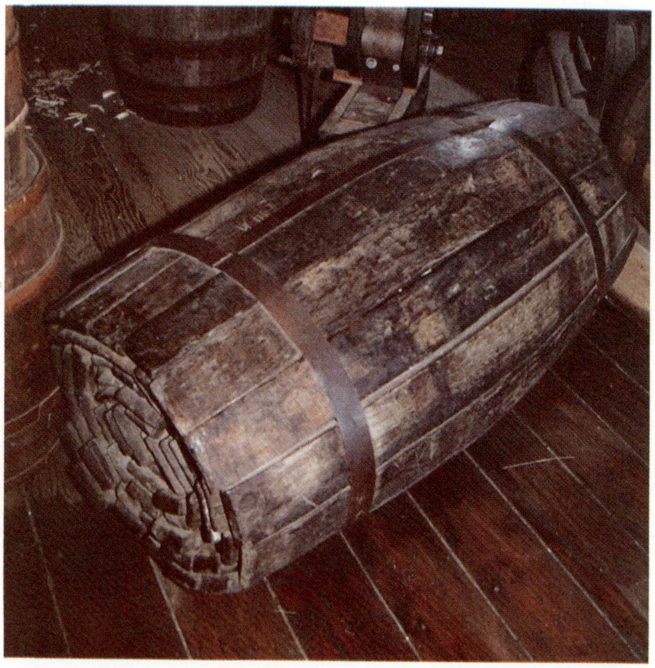

Casks were knocked down, or "shooked," to save space below decks. They were reassembled by the ship's cooper when needed. *Courtesy of the Mystic Seaport Museum*

> The cooper....was quite a skillful "scrimshawer" and made a variety of articles, such as tatting shuttles of tortoiseshell, crocheting needles of whalebone with carved heads, canes of the jaw bone of the sperm whale, and of the heart of the coconut tree, with various shaped heads made from sperm whale's teeth, all of excellent design and beautifully finished....Some of the foremast hands made various articles...but the cooper was the real artist.[35]

William H. Chappell, cooper aboard the ship *Saratoga* remarked on February 16, 1854:

> ...have been scrimshanting all day making a few fancy articles for the lovely ones at home.[36]

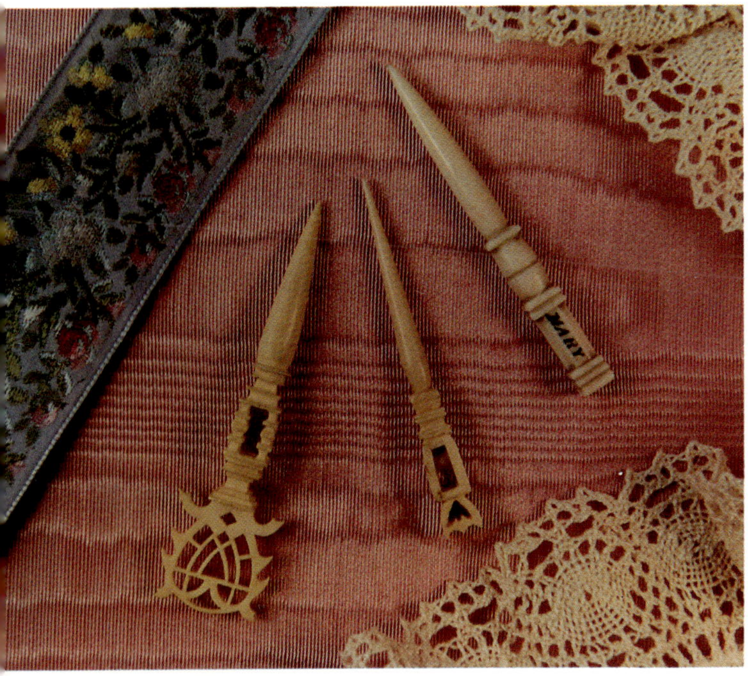

These whale ivory bodkins are representative of the many types of "fancy articles" created by William Chappell and his contemporaries. *Collection of Curtis Nyquist, B.M.N.*

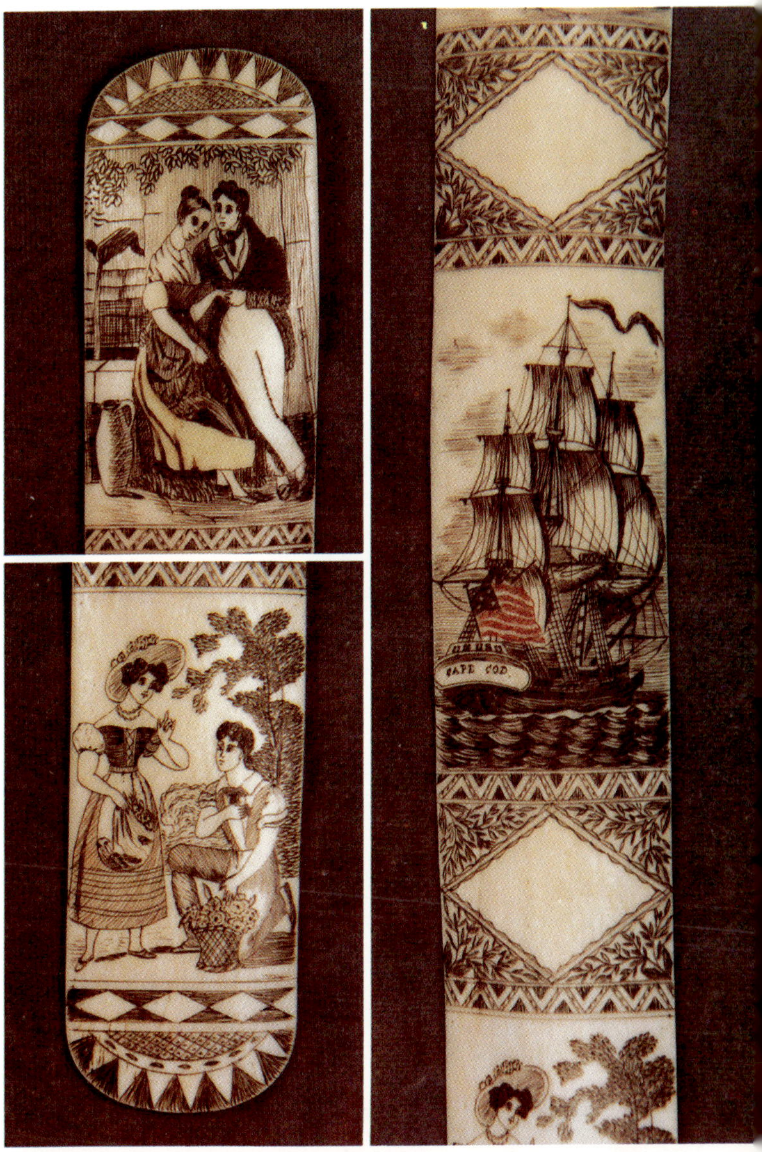

Despite the fact that scrimshaw was executed on all parts of the ship, popular images of homesick whalemen patiently fashioning remembrances for loved ones remain inextricably entwined with scenes of the foc'sle. And indeed, whether a single attempt or one of many, numerous pieces of scrimshaw, some utilitarian, some highly decorative, were produced by the men of the foc'sle.

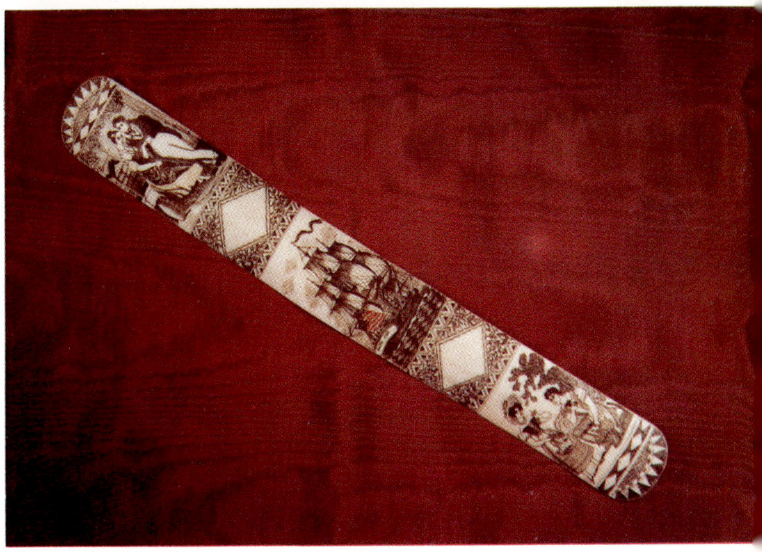

This whalebone busk, designed for insertion in the front of a lady's corset, depicts romantic images often seen in scrimshaw. *Madden Collection*

The crew of an American whaler was usually quite varied ethnically—especially as the nineteenth century wore on. Yankees, Native Americans, Europeans, Cape Verdeans and South Pacific islanders were some of the many backgrounds represented in the foc'sle. Home to twenty or more seamen, the foc'sle, or forecastle, was a cramped triangle nestled in the ship's bow. The meager floor space available was further minimized by the invasion of the foremast as it passed from the main deck above to the hold of the ship below. The only blessing, logistically, was that one third of the men were always above on watch.

Each man was allotted a bunk and floor space for his seaman's chest which served as table, chair and storage. Nelson Cole Haley described the foc'sle of the *Charles W. Morgan*:

> There twenty-five men lived in quarters so small that it was impossible for all of them to find standing room at one time without standing on their sea chests as close as possible.[37]

Minimal ventilation and light came from a hatch cover on the main deck. Heavy seas, or inclement weather resulted in an airless, dark cave, filled with perpetually damp and odorous clothing.

> The decks were dry for the first time in over two weeks. Clothes were brought out of the steaming forecastle and spread on the tryworks and hung in various parts of the riggin', many of the men having had no dry clothes for a week past.[38]

Unpleasant in most situations, the foc'sle became a sweltering hole during times of trying-out:

> Almost under the try-pots, and with the floor buried in a heap of musty and mildewed garments, wet and oily from constant duty overboard and contact with the dripping blubber, the forecastle was a veritable hell.[39]

Here in the foc'sle were the visions of home dreamed, the stories of whale hunts retold, the plan for an incipient piece of scrimshaw envisioned. As elsewhere aboard ship, pent-up feelings of longing were coupled with the desire for beauty and expression. In addition, there was abundant free time, availability of interesting materials, and an ingrained pattern of puttering, repairing and conserving. As a result, by the early nineteenth century,

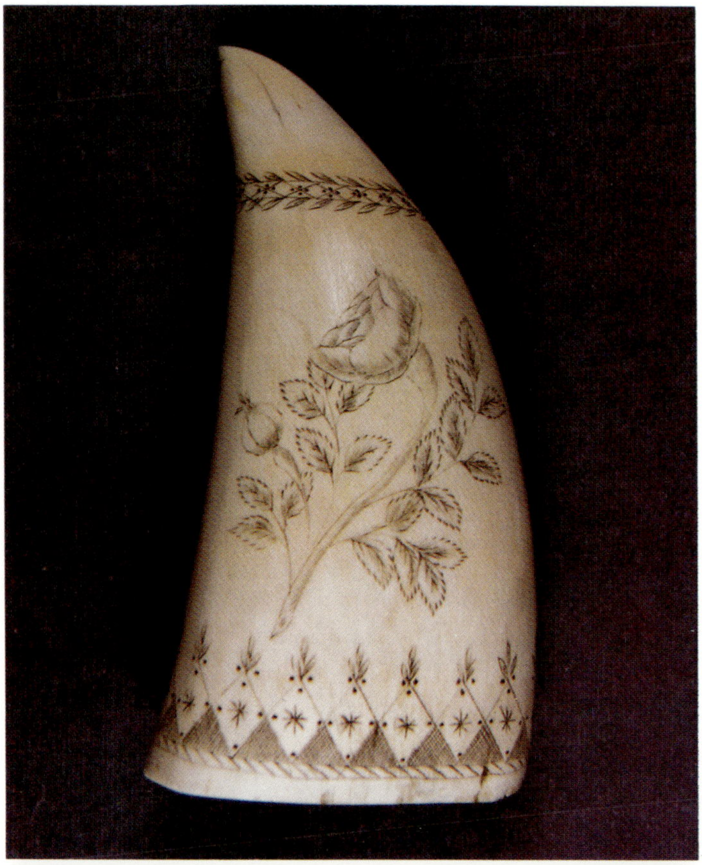

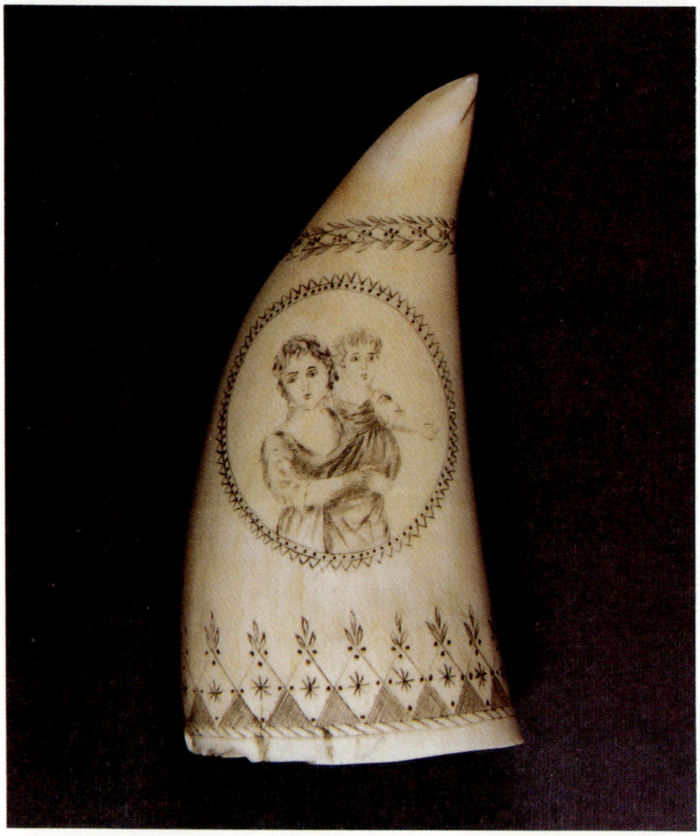

The quintessential romantic imagery associated with scrimshaw graces this lovely work. *Courtesy of the Nantucket Historical Association*

scrimshaw had begun to emerge from all quarters of the ship, from the Captain's sitting room to the seamen's foc'sle.

In the isolated world of the whaling community, scrimshaw flourished as outlet, pastime, and art. As sailors changed ships at the end of a voyage and different crews were formed, techniques, skills and designs were exchanged and incorporated into new pieces, leaving a body of work that, despite individual differences, shares common themes and styles.

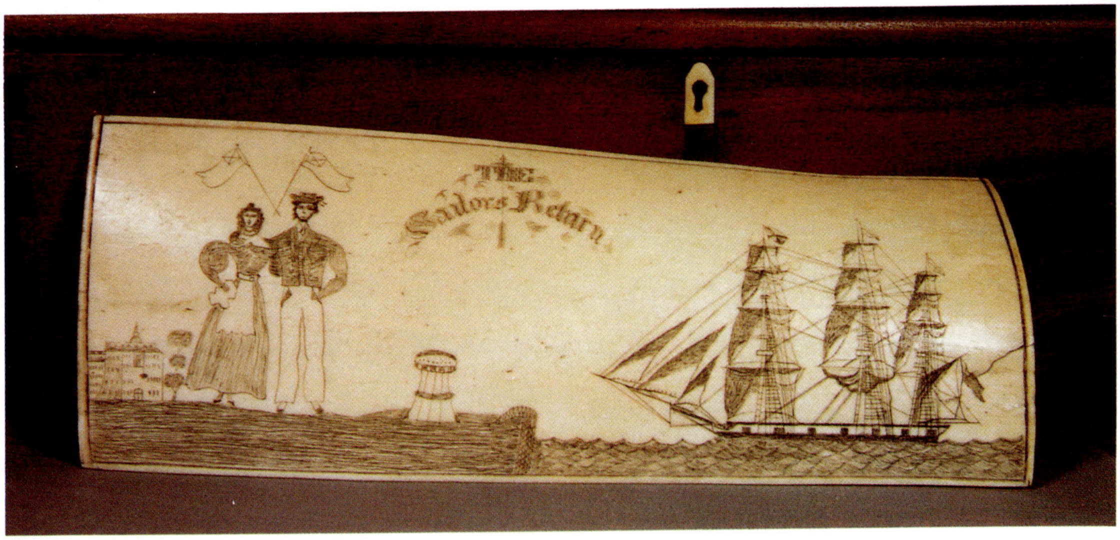

The longed-for day of return is beautifully evoked on this engraved panbone. *Courtesy of the Nantucket Historical Association*

01 Frank T. Bullen, *Cruise of the "Cachalot"* (Philadelphia, Penn.: David McKay Publisher, 1899), 2.

02 Nelson C. Haley, *Whale Hunt* (Mystic, Conn.: Mystic Seaport Museum, Inc., 1990), 205.

03 John M. Bullard, ed., *Captain Edmund Gardner* (Milford, N.H.: The Cabinet Press, 1958), 51.

04 Mary C. Lawrence, *The Captain's Best Mate* (Providence, R.I.: Brown University Press, 1966), 103.

05 Clifford W. Ashley, *The Yankee Whaler* (Boston, Mass.: Houghton Mifflin, 1938), 12.

06 Joseph E. Ray, "Logbook of the Ship *Edward Cary* 1854-1858" (Nantucket, Mass.: Nantucket Historical Association).

07 Ashley, *The Yankee Whaler*, 82.

08 Edouard A. Stackpole, "The *Ann Alexander*'s Scrimshaw Set," *Historic Nantucket* (January, 1980).

09 Ashley, *The Yankee Whaler*, 12-13.

10 Richard Ellis, *Men and Whales* (New York: Alfred A. Knopf, 1991), 31.

11 Ben-Ezra Stiles Ely, *There She Blows* (Middletown, Conn.: Wesleyan University Press, 1971), 48.

12 Bullen, *Cruise of the "Cachalot"*, 223

13 Francis A. Olmstead, *Incidents of a Whaling Voyage* (Rutland, Vt.: Charles E. Tuttle Co., Inc., 1969), 63.

14 Harold W. Williams, ed., *One Whaling Family* (Boston, Mass.: Houghton Mifflin, 1964), 26.

15 Bullen, *Cruise of the "Cachalot"*, 49.

16 Annie H. Ricketson, *Journal on the Whaleship "A.R. Tucker"* (New Bedford: Old Dartmouth Historical Society, 1958), 15.

17 Bullen, *Cruise of the "Cachalot"*, 196.

18 Ashley, *The Yankee Whaler*, 8.

19 Haley, *Whale Hunt*, 109.

20 William H. Tripp, ed., "Extracts from Whaling Log-Books, New Bedford Whaling Museum" (Sharon, Mass.: The Kendall Whaling Museum).

21 Olmstead, *Incidents of a Whaling Voyage*, 82.

22 John S. Coquin, "A Journal on board the Bark *Globe*" (New Bedford, Mass.: Old Dartmouth Historical Society).

23 Margaret S. Creighton, *Dogwatch and Liberty Days* (Salem, Mass.: Peabody Museum of Salem, 1982), 22.

24 Stuart M. Frank, *Dictionary of Scrimshaw Artists* (Mystic, Conn.: Mystic Seaport Museum, 1991), 41.

25 William M. Davis, *Nimrod of the Sea* (North Quincy, Mass.: The Christopher Publishing House, 1972), 265.

26 Frank, *Dictionary*, 178.

27 Coquin, "Journal on board the *Globe*".

28 William M. Manchester, "Logbook of the Bark *Palmetto*" (New Bedford, Mass.: Old Dartmouth Historical Society).

29 Lawrence, *The Captain's Best Mate*, 210.

30 Ibid., 232.

31 Frank, *Dictionary*, 59-60.

32 Edouard A. Stackpole, *Scrimshaw at Mystic Seaport* (Mystic, Conn.: The Marine Historical Association, Inc., 1958), 31.

33 Warren P. Tobey, *The Cabin Boy's Log* (Boston, Mass.: Meador Publishing Co., 1932), 86.

34 Ashley, *The Yankee Whaler*, 97.

35 Williams, *One Whaling Family*, 268.

36 Sotheby Park Bernet, Inc., *Barbara Johnson Whaling Collection — Part IV*.

37 Haley, *Whale Hunt*, 49.

38 Ibid., 48.

39 Ashley, *The Yankee Whaler*, 19.

4. The Raw Materials of Scrimshaw

Unless there was commercial demand for a specific substance, the physical materials necessary to create scrimshaw were abundantly available to the average whaleman by the early part of the nineteenth century. He could choose among teeth, whalebone, baleen, exotic woods, shells and more. Conscious of both the suitability of the materials to the task and a harmonious relationship among the parts, the nineteenth century scrimshander created a diverse array of incredible pieces from substances that would have been wasted, or at best unappreciated.

Because right whaling preceded sperm whaling by a number of years, baleen was the first material readily available to scrimshanders. Although a commercial market for baleen existed, the supply garnered from the right whale fishery was far greater than the late eighteenth and early nineteenth century demand. As the nineteenth century unfolded, however, sperm whale teeth and bone became more common aboard a whaler. In addition, commercial demand for baleen soared, eventually eclipsing that of whale oil. Thus large amounts of baleen were no longer available to the scrimshanders, leading scholars to conclude that "baleen scrimshaw remains primarily a phenomenon of the early 19th century."[1]

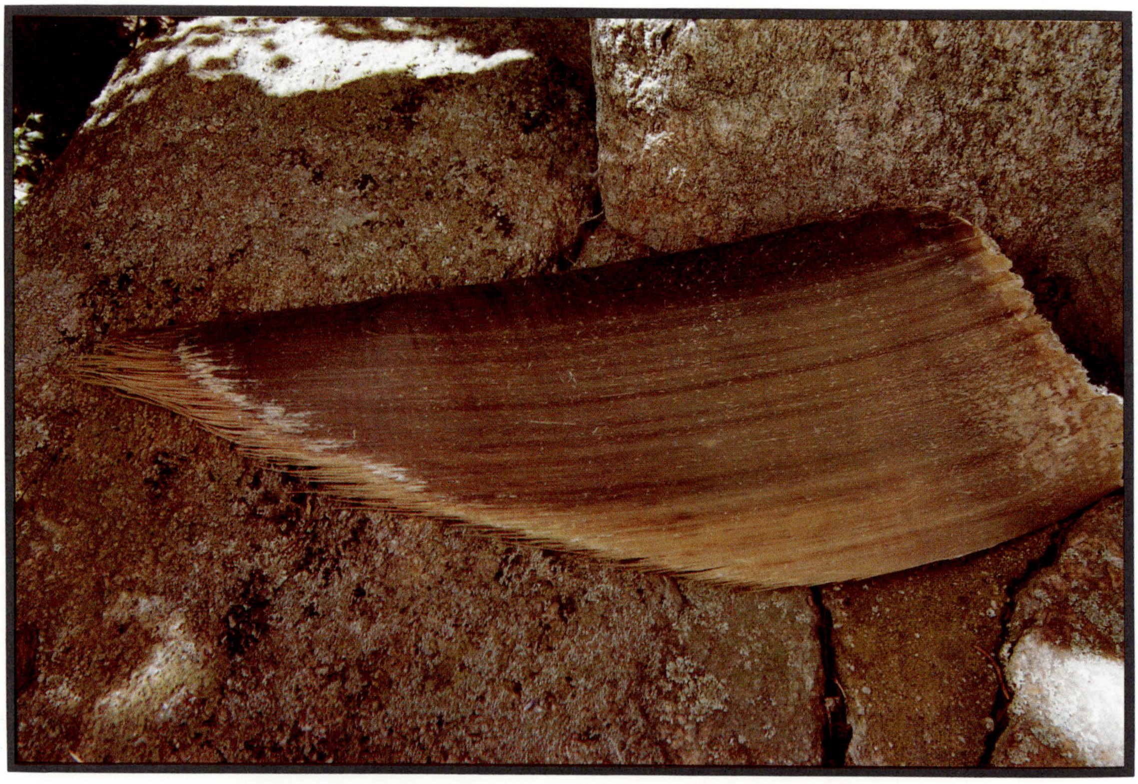

The fringed, lower section of a baleen plate. *Collection of Gladys Sherman Ellis*

Baleen was referred to by the whalers as "whalebone." In current usage however, whalebone denotes skeletal bone, usually that of the sperm whale; and baleen is referred to by its given name. The same flexible properties that made baleen so valuable to manufacturers were also appreciated by scrimshanders. Even more malleable when heated, the baleen could be bent into round or oval boxes. The long, horn-like plates were vertically grained and could be split easily into any width. The flat lengths were perfect for the construction of busks; and no doubt the flexibility of a baleen busk made it a more welcome gift than one of wood or whalebone.

The tooth of the sperm whale remains today the most readily recognizable form of scrimshaw. A tooth was the most difficult surface on which to etch because of its curved surface, but it was also the most popular as it was a trophy of the hunt and testament to the bravery and skill of the hunter. Not only did the dense ivory provide an excellent surface for engraving, but teeth were also carved into cane heads, pie crimpers, bodkins, pick-wicks and more. Wasting not, the carvers saved small, unused pieces for inlays in later works.

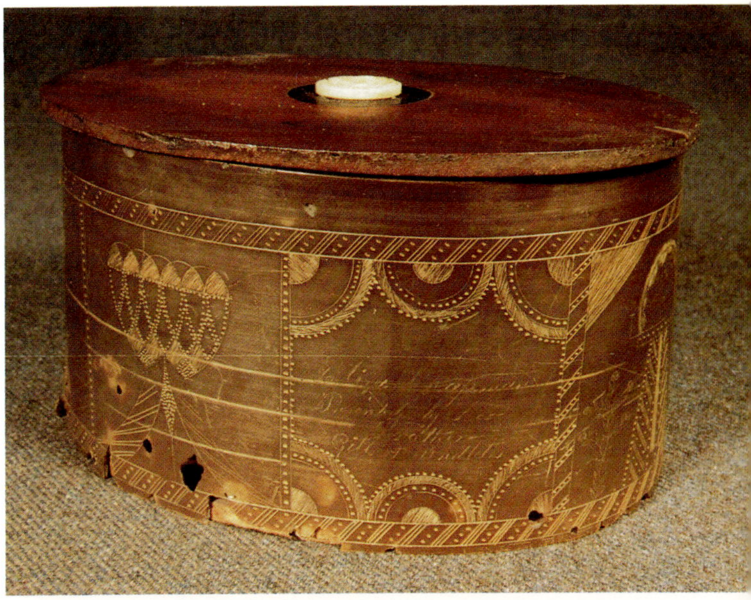

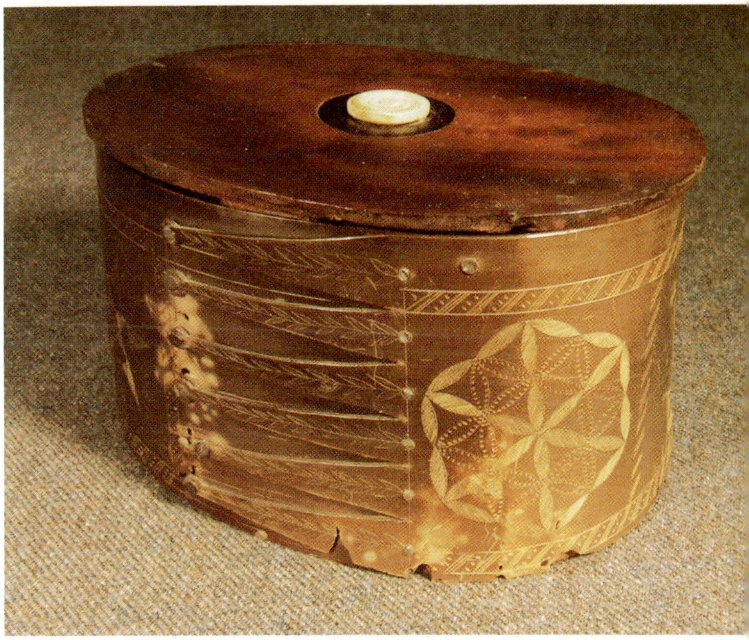

The inscription on this wooden-topped baleen box reads "Eliza Chapman, presented by her brother Gilbert Pendleton." Pendleton was a whaling captain who sailed from Stonington, Connecticut. *Collection of Raymond and Elizabeth De Lucia*

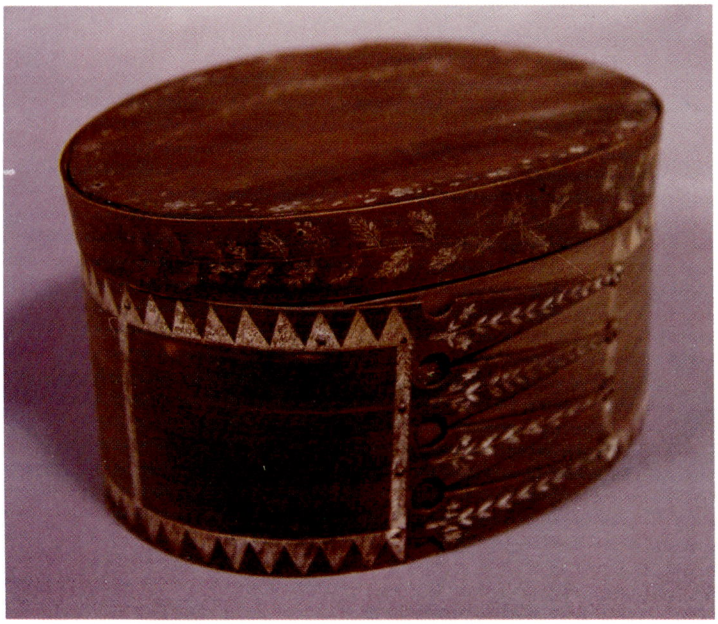

Oval workbox of carved and engraved baleen. *Collection of the Nantucket Historical Association*

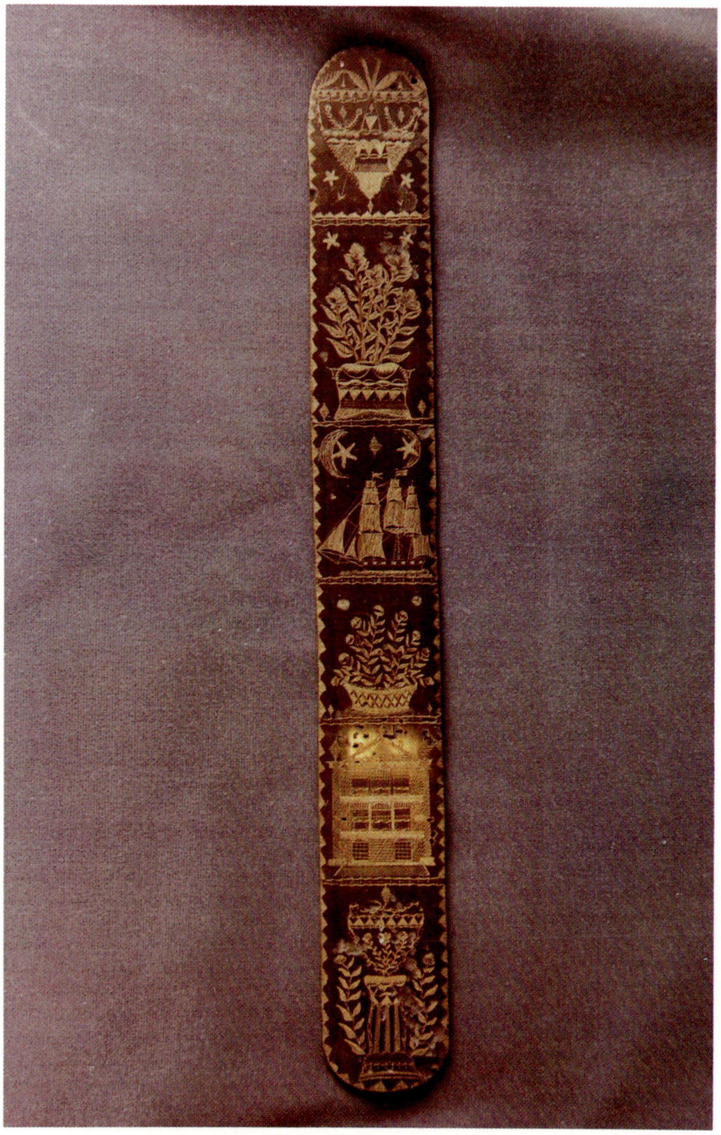

This early baleen busk is adorned with classic motifs. *Collection of the Nantucket Historical Association*

The lower jaw of a good-sized sperm whale averaged about nineteen feet in length and in one might be imbedded from twenty to fifty teeth. Only a third of the tooth was visible above the gum line, and the whole tooth, when extracted, measured between four and ten inches. After the cutting-in, the head was hoisted aboard ship so that spermaceti could be bailed from the head case. The jaw was then available for division among the crew.

On June 29, 1843, Joseph Bogart Hersey described in some detail the final disposition of the whale caught by the crew of the *Esquimaux.*

> At sunrise we commenced cutting in the remains of our whale and finished before breakfast, after which we sheared the jaws and diped the Case. The length of the jaw was eleven feet and contained fourty-two teeth. These we extracted with great dispatch and took particular care of, thinking how suitable they would be for *haberdashing.*[2]

Although American sperm whaling evolved in the early eighteenth century, it is now believed that teeth were not available for scrimshaw prior to 1815 because they were saved for sale in the Pacific islands where they were considered items of great status and worth.[3]

Whaleman William Cary, wrecked in the Fiji Islands in 1825, described the tooth of the sperm whale as "the most valuable article they have among them."[4]

Indeed a mere tooth could serve as a fine levied for offenses as grievious as murder and adultery. Cary described the defeated warriors of an intertribal battle as so frightened that they "made offers of peace, offering all their whales' teeth and the chief's daughter."[5]

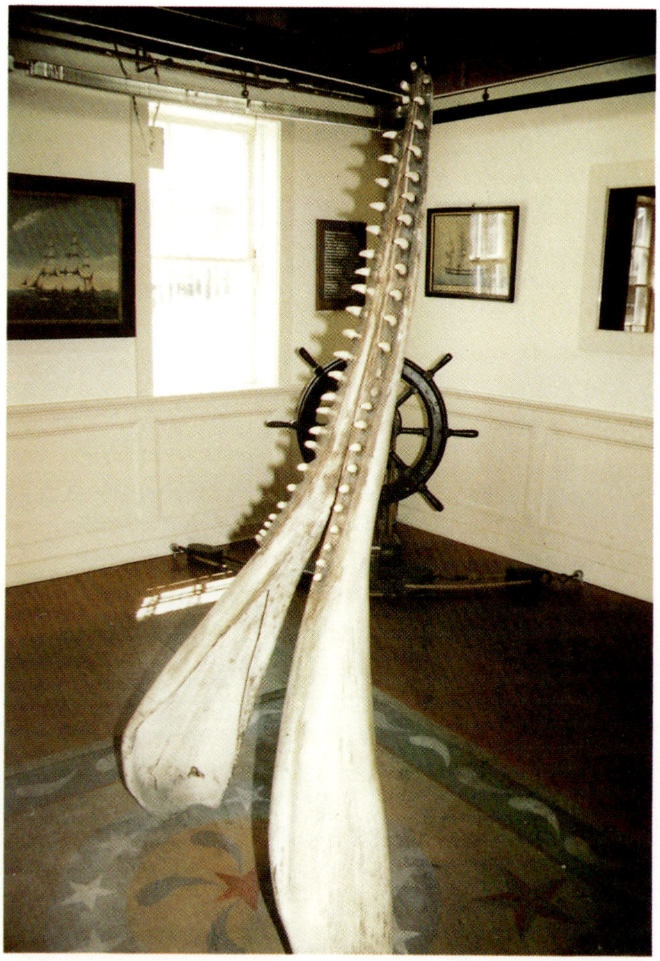

Lower jaw of a young sperm whale. *Courtesy of the Nantucket Historical Association*

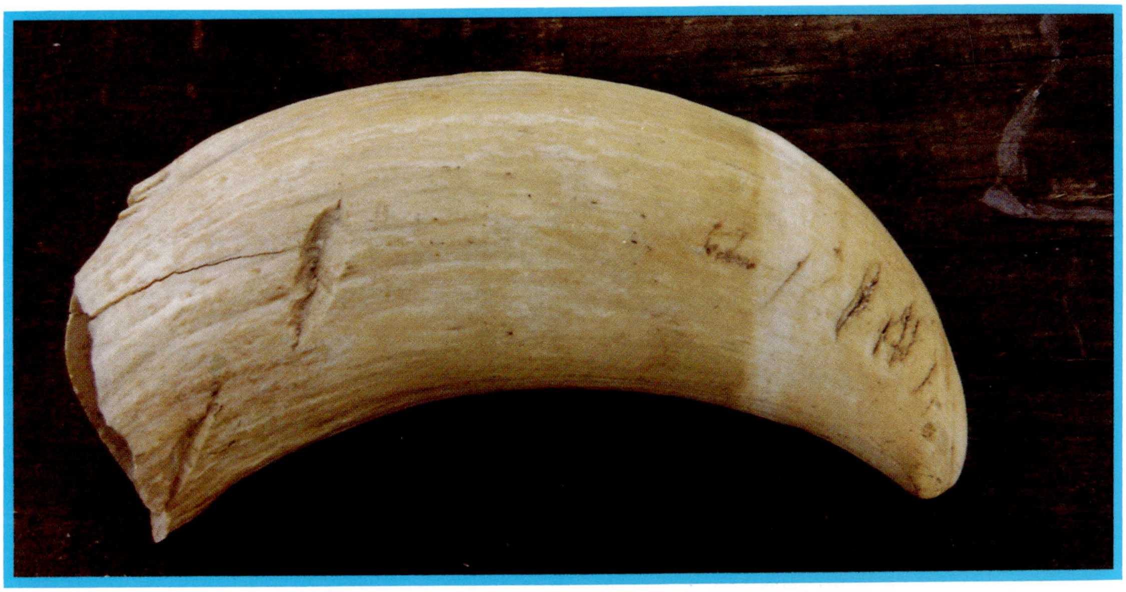

This sperm whale's tooth reveals the spade marks incurred when it was dug out of the animal's jaw. Before removal, the lighter-colored tip was the only section of the tooth that was visible. *Collection of Charles A. Manghis*

Inhabitants of the Hawaiian Islands similarly revered the teeth. There, they were a sign of status, incorporated into necklaces of braided human hair called Lei Nehi Palaoa which were worn by tribal chiefs.

In the late eighteenth and early nineteenth centuries, astute merchants of the China trade, aware of this potential market, purchased all the teeth the whaling industry could supply in order to trade them at various islands on their passage across the Pacific. Just as commercial demand for baleen increased throughout the nineteenth century, leaving little for use by sailors, this earlier market for teeth limited their availability to the whalemen. Although the teeth remained precious to the islanders into the time of Cary's journal and many years thereafter, by 1815 there was a surplus and the traders began to find beads and other trinkets more lucrative items of barter. Teeth that would have previously been sold to China traders were then available to the average seaman wishing to pass the time with scrimshaw.[6]

Barter was by no means limited to commercial merchantmen. When the jaw and teeth were divided on deck among the crew, many sailors who partook of the whalebone were not planning to work it themselves, but rather to trade it with shipmates more inclined to the craft. "I have seen men swap tobacco, the universal currency aboard a whaler, wash clothes and do other menial tasks in order to gain coveted pieces."[7]

If a piece of ivory was acquired by someone unskilled in scrimshaw, he might consign it to the ship's outstanding scrimshander to craft a special memento or gift. Such an artist was Lyman B. Cook, who sailed aboard the whaleship *Logan* between 1828 and 1830. Cook noted in his journal, "I am skrimshonting what time I can get below now but I have so much to do for the rest of the crew that I can't do much for myself."[8]

The panbone or lower jaw bone of the sperm whale was the only skeletal bone dense enough for use as scrimshaw. From the pan bone were produced large pieces such as walking sticks, panoramic engraved wall plaques as well as smaller items such as busks and swifts. Within each panbone were sections that were harder and more finely grained than others and could be buffed to appear almost as glowing and translucent as the ivory of the teeth. These pieces were often saved for decorative work such as swifts and busks while more coarsely grained pieces were incorporated into sailors' tools or other items whose function was more important than appearance. In addition, when

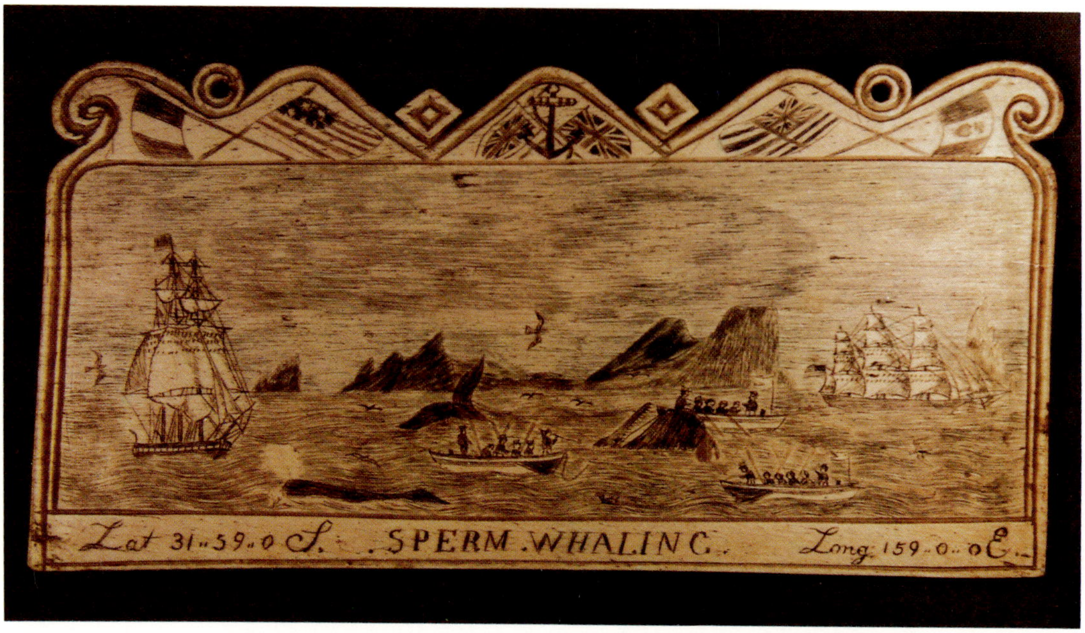

Panbone provided the artist a surface large enough to include all the elements of this panoramic scene. It was not uncommon to find a number of ships whaling in the same location at the proper time of the year. The latitude and longitude place this scene a few hundred miles off the southeast coast of Australia. The panoply of flags gives a sense of the international composition of the whaling fleet. *Courtesy of the Nantucket Historical Association*

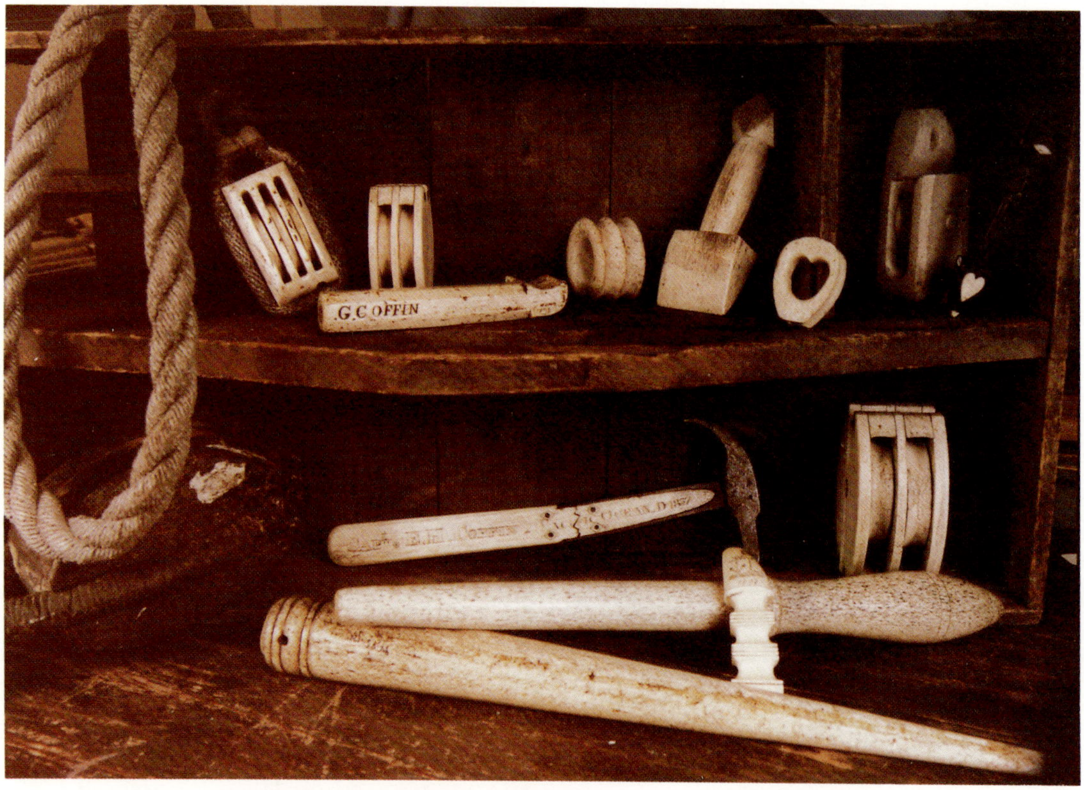

Encouraged by their captains, crew members turned "waste" whalebone into shipboard tools. *Courtesy of the Nantucket Historical Association*

The advent of Arctic whaling brought contact with Eskimos, and for the scrimshanders the acquisition of walrus tusks. Mary Lawrence noted in her journal entry of July 13, 1858:

> We had Eskimos in great numbers on board through the day, men, women, and children...Samuel purchased about eighty pounds of walrus teeth and two splendid bearskins of them.[10]

Although walrus tusks were more coarsely grained than sperm whale teeth, their lengths of up to thirty inches made them perfect surfaces for the scrimshander to apply either one panoramic or many varied designs. During the 1870s, when much of the fleet was California-based, walrus tusks were in plentiful supply and were worked into many pieces of scrimshaw.

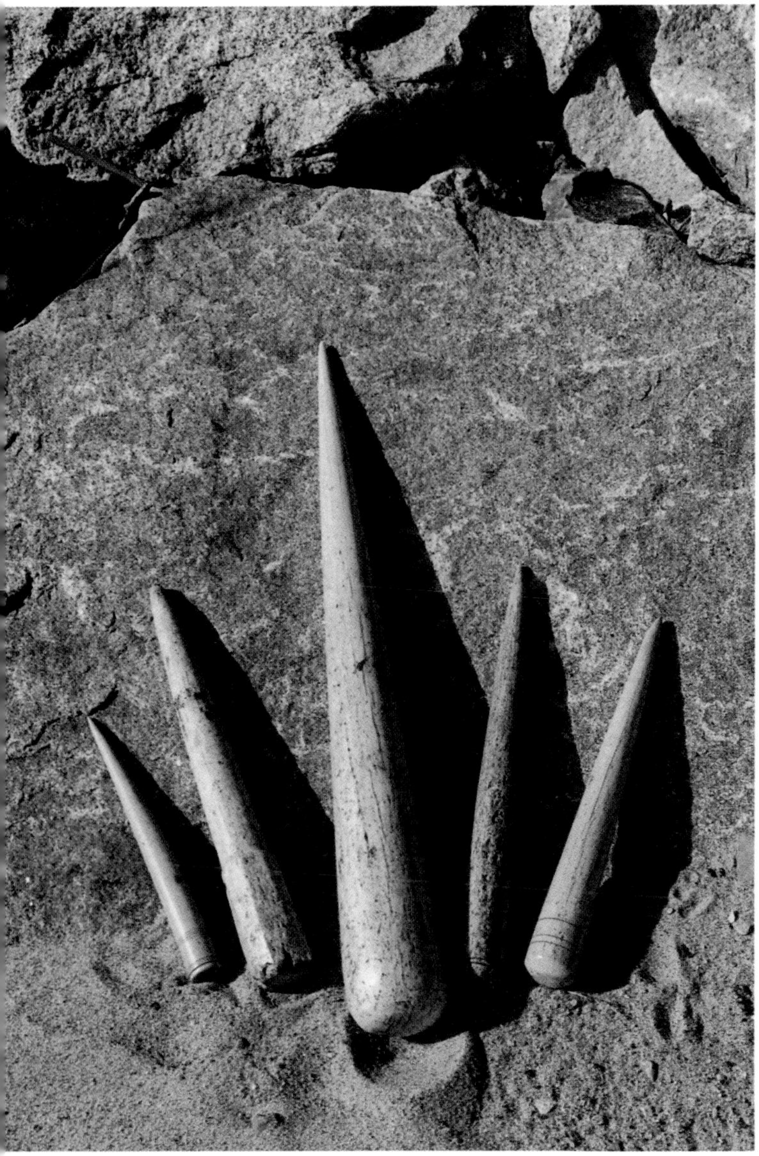

These whalebone fids were used for splicing line and other rigging work. *Private Collection*

fresh and relatively soft, the panbone could be sectioned into thin slices which could be steamed and bent into oval work boxes.

Joseph Bogart Hersey described towing the panbone in the sea to whiten it. After it was hauled aboard the *Esquimaux*:

> We then began to saw up and divide the bone, scarcely any of which but was held in such high estimation as to prevent it from being wasted. The jaw and the pans were dissected to such an advantage that nearly all had a piece which would answer to make a busk, or cane, and some were fortunate enough to get both.[9]

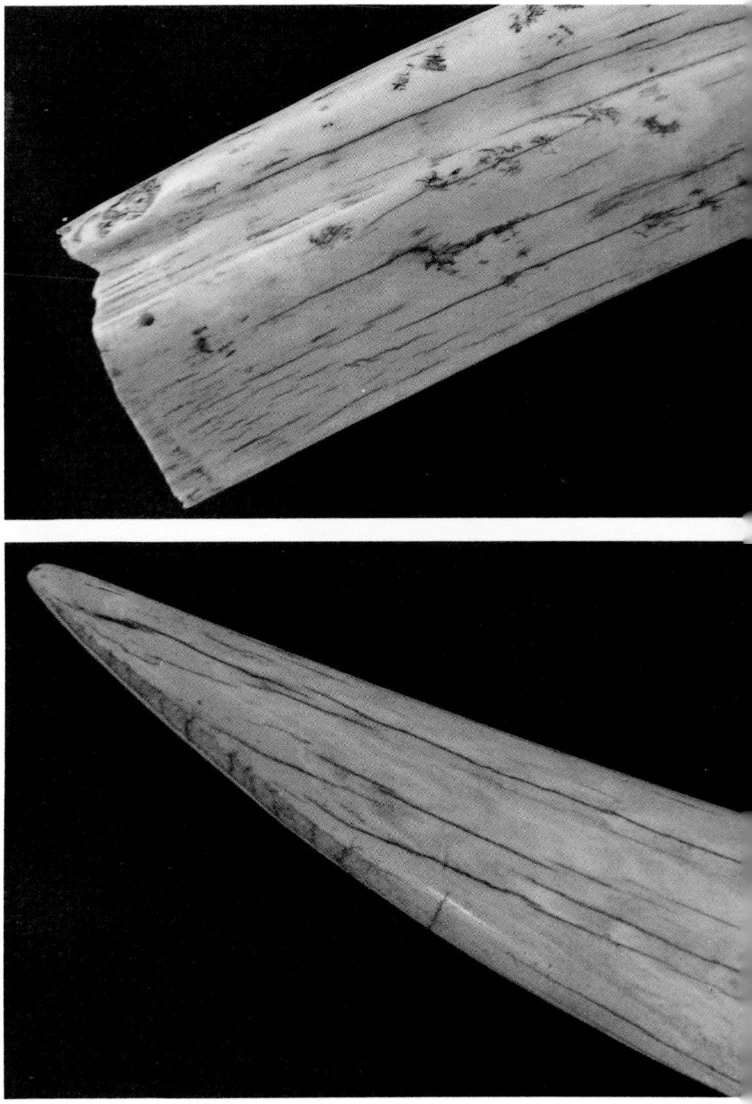

A polished walrus tusk, ready to be worked. *Collection of Charles A. Manghis*

In 1868, Ambrose H. Bates of the brig *Isabella* witnessed just such a creation:

> While I am at this table writing there is another man at the opposite end of said table making pictures upon walrus tusks. Now this man seems completely satisfied that the world is just right and was got up just to his own idea.[11]

Rare and desirable, the naturally scrolled tooth of a fifteen foot narwhal, *Dentes balaenarum*, could measure eight feet. As it was difficult for a scrimshander to improve upon the natural lines of narwhal tusks, they are usually found intact, incorporated into walking sticks or decorative accents in large pieces.

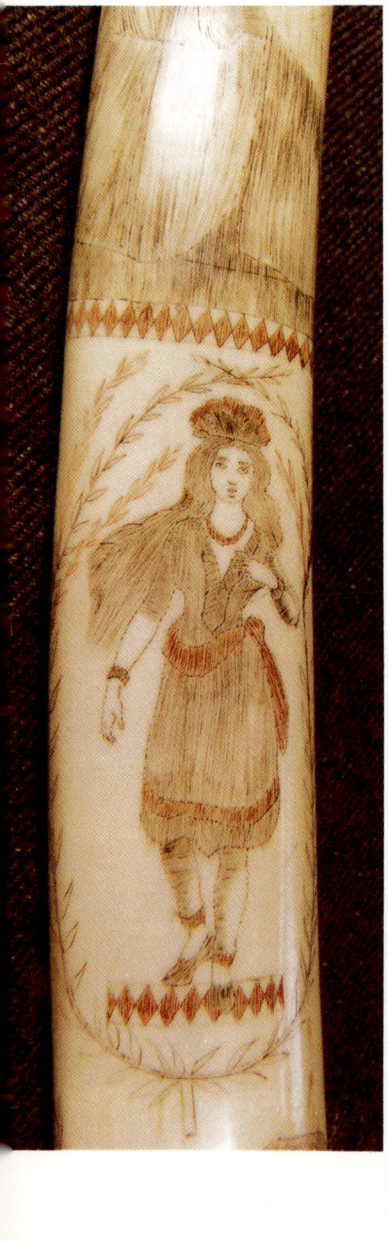

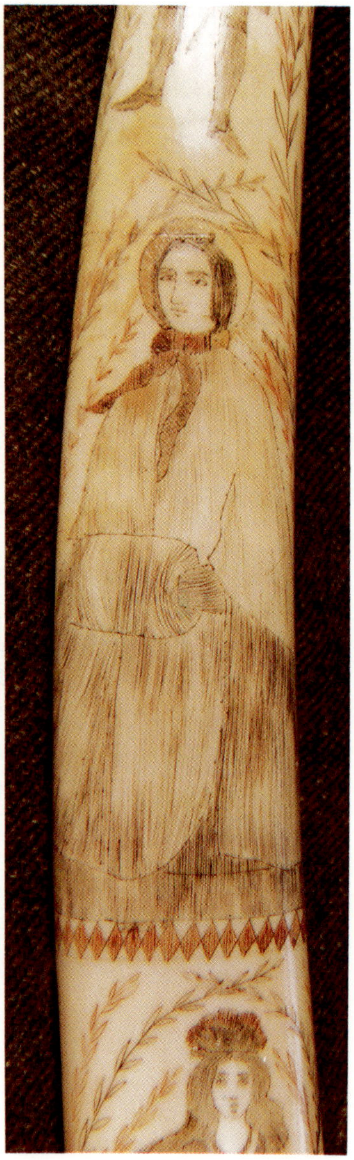

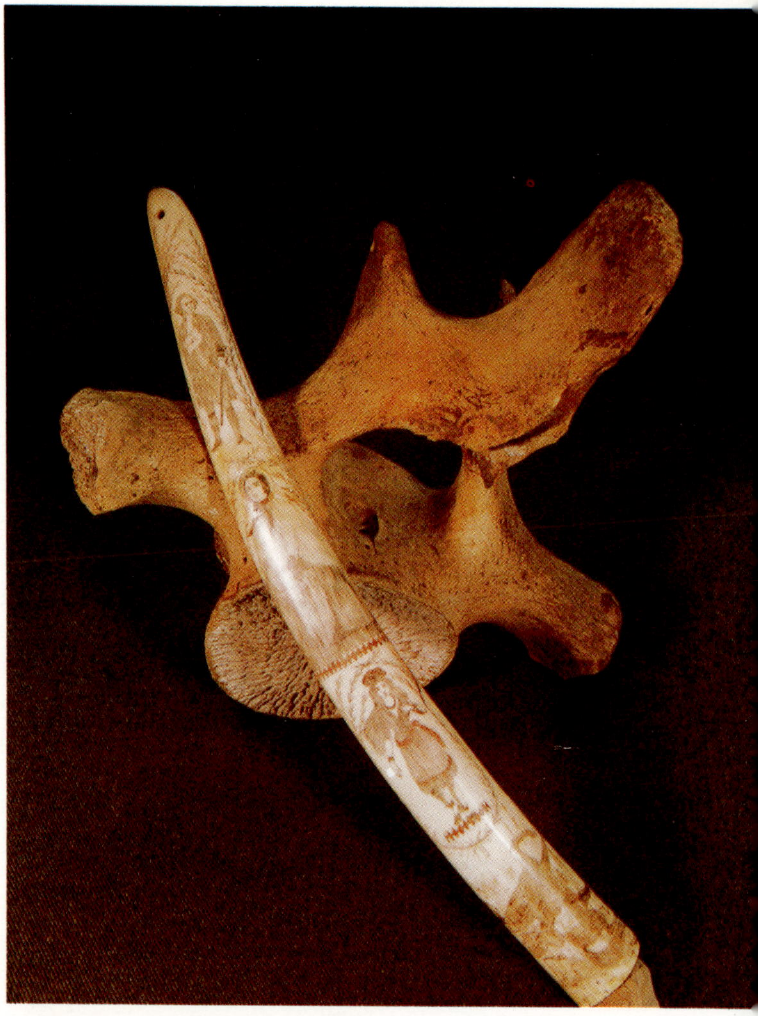

A whale vertebra supports this handsome walrus tusk whose four polychrome figures are engraved with the pin-prick technique. *Collection of Raymond and Elizabeth De Lucia*

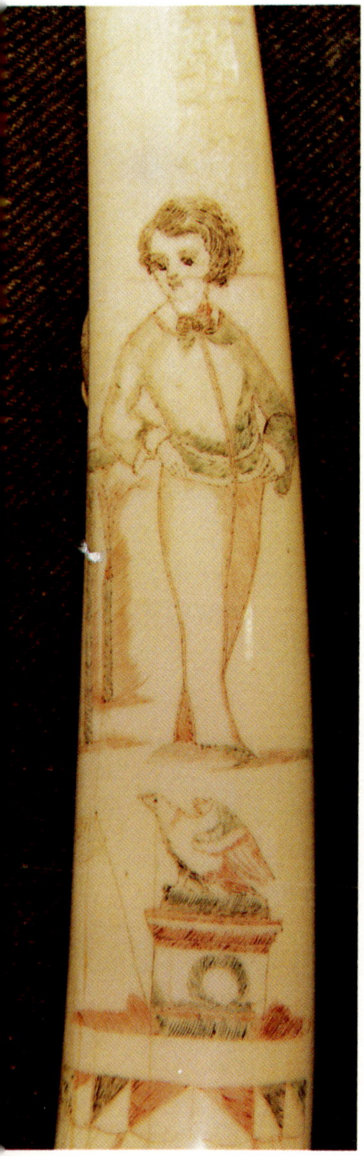

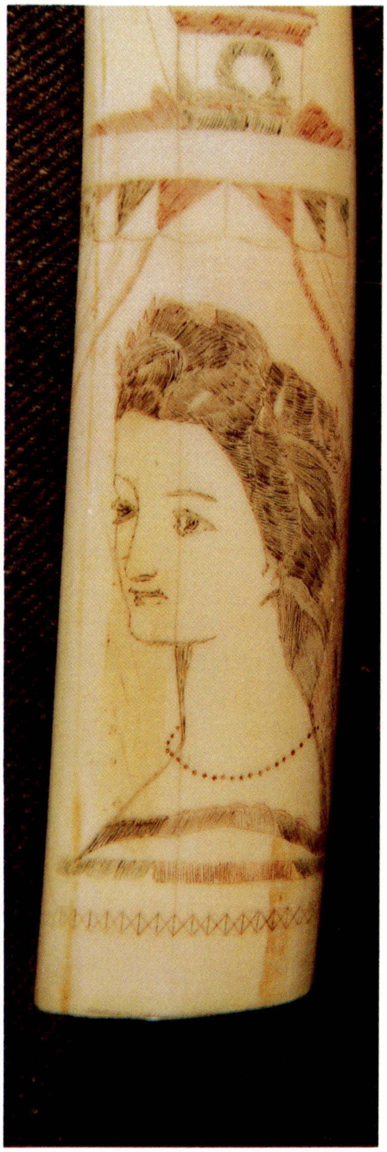

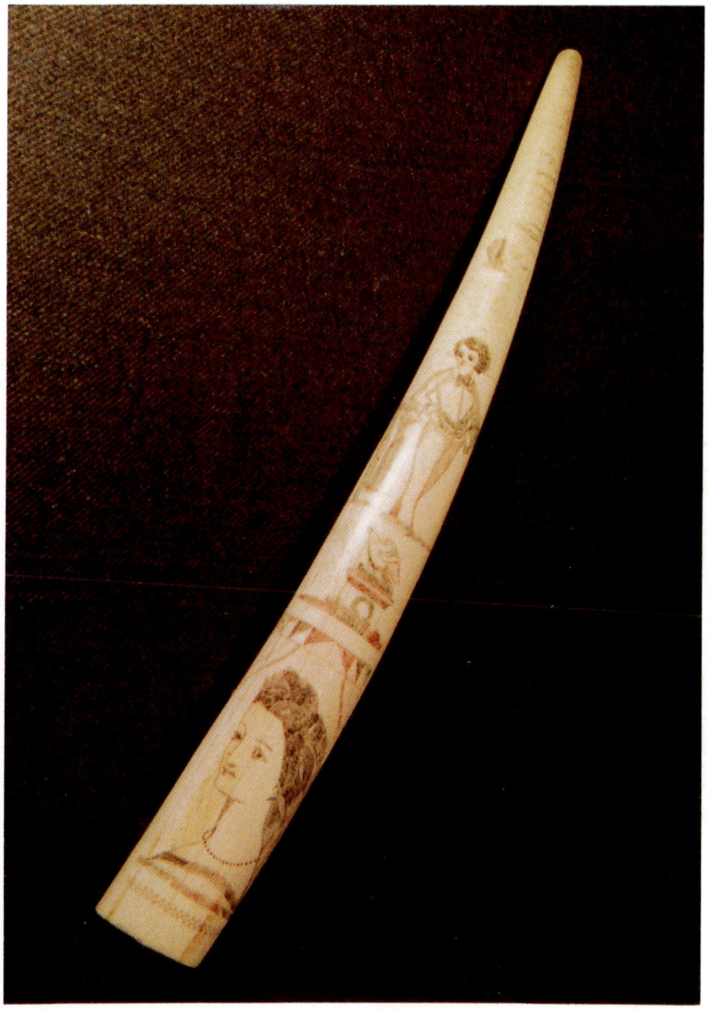

Red and green coloring highlight the renderings on this delicately worked walrus tusk. *Collection of Raymond and Elizabeth De Lucia*

Shells, exotic woods, tortoise shells and coconut shells were incorporated routinely into scrimshaw, sometimes subordinated to the ivory, sometimes making up the majority of the piece. Whaleman William Davis described such a find in Colombia's Selango Bay:

> Great heaps of large and exquisite mother-of-pearl shells were to be seen, and we selected a fair number of the choicest...We also took pains to secure some of the beautiful ornamental wood for canes and general whittling.[12]

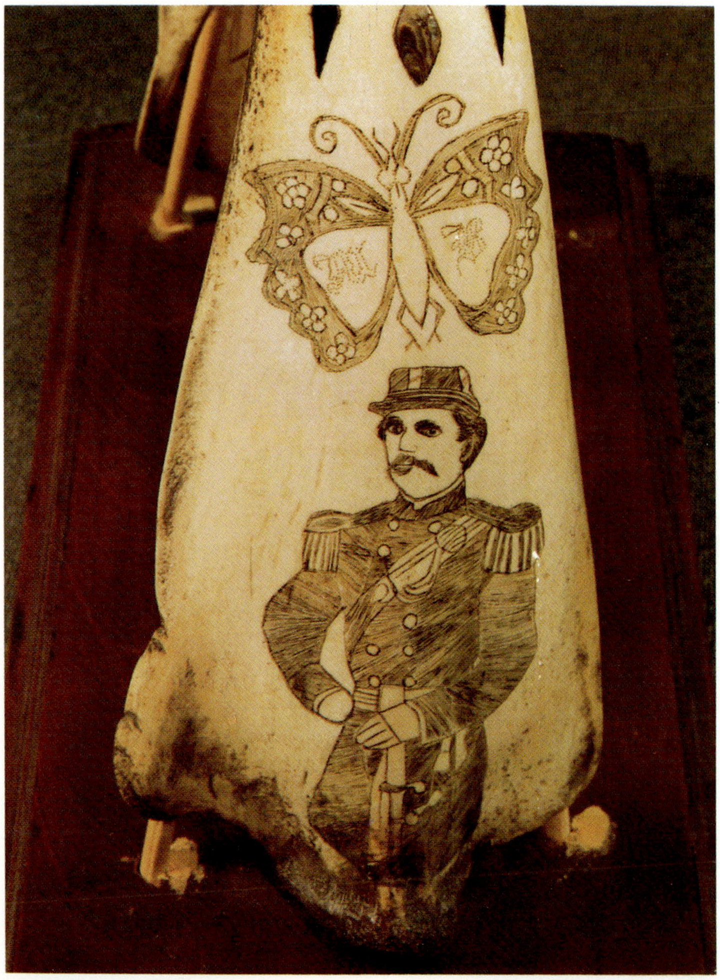

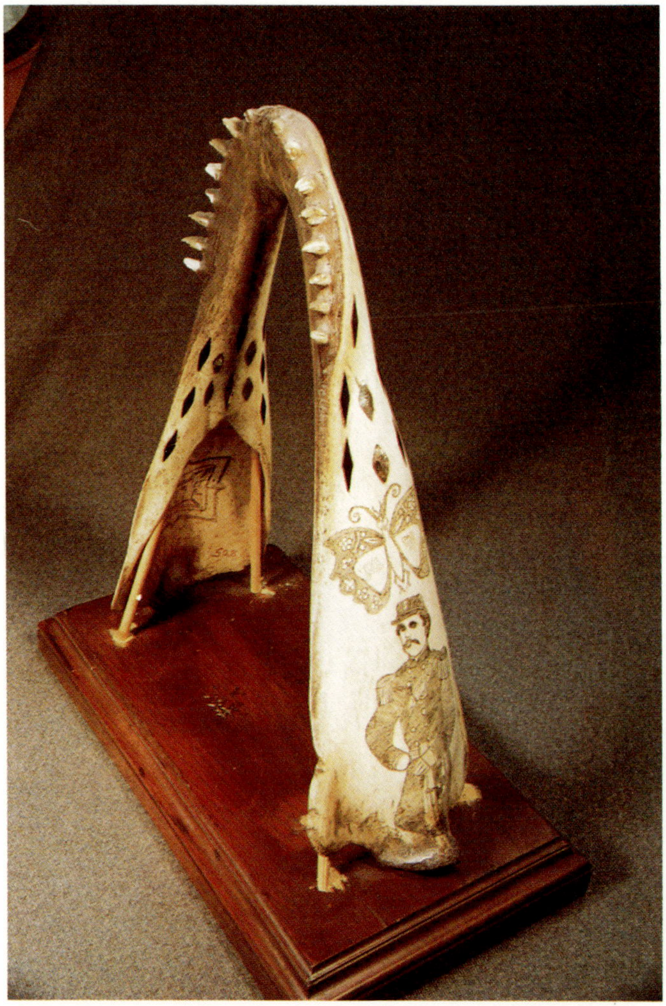

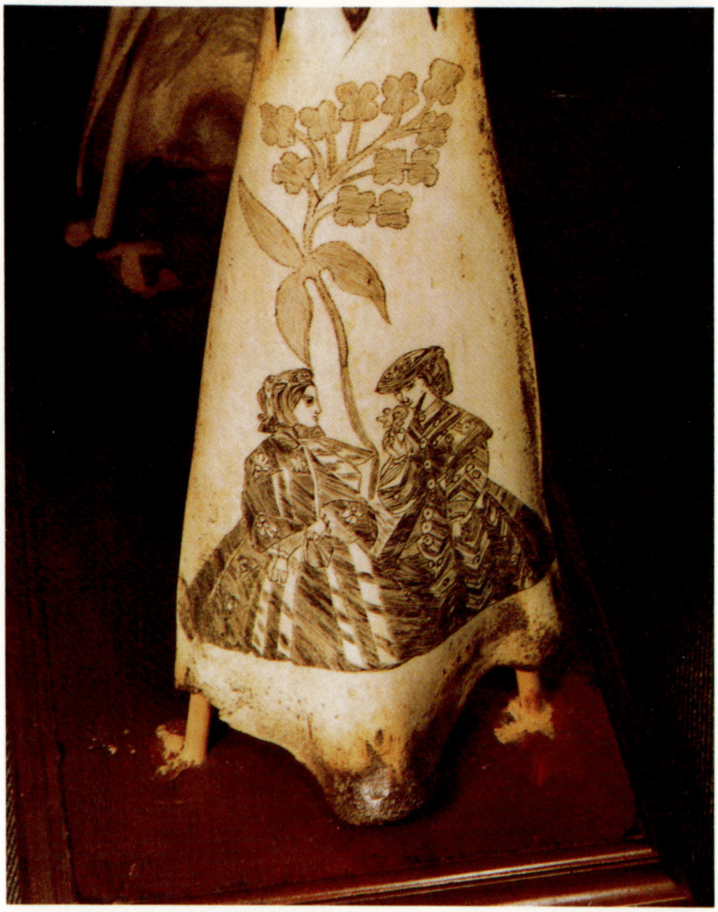

Blackfish, or pilot whales, were sometimes taken by whalers. Here, the jaw of one has been engraved with two fashionable women on one side and a one-handed Union soldier on the other. The jaw is inlaid with abalone and baleen. *Collection of Raymond and Elizabeth De Lucia*

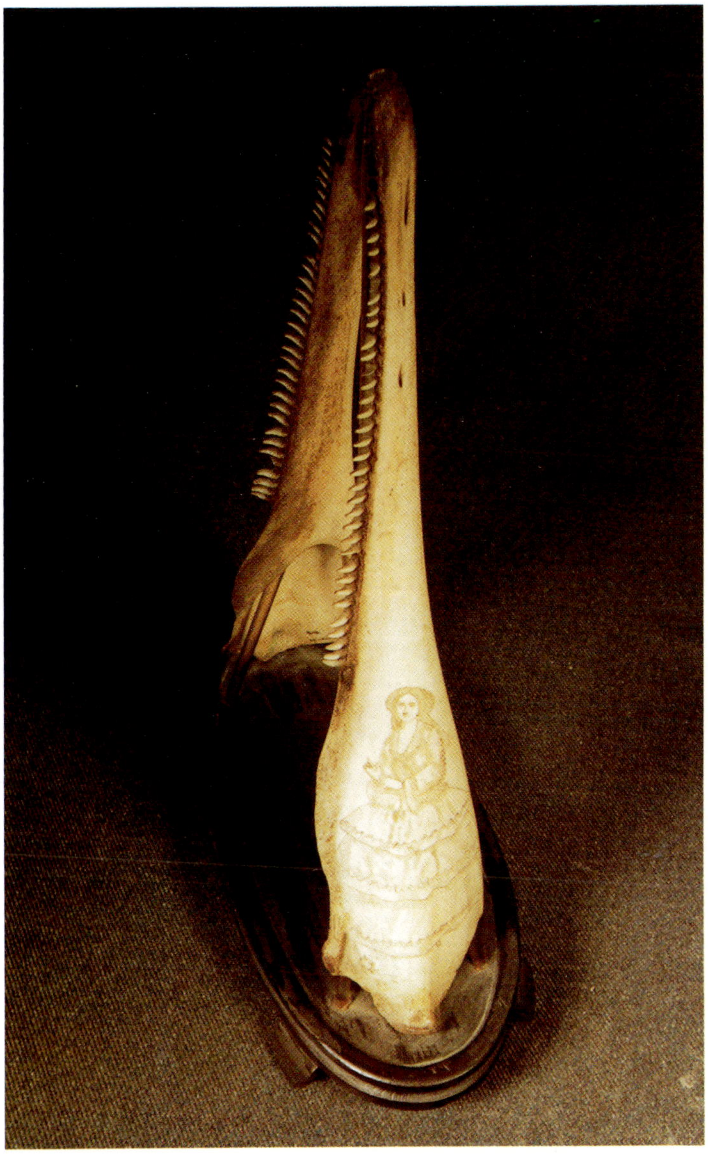

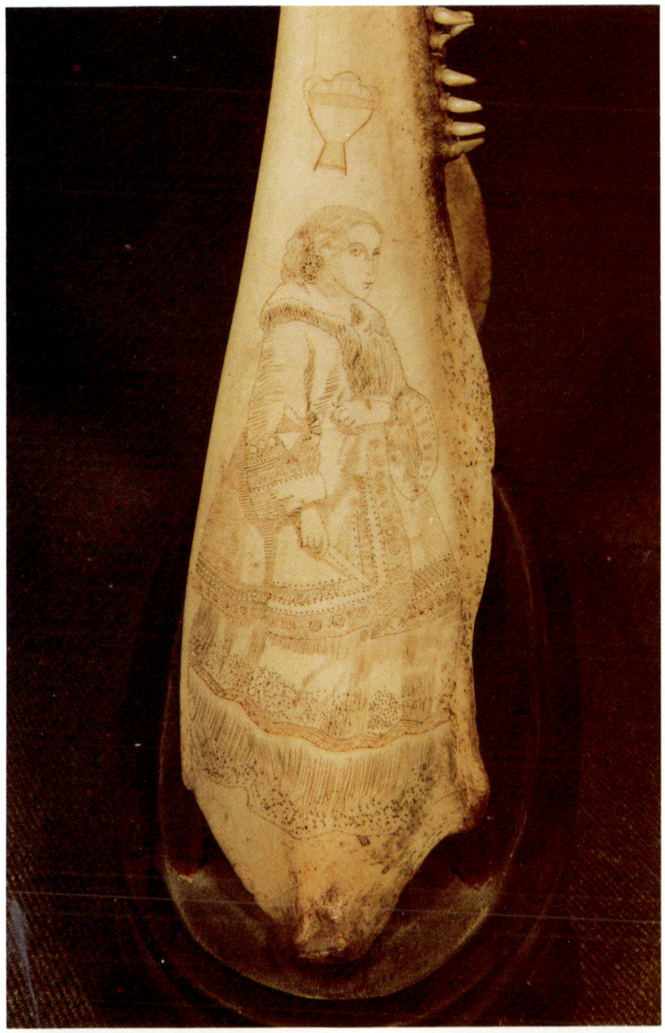

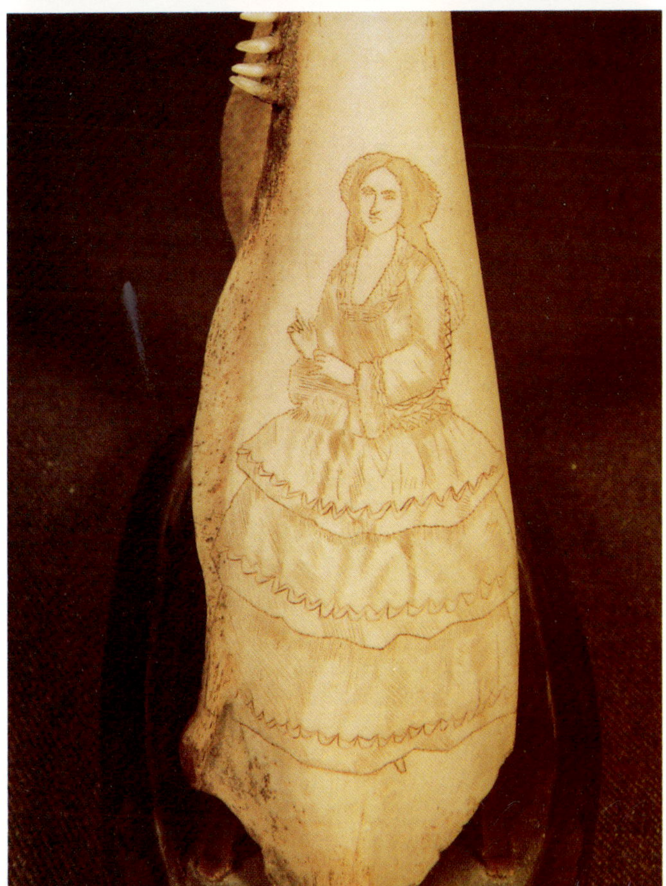

A porpoise jaw was the medium chosen by this scrimshander to depict two elaborately dressed women. Their ruffles and ribbons appear somewhat out of place on the toothy jaw. *Collection of Raymond and Elizabeth De Lucia*

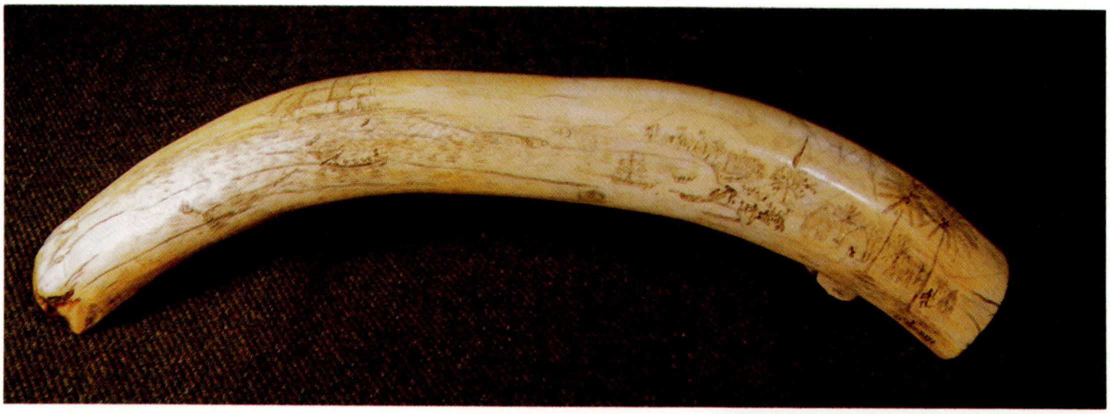

Hippopotamus tusks were also occasionally used for scrimshaw. On this example, the artist has engraved a panoramic scene showing both a whale hunt and a tropical village whose inhabitants are running toward the beach to meet the incoming sailors. *Collection of Raymond and Elizabeth De Lucia*

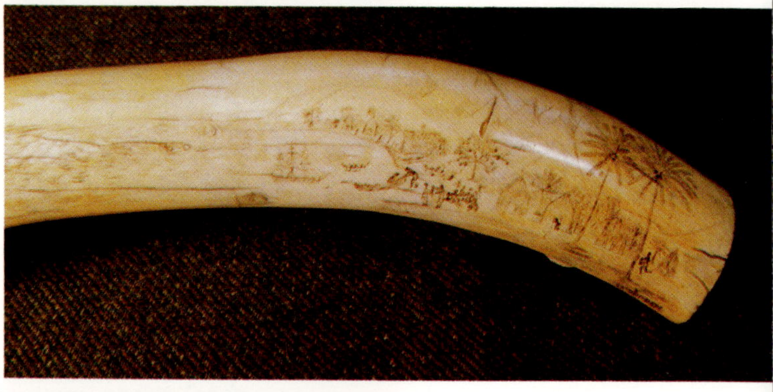

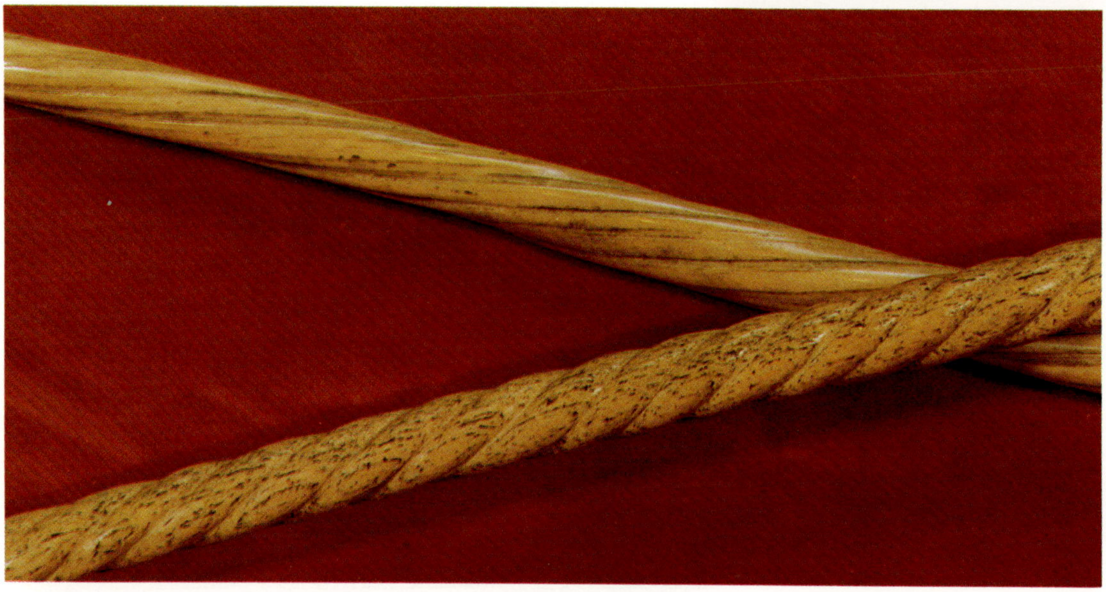

The shaft of the lower cane is whalebone, carved to resemble rope. The other, however, is a narwhal tooth in its natural state. *Collection of Raymond and Elizabeth De Lucia*

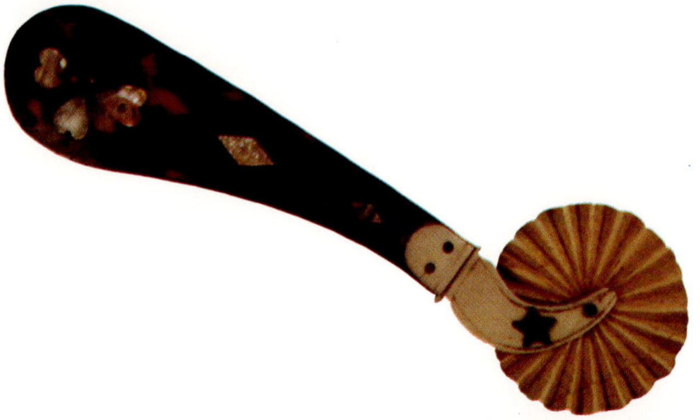

The tortoise shell handle of this pie crimper is inlaid with abalone. *Courtesy of the Nantucket Historical Association*

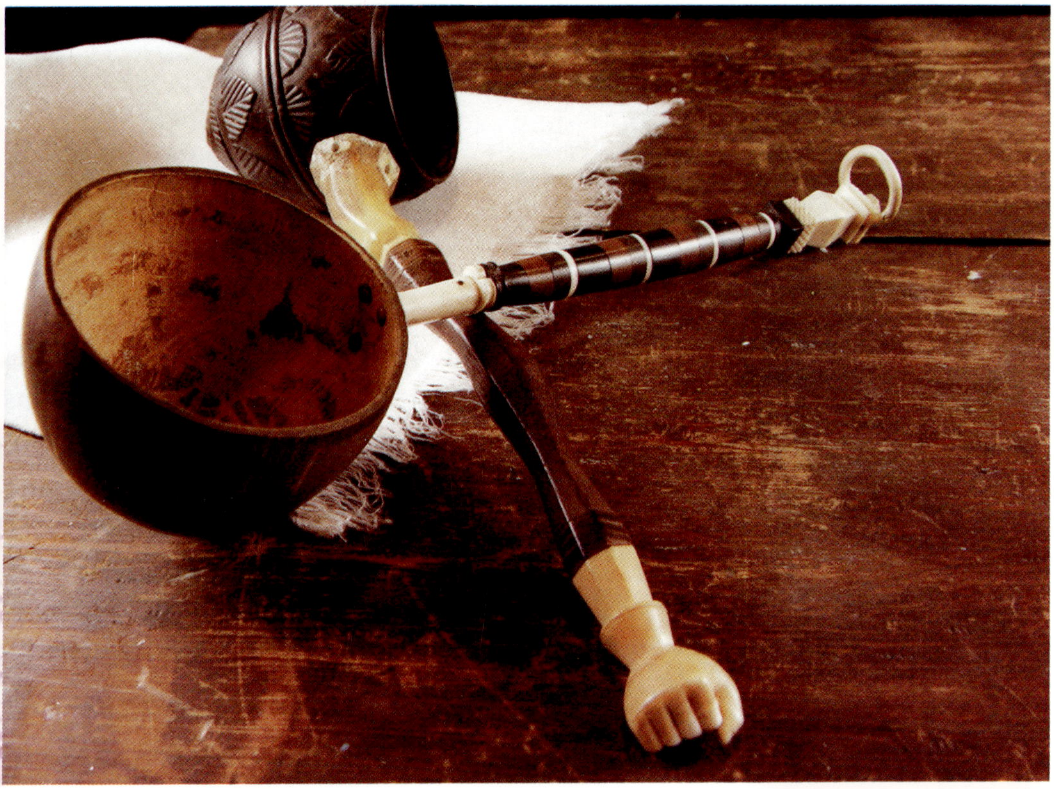

These beautifully carved coconut shell ladles incorporate tropical woods and whale ivory into their design. *Courtesy of the Nantucket Historical Association*

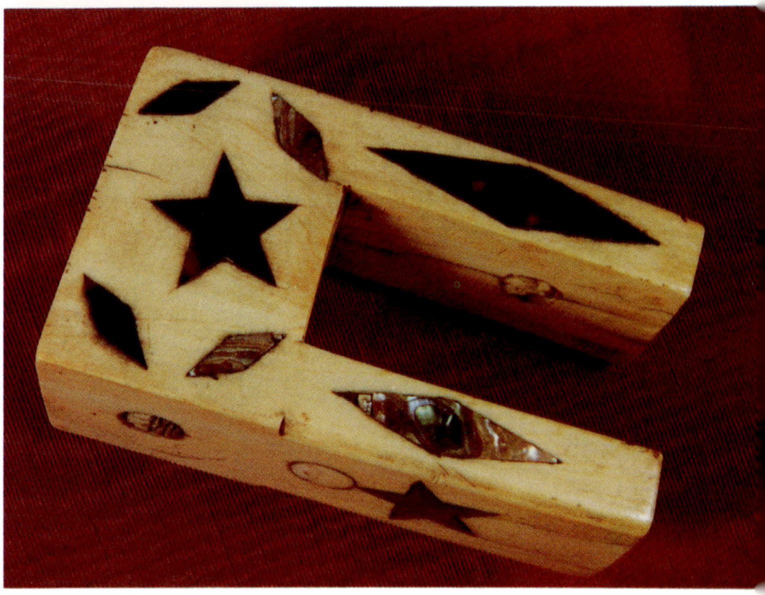

"In scrimshoning, we carve and work much in the ivory of whales' teeth, and by inlaying with pearl, some beautiful objects are wrought." (William Davis, *Nimrod of the Sea*, p. 265) Beautiful inlays of tortoise shell and abalone decorate this whale ivory swift clamp. *Collection of Raymond and Elizabeth De Lucia*

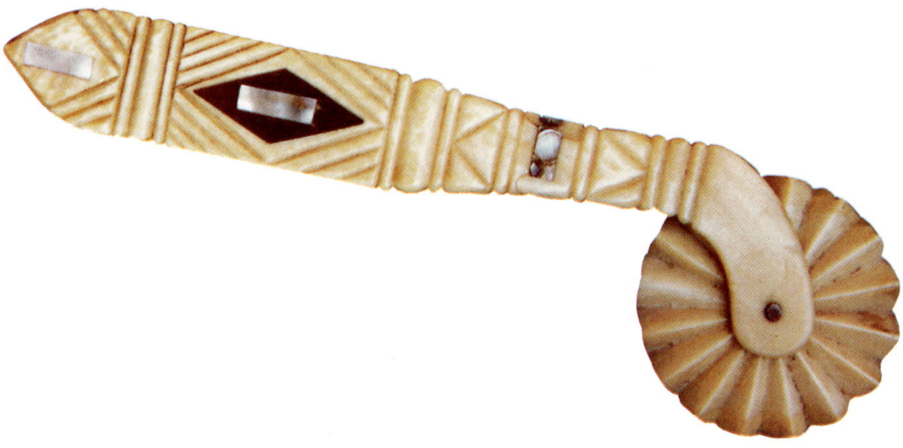

This sturdy, whale ivory pie crimper is inlaid with abalone and tortoise shell. *Collection of Charles A. Manghis*

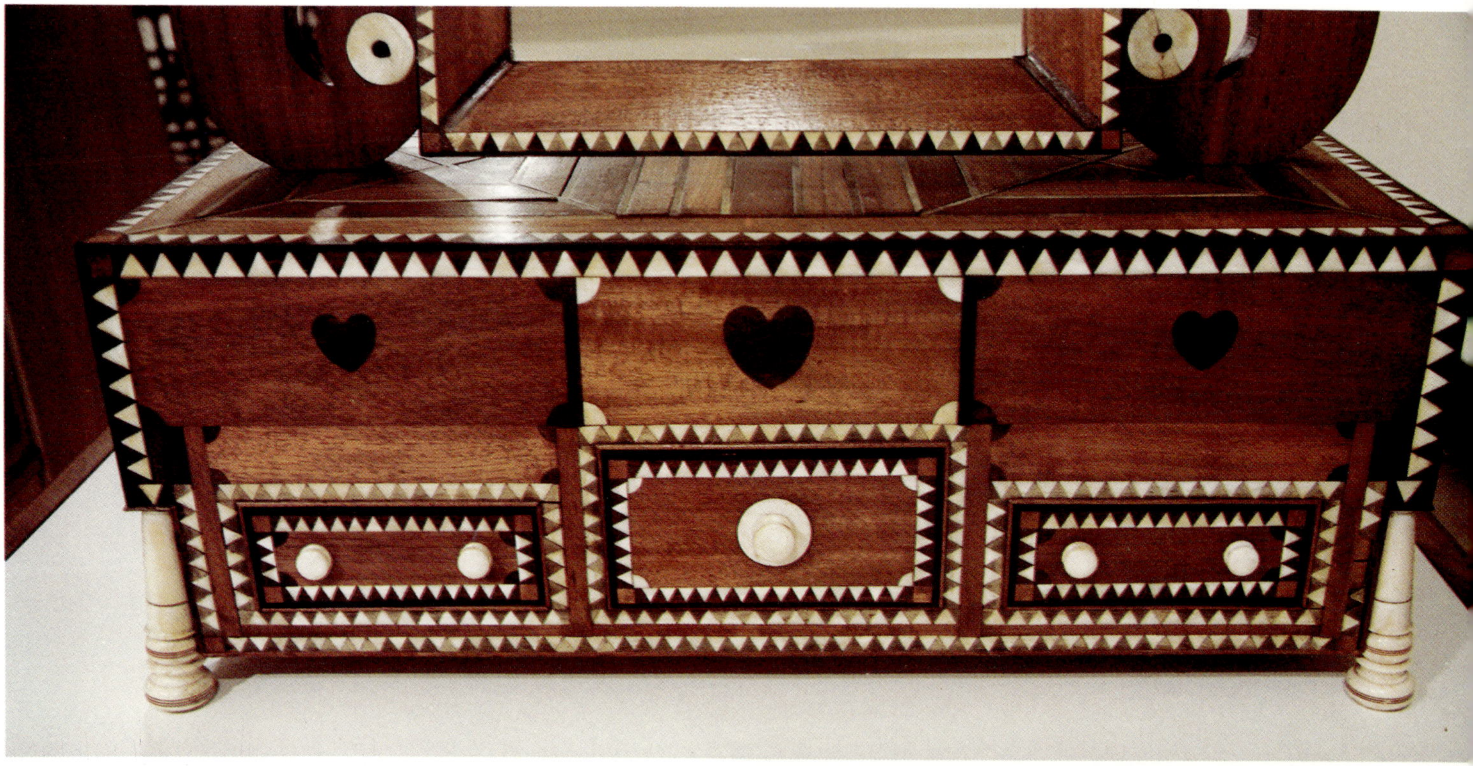

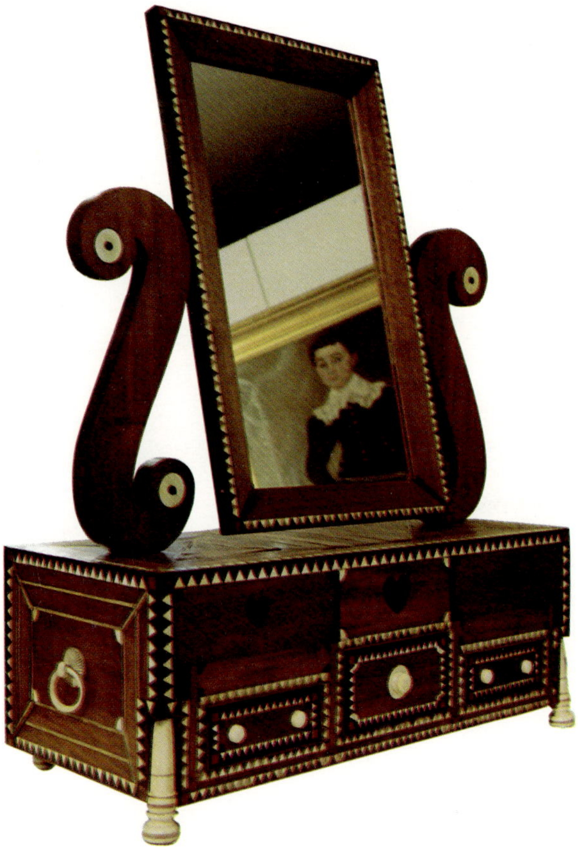

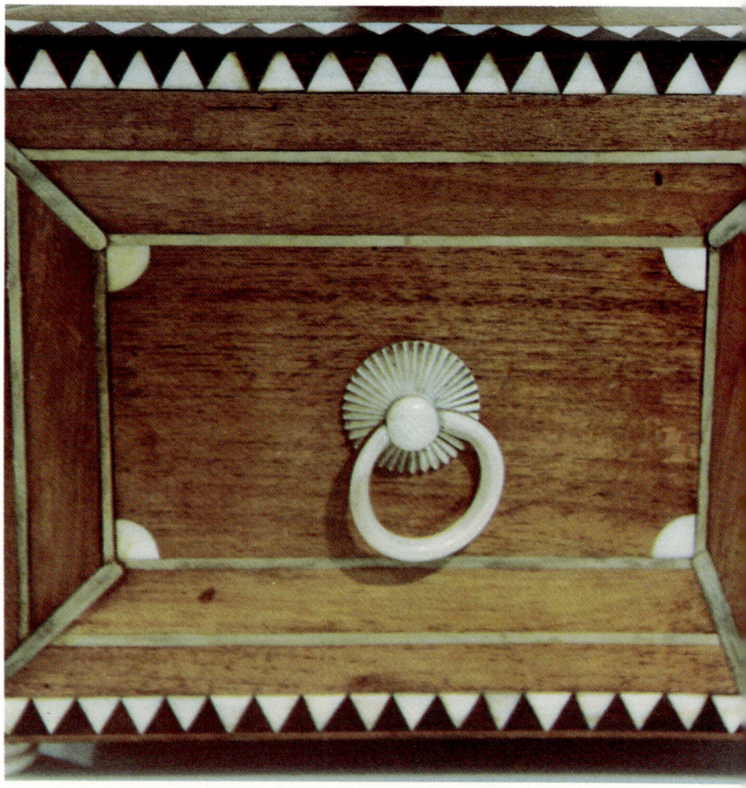

Captain James Archer constructed this beautiful dressing case for his wife Mary while sailing on the bark *Afton* between 1853 and 1856. The mahogany chest is inlaid with ebony, rosewood, whalebone, and whale ivory and is adorned with intricately carved knobs and legs of whale ivory. *Courtesy of the Nantucket Historical Association*

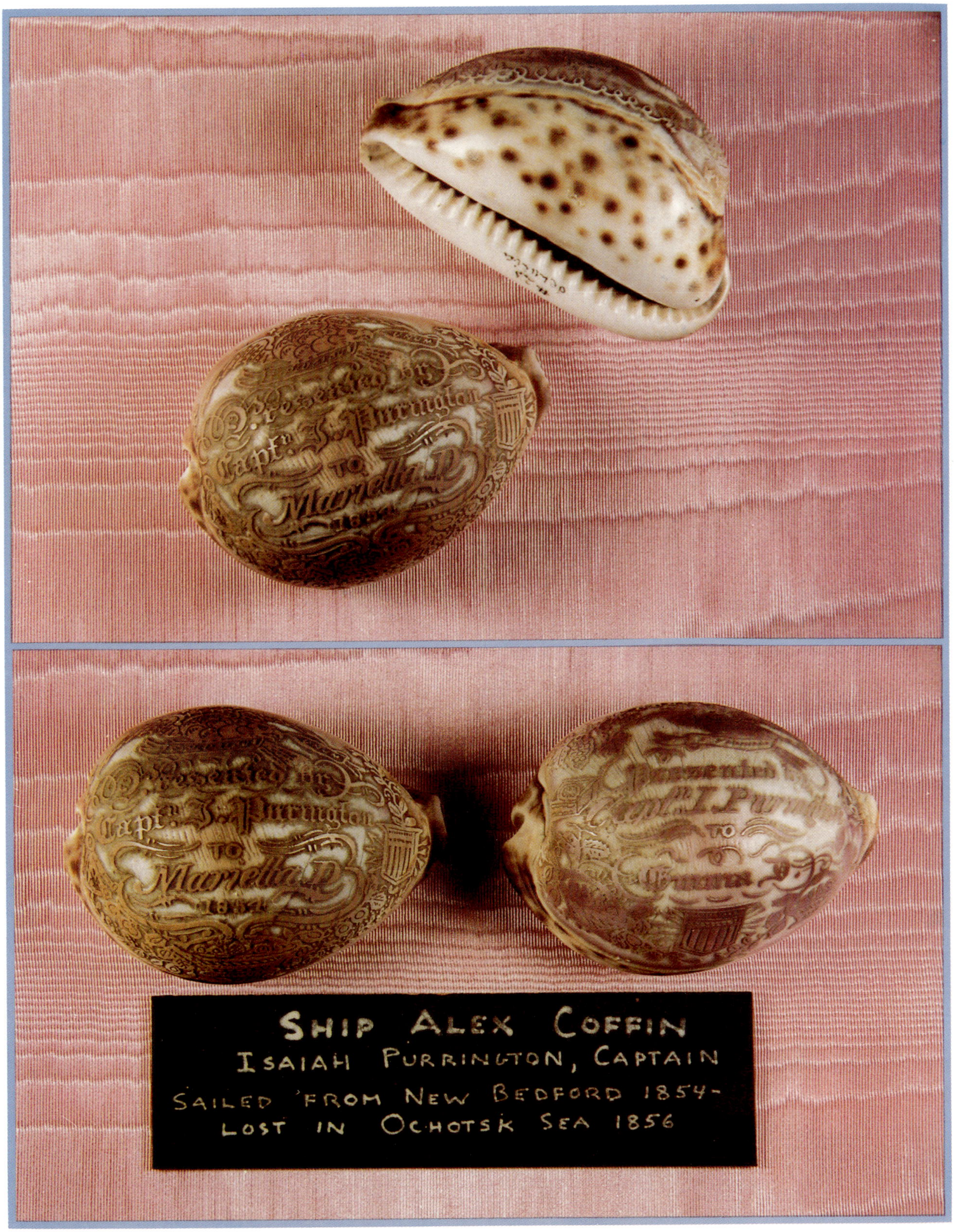

These cowrie shells were probably not carved by shipboard scrimshanders but rather by Pacific islanders encountered on the voyage. This pair was presented by Captain Isaiah Purrington of the ship *Alex Coffin* to two ladies, Emma and Marietta. *Collection of Raymond and Elizabeth De Lucia*

Before beginning the fine work of engraving, the scrimshander filed, sanded and polished a tooth. Sharkskin was used for sanding because, as Francis Olmstead noted, "The skin of the shark is very hard and rough like a file, which renders it an excellent substance for sandpaper in smoothing wood work."[13] Finer abrasion was achieved by buffing the work with wood ashes or pumice and a final polish was attained by vigorous hand rubbing.

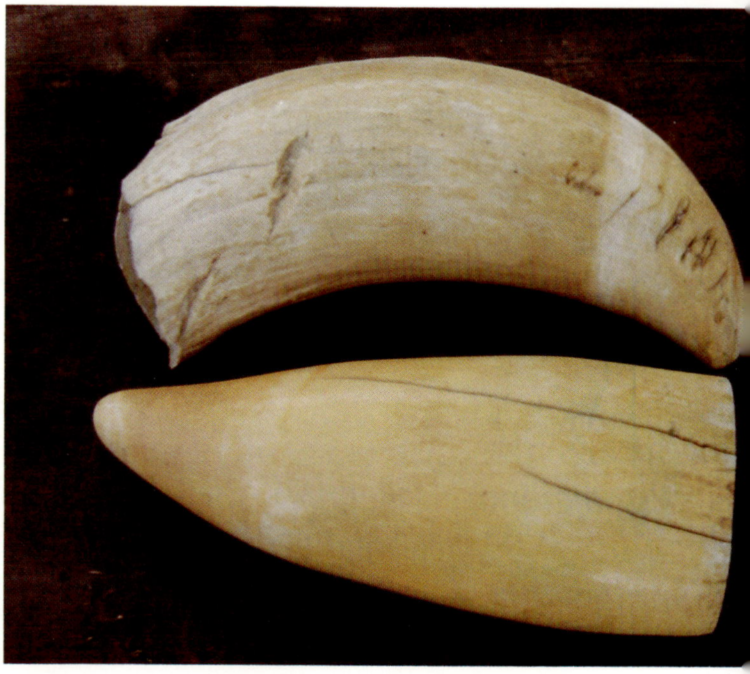

The tooth above remains in its natural state, while the one below has been filed and polished and is ready to work. *Collection of Charles A. Manghis*

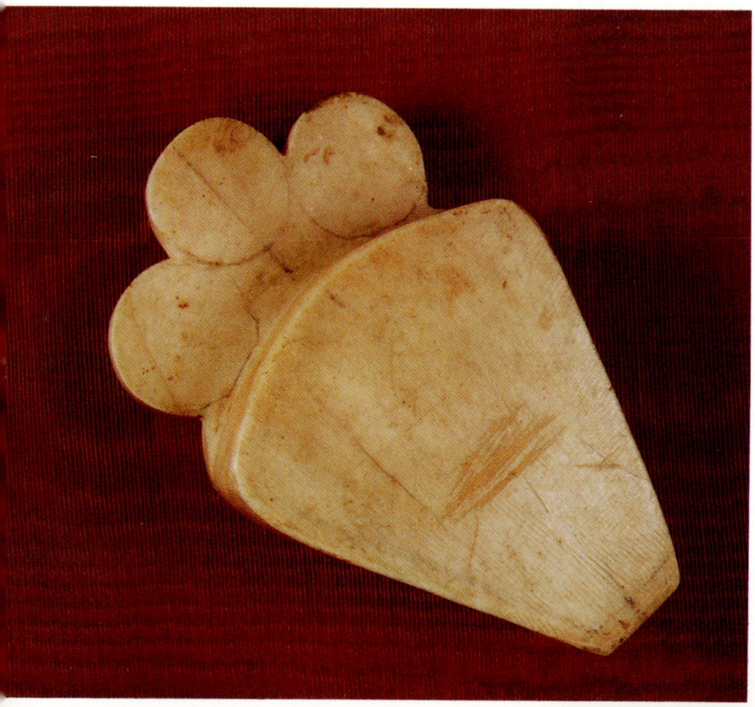

Over the years the artist's pencil marks have remained, indicating the manner in which he intended to carve this incipient whale ivory swift clamp. *Collection of Raymond and Elizabeth De Lucia*

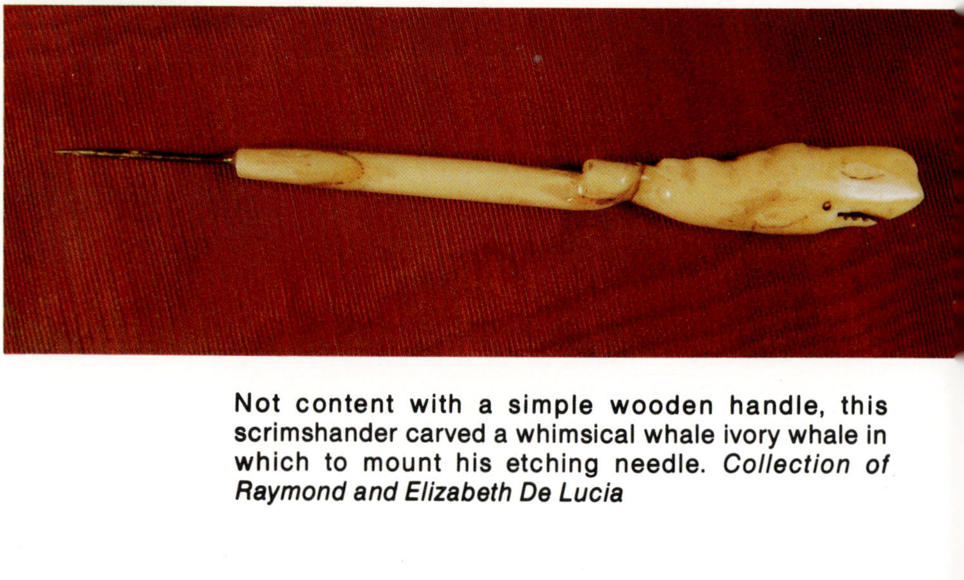

Not content with a simple wooden handle, this scrimshander carved a whimsical whale ivory whale in which to mount his etching needle. *Collection of Raymond and Elizabeth De Lucia*

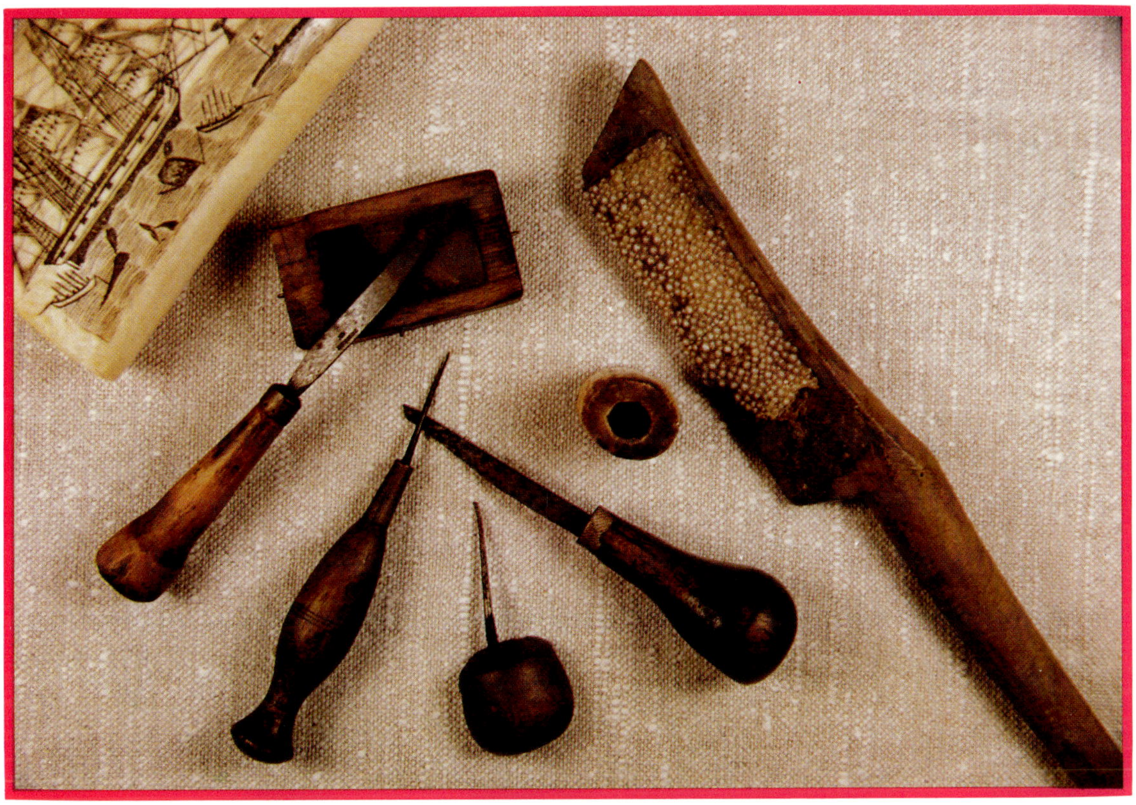

These simple tools are the sort used by nineteenth century scrimshanders. They include awls, files, sail needles set in handles, a whetstone, a sharkskin sander, and an inkwell carved from a small whale's tooth. *Courtesy of the Nantucket Historical Association*

Difficult as it is to believe when viewing the intricate work of a nineteenth century scrimshander, his principal tool for both engraving and carving was an ordinary jackknife. Additional assistance in engraving was provided by awls and sail needles imbedded in handles. The file was an important tool, used not only for smoothing, but also to achieve the same effect as scroll sawing.

Some ships had turning lathes for use by their coopers and carpenters and these were available to the crew. By modern standards, however, these machines, powered by foot treadles, were primitive at best; and not everyone who approached a lathe was rewarded with a work of art, as Mary Lawrence described on December 27, 1859:

> Captain Willard came on board today with his carpenter, that he might use our turning lathe, but he was not at all successful. Samuel turned two ivory lamp picks for him.[14]

As was the case with Captain Willard's vessel, not all ships carried lathes and much of what appears to be carefully turned lathe work is, actually, incredibly accurate hand carving and filing. Such was the situation aboard Bullen's *Cachalot*:

> The work turned out would, in many cases, take a very high place in an exhibition of turnery, though never a lathe was near it.[15]

As with tools and materials, the pigments chosen to color engraved pieces of scrimshaw were dictated by their availability. For monochrome work, lampblack and soot from the tryworks were always on hand. India ink was also used, although to a lesser degree. Natural dyes, oil paints, water color paints and sealing wax were used for polychrome engraving. Although surviving monochrome works greatly outnumber polychrome ones, more colored pieces of scrimshaw may have been produced than the current supply indicates. Some researchers believe that as the ivory dried over the years, waterbased pigments may have been absorbed into the tooth and faded.[16]

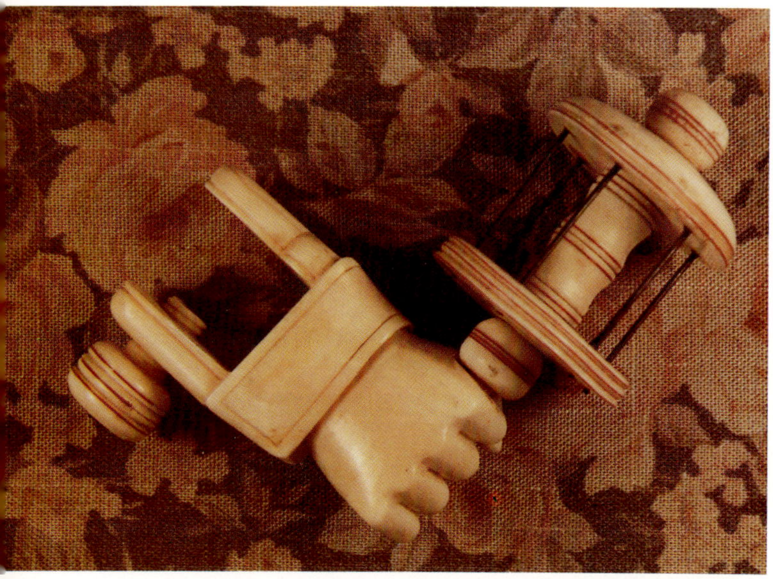

A beautifully carved and turned whale ivory swift clamp, literally grasping a silk spool holder, is colored with red sealing wax. *Courtesy of the Nantucket Historical Association*

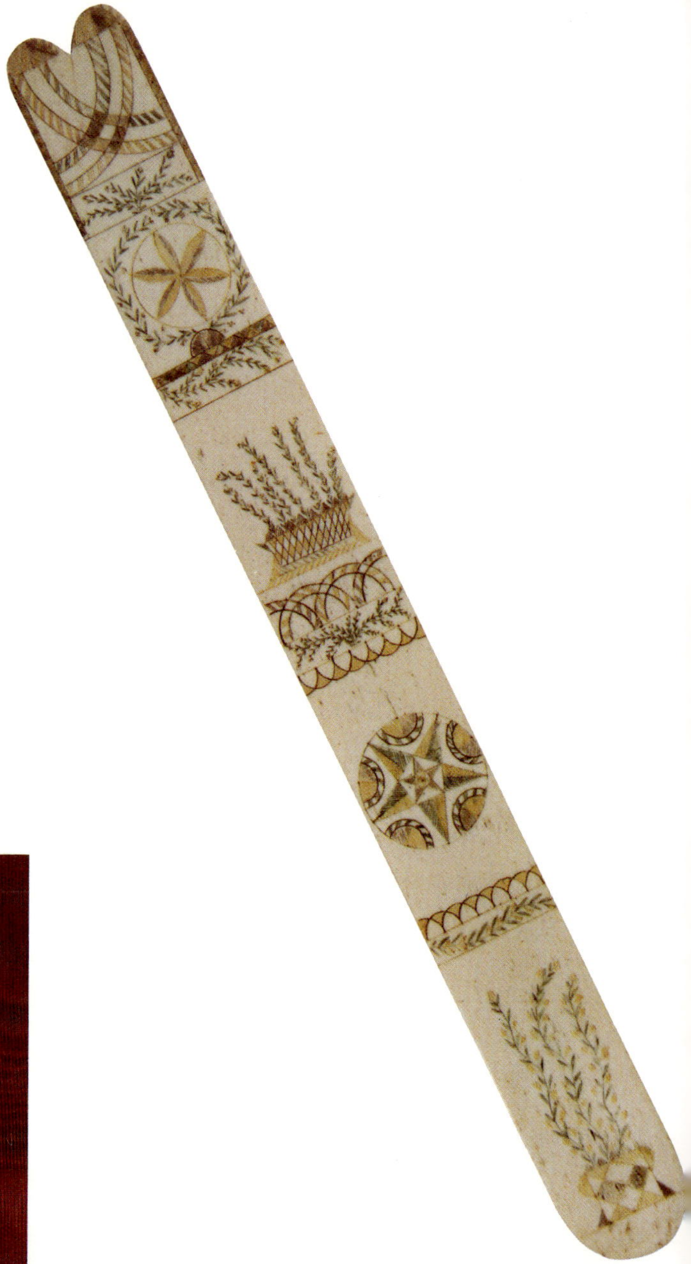

The creator of this lovely whalebone busk chose ochre and green pigments to highlight his work. *Private Collection*

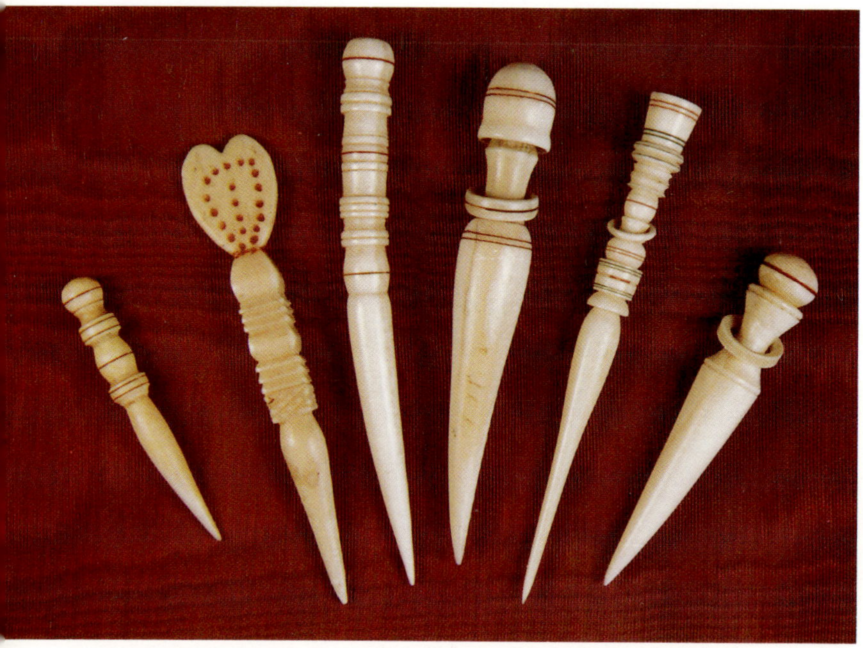

Red and green sealing wax coloring emphasizes the carving in this group of whale ivory bodkins. *Collection of Curtis Nyquist, B.M.N.*

[01] Stuart M. Frank, *Dictionary of Scrimshaw Artists* (Mystic, Conn.: Mystic Seaport Museum, 1991), 172.

[02] Ibid.

[03] Stuart M. Frank, Presentation at the Kendall Whaling Museum's Fourth Annual Scrimshaw Collectors' Weekend, April 24, 1992.

[04] William S. Cary, *Wrecked on the Feejees* (Nantucket, Mass.: The Inquirer and Mirror Press, 1949), 23.

[05] Ibid., 33.

[06] Frank, Presentation at the Kendall Whaling Museum.

[07] Clifford W. Ashley, *The Yankee Whaler* (Boston, Mass.: Houghton Mifflin, 1938), 113.

[08] Frank, *Dictionary*, 37.

[09] Ibid., 172.

[10] Mary C. Lawrence, *The Captain's Best Mate* (Providence, R.I.: Brown University Press, 1966), 108.

[11] Frank, *Dictionary*, 178.

[12] William M. Davis, *Nimrod of the Sea* (North Quincy, Mass.: The Christopher Publishing House, 1972, 130.

[13] Francis A. Olmstead, *Incidents of a Whaling Voyage* (Rutland, Vt.: Charles E. Tuttle Co., Inc., 1969), 184.

[14] Lawrence, *The Captain's Best Mate*, 210.

[15] Frank T. Bullen, *The Cruise of the "Cachalot"* (Philadelphia, Penn.: David McKay Publisher, 1899), 84.

[16] Desmond Liddy, Presentation at the Kendall Whaling Museum's Fourth Annual Scrimshaw Collector's Weekend, April 25, 1992.

5. Themes and Techniques

The scrimshander's craft often reflected the best of his world and was a reaction to the worst of it. Working on a cleanly executed, intricately designed piece of scrimshaw was certainly a counterpoint to moments when the pitching decks ran with oil and blood. Etching a message of love to a sweetheart was a soothing alternative to the cramped, rough world of the foc'sle; and, after months surrounded only by water, many a sailor found joy by detailing the lines of a trim New England village or bucolic farm scenes. Yet despite his yearning for home, much pride and professional satisfaction derived from the ability to render perfectly the ship on which he sailed, each line exactly placed, each sail properly set. In addition, hours spent meticulously reproducing every detail of the most recent whale hunt recorded for posterity the artist's personal role in the drama and danger.

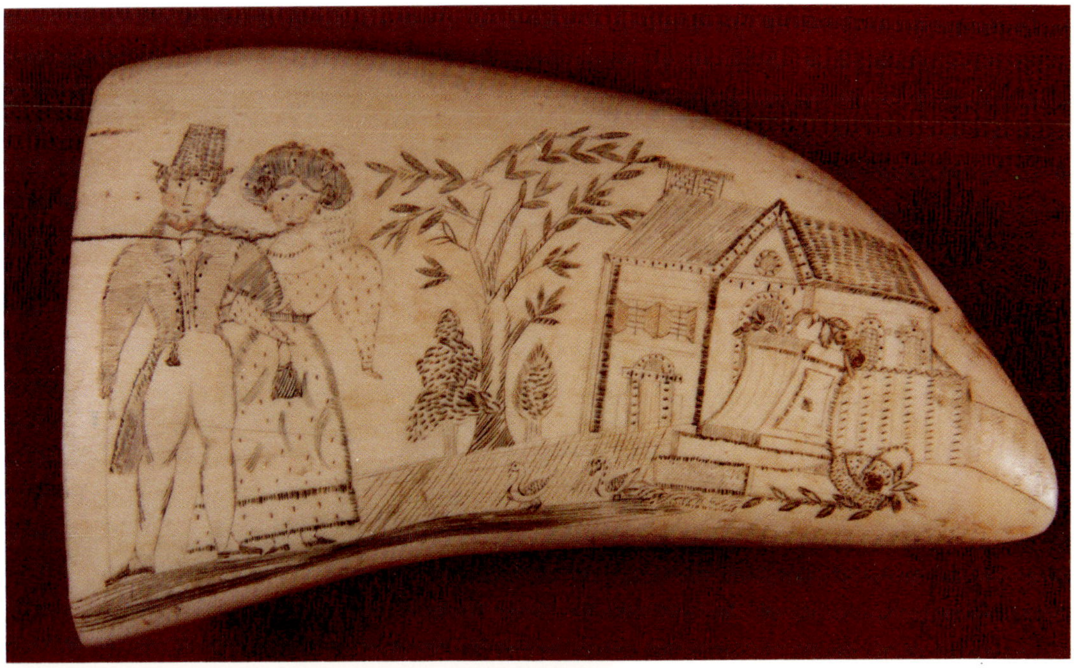

This delightful tooth epitomizes the dreams of home and family shared by all the men aboard ship. *Madden Collection*

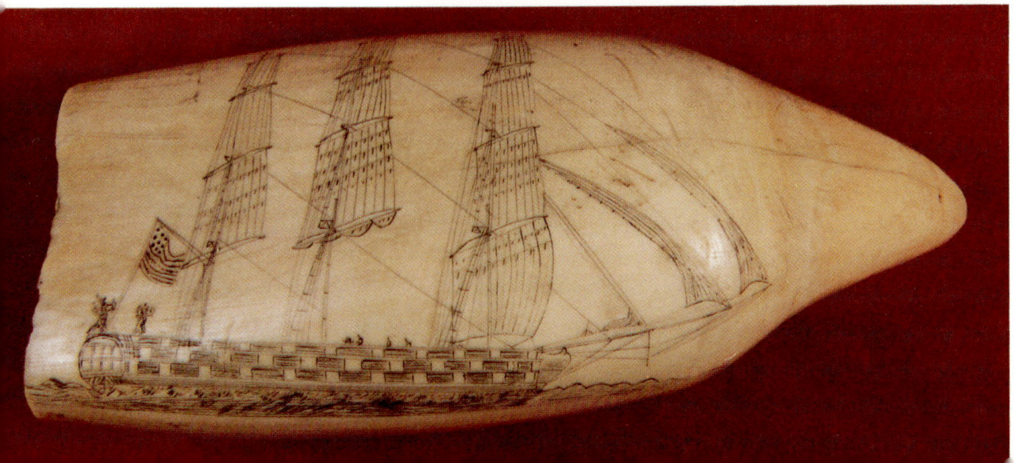

On the stern of the American frigate engraved on this tooth, two officers are holding quadrants, thus lending to this piece the name "Navigator Tooth." *Private Collection*

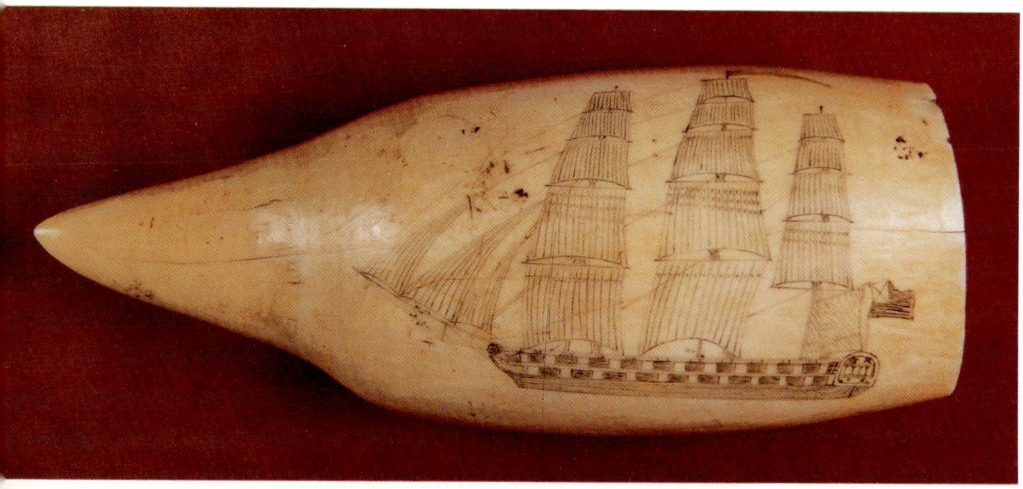

An English frigate sails a waterless ocean on the reverse of the "Navigator Tooth". *Private Collection*

The great era of scrimshaw closely paralleled the Golden Age of whaling. Between 1830 and 1850, scrimshaw had become a stylized and structural form with common themes, motifs and engraving techniques. Yet within these structured boundaries, the more practiced artisans developed their own styles and techniques enabling attribution today to either identified scrimshanders or at least anonymous artists to whom certain bodies of work can be ascribed.

By the 1830s, new printing techniques had greatly increased the amount of illustrated material available to the common man. The scrimshander could choose among lithographs, fashion plates, advertising placards and other illustrated material for either inspiration or, more often, sources of outright copying.

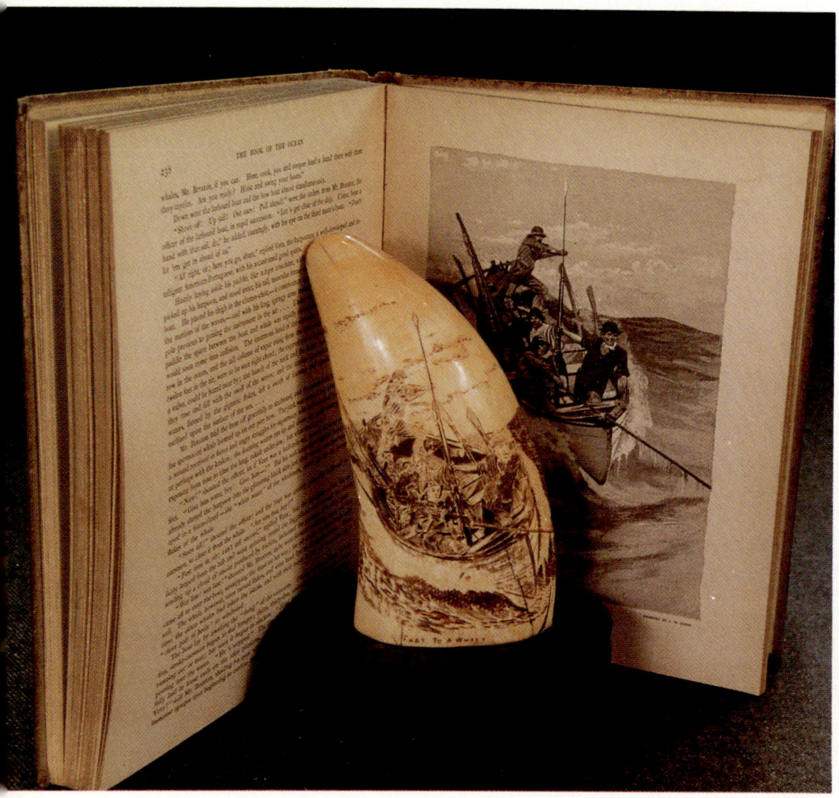

The scrimshawed scene "Fast to a Whale" was obviously a reproduction of this engraving by J. W. Evans. *Collection of Raymond and Elizabeth De Lucia*

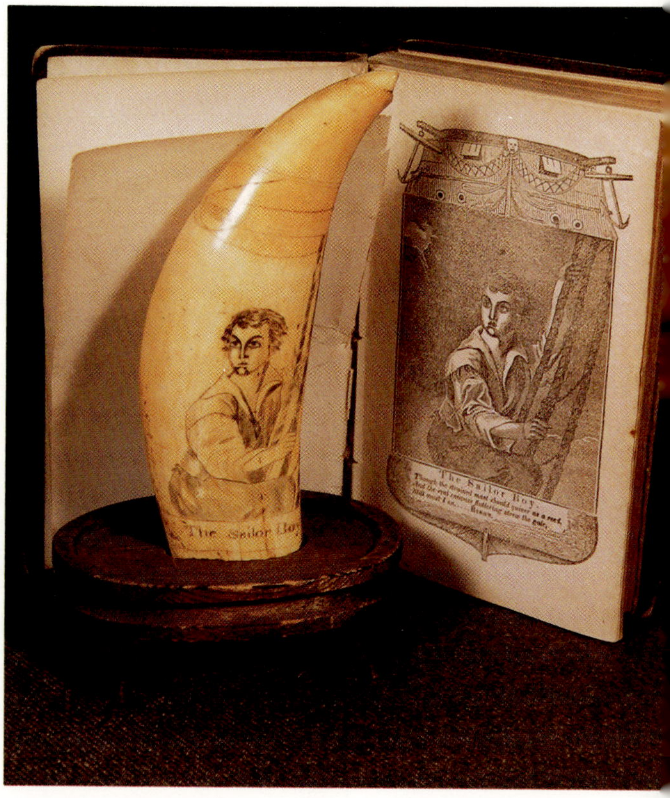

The inspiration for "The Sailor Boy" can be found on the frontispiece of *Shipwrecks and Disasters at Sea* published in 1836. *Collection of Raymond and Elizabeth De Lucia*

Engraved scrimshaw includes a wide variety of repeating themes. Patriotic renderings included national leaders, naval engagements, the female embodiment of liberty and references to both the War of 1812 and the associated threats posed to sailors' rights. Also popular were literary characters, fashionable women of the period, and flora and fauna. The marine animals encountered daily were well documented. "Even though a few seamen dismissed the ocean as a wide desolate waste, others found it teeming with inspiration."[1]

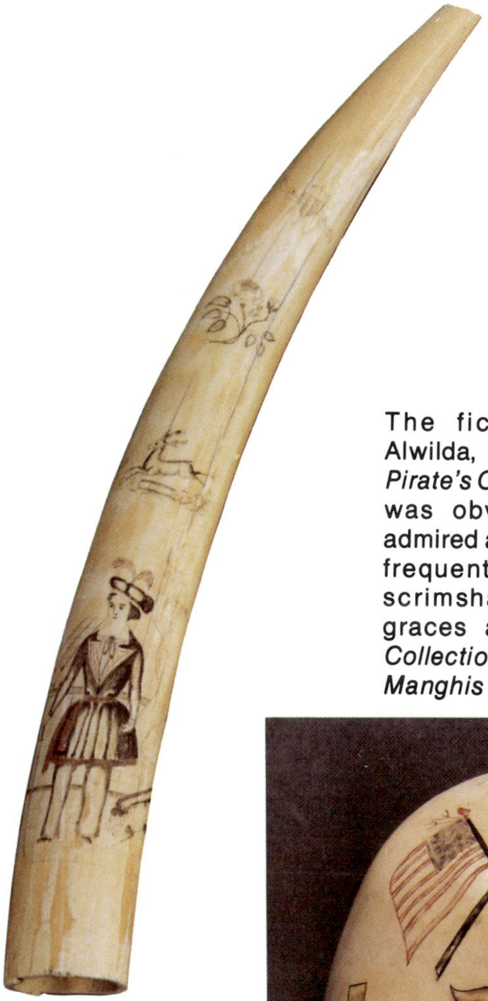

The fictional pirate, Alwilda, heroine of *The Pirate's Own Book* (1837), was obviously greatly admired as she appeared frequently in pictorial scrimshaw. Here she graces a walrus tusk. *Collection of Charles A. Manghis*

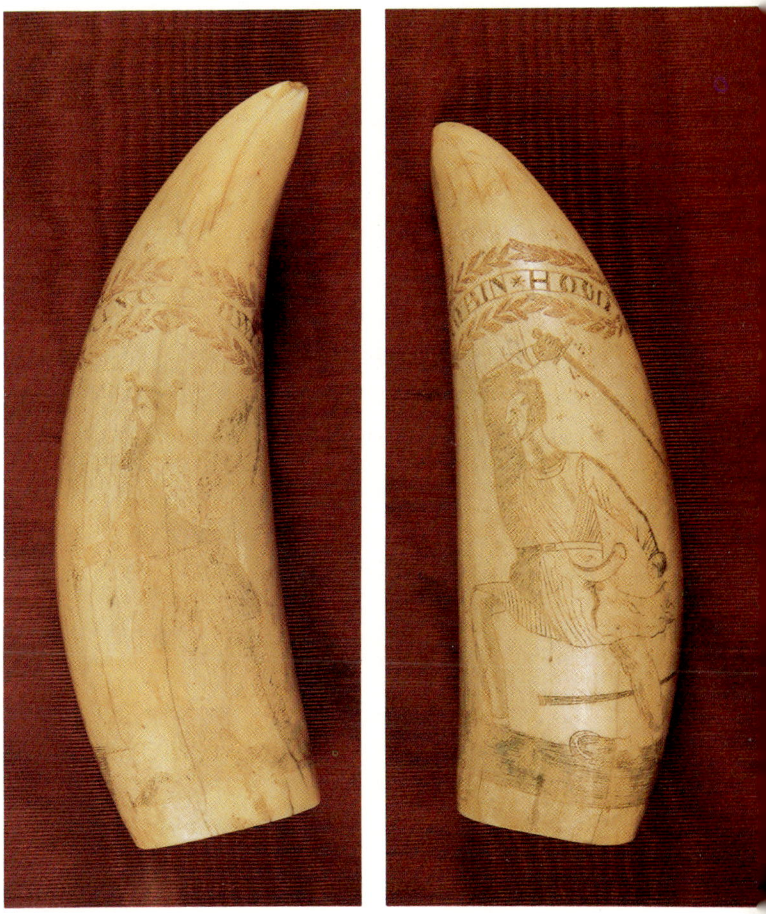

A nineteenth century theatrical publication may have served as the model for this dramatic "Robin Hood". Although the engraving is worn, King Edwin can still be discerned on the reverse of the tooth. *Collection of Charles A. Manghis*

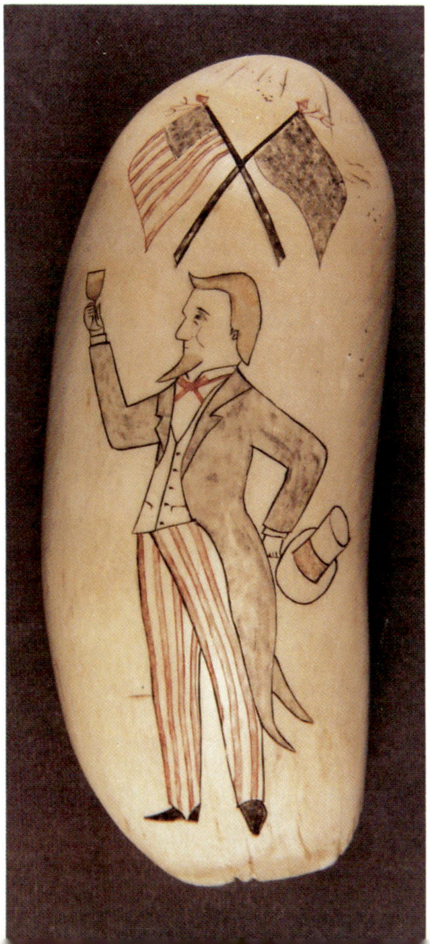

A colorful Uncle Sam toasts to Liberty. *Courtesy of the Nantucket Historical Association*

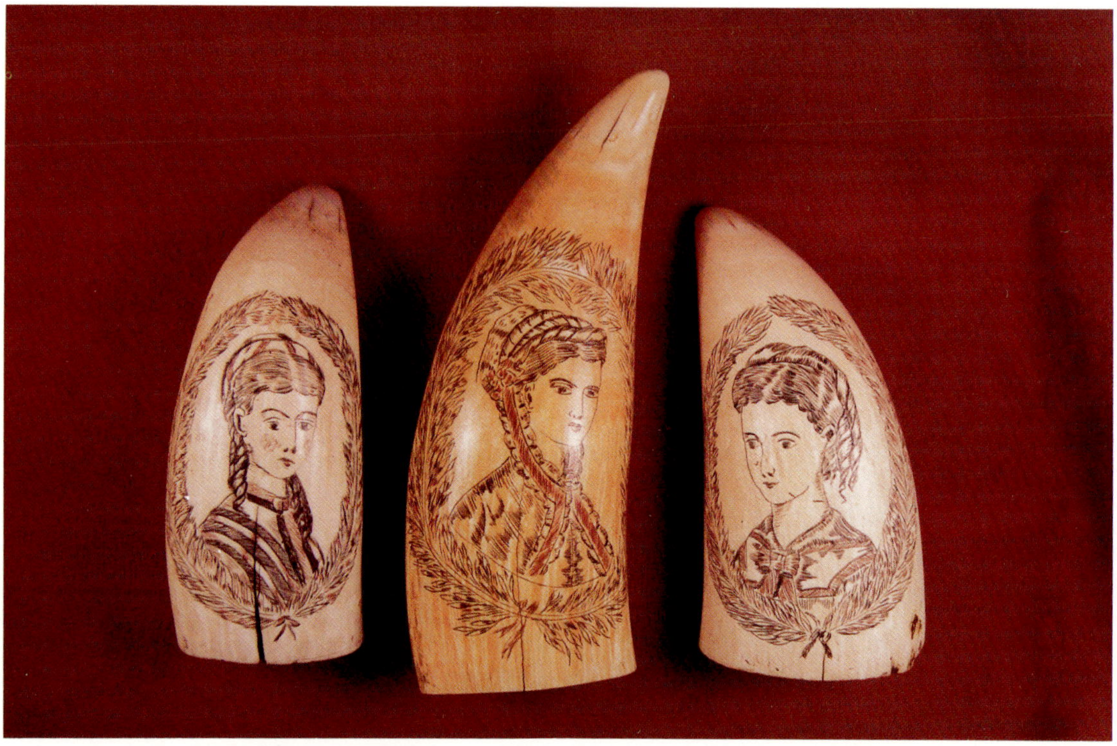

Beautiful women were a favorite subject for lonely scrimshanders. These three teeth are attributed to the same artist. The reverse of the middle tooth is illustrated on page 124. *Madden Collection.*

Ports of call and their inhabitants and noteworthy sights were also attempted by scrimshanders courageous enough to draw freehand from observation. One such popular "tourist" stop for whalemen was Napoleon's tomb on St. Helena. When the *Globe* called at the island, John Coquin, like many whalers before him, made the visit: "St. Helena, April 10, 1870....I went over to Napoleons tomb...saw the House and rooms that he died in..."[2]

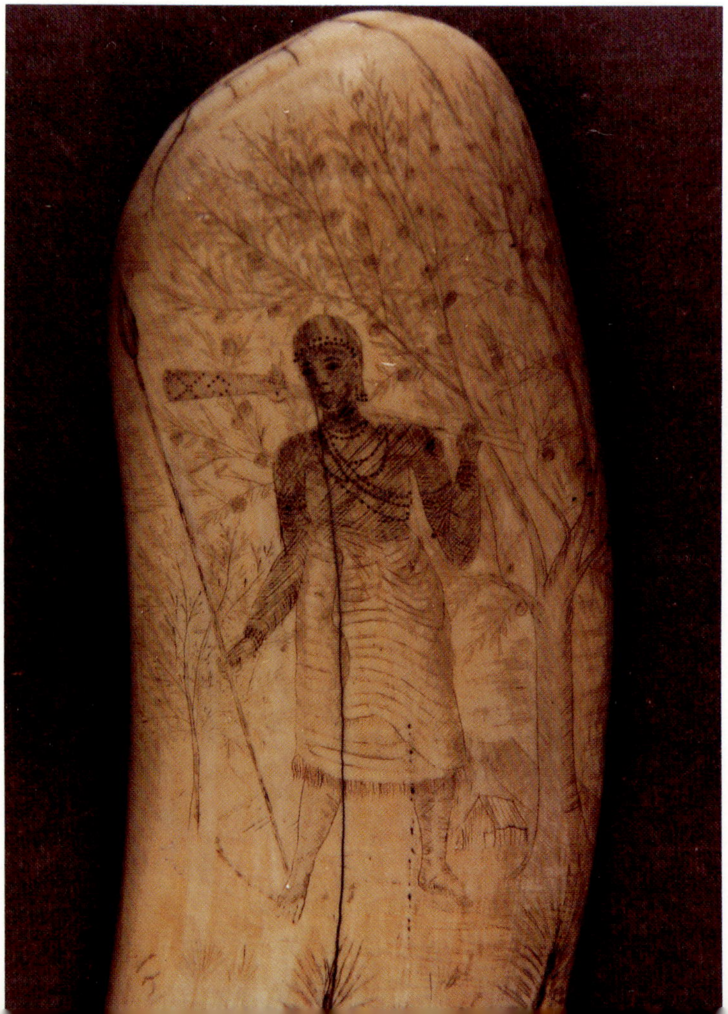

Brandishing both a spear and a gun, this well-armed Polynesian native was recorded for posterity —possibly by George Hilliot, whose biographical history is unknown. A tooth signed by Hilliot is in the collection of the Kendall Whaling Museum and is similar in style. *Courtesy of the Nantucket Historical Association*

Considering the longing for home experienced by so many of the men aboard ship, it is not surprising that idealized scenes of domestic bliss feature heavily in engraved work. The pain of separation was described succintly by Captain Samuel Braley in 1849: "Oh God! my wife. Talk about dieing. I hope that I shal never suffer any keener pangs than those that now pierce my heart."[3] As a result of such emotions, courting lovers, married couples, happy children, and cozy homes were repeatedly depicted on illustrated scrimshaw.

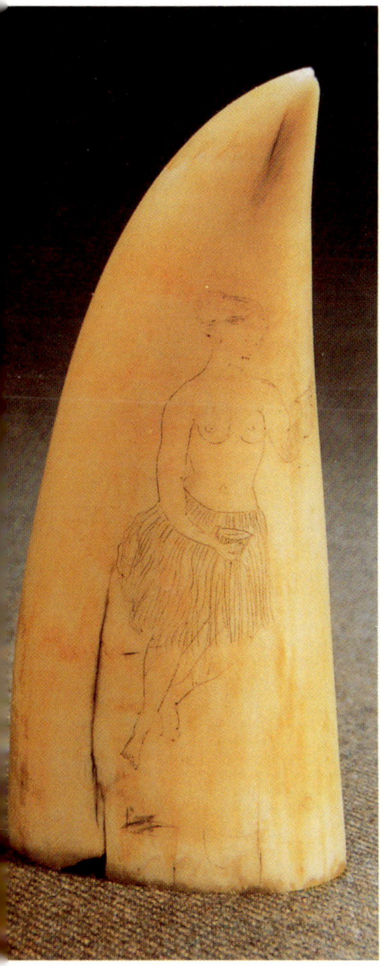

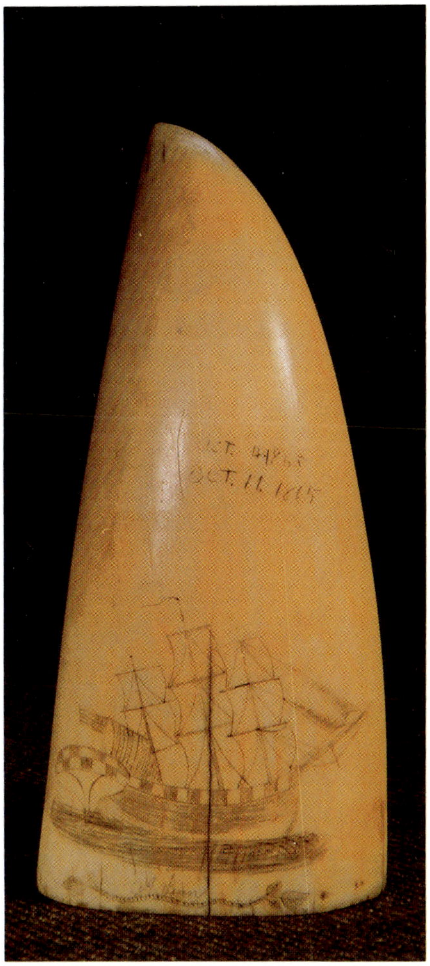

Although many foreign scenes such as this Pacific maiden etched by A. B. Bean were created during a whaleman's sojourn in that part of the world, it is believed that this piece was executed in New Haven after Bean had permanently retired from the sea. *Collection of Raymond and Elizabeth De Lucia*

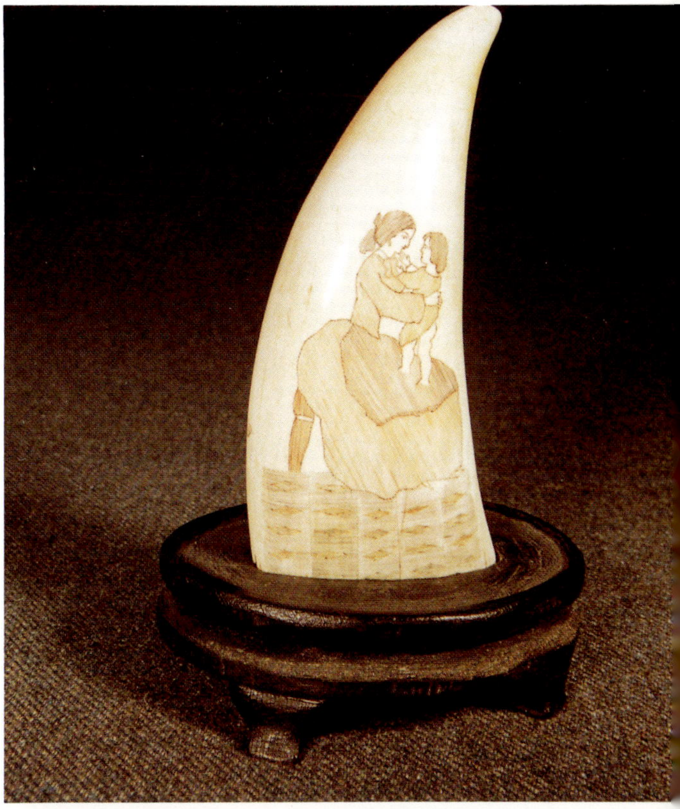

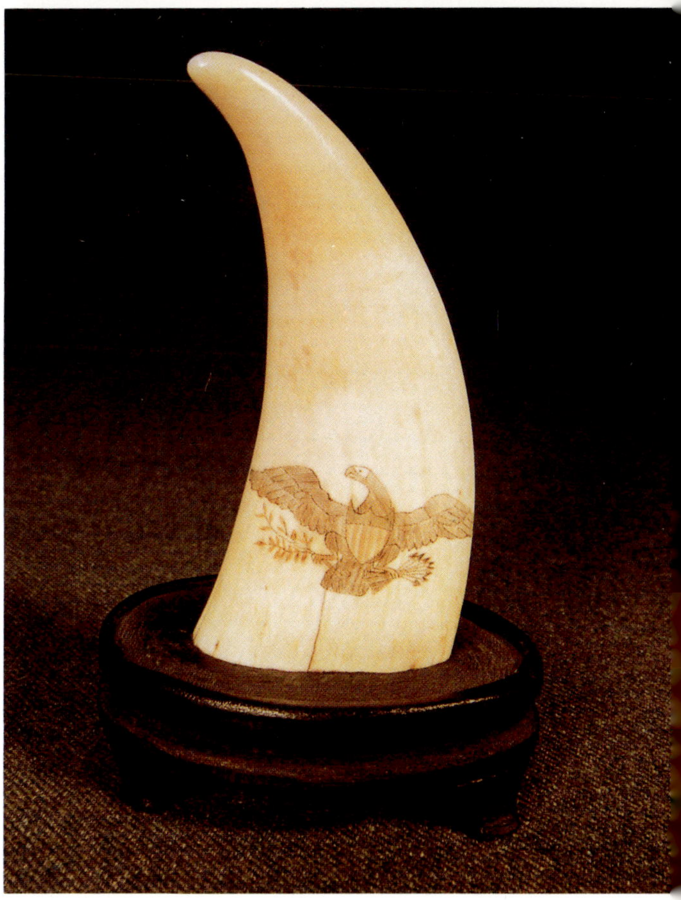

This lovely polychrome tooth represents two favorite themes of whalemen—family and patriotism. *Collection of Raymond and Elizabeth De Lucia.*

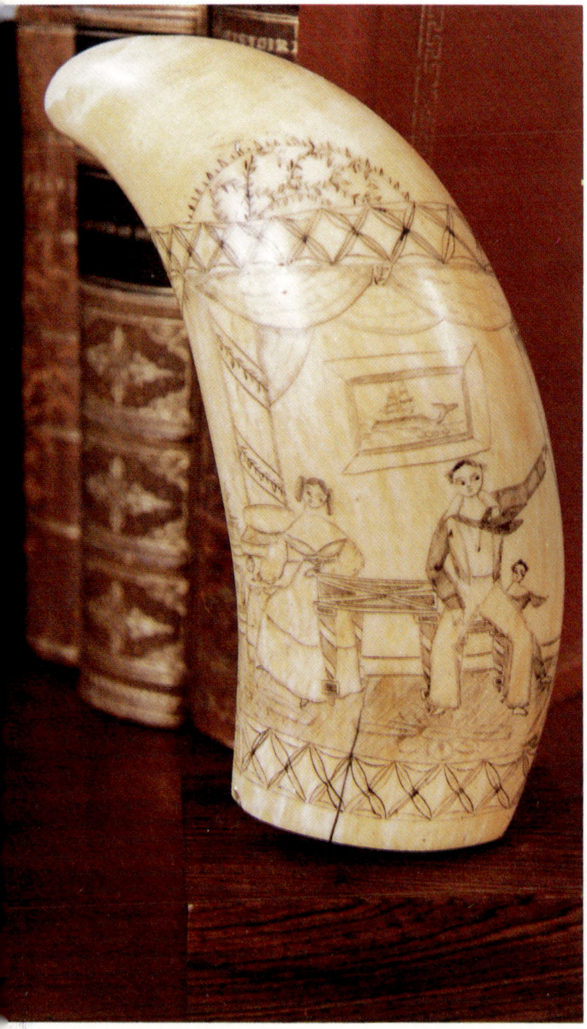

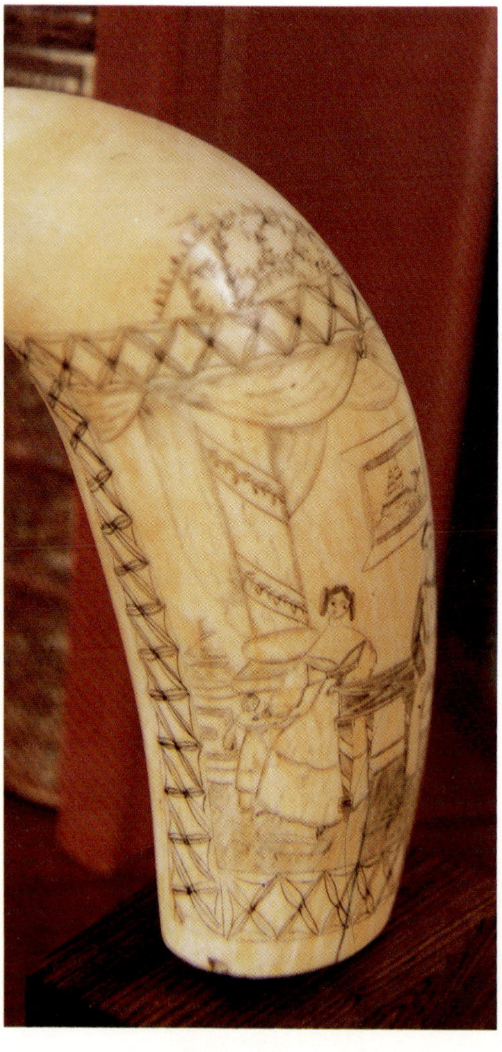

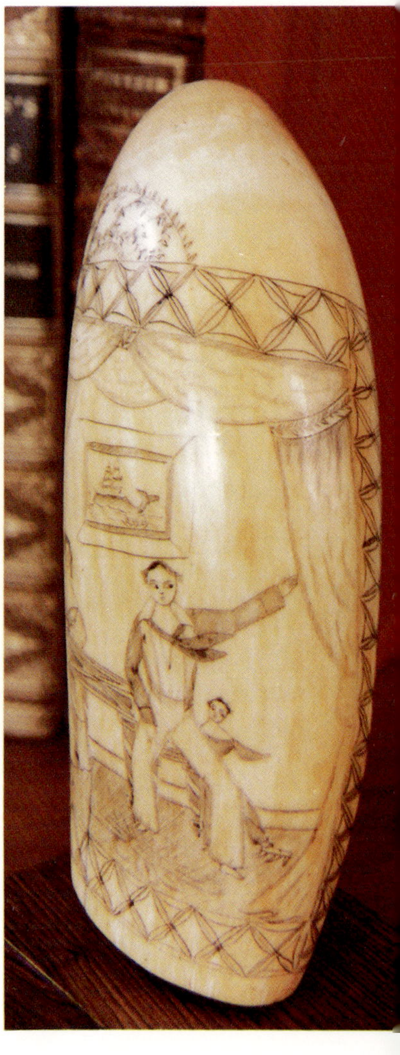

On this tooth, the *Ceres* artisan places his frequently portrayed seaman in a domestic setting where a portrait of a whaleship adorns the wall of the handsome parlor. In this scene, the sailor's familiar gesture is directed toward the window where his ship presumably awaits him. Other similar *Ceres* teeth are referred to as the "Domestic Happiness" group. *Madden Collection*

Another hauntingly recurrent theme was that of death. With the number of fatalities common aboard any nineteenth century ship, even one not engaged in the hazardous business of whaling, it is small wonder that the sailor's mind would turn to thoughts of his own mortality and the reactions to his death by loved ones at home. Perhaps an envisioned scenario would be similar to one passed down in Nantucket lore of the day Mrs. Samuel Joy observed a carriage arriving at her door. As two shipmasters made their way up the walk, she reportedly turned to her two sons and quietly said, "Thee must prepare yourself for sad news, my sons, I know why these men have come—they are going to tell me thy father has been lost at sea."[4]

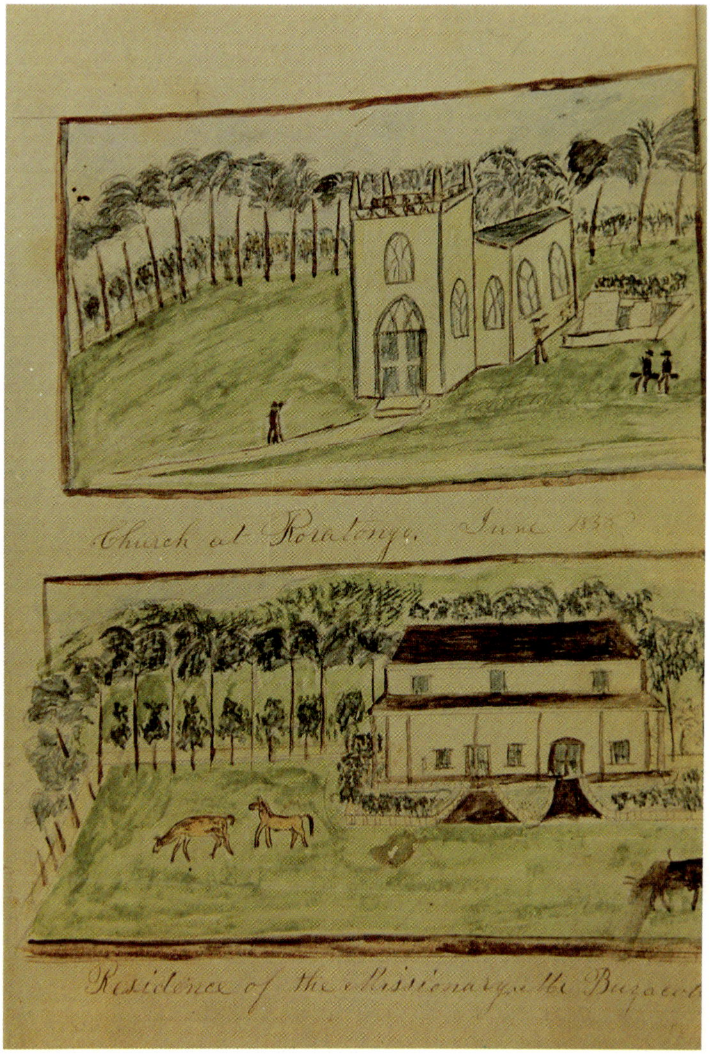

In the log of the *Edward Cary*, Joseph Ray describes in great detail a visit to the graveyard at Roratonga where lay the bodies of Elizabeth Nicholson, wife of a Nantucket whaling captain, and their baby daughter Eliza. He concludes, "I returned to the Ship at night feeling lonely and sad, after viewing the last resting place of those but who a [few] short months before I saw in the bloom of health and loveliness." *Collection of the Nantucket Historical Association*

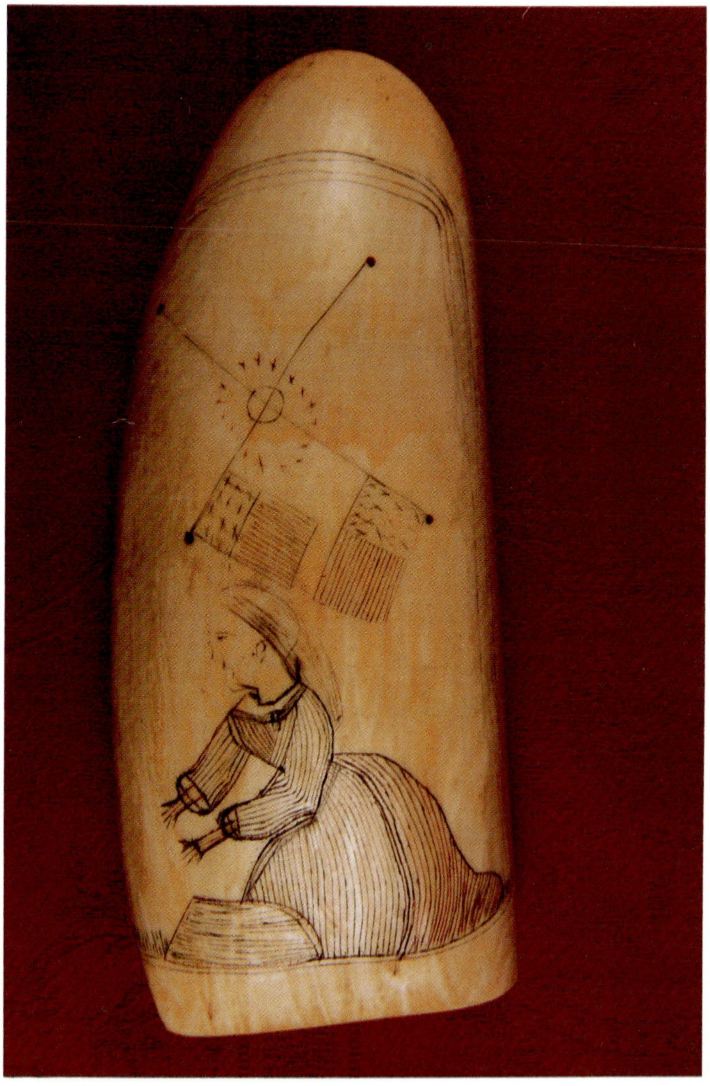

The crossed, inverted flags suggest that the woman pictured on this polychrome tooth is mourning a loved one. *Private Collection*

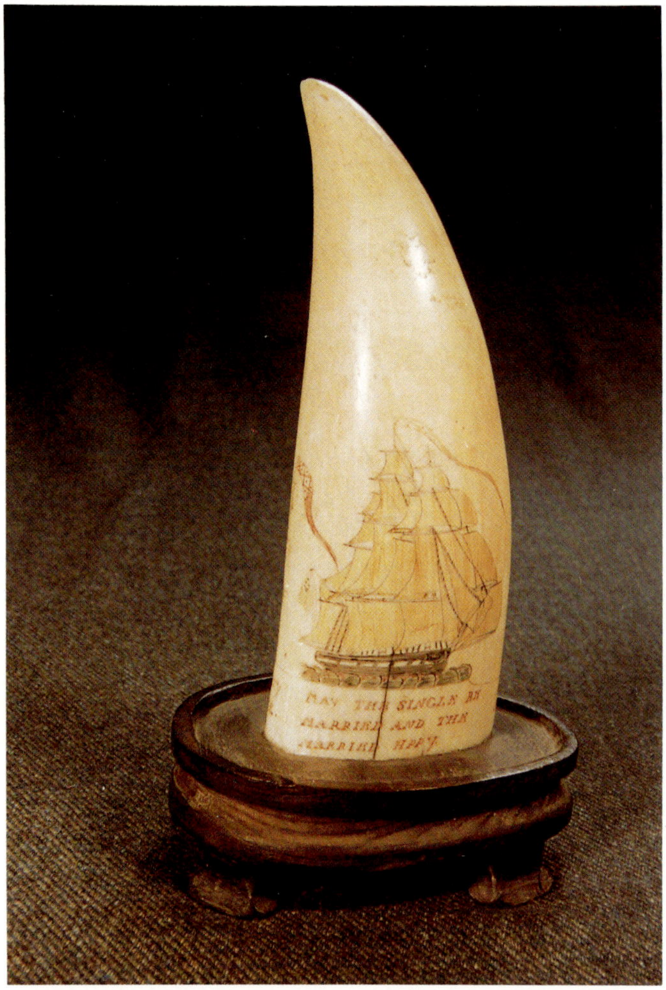

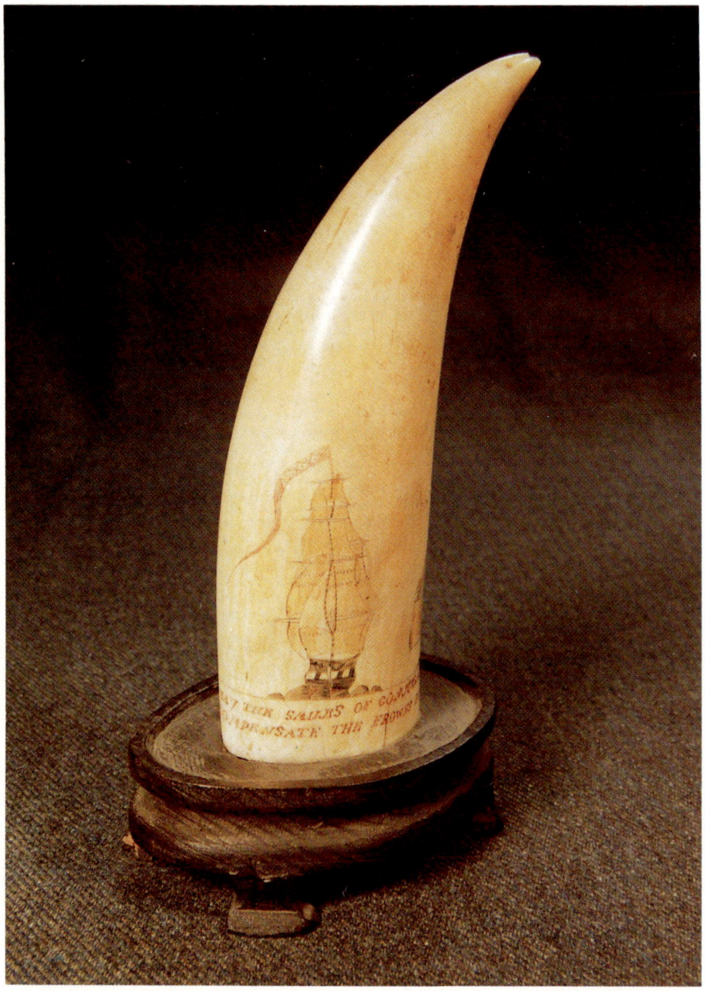

Domestic bliss was also on the mind of the artist who engraved these two views of a ship under sail. Around the base of the tooth he inscribed, "May the single be married and the married h(a)ppy," and "May the smiles of conjugal felicity compensate the frowns of fortune." *Collection of Raymond and Elizabeth De Lucia*

Fear of death also centered on family members left at home. The third mate of the bark *Emily* recorded what was undoubtedly an all too familiar story, "Captain Luce read today the letters he received from home....and by them learned that his wife was dead." More unusual was the fact that, with a sense of foreboding, Luce had left the letters unopened for twenty days as if to thereby prevent the intrusion of reality.[5] In addition, childhood mortality was common, and a father who sailed away for four years on a whaler might have a child be born and die in his absence.

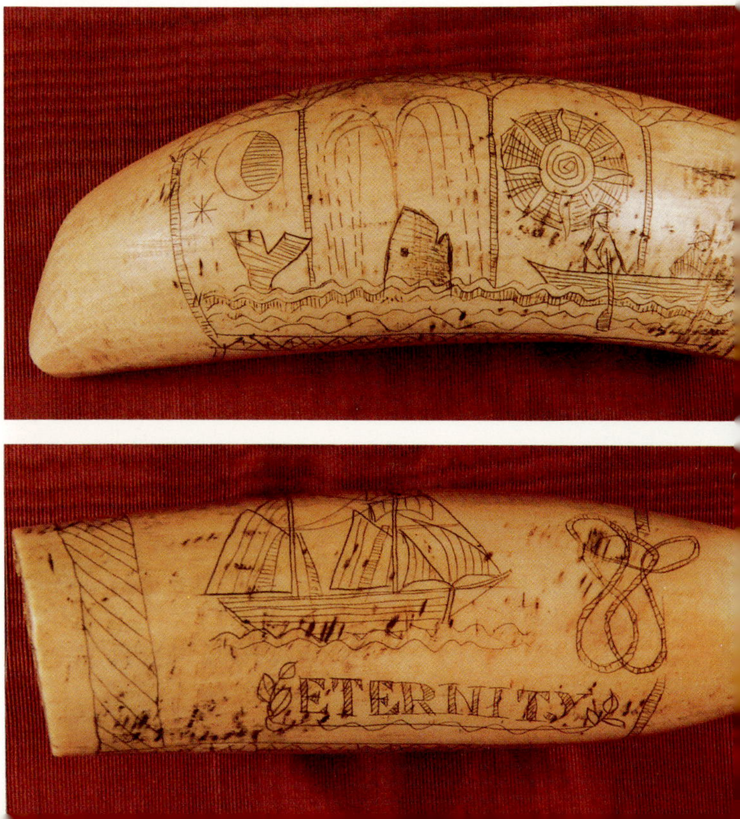

Perhaps the inscription, "eternity," engraved on this wonderful primitive tooth refers to the artist's estimation of the time he would spend at sea. *Collection of Raymond and Elizabeth De Lucia*

On a more life-affirming note, some scrimshanders attempted renderings of classical female nudes or, occasionally, even more erotic images. The latter were certainly unsuitable as gifts however; and it is theorized that before the ship arrived home, most scrimshaw with sexual themes was either reworked or tossed overboard, thus explaining why so few examples remain today.

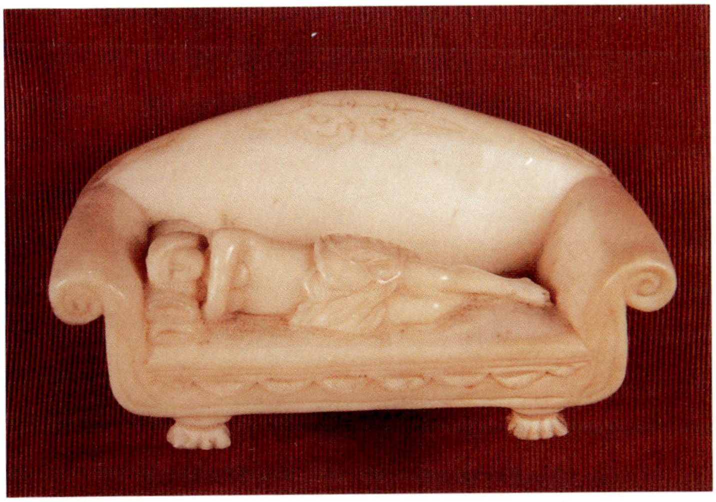

In this rare ivory carving, a more modest maiden is found in repose. *Courtesy of the Nantucket Historical Association*

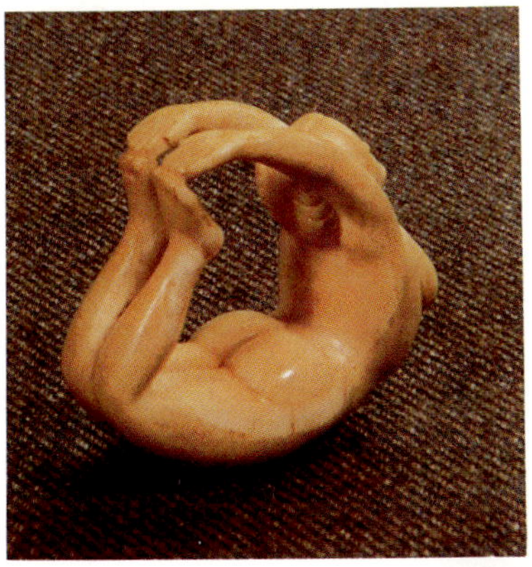

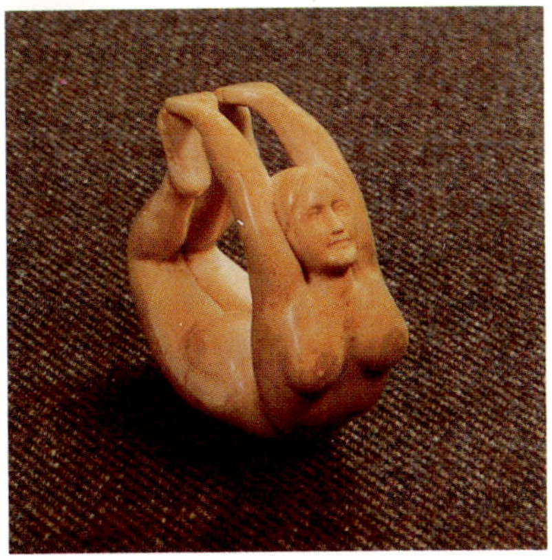

This nimble woman beautifully carved of whale ivory may have served as a napkin ring for some discriminating diner. *Collection of Raymond and Elizabeth De Lucia*

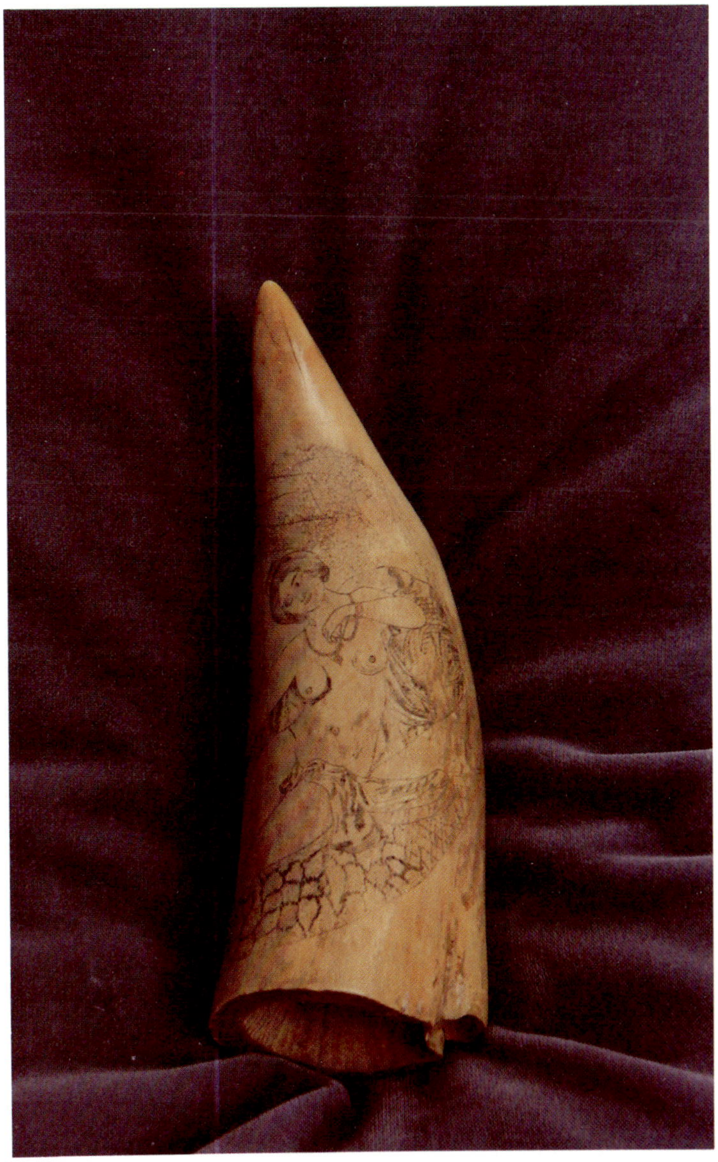

Unlike many females depicted by scrimshanders, this polychrome nude appears to have been engraved freehand rather than copied. *Collection of Charles A. Manghis*

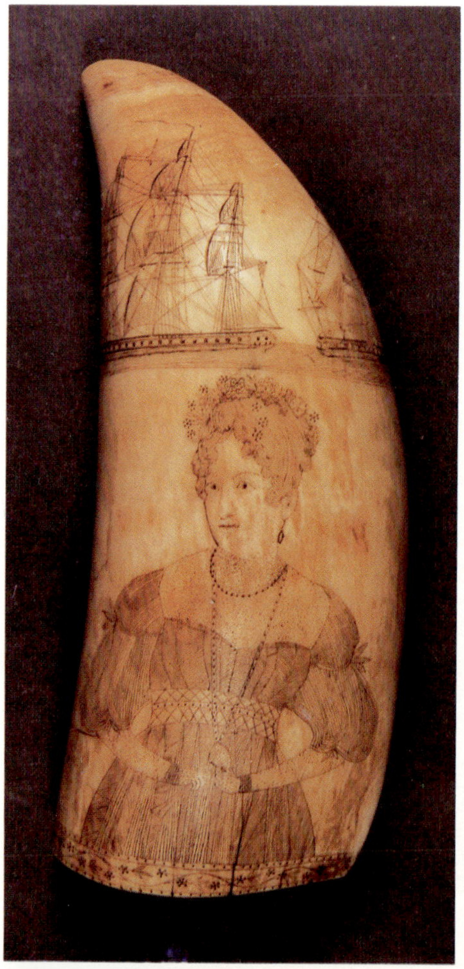

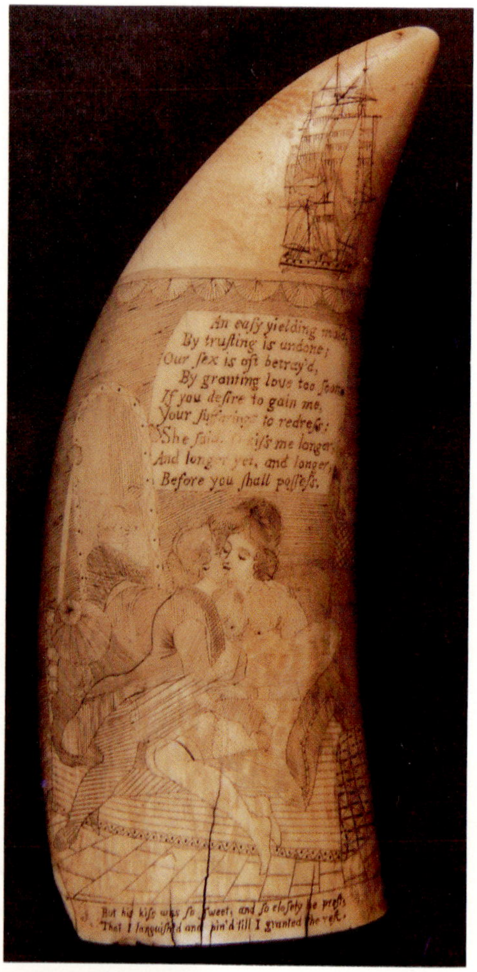

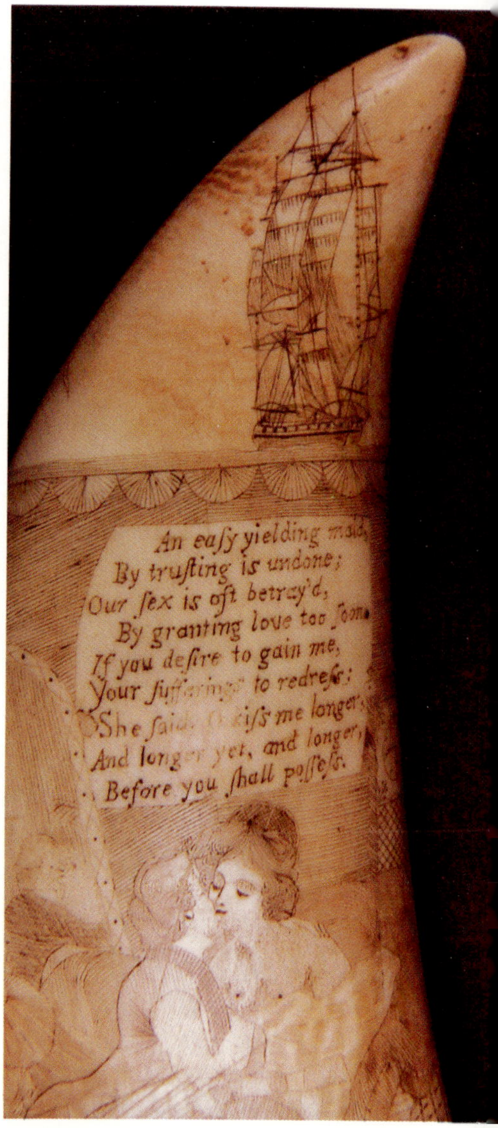

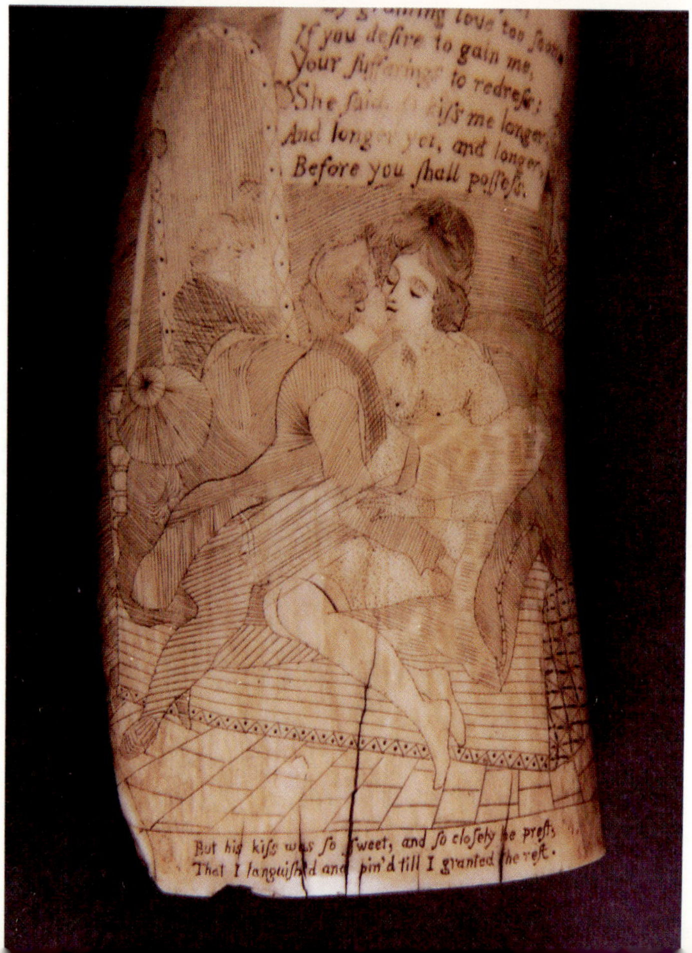

The demure lady etched on one side of this tooth gives no indication of the erotic scene on the reverse, which is partially scratched out. It is not known whether the correction was made by a repentent artist or a later censor. The inscribed verse records the fall of one fair maiden:

An easy yielding maid,
By trusting is undone;
Our sex is oft betrayed,
By granting love too soon.
If you desire to gain me,
Your sufferings to redress;
"She said, o kiss me longer,
And longer yet, and longer,
Before you shall possess.
But his kiss was so sweet, and so closely he prest,
That I languish'd and pin'd till I granted the rest.

Courtesy of the Nantucket Historical Association

One of scrimshaw's most popular themes involved recording the whalemen's life at sea. Ships, whale hunts, cutting-in scenes, and anatomical representations of the whale itself were frequently and accurately rendered.

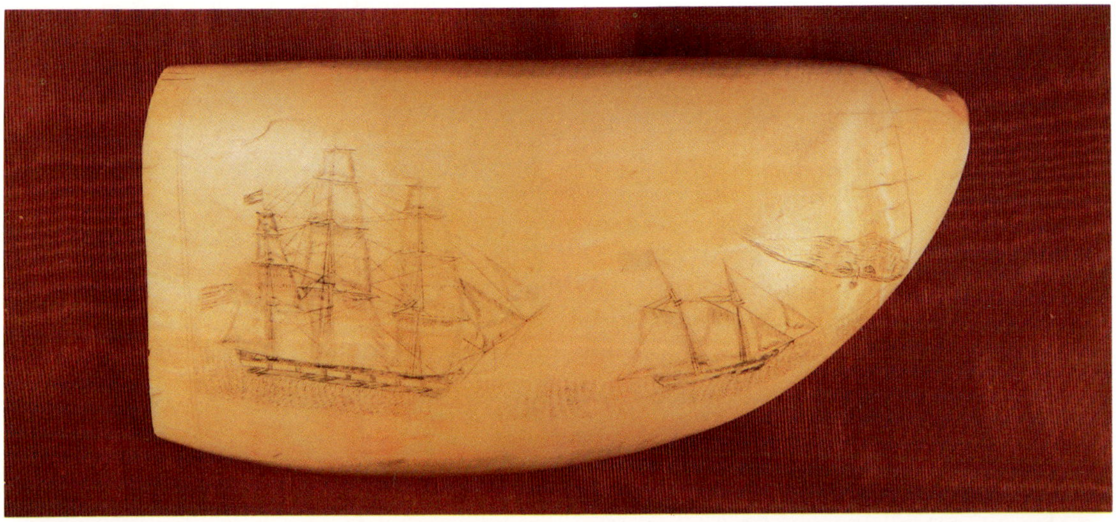

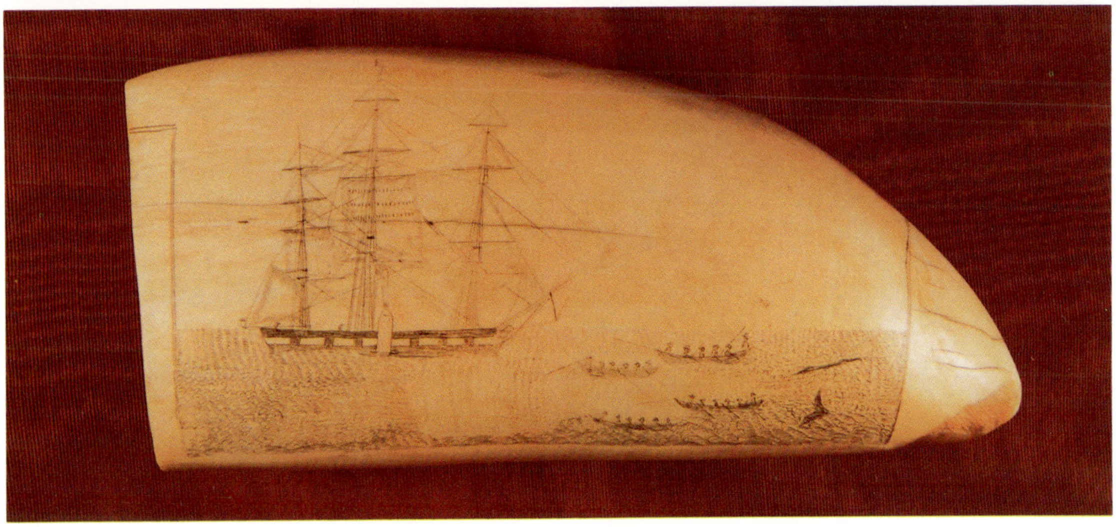

On this large tooth, the artist has rendered a detailed scene of a whaling ship, complete with figurehead, following a pilot boat into an island harbor. The reverse shows whaleboats engaged in the hunt and the mother ship involved in cutting-in. *Collection of Raymond and Elizabeth De Lucia*

In addition to these central scenes were repetitive ancillary motifs and border designs. Borders were inspired by flowers, vines, lacework, tombstone engravings, embroidery patterns, wrought iron and rope. Peripheral motifs included patriotic images such as flags, eagles, drums and banners as well as birds, flowers, hearts, anchors, rope, compass roses and intricate geometric patterns. Joseph Bogart Hersey described some of his designs on August 31, 1843:

> I employed a part of my time in engrav(ing) or flowering two busks. Being slightly skilled in the art of flowering; that is drawing and painting upon bone; steam boats, flower pots, monuments, balloons, landscapes &c &c &c; I have many demands made upon my generosity, and I do not wish to slight any; I of course work for all.[6]

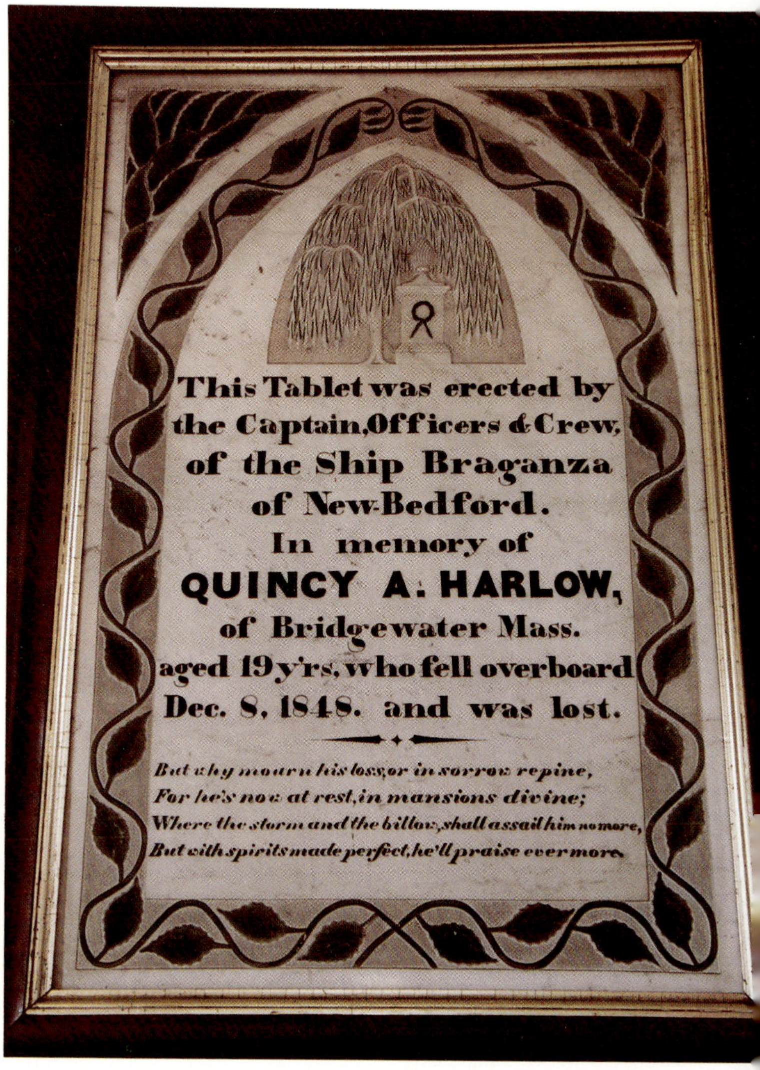

The artwork on this cenotaph in New Bedford's Seamen's Bethel is similar to much of the iconography found in contemporaneous scrimshaw. *Courtesy of the New Bedford Port Society*

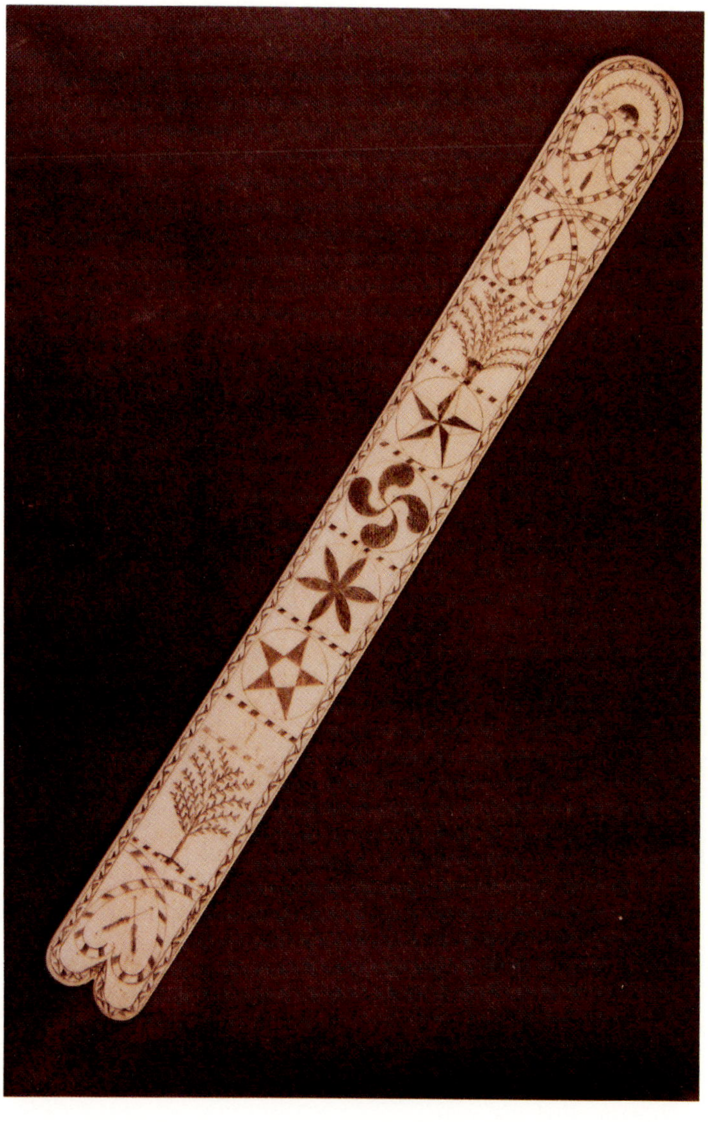

Classic black and ochre geometric motifs —often learned and practiced in mid-nineteenth century school houses, adorn this whalebone busk which is very representative of scrimshaw work of the period. *Courtesy of the Nantucket Historical Association*

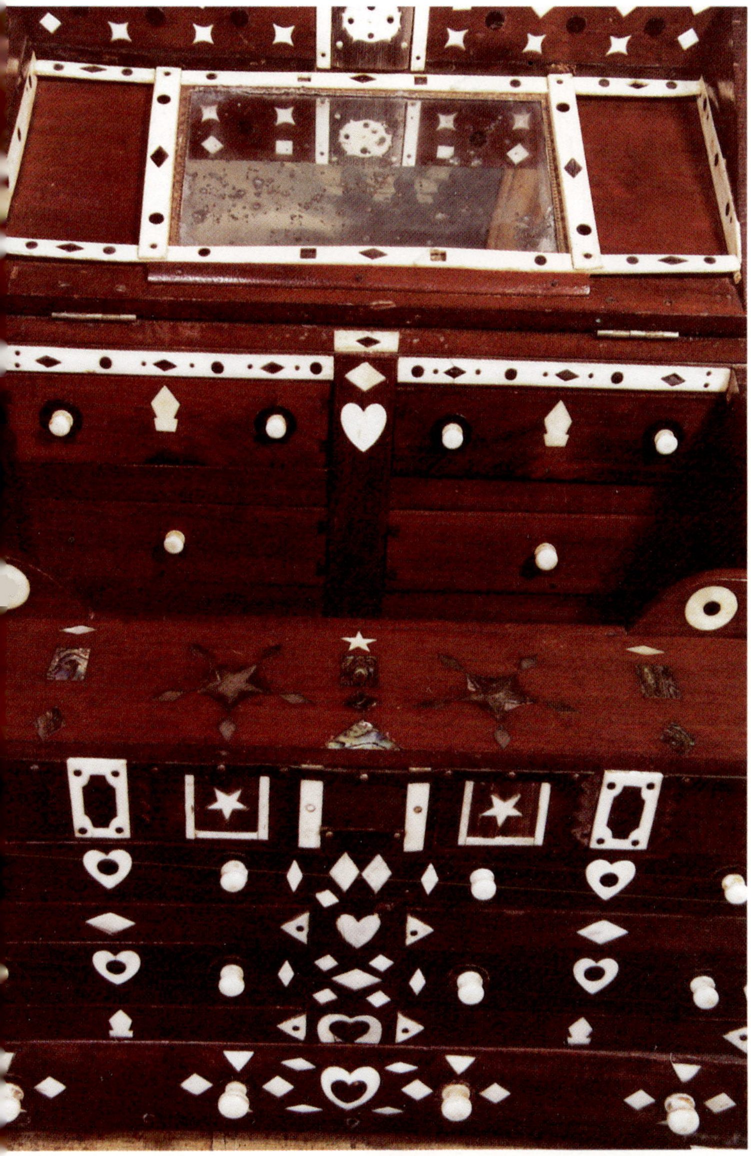

Inlaid stars, hearts, diamonds, and other geometric forms repeat endlessly in these inlaid chests. (above) *Private Collection.* (below) *Courtesy of the Nantucket Historical Association*

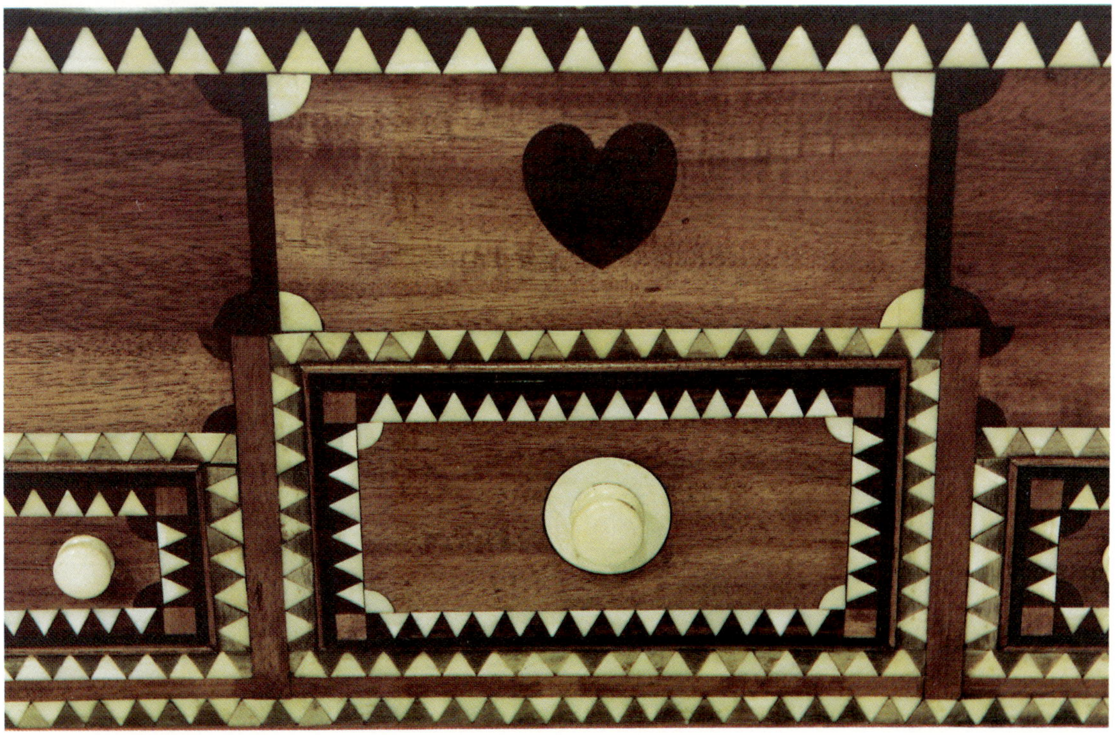

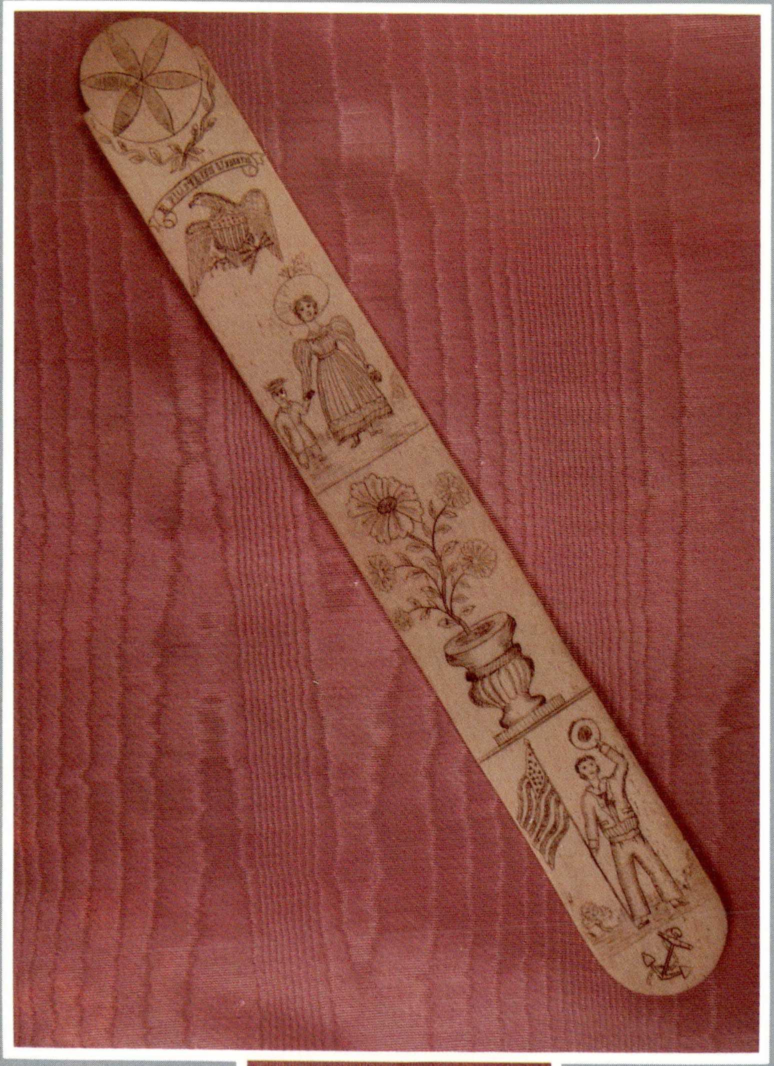

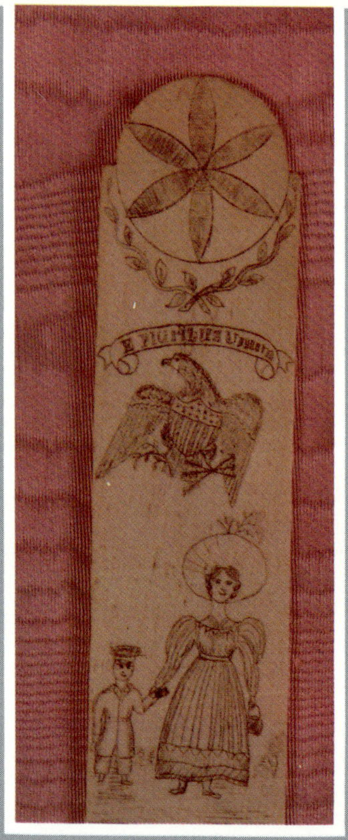

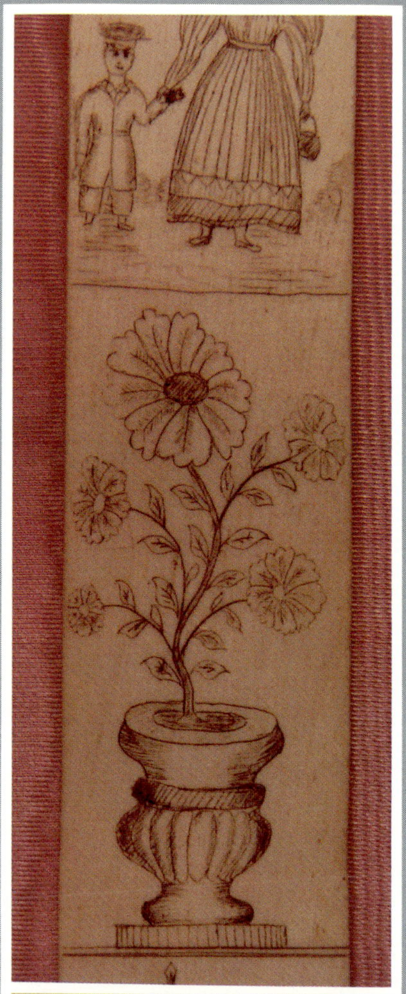

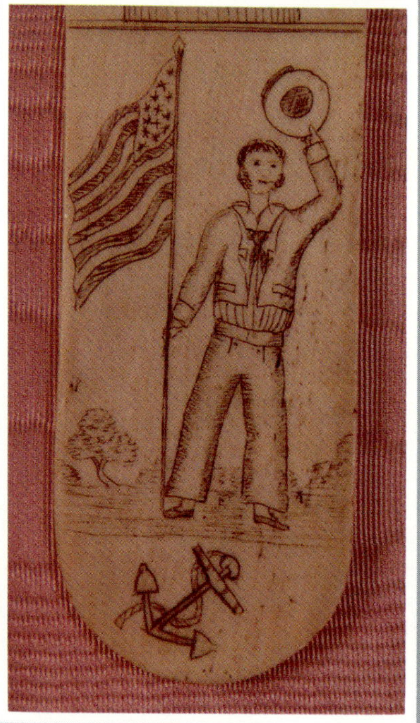

The scrimshander who "flowered" this whalebone busk incorporated many motifs. A busk's long, flat surface was a perfect practice area for different types of designs. *Private Collection*

Except for a very few artists, the average scrimshander had no artistic training. Consequently, as in much folk art, perspective was haphazard, figures were primitively rendered, and a properly executed portrait was often the result of direct tracery. Such copying was common and involved pasting an illustration over the ivory and pricking holes along the lines of the picture to mark its outline. The illustration was then removed and the scrimshander engraved lines to connect the holes, recreating the original design. Popular sources for illustrations of fashionable ladies were *Harper's Weekly* and *Godey's Lady's Book*. It is especially ironic to picture the seasoned sailor dressed in patched and repatched clothing eagerly replicating every detail of the latest fashion of the day.

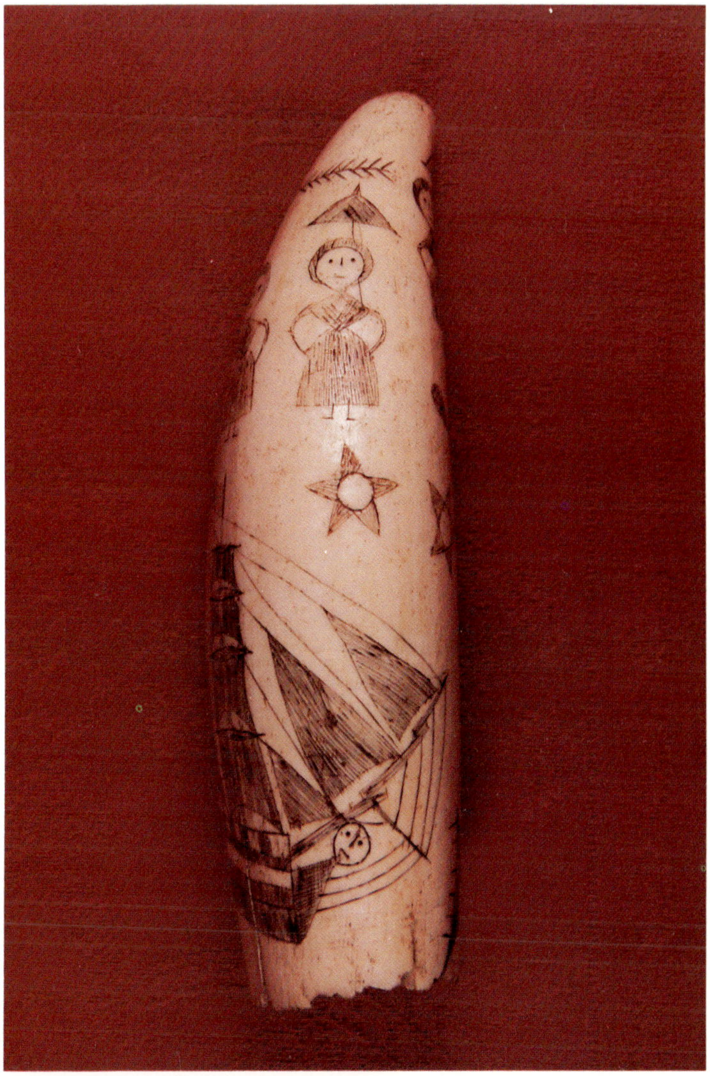

These two primitively engraved polychrome teeth are believed to be the work of the same scrimshander. The main theme portrayed on the top tooth is a whaleboat's capture of a one hundred and ten barrel sperm whale and includes wonderful details such as the "figurehead" on the mother ship. The unfortunate sailor in the whale's mouth is hopefully a symbolic reference to the danger posed by the whale hunt rather than the recording of an actual fatality. Why the sedate couples and awkward birds are in the midst of this busy scene is a question only the artist could answer. The lower tooth, inscribed with the letters "M.R.J.R.G.C.R.," shows a whaleboat pulling up to a harpooned whale, the officer ready to lance the wearied animal. *Madden Collection.*

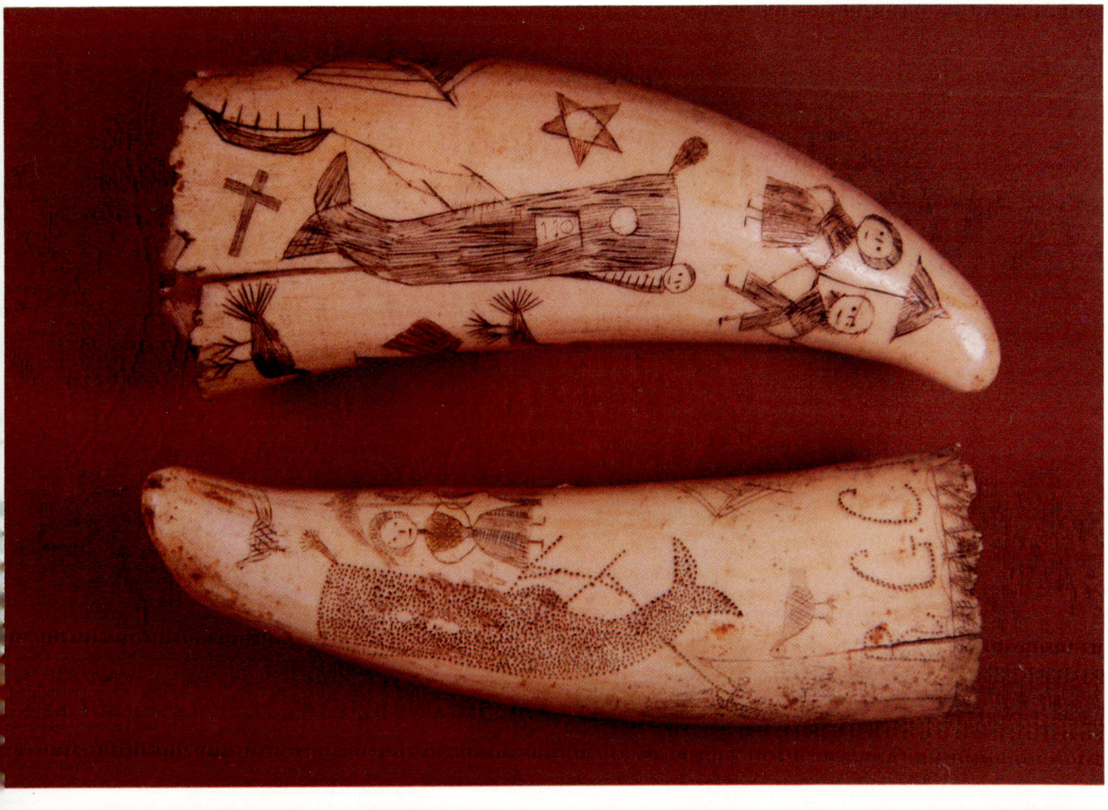

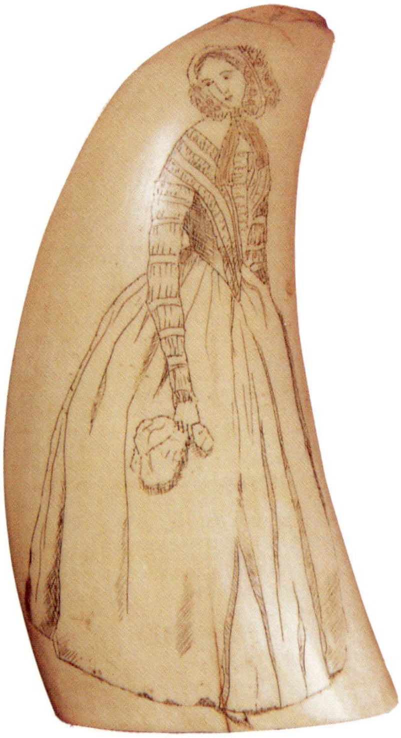

This graceful woman was transferred from the pages of a fashion magazine to the unlikely surface of a sperm whale's tooth by utilizing the pinprick method of copying.
Private Collection

The pinpricks which form the outline of the designs on this polychromed walrus tusk can be readily observed.
Collection of Raymond and Elizabeth De Lucia

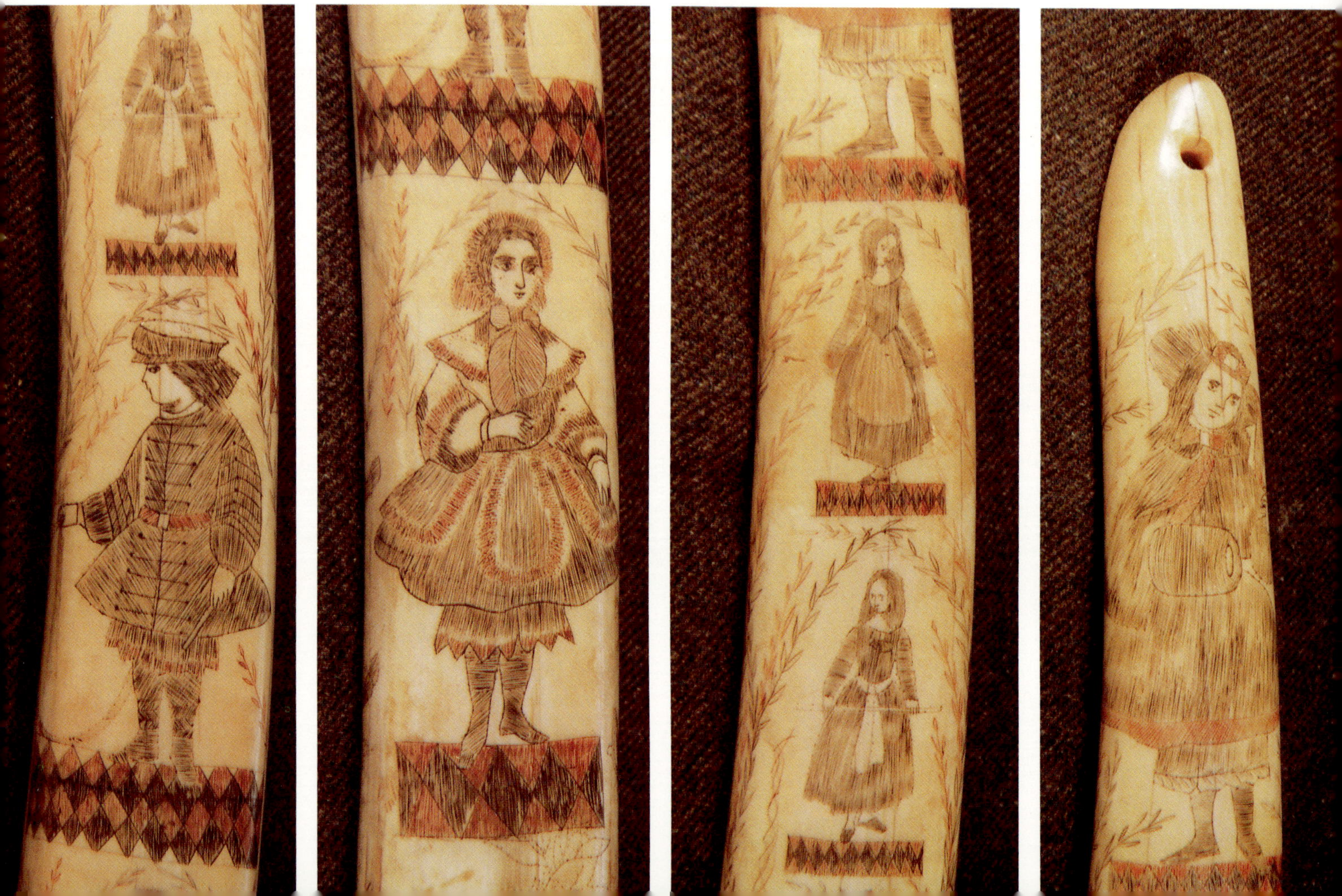

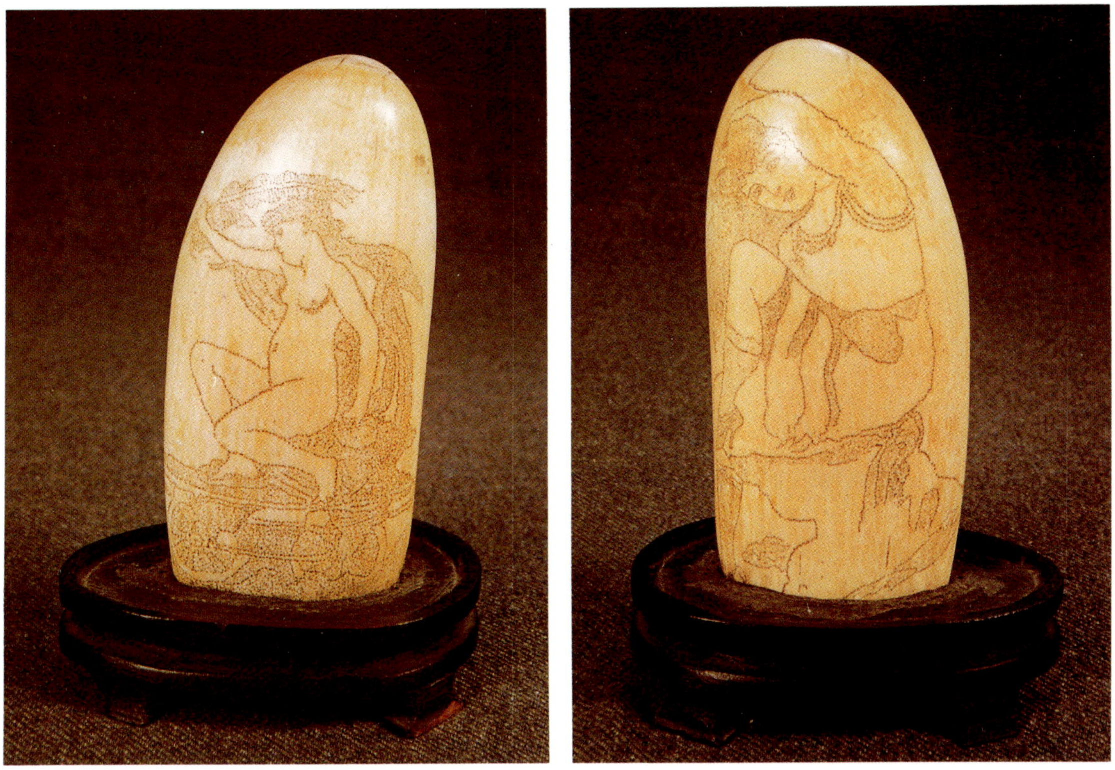

Stippling was the technique used to create the mariner's fantasies illustrated on this tooth. *Collection of Raymond and Elizabeth De Lucia*

Within the surviving body of illustrated scrimshaw are found varying degrees of artistic sophistication. The most basic engraving technique was achieved by incising a simple outline with a knife or sail needle. This image, however, lacked any depth or rounding and did not satisfy those desiring to achieve the photographic realism popular at the time. The placement of additional linear cuts in areas to be shaded achieved a modest rounding, while more sophisticated results were accomplished by cross-hatching, in which numerous intersecting lines were etched. Stippling with varied concentrations of tiny dots provided an even greater degree of depth and rounding, with more subtlety. Although rare, both intaglio (a technique in which the ivory was carved out and then heavily inked) and relief carving were also employed.

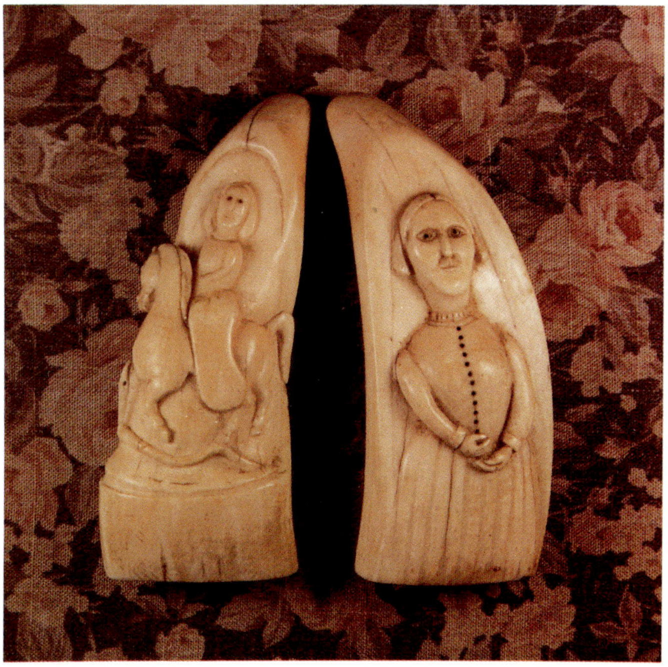

Relief carvings such as those worked on this pair of teeth are rare. *Courtesy of the Nantucket Historical Association*

The varying artistic results evident in pictorial scrimshaw were due not only to such esoteric concerns as training, talent or technique, but also to more mundane realities such as a lurching ship, weather or lack of proper light. William Chappell, cooper aboard the *Saratoga* described one difficulty typical of his location in the Kamchatka Sea, the numbing cold:

> On April 21 in 1854...spent my time below at the lathe an uncomfortable job in this weather...of importance was to set up the stove in the cabin...while I continue to scrimshand.[7]

For the scrimshander working in the cramped space of the foc'sle, or even the slightly roomier quarters of a mate or boatsteerer's cabin, the light was extremely poor. Not only was magnification, an accepted aid in contemporary work, unavailable, but an artist unfortunate enough to possess less than perfect eyesight did not have access to correctional lenses. In addition to these obstacles, the scrimshander had to accommodate his cuts to the rolling and swaying of the ship.

Affixed to the bottom of a wonderfully constructed and intricately turned ivory and mahogany "picture show case" is a message from its maker William Chappell, again in the Kamchatka Sea:

> Sept. Ist, 1855. This miniature "Show Case" was designed and Manufactured by the undersigned during a whaling voyage in the Northern Ocean and under many disadvantages; hence the Charitable will overlook the many imperfections. Wm. H. Chappell, Cooper.[8]

Given the handicaps encountered, it is easy to understand why engraved cuts within a work of scrimshaw are often of differing length or depth and why lines connecting pinpricks occasionally bypass rather than join the holes. And, one need not be remotely "charitable" to stand in awe of the fine examples produced in such circumstances or to marvel at the poor fellow whose work achieved any resemblance to the scene he was trying to reproduce.

Varying quality of work, differing styles of engraving and individual affinity for repetitive themes and motifs are interesting not only in their own right, but also as bases on which scholars are today attempting to attribute different pieces of scrimshaw. Occasionally works appear which are dated or signed, but, as with most folk art, such finds are rare. However, through exacting research and careful visual analysis a surprising number of pieces have been attributed to identified scrimshanders. There are also groups of work ascribed to the hands of anonymous artists known only by designations that have become attached to them over the years such as the "*Ceres* Artisan," the "Eagle Portraitist," and the "Banknote Engraver." By establishing such visual methods to evaluate scrimshaw and discover relationships between pieces, students of the subject can carefully begin the process of attribution without waiting for the exceedingly rare "signed" piece of scrimshaw.

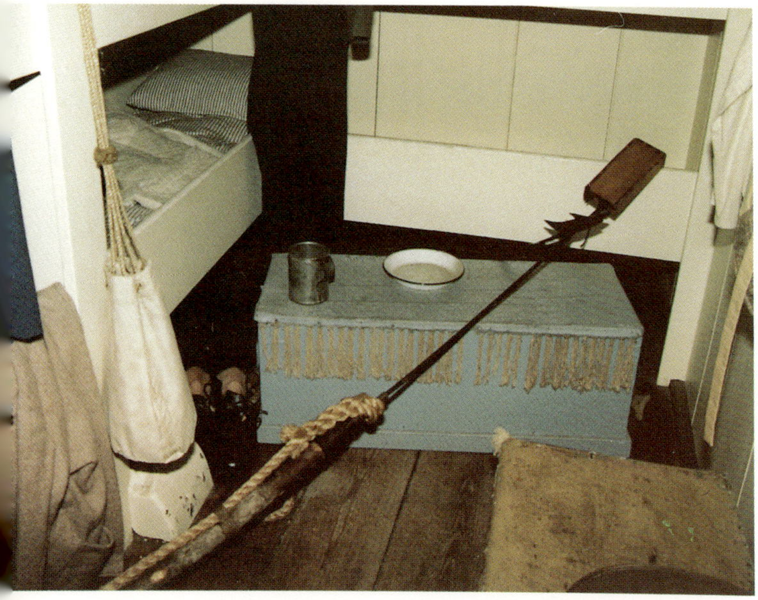

The *Charles W. Morgan's* cramped steerage offered little space for scrimshanding. *Courtesy of the Mystic Seaport Museum.*

01 Margaret S. Creighton, *Dogwatch and Liberty Days* (Salem, Mass.: Peabody Museum of Salem, 1982), 69.

02 John S. Coquin, "A Journal on board the Bark *Globe*" (New Bedford, Mass.: Old Dartmouth Historical Society).

03 Creighton, *Dogwatch and Liberty Days.*

04 Edouard A. Stackpole, *The Sea Hunters* (Philadelphia, Penn.: J.B. Lippincott Co., 1953), 404.

05 Emma M. Whiting and Harry B. Hough, *Whaling Wives* (Boston, Mass.: Houghton Mifflin, 1953), 3.

06 Stuart M. Frank, *Dictionary of Scrimshaw Artists* (Mystic, Conn.: Mystic Seaport Museum, 1991), 68.

07 Sotheby Park Bernet, Inc., *Barbara Johnson Whaling Collection — Part II.*

08 Ibid., Part III.

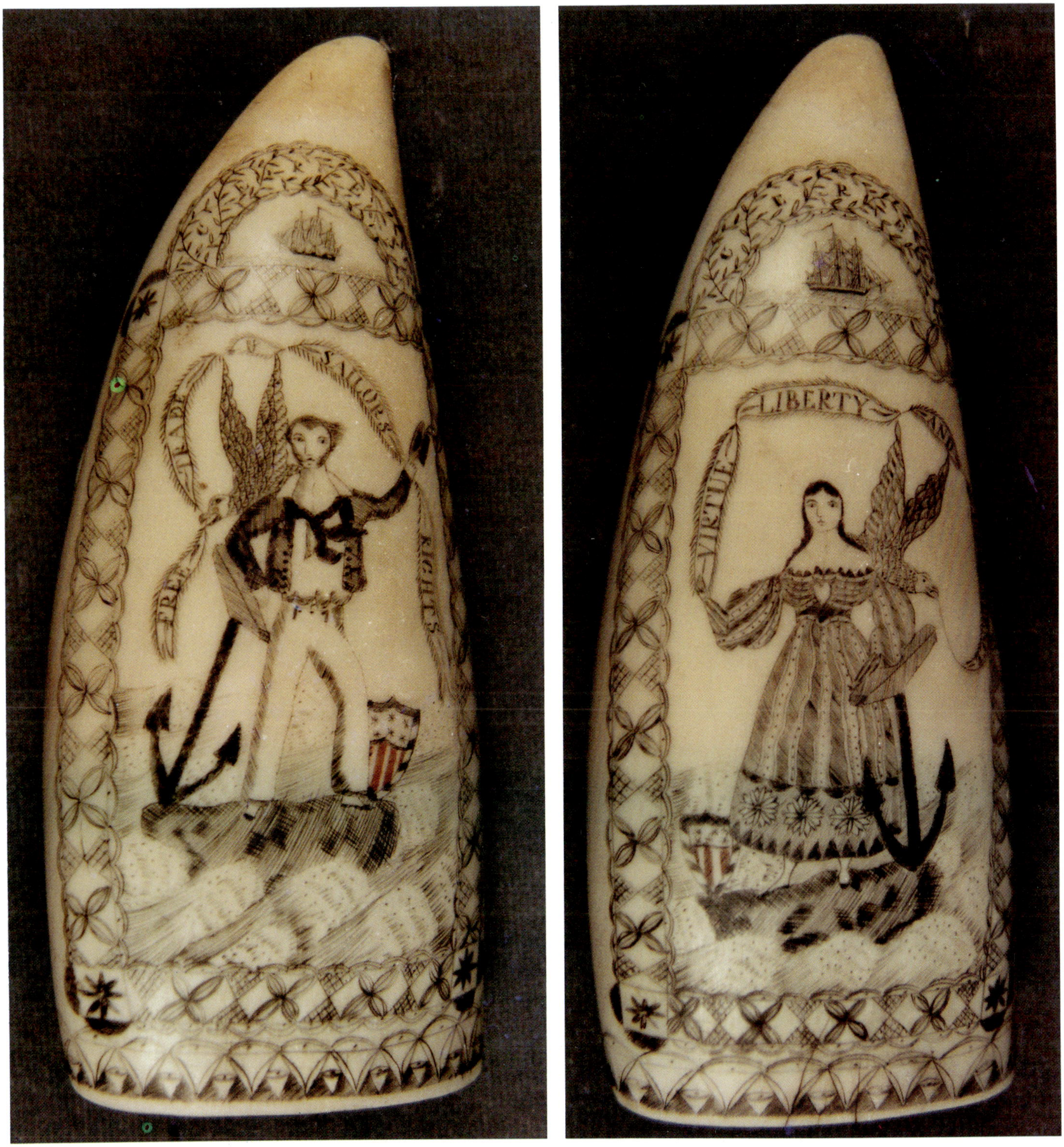

These two teeth are wonderful examples of the work of the *Ceres* artisan who often engraved matched sets of teeth, one showing a jaunty sailor with outstretched arm and the other a fancily dressed woman. In addition, patriotic designs and messages such as "Free Trade" and "Sailors' Rights" were routinely incorporated into his work. Another distinguishing feature evident in this pair is the detailed decorative border topped by a semicircular arch. *Courtesy of the Nantucket Historical Association*

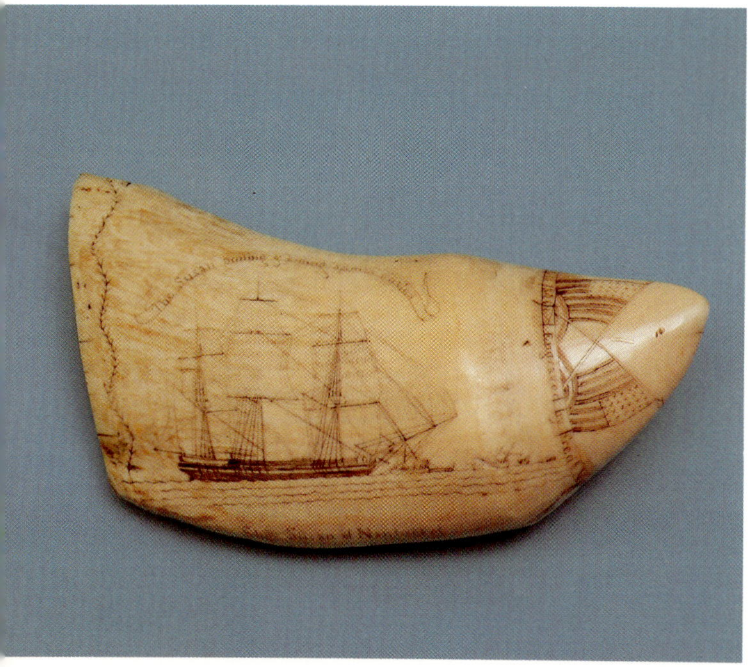
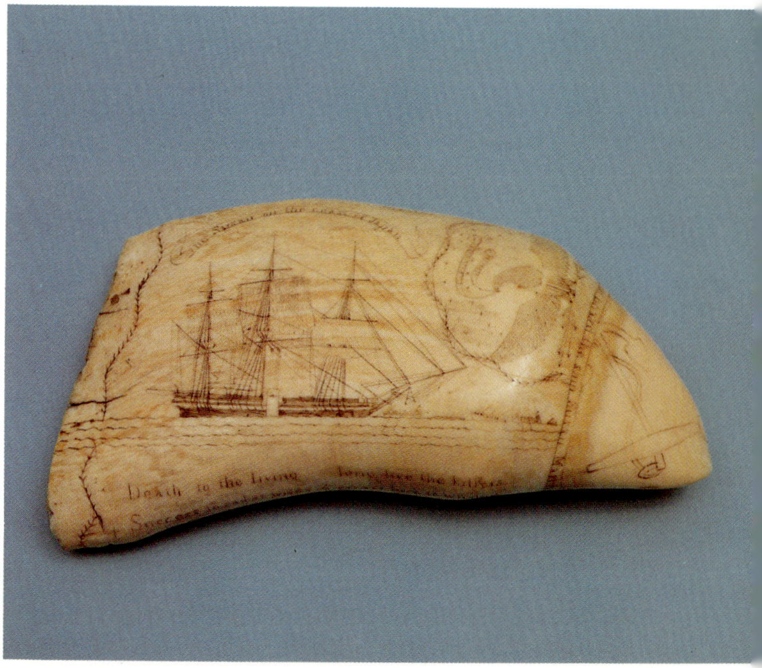

This tooth, dated March 4, 1829, is one of the series of over twelve teeth engraved by Frederick Myrick aboard the ship *Susan*. Both scenes feature ongoing whale hunts, while one view shows the ship cutting-in a whale and the other depicts smoke billowing from the tryworks where blubber is being boiled. Like the *Susan*'s tooth in the collection of the Nantucket Historical Association dated a month earlier and illustrated on pages 21 and 22, this tooth is inscribed with wishes for long life and greasy luck to whalers as well as success to their wives. Although Edward Burdett is believed to have been working pictorial scrimshaw as early as 1823, Frederick Myrick is the first scrimshander to sign and date his work. As a result, his beautifully engraved pieces are extemely valuable and, unfortunately, frequently the subject of forgery. *Courtesy of Richard A. Bourne Co., Inc.*

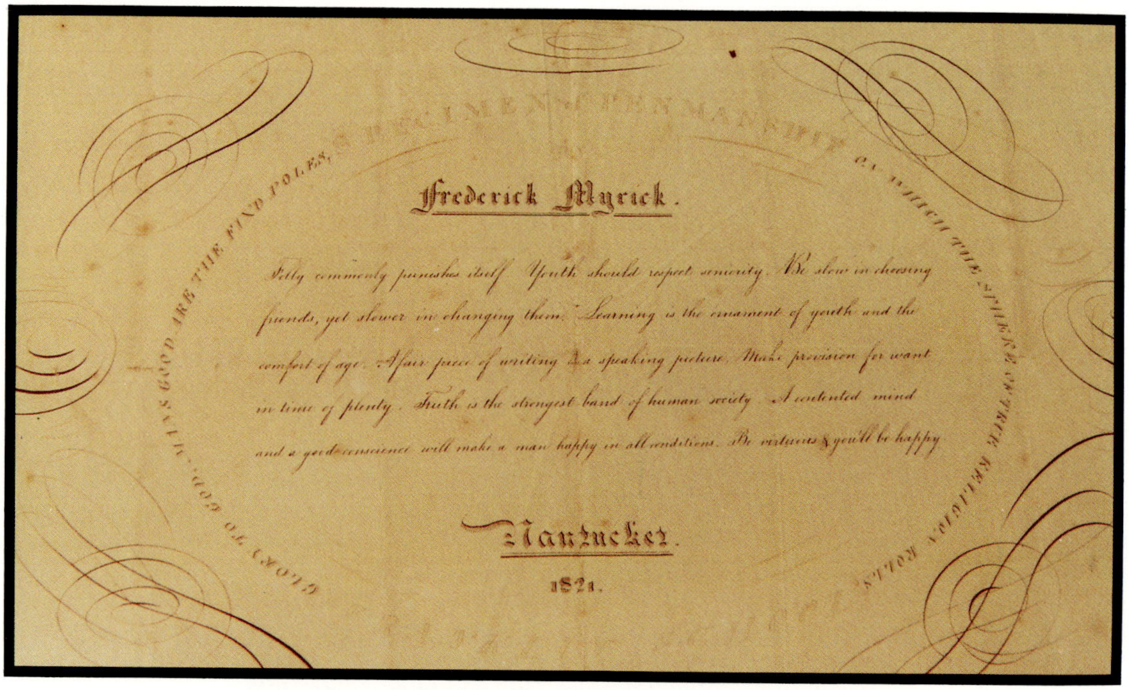
Frederick Myrick.

Folly commonly punishes itself. Youth should respect seniority. Be slow in choosing friends, yet slower in changing them. Learning is the ornament of youth and the comfort of age. A fair piece of writing is a speaking picture. Make provision for want in time of plenty. Truth is the strongest band of human society. A contented mind and a good conscience will make a man happy in all conditions. Be virtuous & you'll be happy.

Nantucket.

1821.

A specimen of Frederick Myrick's penmanship, executed at the age of thirteen during his days at Nantucket's Franklin School, displays the fine hand that would later record the era of deep-sea whaling on pictorial scrimshaw. *Courtesy of the Nantucket Historical Association*

6. Scrimshaw in the Home

The incredible variety of implements produced aboard ship are a testament to the scrimshanders' imagination, as well as the suitability of whalebone and ivory for a multitude of tasks. It is believed that the first pieces of scrimshaw constructed aboard whalers were tools turned out in the late eighteenth century at the captain's behest. Not only was whalebone readily available, it was often better suited for its intended purpose than wood. For instance, a bone belaying pin was more resistant to wear than a wooden one, and a whalebone fid was not only strong but self-lubricating as well. The hard, durable bone of the sperm whale was incorporated into many ship-board items: fids, belaying pins, blocks, scribers, cleats, seam rubbers, navigational tools, serving mallets, measuring sticks, and needle cases. In addition to tools, items for shipboard recreation such as cribbage boards, dominoes, checker sets, whistles, and noisemakers poured from the creative hands of the whalemen.

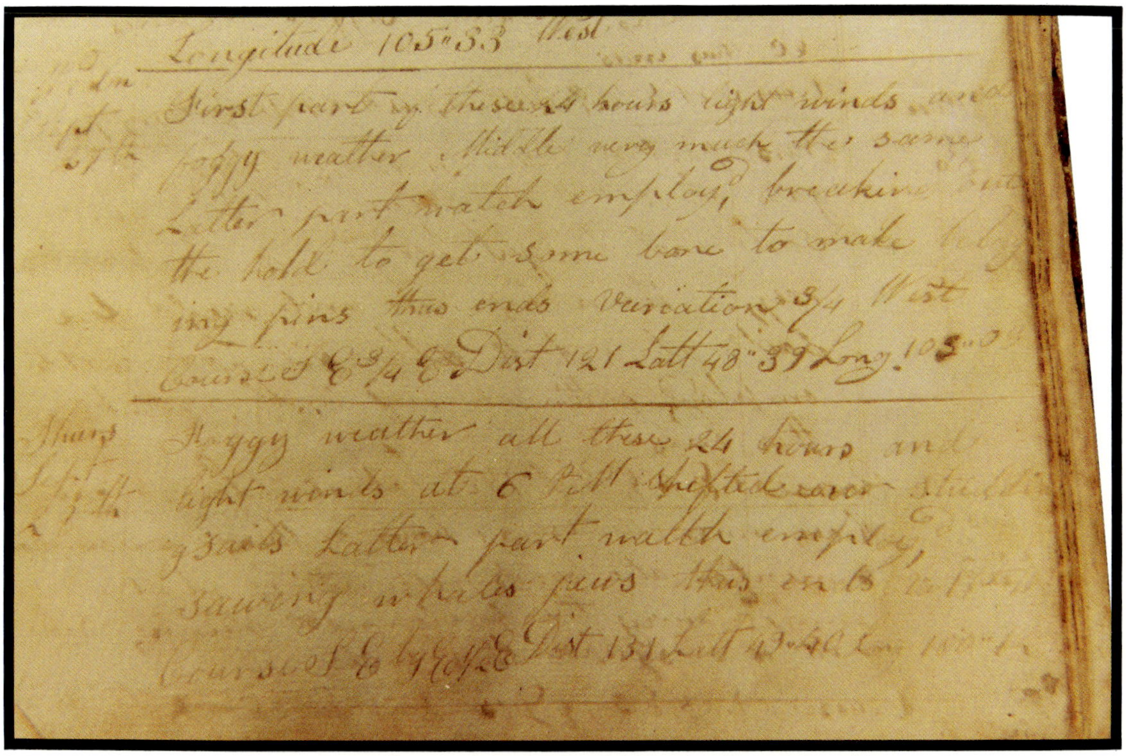

Longitude 105"33 West

First part of these 24 hours light winds and foggy weather Middle very much the same Latter part watch employ'd breaking out the hold to get some bone to make belaying pins thus ends Variation 3/4 West

Course S E 3/4 E Dist 121 Latt 48"39 Long 103"

Foggy weather all these 24 hours and light winds at 6 PM shifted our studding sails Latter part watch employ'd sawing whales jaws thus ends

Course S E by E Dist 131 Latt

An entry on September 27th, 1826 in the log of the ship *Almira* testified to the disposition of whalebone on that vessel: "Latter part watch employ'd breaking out the hold to get some bone to make belaying pins." And log keeper Henry Marchant added the following day: "Latter part watch employ'd sawing whales jaws." *Courtesy of the Nantucket Historical Association*

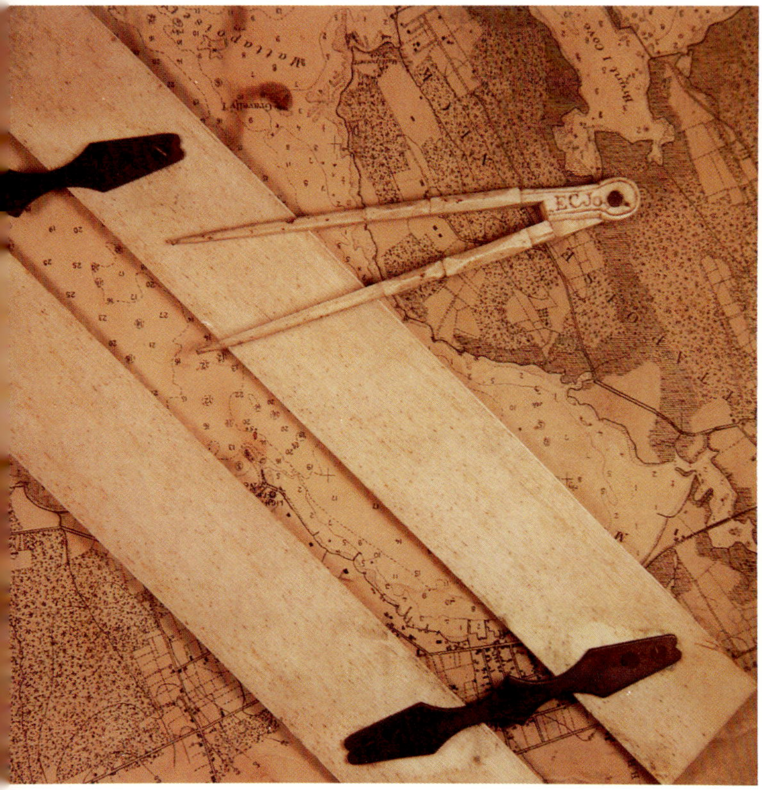

A whalebone parallel rule and dividers belonging to E. C. Joy. *Courtesy of the Nantucket Historical Association*

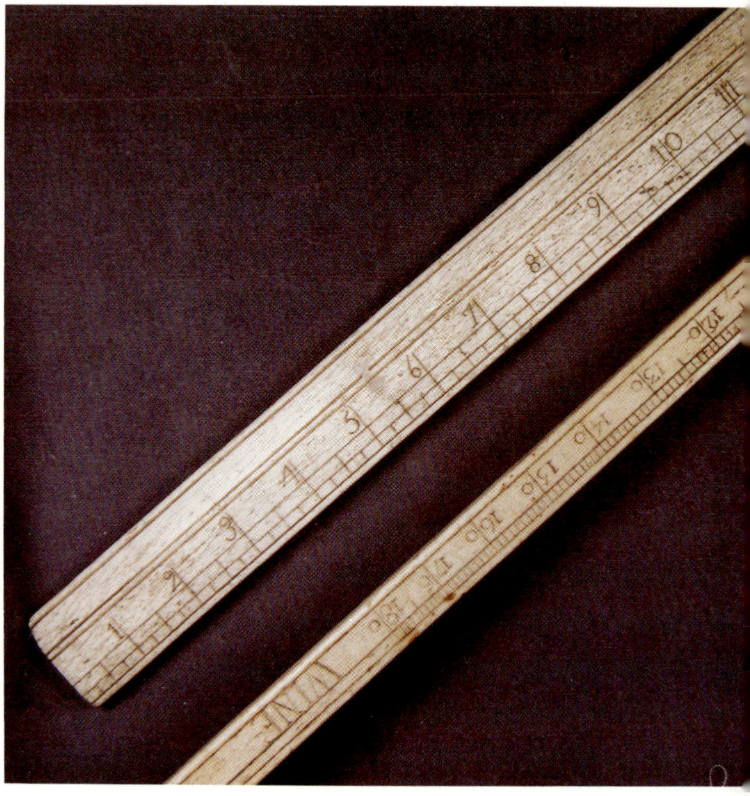

A whalebone wine measure and yardstick. *Courtesy of the Nantucket Historical Association*

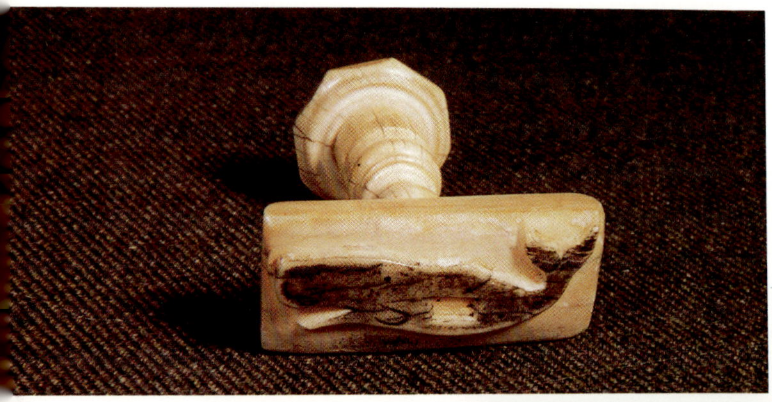

The rectangular cutout on this whalebone stamp allowed the log keeper to record the number of barrels of oil the captured whale produced. *Collection of Raymond and Elizabeth De Lucia*

Two thimbles, a sturdy seam rubber and a snatch block, all carved from whalebone, are flanked by a more decorative inlaid wooden seam rubber. *Courtesy of the Nantucket Historical Association*

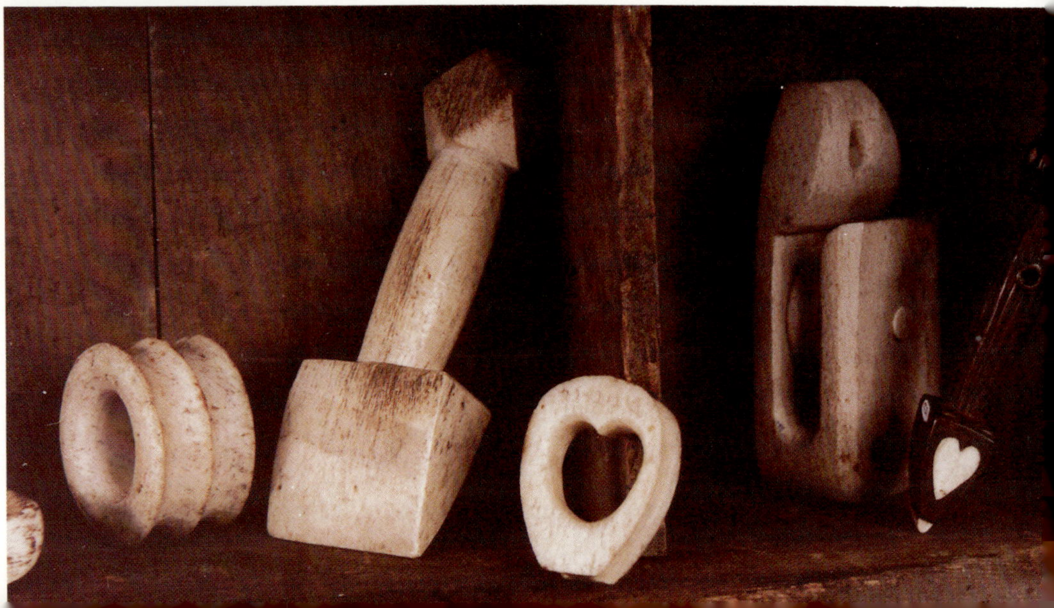

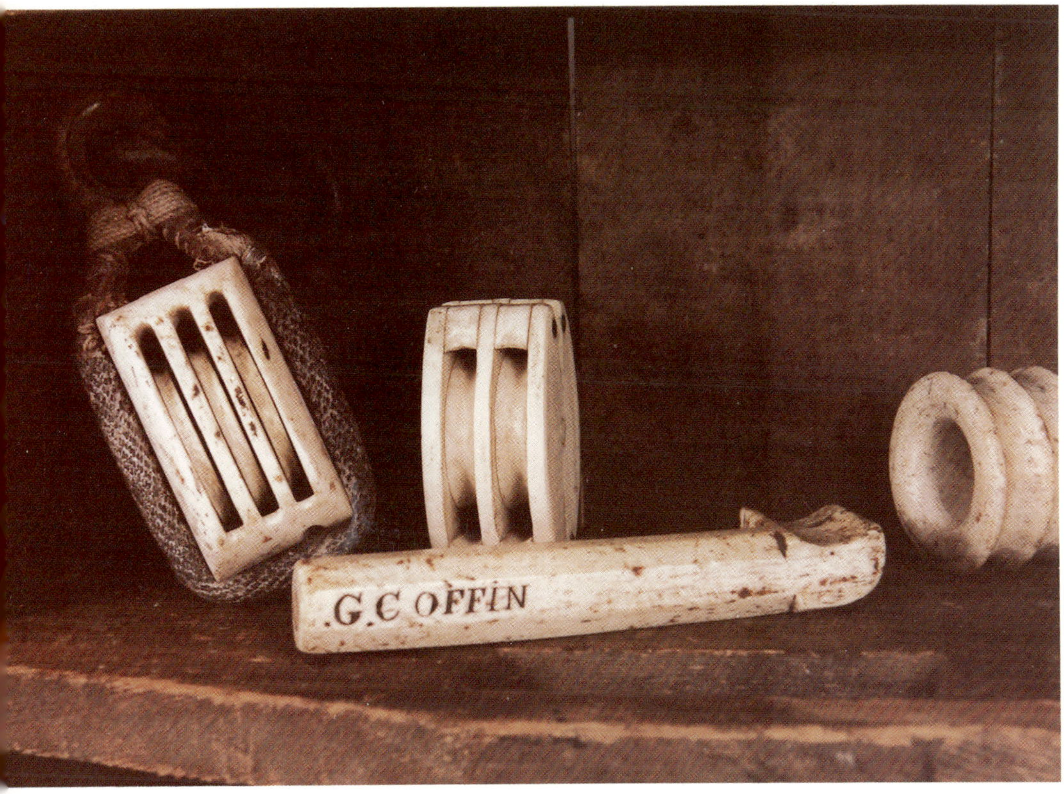

Two whalebone blocks are joined by a whalebone serving mallet belonging to George Coffin, cooper on the Nantucket whaleship *Barclay* on her 1847 voyage. A serving mallet was used to wind line around the standing rigging. *Courtesy of the Nantucket Historical Association*

A netting shuttle enhanced with delicate decorative engraving. *Courtesy of the Nantucket Historical Association*

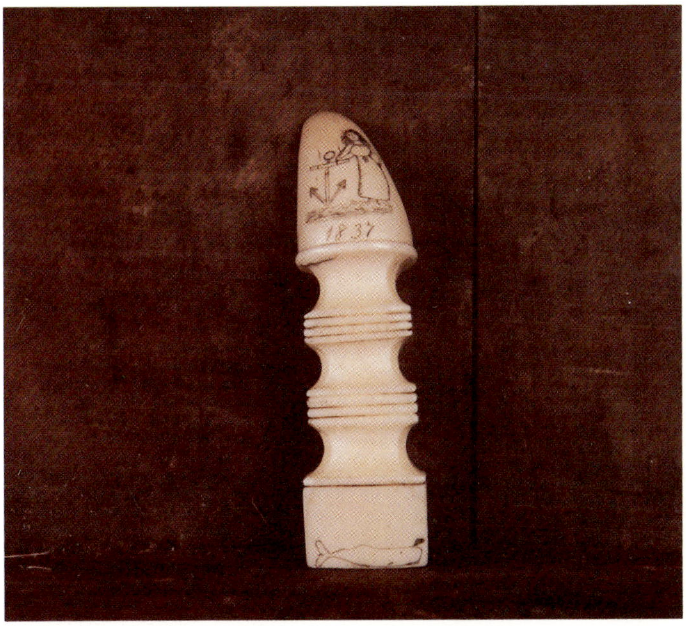

This delicate seam rubber, adorned in 1837 with a young woman, anchor and sperm whale, was perhaps intended for decoration as it is too small for a seam rubber's intended purpose of creasing the heavy canvas sails as they were taken down and furled. *Nantucket Historical Association*

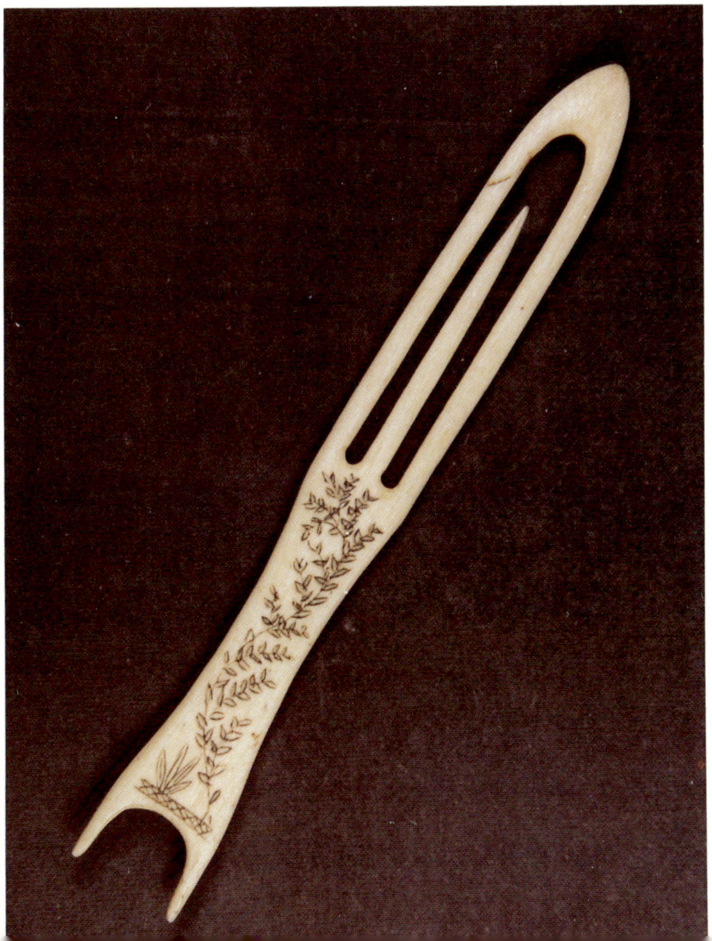

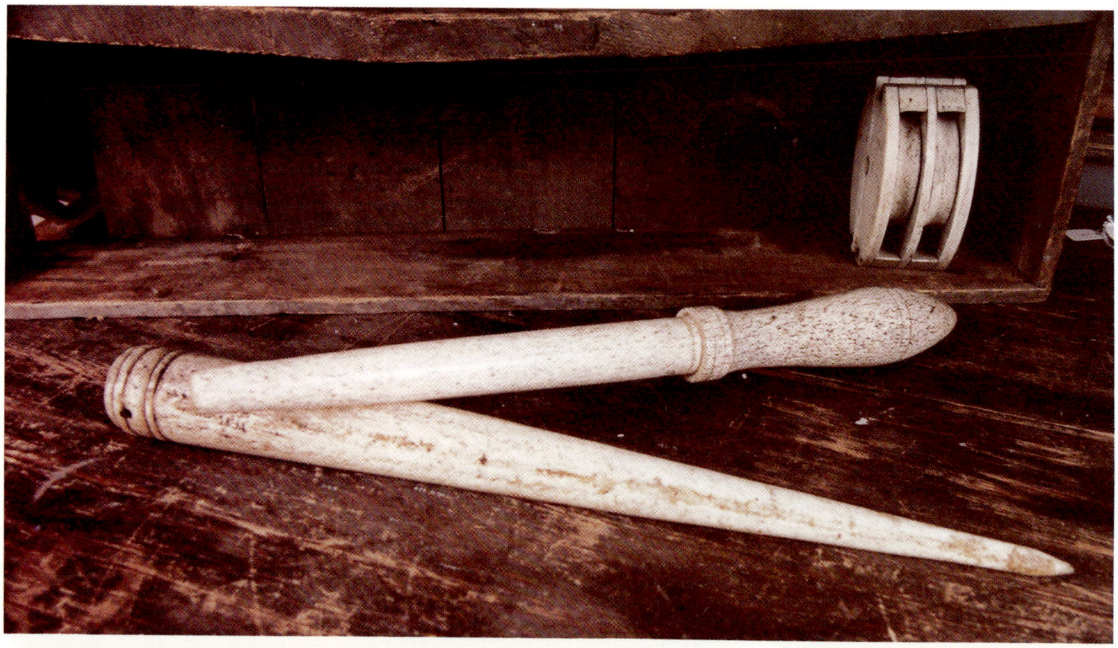

This fid, belaying pin and block were all crafted from whalebone. *Courtesy of the Nantucket Historical Association*

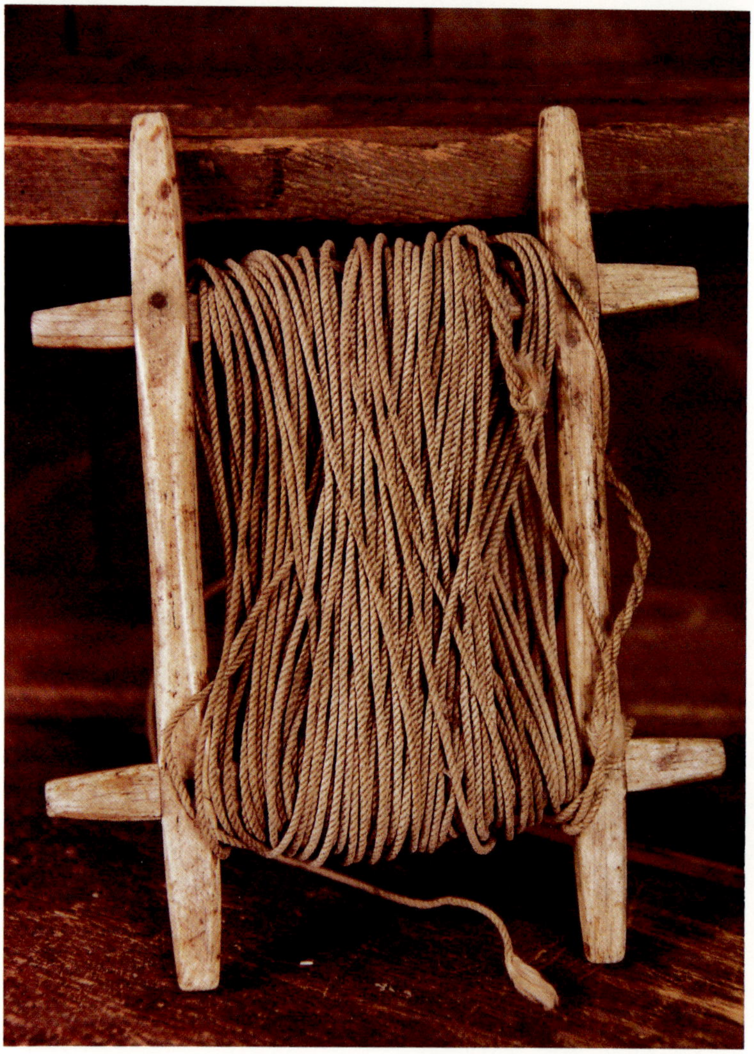

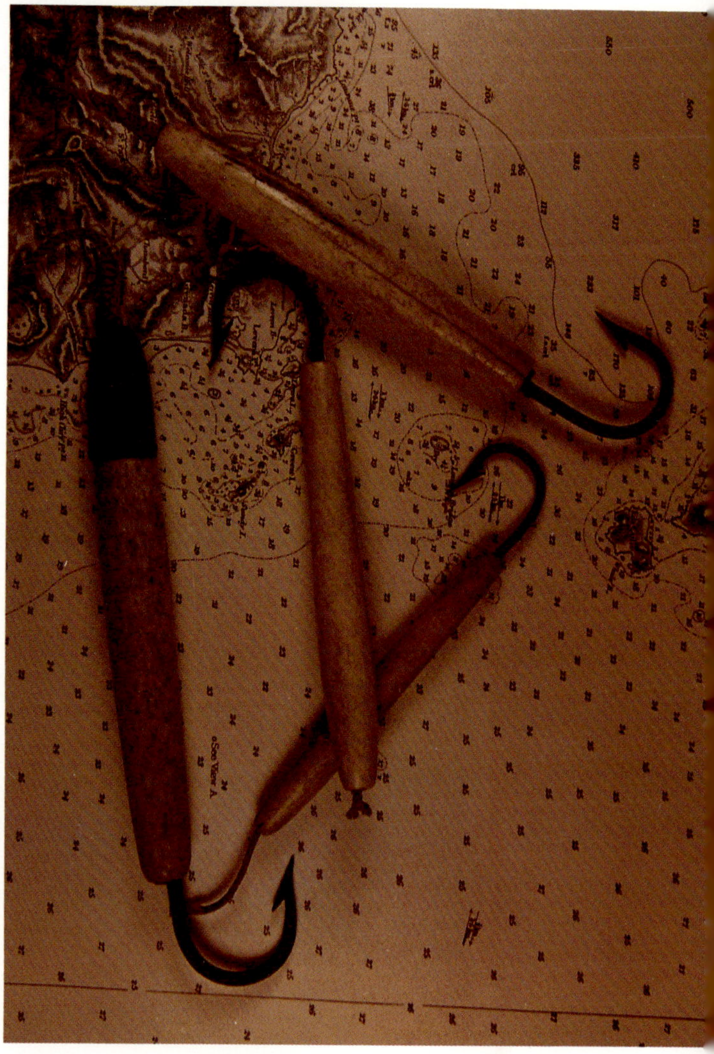

Whalebone was also incorporated into gear used for capturing lesser "fish". Left, *Courtesy of the Nantucket Historical Association* and Right, *Private Collection*

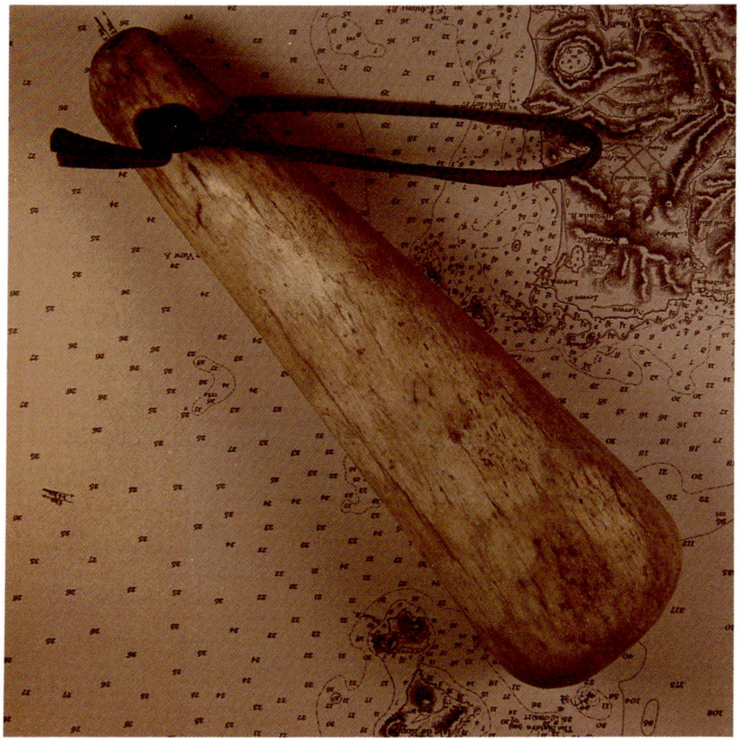

Whalebone club *Private Collection*

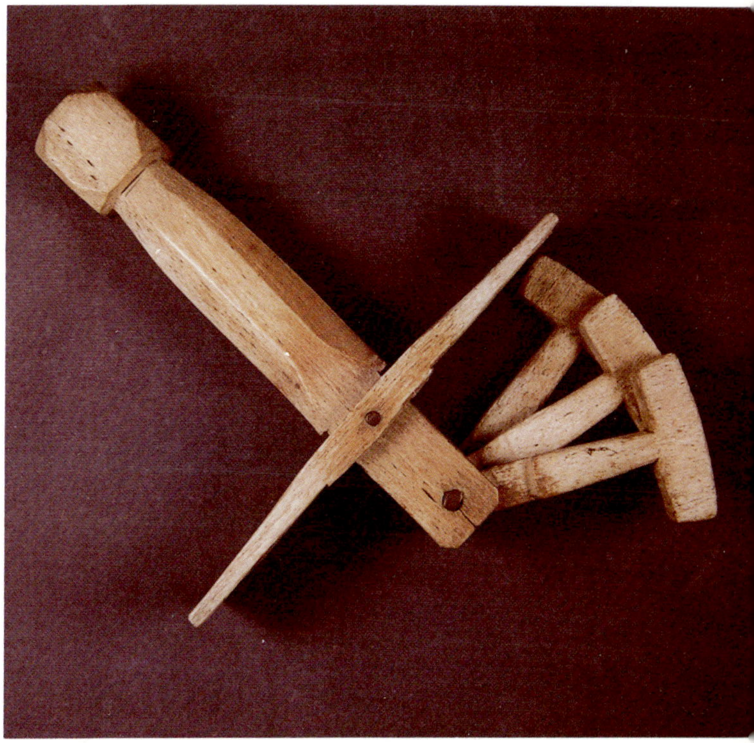

A whalebone clapper could serve as a rhythm instrument when music broke out during the evening watch. *Courtesy of the Nantucket Historical Association*

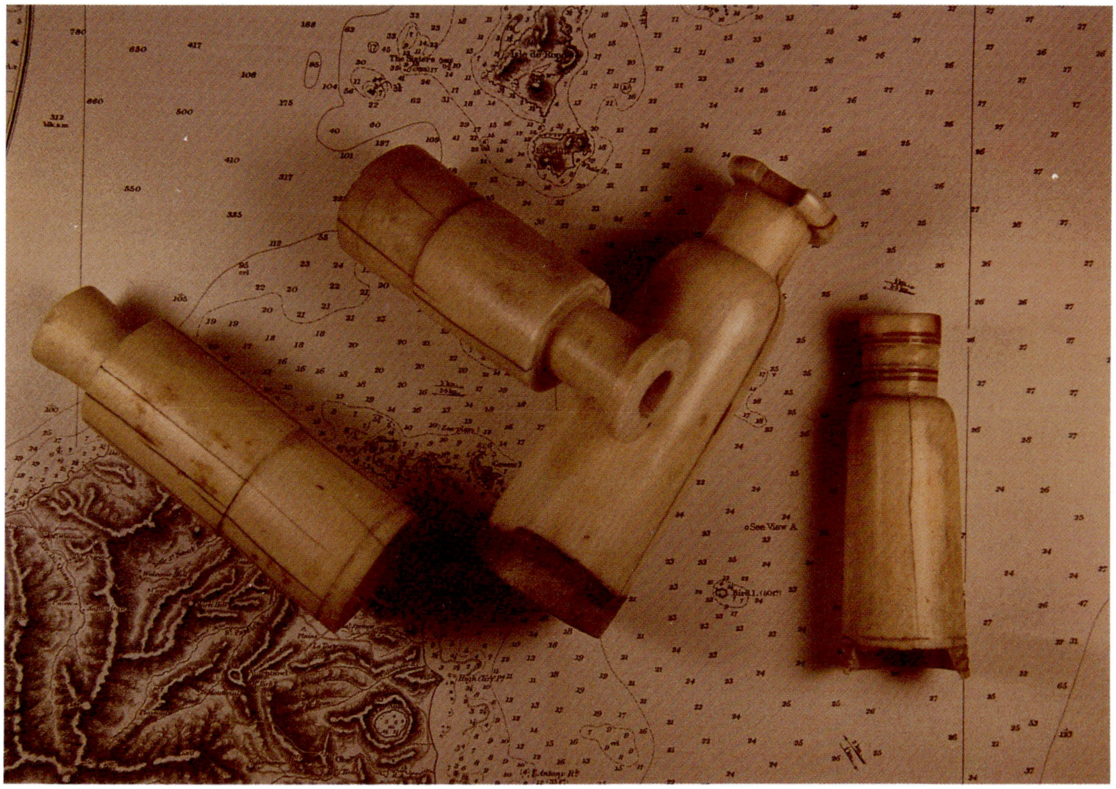

These whale's teeth were carved to serve as vials, perhaps for medicinal powders. *Private Collection*

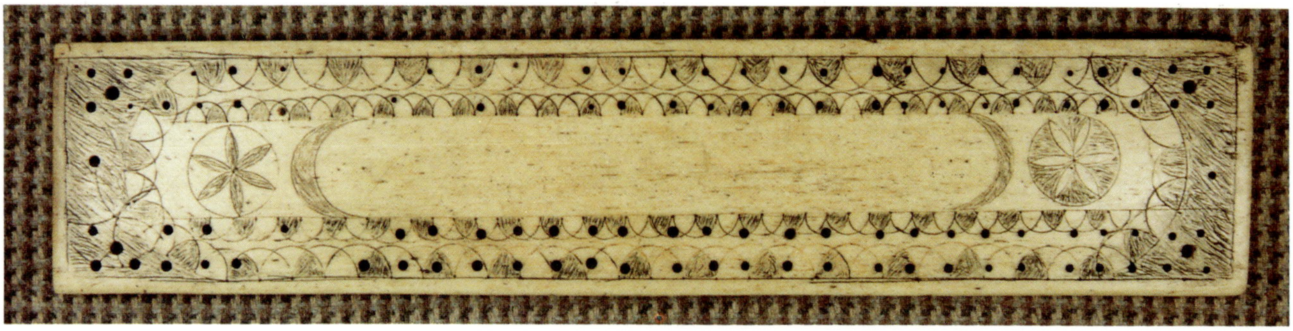

A cribbage board such as this engraved whalebone example provided diversion first in its construction and then once more in its use. *Madden Collection*

Although much scrimshaw evolved from this practical incorporation of an abundant material into necessary shipboard items, the majority of pieces were produced as mementos for those at home. The ability to create something both lovely and useful from the very prey whose pursuit caused the long separation from loved ones perhaps somewhat compensated for the years of danger, drudgery and loneliness.

When the gifts eventually arrived in the hands for whom they were intended, they were no doubt treasured and appreciated aesthetically. It is easy to forget, however, that these now priceless artifacts were not intended to glisten idly in antiseptic cases, but to assume a life of service in the daily routines of nineteenth century homes.

Courtesy of the Nantucket Historical Society

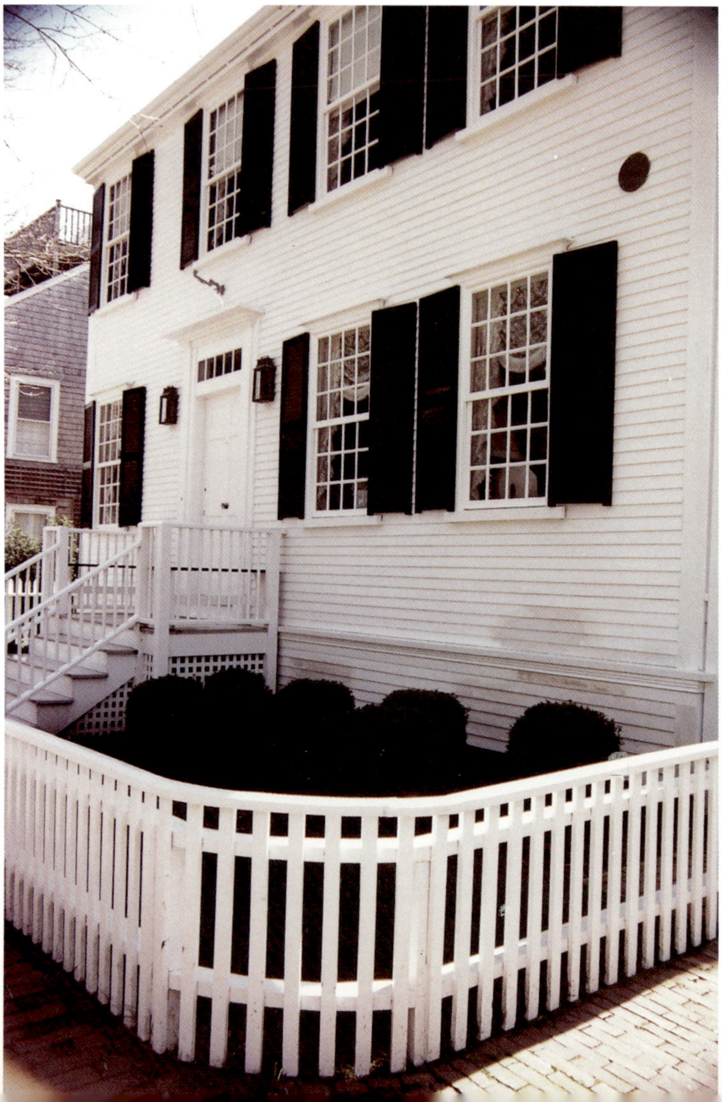

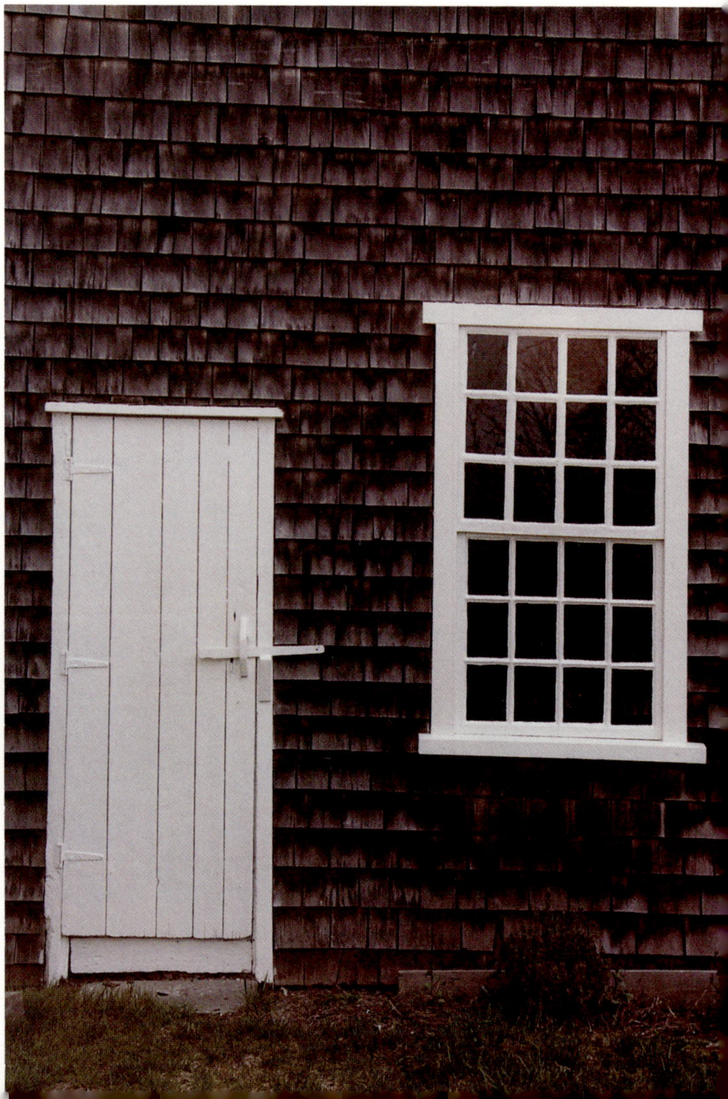

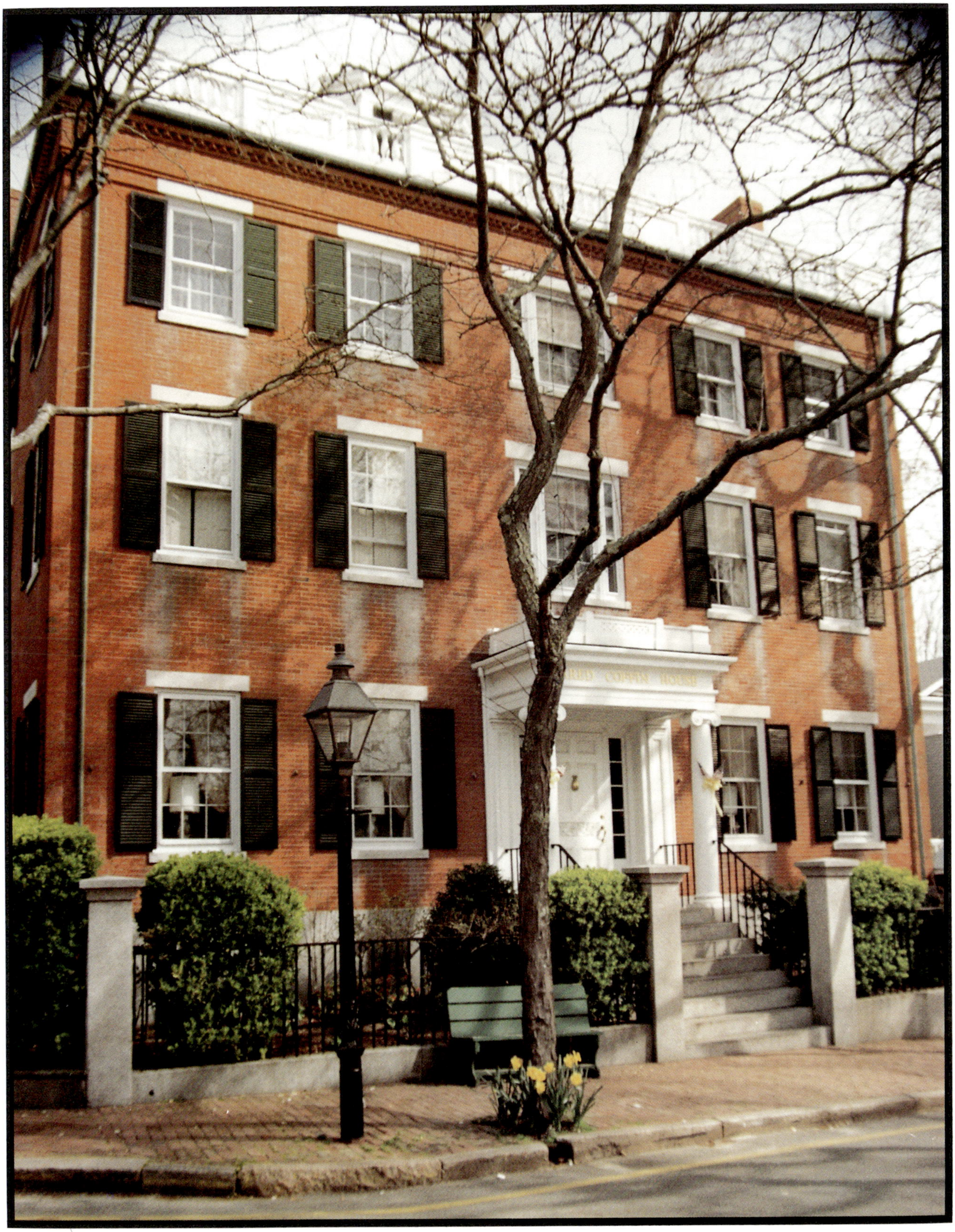

Opposite page and above:
Scrimshawed items of function and beauty could be found in many Nantucket homes.

From the kitchen to the parlor, scrimshaw was an integral part of a whaling home, be it a ship owner's mansion or a picket-fenced cottage. As so many of the gifts were intended for a mother, sweetheart or wife, it is not surprising that much of the scrimshaw inhabited the woman's domain. Many implements were designed for assistance in the kitchen. Among these were rolling pins, which ranged from simple wooden cylinders classically accented with whale ivory handles to elaborately inlaid creations. The ingenious artists also fashioned whalebone choppers, mortars and pestles, spoons and butter stamps; carved coconut-shells were converted to cups, bowls and ladles. Clothespins of various sizes were carved from whalebone, either for home or use aboard ship.

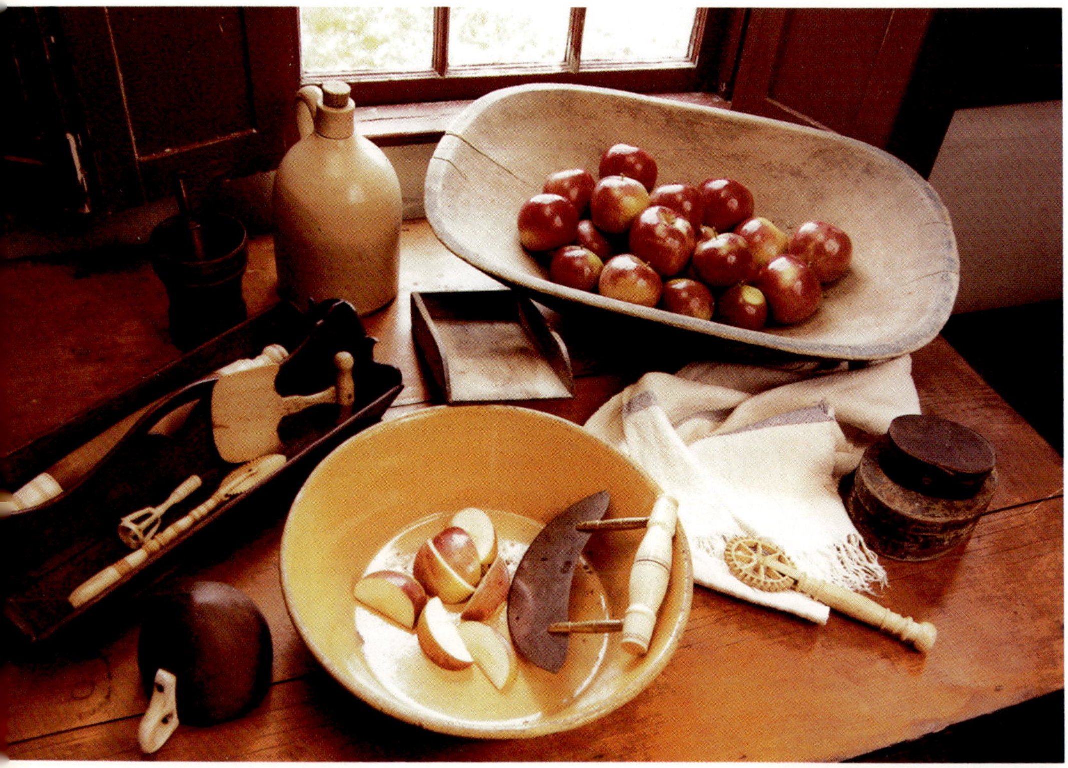

Various scrimshawed kitchen implements appear at home in the kitchen of the Nantucket Historical Association's "1800 House." *Courtesy of the Nantucket Historical Association*

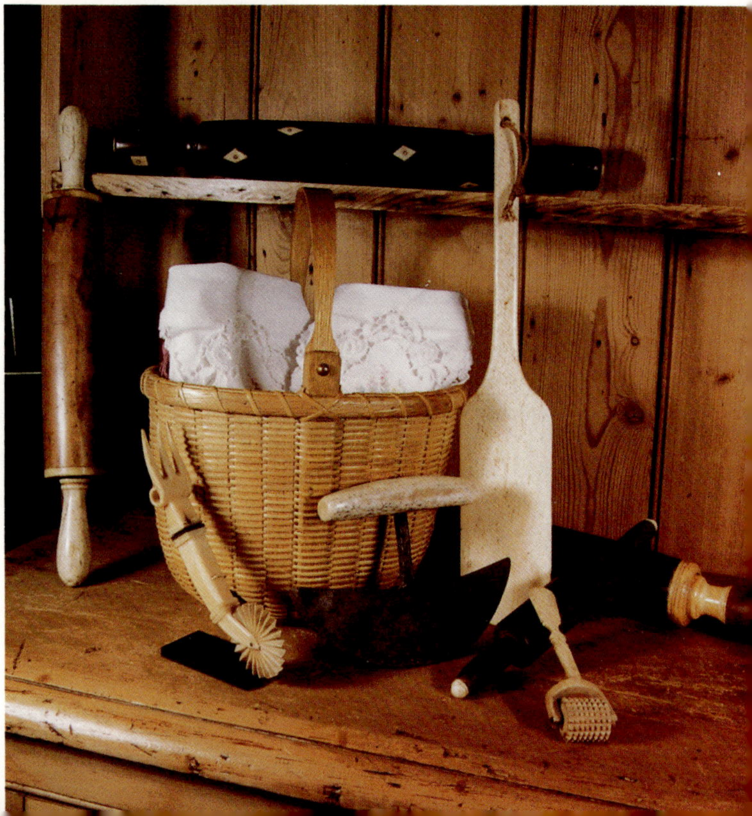

Homely articles made beautiful by a scrimshander's creativity. *Private Collection*

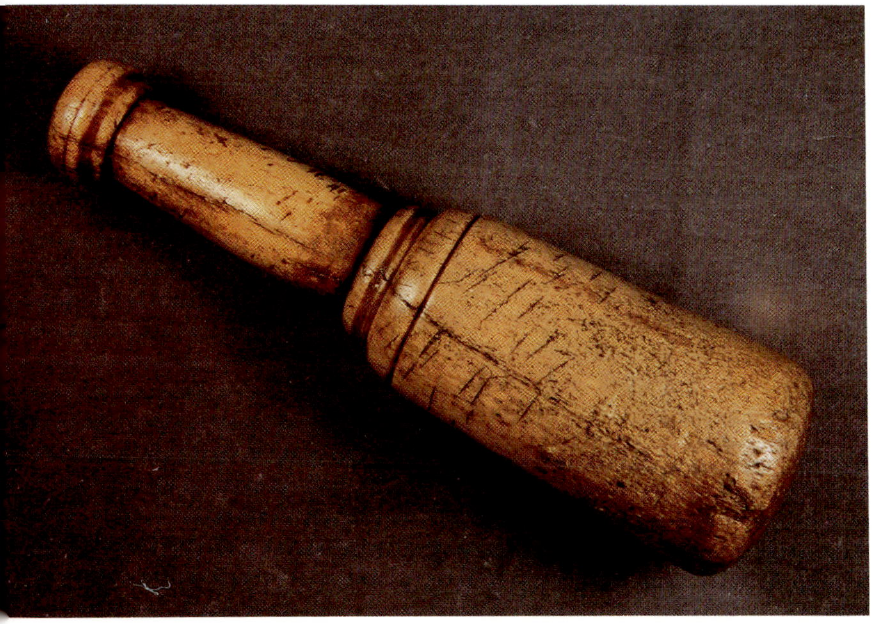

This heavy whalebone pestle gives evidence of many years of use. *Madden Collection*

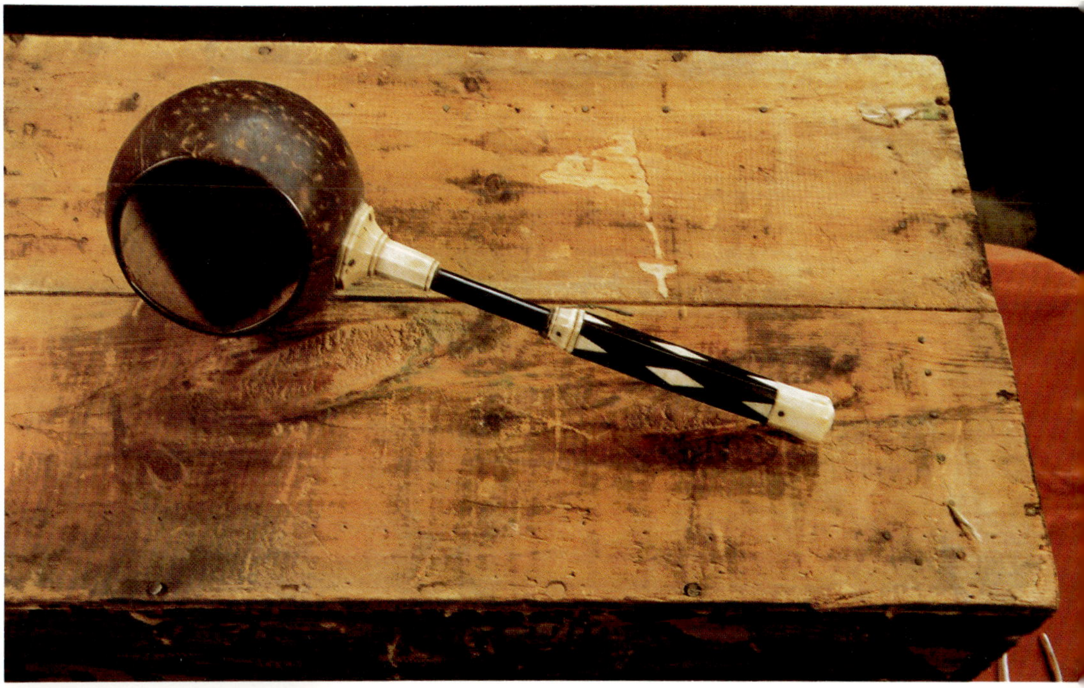

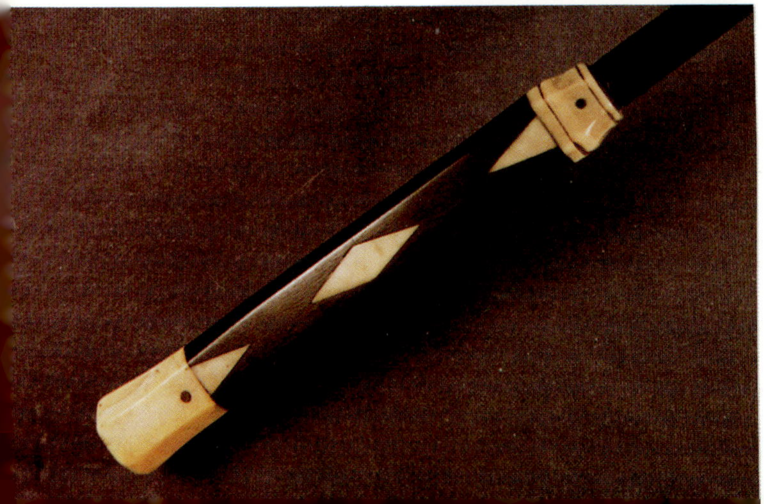

A finely finished coconut shell was fashioned into an elaborate dipper by the addition of a beautiful ebony handle inlaid and decorated with whale ivory. A very similar dipper in the collection of the Kendall Whaling Museum is attributed to Captain John Marble, while he was master of the bark *Kathleen* between 1857 and 1860. *Collection of Raymond and Elizabeth De Lucia*

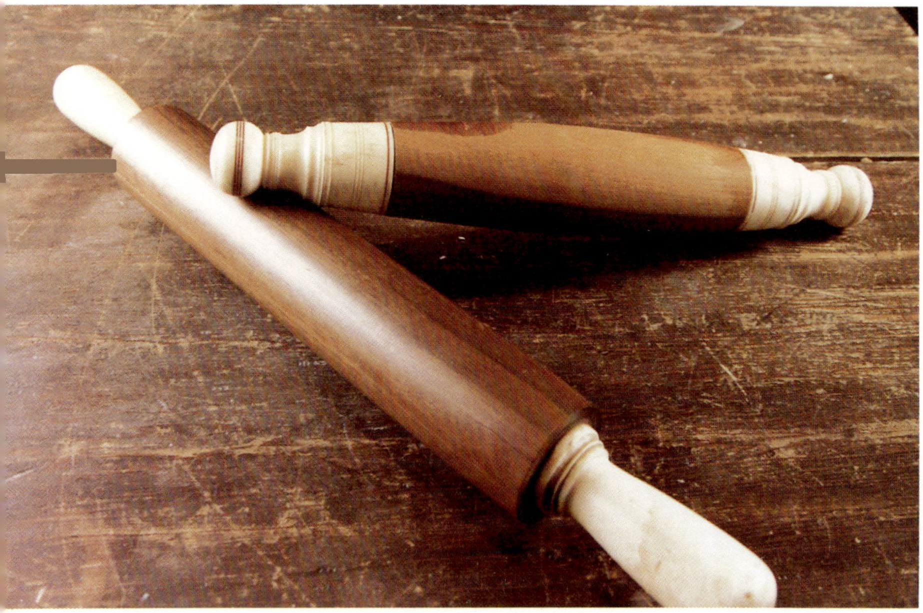

On May 31, 1861, Eliza Williams wrote in her journal, "My Husband has been turning me a rolling Pin of yellow Ebony. It is very pretty." (Harold Williams, *One Whaling Family*, p. 179) These rolling pins are embellished with whale ivory handles. *Courtesy of the Nantucket Historical Association*

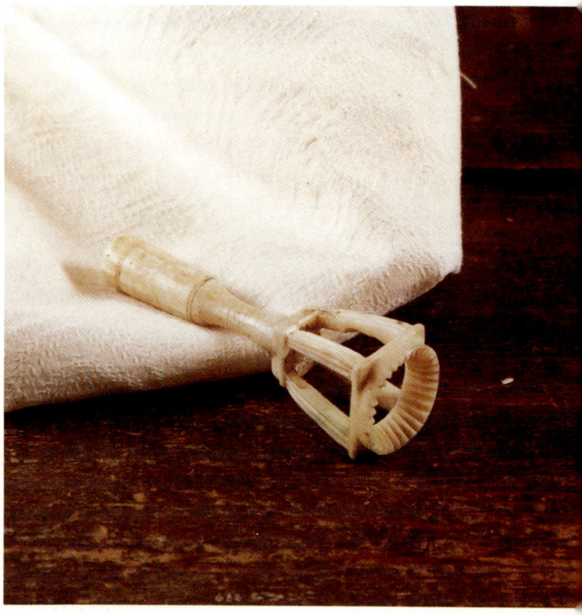

Whalebone pastry tool *Courtesy of the Nantucket Historical Association*

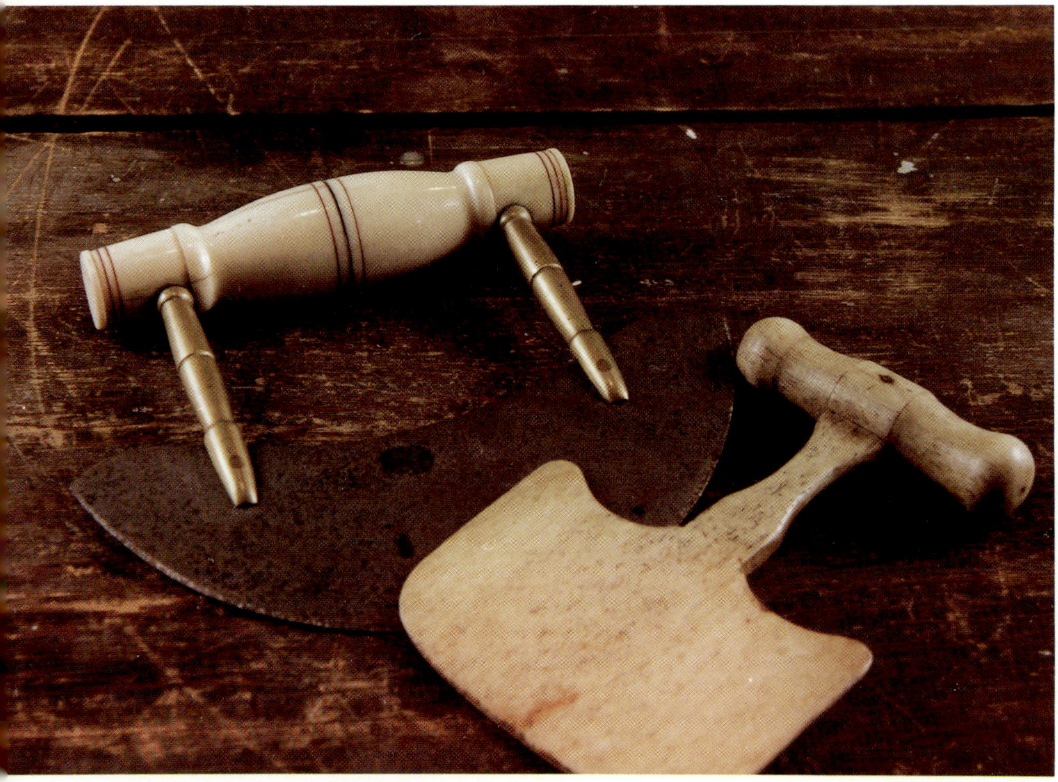

This sturdy whalebone food chopper is paired with a more elegant example whose whale ivory handle is decorated with red and green sealing wax. *Courtesy of the Nantucket Historical Association*

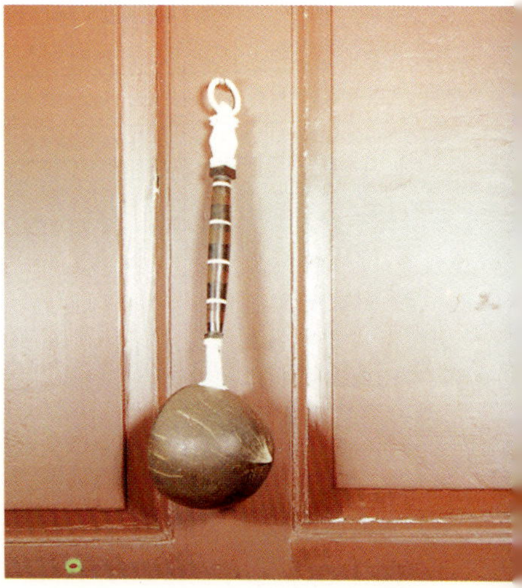

A coconut shell dipper hangs beside the hearth in the kitchen of the "1800 House" *Courtesy of the Nantucket Historical Association*

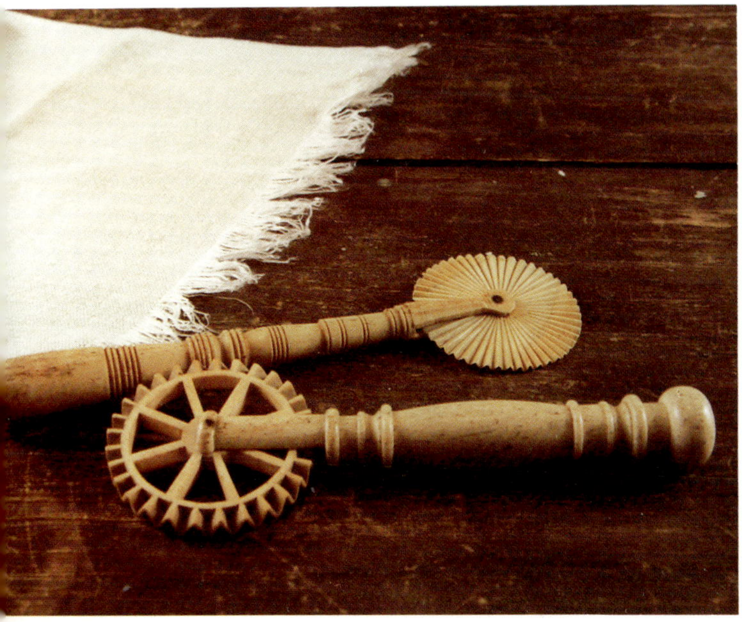

The whale ivory jagging wheels of these two classic kitchen pie crimpers are attached to turned, whalebone handles, one of which is colored with red sealing wax. *Courtesy of the Nantucket Historical Association*

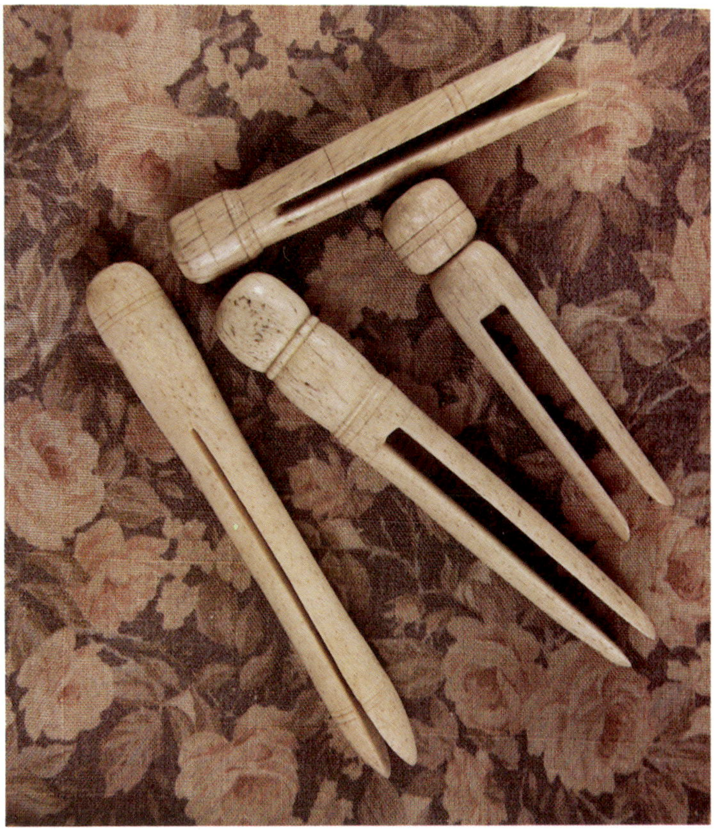

Carving whalebone clothespins was a common pastime for resourceful whalemen. *Courtesy of the Nantucket Historical Association*

One need not be an anthropologist to deduce that Yankee whalemen enjoyed, perhaps even lusted for, good pie. In testament are the plethora of surviving pie crimpers, or jagging wheels, which only hint at the number originally carved. Crimpers also provided boundless opportunity for innovation and design and a challenging means of competition between shipboard artists. Used to cut and decorate pastry, surviving crimpers include sturdy, functional utensils as well as fanciful, incredibly wrought, multi-wheeled creations that probably never touched a piece of dough. Sometimes ingeniously carved from one tooth, often inlaid with shells or woods, the crimper usually included at least one carved fork to pierce the bubbling delicacy.

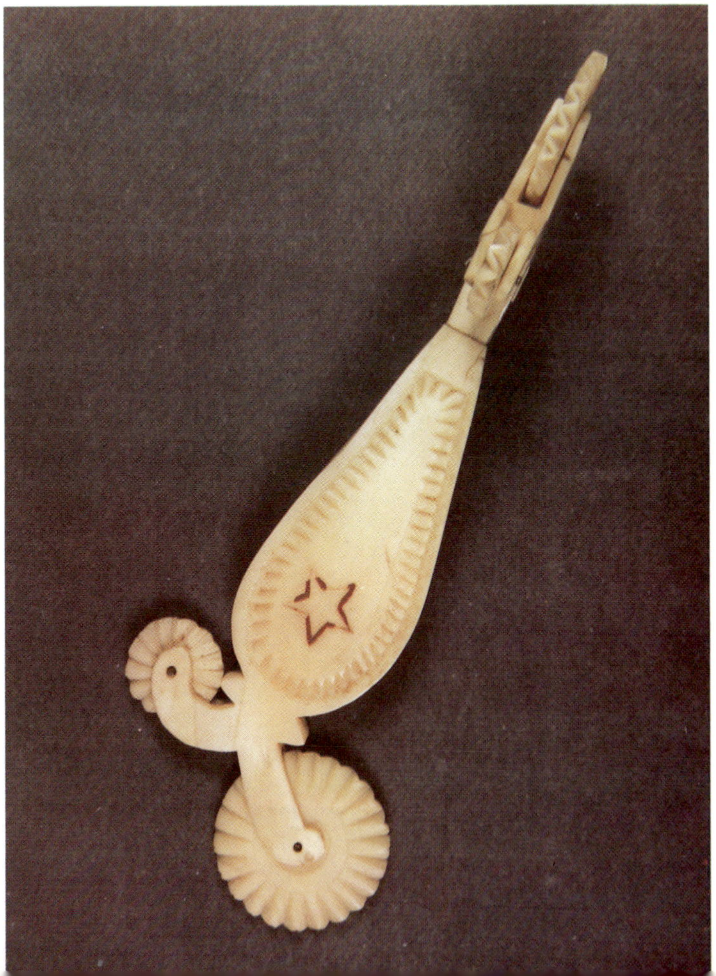

This decorated whale ivory pie crimper has a wheel for every task. *Courtesy of the Nantucket Historical Association*

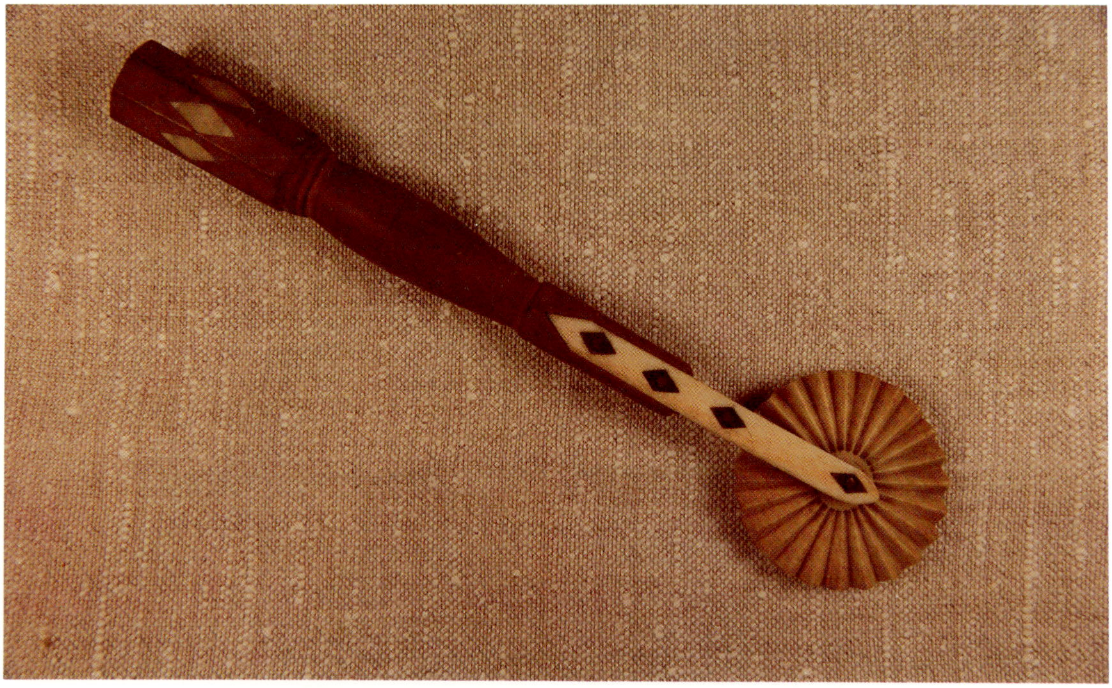

This graceful old wooden-handled crimper is inlaid with abalone and baleen. *Courtesy of the Nantucket Historical Association*

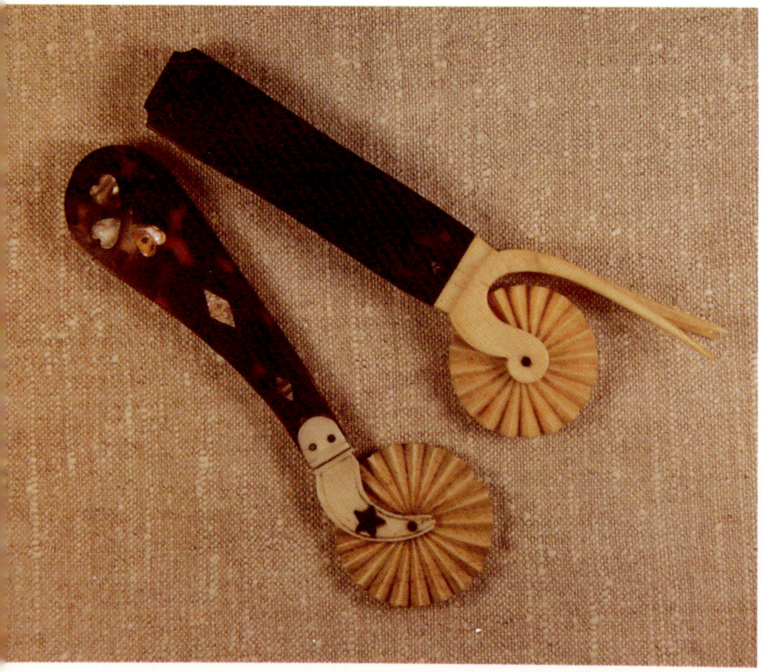

A whale ivory bird's head grasps the jagging wheel as its body evolves into the crimper's fork. The handle is tortoise shell as is the second crimper, which is inlaid with abalone. *Courtesy of the Nantucket Historical Association.*

Much planning went into the execution of this lovely pierced whale ivory jagging wheel. *Courtesy of the Nantucket Historical Association*

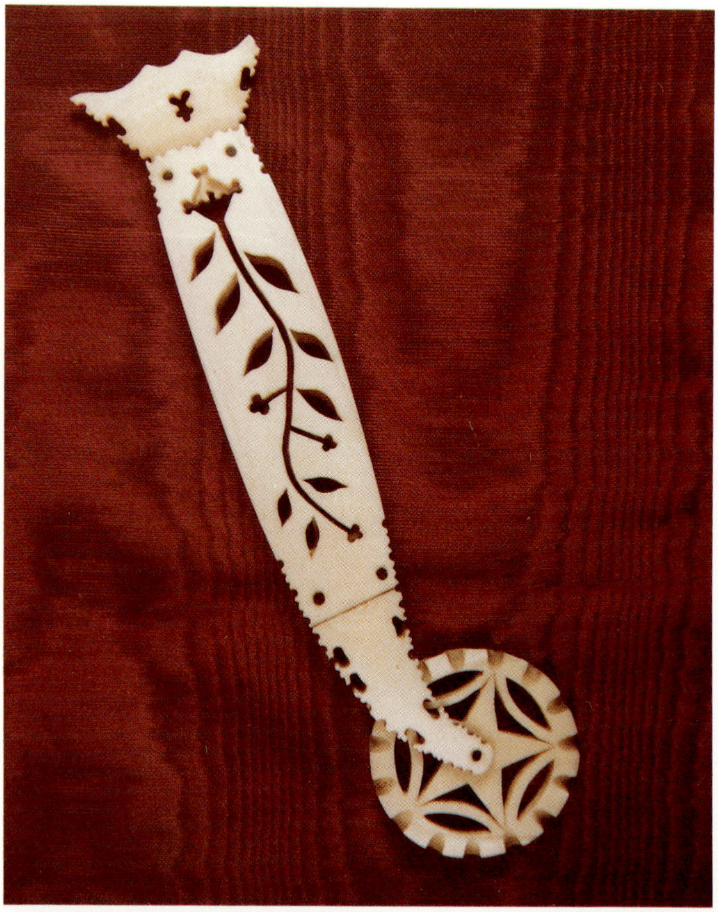

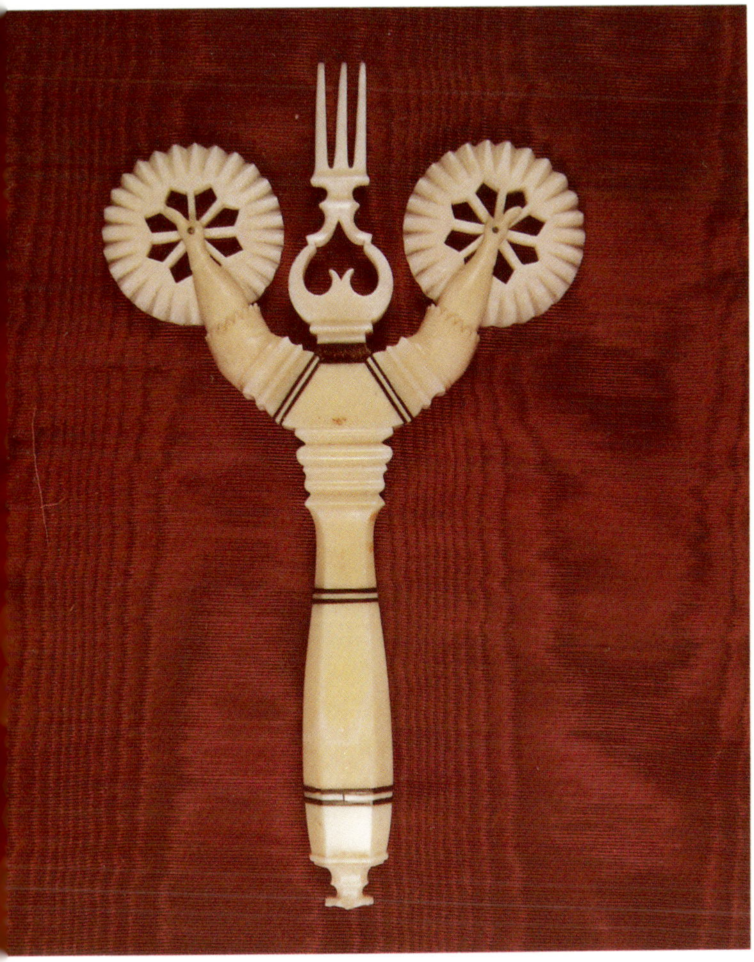

The wheels of this classically-shaped, whale ivory pie crimper at first appear to be clasped by two delicate birds. When the piece is reversed, however, dainty feet attached to two voluptuous legs emerging from lacy bloomers are clearly doing the job. The inlays are baleen. *Courtesy of the Nantucket Historical Association*

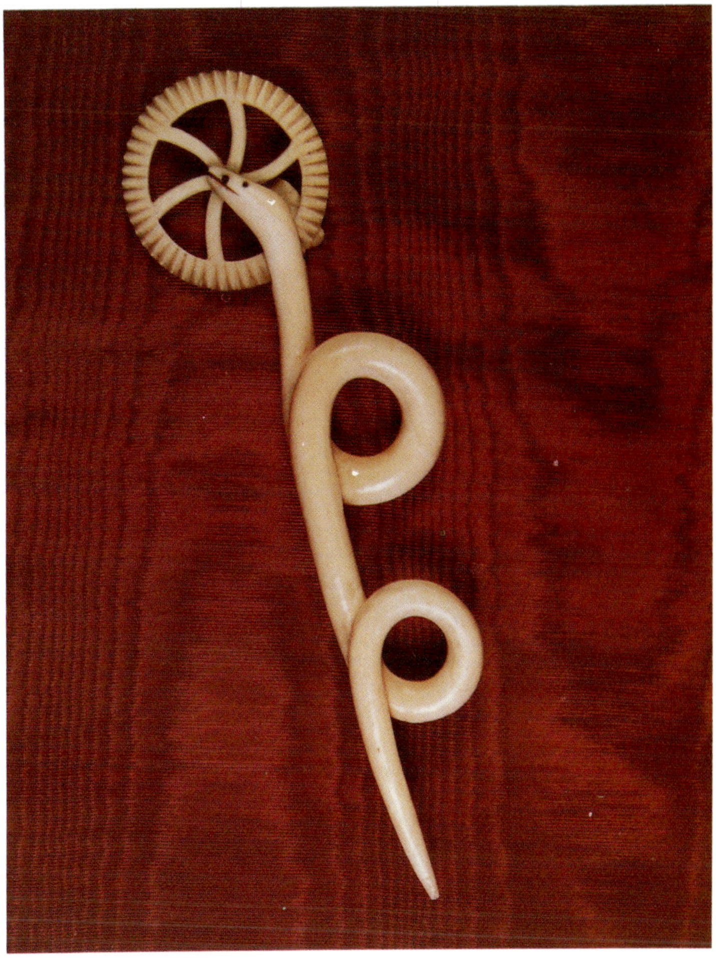

A sinuous serpent comprises the handle of this whale ivory jagging wheel. *Courtesy of the Nantucket Historical Association*

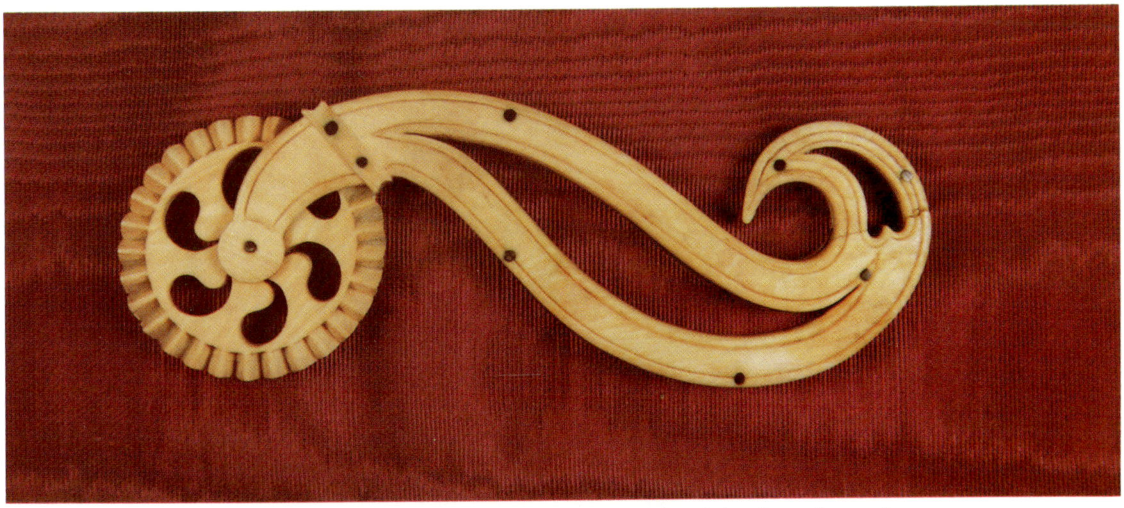

Simple, well-proportioned curves blend the handle and wheel of this whale ivory pie crimper into a beautifully unified piece. *Courtesy of the Nantucket Historical Association*

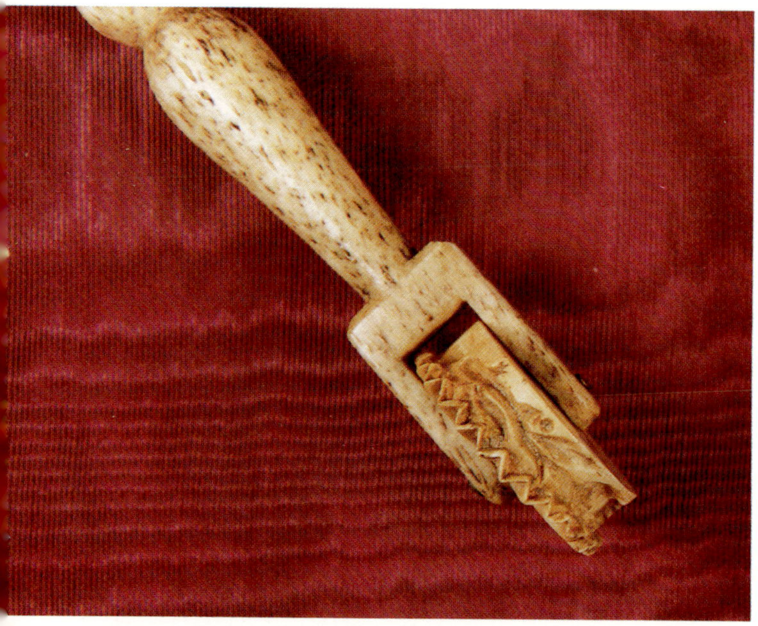

A sturdy, whalebone handle grasps a jagging wheel whose relief-carved pattern would leave a flower and vine design on the pastry crust. *Courtesy of the Nantucket Historical Association*

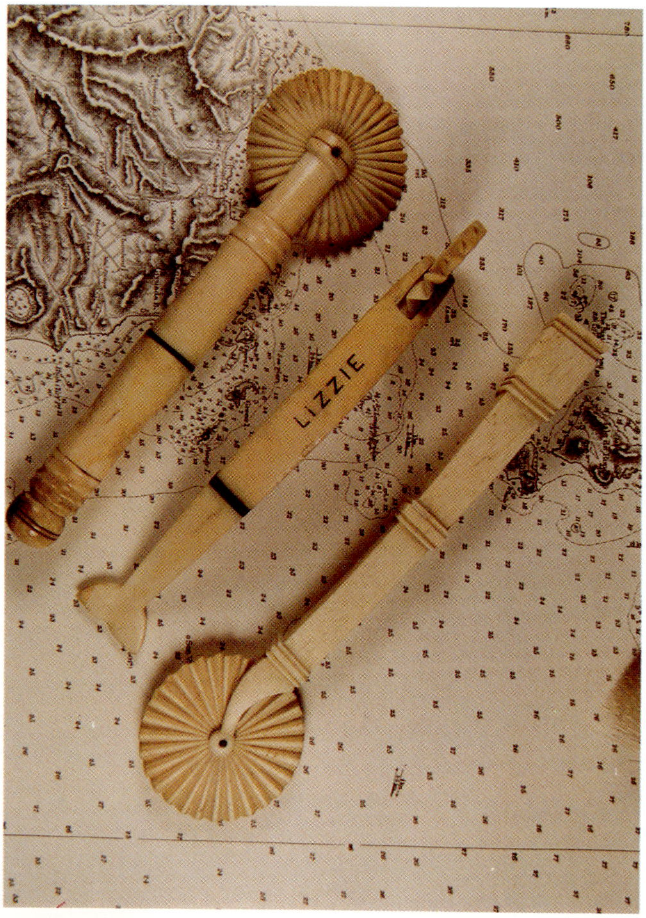

Turned, carved, inlaid, inscribed, or decorated with a whale's tail, each pie crimper reflected the ingenuity of its maker. *Private Collection*

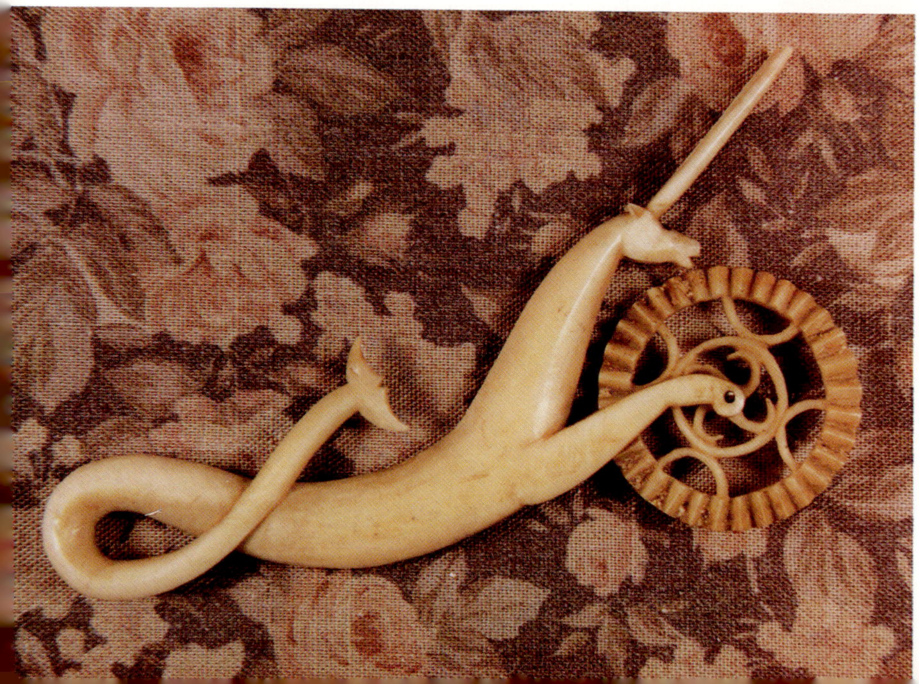

A mythical whale ivory creature grasps this delicate crimping wheel. *Courtesy of the Nantucket Historical Association*

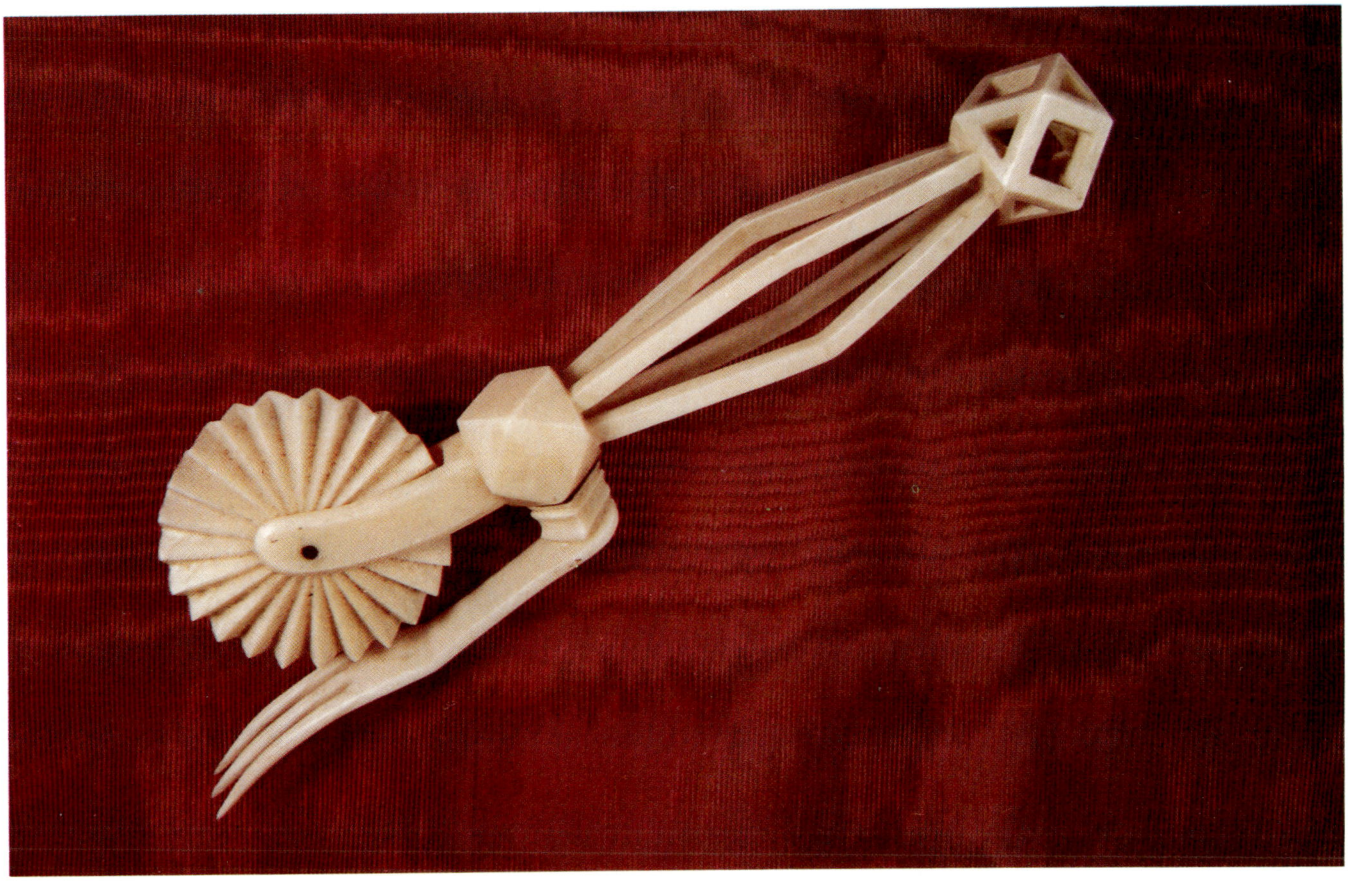

The solid polyhedron knob of this incredibly well-planned and executed whale ivory pie crimper is mimicked at handle's end by a hollow version of its shape. *Courtesy of the Nantucket Historical Association*

Scrimshawed articles were also abundant in the lady's sewing area. As she sat down to her needlework, she could reach for a carved ivory bodkin in an inlaid box of tropical wood or find neatly arranged threads and needles in an ornately tiered spool holder. A bone work box, carefully steamed, bent, fastened and decorated might hold scraps of material or yarn, ready for mending. Knitting needle sheaths, crochet hooks, knitting needles, and bodkins were common instruments raised above mere utilitarianism by the workmanship of their creators. Just as crafting a gift for a loved one brought home closer to the scrimshander, handling the everyday implements lovingly fashioned by a husband or brother could foster a reassuring connection for the woman at home.

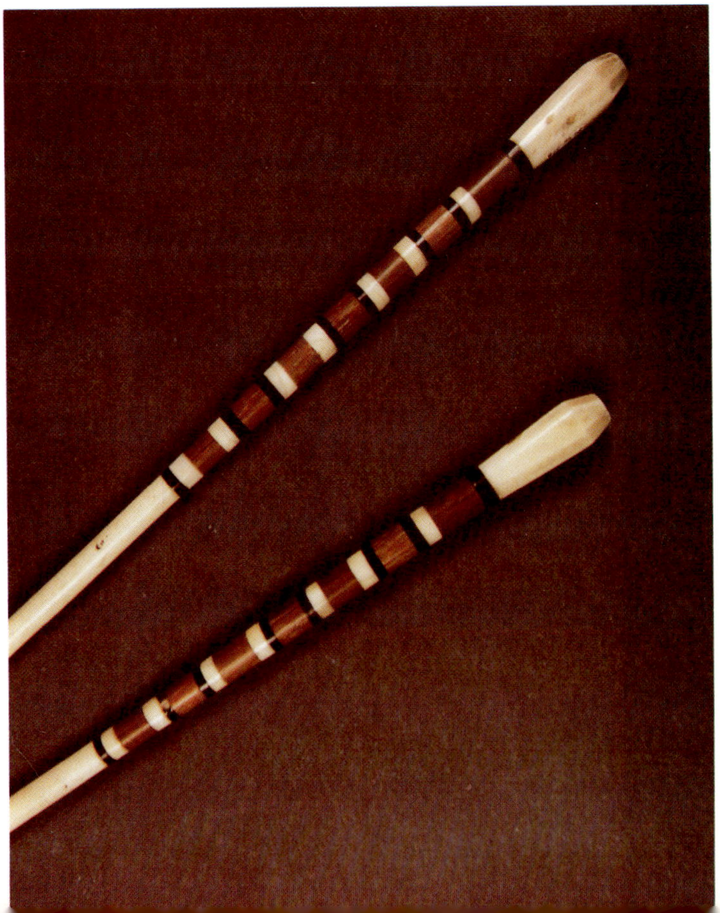

These elegant knitting needles are constructed of whalebone, whale ivory, tropical wood and baleen. *Courtesy of the Nantucket Historical Association*

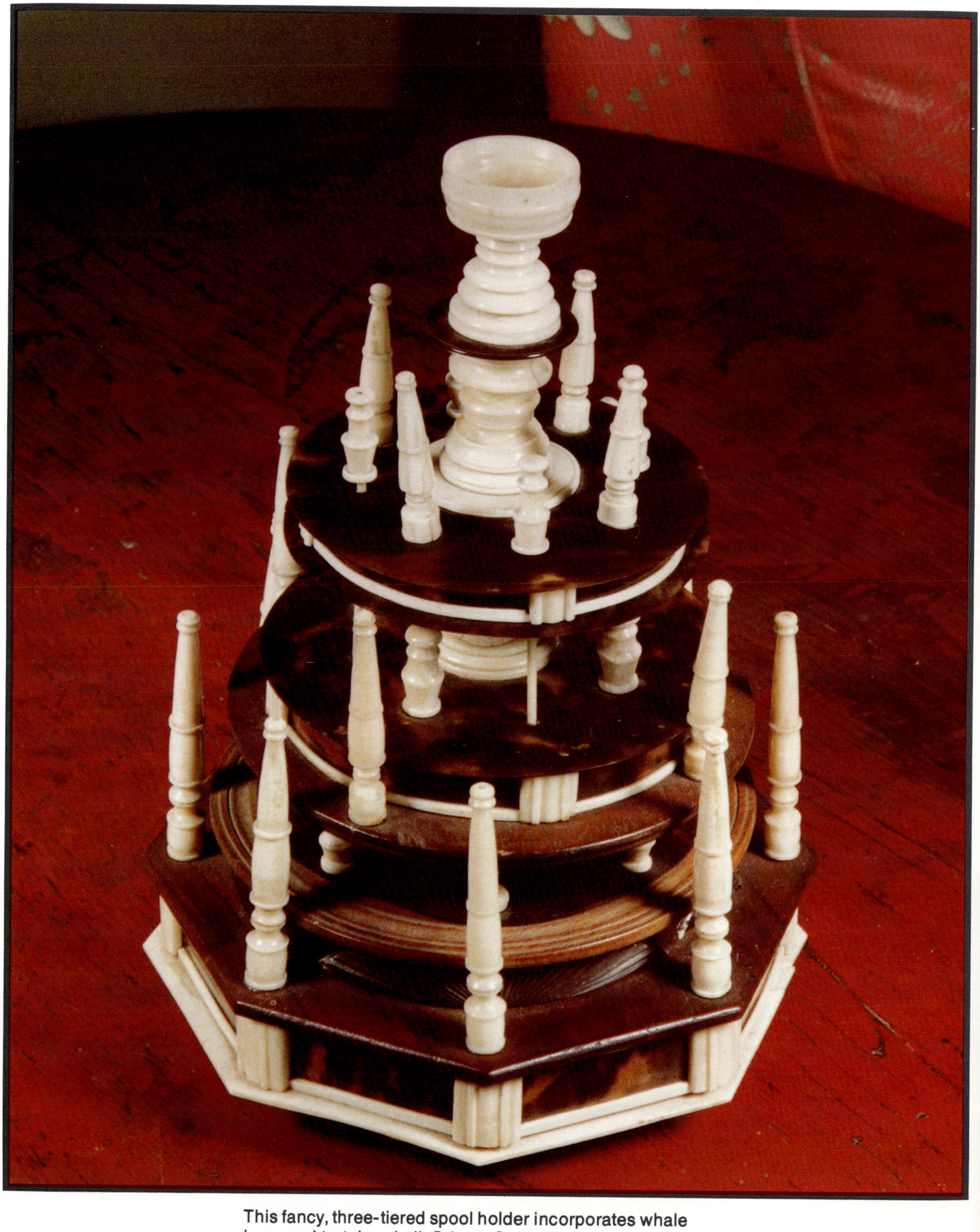

This fancy, three-tiered spool holder incorporates whale ivory and tortoise shell. *Private Collection*

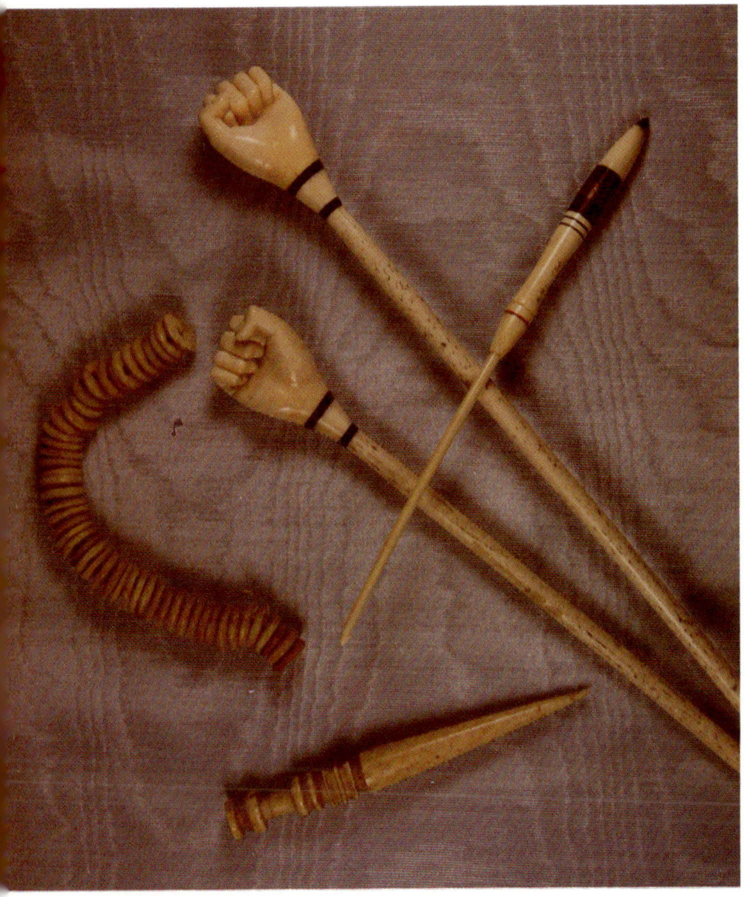

This assortment of items might have been found in a typical nineteenth century sewing basket. Included is a handsomely carved set of whalebone knitting needles topped by finely detailed whale ivory hands. *Private Collection*

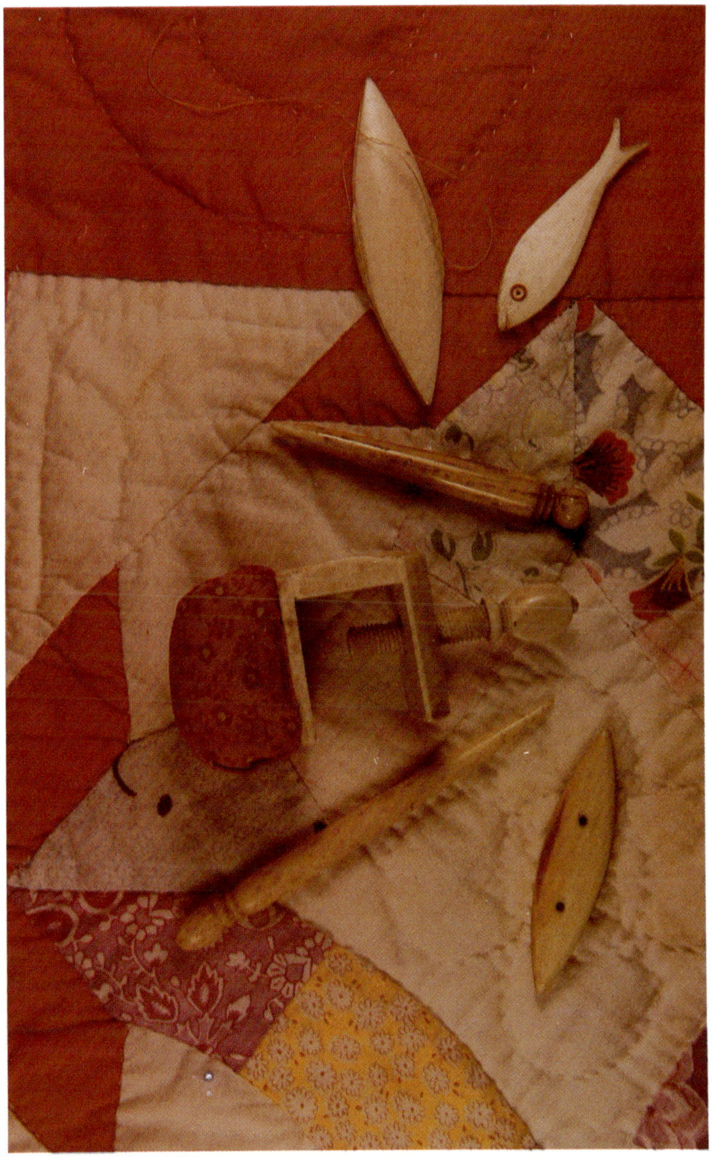

Three whale ivory shuttles, one in the shape of a fish, are joined by two whalebone bodkins and a pincushion supported by a whalebone clamp. *Private Collection*

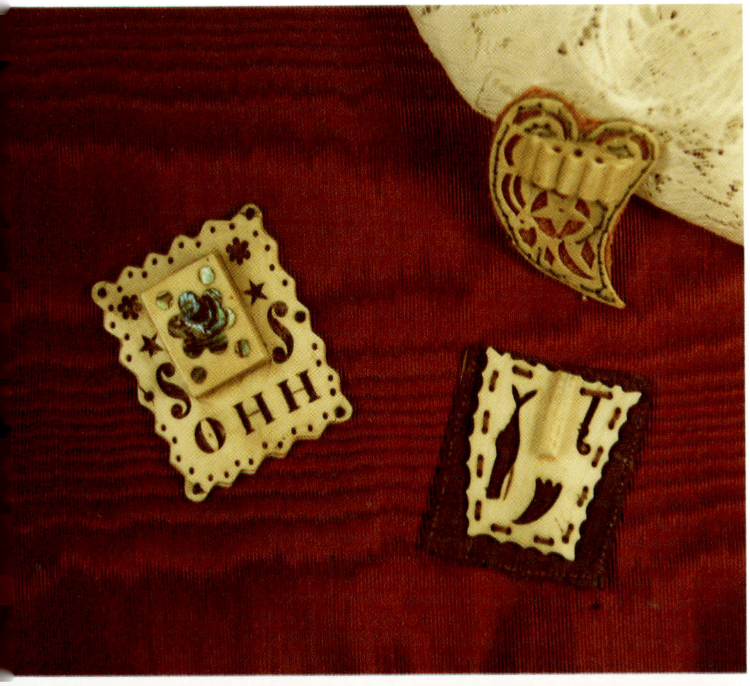

No details were overlooked in the creation of these fancy needleholders. *Collection of the Nantucket Historical Association*

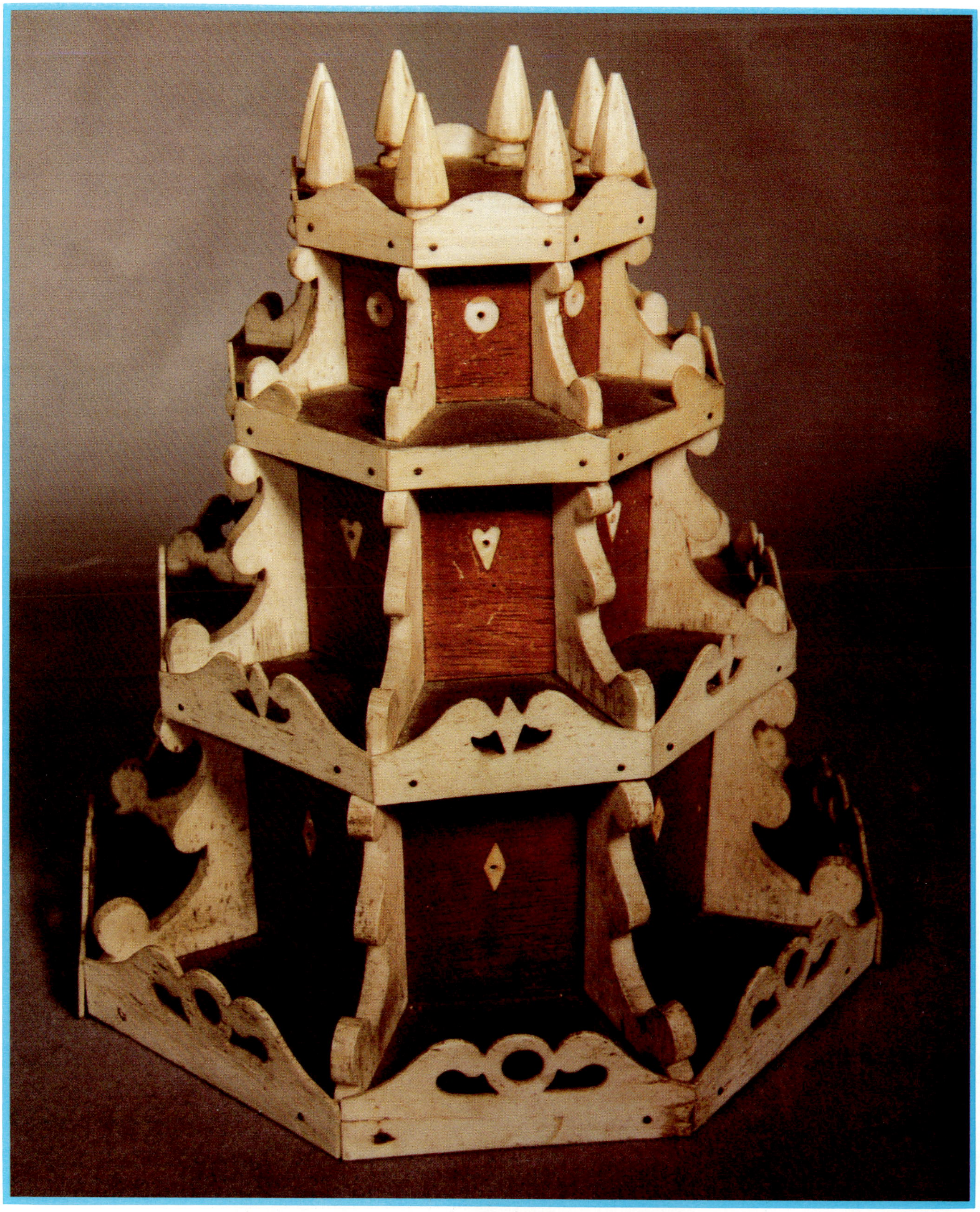

Thread is stored inside this elegant wood and whalebone spool holder and passed through the holes in the inlaid whale ivory hearts, diamonds and circles. *Courtesy of the Nantucket Historical Association*

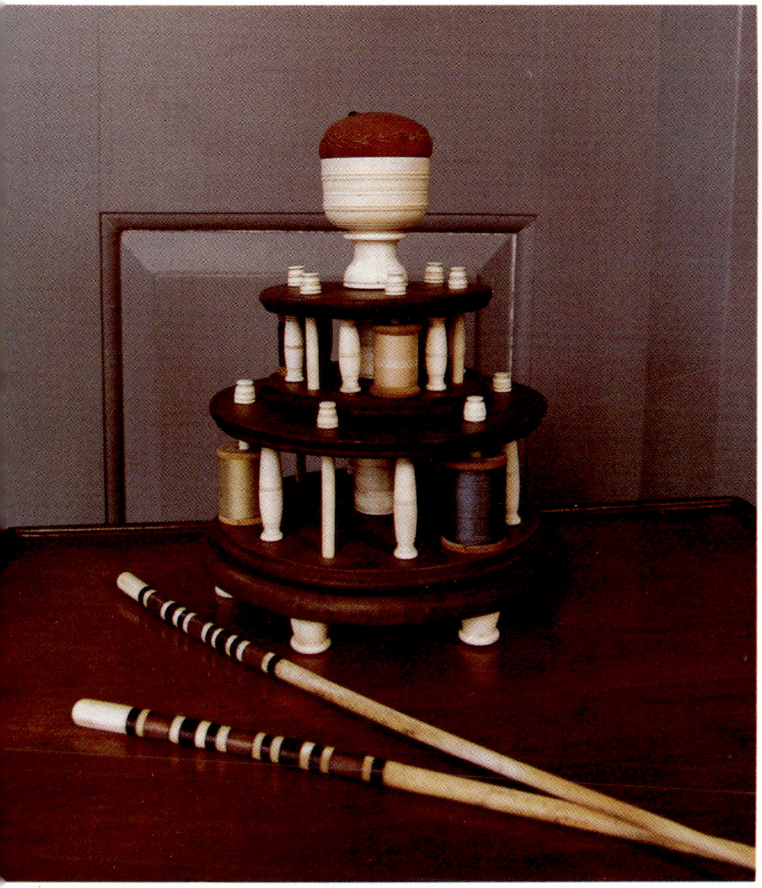

Classic wood and whale ivory spool holder, topped with a red pincushion, is flanked by whalebone, whale ivory, baleen and mahogany knitting needles. *Madden Collection*

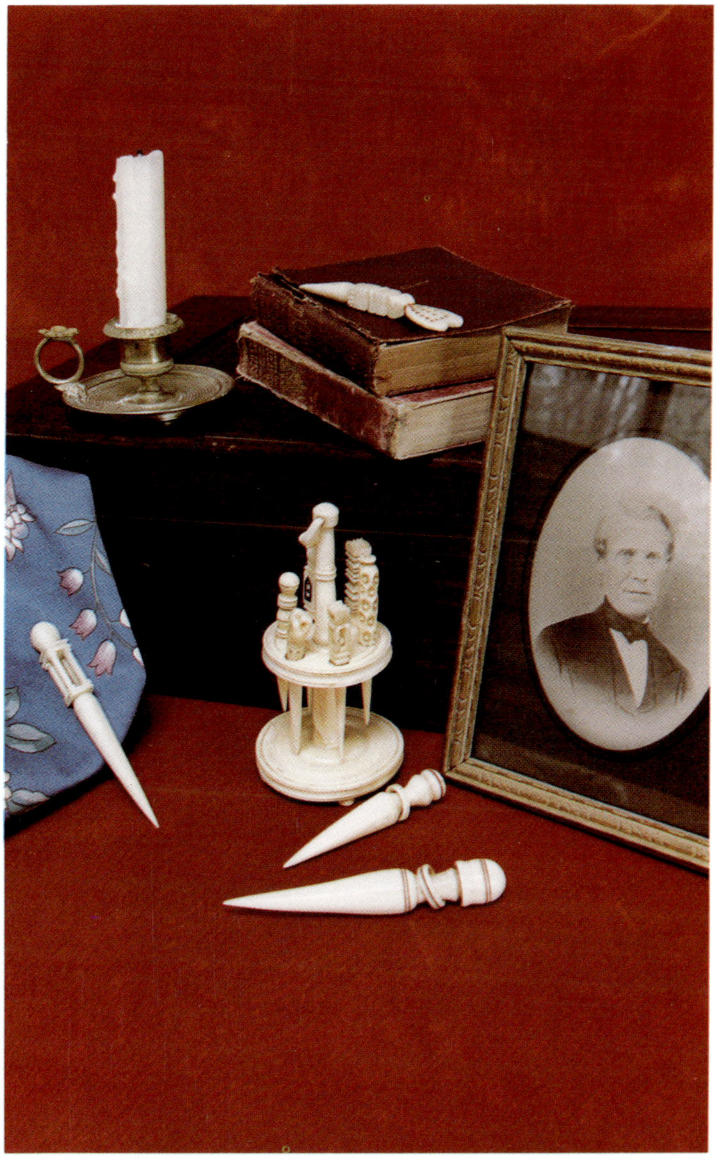

Only the scrimshander's imagination limited the variety of bodkins he might produce. *Collection of Curtis Nyquist, B.M.N.*

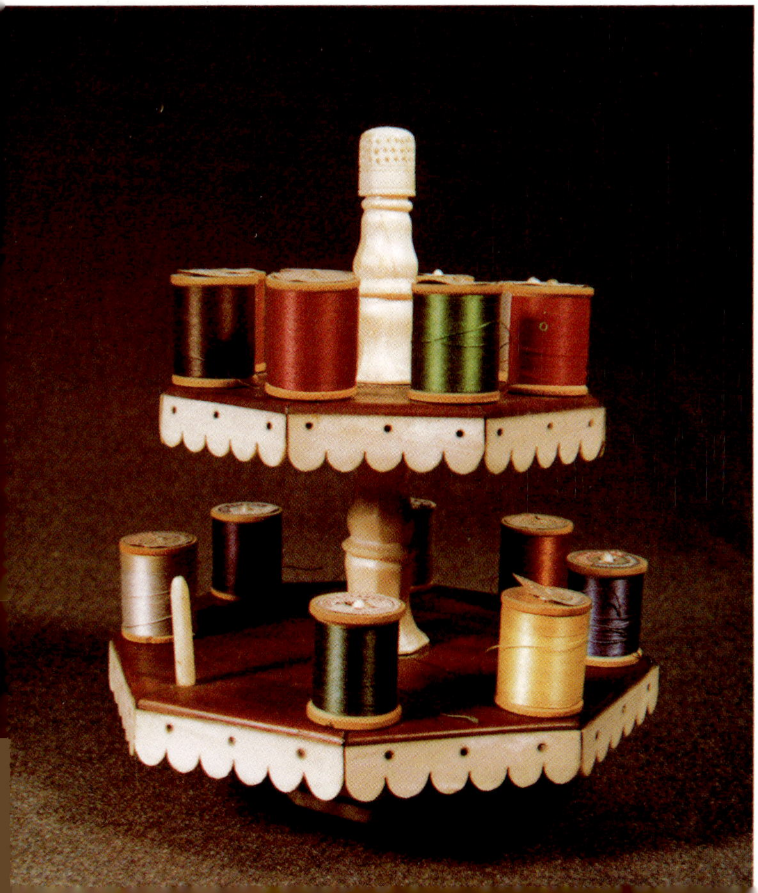

A removable thimble tops this scalloped whale ivory and wood, spoolholder. *Collection of Raymond and Elizabeth De Lucia*

Bodkins ranged from sturdy workhorses to more delicately wrought creations. They were used in sewing for piercing holes and threading ribbon and could also double as attractive hair ornaments. *Collection of Curtis Nyquist B.M.N.*

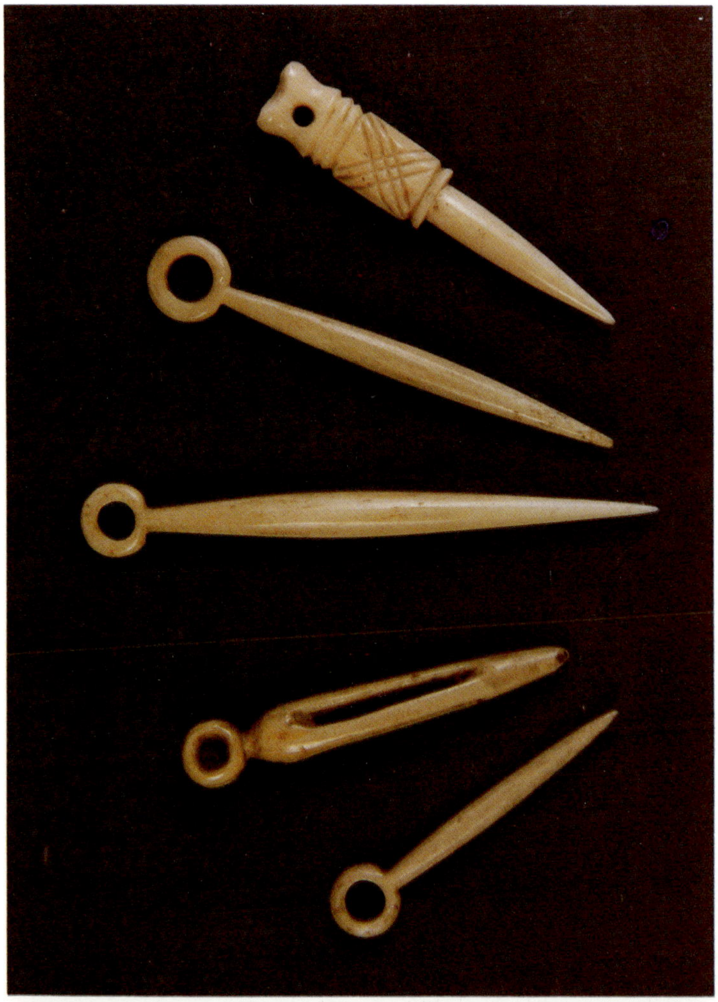

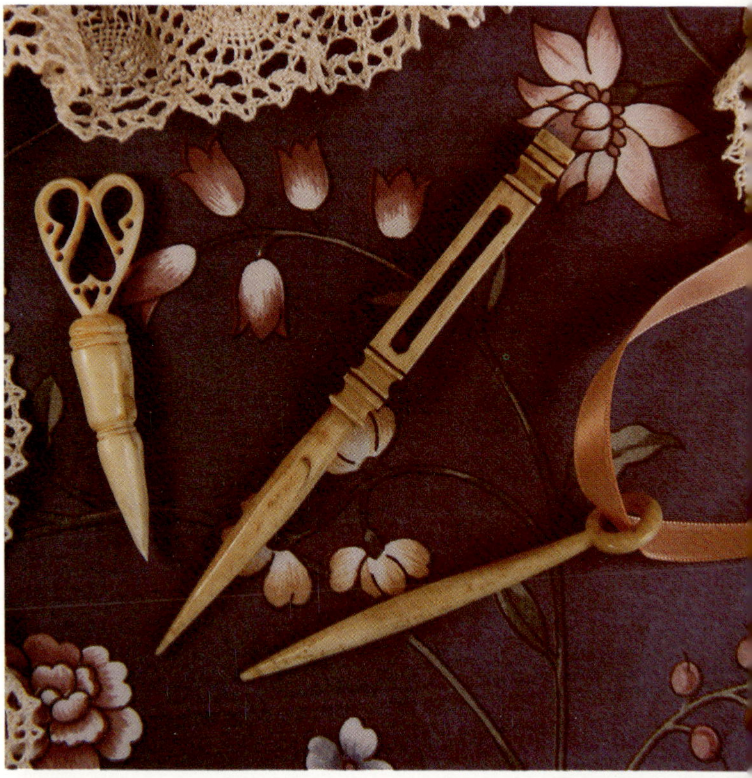

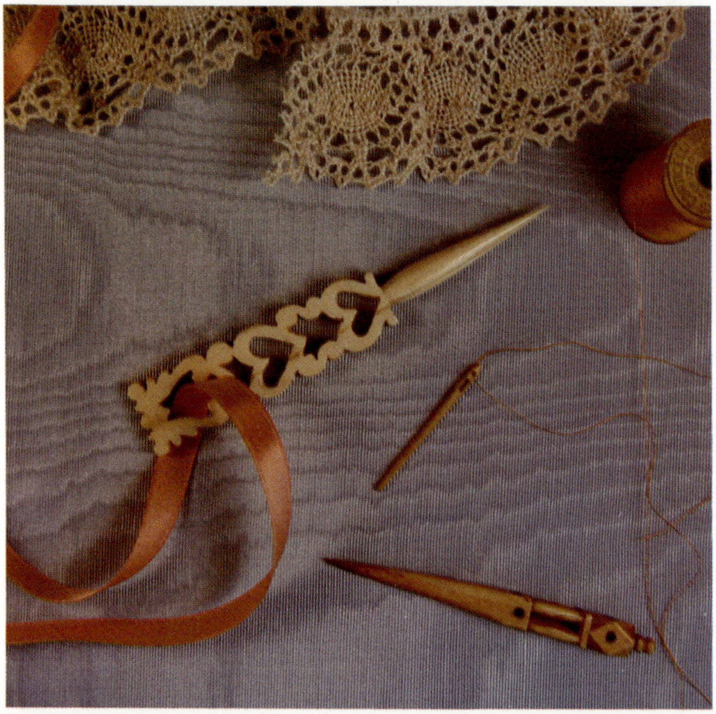

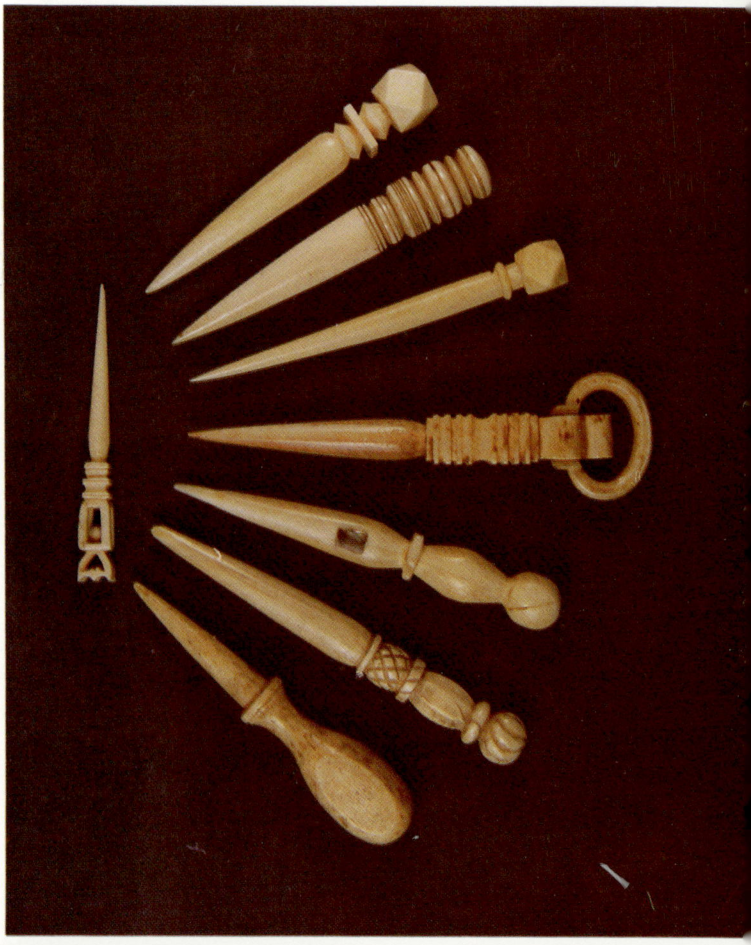

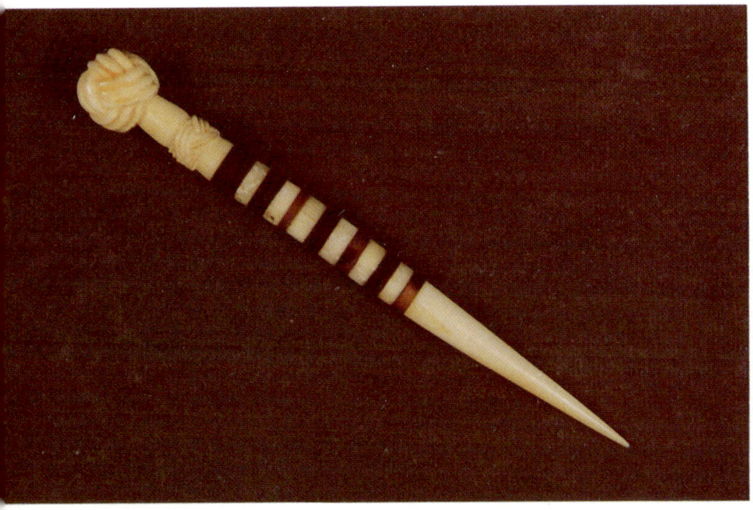

Detailed ropework carving accented with wood and baleen spacers decorate this whale ivory treasure. *Collection of Curtis Nyquist, B.M.N.*

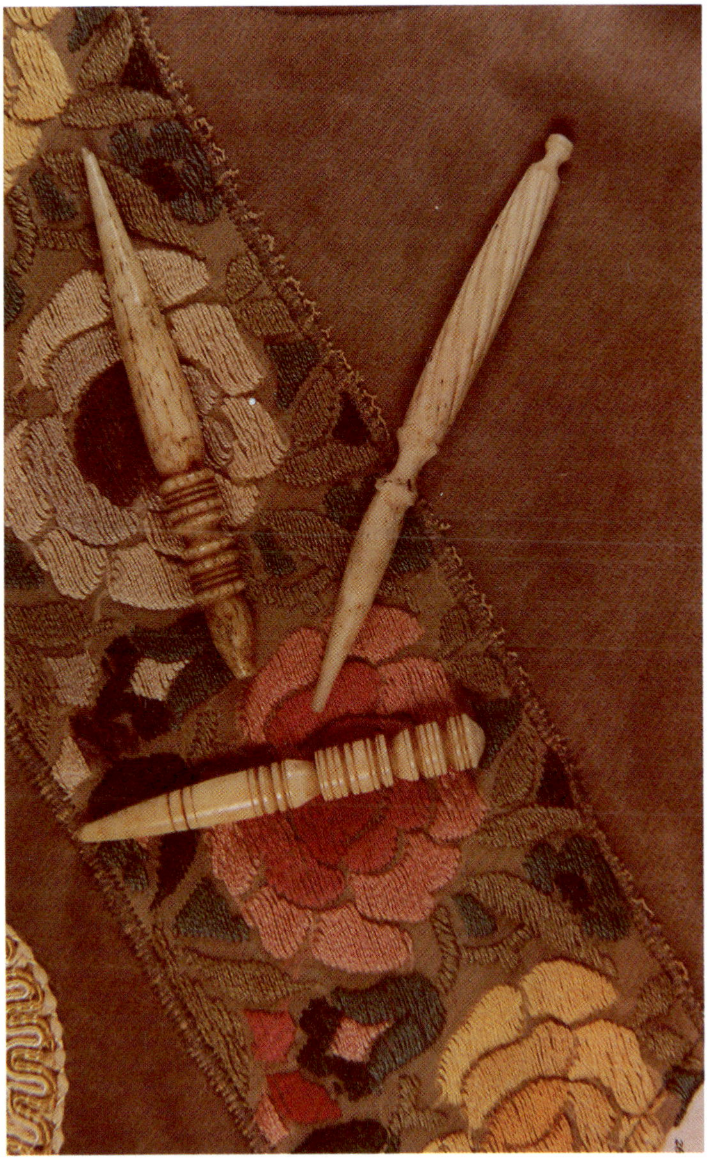

Well-worn whalebone and whale ivory bodkins yielded many years of good use. One is carved in the manner of a narwhal tooth. *Private Collection*

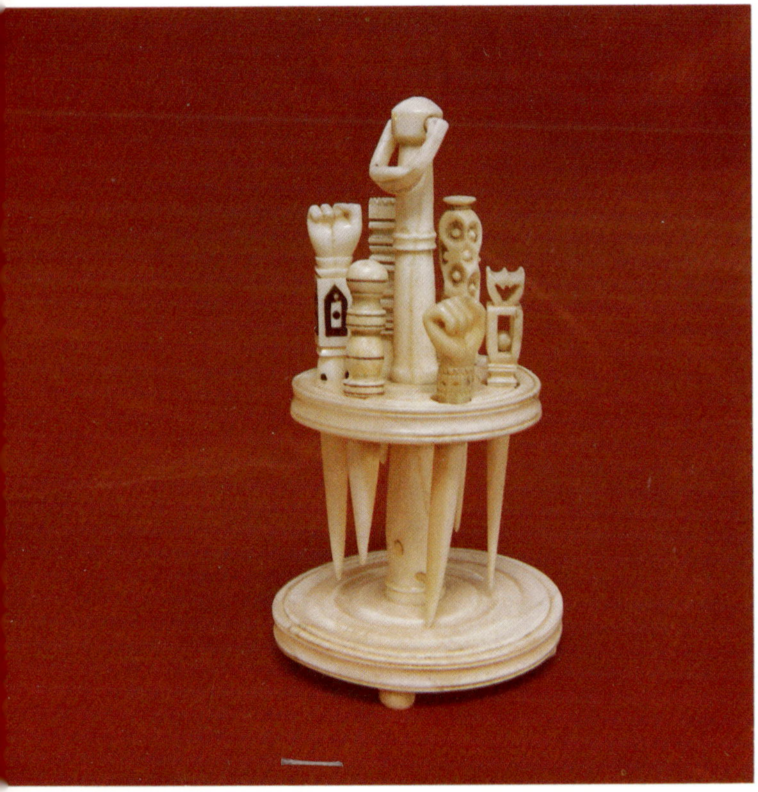

This classically-turned whale ivory bodkin holder is a rare find. *Collection of Curtis Nyquist, B.M.N.*

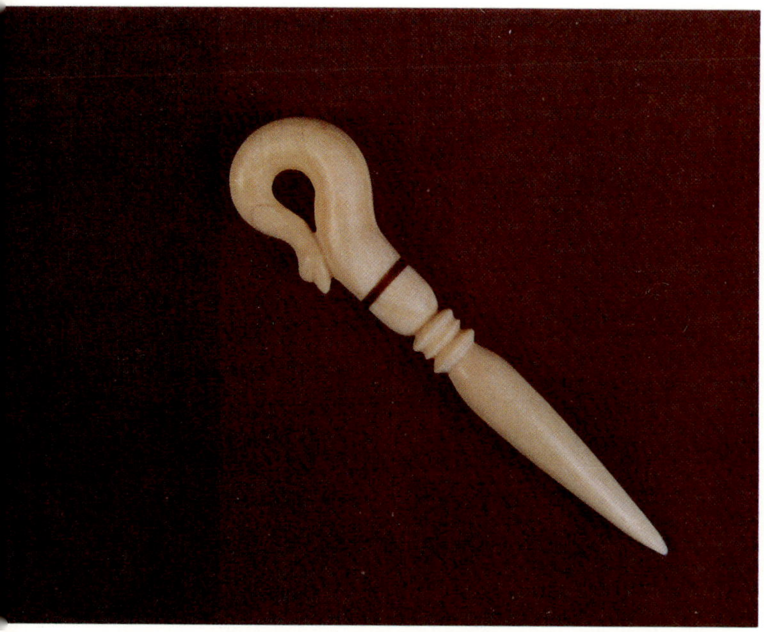

The curvaceous neck of a curious bird tops this whale ivory bodkin. *Collection of Curtis Nyquist, B.M.N.*

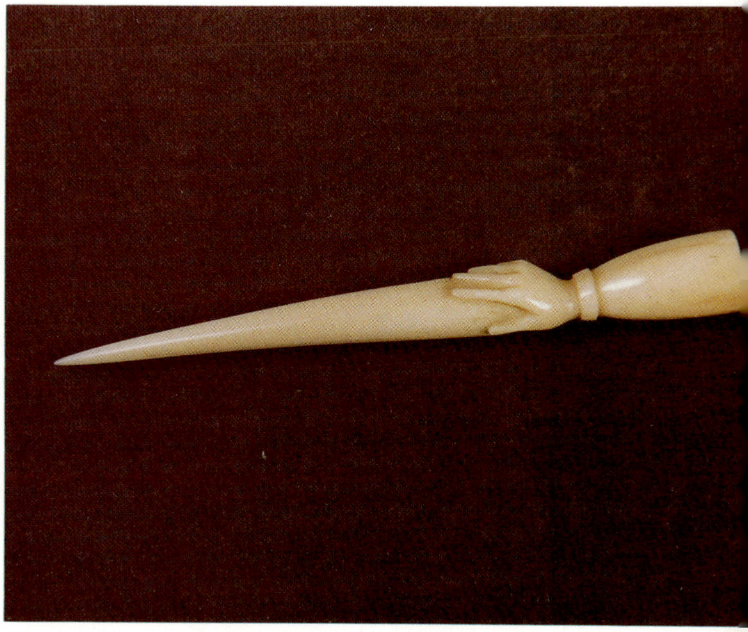

The woman who received this whale ivory gift could not help but be reminded of its maker as the bodkin replicates a hand holding a seaman's fid. *Collection of Curtis Nyquist, B.M.N.*

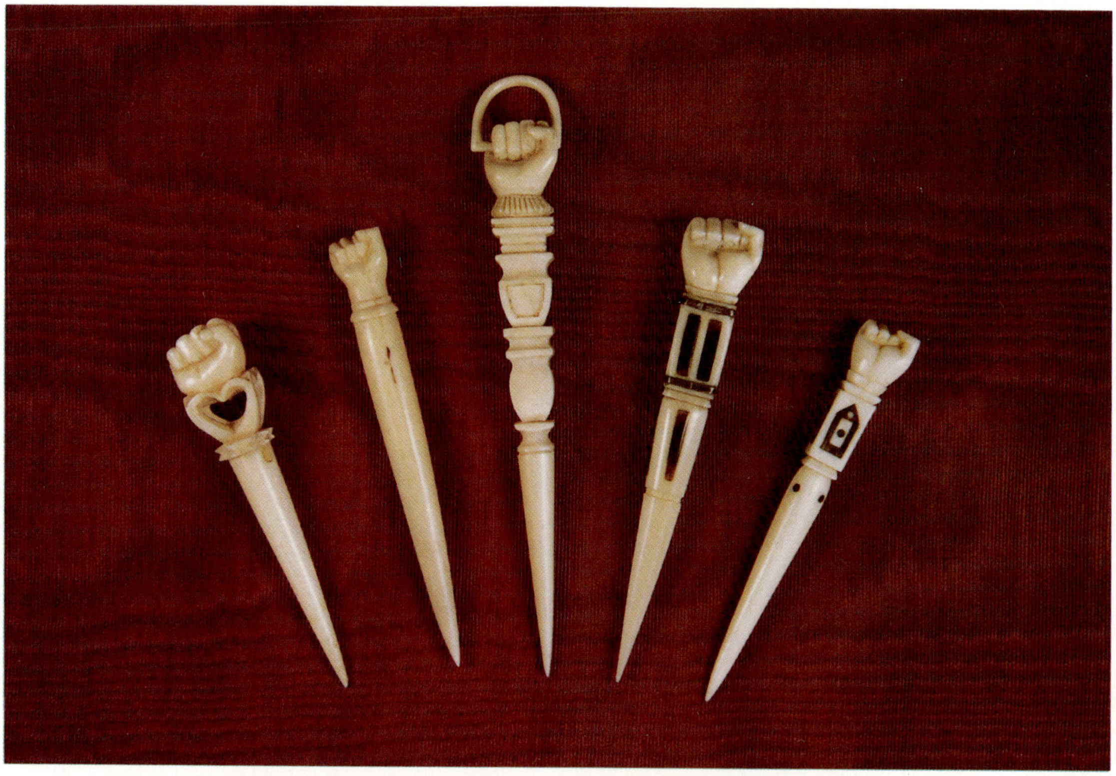

On June 2, 1878, Louis Jennings, serving aboard the New Bedford bark, *Sea Ranger*, wrote to his sister Antionette, "I have made you an Ivory bodkin and an Ivory crochet needle. The bodkin has a fist for a head and the needle has a diamond head. I will make you more things if I can think what to make." (Stuart Frank, *Dictionary of Scrimshaw Artists*, p. 73) *Collection of Curtis Nyquist, B.M.N.*

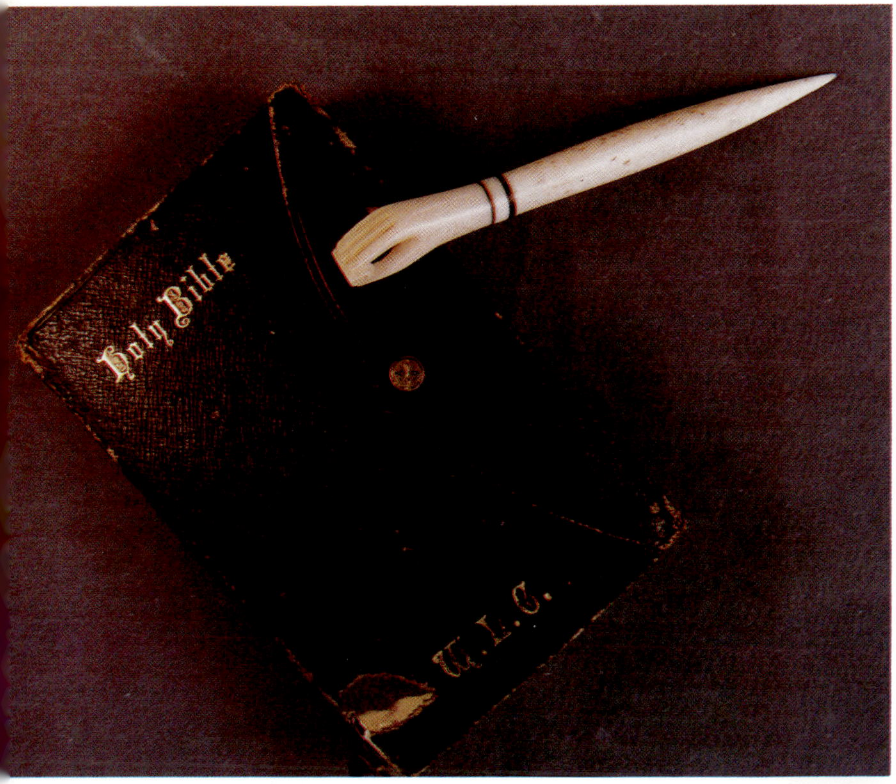

This whalebone bodkin, set with baleen spacers, is topped with a whale ivory hand clasping a book. *Collection of Curtis Nyquist, B.M.N.*

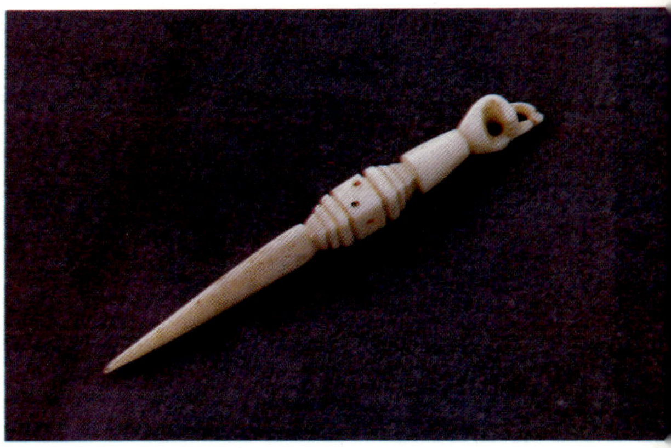

Dots of red and green sealing wax trim this small whalebone bodkin which is topped with a delicately carved hand. *Collection of Charles A. Manghis*

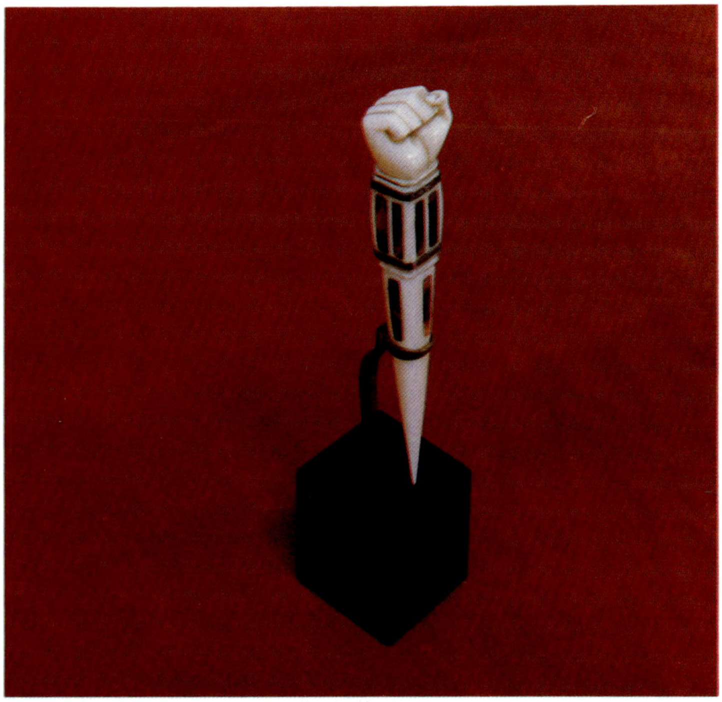

At first glance it is easy to appreciate the lovely design and fine carving of this handsome whale ivory bodkin. However, further inspection reveals a hollow shaft, which allows light to pass through its sheer tortoise shell "windows". *Collection of Curtis Nyquist, B.M.N.*

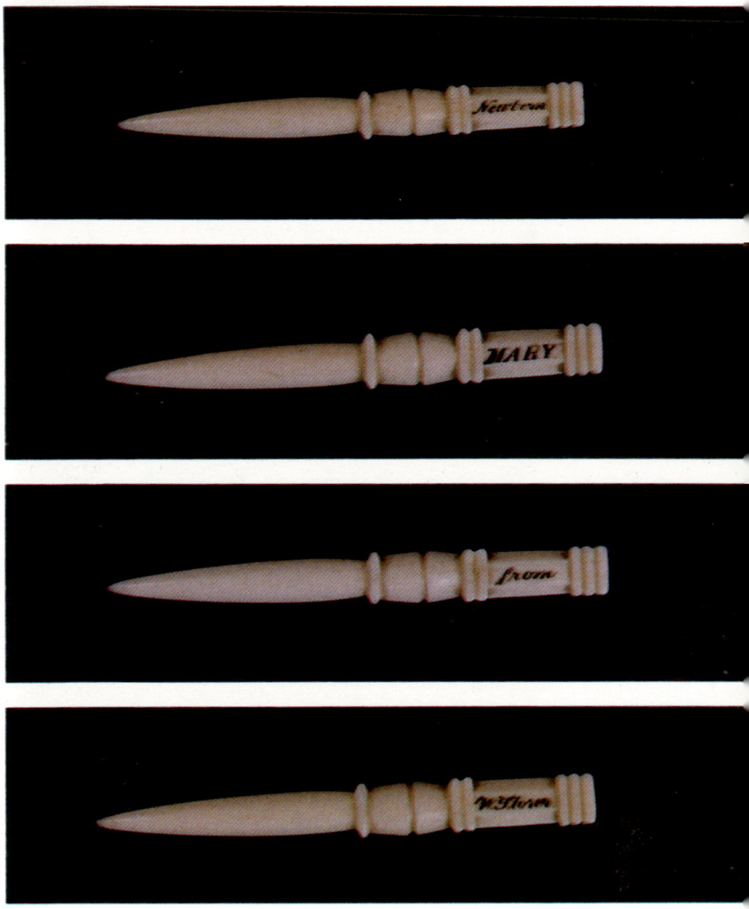

The inscription etched on the four sides of this charming whale ivory bodkin reads, "Newborn Mary from W. Storer, May 1863" *Collection of Curtis Nyquist, B.M.N.*

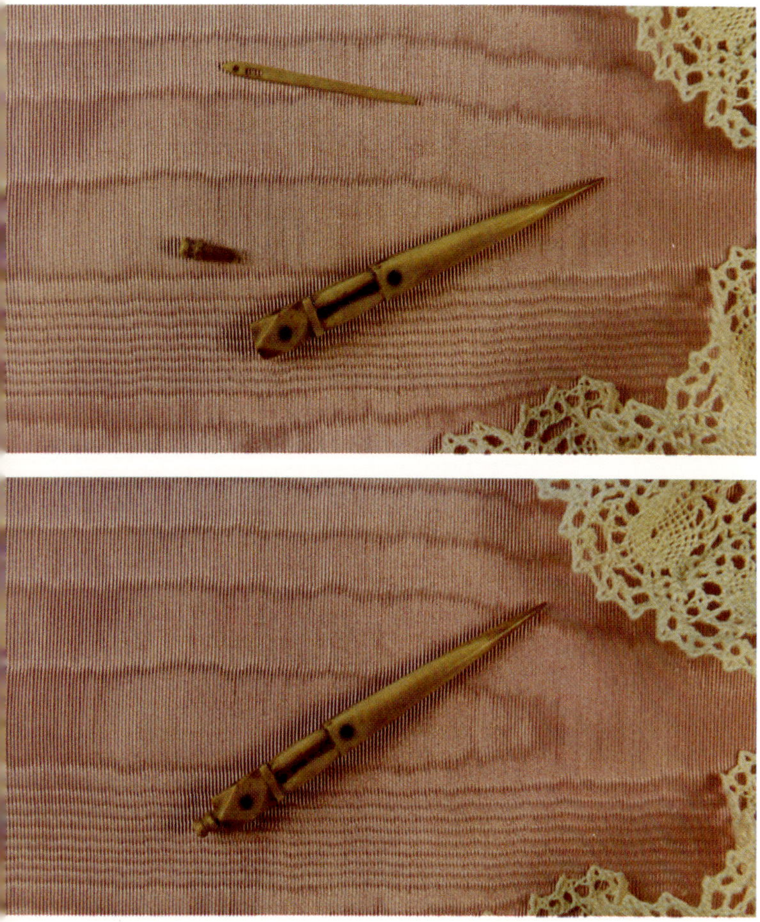

When the top of this whale ivory bodkin is removed, a sewing needle is found contained in its shaft. *Collection of Curtis Nyquist, B.M.N.*

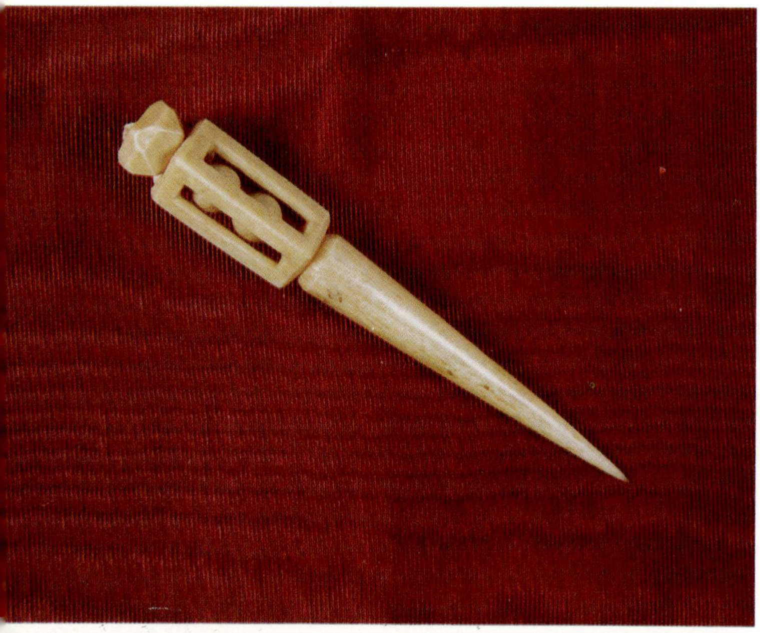

Not satisfied with demonstrating the virtuosity necessary to carve one ball in a cage, the scrimshander who created this whale ivory bodkin decided to include two. *Collection of Raymond and Elizabeth De Lucia*

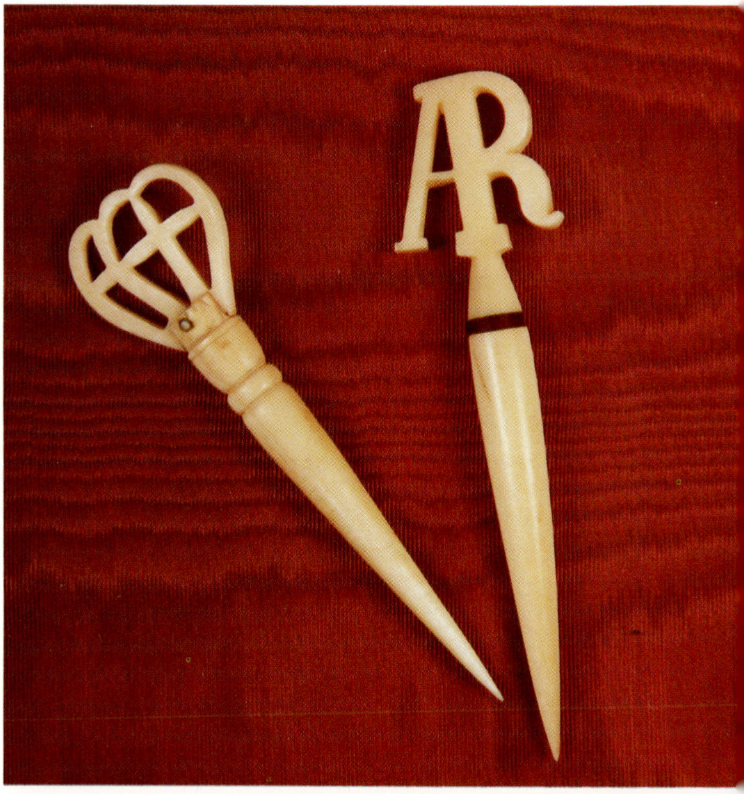

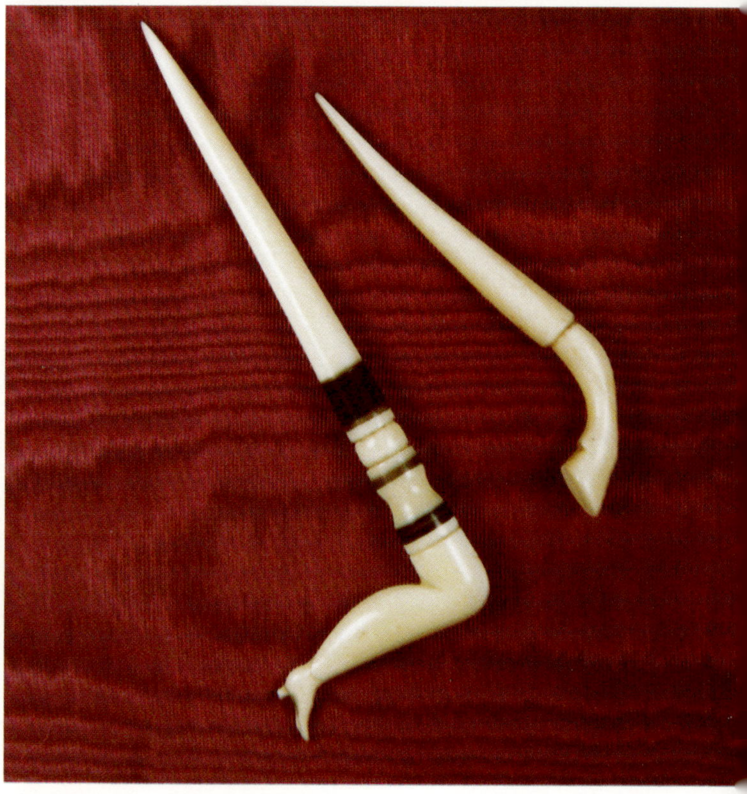

These lovely whale ivory bodkins illustrate once more the seemingly boundless creativity of the scrimshanders fabricating them. *Courtesy of the Nantucket Historical Association.*

Attached to either the lady's work table or to its own custom made case was the swift, an expandable cage of whalebone staves wired to sliding cage collars and used for winding yarn. The swift was to sewing what the pie crimper was to cooking—a fantastically designed, engineered, crafted and decorated item of service. The top could be adorned with an elaborate finial or a simple turned cup intended to hold a ball of yarn. Clamps and their filed or turned thumb screws were not mere methods of attachment, but opportunities for further creativity. The exclusively American swift, a housewife's yarnwinder, epitomizes the brilliant blending of function, design, and execution common to so much nineteenth century scrimshaw.

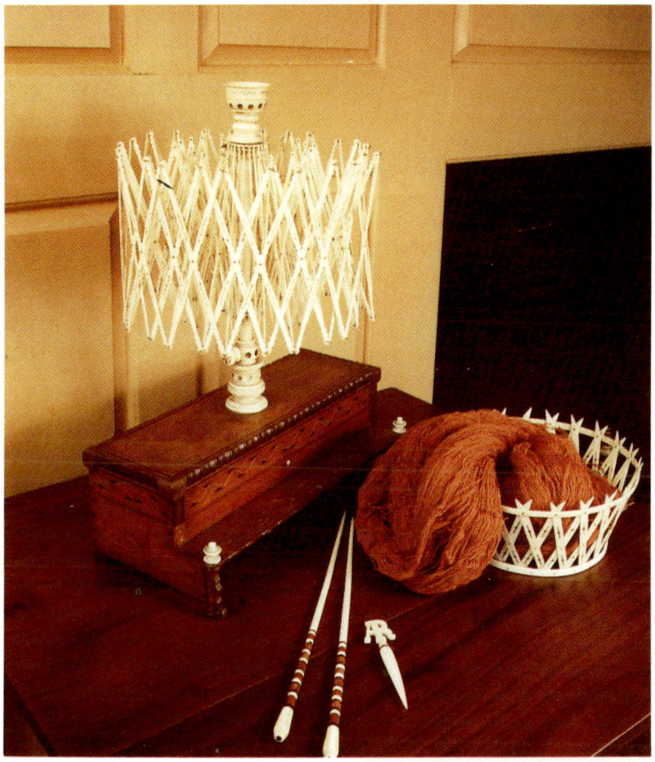

This classic whalebone and whale ivory swift is mounted on a beautifully inlaid work box. It joins other sewing implements in the Nantucket Historical Association's "1800 House". *Courtesy of the Nantucket Historical Association*

Like prematurely decommissioned soldiers ready to return to their duties, these antique swifts are fully operational and able to resume their lives of service. *Collection of Charles A. Manghis*

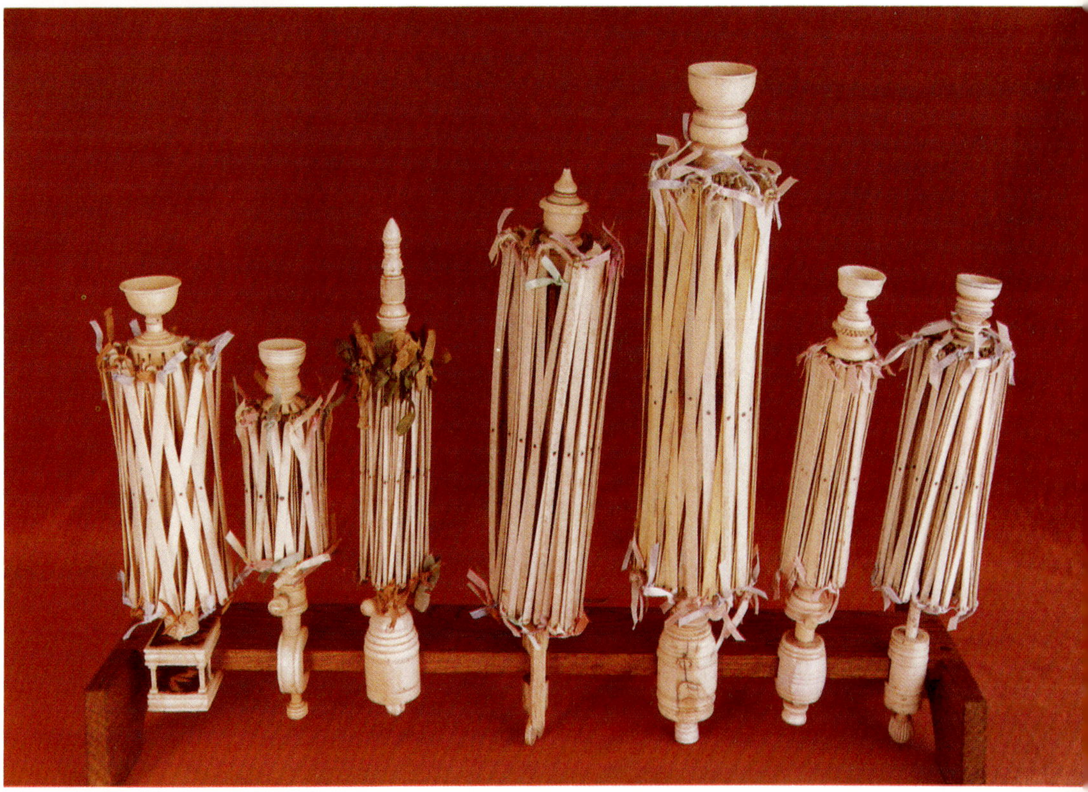

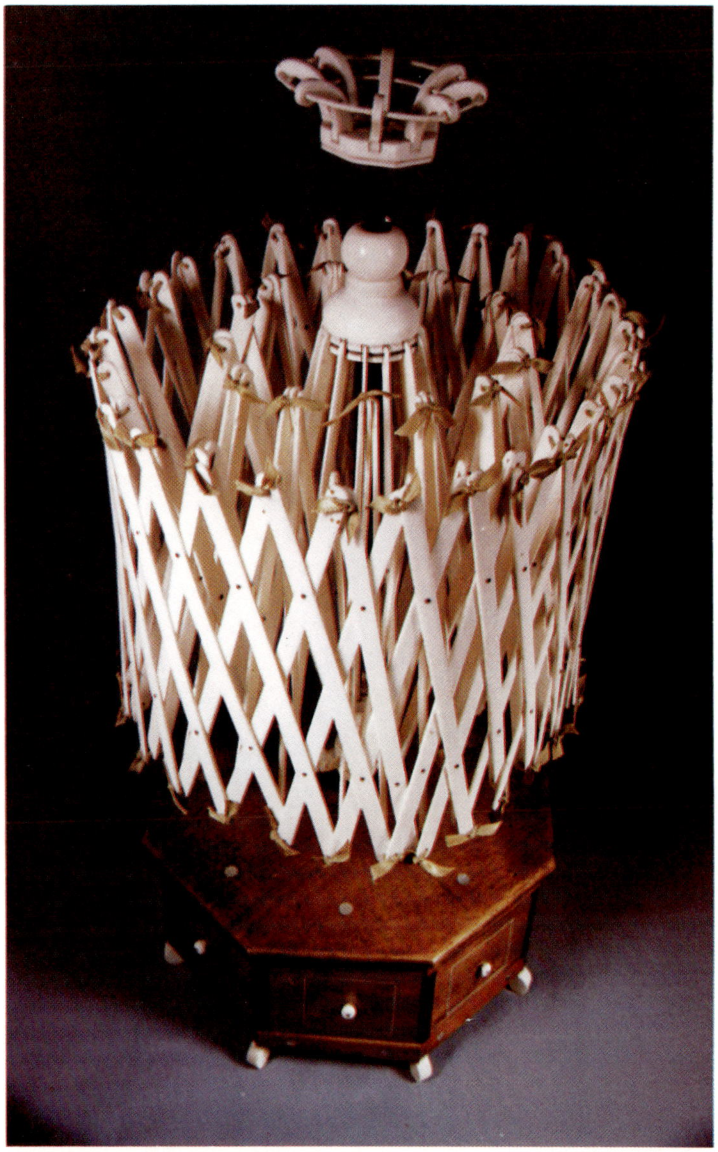

This exquisite whale bone swift is permanently mounted on an octagonal box featuring mother of pearl inlays and eight operating drawers. The unusually carved whale ivory finial repeats the theme of eight. *Courtesy of the Nantucket Historical Association*

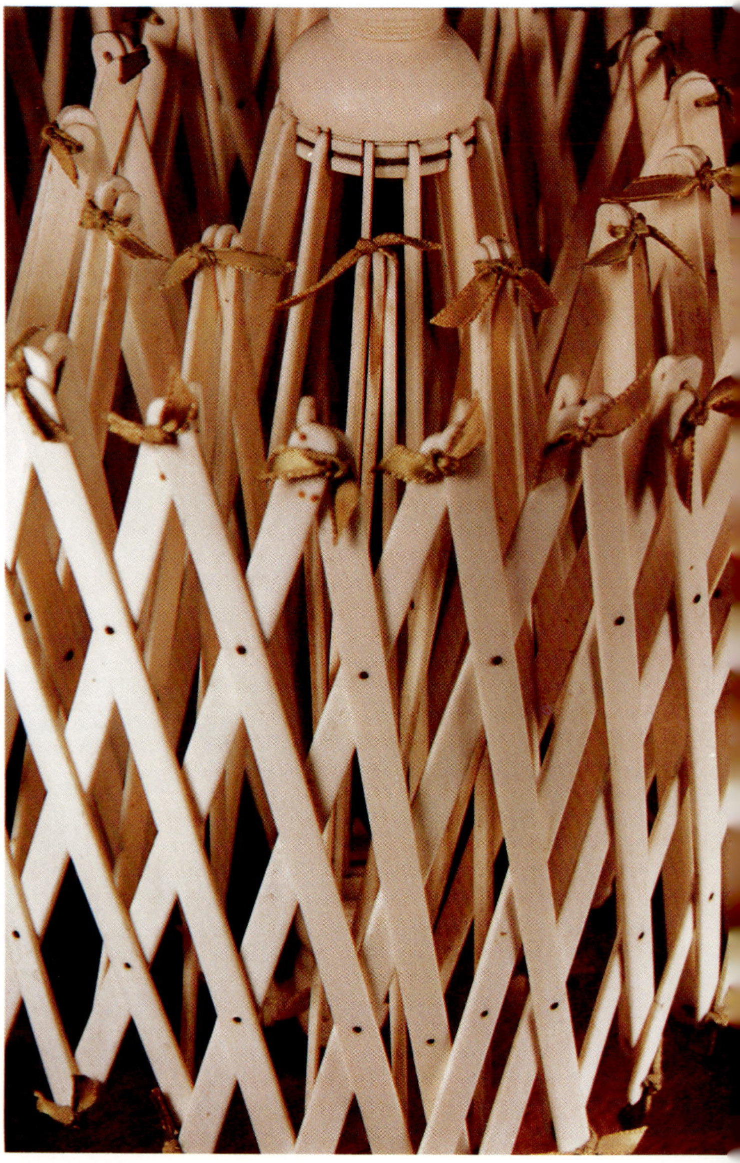

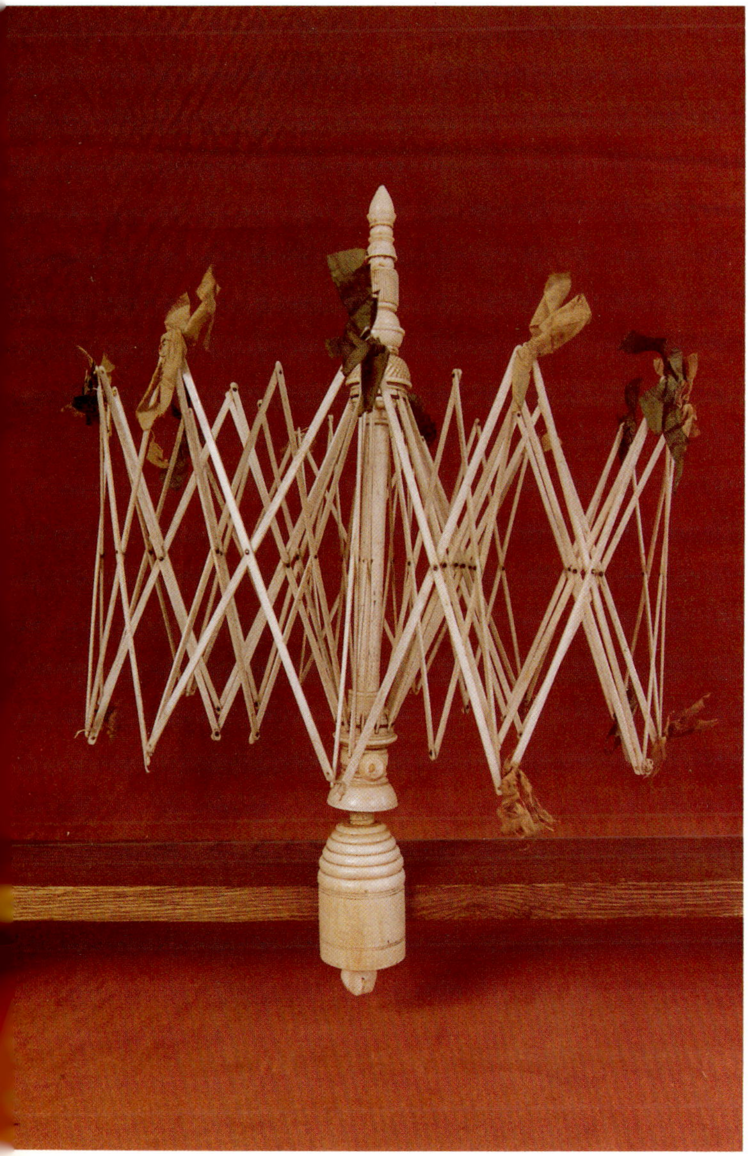

This extremely dainty whalebone and whale ivory swift is tied with its original ribbons and features a beehive clamp and a turned finial further decorated with hand carvings. *Collection of Charles A. Manghis*

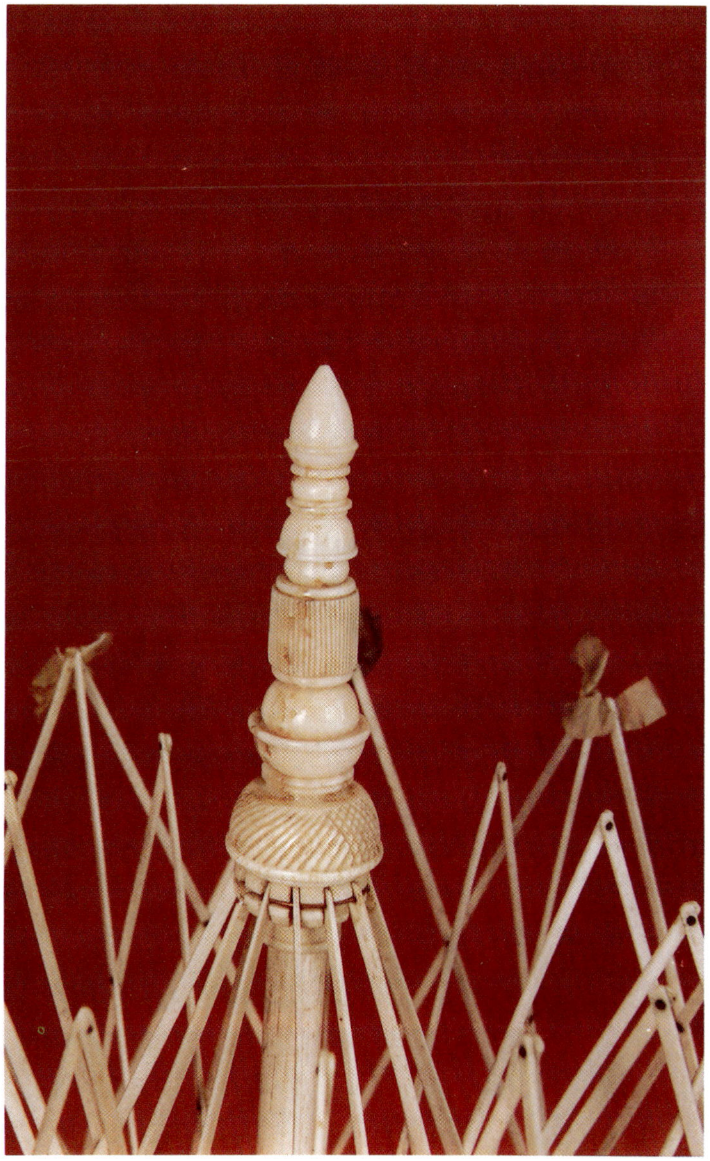

In this "double" whalebone and whale ivory swift, two staves are positioned in each groove of the cage collar where one stave would normally be found. A handsome whale ivory "C" clamp and turned finial complete the intricate piece. *Collection of Charles A. Manghis*

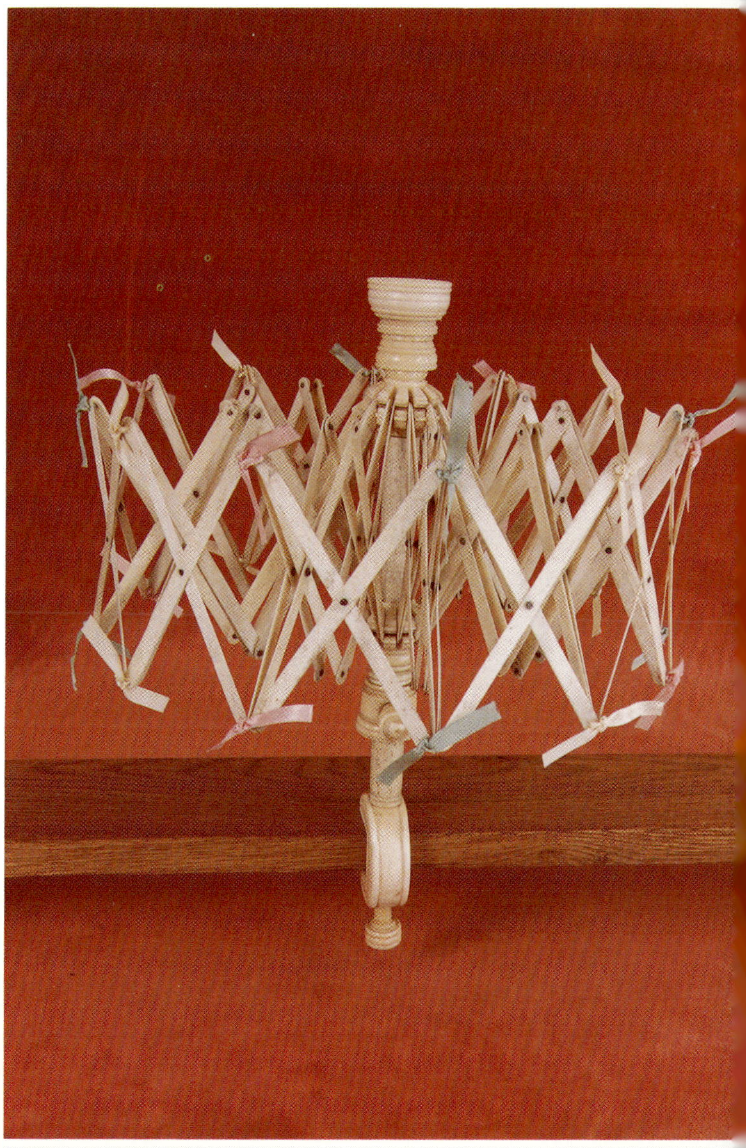

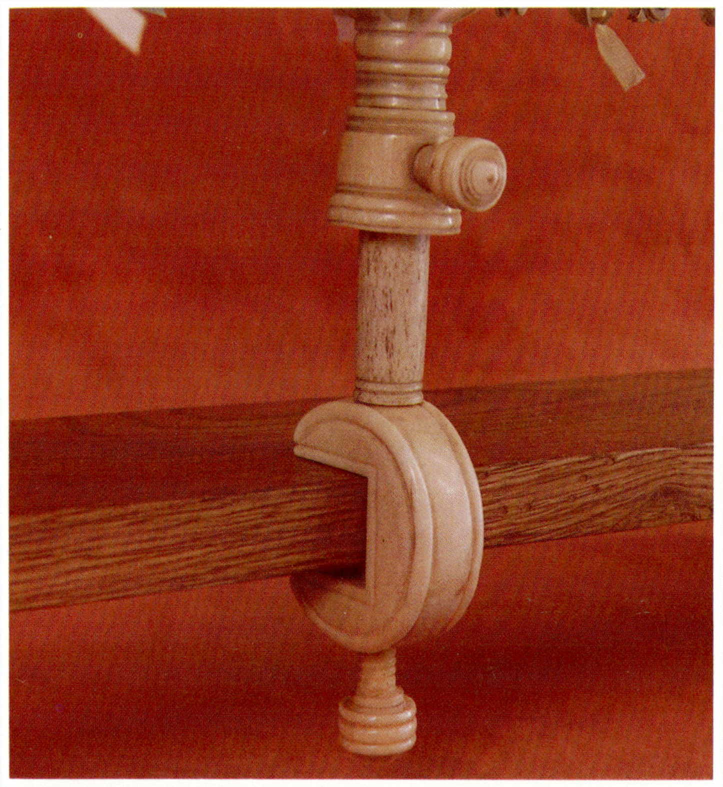

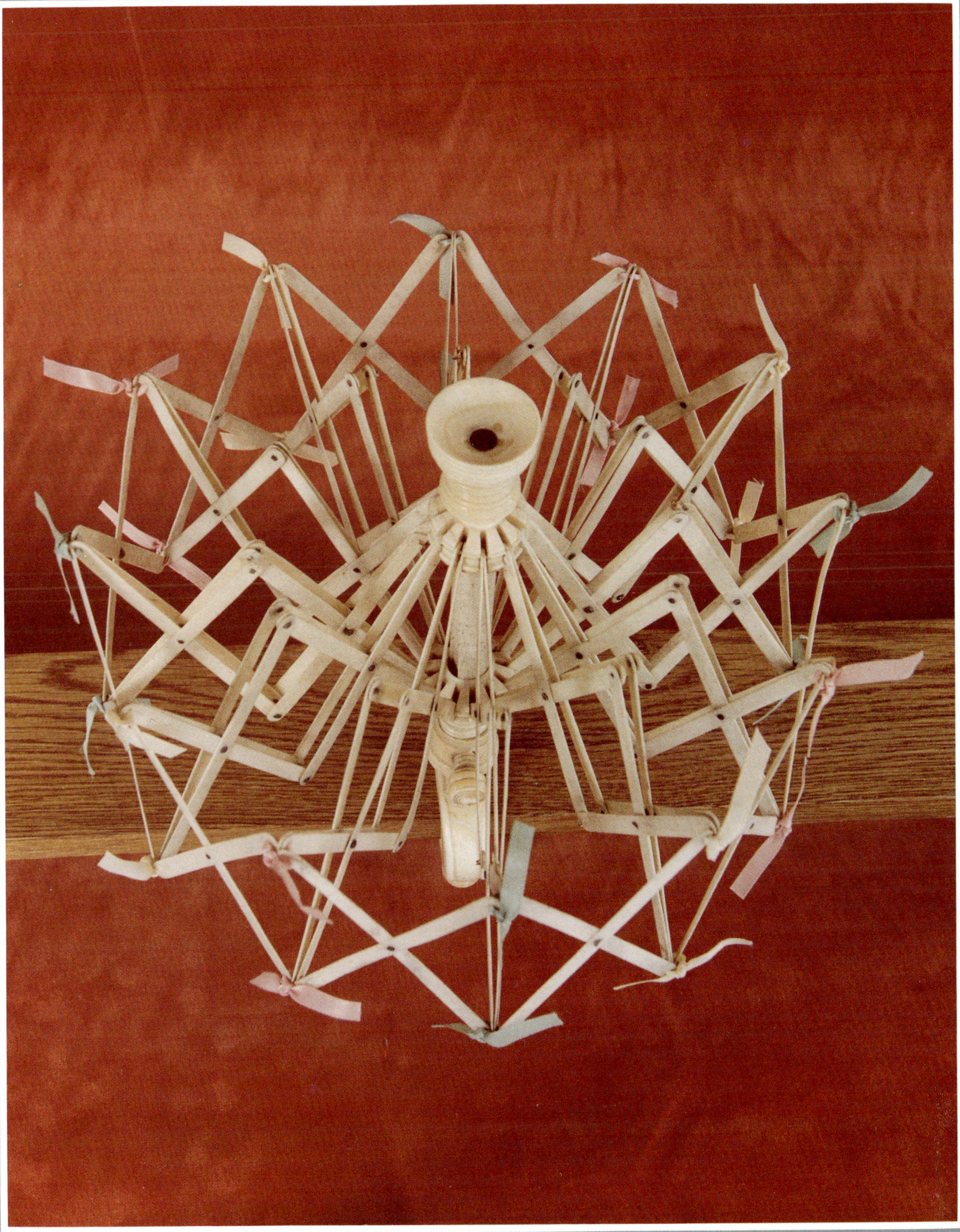

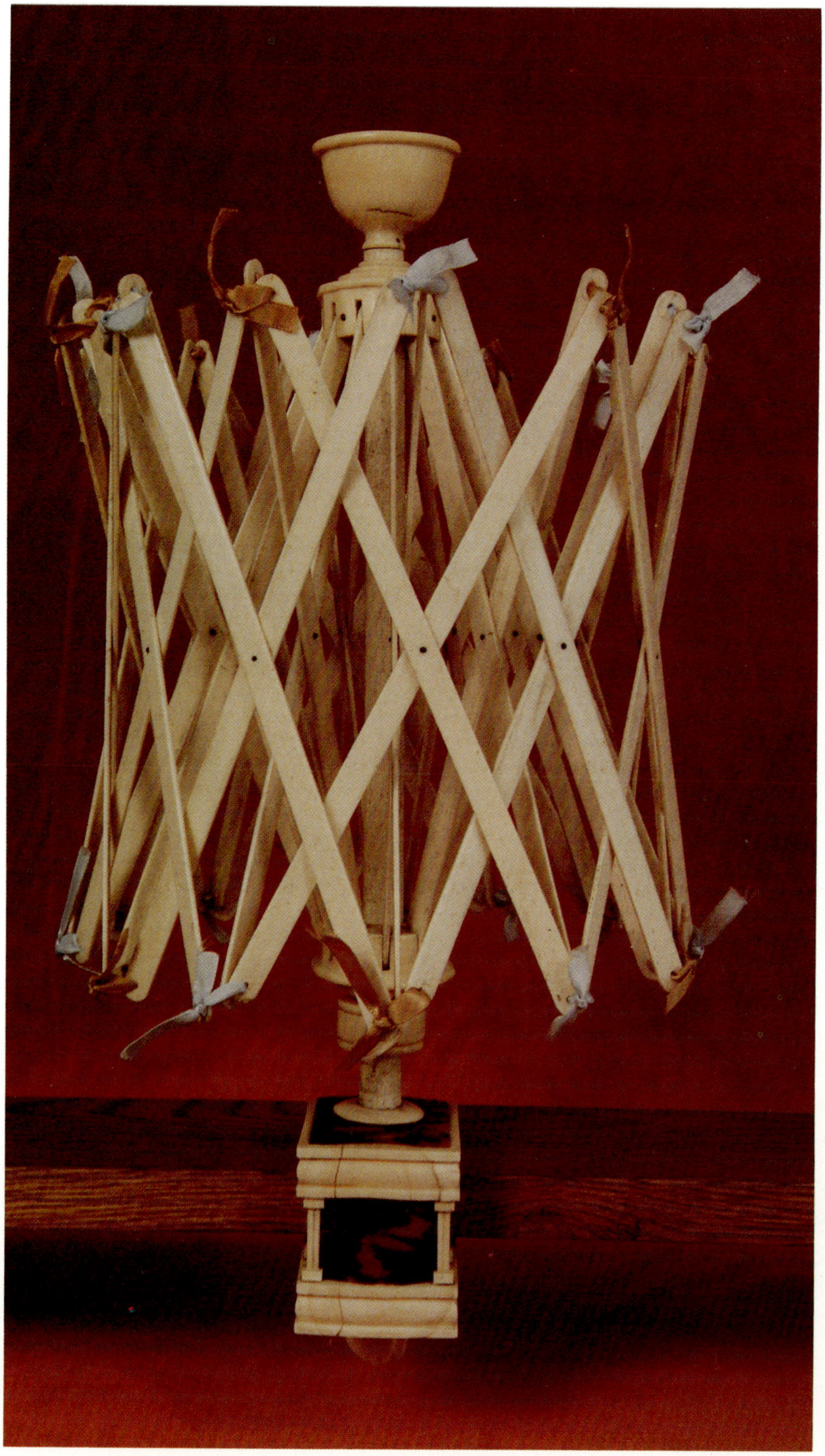

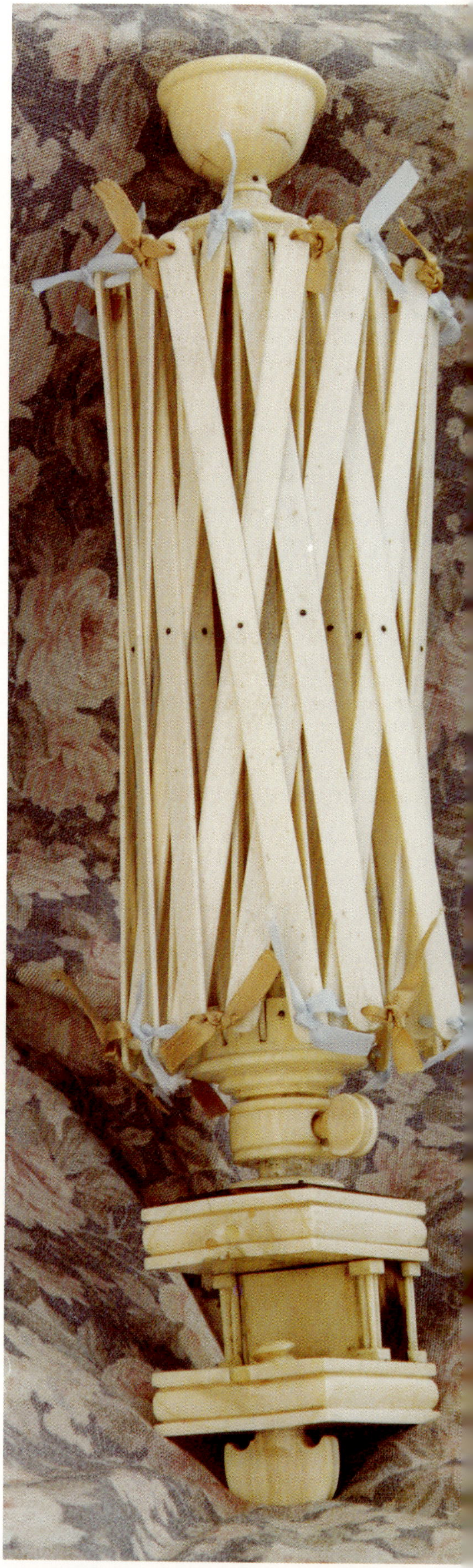

The classical, columned clamp of this whalebone and whale ivory swift is inlaid with tortoise shell. The finial is hand carved despite its lathe-turned appearance. *Collection of Charles A. Manghis*

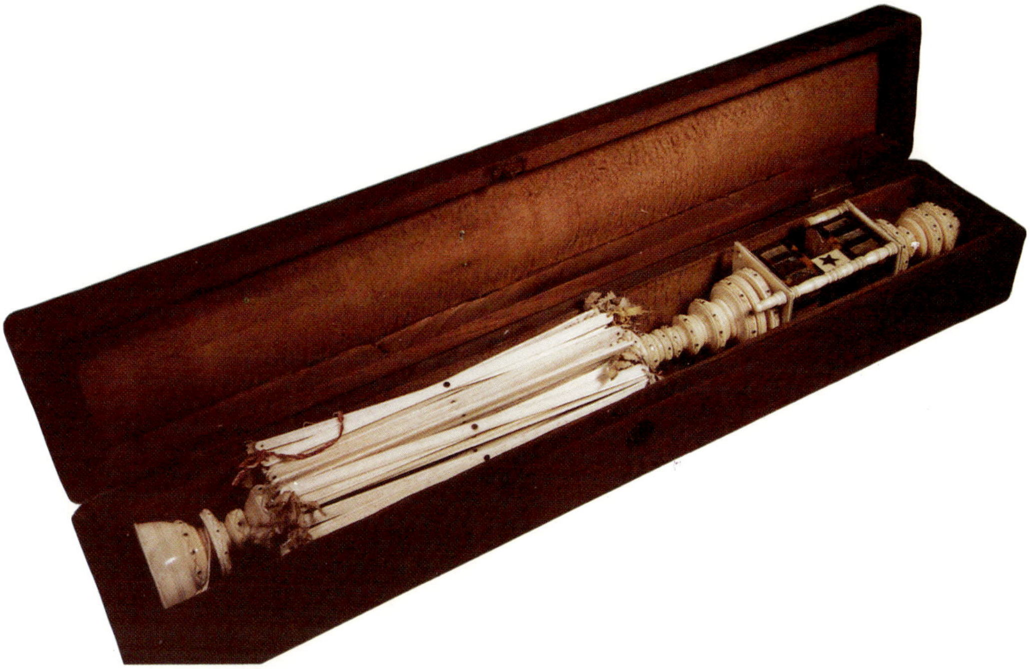

This swift whose elaborate clamp is inlaid with abalone, tortoise shell and baleen was made aboard the ship *Java* of Fairhaven between 1835 and 1838 by her master, Randall Kelley, for his wife Charlotte. *Courtesy of the Nantucket Historical Association*

This whale ivory swift clamp is carved in the shape of a man's wedding-ringed hand and could symbolically support his wife's work during his absence at sea. Green and red sealing wax further adorn the piece. *Courtesy of the Nantucket Historical Association*

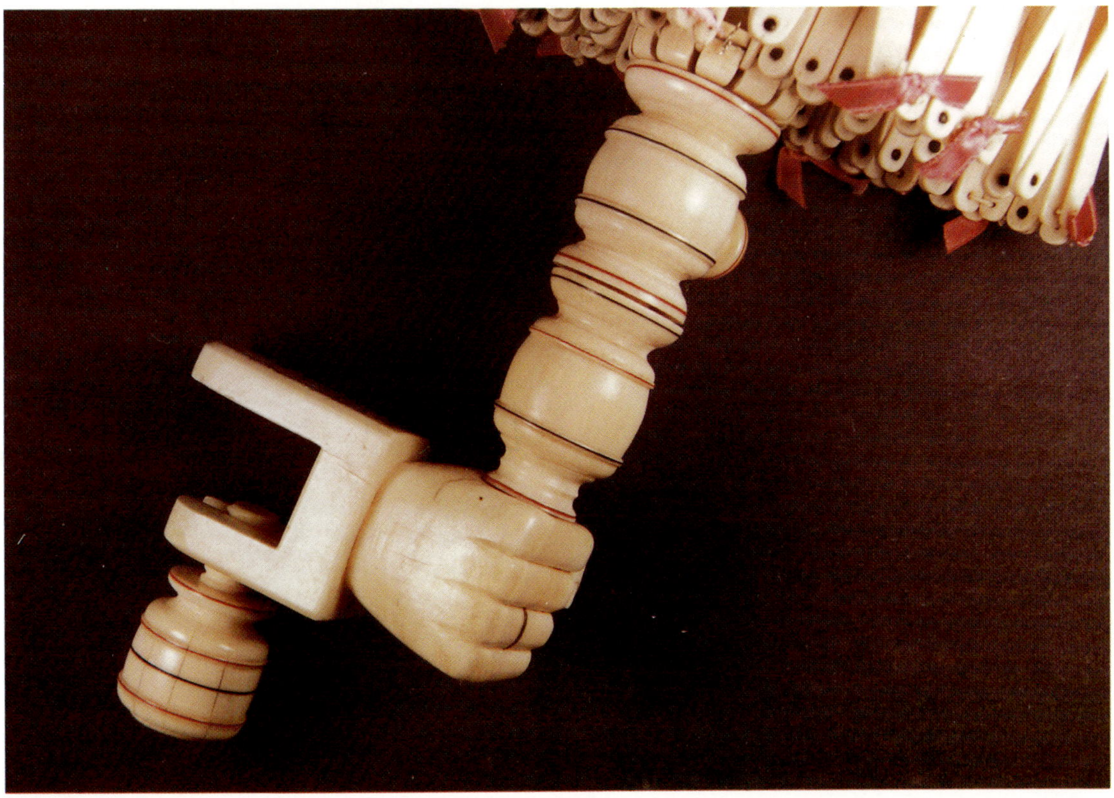

In the front hallway were stored scrimshawed walking sticks. Some were beautifully turned pieces of tropical wood, inlaid with whale ivory, baleen, and mother of pearl; others were fashioned completely of whalebone and topped with carvings of eagles, whales, clenched fists or women's curvaceous, but discreetly shod, legs. Although the shafts of most walking sticks were carved from one piece of wood or bone, occasionally carved pieces of teeth or even shark vertebrae were threaded over an iron shaft. Ivory simulations of rope and knots were popular decorations for walking sticks as the scrimshander had ample opportunity to analyze their structure and correctly reproduce them.

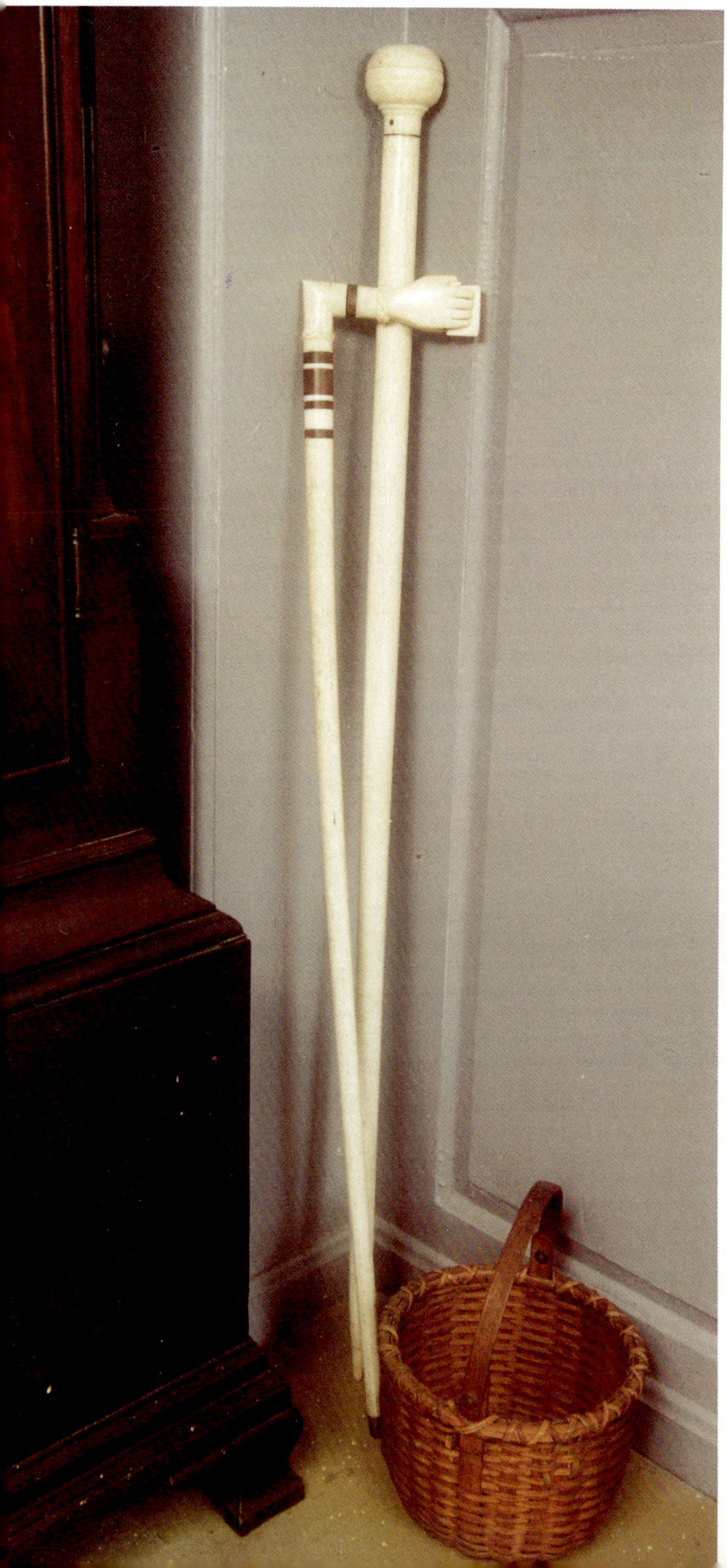

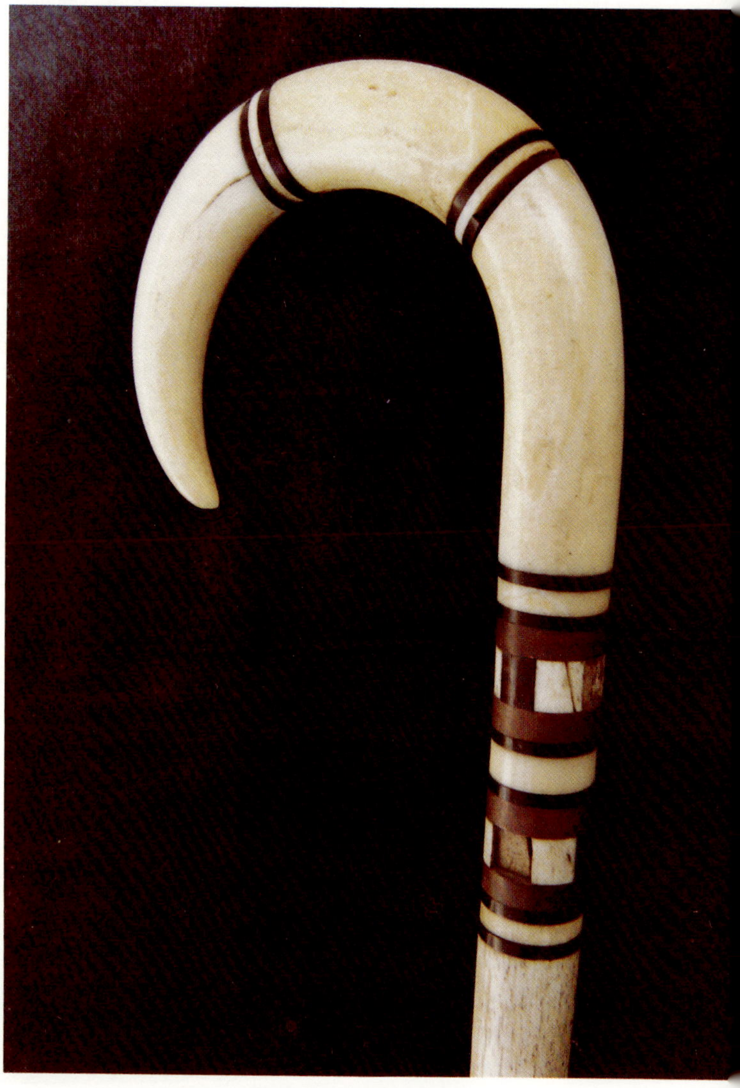

This whalebone walking stick carries an unusual crooked, whale ivory handle, spaced with baleen and inlaid with both coconut wood and rosewood. *Collection of Charles A. Manghis*

On February 10th, 1844, Joseph Dias, boatsteerer and keeper of the log of the whaler *Clifford Wayne*, complained, "Nothing to do but make Canes to support our dignity with when we (are) home." Perhaps these graceful walking sticks were the result of the sort of ennui described by Dias. *Courtesy of the Nantucket Historical Association*

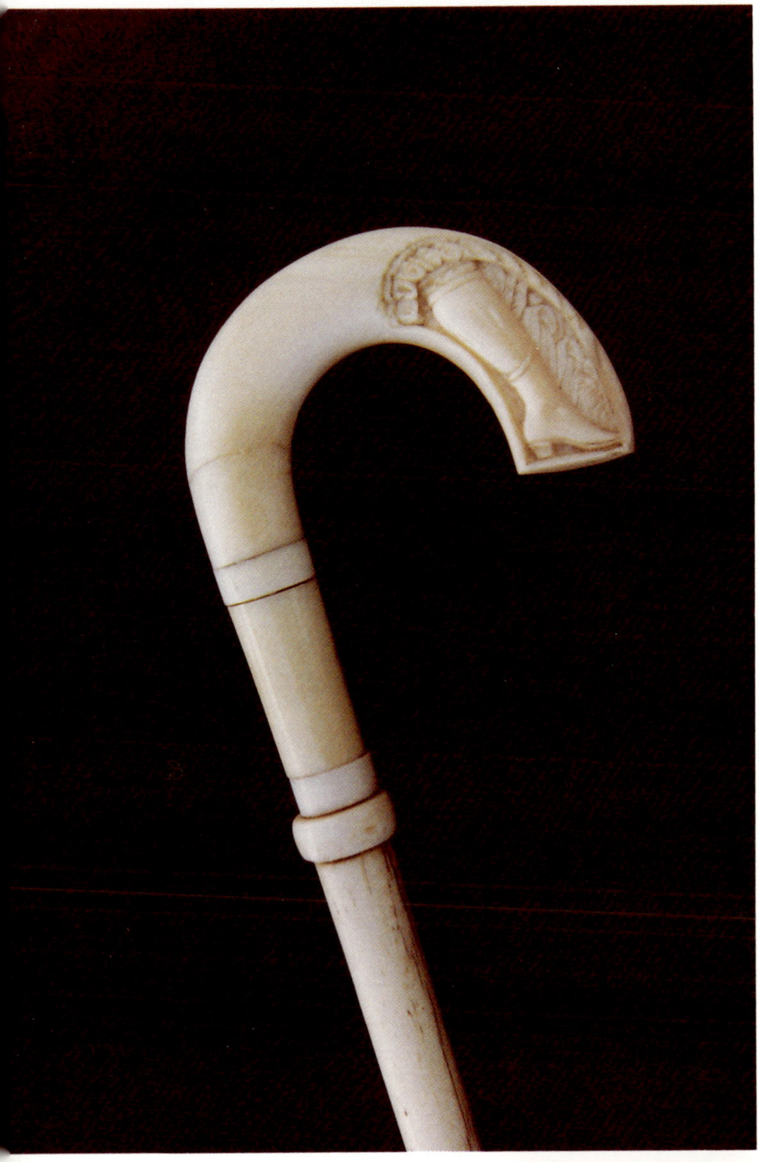

A relief-carved, beruffled leg nicely trims the whale ivory handle of this cane. *Collection of Charles A. Manghis*

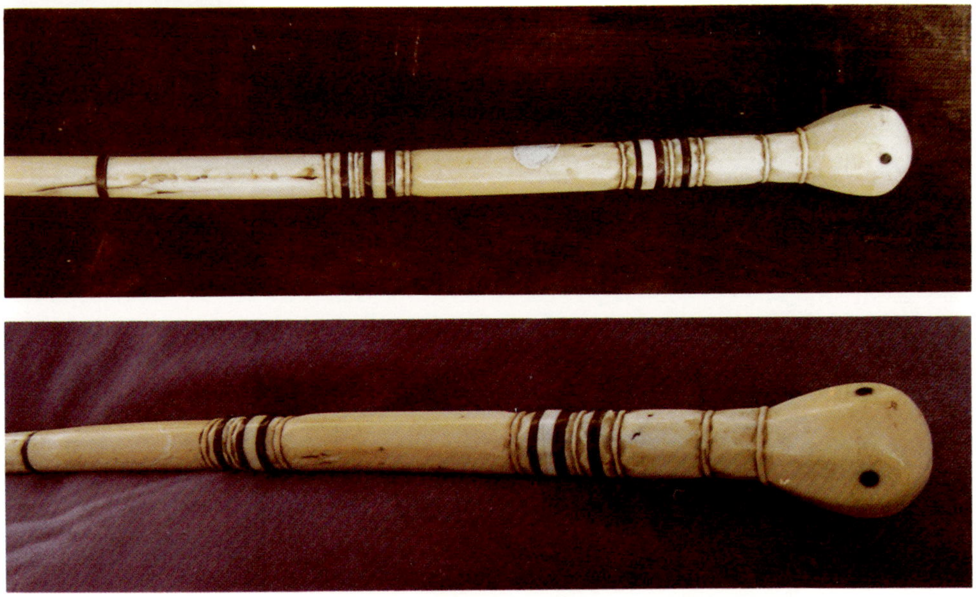

The shaft of this unusual walking stick is constructed of a series of turned and graduated whale's teeth, threaded on an iron rod and decorated with baleen spacers. The majority of canes were created from one piece of whalebone. *Collection of Charles A. Manghis*

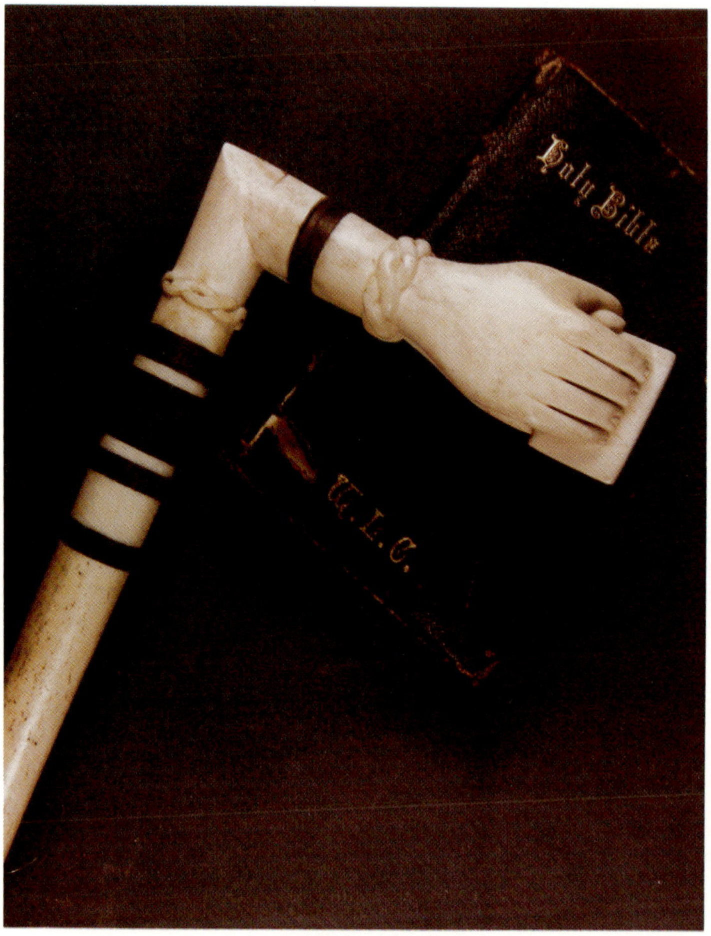

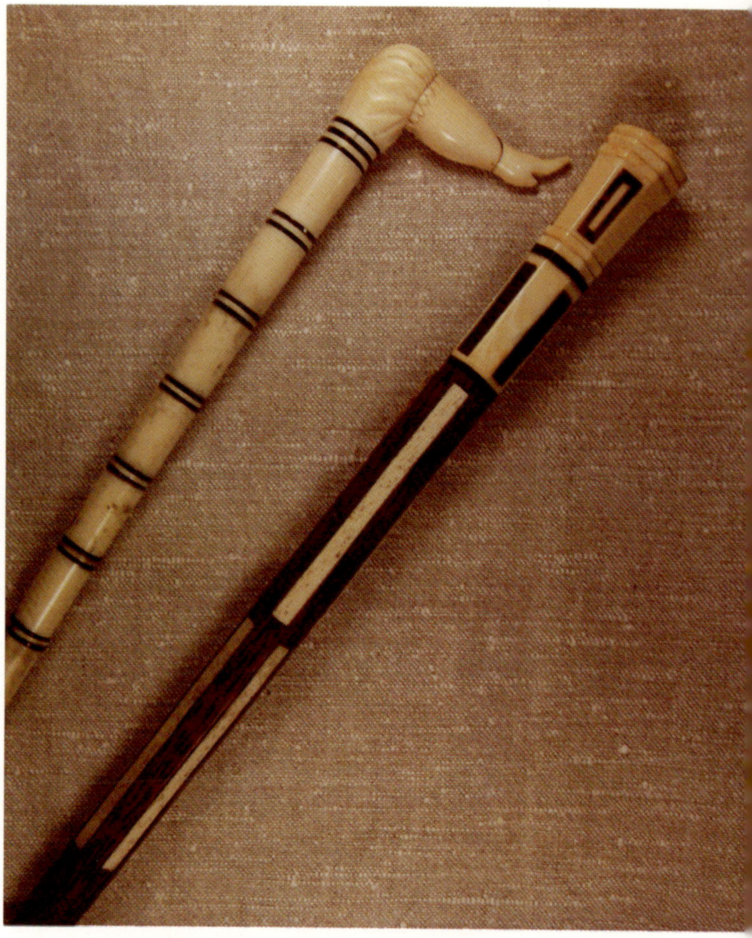

A striking whalebone walking stick features a whale ivory handle carved into a detailed hand clasping a book. Ropework carving and baleen spacers further decorate this piece. *Courtesy of the Nantucket Historical Association*

The unique walking stick on the left is another example of one constructed from a series of graduated whale's teeth separated by baleen spacers. The wooden shaft of the accompanying stick is inlaid with whalebone and topped with a whale ivory head. *Courtesy of the Nantucket Historical Association*

Exquisite carving, baleen spacers and red and green sealing wax highlight this trio of whalebone and whale ivory walking sticks. *Courtesy of the Nantucket Historical Association*

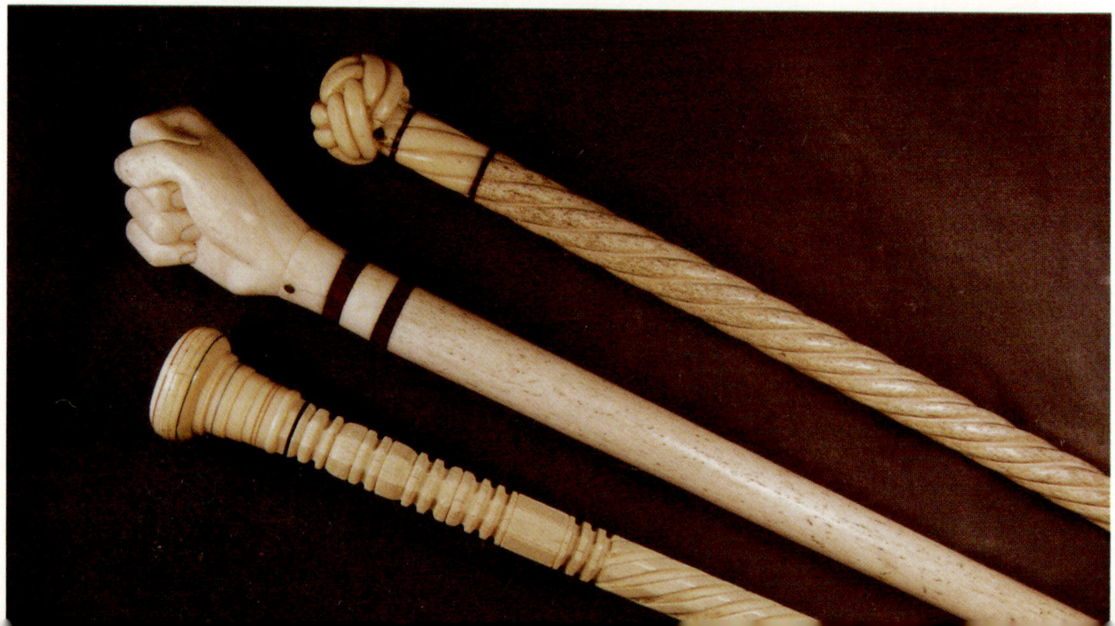

The more strictly decorative pieces of scrimshaw were displayed in the parlor. These included panoramic scenes filling large pieces of panbone, engraved teeth, and perhaps an especially elaborate swift.

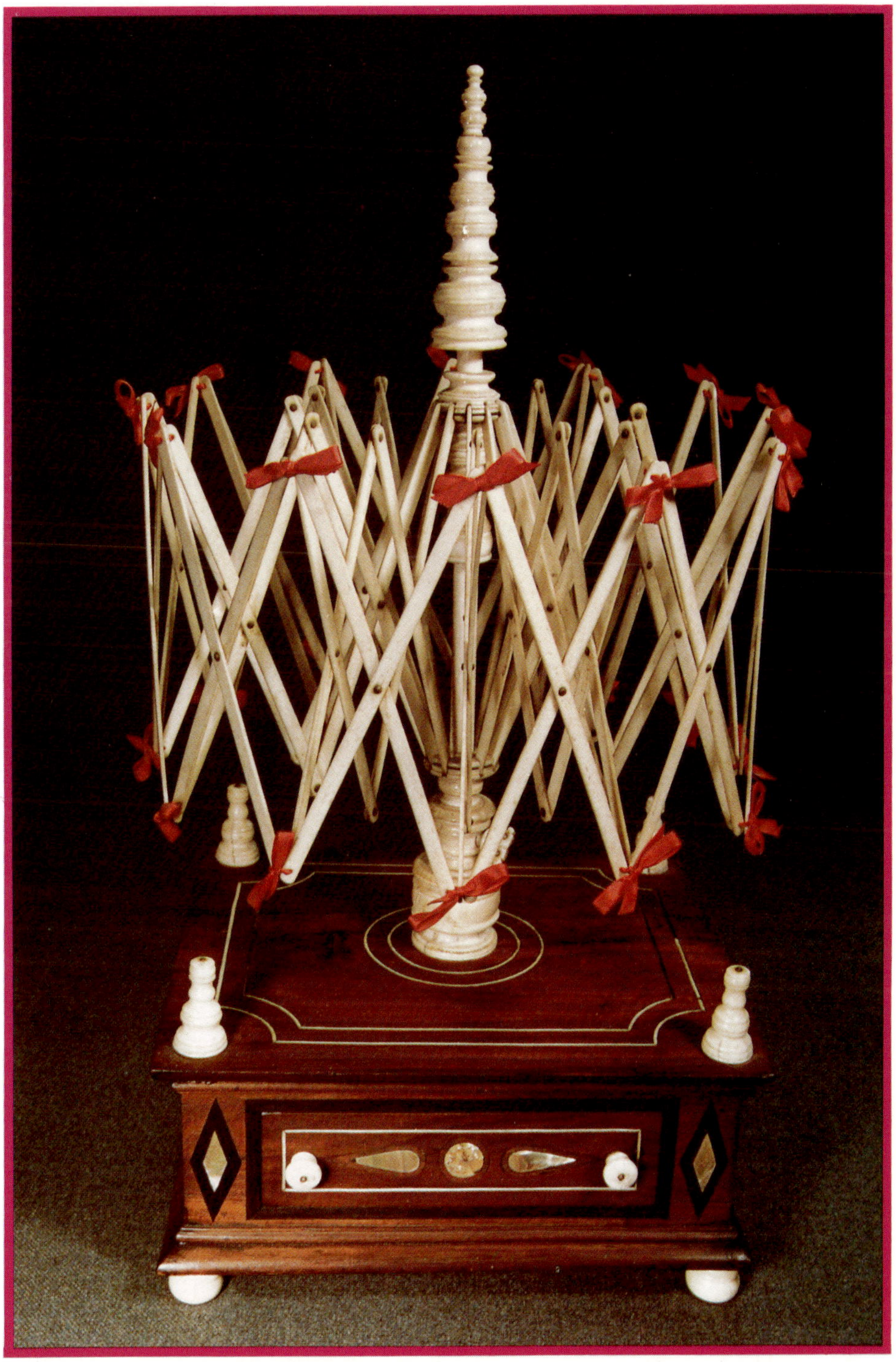

Such an elaborate swift with its beautifully turned whale ivory finial was the sort which might have graced a nineteenth century parlor. The mahogany base is exquisitely inlaid with ebony, abalone and whalebone. *Collection of Raymond and Elizabeth De Lucia*

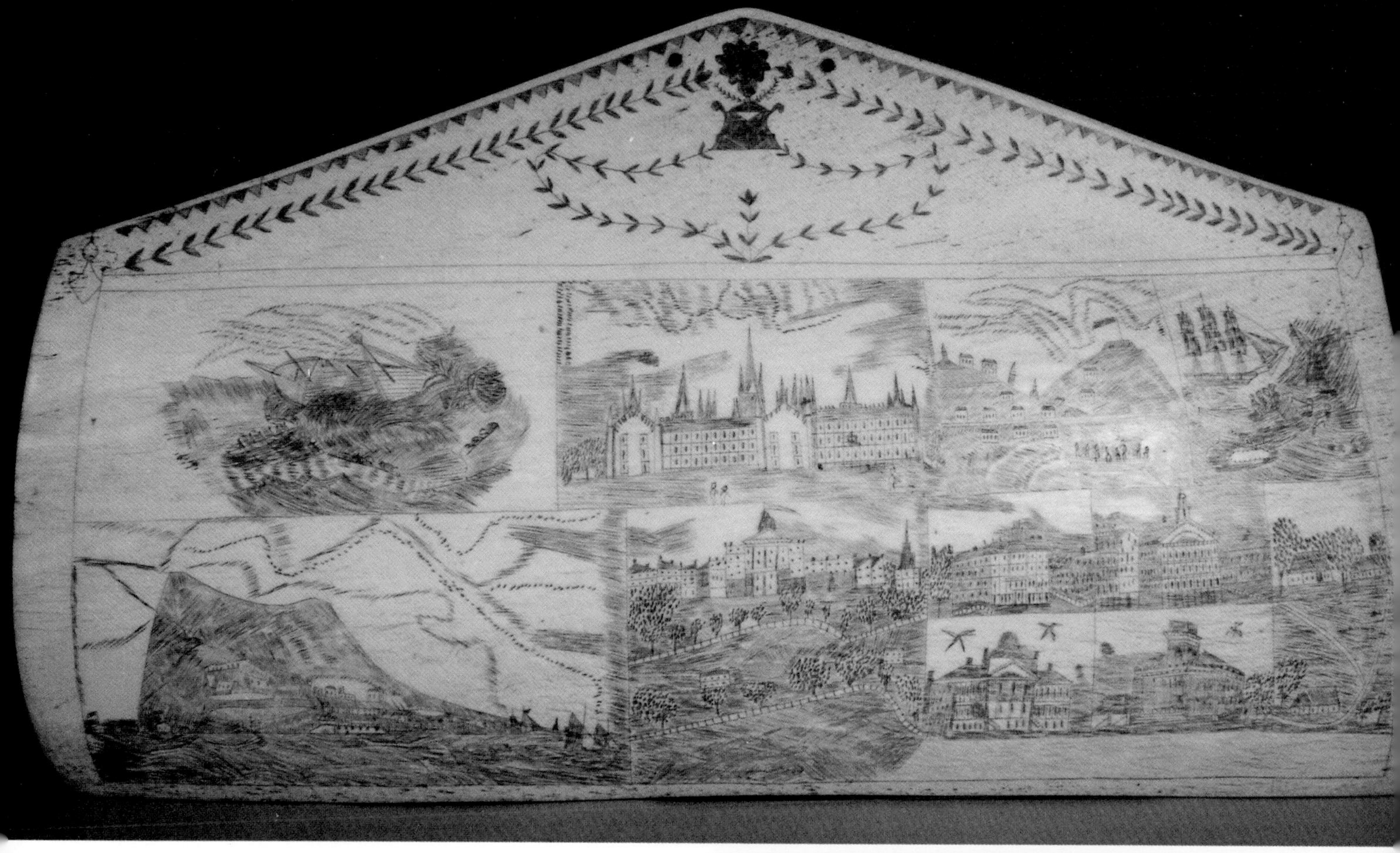

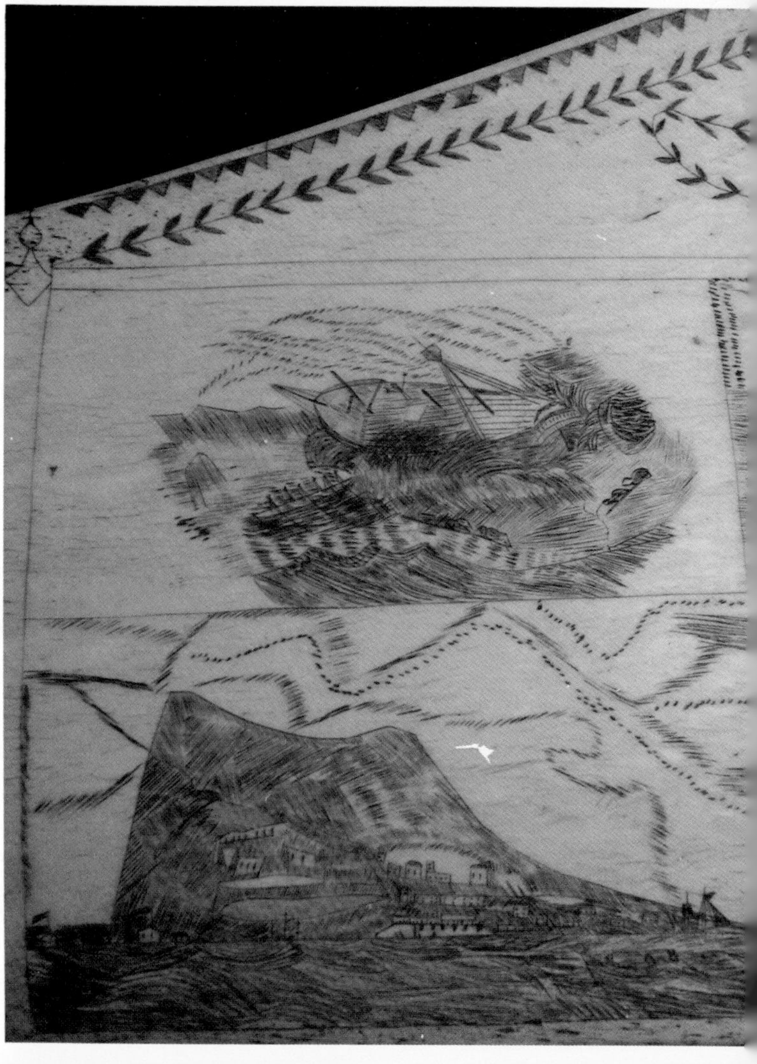

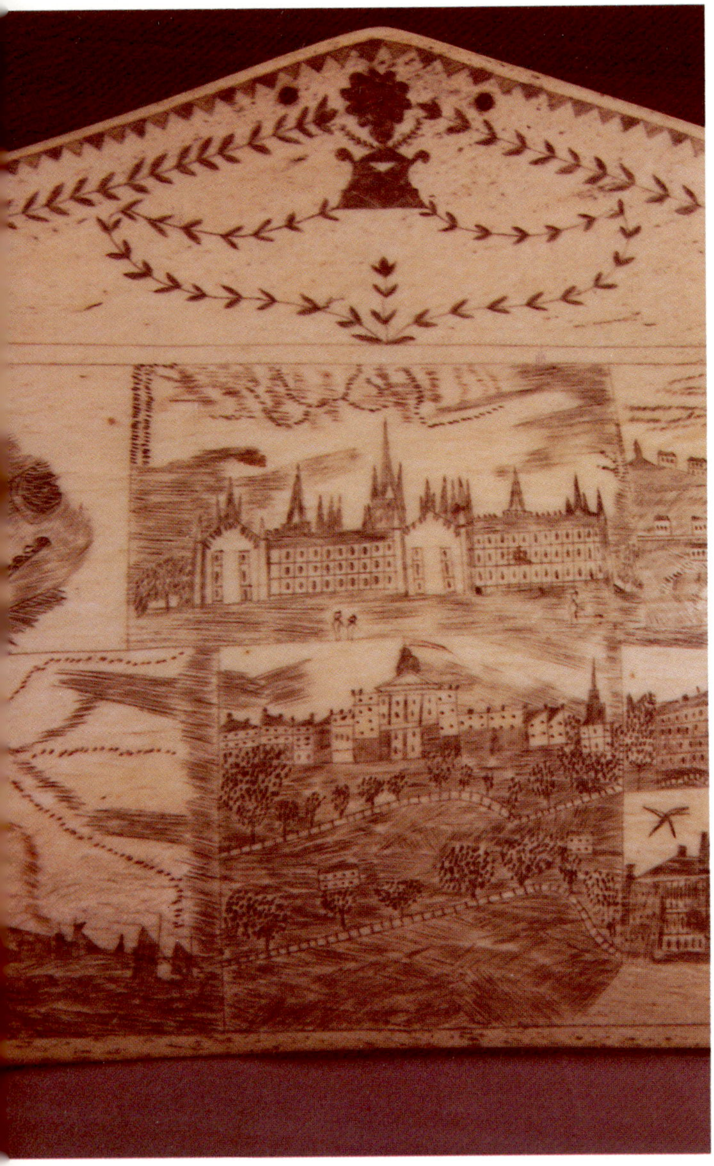

This panbone abounds with scenes as diverse as a dramatic whale hunt, foreign vistas and a country home. *Courtesy of the Nantucket Historical Association*

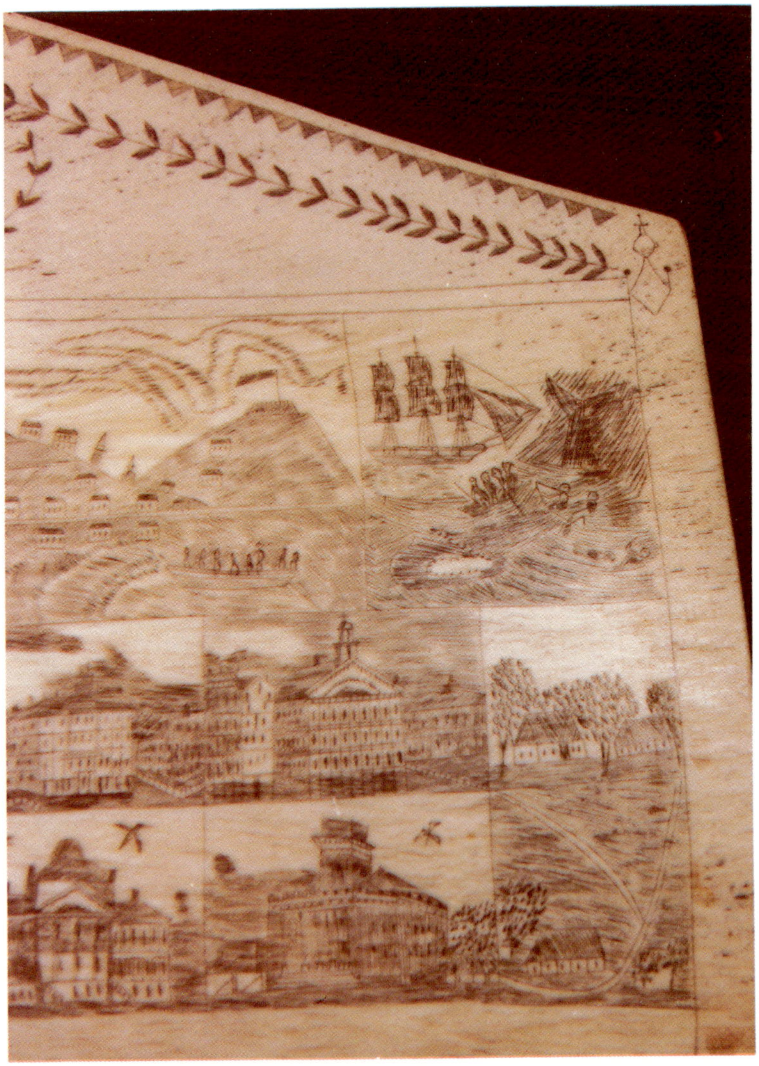

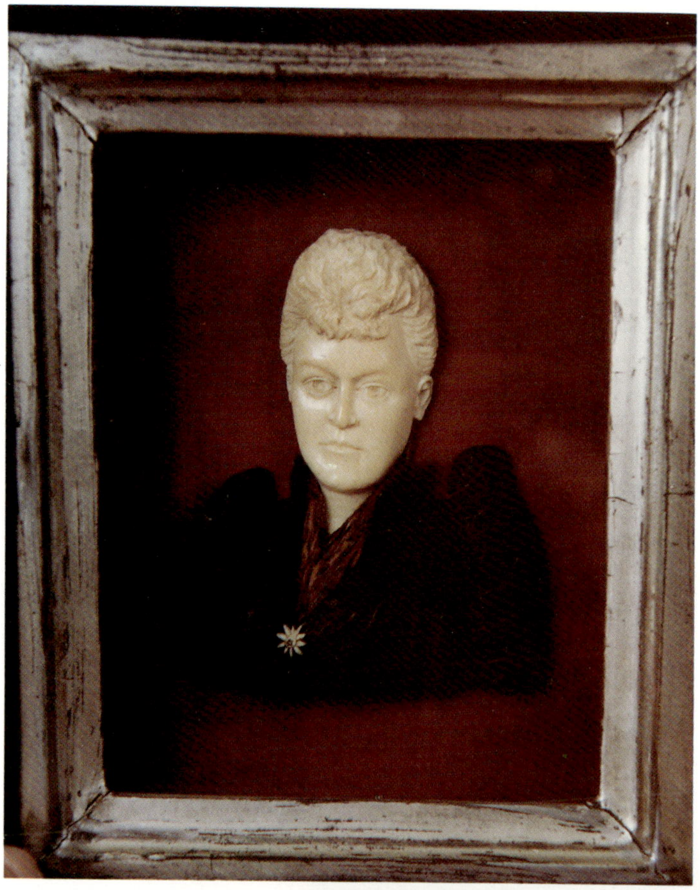

This highly unusual whale ivory carving rests inside a shadow-box frame. *Madden Collection*

"The Proposal," a rare whale ivory carving, depicts a lovestruck young man and the lady he is courting. *Courtesy of the Nantucket Historical Association*

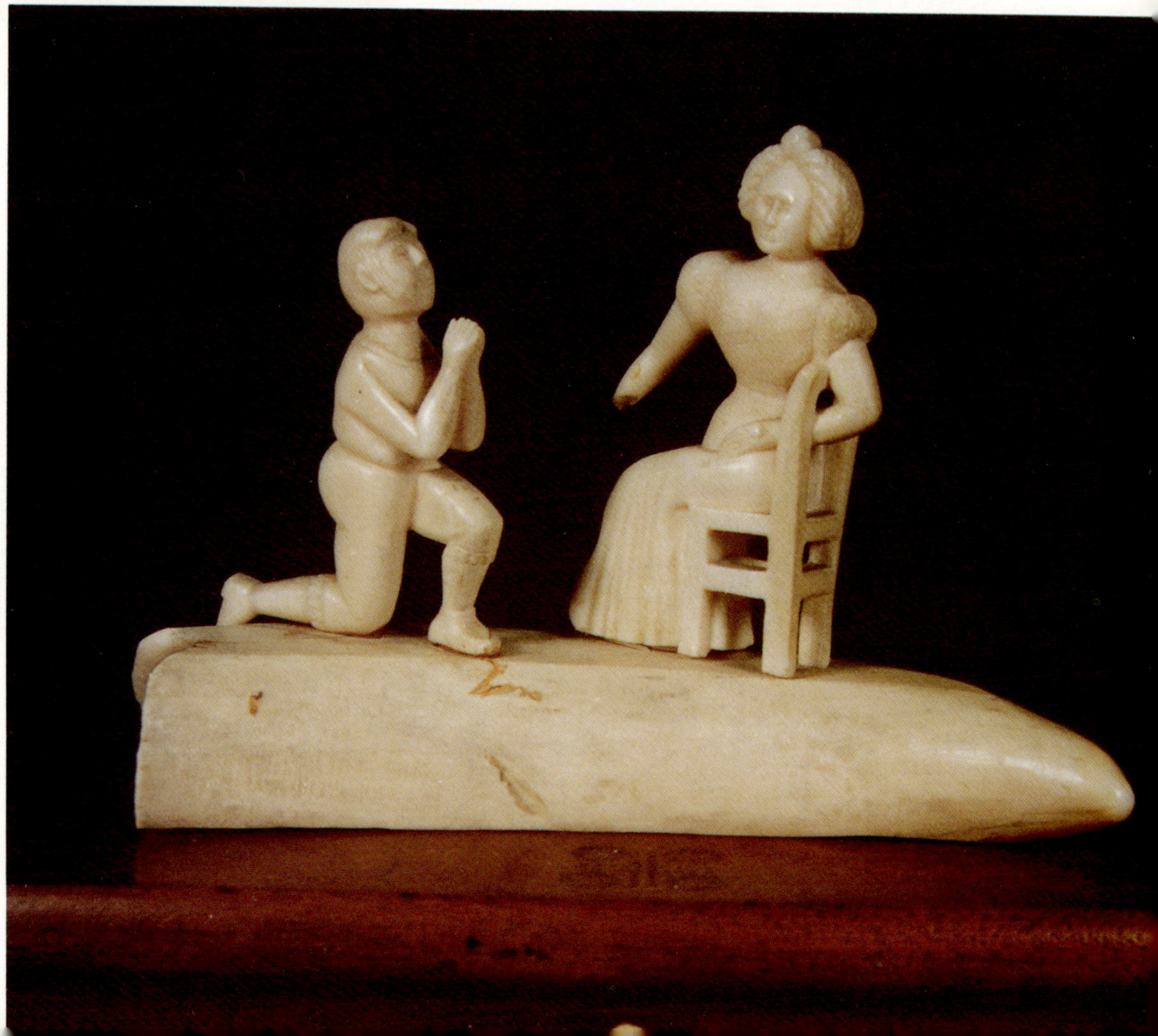

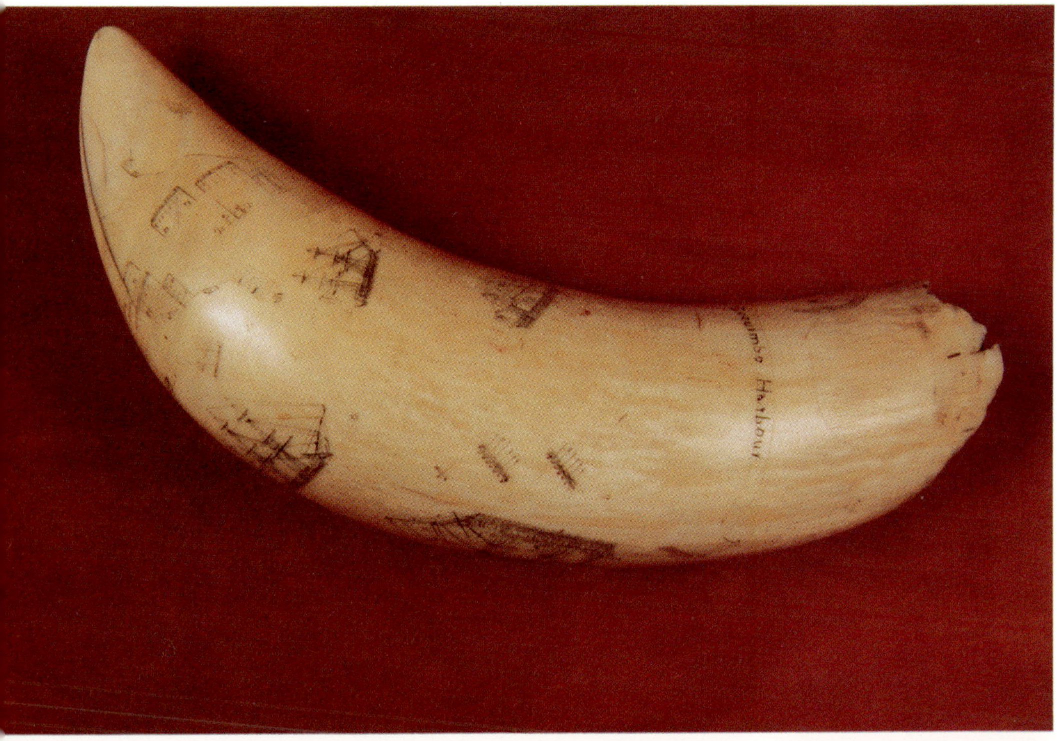

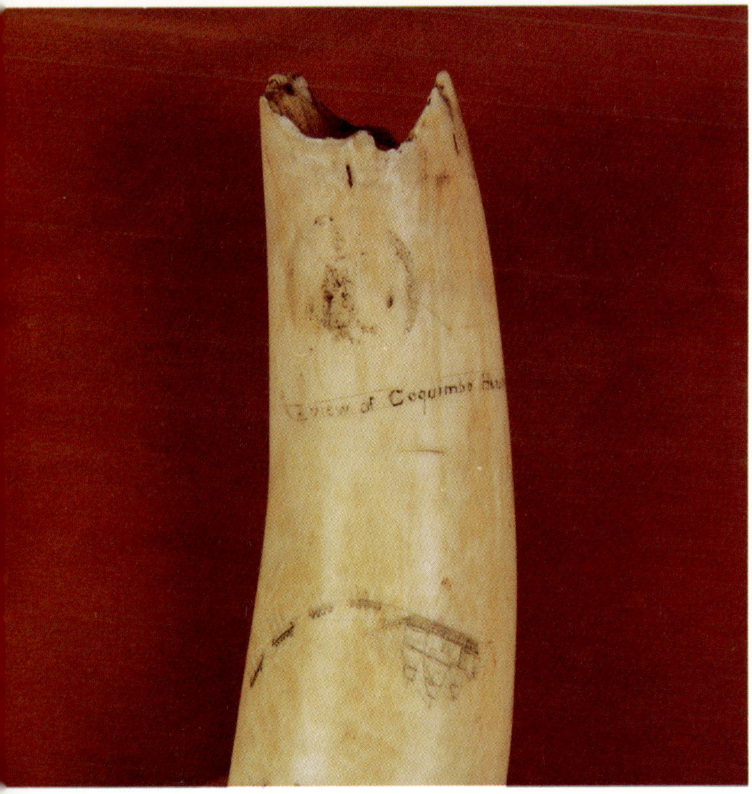

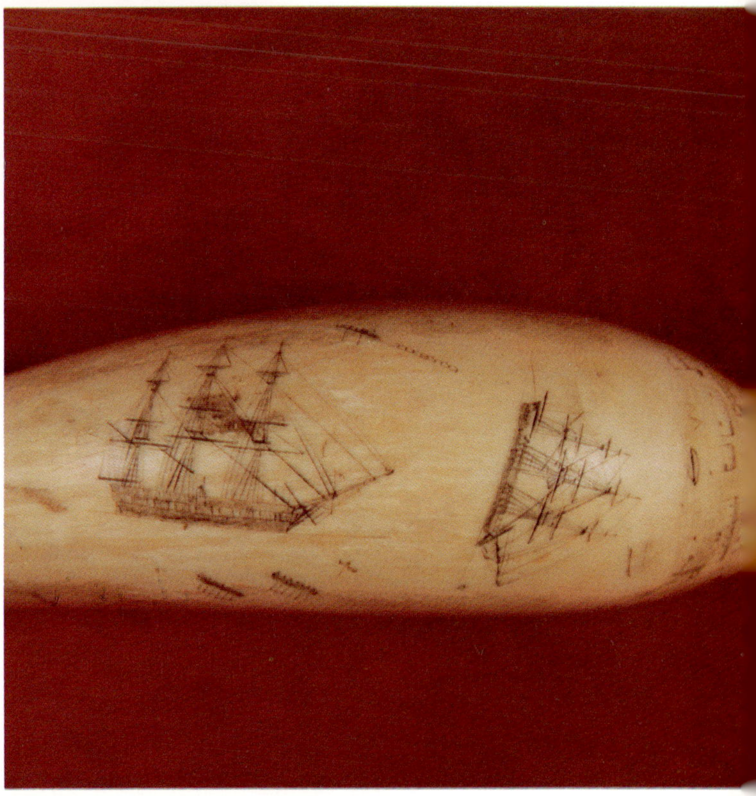

Unlike the carefully planned designs engraved by Frederick Myrick in his *Susan* series, the renderings on this tooth, attributed to Myrick, comprise a pastiche of scenes. Labeled "A view of Coquimbo Harbour," the tooth pictures the busy Chilean port filled with whaleships, one of which is being towed by its own four whaleboats. *Private Collection*

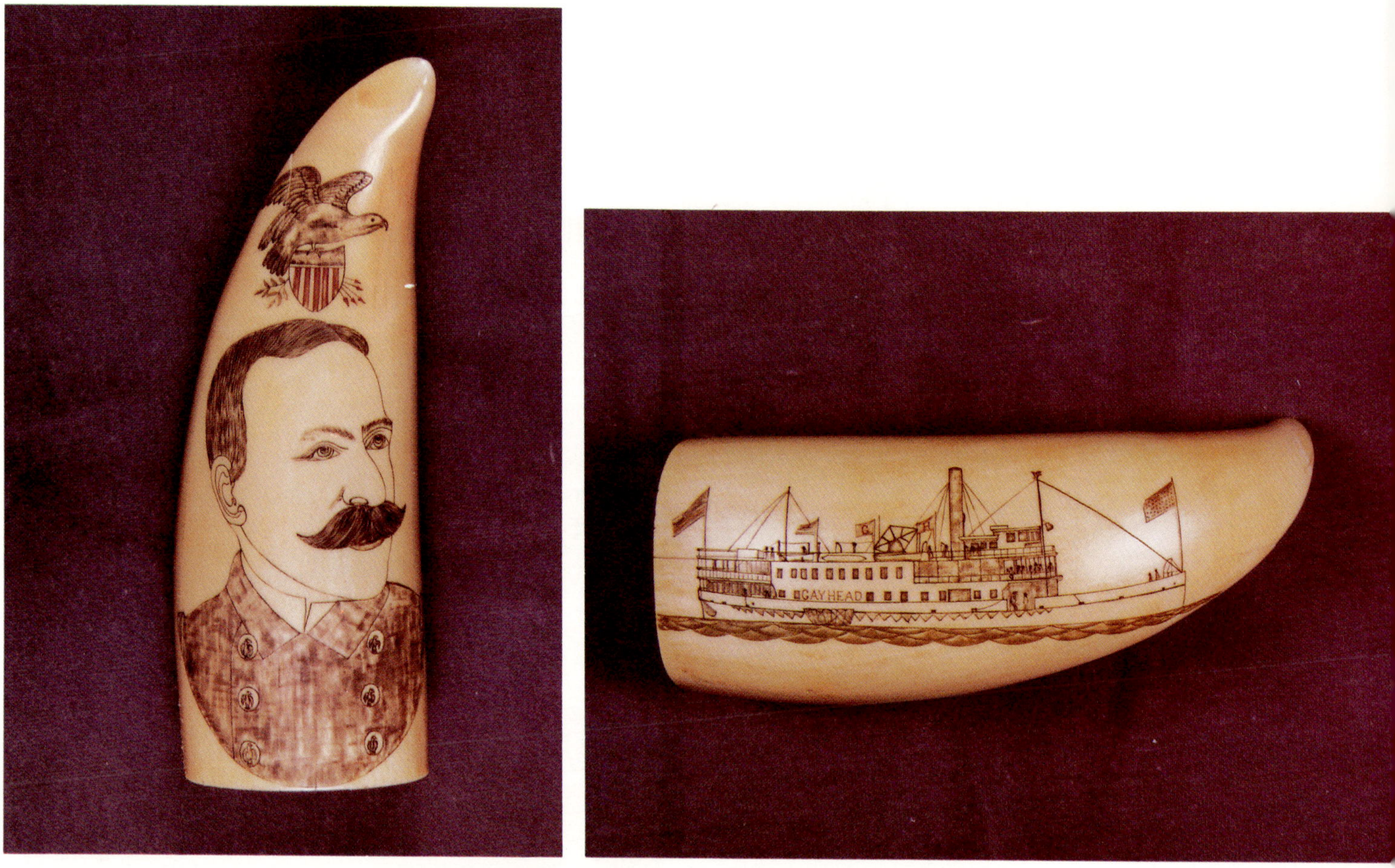

Admiral George Dewey, commander of the American naval forces responsible for the defeat of the Spanish in Manila Bay, is cleanly rendered on one side of this sperm whale tooth. The steamship *Gayhead* is portrayed on the reverse. *Madden Collection*

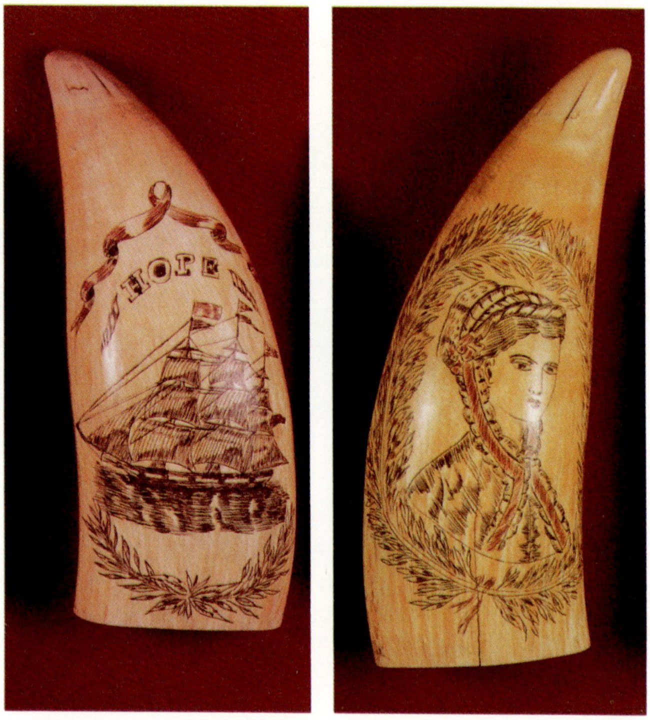

"Hope" is the ambiguous sentiment surmounting the ship on this lovely polychrome tooth. Perhaps the beautiful young woman on the reverse was the inspiration for the inscription. *Madden Collection*

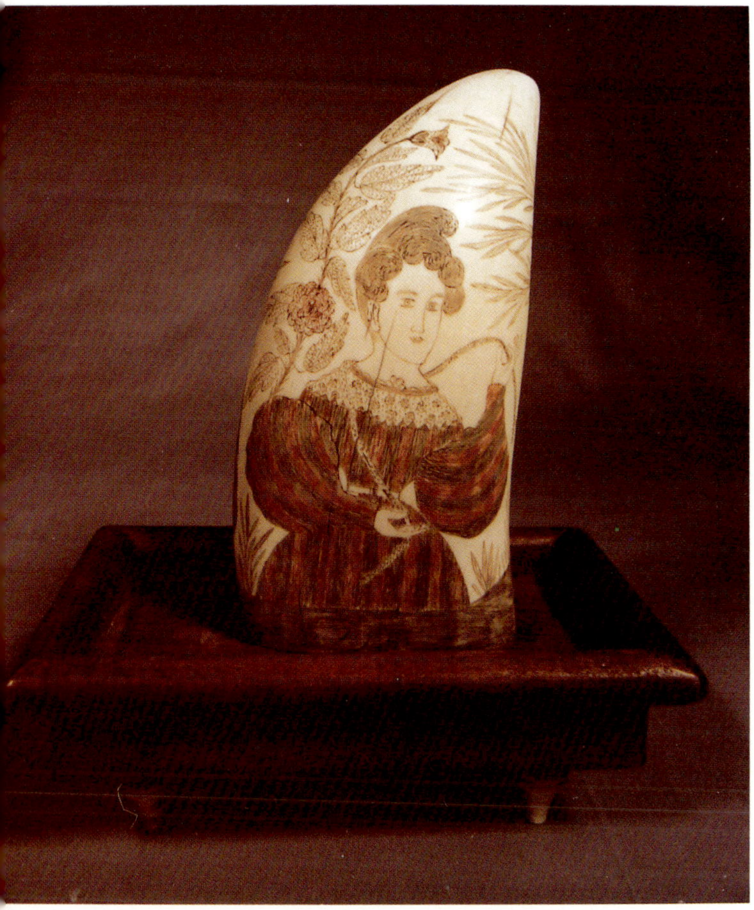

The fashionably attired woman on this polychrome tooth is cast in a flowery setting. *Courtesy of the Nantucket Historical Association*

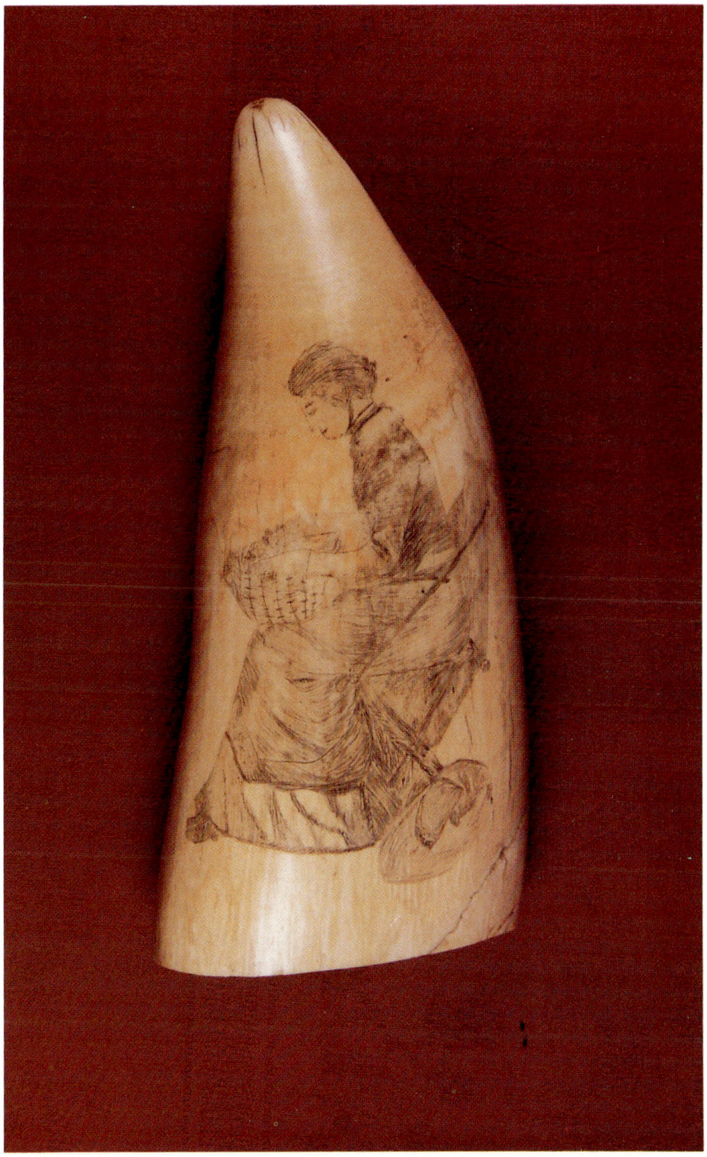

Rather than a fashion plate, this scrimshander chose to portray an image of woman perhaps more familiar to him. *Private Collection*

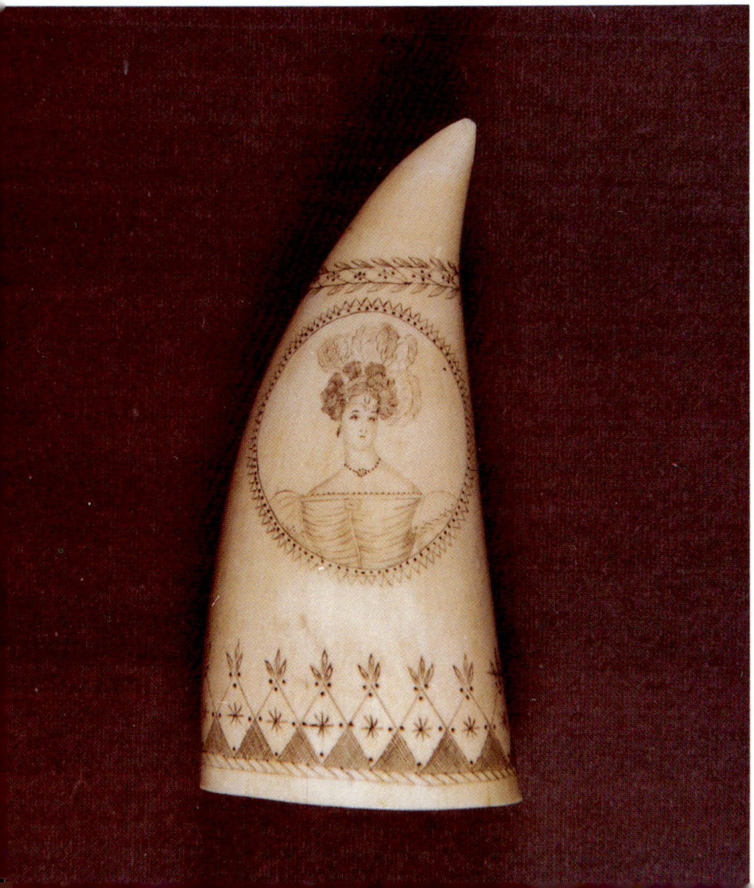

Even the graceful shape of the tooth itself blends with the delicate border designs and cameo portrait engraved on this piece. Another tooth, picturing a mother and child and illustrated on page 46 is by the same hand. *Courtesy of the Nantucket Historical Association.*

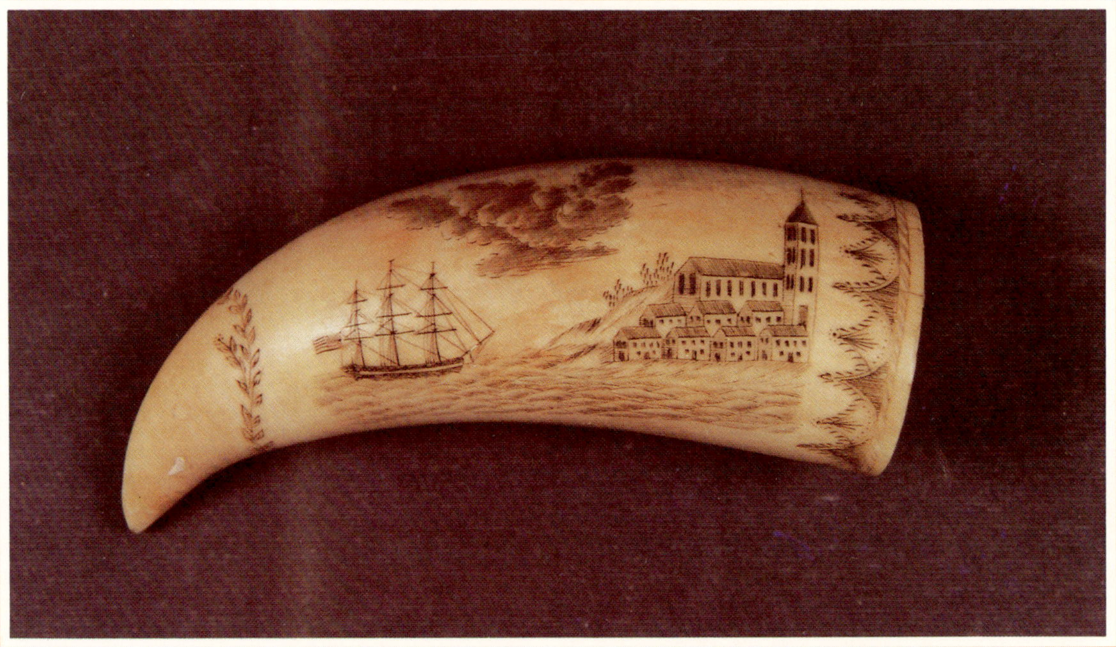

An American ship entering a foreign port. *Courtesy of the Nantucket Historical Association*

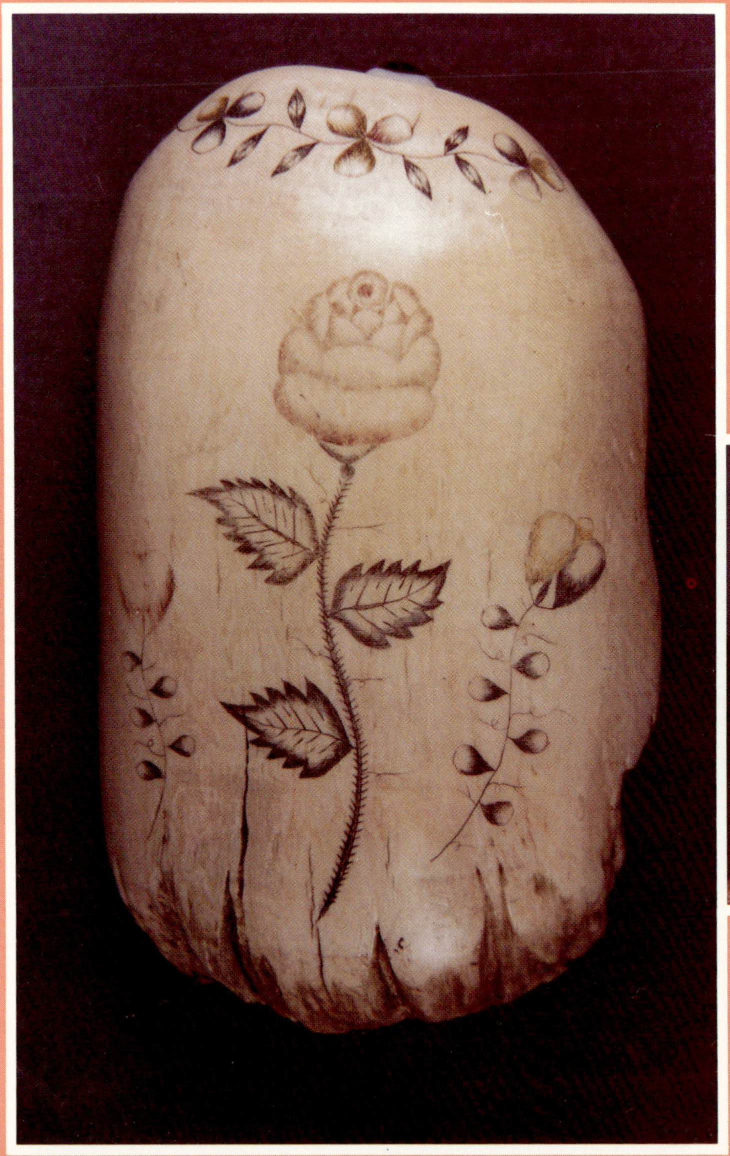

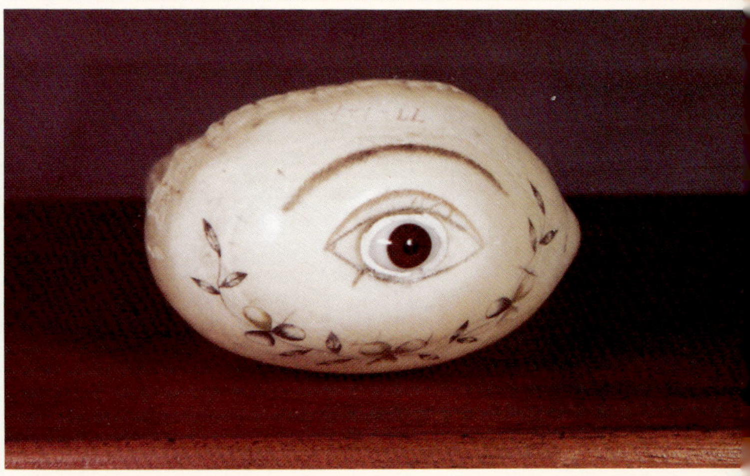

The creator of this fabulous piece of scrimshaw must have enjoyed a good sense of humor as well as a talent for his craft. *Courtesy of the Nantucket Historical Association*

Much action is portrayed in this detailed harbor scene.
Courtesy of the Nantucket Historical Association

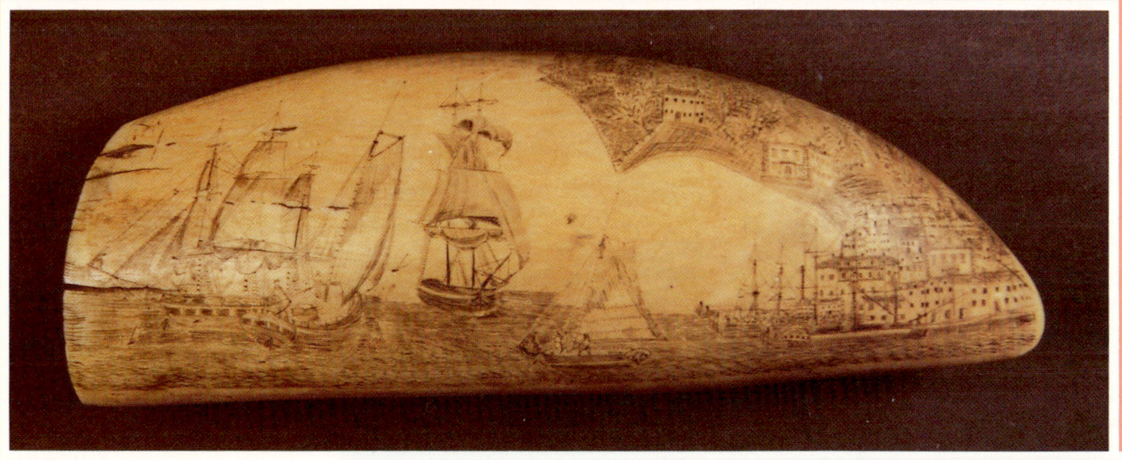

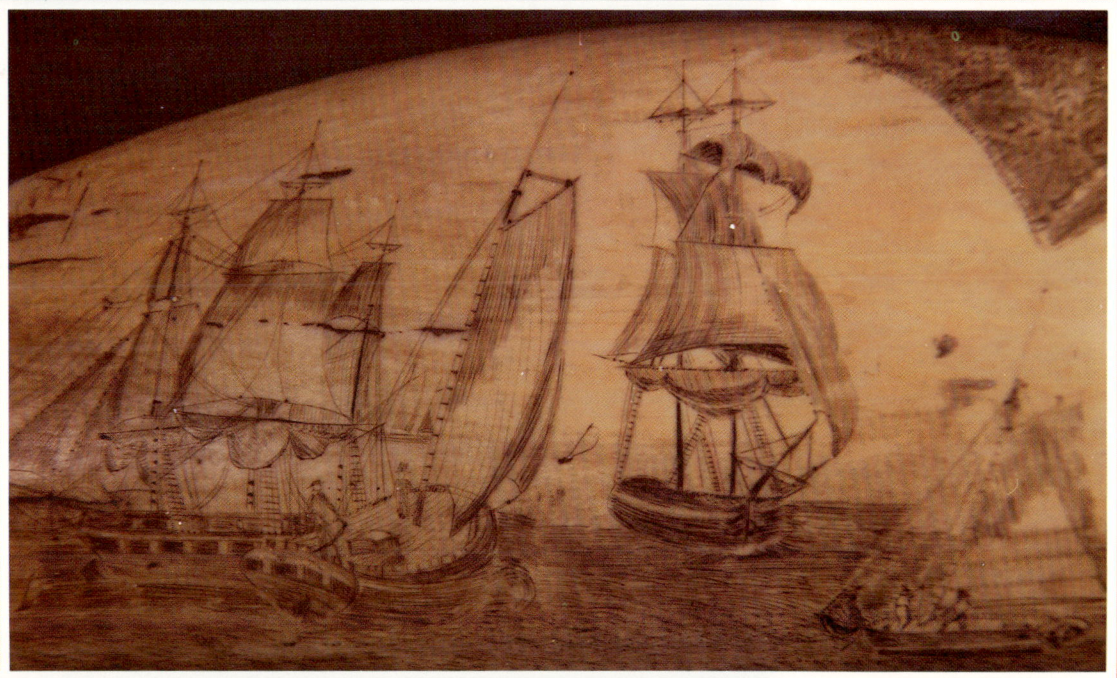

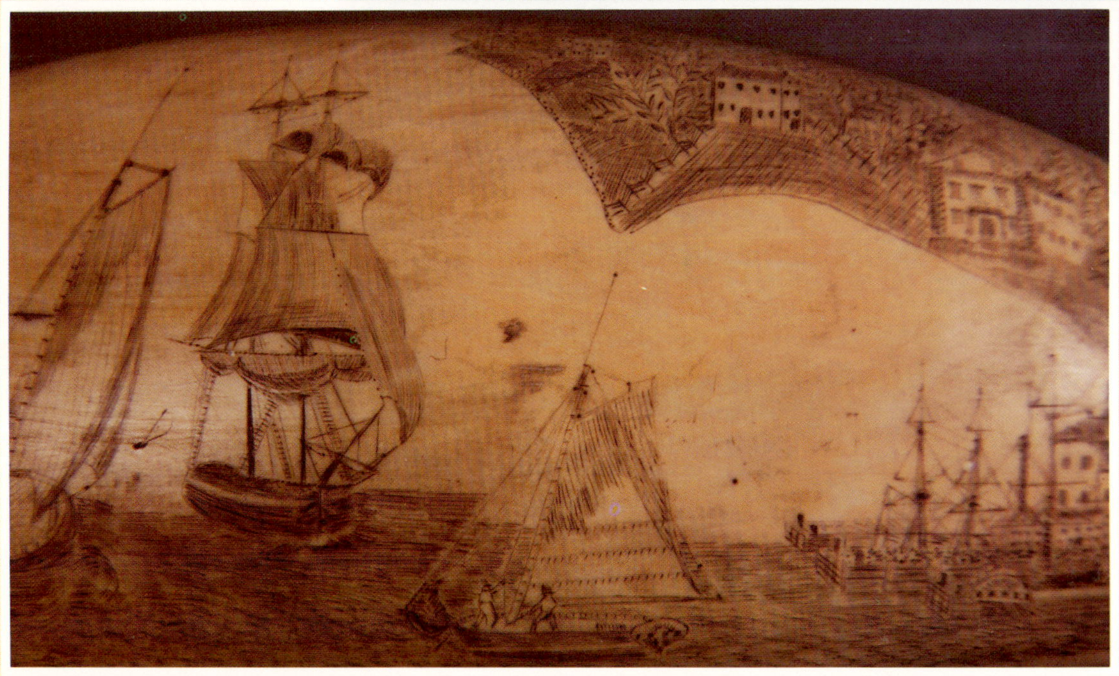

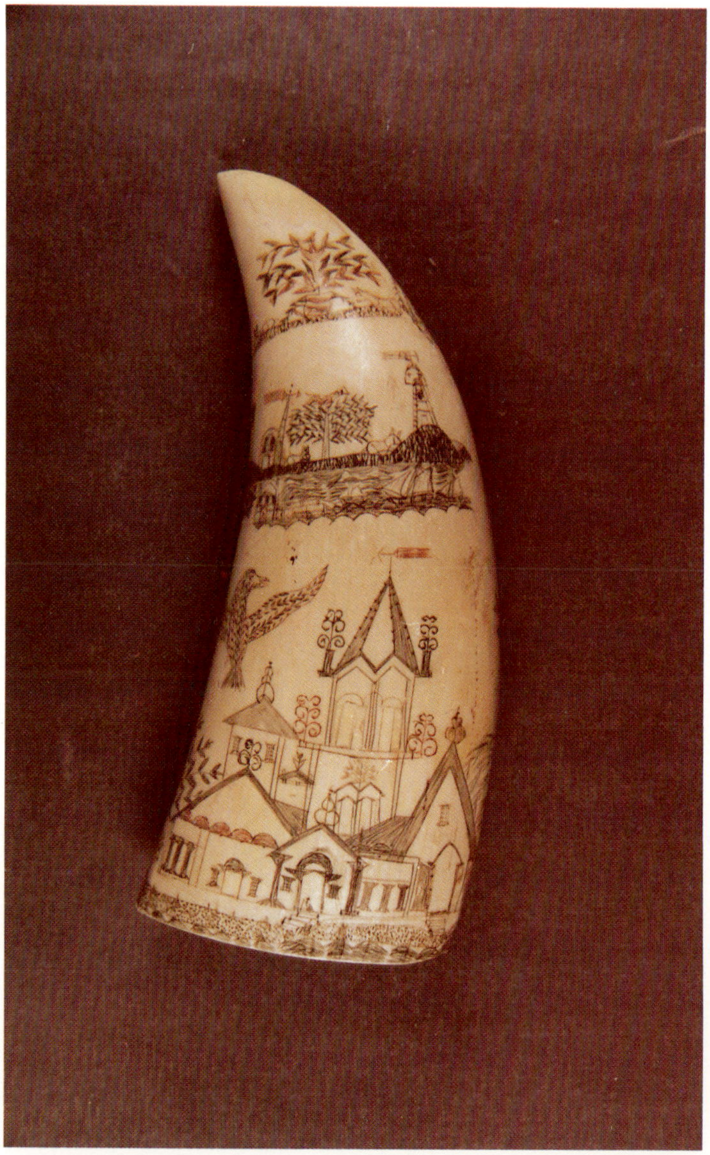

Recording his journey for posterity, an unknown seaman rendered these vignettes of the Azores and included a typical island windmill. *Courtesy of the Nantucket Historical Association*

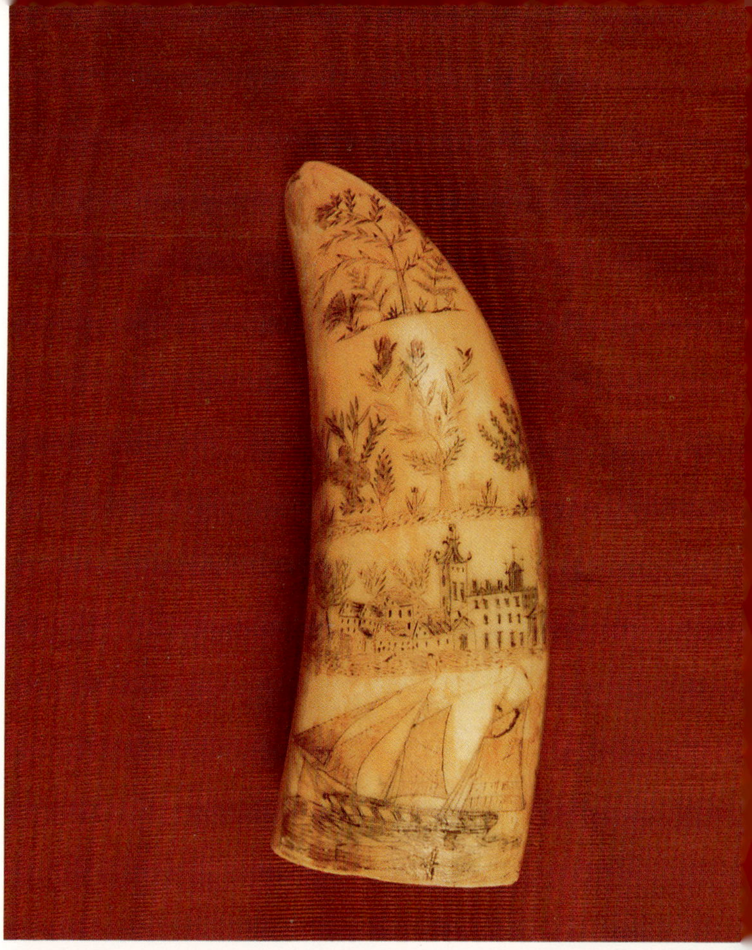

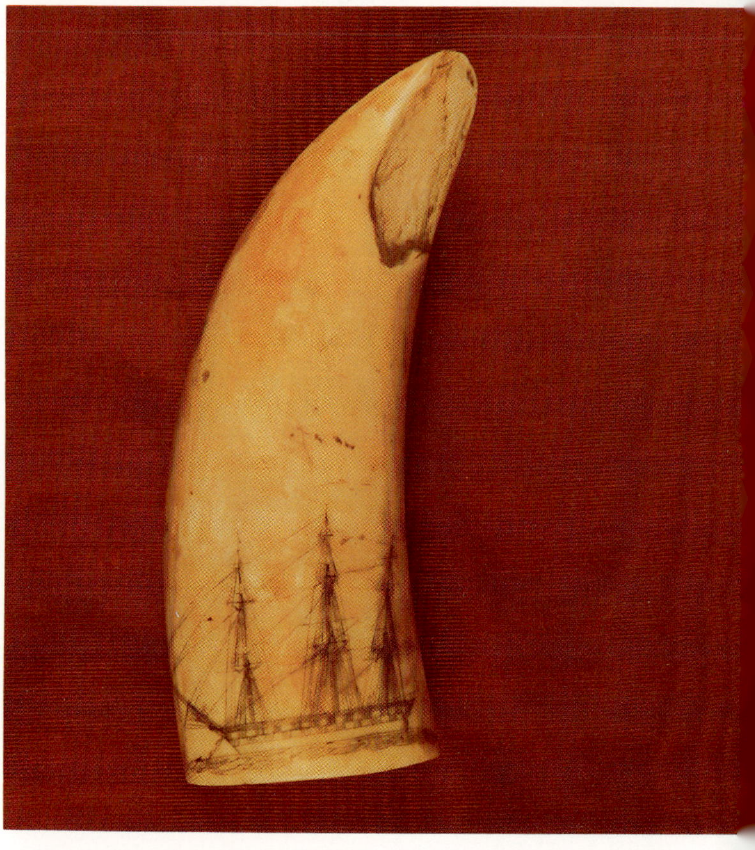

Another scrimshander's view of the Azores includes colorful floral motifs as well as a schooner whose journey apparently has been joined by a sperm whale swimming below the vessel. A lone ship is all that was engraved on the tooth's reverse. *Collection of Charles A. Manghis*

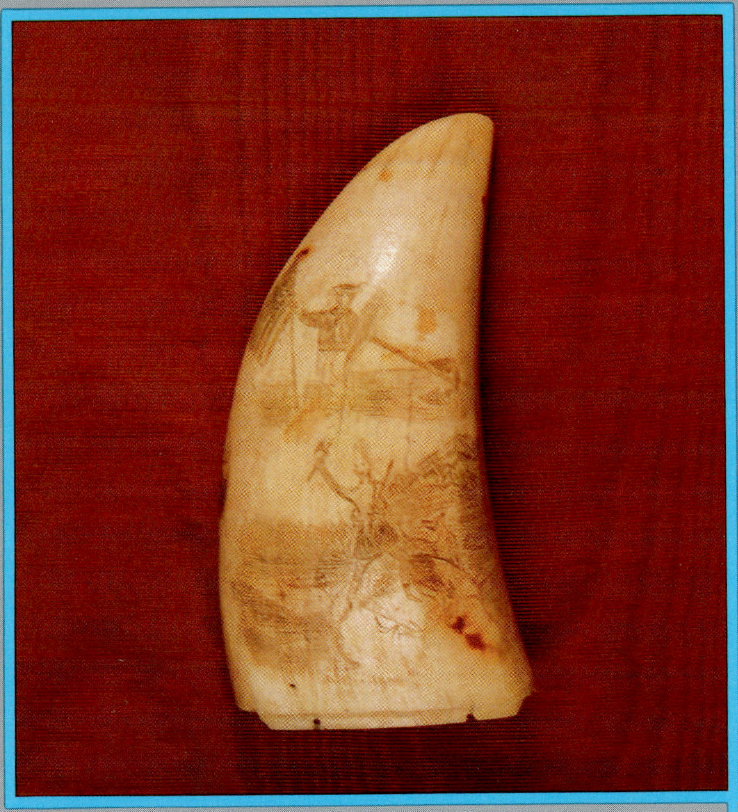

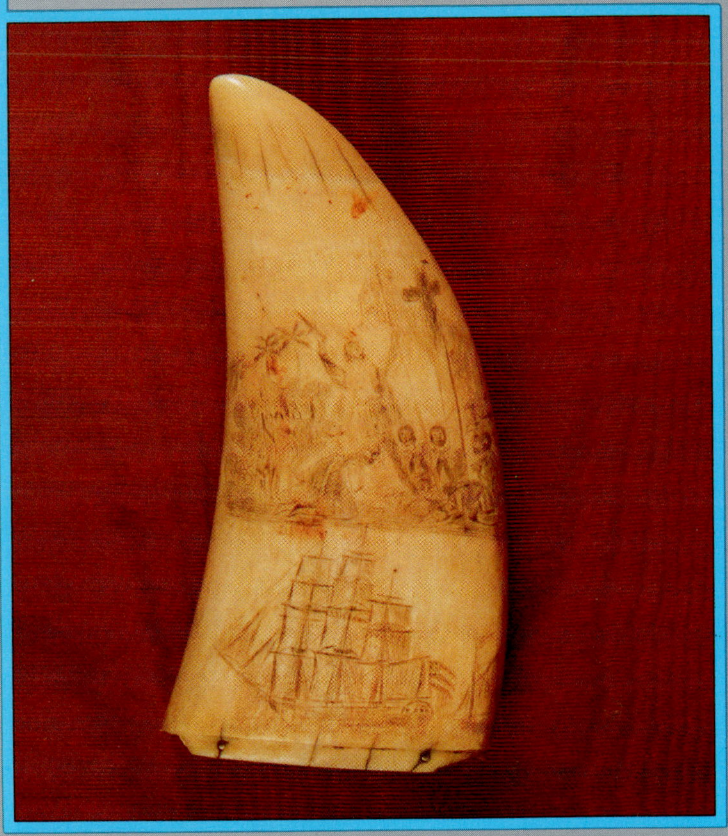

The scenes engraved on this tooth are unusual in that they depict not only the common seaman, but also a hatchet-wielding Native American. Behind him two men paddle a canoe. The engraving on the reverse appears to portray a European explorer bringing both the sword and cross to the New World. *Collection of Charles A. Manghis*

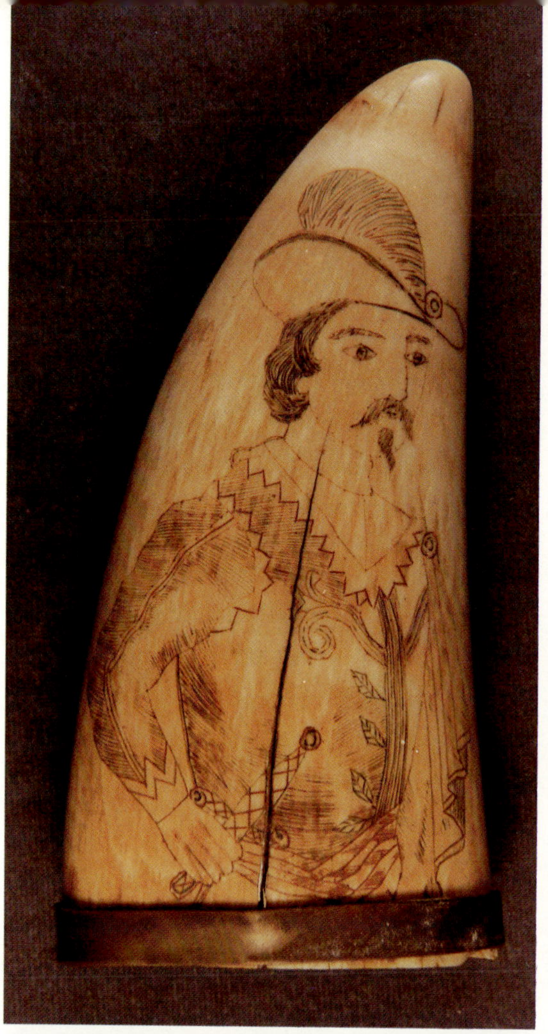

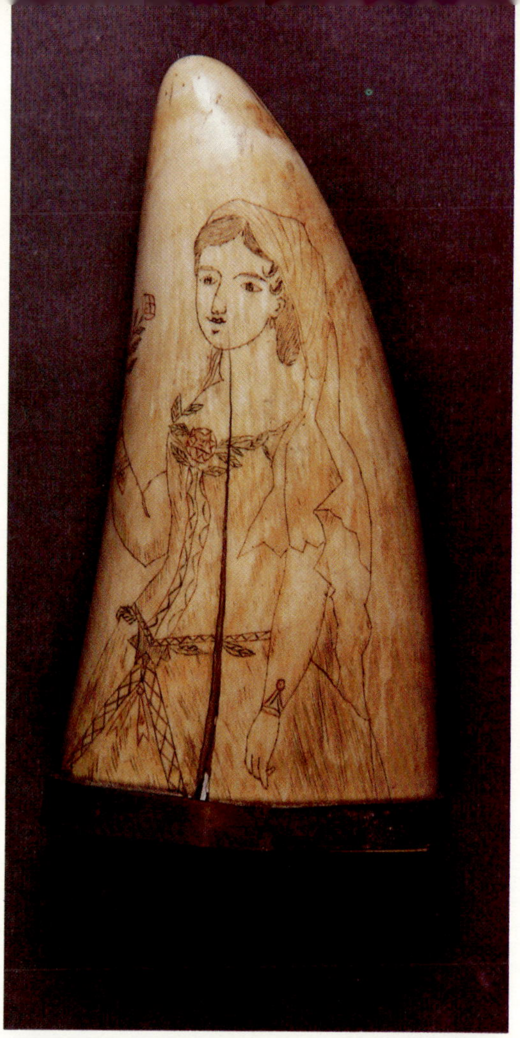

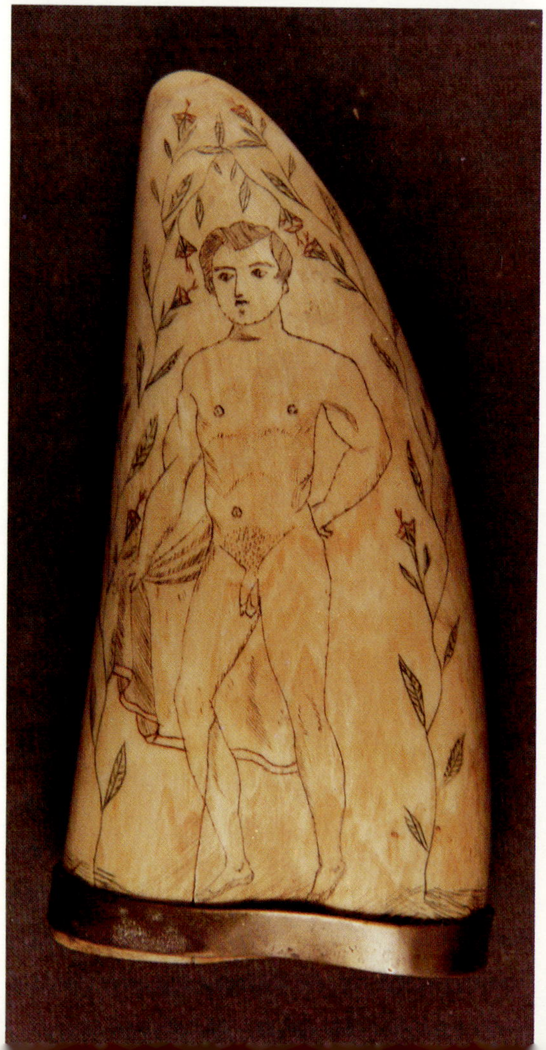

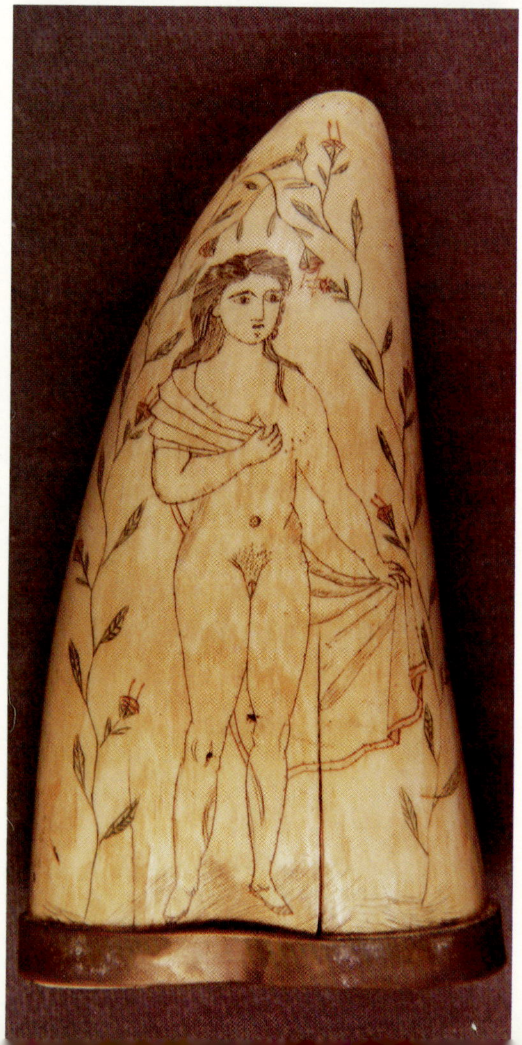

The handsomely dressed man and woman engraved on these silver-banded polychrome teeth give no indication of the less inhibited couple found on the reverse sides. *Courtesy of the Nantucket Historical Association*

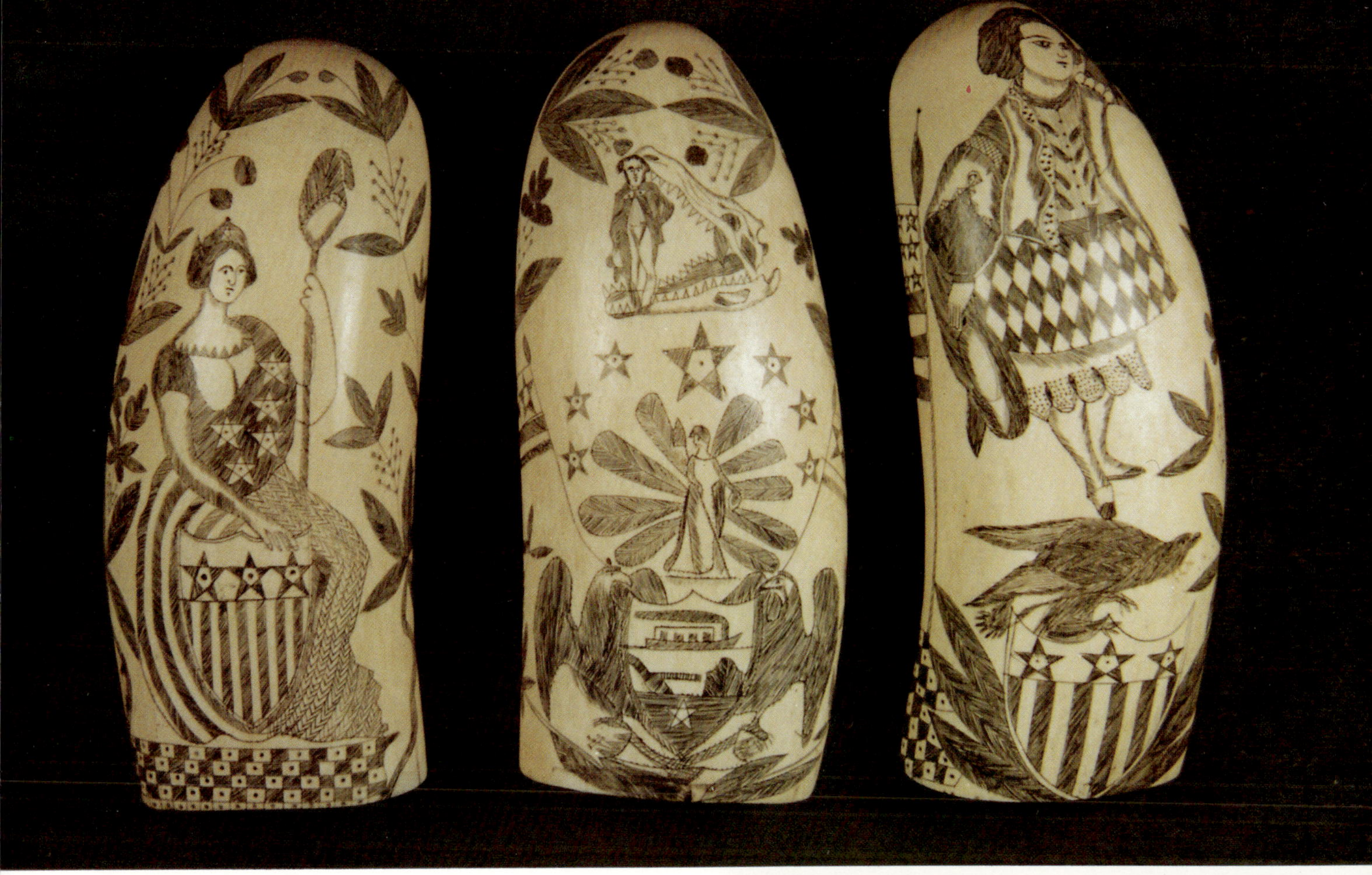

A trio of teeth display a variety of designs ranging from the patriotic to the whimsical. *Courtesy of the Nantucket Historical Association*

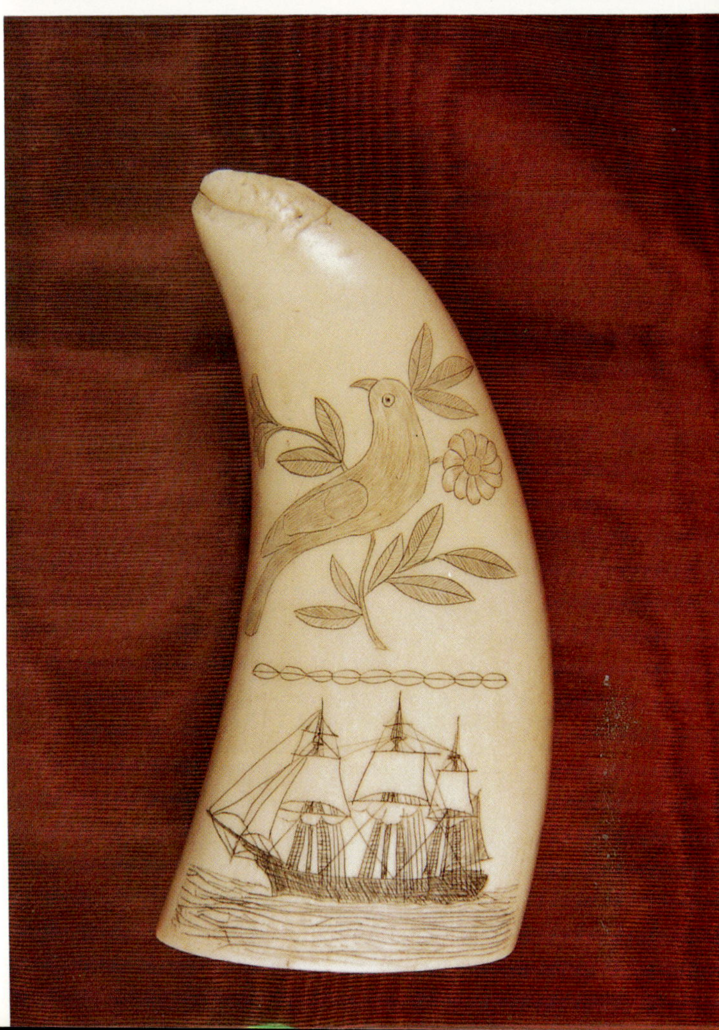

This pleasingly simple, polychrome design is found on the reverse of the tooth gracefully portraying a fashionable young woman, illustrated on page 80. *Private Collection*

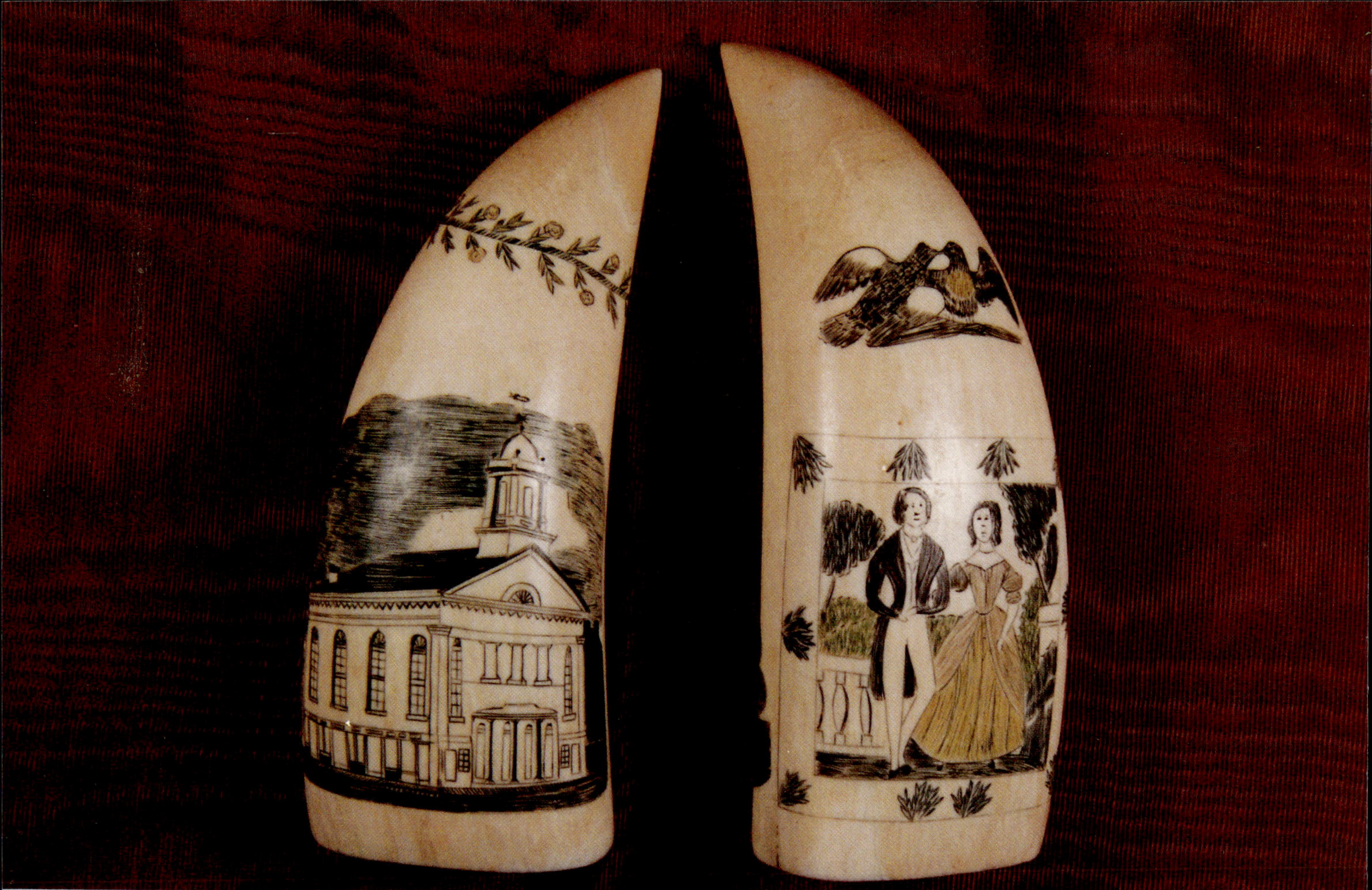

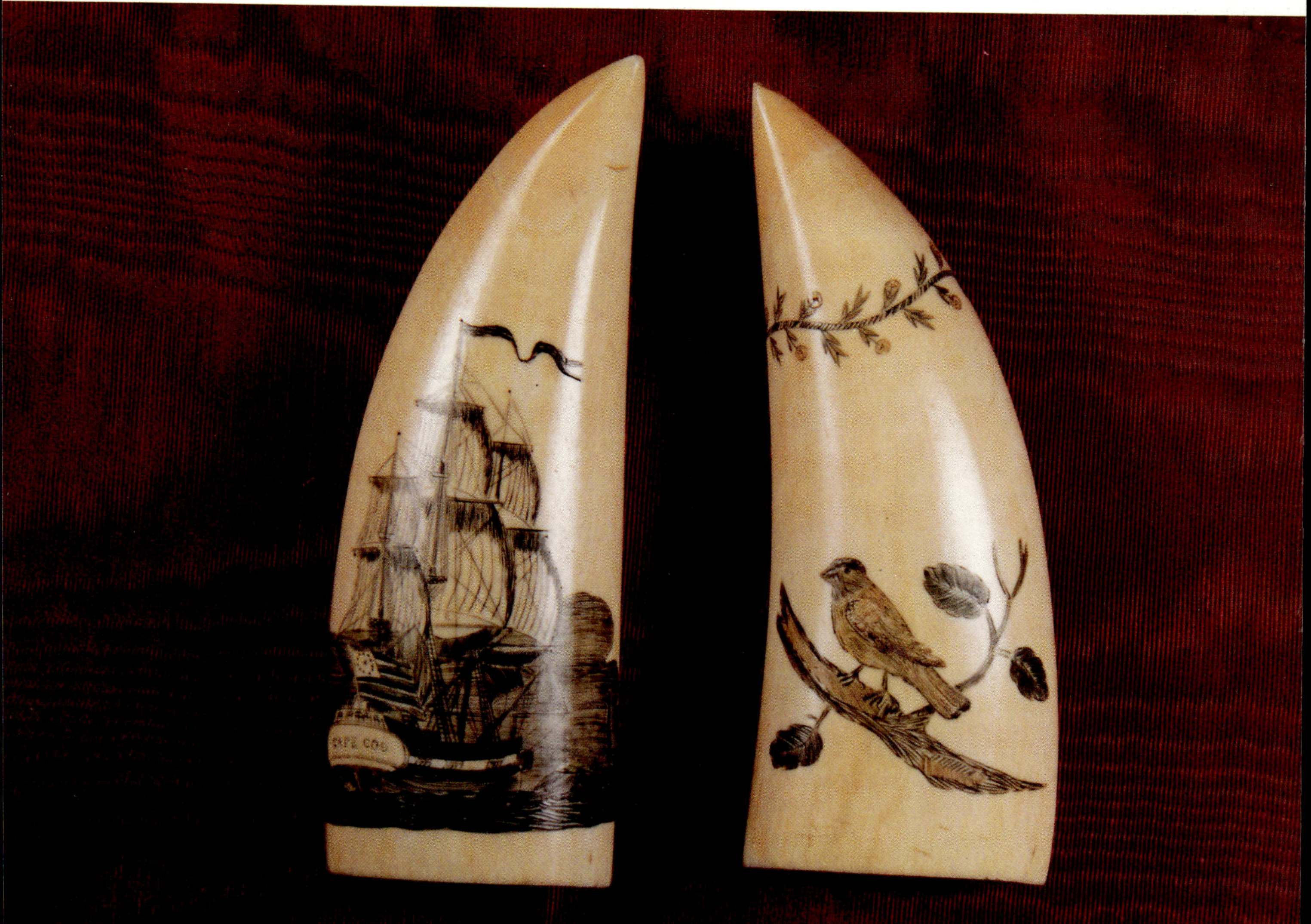
CAPE COD

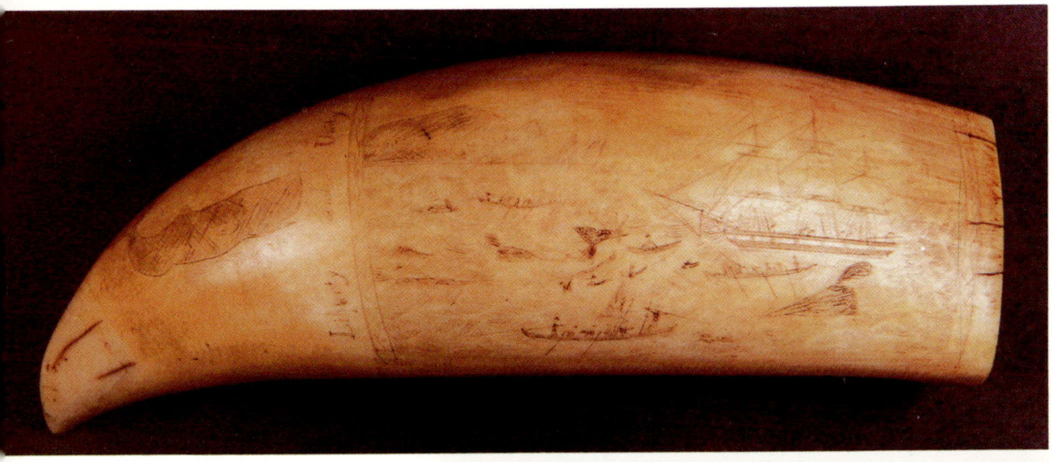

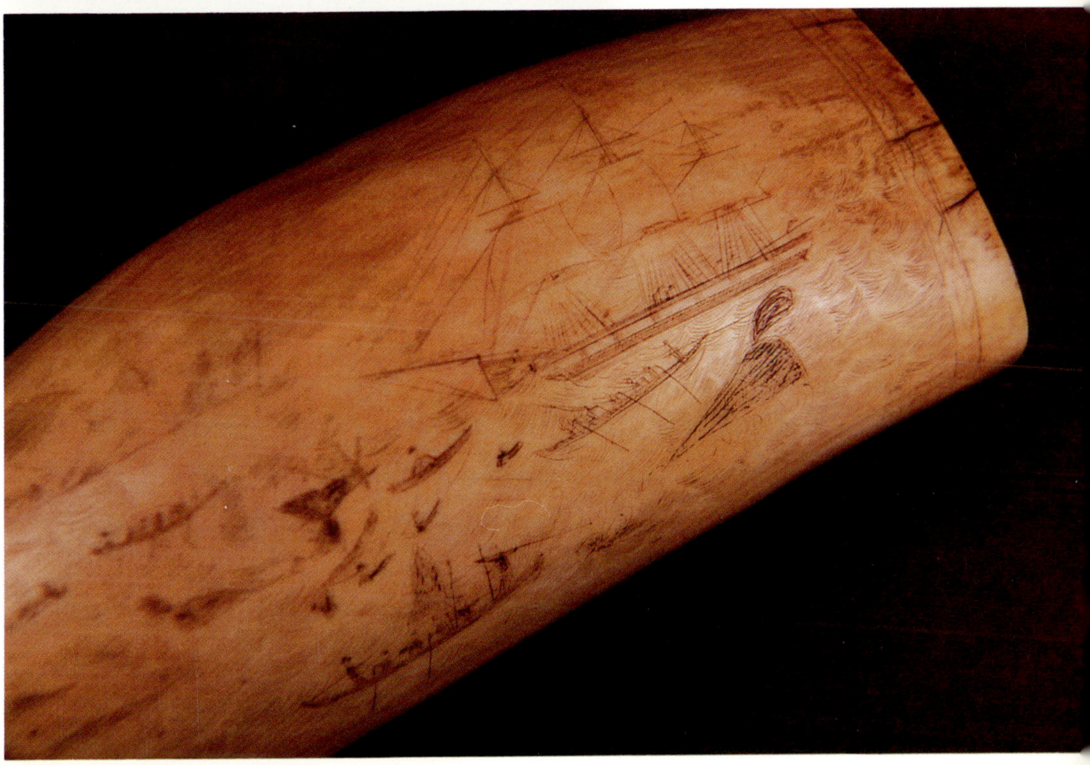

Opposite page:
The artist who engraved these two green and ochre colored teeth is also responsible for the busk shown on page 45. *Madden Collection.*

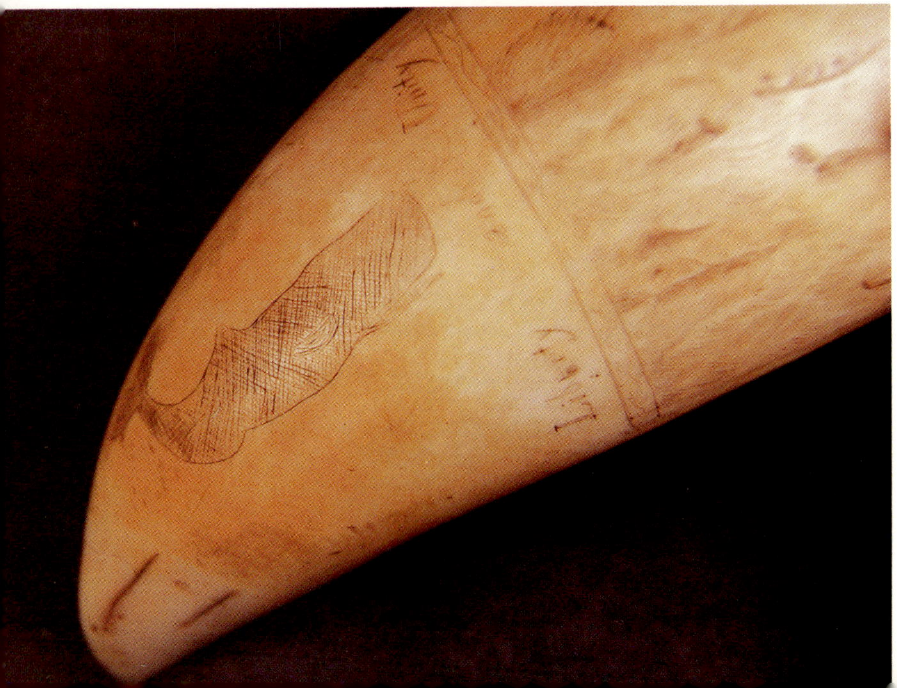

Edward Starbuck engraved this large tooth near the end of a three year voyage aboard the ship *Mariner*. On its surface he included much visual and written material. On this side he rendered the flurry of the whale hunt, a lone sperm whale and the inscription "Liberty and Unity". *Courtesy of the Nantucket Historical Association*

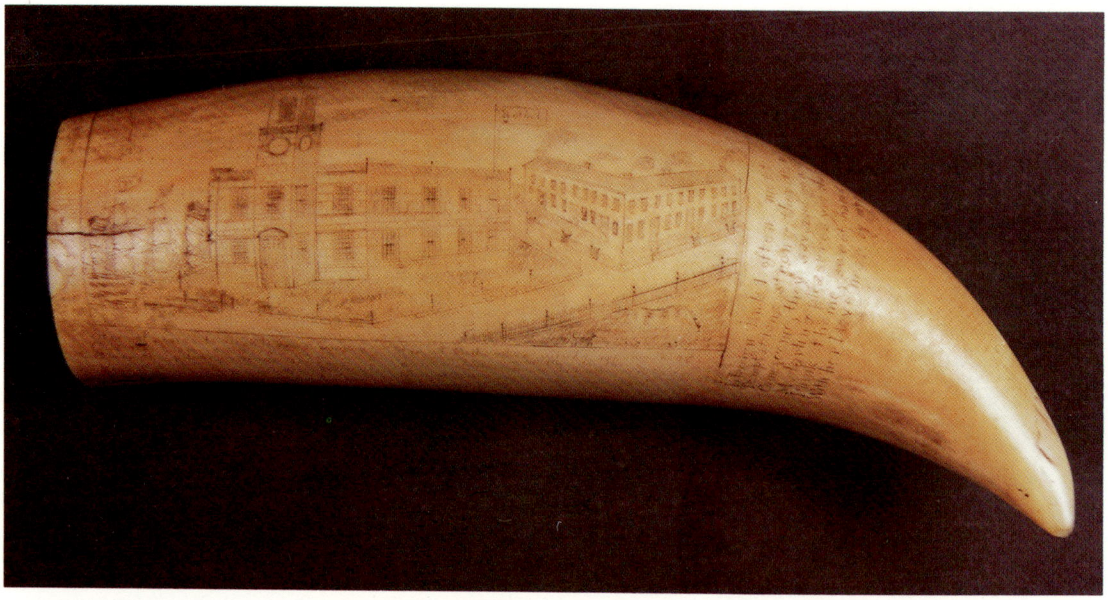

On the tooth's reverse, Starbuck included a similarly detailed scene of a seamen's bethel. Below he signed the tooth, "Edward C. Starbuck on board the Ship *Mariner* Eben Coleman Master bound to Nantucket March 16th 1835 Lat. 24°S Long. 29°W" and then etched a poignant verse:

When will kind fortune set me free,
That I can quit the boisterous sea:
I love my friends I love the shore,
I long to hear the oceans roar:
Then home, sweet home, shall be my pride
With her I love near by my side.

Courtesy of the Nantucket Historical Association

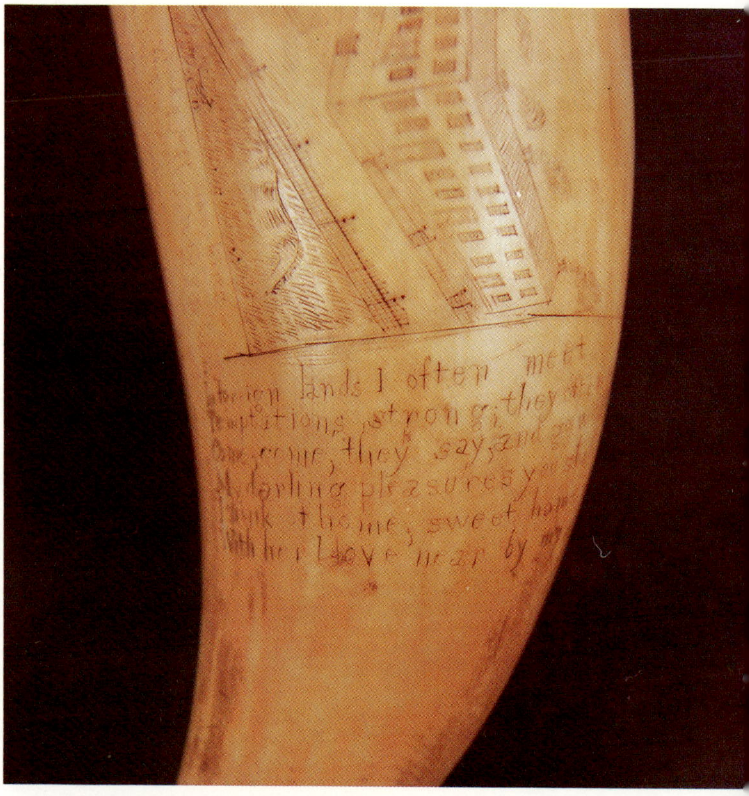

To the right of the bethel scene, Starbuck squeezed in one more verse whose sentiments were hopefully appreciated by his wife Eliza:

In foreign lands I often meet
Temptations strong; they often greet
Come, come, they say, and go with me
My darling pleasures you shall see; —
I think of home, sweet home denied
With her I love near by my side.

Courtesy of the Nantucket Historical Association

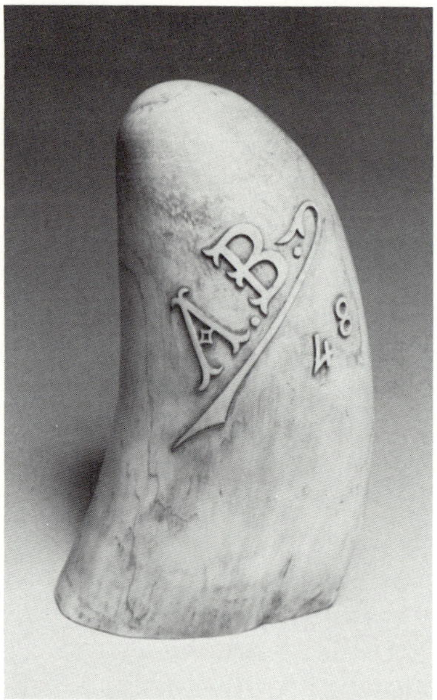

Although this beautifully carved tooth is potentially rich with information, in this instance, the initials and date unfortunately give no clue to the scrimshander. *Courtesy of the West Sea Company*

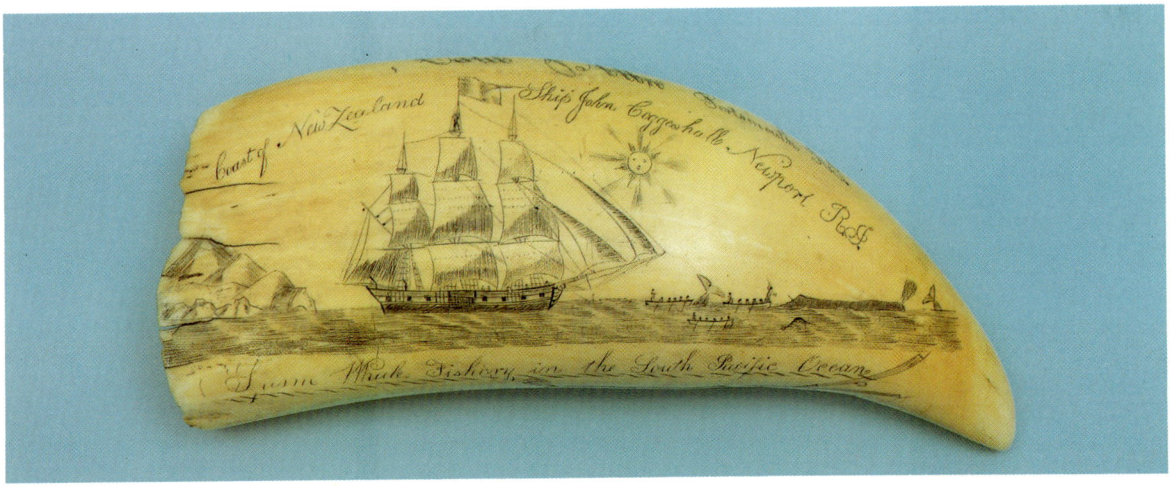

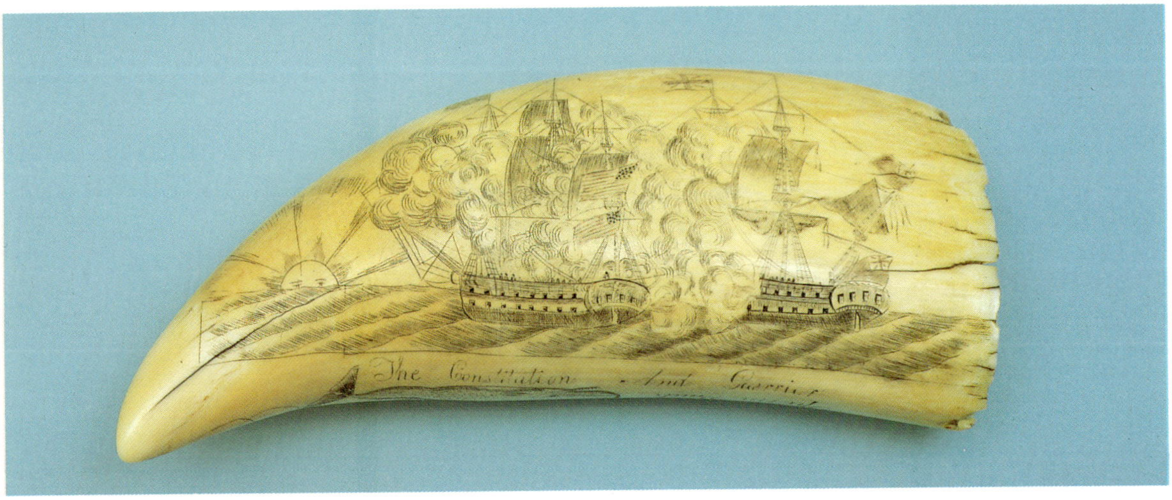

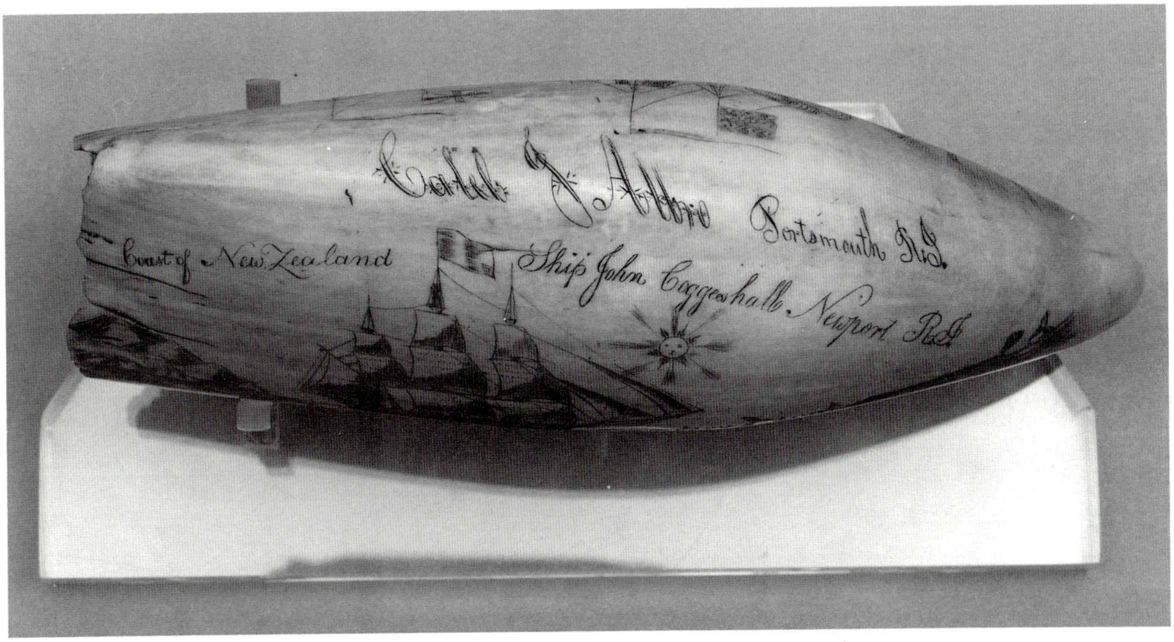

Caleb Albro was the scrimshander who engraved this tooth aboard the ship *John Coggeshall* of Newport. On one side, the *John Coggeshall* is shown whaling off the coast of New Zealand, on the other a naval engagement between the *Constitution* and the *Guerrier*. Caleb Albro sailed on this four year voyage beginning in 1835 as an ordinary seaman. Caleb's brother, Thomas, served as steward on this and other voyages of the *John Coggeshall* and is the author of engraved teeth very similar in style to those of his brother. *Courtesy of Richard A. Bourne Co., Inc.*

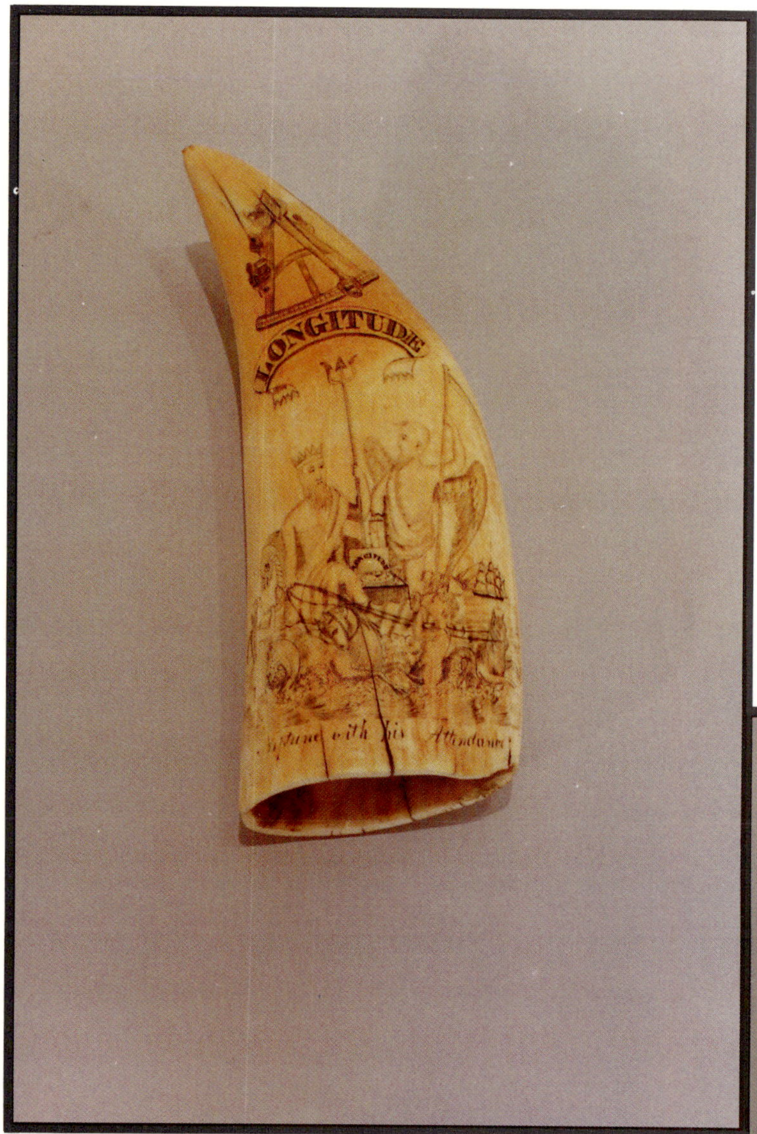

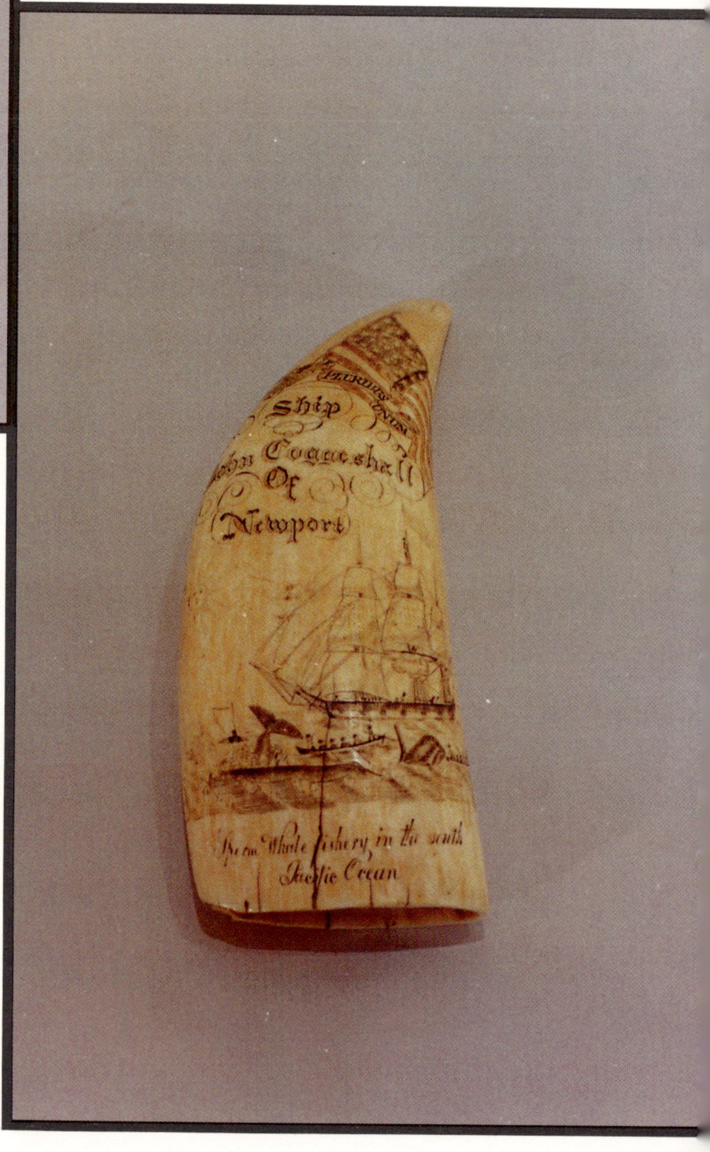

The *John Coggeshall* is again featured in this remarkable tooth whose reverse depicts King Neptune in his glory. Because the works of Caleb and Thomas Albro are so similar, it is not certain which brother engraved this unsigned tooth. However accurate renderings of navigational equipment, such as the ship's chronometer and octant depicted on this tooth, are extremely rare. Some collectors familiar with this tooth theorize that Thomas, in his position as steward, would have had more opportunity to observe and appreciate these instruments than his brother and is thus more likely to have been the artist. *Courtesy of the West Sea Company*

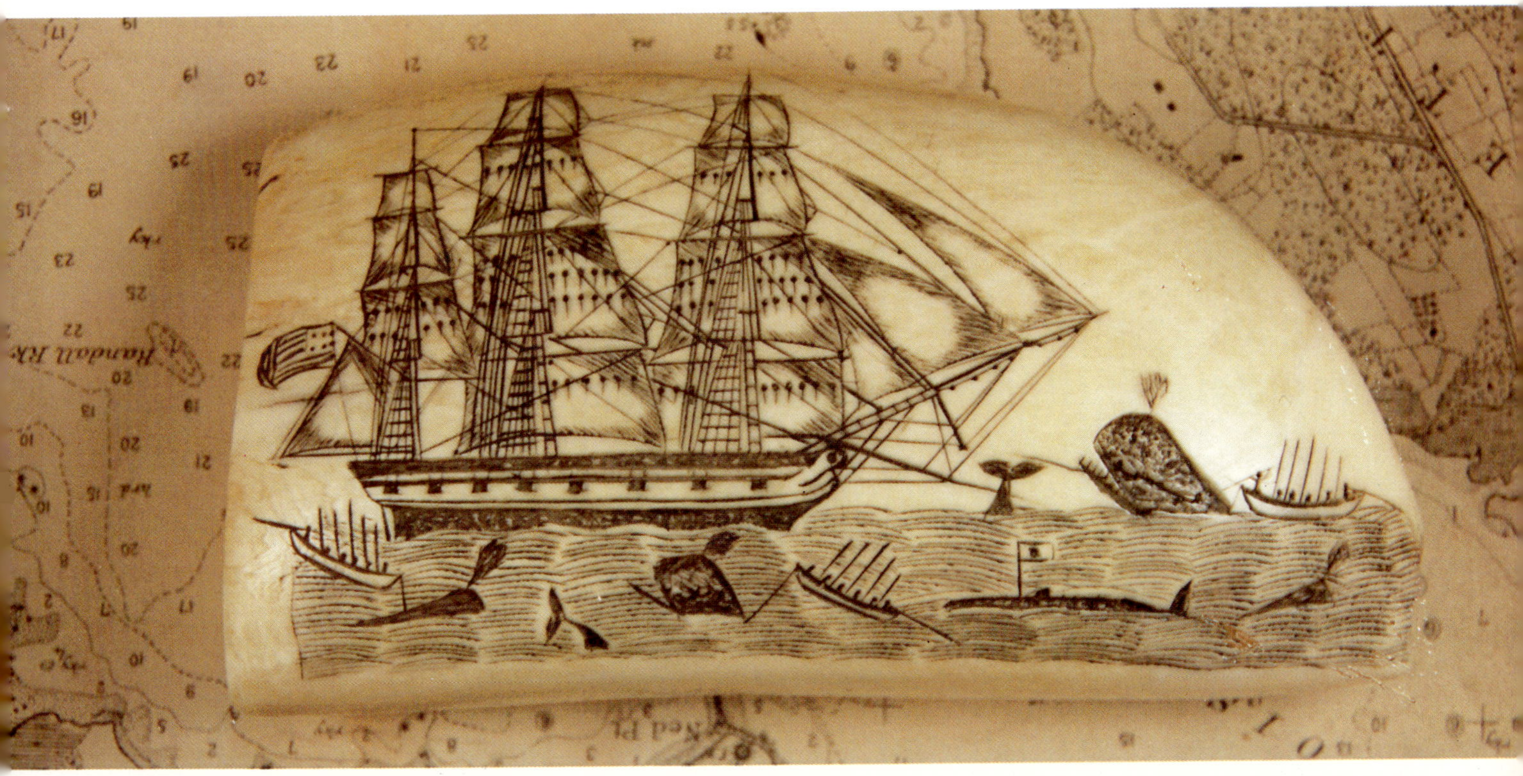

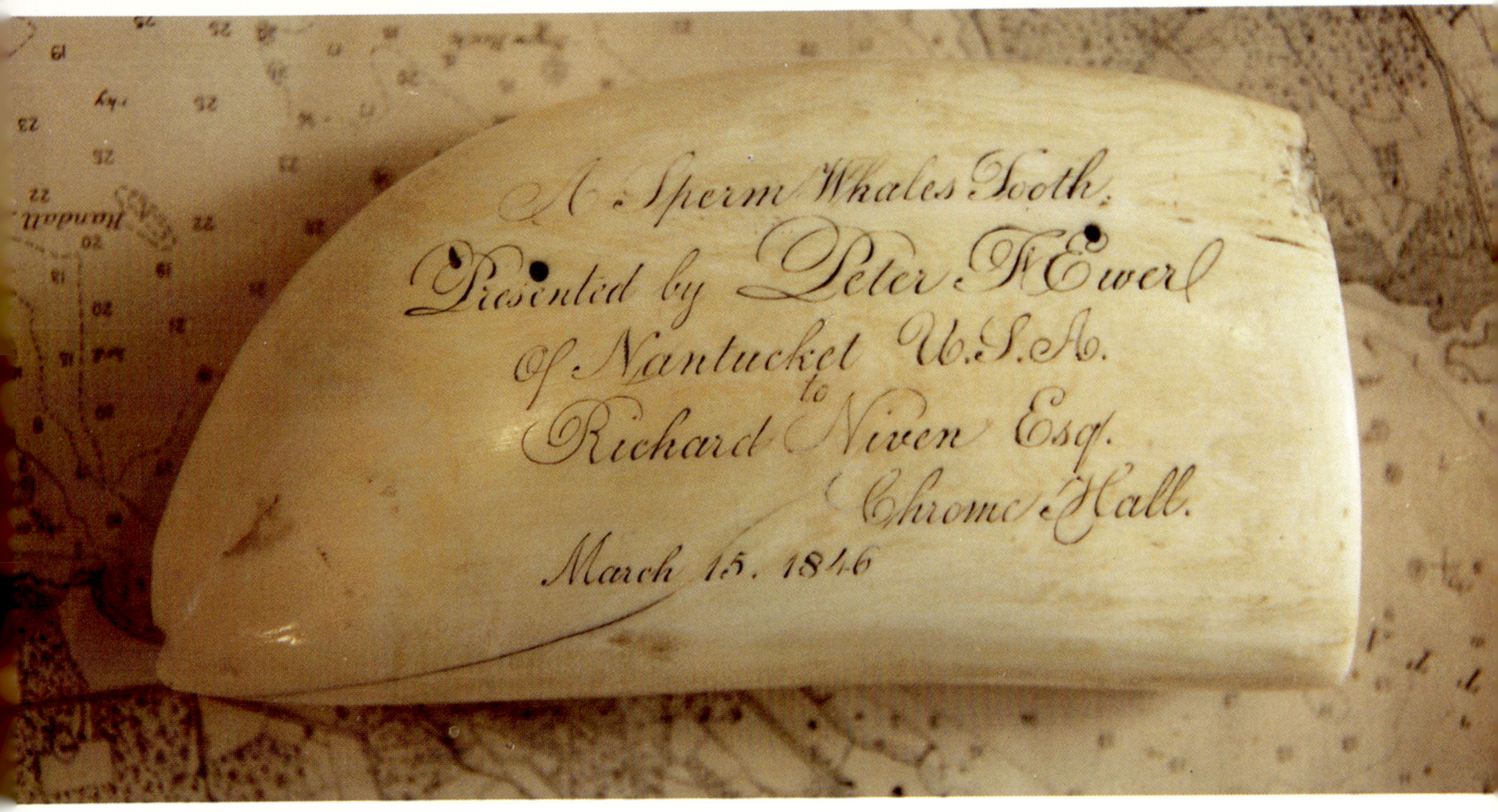

The wonderful whaling scene on this "presentation tooth" was executed by Edward Burdett and includes his identifying intaglio engraving technique. In 1846, more than a decade after Burdett's death, the tooth was presented by Peter F. Ewer who had adapted a Dutch version of floating drydocks for use in Nantucket Harbor. These "camels" were intended to move whaling vessels whose increasing capacity rendered them unable to clear the shallow sandbar at the harbor's entrance. Ewer's design was not a success, however, and the inability of many whalers to enter the harbor was a primary reason the island lost its ranking as the nation's busiest whaling port to the city of New Bedford. *Courtesy of the Nantucket Historical Association*

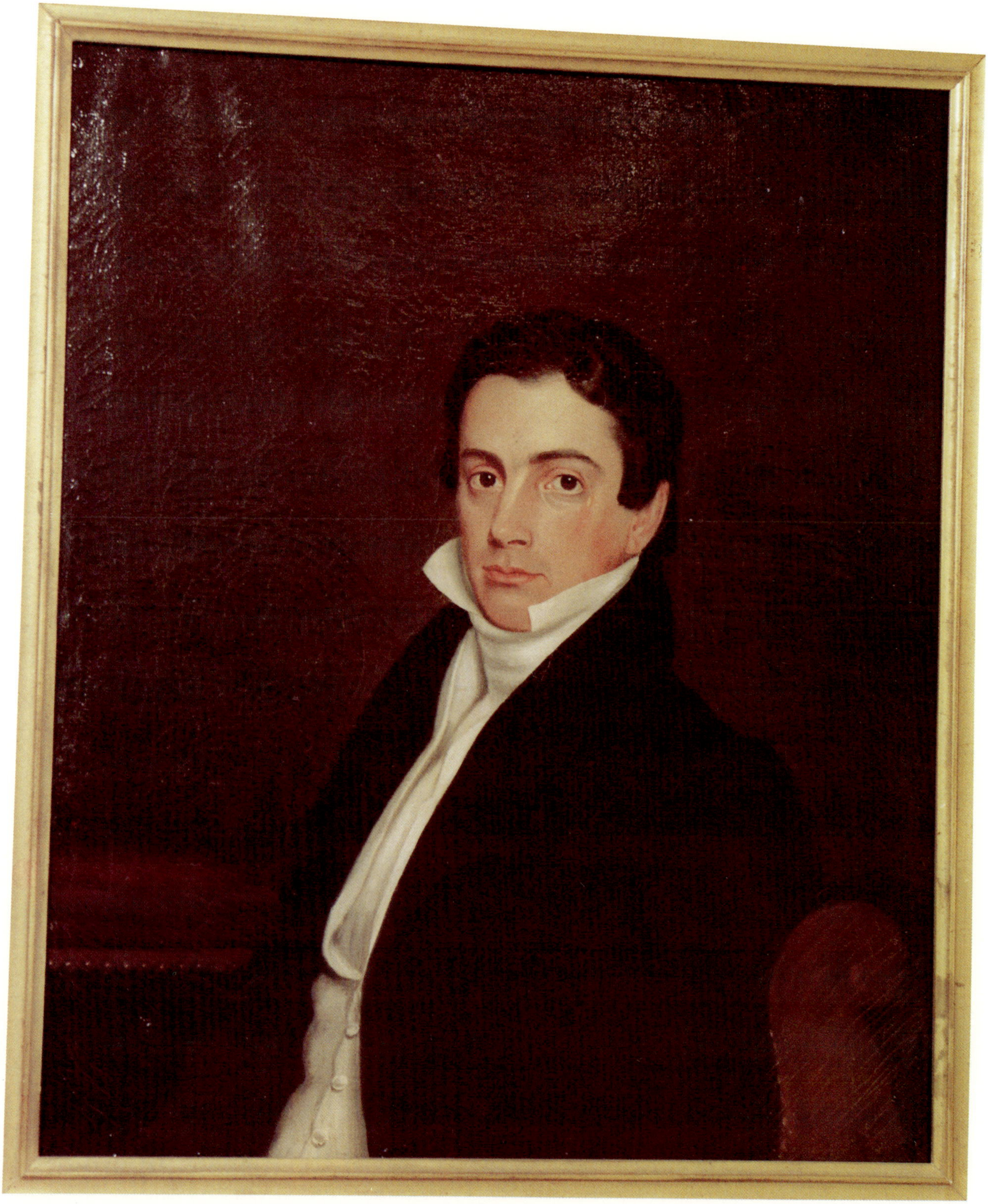

Peter F. Ewer as painted by William Swain *Courtesy of the Nantucket Historical Association*

Also gracing the mantel or tables of this "best" room of the house were many functional items made worthy of display by the scrimshander's skill. Well-proportioned, turned pickwicks pleased the eye as well as fulfilling their purpose of raising the wick in the parlor's oil lamp. Writing boxes fashioned of glowing tropical woods and embellished with a multitude of wonderful inlays shared space with whale ivory ink stands, seals, and sanders. Marvelously delicate pierced and lattice whalebone baskets served decorative as well as useful roles. A rendering of the absent mariner was safely encased in a scrimshawed picture frame, and an engraved cribbage board awaited his eventual return and respite between voyages.

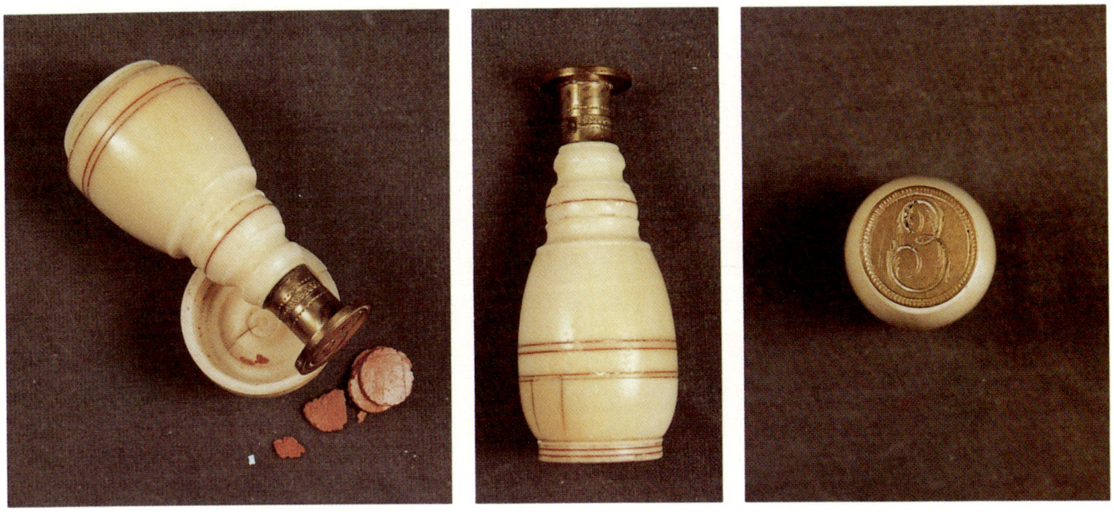

Another piece of scrimshaw owned by Peter Ewer is this lovely sealing stamp carved from a whale's tooth. The sealing wax could be stored in the hollow base of the stamp. *Madden Collection*

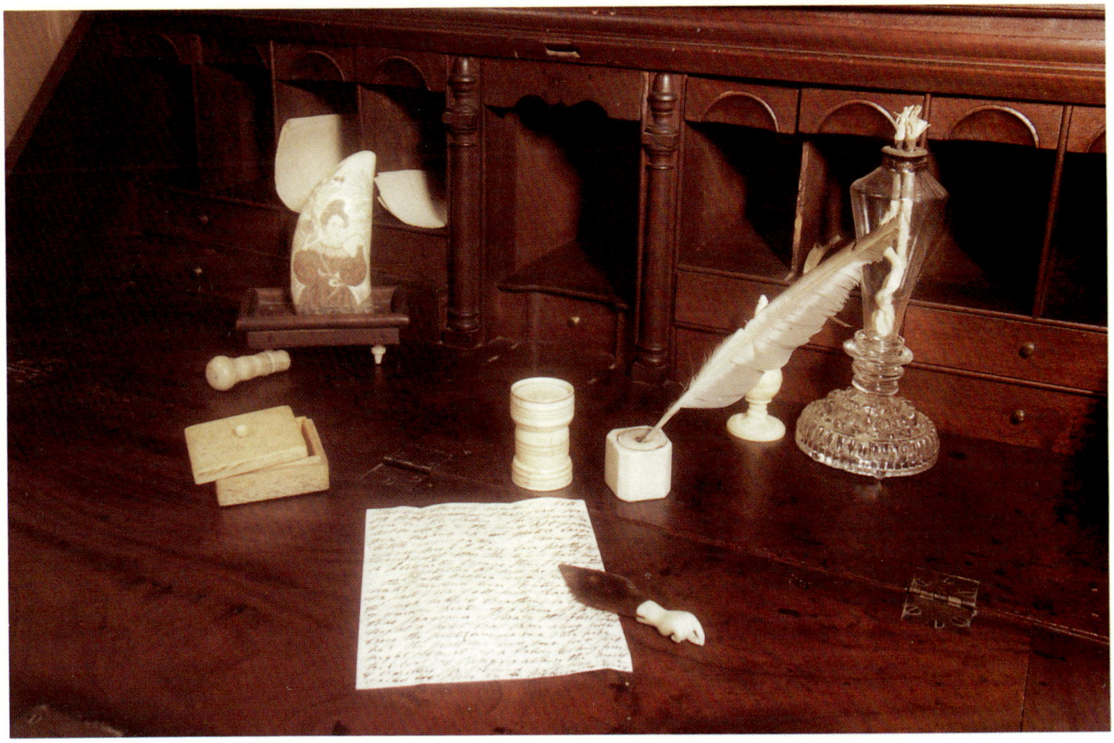

Among their many other uses, whalebone and whale ivory were incorporated into writing accessories. *Courtesy of the Nantucket Historical Association*

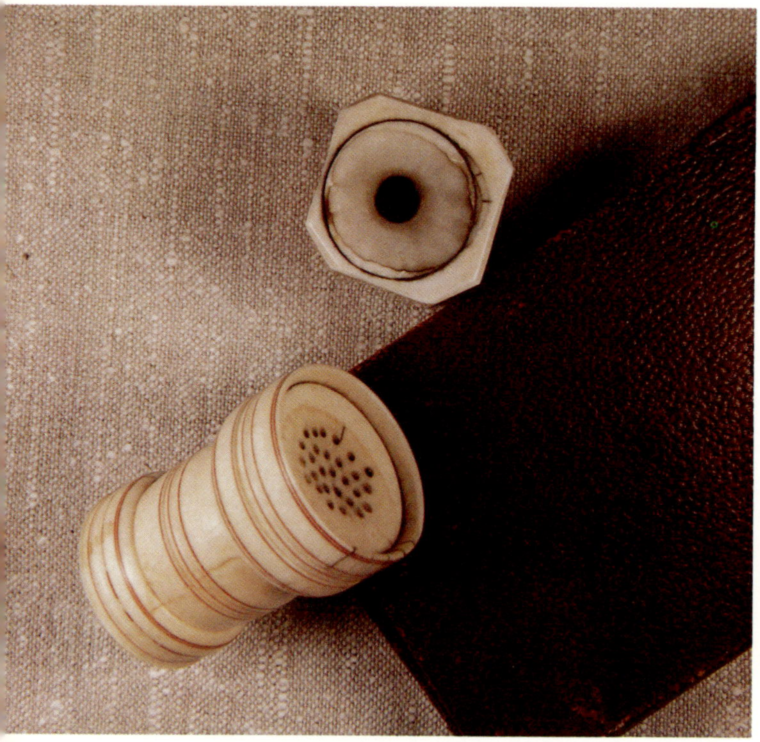

Both this ink well and pounce pot, which held sand for blotting fresh ink, were carved from the teeth of sperm whales. *Collection of the Nantucket Historical Association*

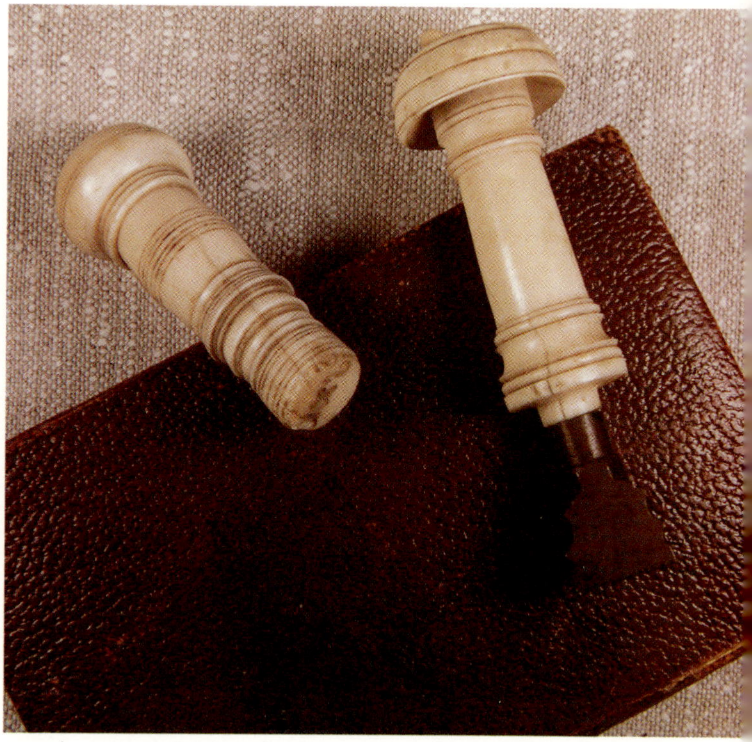

One of these sealing devices is carved completely from whale ivory while the other has a wooden seal attached to the handle. *Collection of the Nantucket Historical Association*

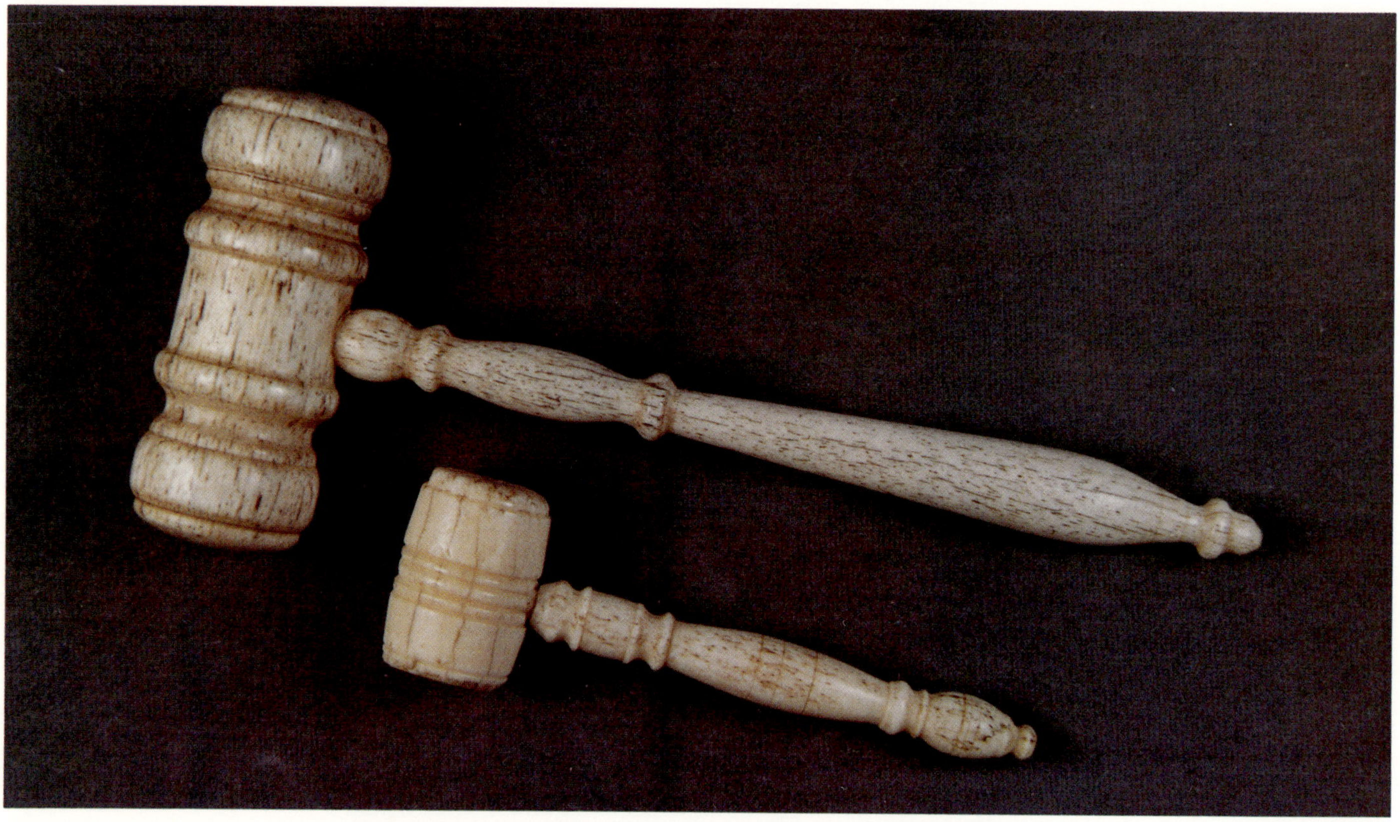

The smaller of these whalebone gavels has a head carved of whale ivory. *Private Collection*

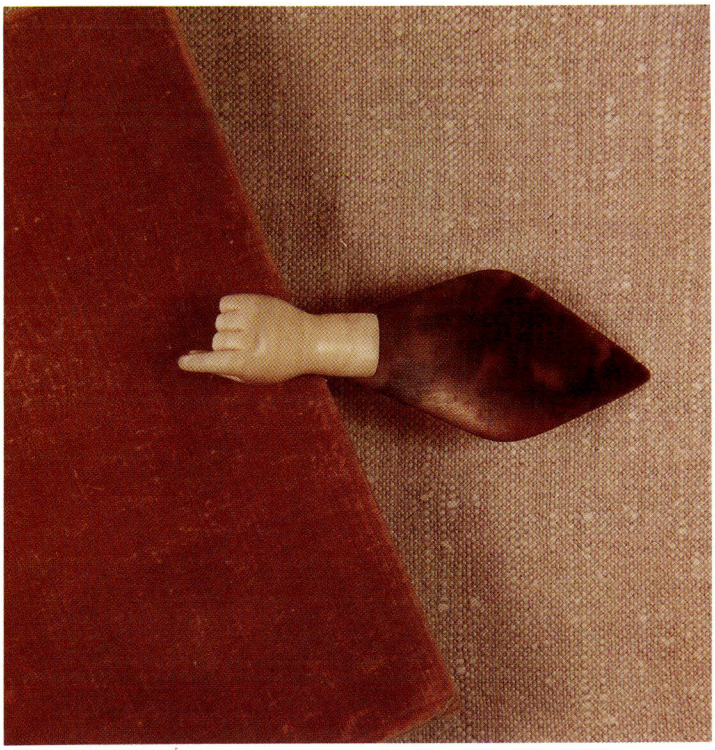

Lovely whale ivory and tortoise shell letter opener *Courtesy of the Nantucket Historical Association*

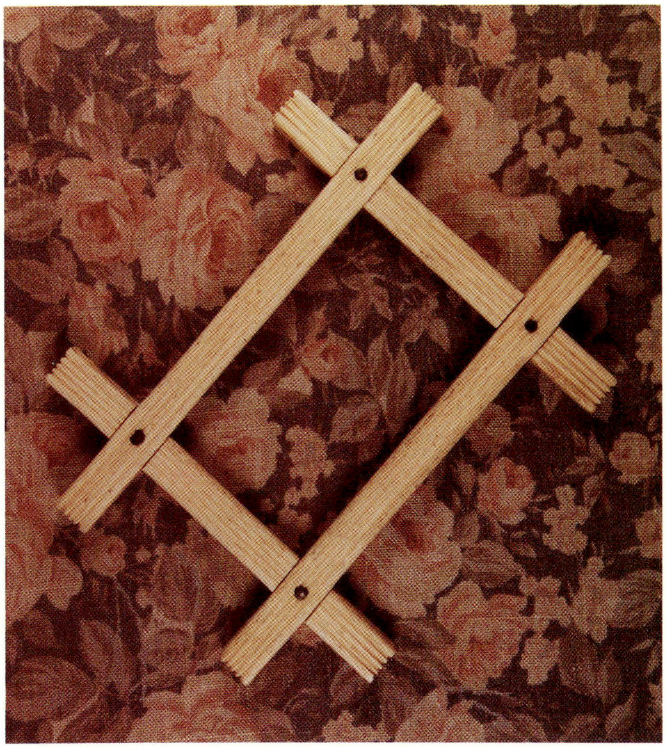

Simple whalebone frame *Courtesy of the Nantucket Historical Association*

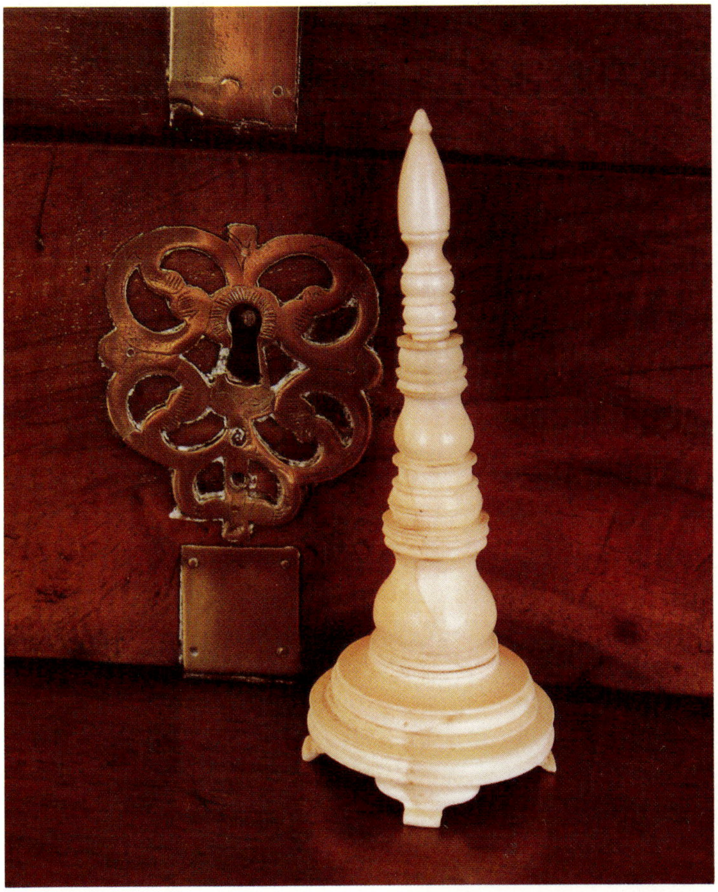

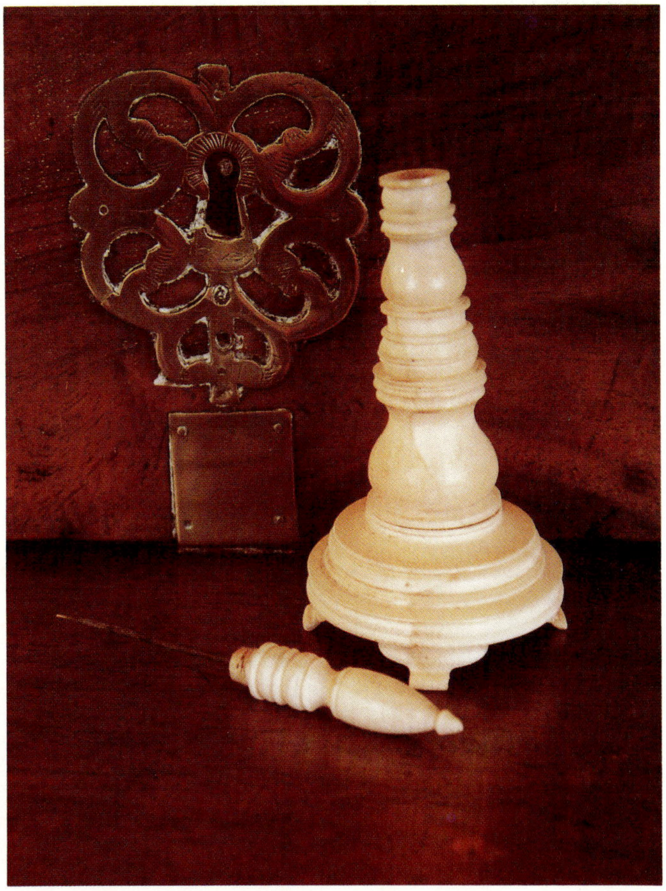

This beautifully turned whale ivory pick-wick reveals its more utilitarian nature when opened. *Madden Collection*

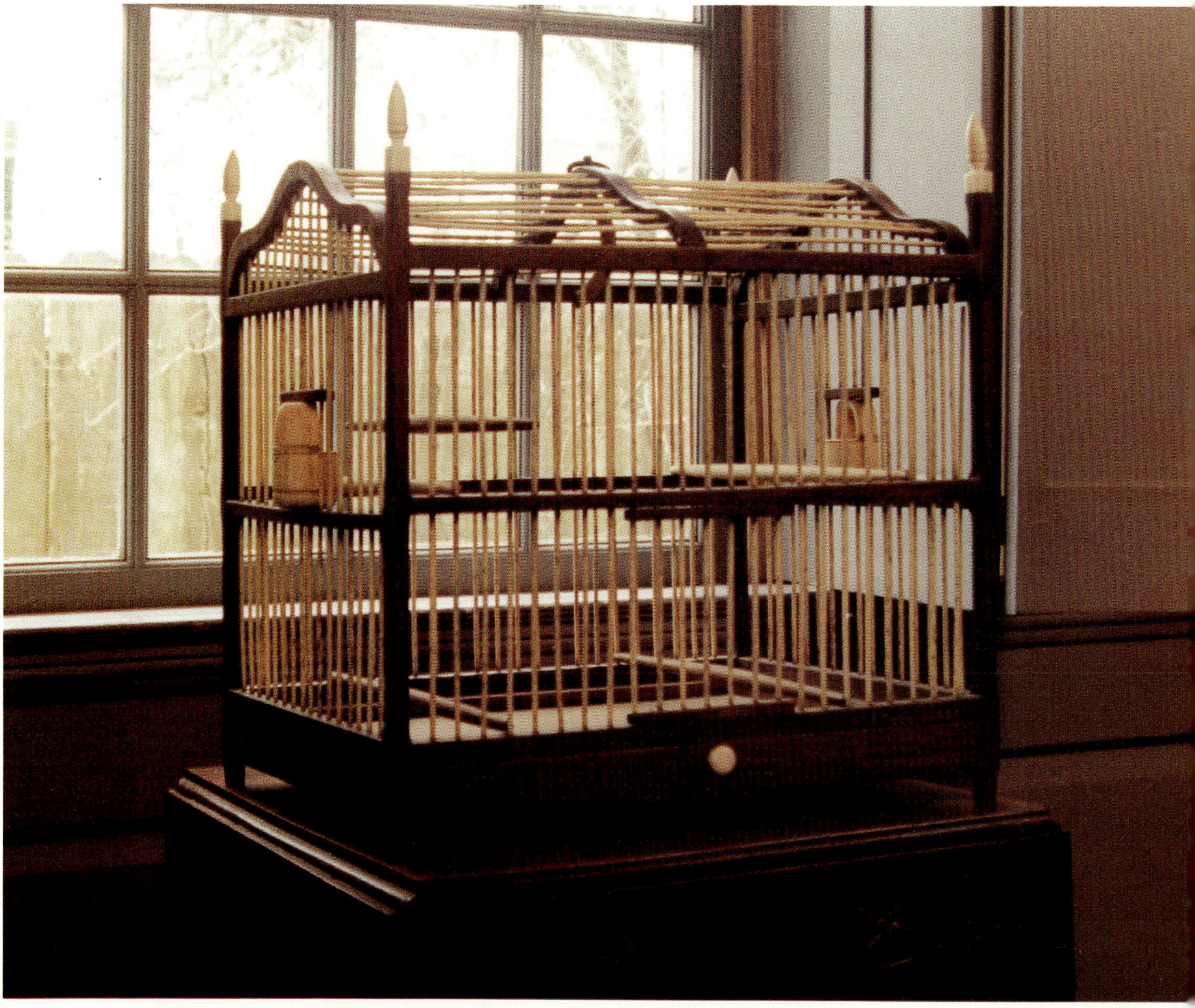

Log-keeper George Blanchard described the activity aboard the whaleship *America* on December 6th, 1841: "Light winds and squally; Work on rigging. Blacksmithing. Skrimshoning. Making Bird Cages." Often, cages such as those referred to by Blanchard and the one illustrated were constructed to house tropical birds captured during the voyage. *Courtesy of the Nantucket Historical Association*

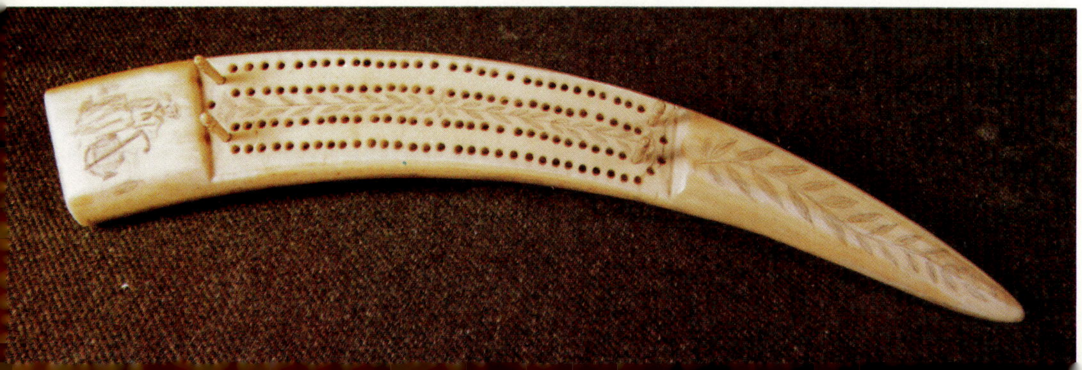

This graceful cribbage board was created from a walrus tusk. *Collection of Raymond and Elizabeth De Lucia*

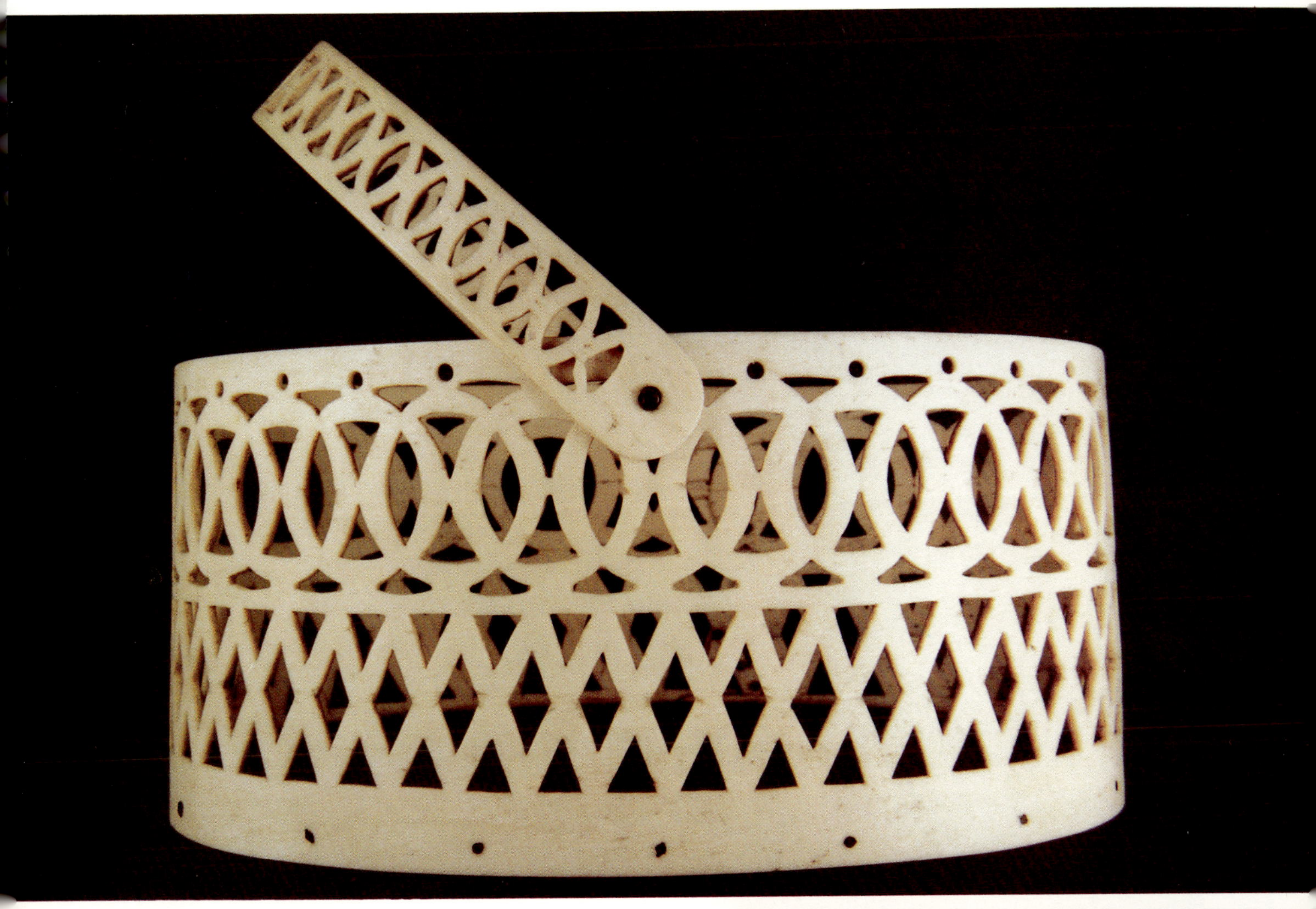

This sampling of wonderfully-carved and constructed whalebone baskets testifies to the skill and ingenuity of shipboard scrimshanders.

Madden Collection

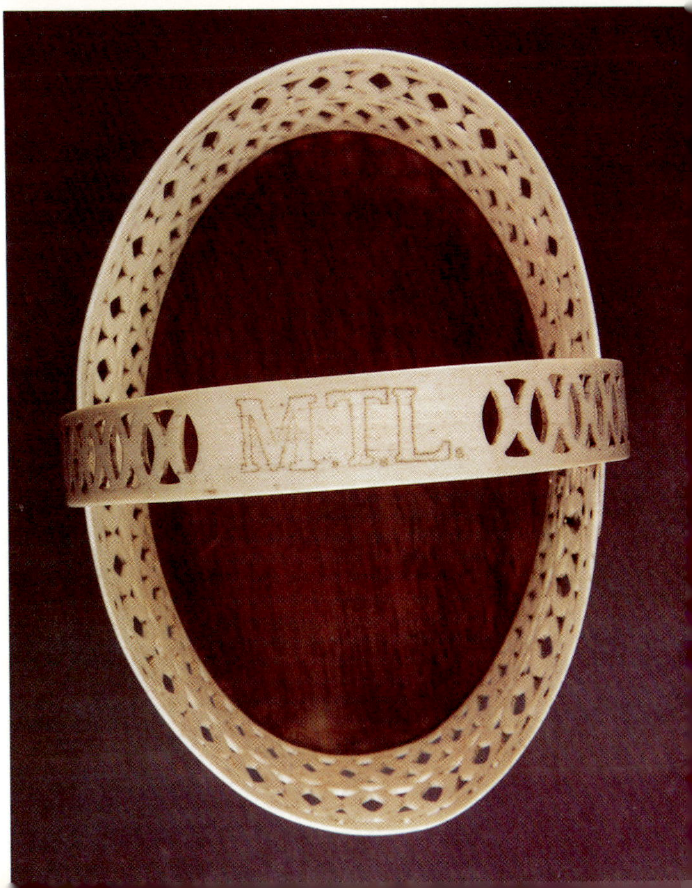

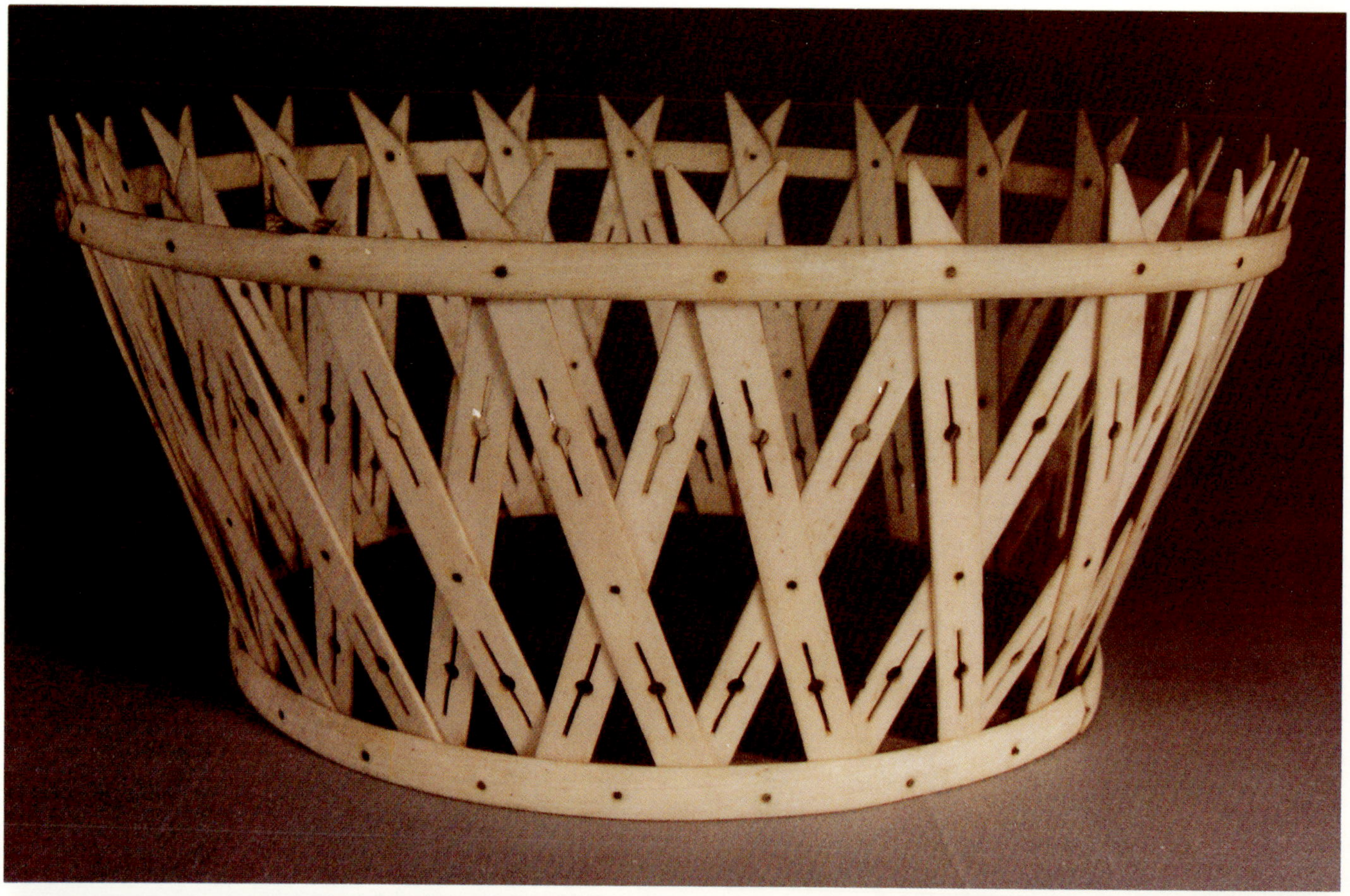

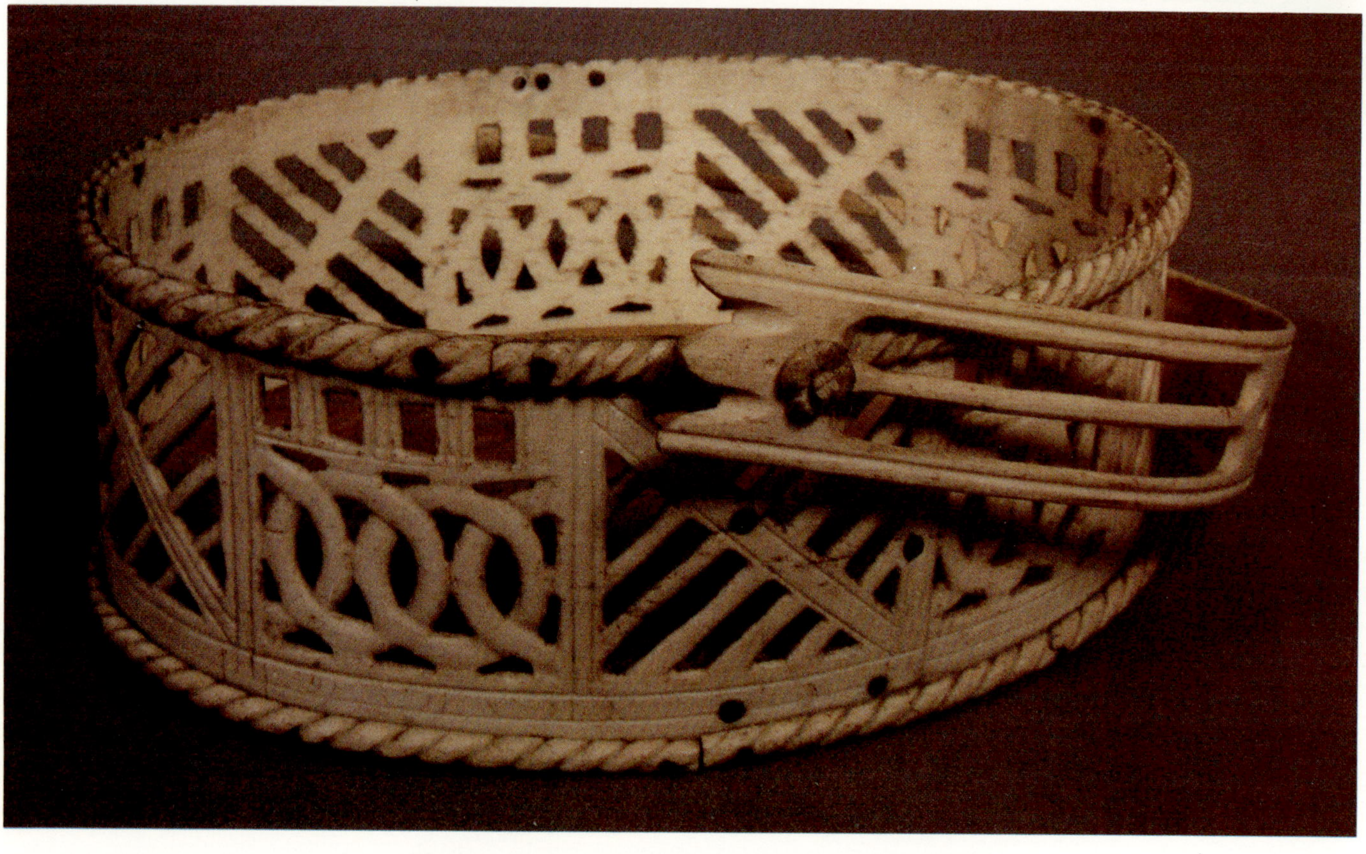

Courtesy of the Nantucket Historical Association

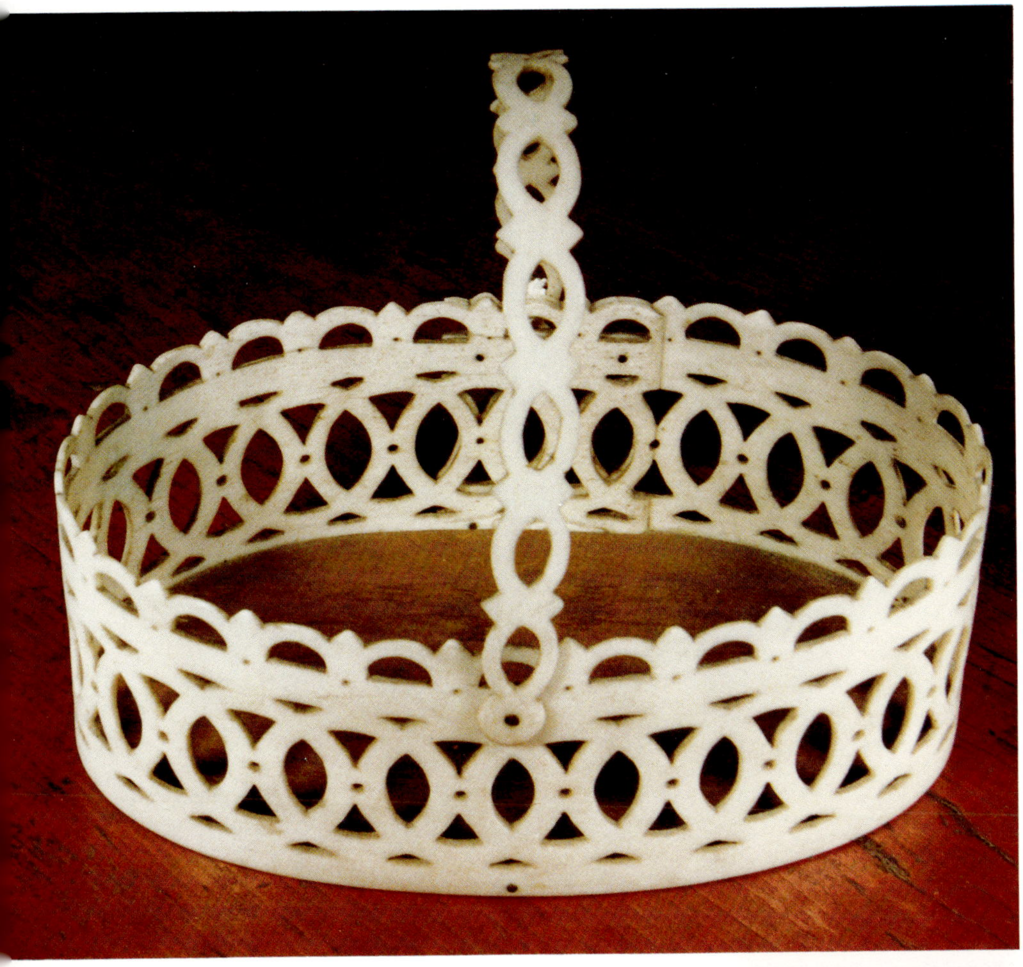

Private Collection

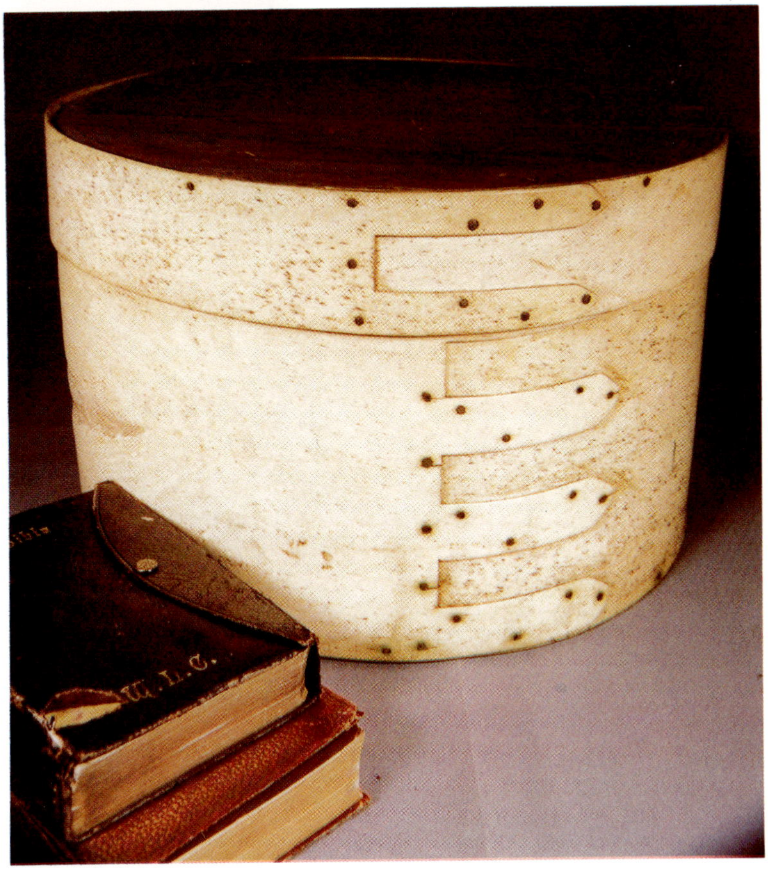

Whalebone work box with wooden lid. *Courtesy of the Nantucket Historical Association*

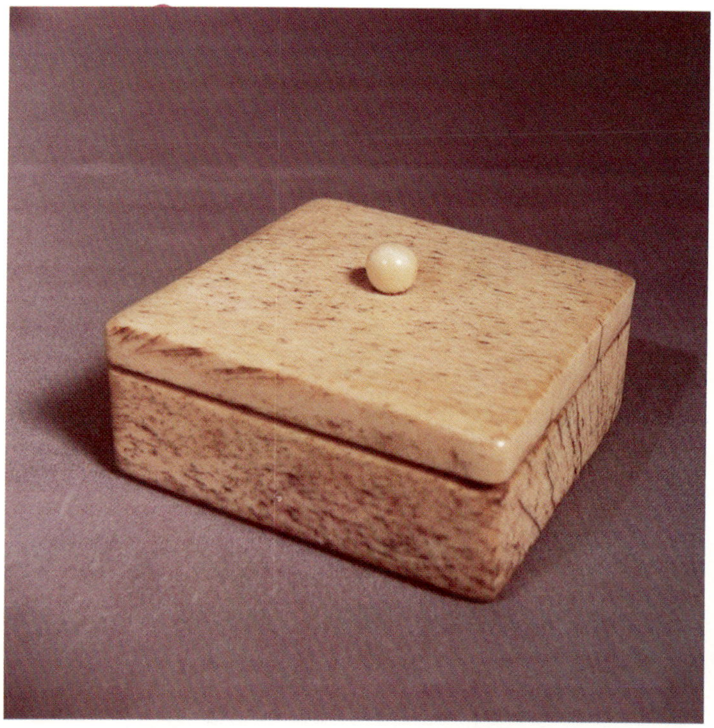

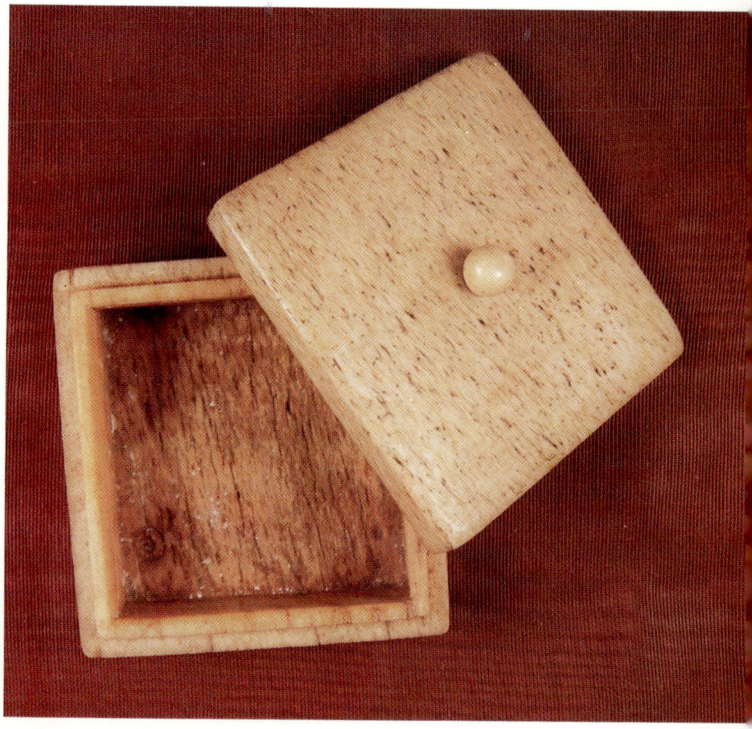

The only adornment added to this small, shallow whalebone box was a simple whale ivory knob. *Courtesy of the Nantucket Historical Association*

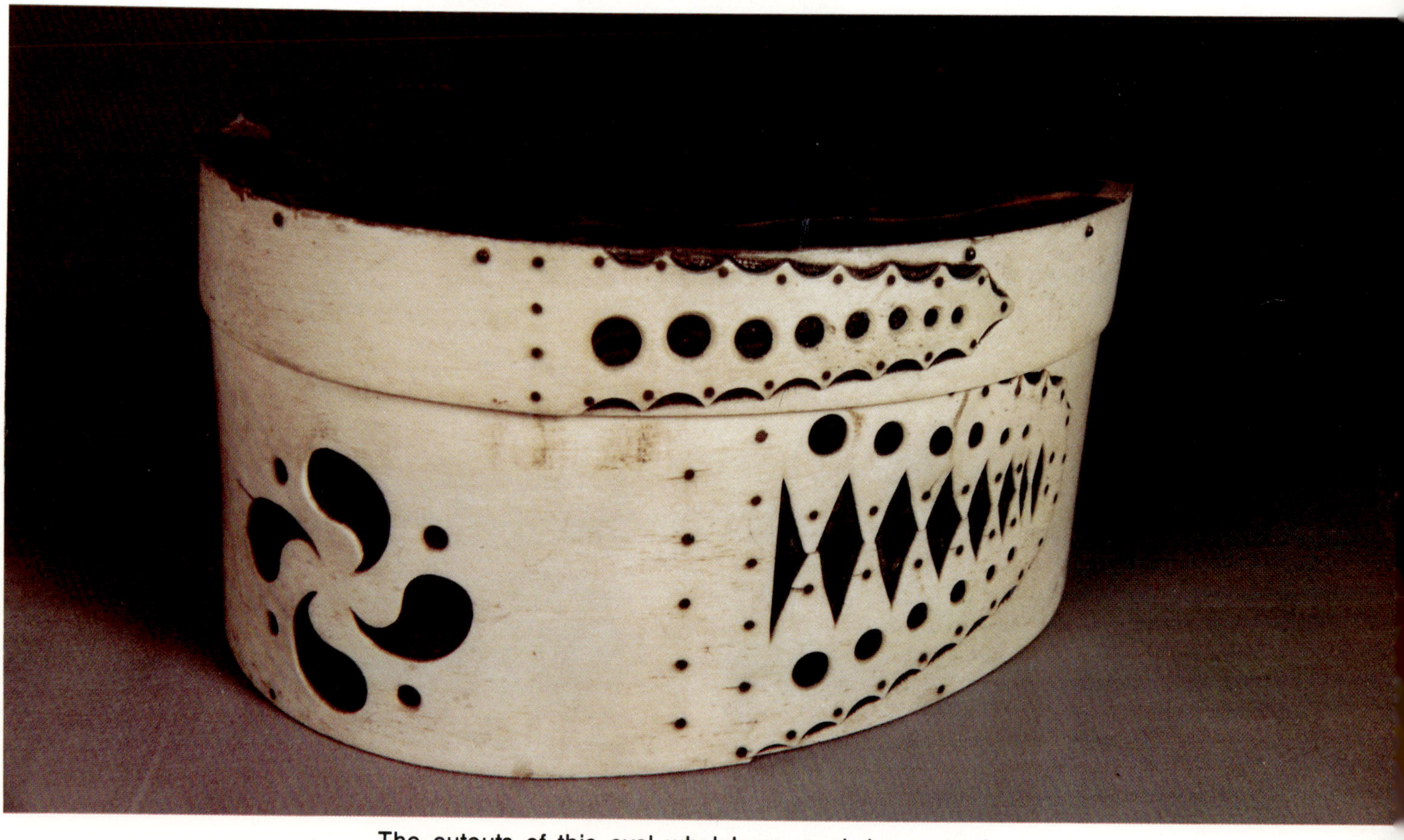

The cutouts of this oval whalebone work box reveal baleen beneath. *Courtesy of the Nantucket Historical Association*

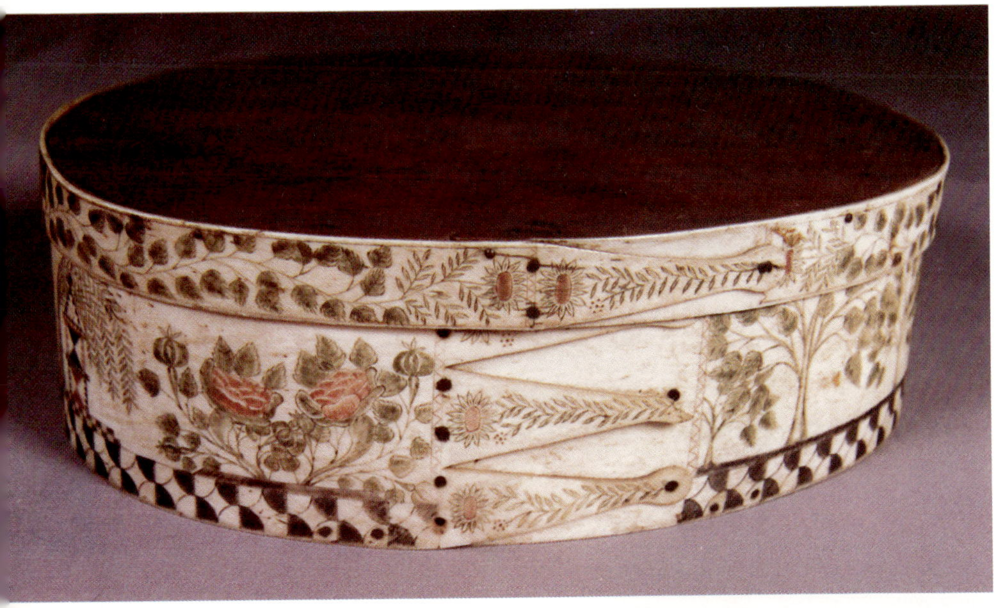

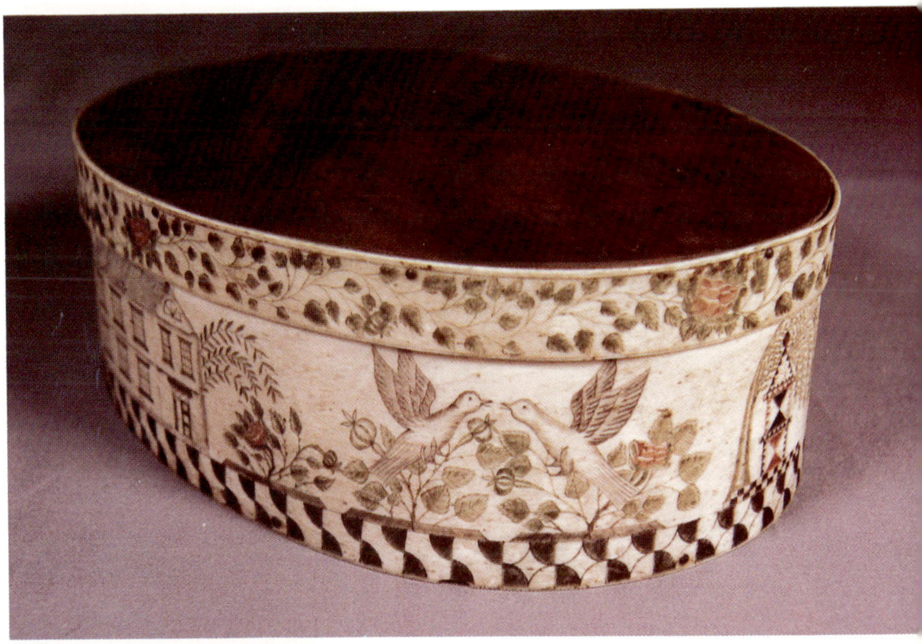

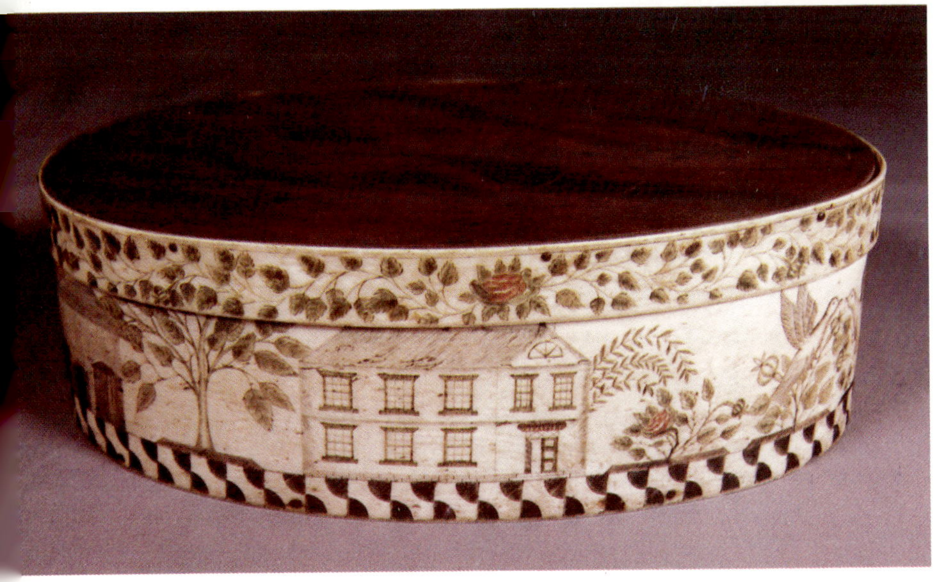

Romantic and nostalgic images abound on this exquisitely engraved polychrome whalebone box. *Courtesy of the Nantucket Historical Association*

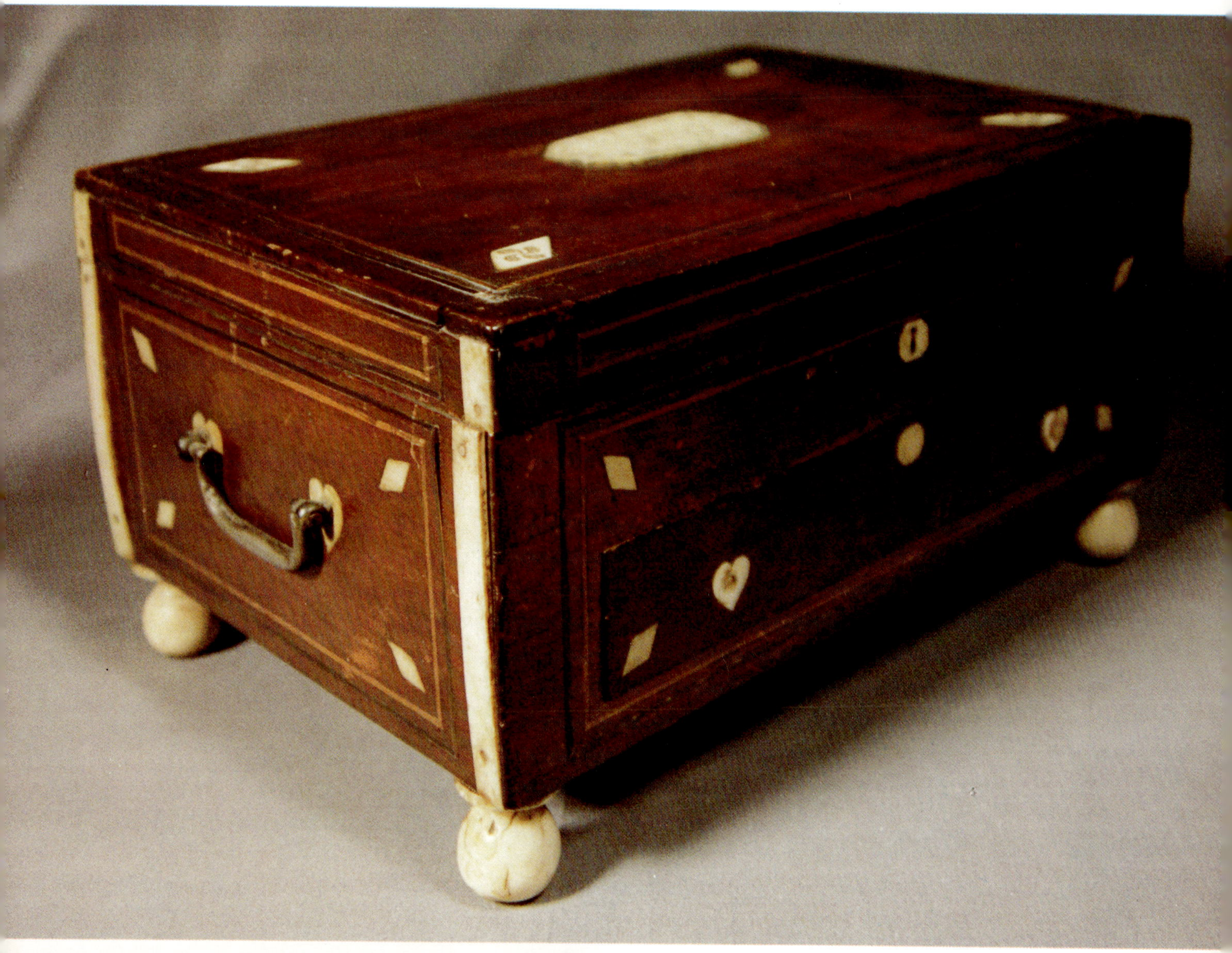

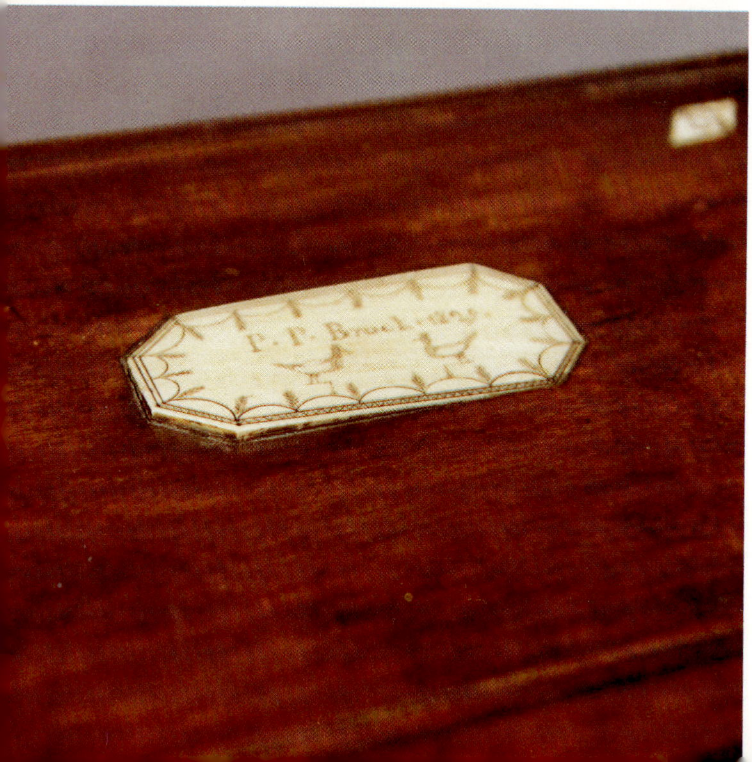

The whale ivory inlay on the top of this box is inscribed "P. P. Brock 1829" and refers to its maker Captain Priam P. Brock of Nantucket who was killed only four years later when he and the five other crewmembers of his whaleboat were lost while hunting a whale. *Courtesy of the Nantucket Historical Association*

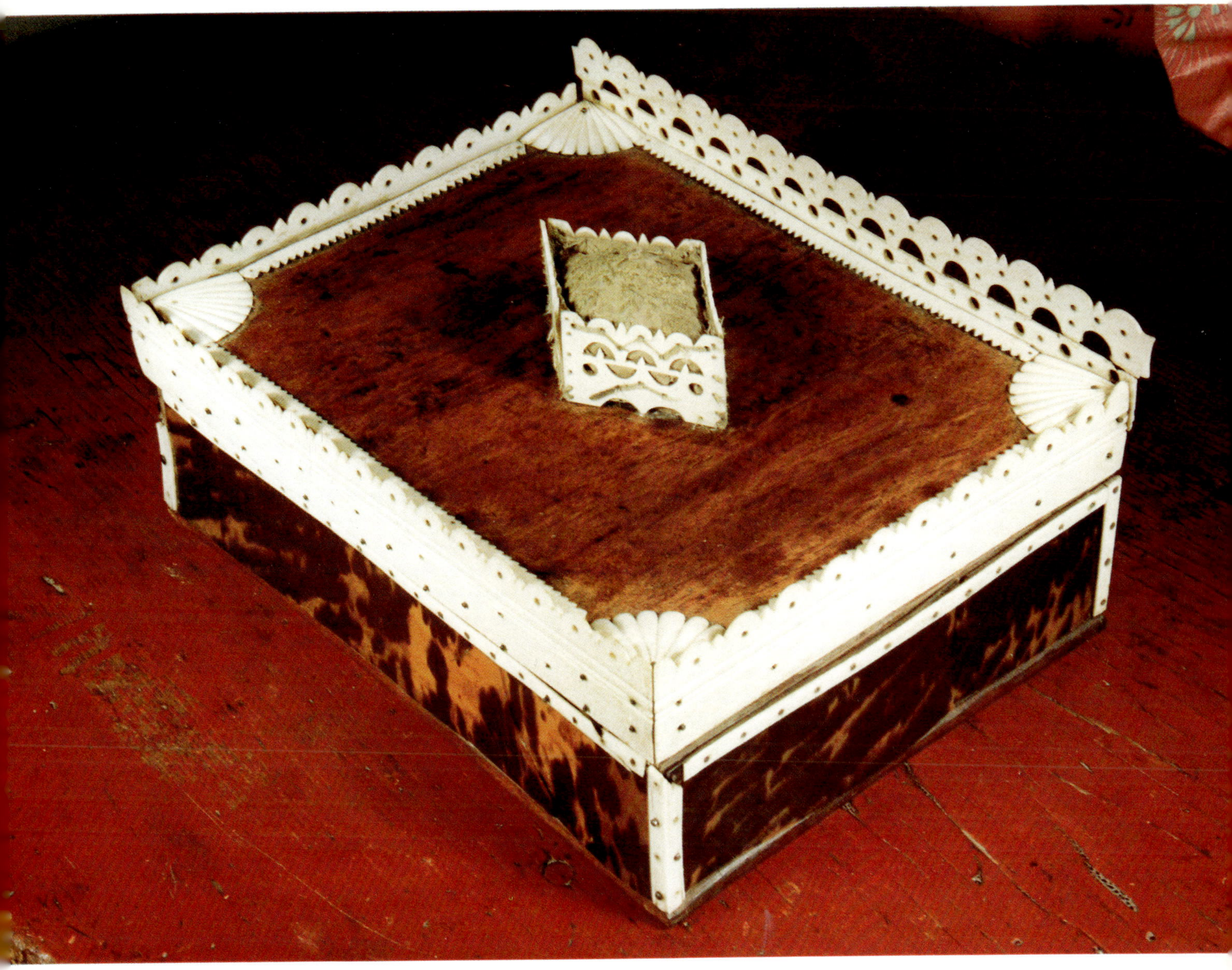

A lace-like trim, carved of whale ivory, adorns this unusual sewing box whose sides are constructed of tortoise shell. A pincushion sits on the wooden top. *Private Collection*

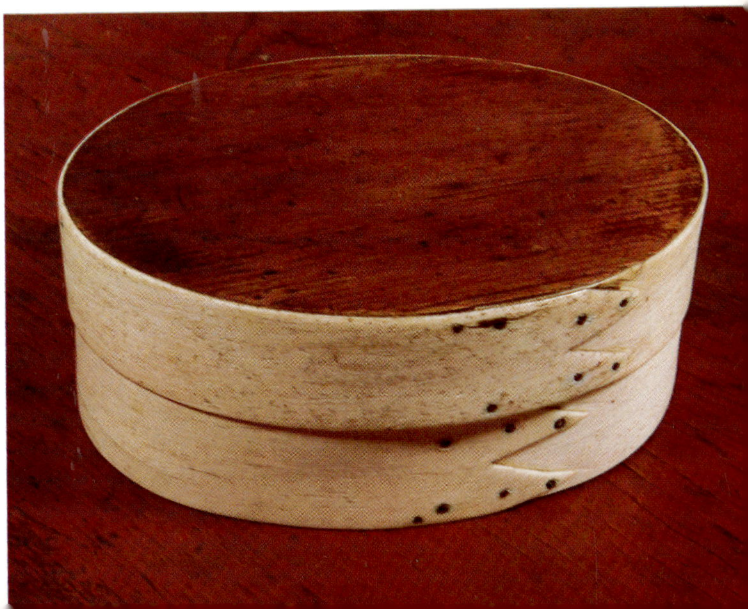

Any embellishment would be superfluous on this simply perfect whalebone box. *Private Collection*

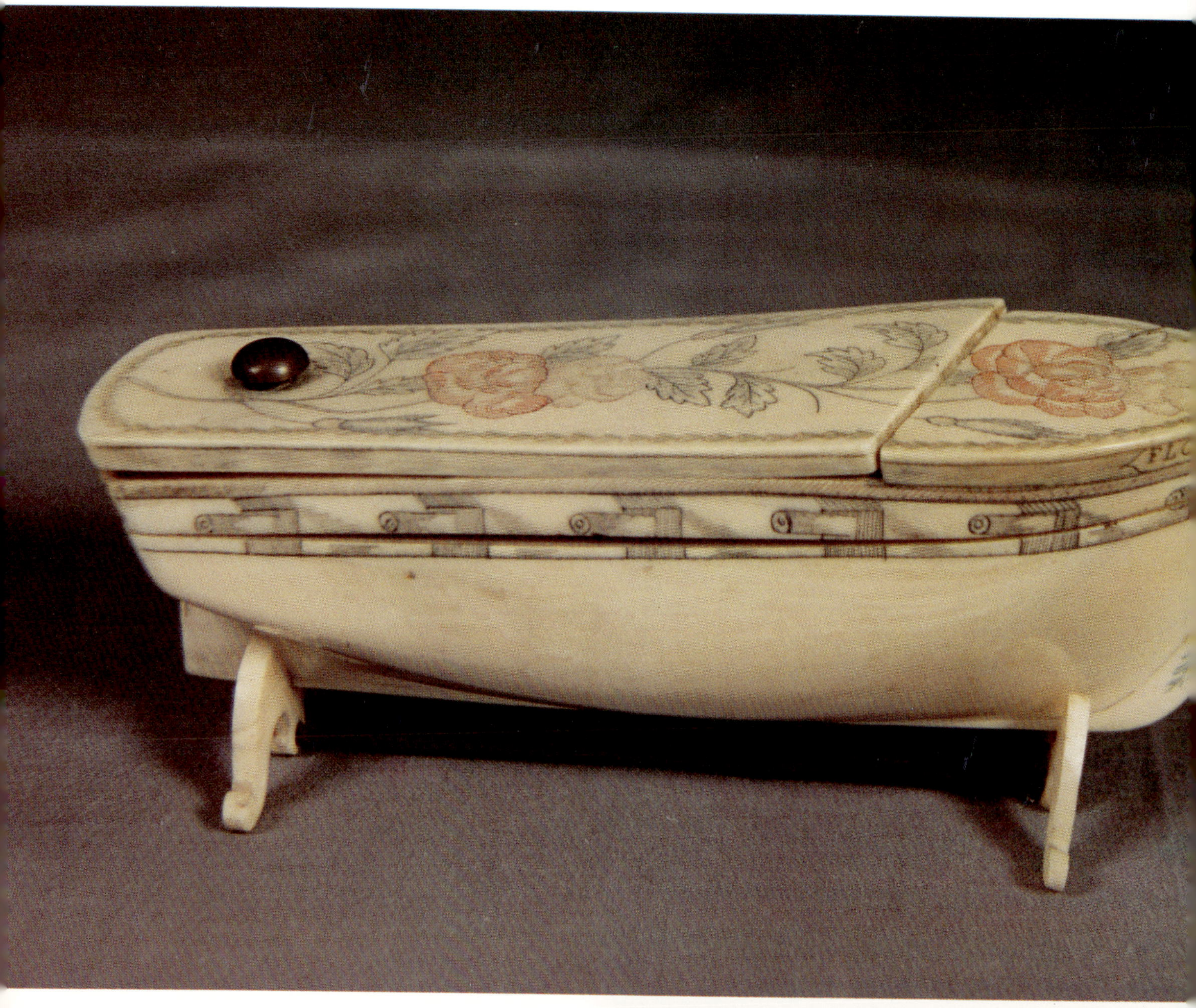

This exquisite, whale ivory treasure box was christened "Florinda" and sits in its own engraved stand. The top slides to the side to reveal the interior. *Collection of the Nantucket Historical Association*

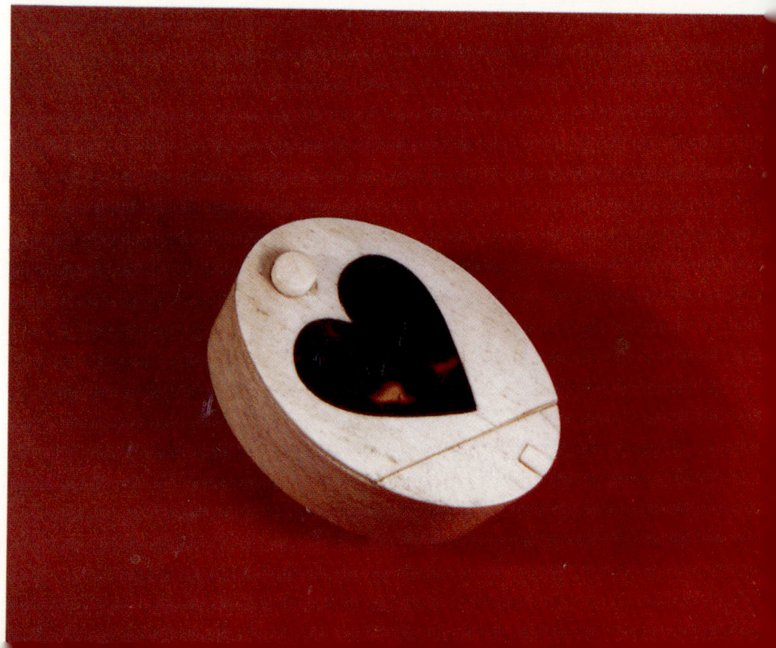

Patience and concentration is required to open this ingenious whalebone puzzle box whose heart-shaped interior exactly repeats the pattern of the tortoise shell inlay on the top. *Madden Collection*

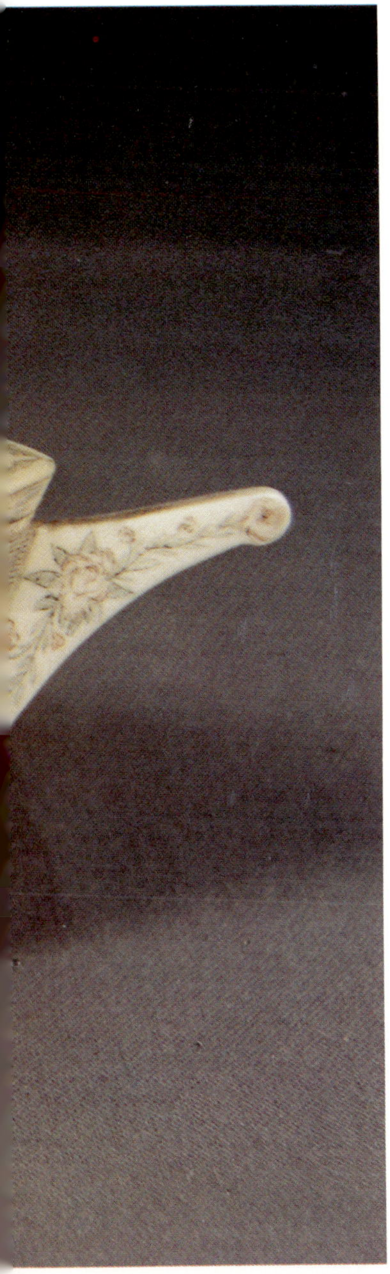

In eighteen hundred twenty-three,
March the twentieth day,
We hauled our larboard tacks aboard,
For home we put away.

-

Out mainmast now being somewhat weak,
We thought it best to fix it,
Lest on our passage round the cape
Some accident should dish it....

-

And having fitted well our ship
To pass Cape Horn again,
Each man then fore and aft the ship,
Scrimshauning did begin.

-

The knitting sheaths and jagging knives
Were cut in every form,
And other trinkets for the girls,
As presents from Cape Horn....

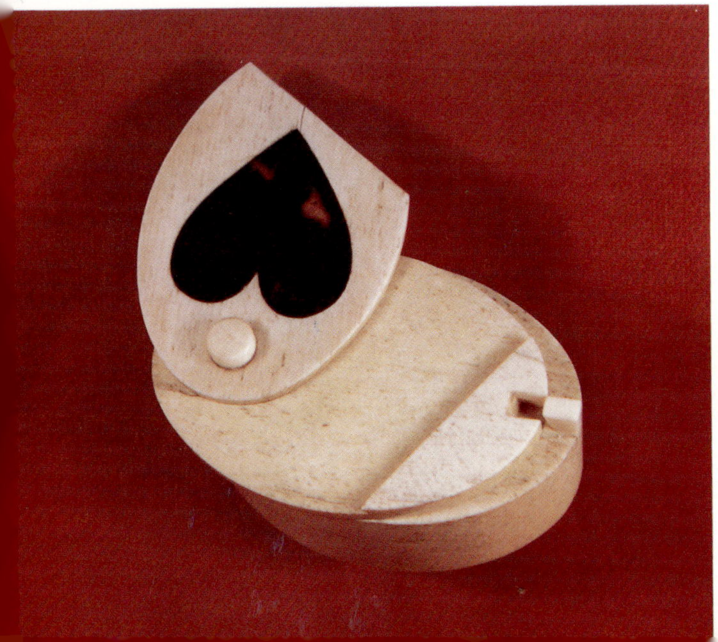

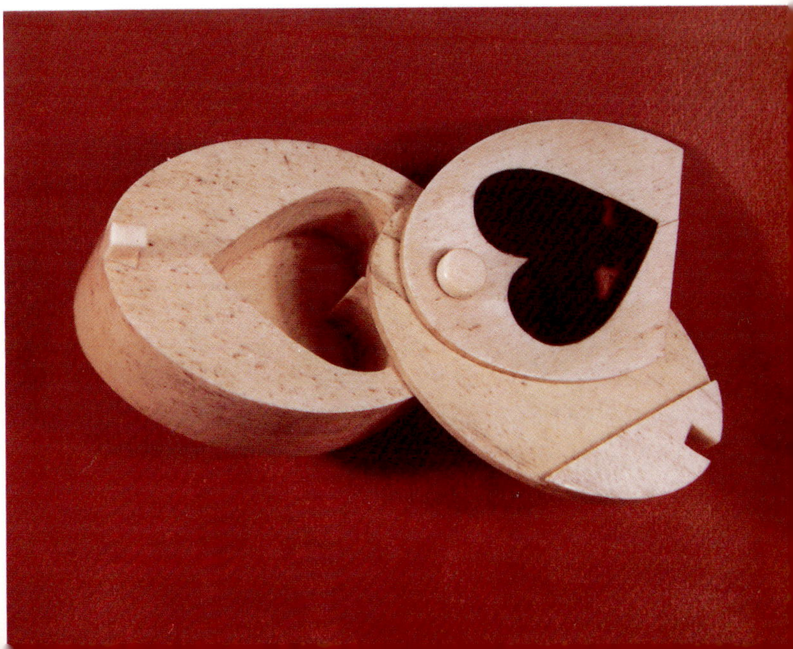

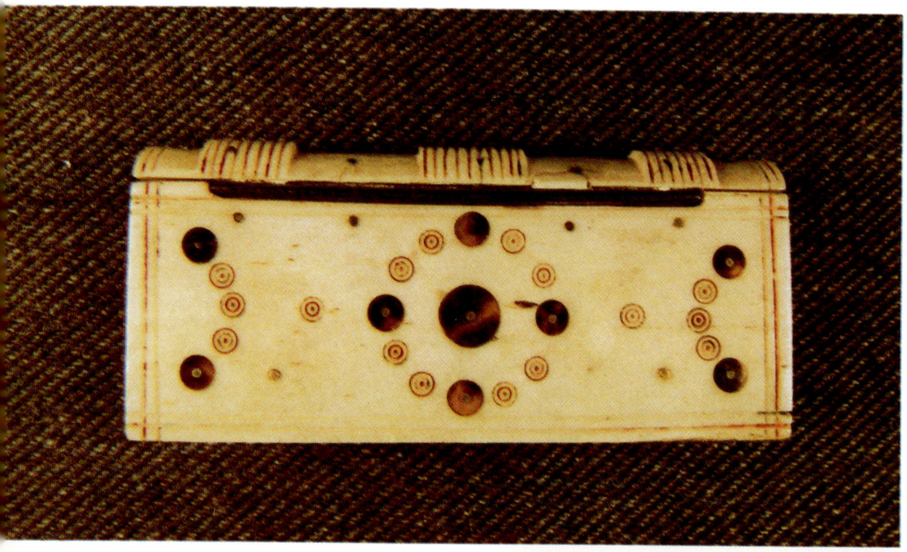

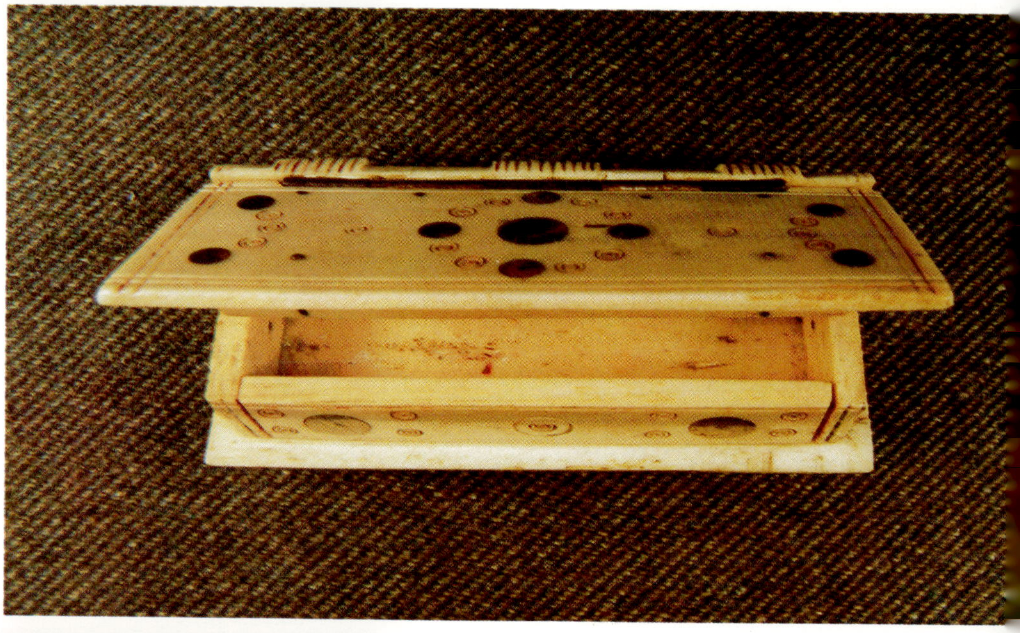

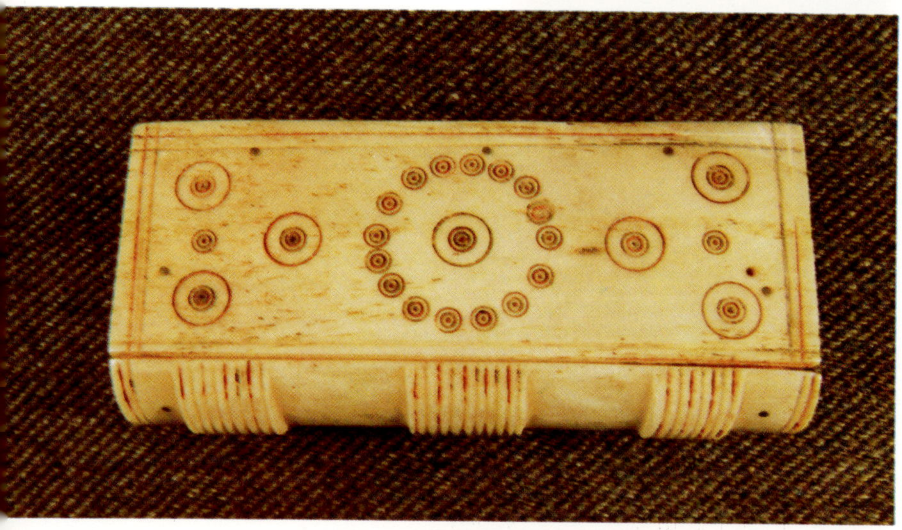

This book-shaped box is inlaid with tortoise shell and colored with sealing wax. *Collection of Raymond and Elizabeth De Lucia*

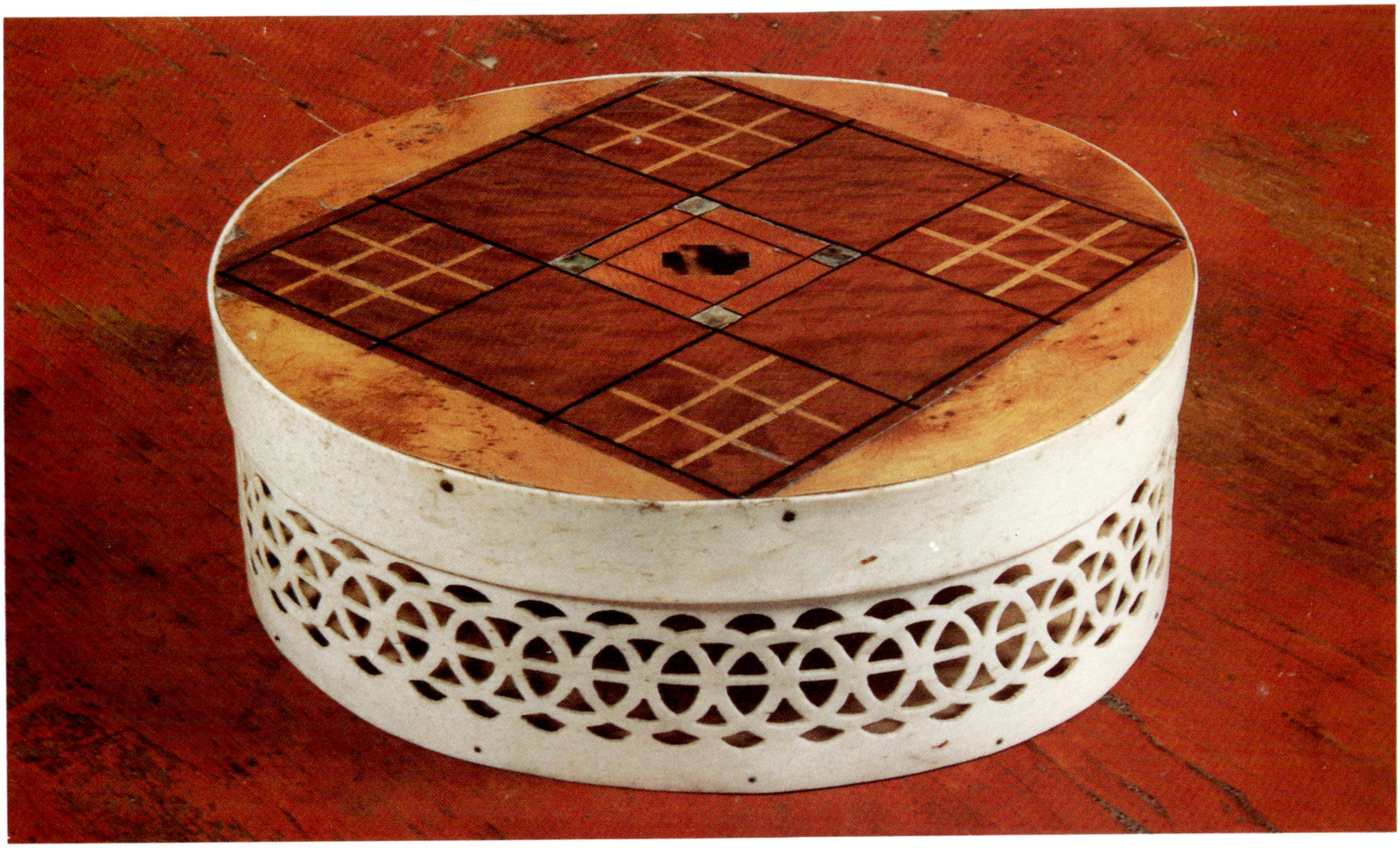

A practiced craftsman constructed this elegant, pierced oval whalebone box whose top is inlaid with various woods, abalone and tortoise shell. *Private Collection*

Scrimshawed toys, blocks, alphabet letters, teething rings, rattles, and dolls' beds resided in the childrens' rooms, clearly indicating the loving thoughts of fathers, uncles, and brothers pursuing their livelihoods at sea. These children's gifts were intended to provide happy hours of enjoyment, and remarkably some have survived their years of use.

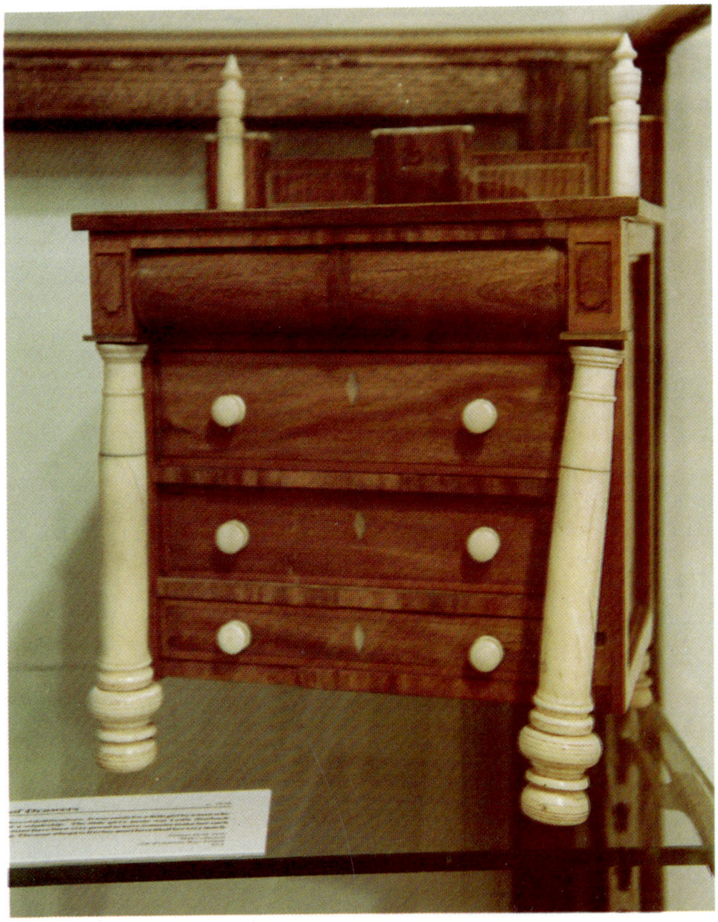

Lydia Starbuck Paddock of Nantucket was the fortunate young lady believed to have received this tamana wood doll's chest adorned with whale ivory. *Courtesy of the Nantucket Historical Association*

Examples of the scrimshander's versatility were also found in the family's private quarters. On a gentleman's dresser rested grooming instruments such as toothpicks, ear cups, brushes, and other useful implements. Another masculine piece was the watch stand which provided a place of display and protection for one of a man's most valuable possessions.

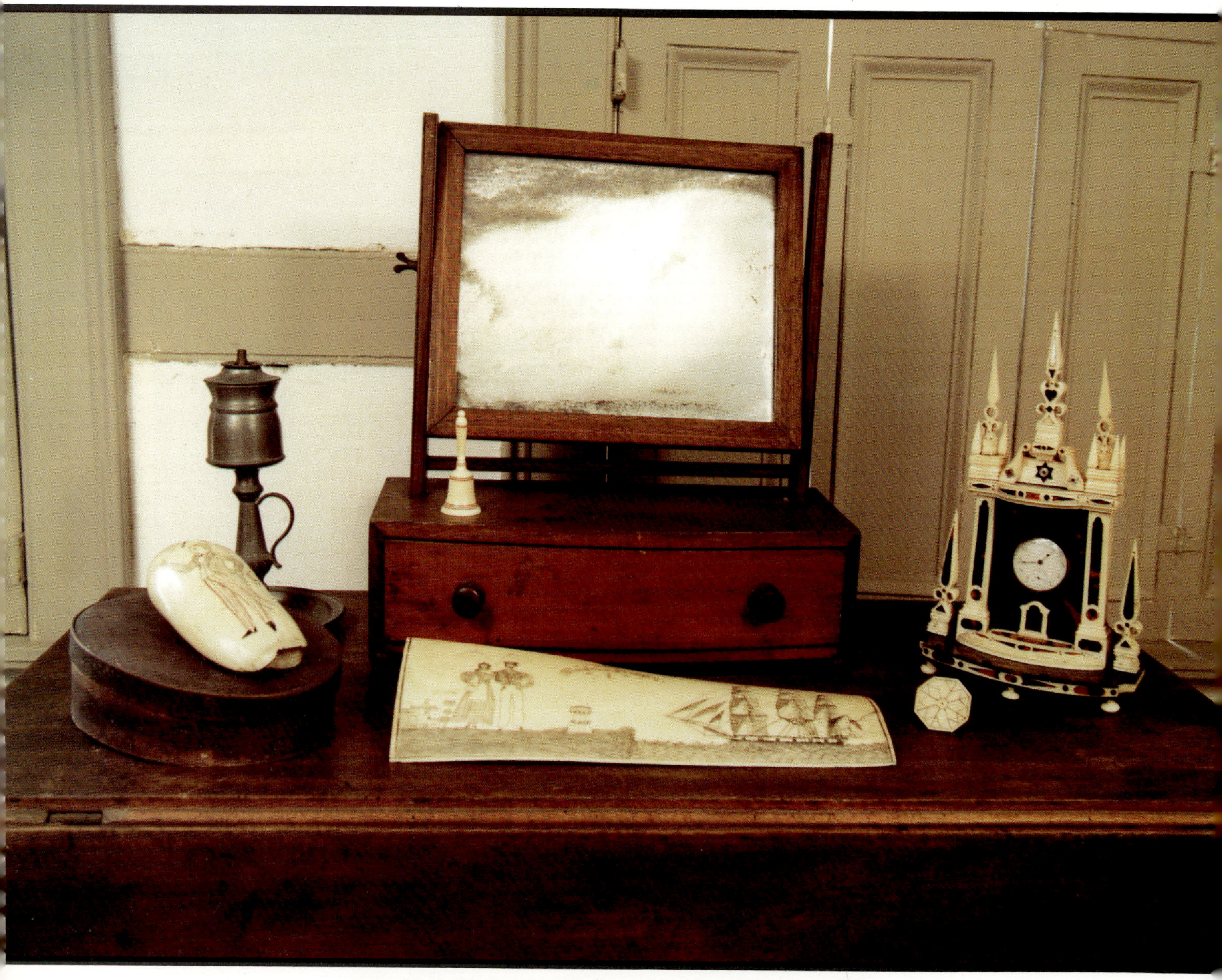

A second floor bed chamber of Nantucket's "1800 House" *Courtesy of the Nantucket Historical Association*

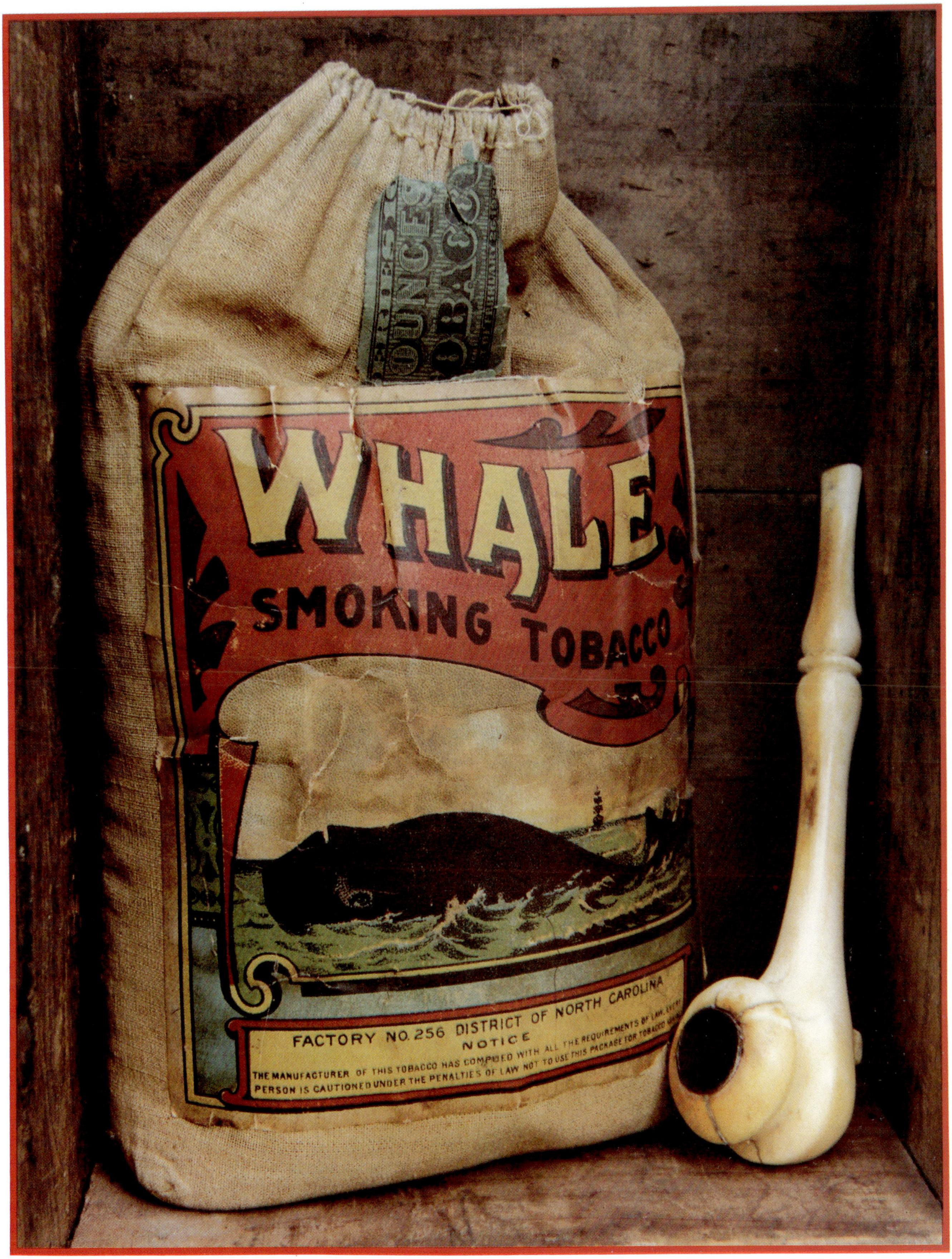

This whale ivory sailor's pipe reflects its years of use.
Collection of Charles A. Manghis

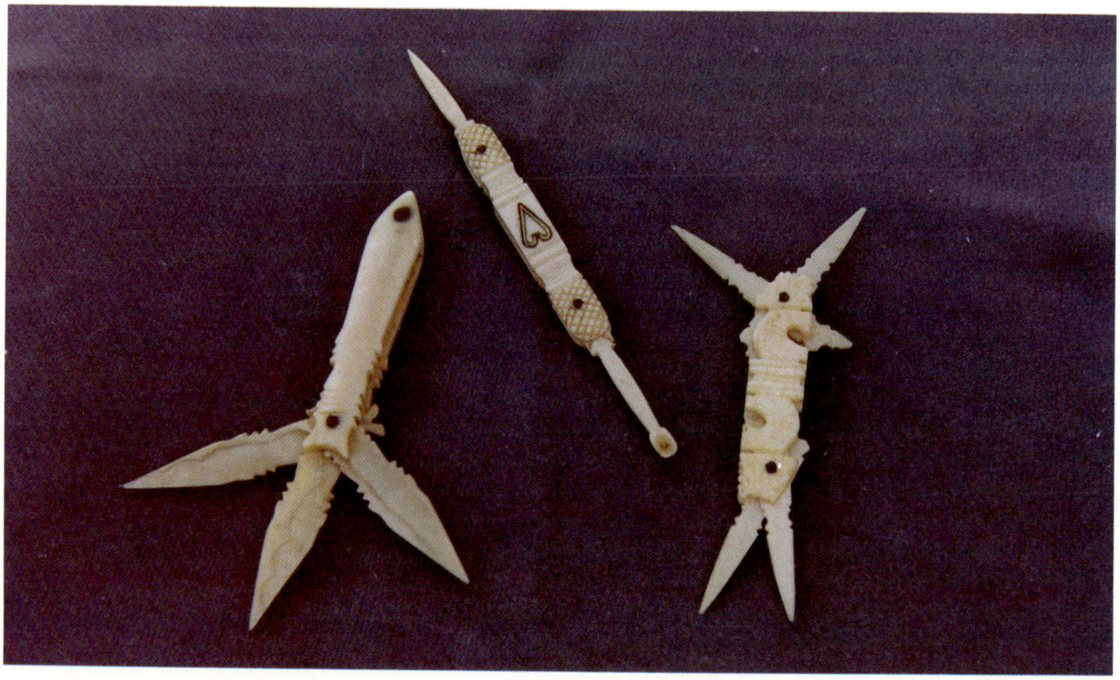

This grouping of toothpicks was carved of both whalebone and whale ivory. One is fitted with a tiny earcup. *Collection of Charles A. Manghis*

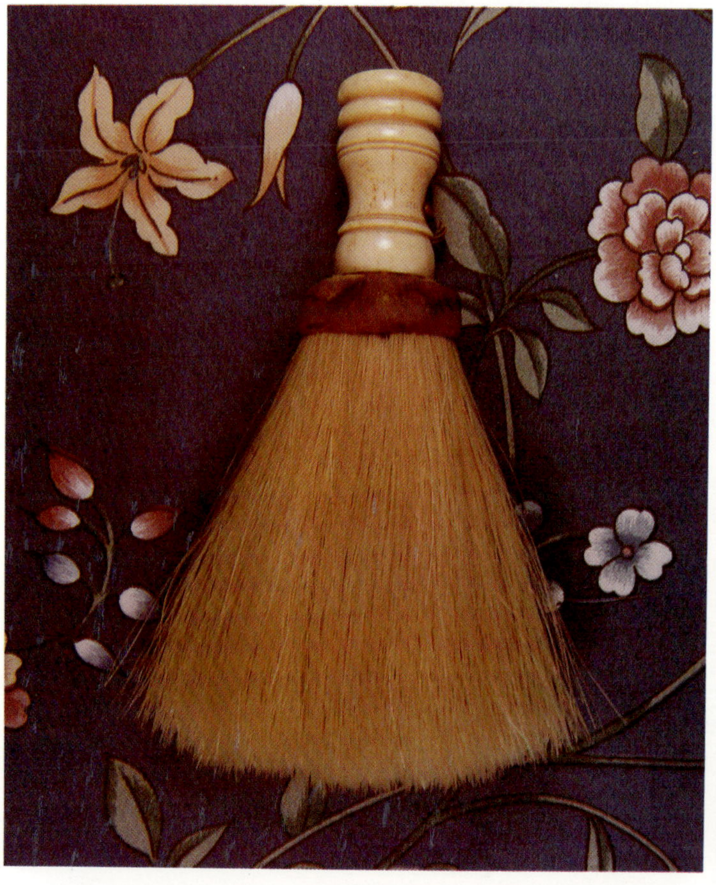

Although possibly produced commercially rather than by a shipboard artist, this brush handle gives evidence to the variety of uses to which whale ivory and whalebone were put. *Private Collection*

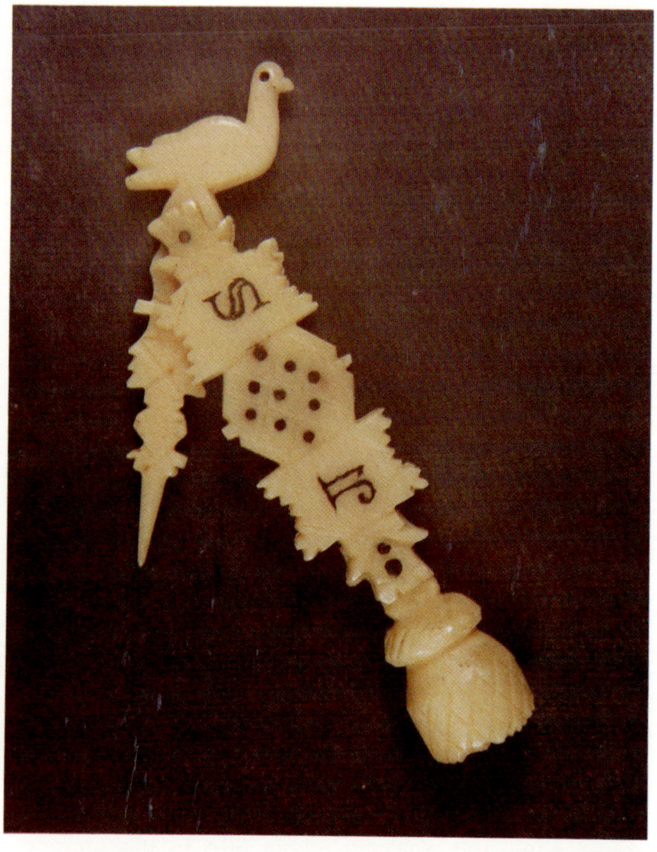

A versatile piece, this bird-topped toothpick inscribed "J. S." doubles as a sealing device. *Private Collection*

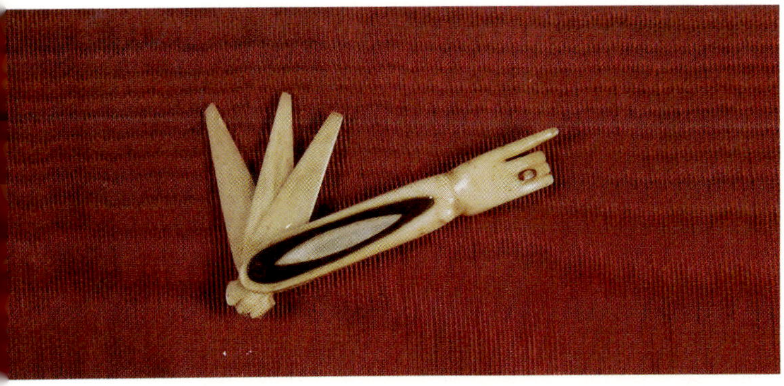

The small size of articles such as toothpicks did not limit the scrimshander's desire to incorporate creative details, as this inlaid whalebone piece attests. The carved hand is fitted with a ring and the handle is inlaid with ebony and mother-of-pearl. *Collection of Raymond and Elizabeth De Lucia*

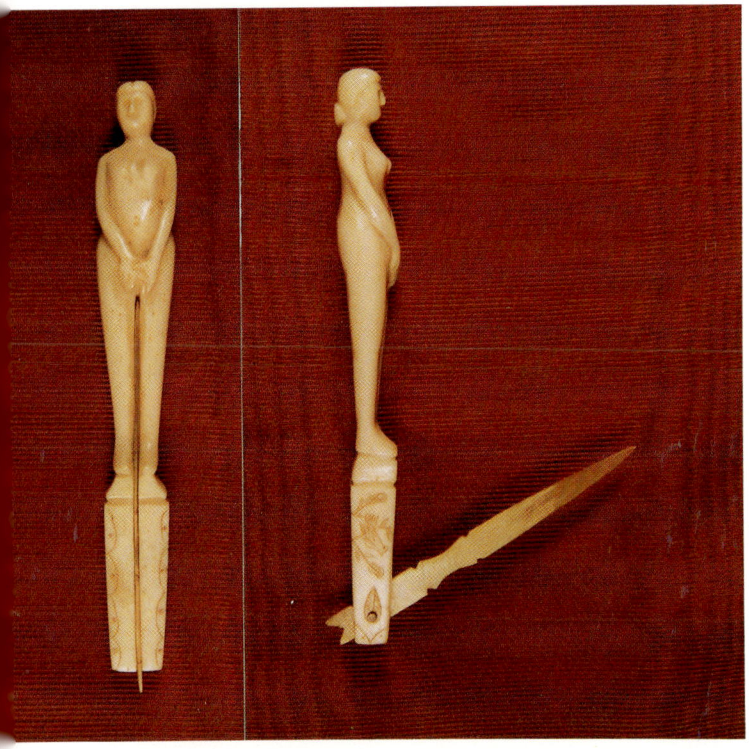

This unusual whale ivory toothpick was no doubt a conversation starter when brought forth for use. *Collection of Raymond and Elizabeth De Lucia*

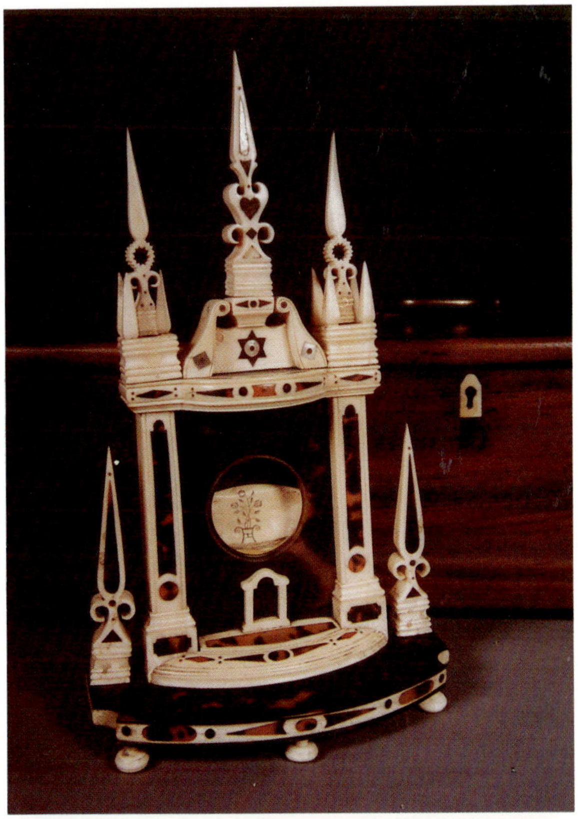

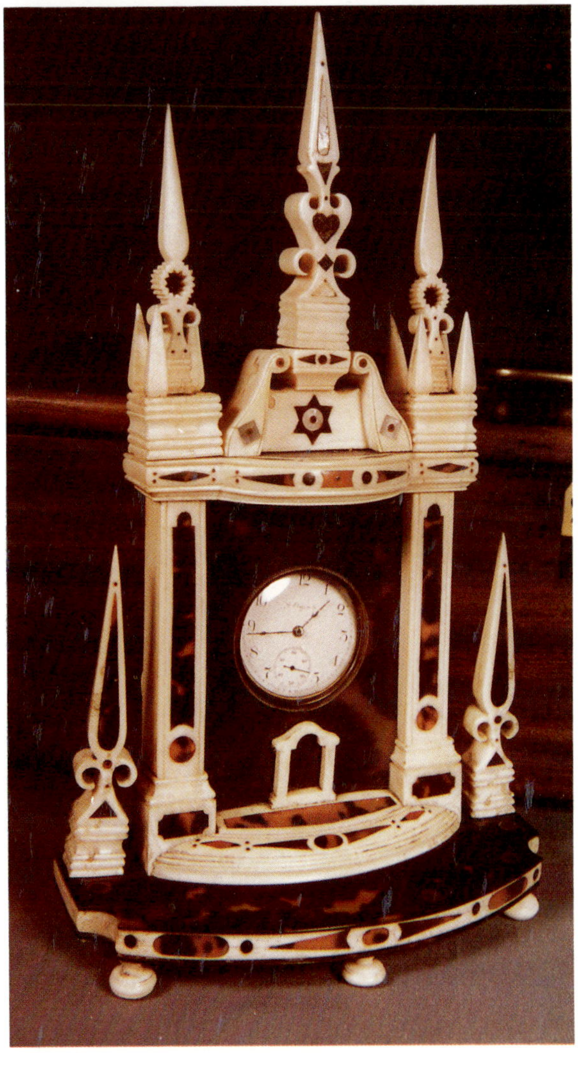

A gentleman's watch stand served not only as an elegant creation in its own right but also as a convenient place to store his timepiece at day's end. In this intricately carved piece, the artist was also concerned with the appearance when the stand was not in use and thus engraved a piece of ivory to decorate the void left by the watch's absence. Tortoise shell and abalone inlays add to the stand's abundant whalebone and whale ivory decorative details. *Courtesy of the Nantucket Historical Association*

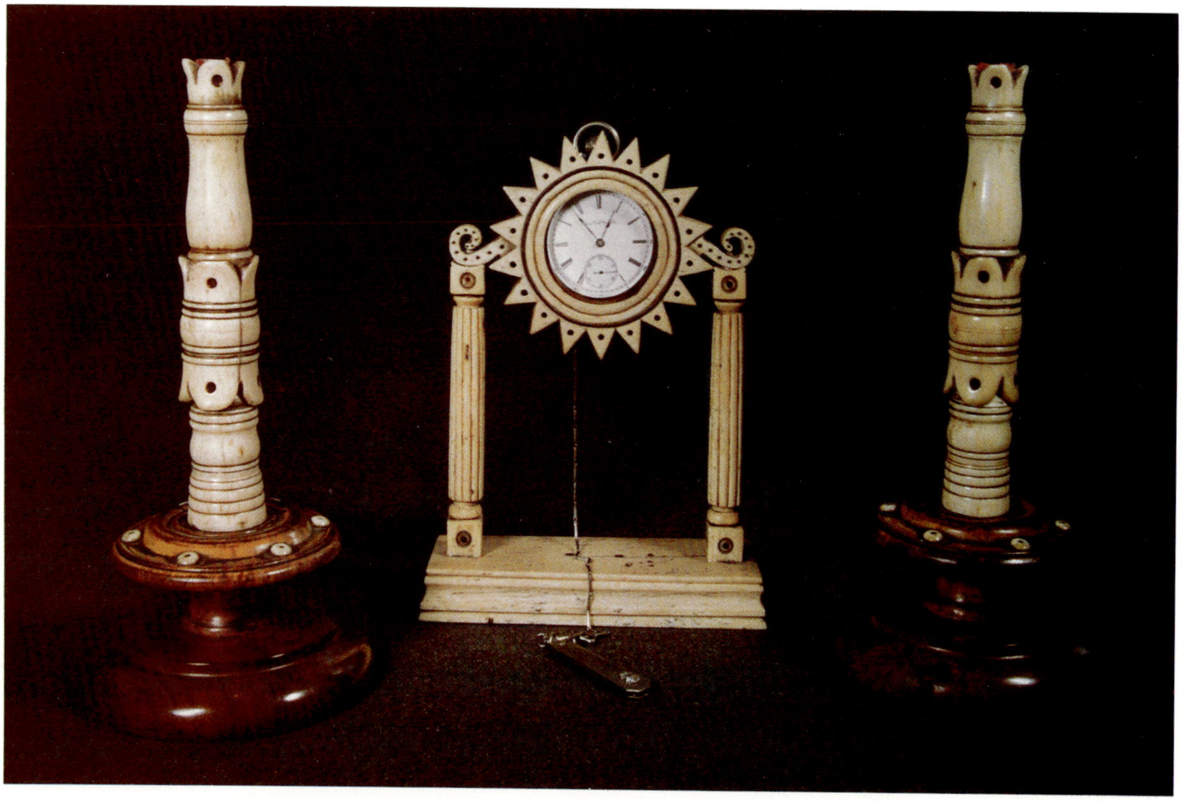

In contrast to more ornate stands, the creator of this whalebone watch stand chose classic lines and simple baleen inlays for his work. Here it is flanked by two mahogany and whale ivory candle sticks. *Collection of Raymond and Elizabeth De Lucia*

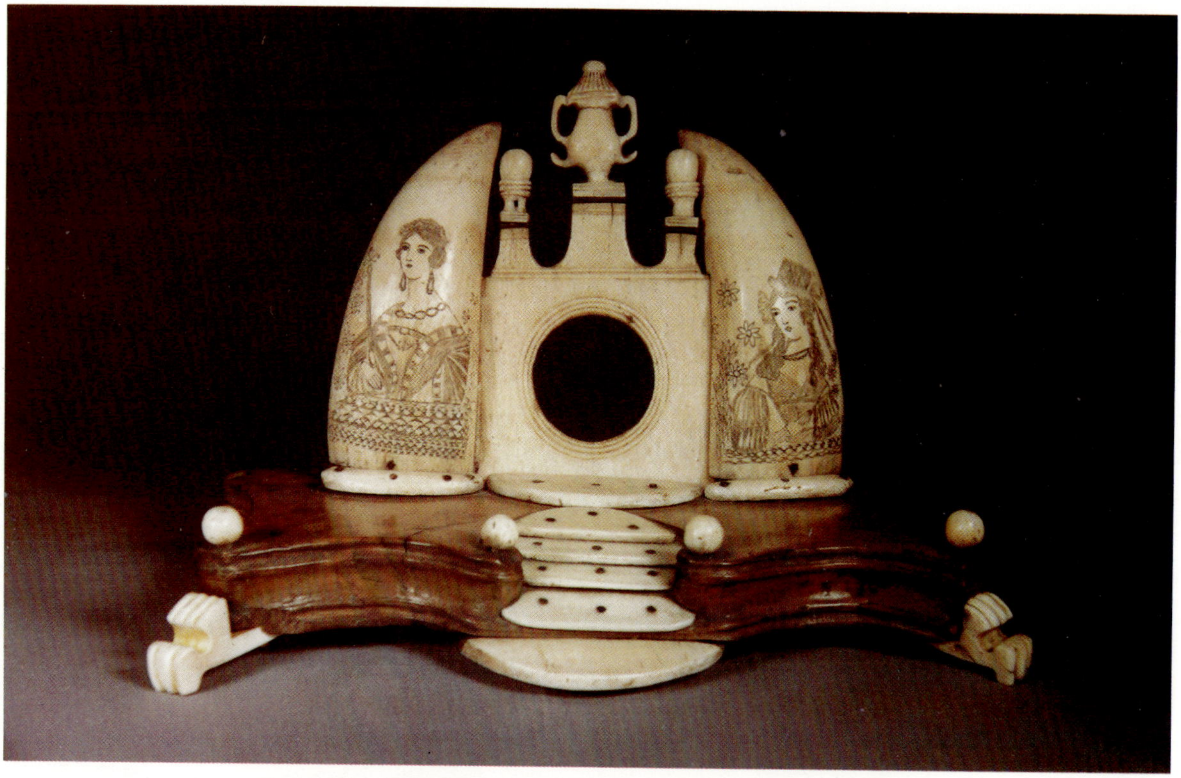

A nicely matched set of teeth combine with carved whalebone in this attractive watch stand. *Courtesy of the Nantucket Historical Association.*

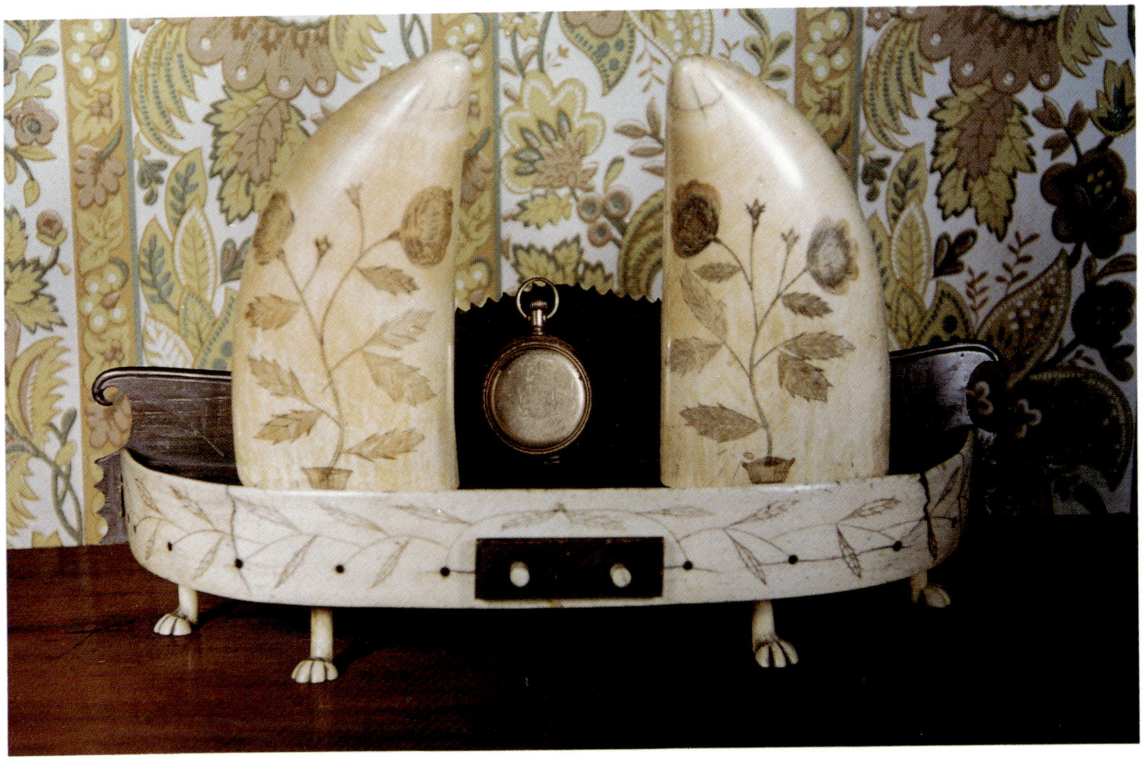

A pair of matching sperm whale's teeth, engraved with polychrome flowers, guard the watch in this wonderful whalebone and baleen stand. Inscribed on the baleen is this verse:

> Now don't put your heart in a flurry
> Nor think me the rashest of men —
> I assure you I am not in a hurry
> But will wait till three score and ten.

On the back of the stand, an only partially visible but obviously negative response to this entreaty is engraved. The story behind the two verses remains a mystery. *Collection of Raymond and Elizabeth De Lucia*

The eight and twentieth day of June
The foggy vapors cleared;
We bore away before the wind,
And for Nantucket steered.

-

The flaming orb of day had passed
Two thirds the vaulted sky,
When, lo! upon our starboard bow
Nantucket then did lie.

-

Same day we anchored at the bar,
Our anxious voyage now o'er;
To see our wives, sweethearts, and friends,
We hastened to the shore.

And now in harbor we've arrived;
All hands are well and stout.
Unbend the sails and take them up,
And next the oil break out.

-

Our oil is sold, and cash is paid;
We'll share it with our friends,
And when it's gone, to sea for more.
And so my voyage ends.

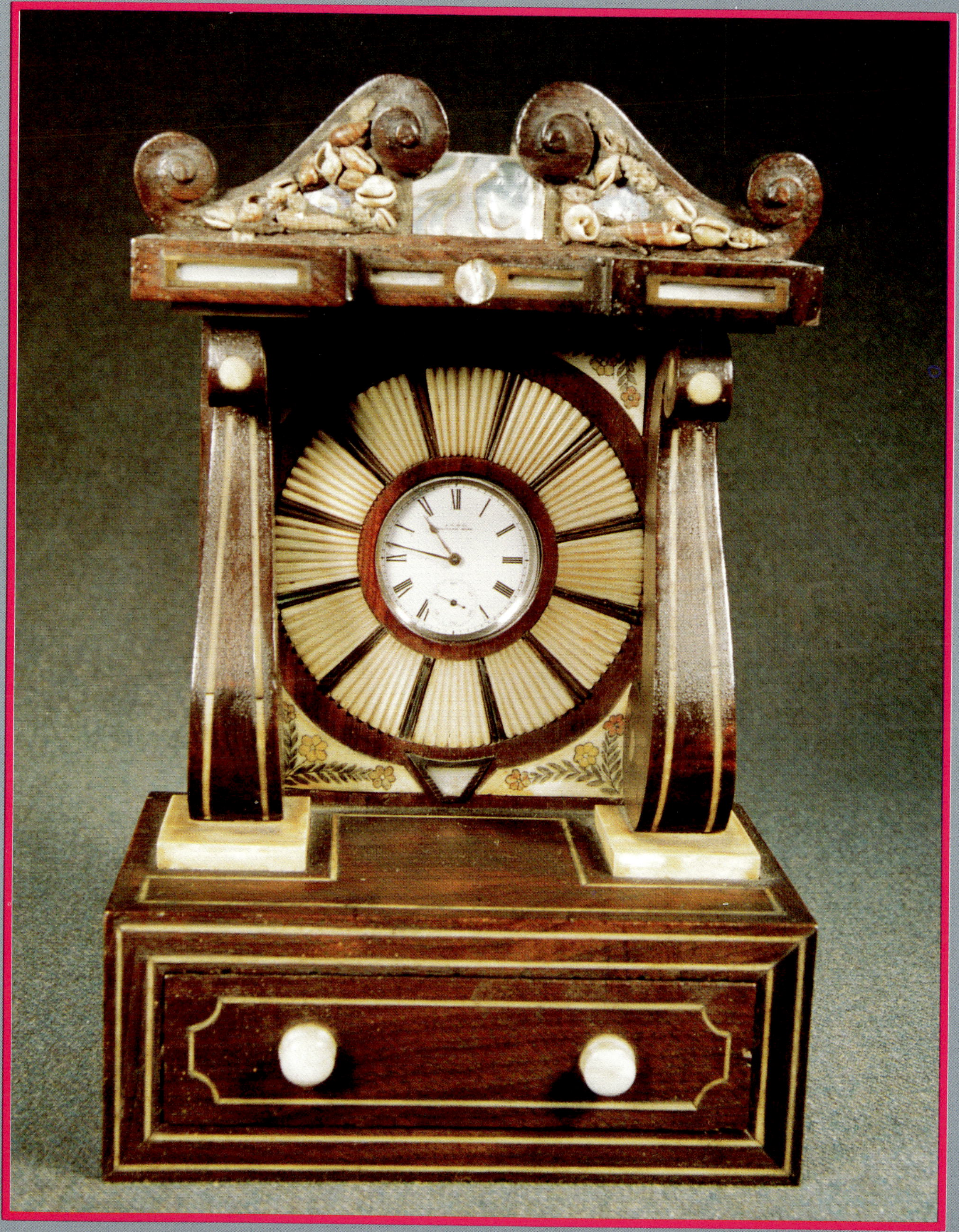

Many elements were incorporated into this incredible mahogany watch stand: abalone, shells, whale ivory, carving, engraving, and inlay work. *Collection of Raymond and Elizabeth De Lucia*

Personal necessities for the lady offered the scrimshander not only more opportunity to create but to do so for someone special. Adorning her dressing table might be found such remembrances as a lovely vanity chest, replete with clever drawers and cubbyholes, or candlesticks turned during her husband's last voyage.

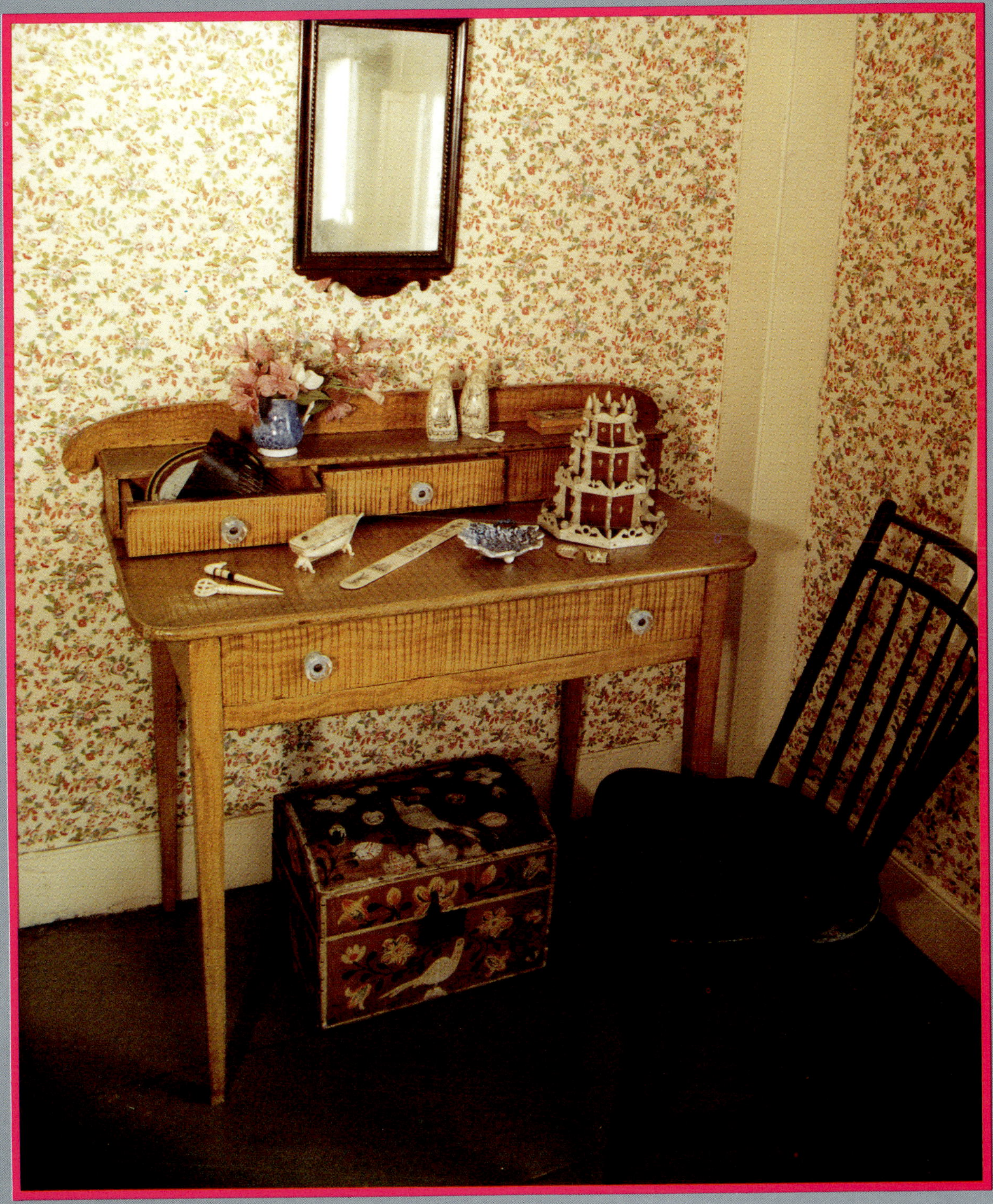

The lady's corner of a bed chamber of Nantucket's "1800 House". *Courtesy of the Nantucket Historical Association*

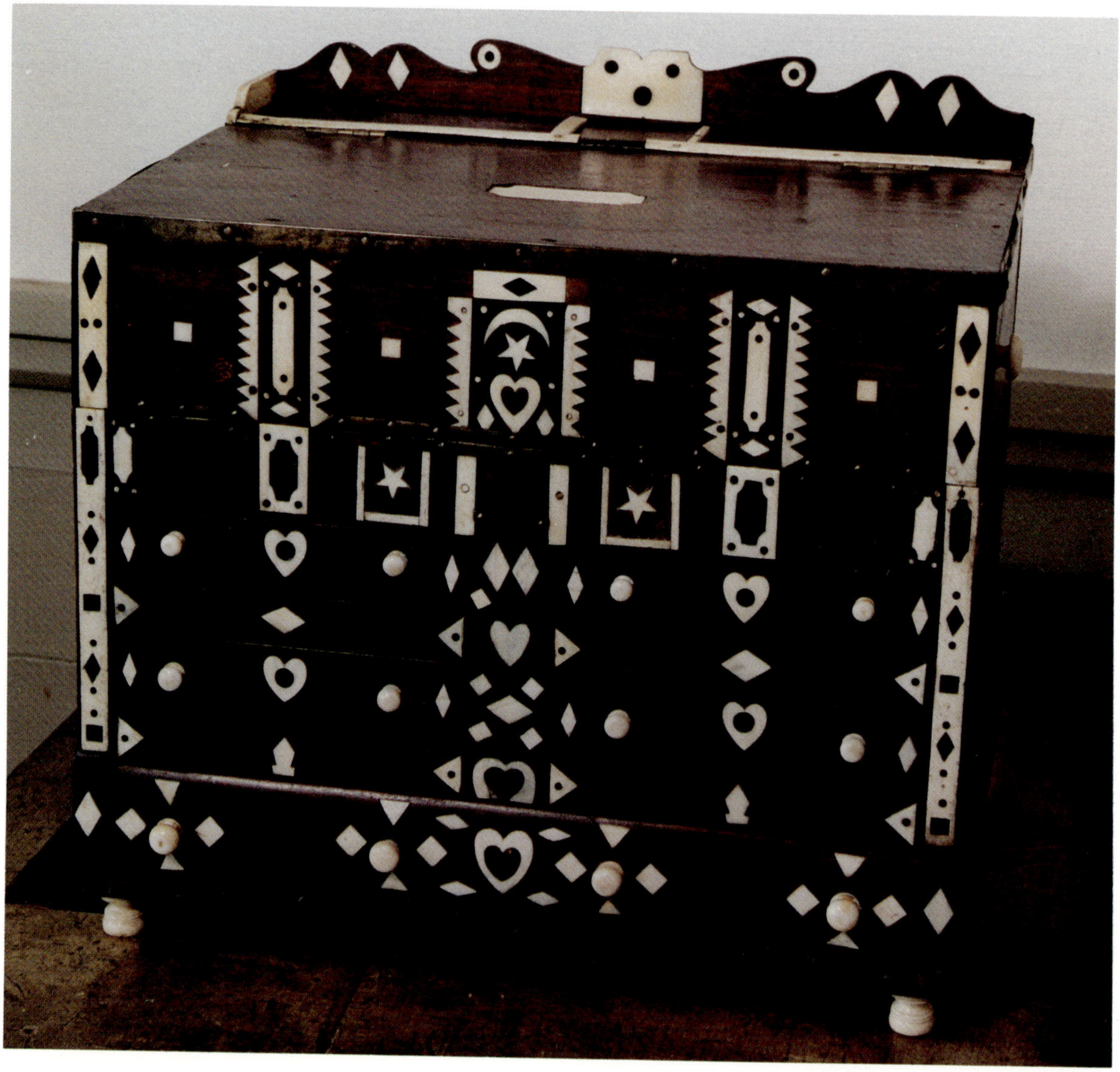

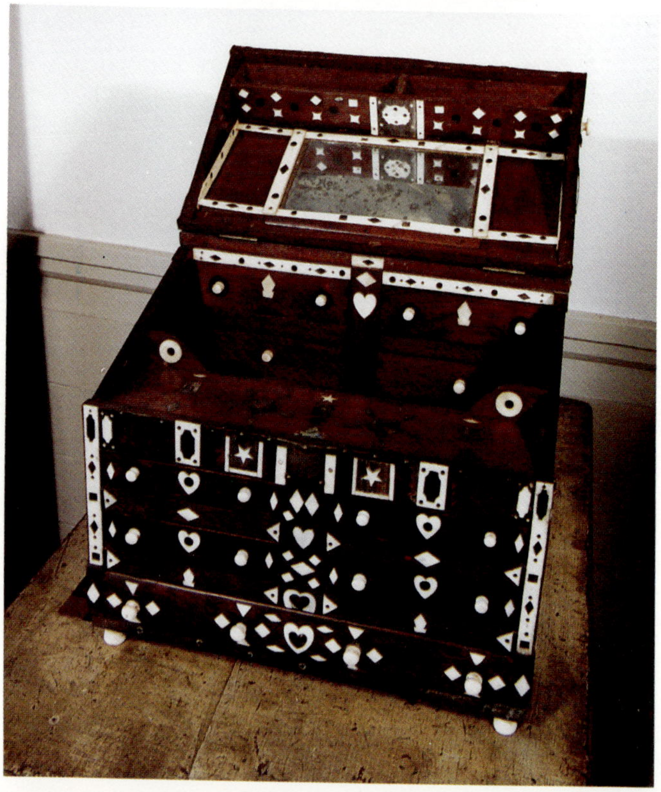

Imagine creating this intricate vanity case in the cramped quarters and poor light of a rolling whaleship. The many inlays in this mahogany chest consist of whale ivory, baleen and abalone. A more detailed view of the inlays is shown on page 77. *Private Collection.*

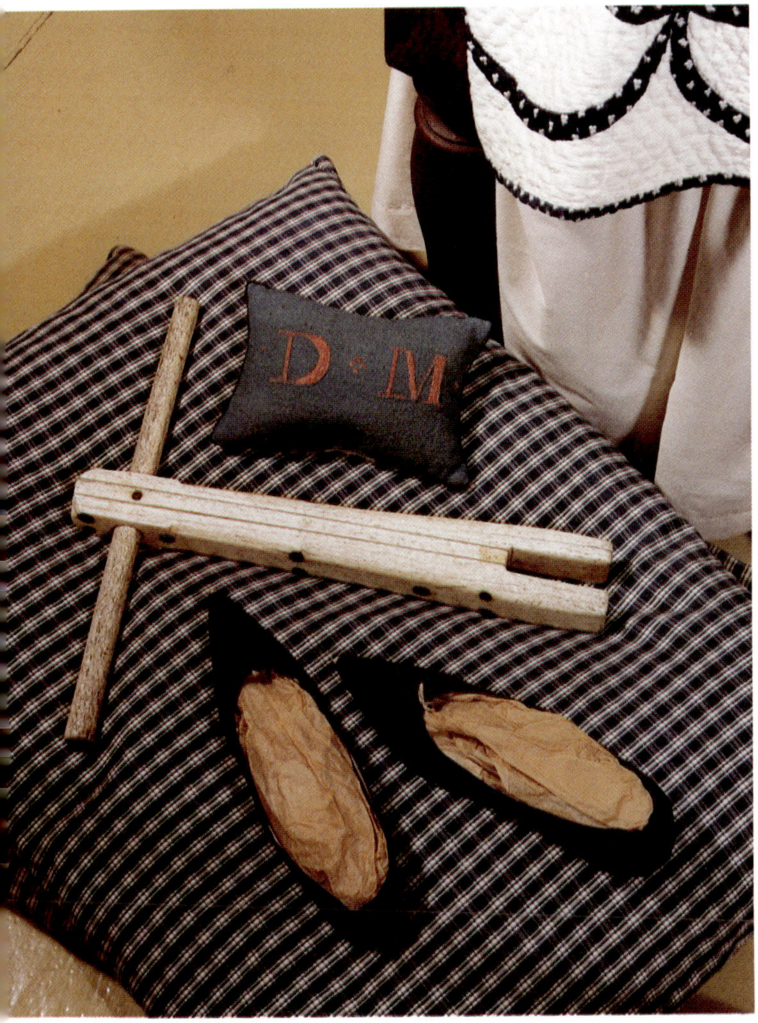

A whalebone bed tightener played an important role in any home furnished with a rope bed. *Madden Collection*

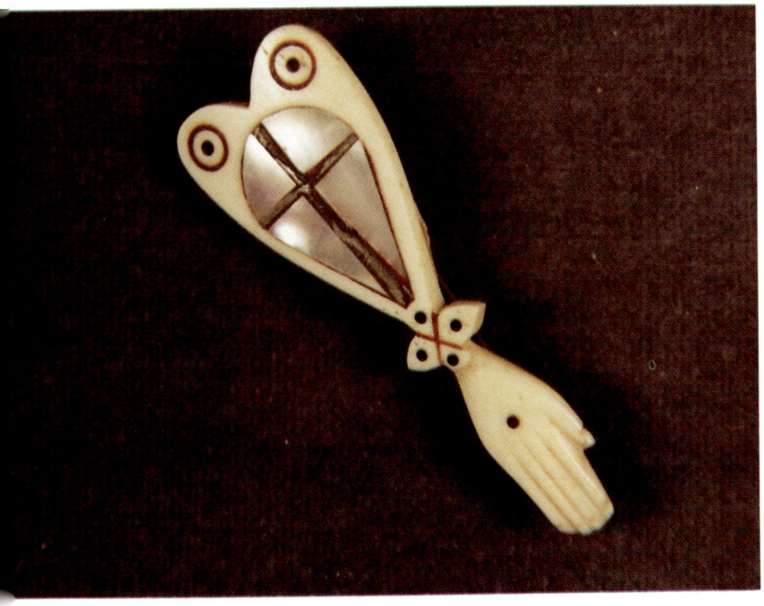

This whalebone pin is inlaid with mother of pearl and decorated with red sealing wax. *Collection of the Nantucket Historical Association*

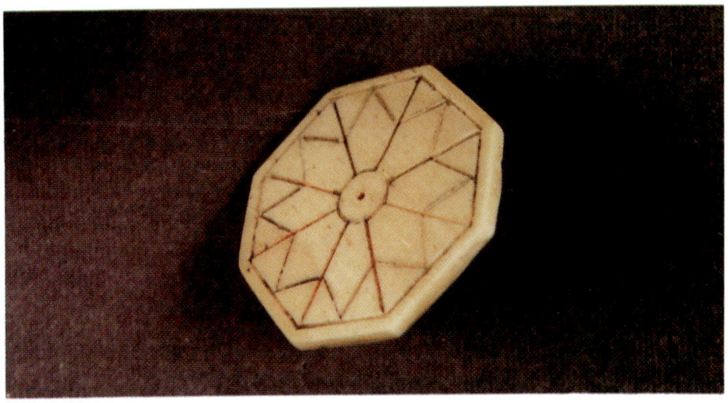

Simply inscribed and colored with red and green sealing wax, this whalebone octagon served as a neckerchief slide. *Courtesy of the Nantucket Historical Association*

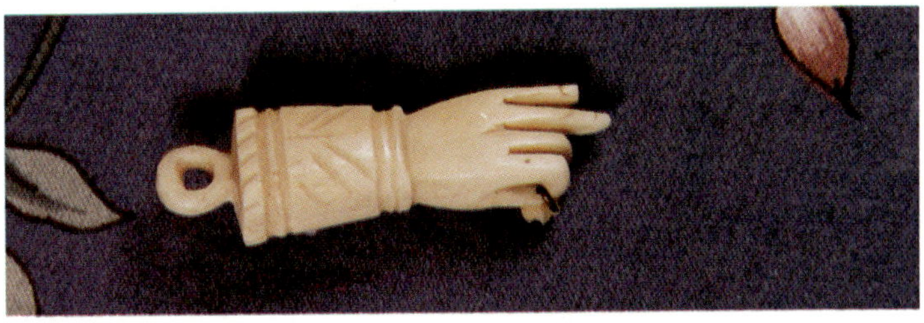

The thumb and forefinger of this whale ivory pendant hold a tiny carved flower. *Private Collection*

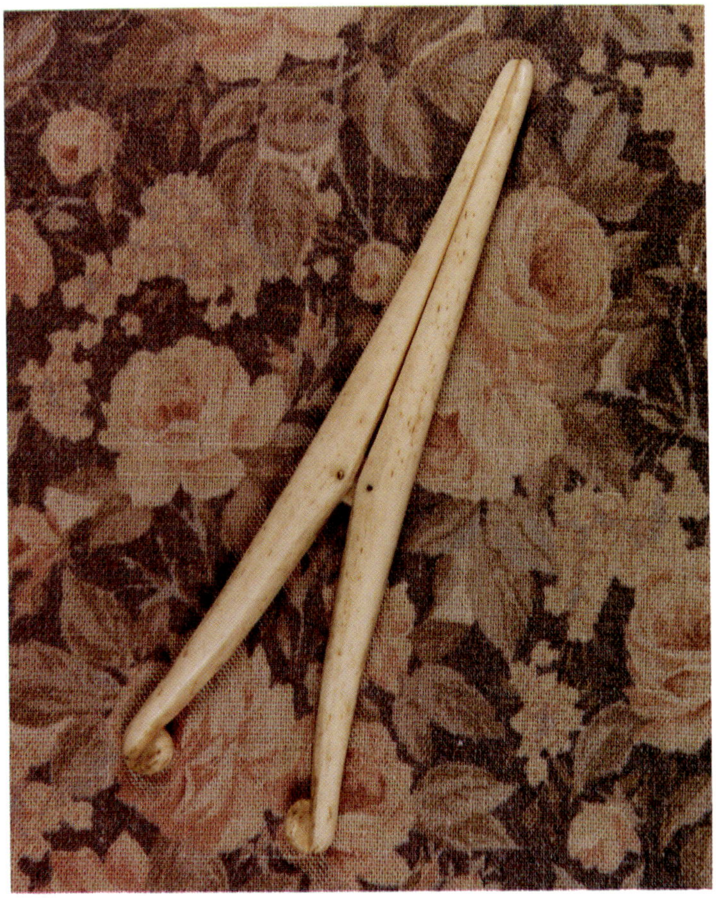

Often commercially produced, these glove stretchers are made of whalebone. *Private Collection*

Also located among the woman's treasures was a very intimate gift, the busk. Given its purpose of straightening and reining in the female figure by its insertion in the front of a corset, the receipt of this foot-long, inch-wide slab of ivory was perhaps a mixed blessing. However, such a presentation apparently confirmed the scrimshander's feelings of longing and tenderness. Moreover, the busk provided the artist with a wonderful flat surface on which he could practice various motifs and borders that he might later incorporate onto the more difficult, curved surface of a tooth. Not only were the scenes often romantic, nostalgic evocations of home, but verses, both original and borrowed, also reinforced his sentiments.

Rest on the bossum of the fair
And softly whisper Peace
Bid every sorrow, every care
And dark foreboding cease.

In many a gale
Has been the whale
In which this bone did rest
His time is past
His bone at last
Must now support thy breast.

From rocks and
Sands and danger far
May God protect
the Yankee Tar.

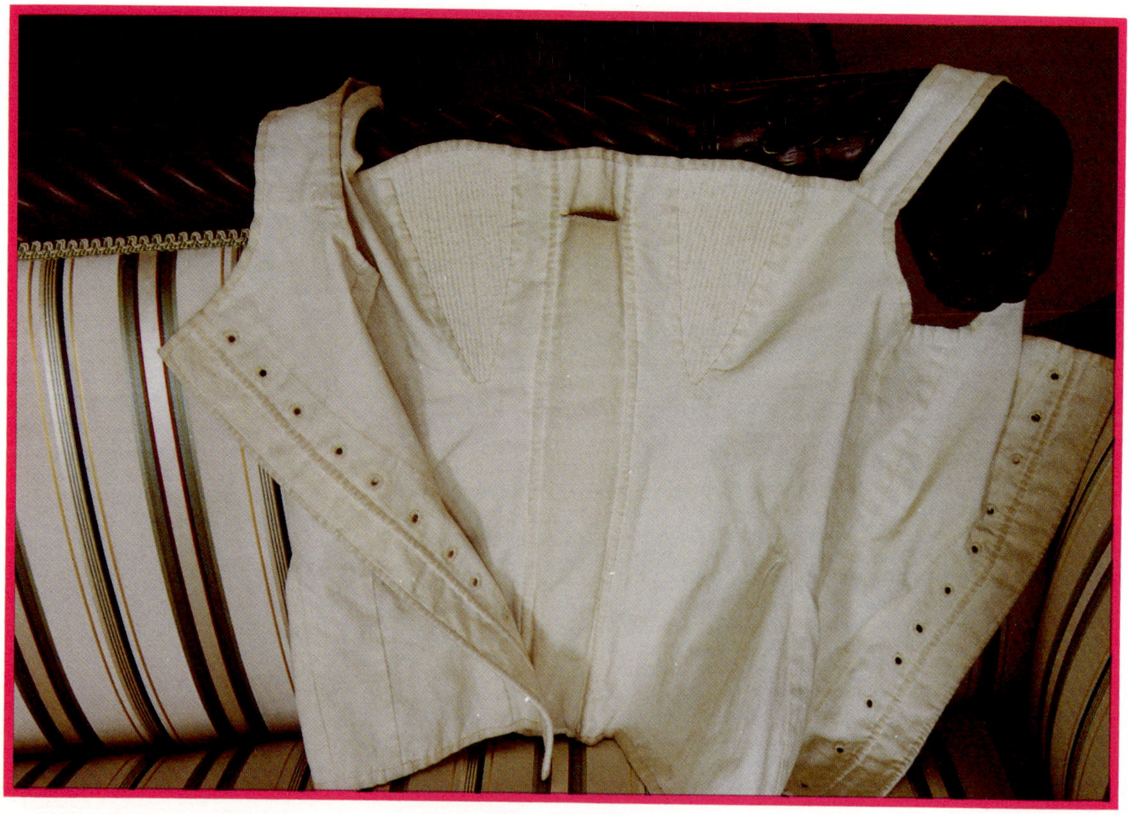

This replica of a lady's corset was made by Judith Lund of the New Bedford Whaling Museum. The corset laces in back. The hole for inserting the busk in its stitched channel can be seen in the center front of the garment. *Courtesy of the New Bedford Whaling Museum*

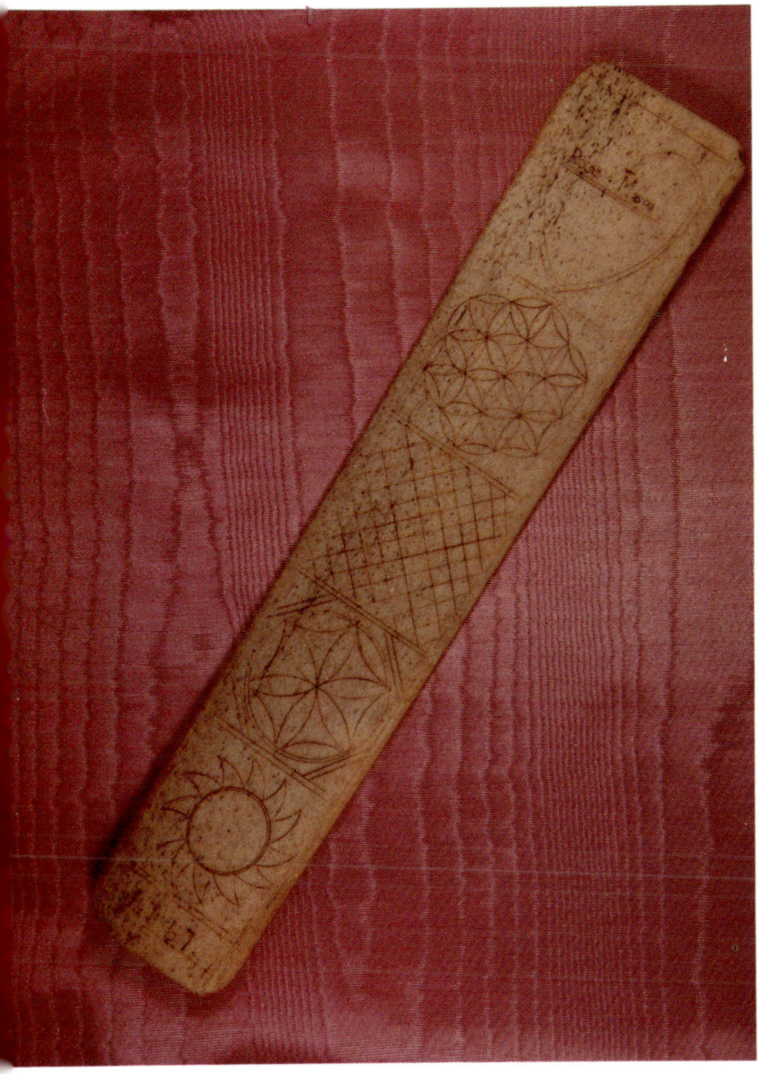

This early, unusually wide whalebone busk is dated 1767 and inscribed "Rose Mason." *Private Collection*

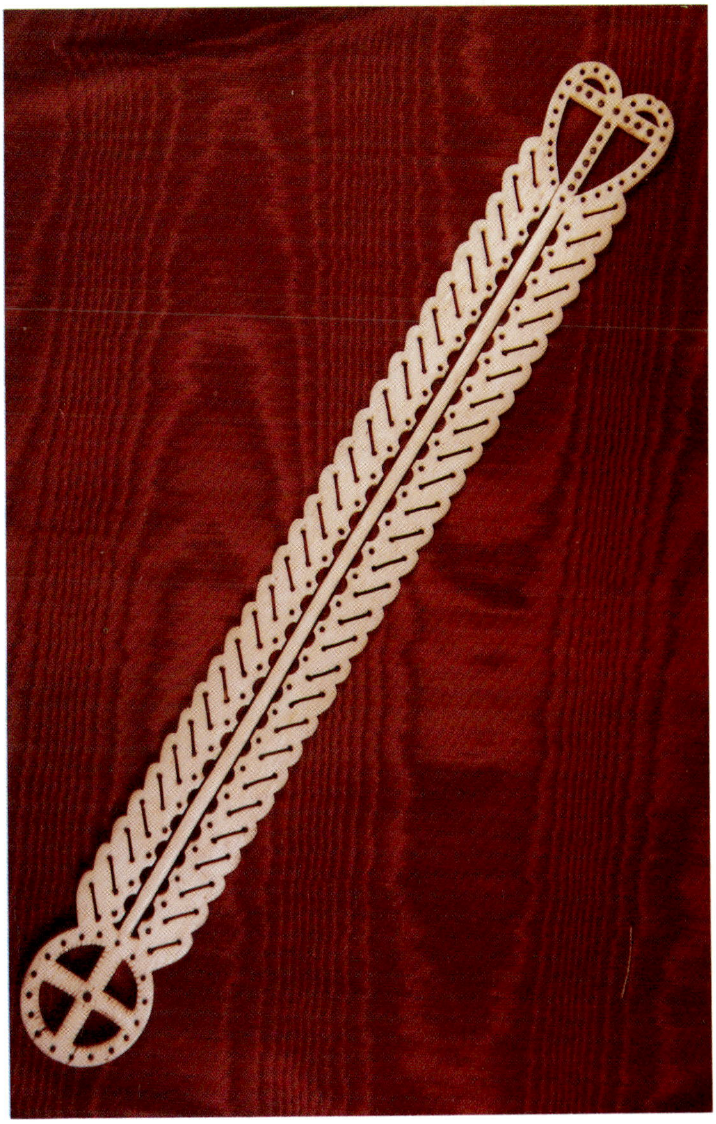

A stunning, pierced whalebone busk *Courtesy of the Nantucket Historical Association*

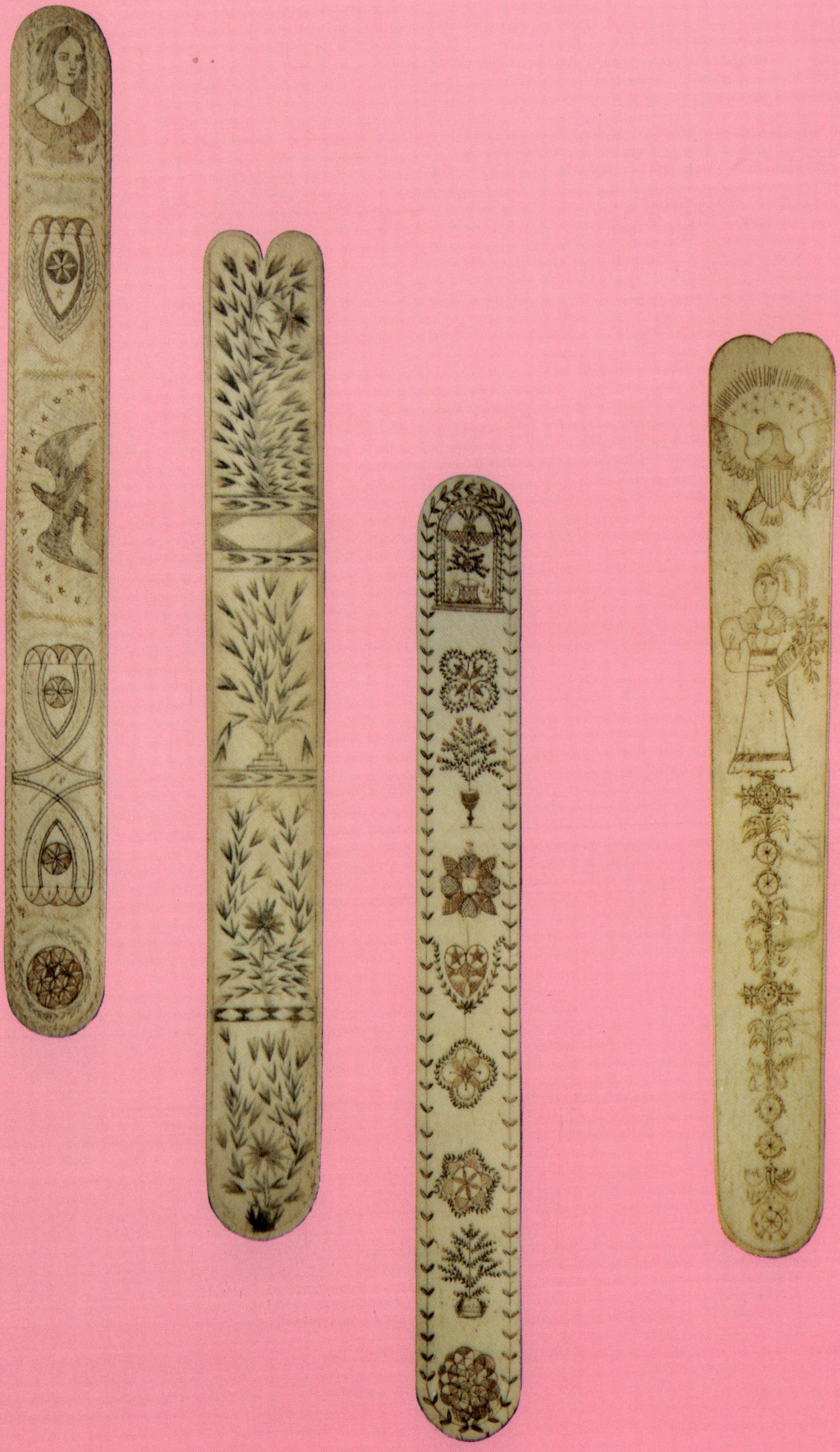

These examples typify the many designs and motifs included by scrimshanders on whalebone busks. *Courtesy of the Nantucket Historical Association*

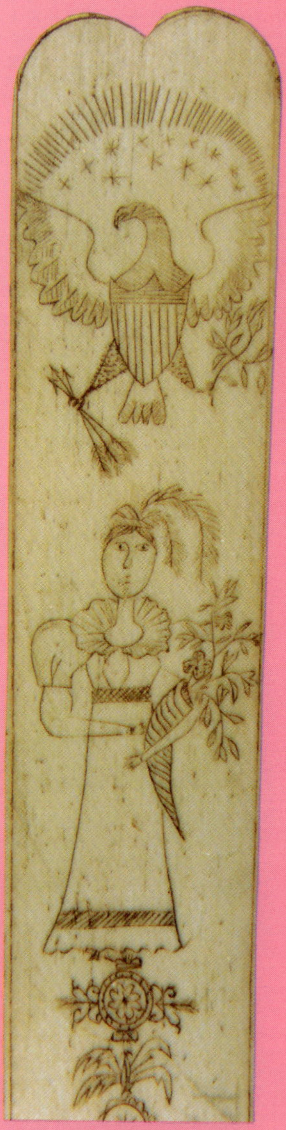

A charming, early whalebone busk *Private Collection*

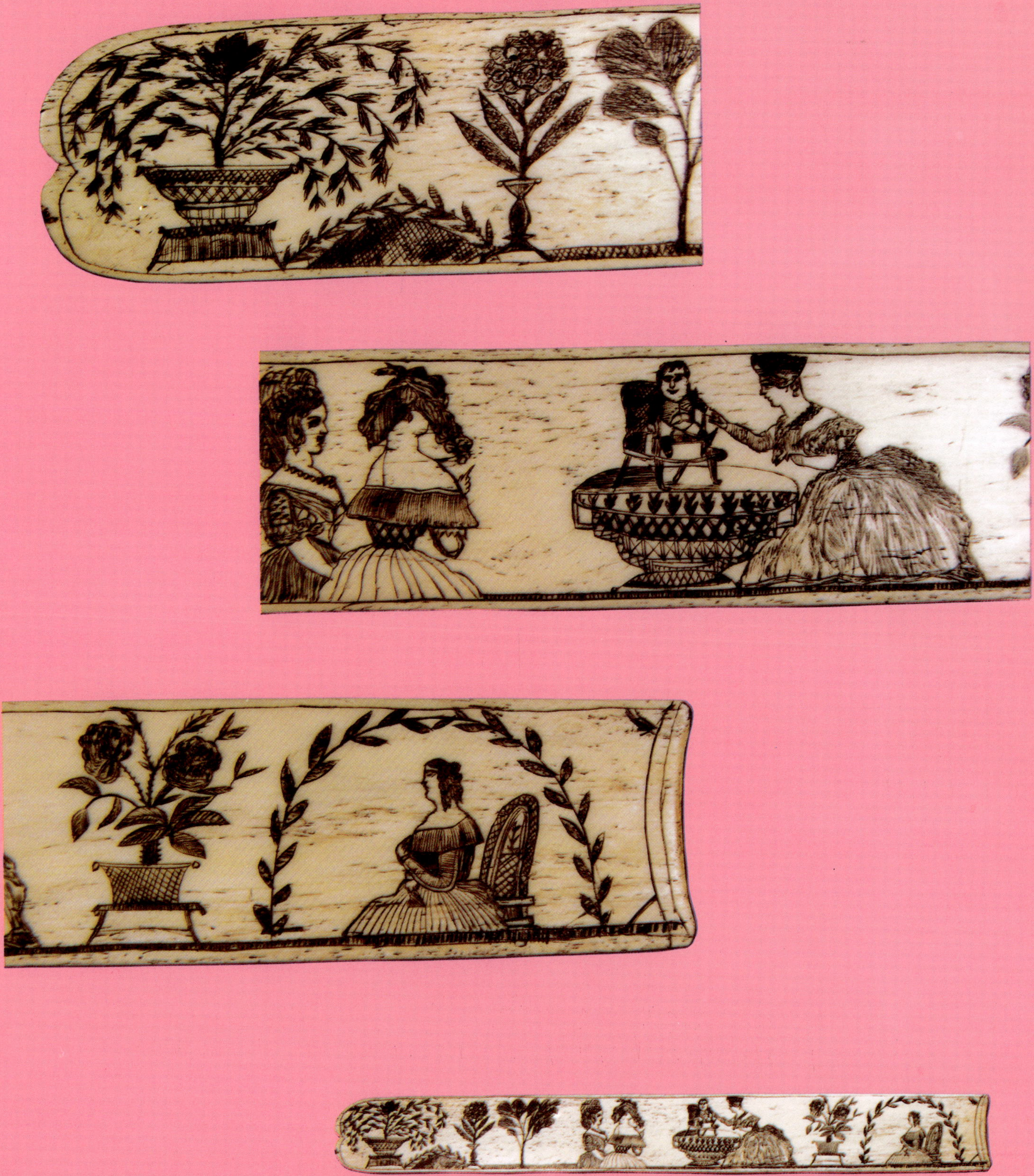

A visit by Tom Thumb to Queen Victoria *Madden Collection*

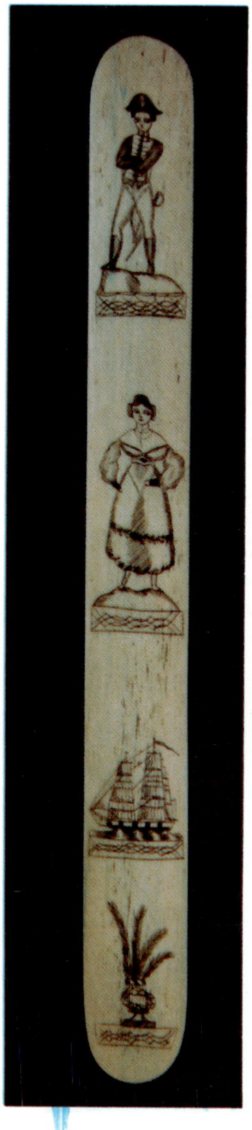

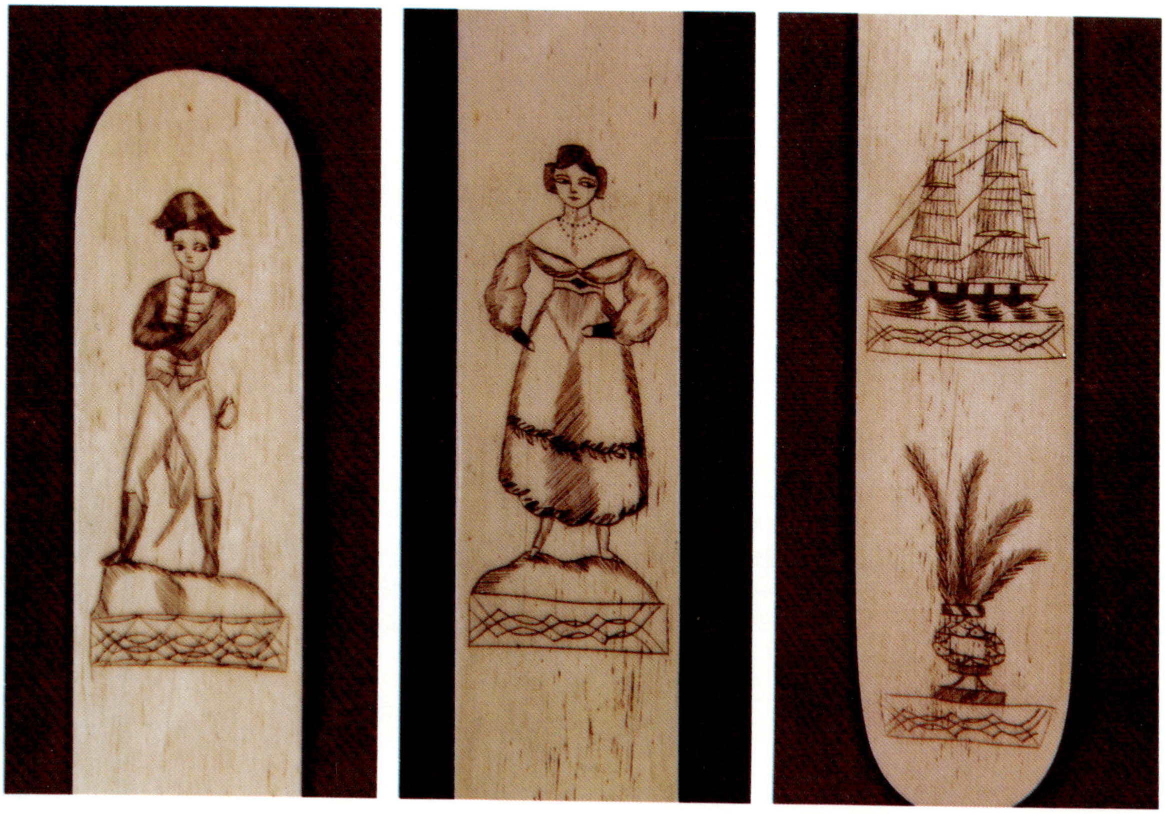

Another work attributed to the *Ceres* artisan *Courtesy of the Nantucket Historical Association*

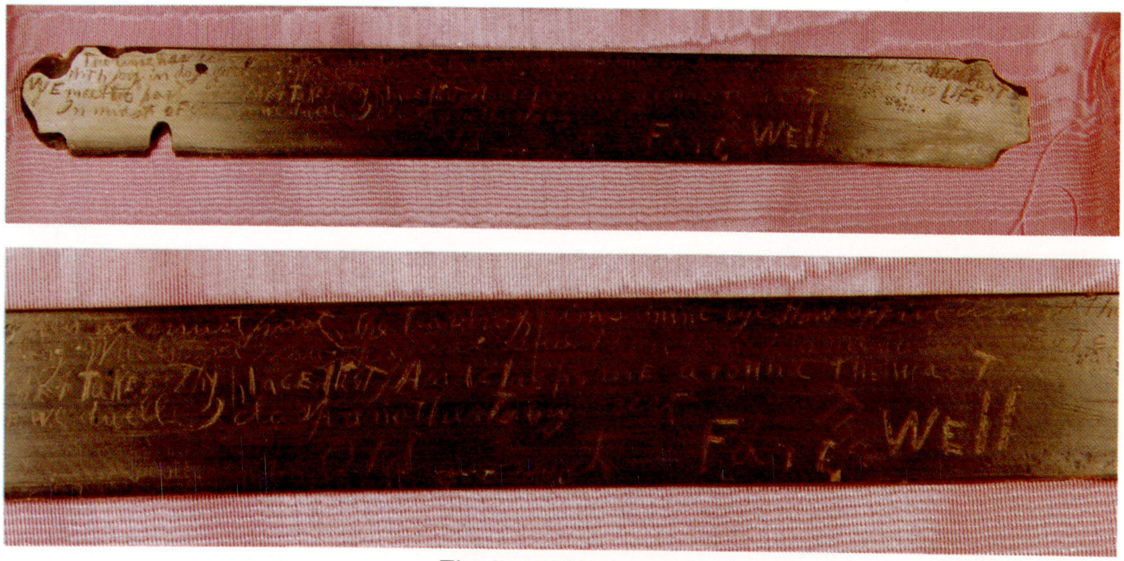

The inscription on this early, baleen busk reads:

> The time has come when we must part. The teardrop dims mine eye. How oft I've claspd thee to my heart with joy in days gone by. When first I saw thee I was sure Thou camst to me to stay. But such is life, we meet to part. Another takes thy place at last and clasps me around the wast. In midst of change we dwell, I clasp another to my brest. Old corset —Fare Thee Well

Collection of Raymond and Elizabeth De Lucia

7. The Legacy Preserved: Scrimshaw Collectors

Prior to the 1960s, antique scrimshaw was relatively unappreciated, and fine pieces languished in attics or were sold at auction for what now seem laughably low prices. As popularity and values have risen, only a few collectors have the resources required to put together vast collections representing all areas of the craft. The wide array of scrimshawed implements, however, makes specialized collecting more achievable, and there are many who seek out only whalebone tools, sewing implements, or kitchen paraphernalia.

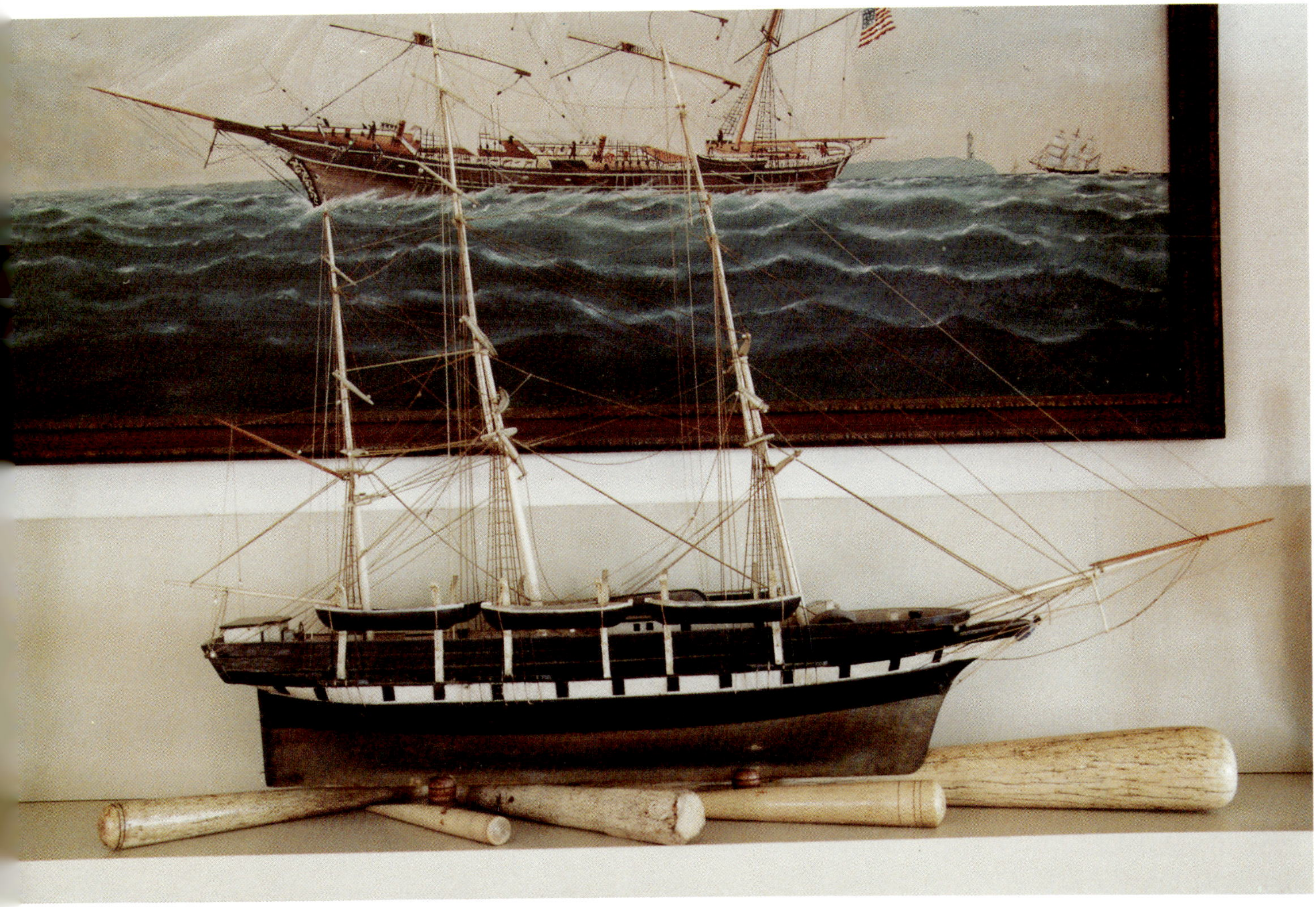

Scrimshaw collectors often surround themselves with articles associated with the sea in general or whaling in particular such as this model of a whaleship and marine painting. *Private Collection*

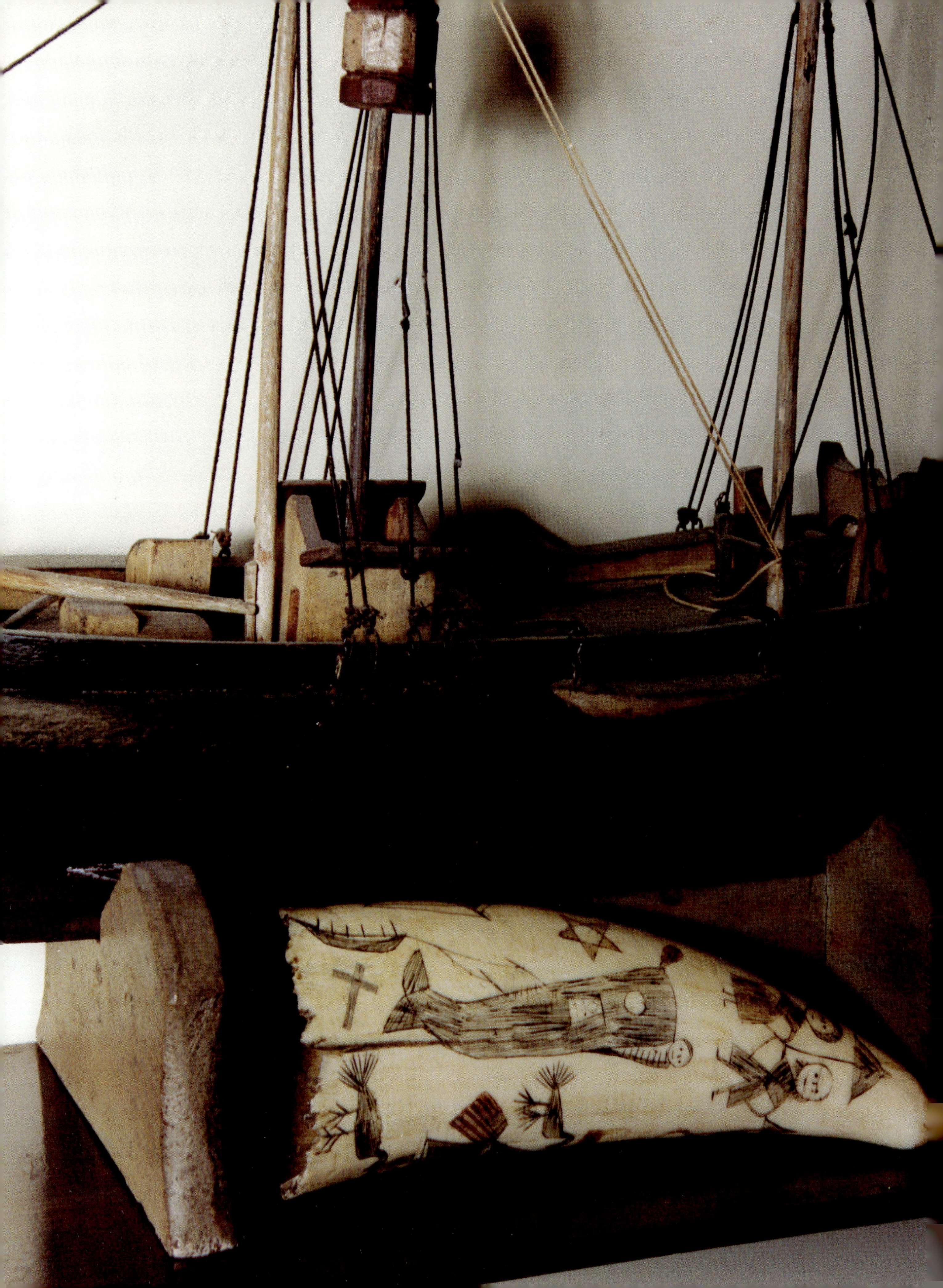

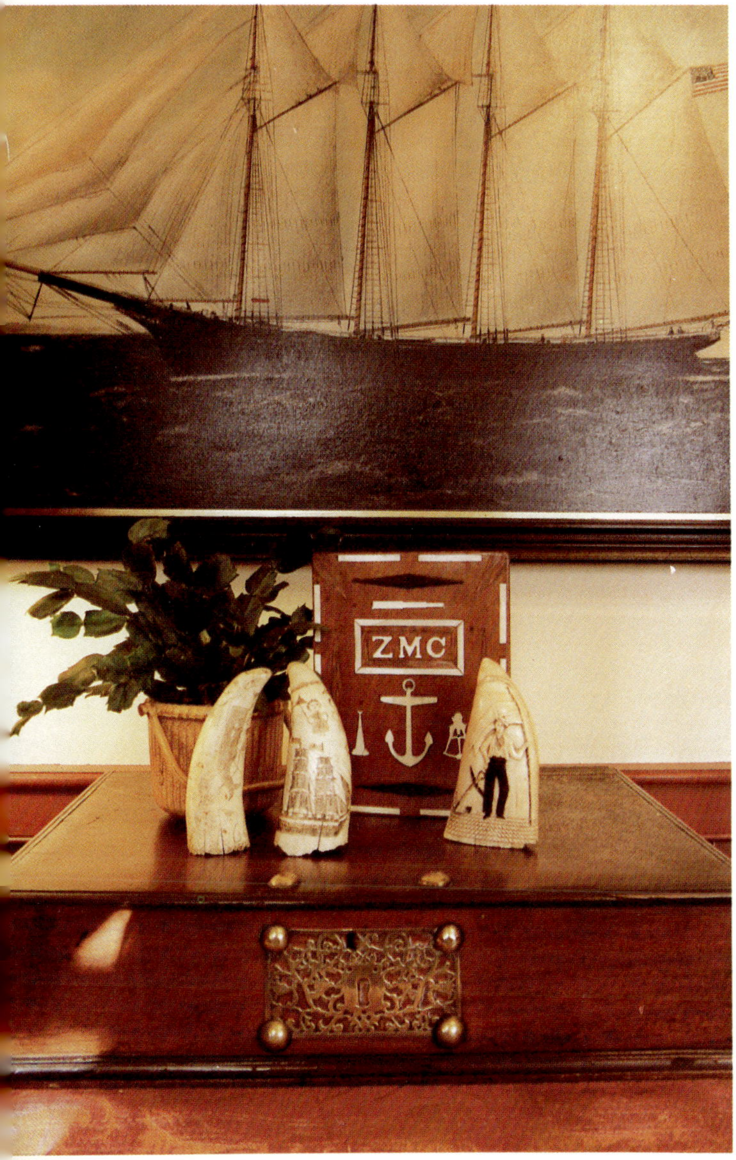

The grooming box in the background of this nautical grouping is inlaid with whale ivory and baleen and opens to reveal a shaving mirror. *Madden Collection*

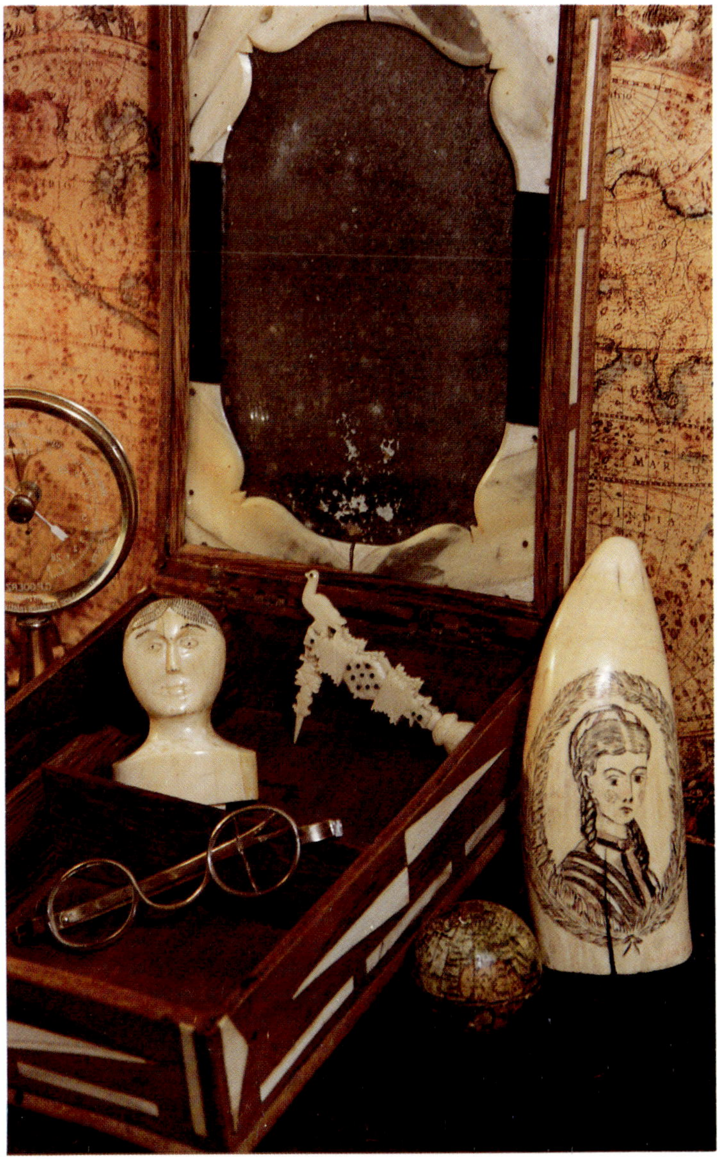

Opposite page:
This primitive tooth is nestled beneath a model of a nineteenth century lightship. *Madden Collection*

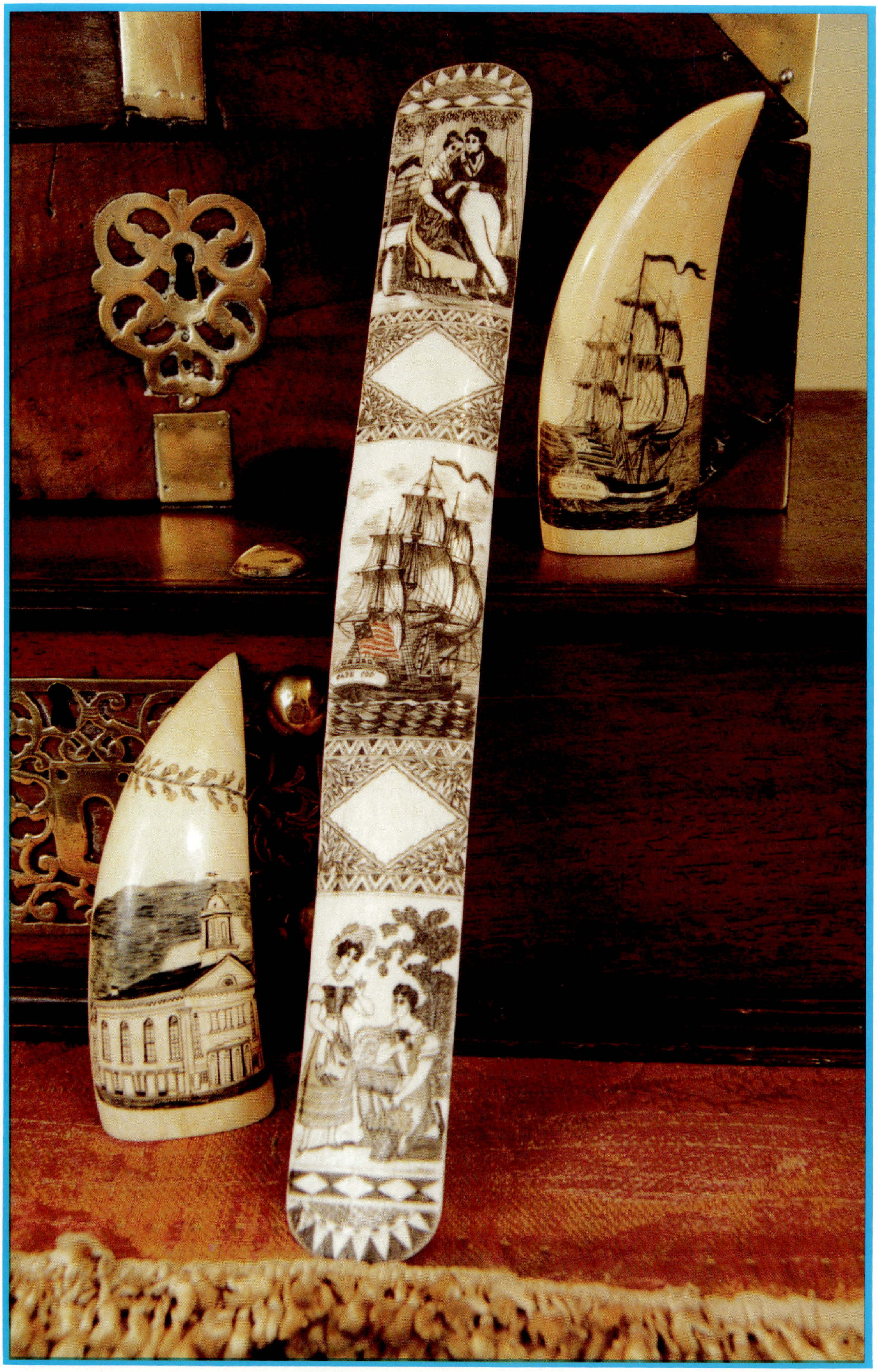

Madden Collection

Although many private collections are housed as correctly as they would be in a museum, others are scattered throughout a home, tangible components of a household once more. Whaling artifacts—harpoons twisted by the gyrations of an angry whale, advertising cards featuring the virtues of sperm whale oil, marine paintings, or whaling logs and journals often round out a collection of scrimshaw.

Unfortunately scrimshaw collecting can be a treacherous field for the uninitiated. The development of polymer "scrimshaw" has made ownership possible without the monetary or ecological concerns associated with real scrimshaw. However some polymer pieces are not labeled as reproductions and are offered as "real" for inflated prices.

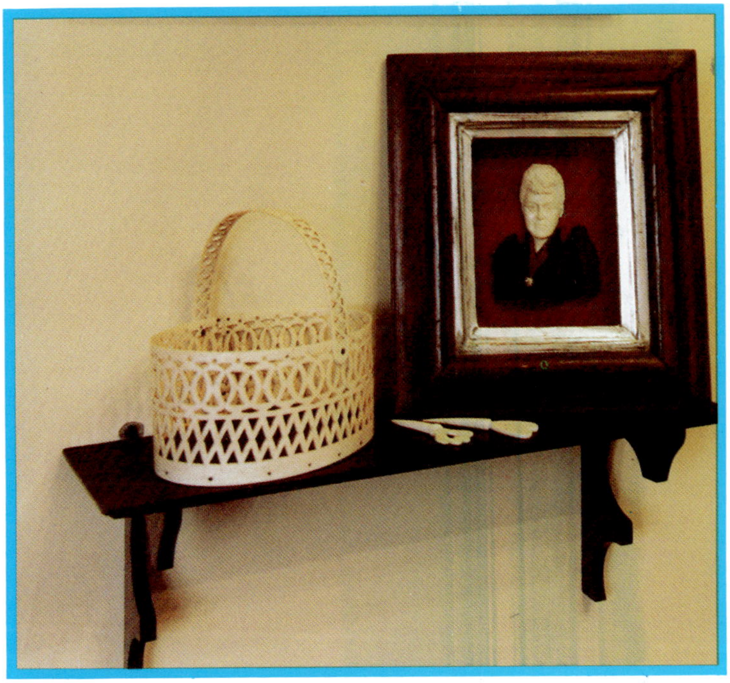

Madden Collection

Admiral Dewey appears pleased to have been placed in such charming company. Behind the teeth is a sailor's valentine, a shell creation probably created in Barbados, W.I., rather than by shipboard sailors as previously believed. *Madden Collection*

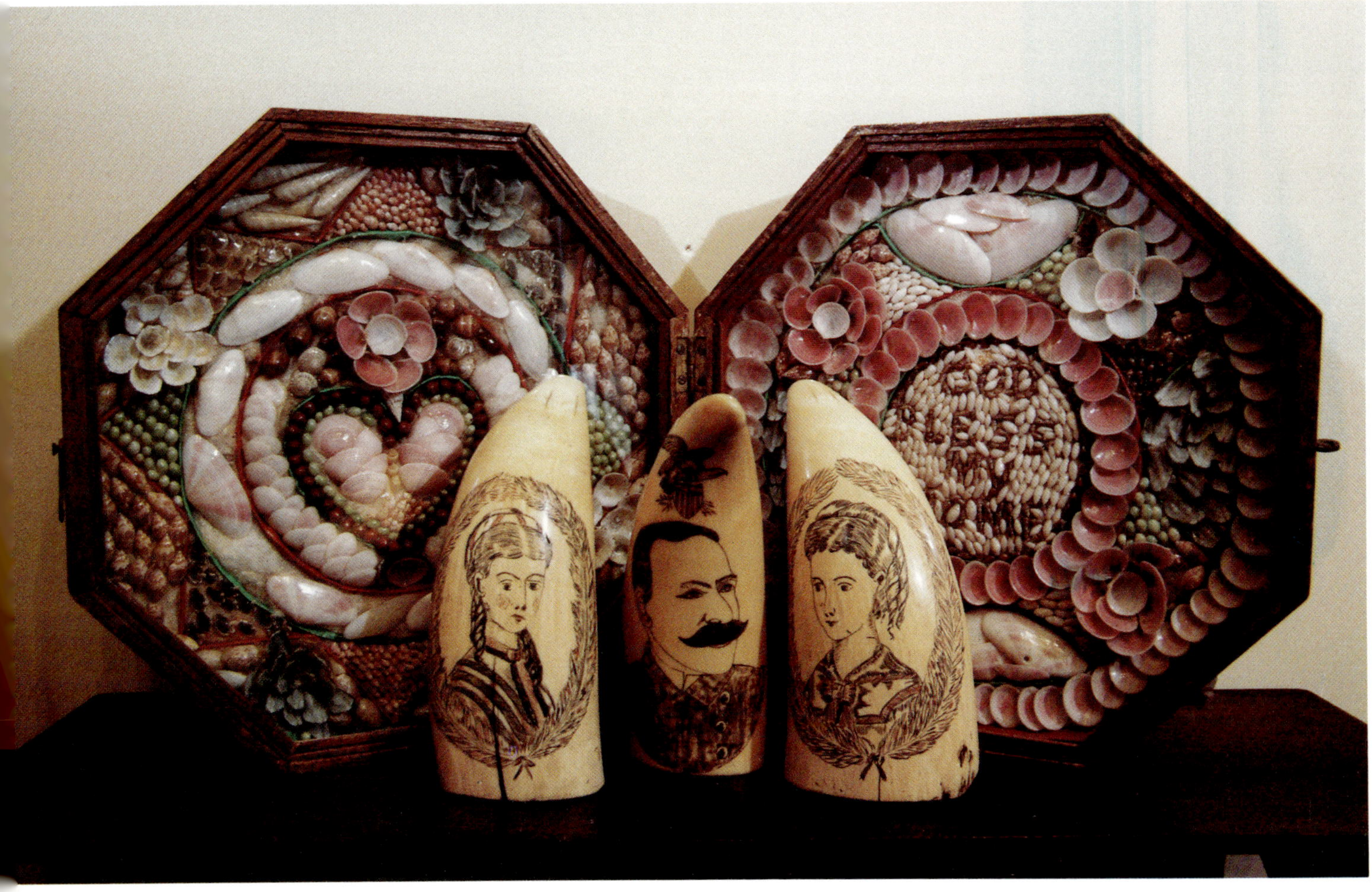

All "fake" scrimshaw is not plastic however. Unscrupulous forgers also copy antique scenes on real ivory. Teeth are a favorite of forgers; while the teeth themselves are truly ivory, perhaps even antique, the work upon them is contemporary. Yet such fakes will be offered to the unsuspecting purchaser as authentic nineteenth century works, carrying commensurately high price tags.

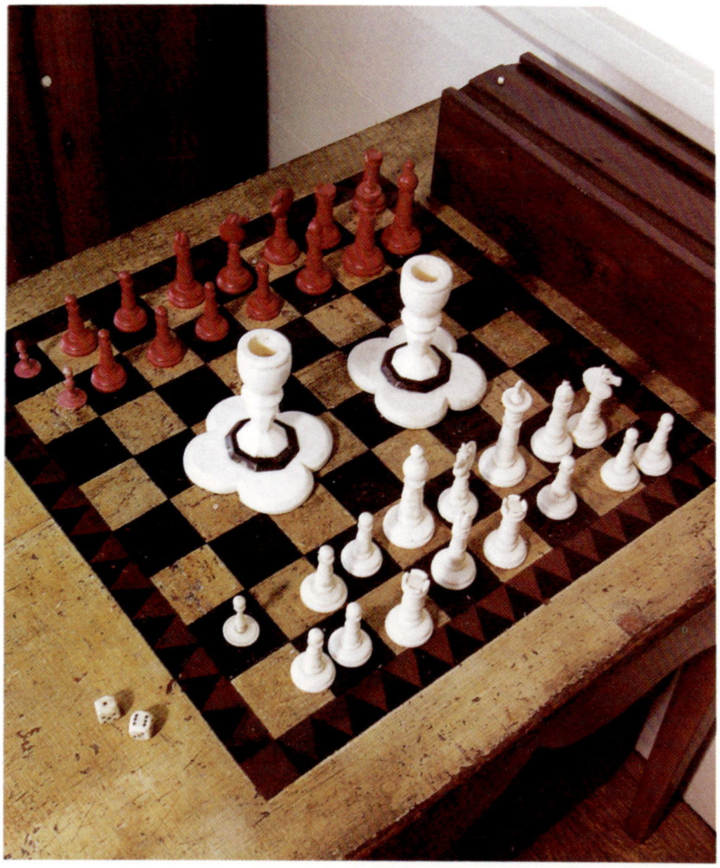

Handsome whalebone candlesticks are complemented by an old elephant ivory chess set. *Private Collection*

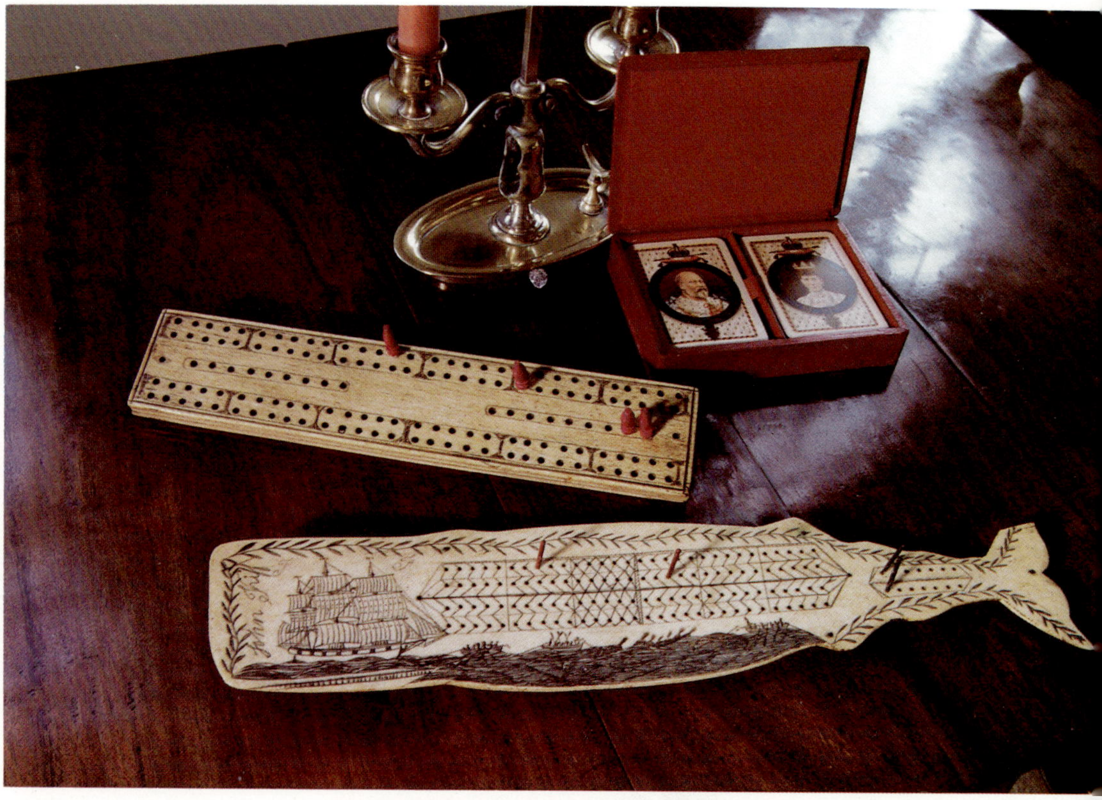

Whalebone cribbage boards. *Madden Collection*

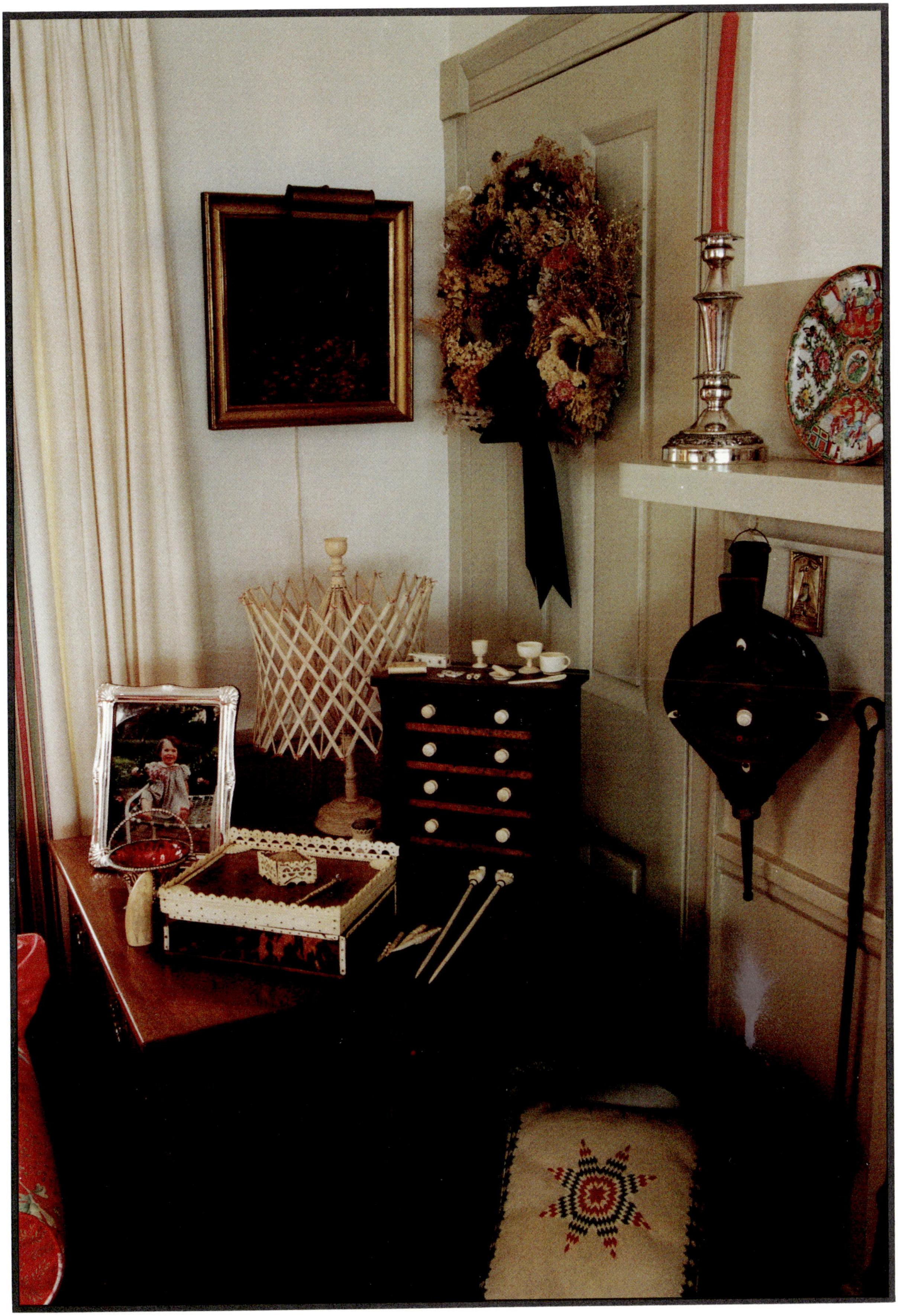

Private Collection

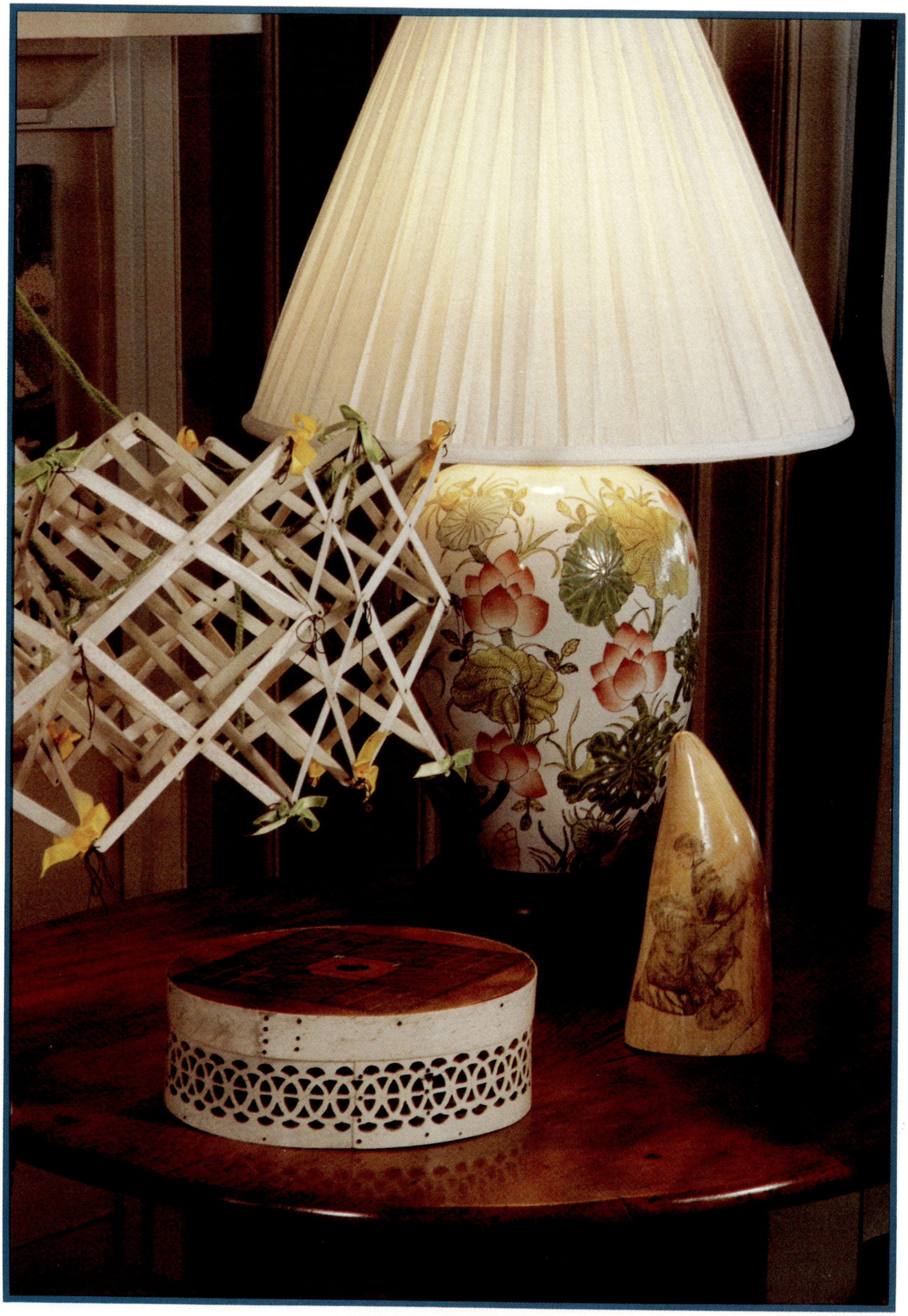

Private Collection.

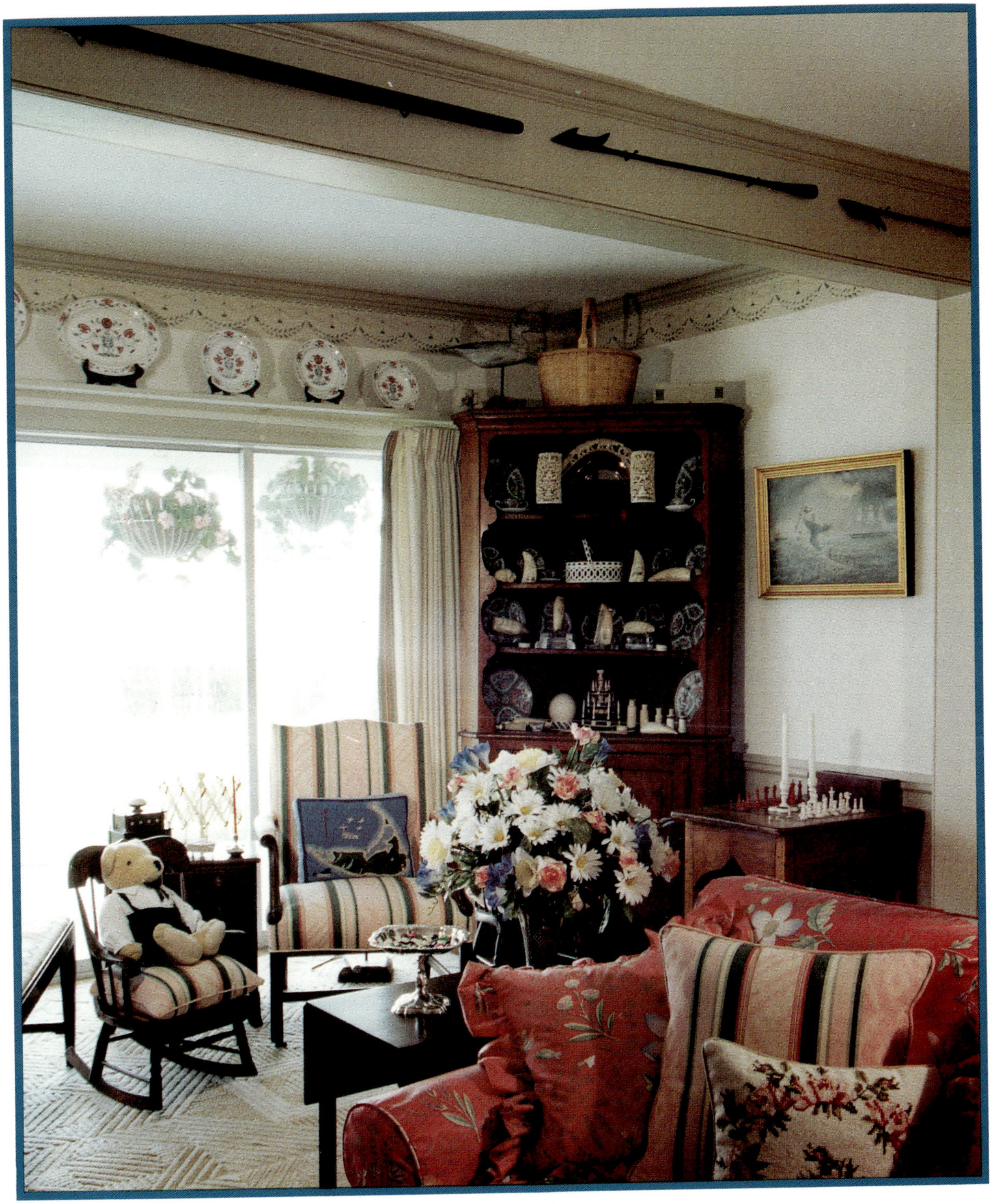

Private Collection.

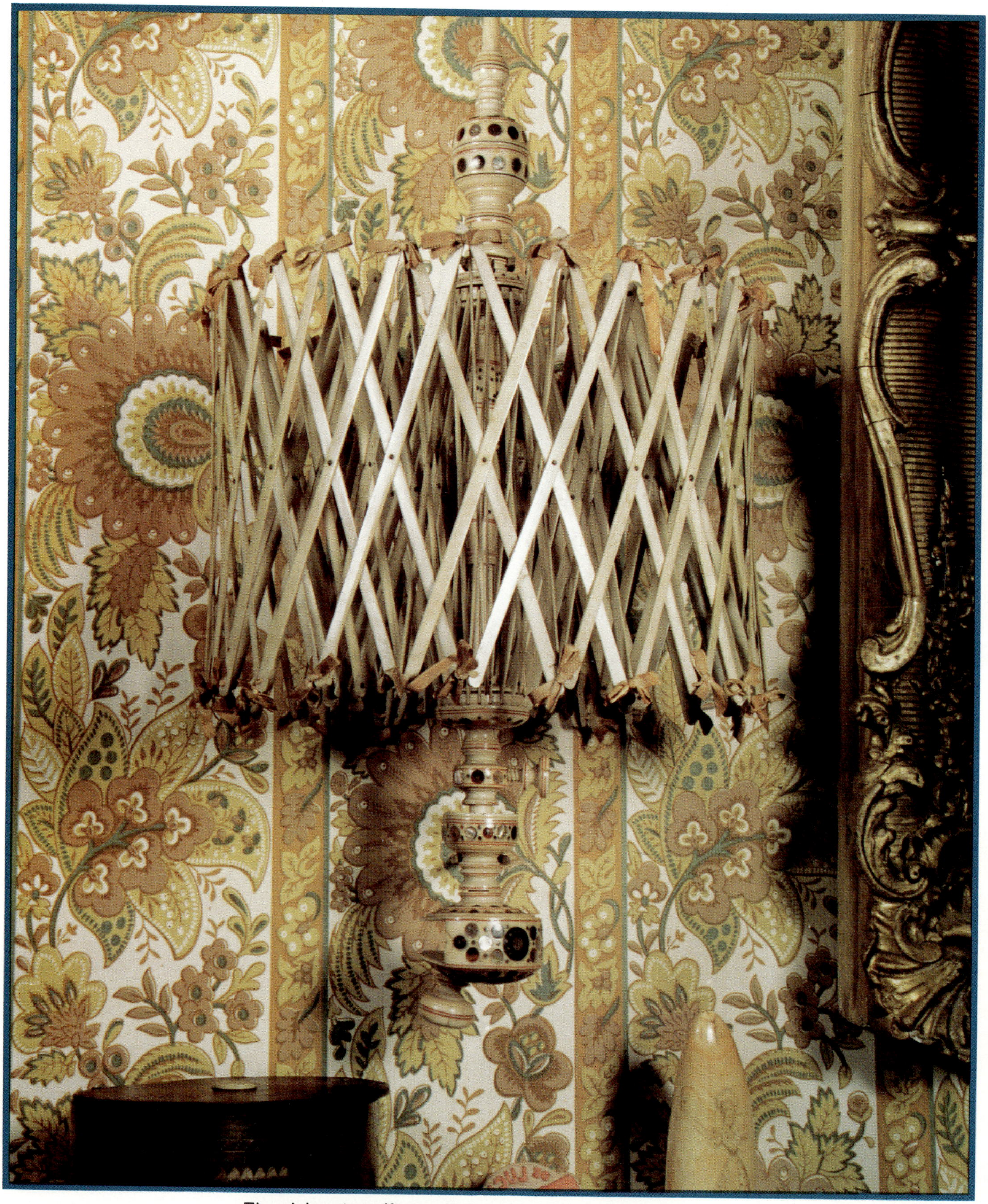

The elaborate swift mounted on the wall of this home is inlaid with abalone, mother of pearl and tortoise shell. *Collection of Raymond and Elizabeth De Lucia*

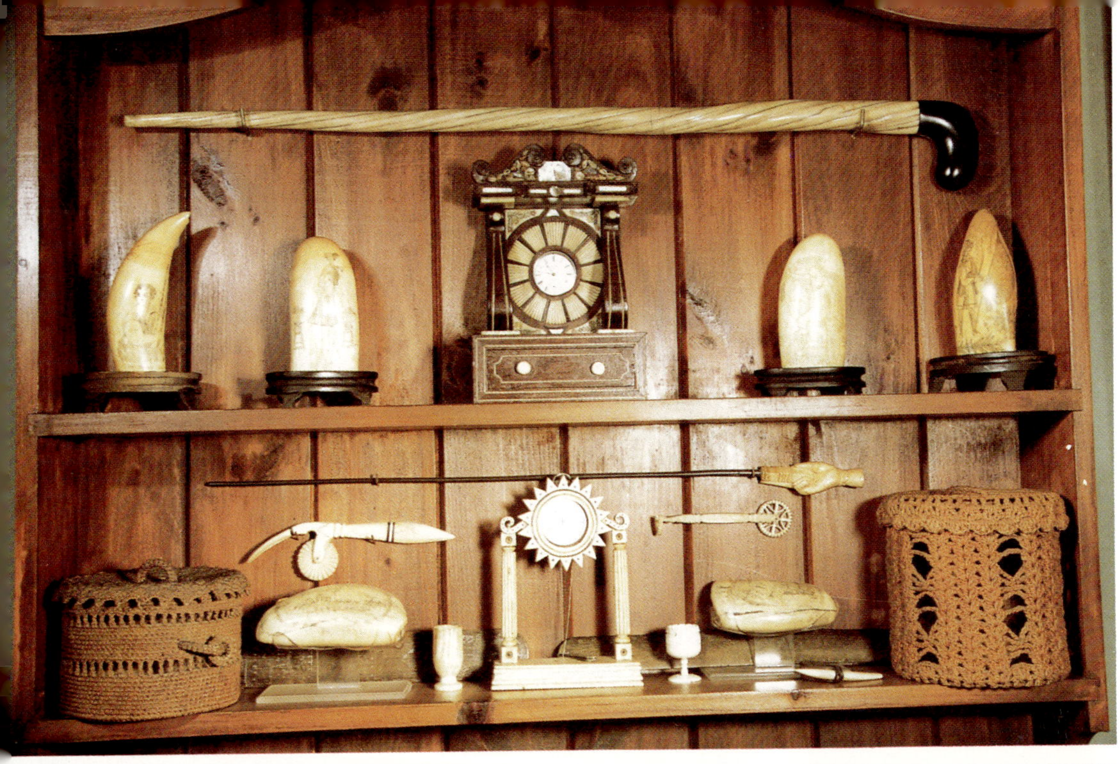

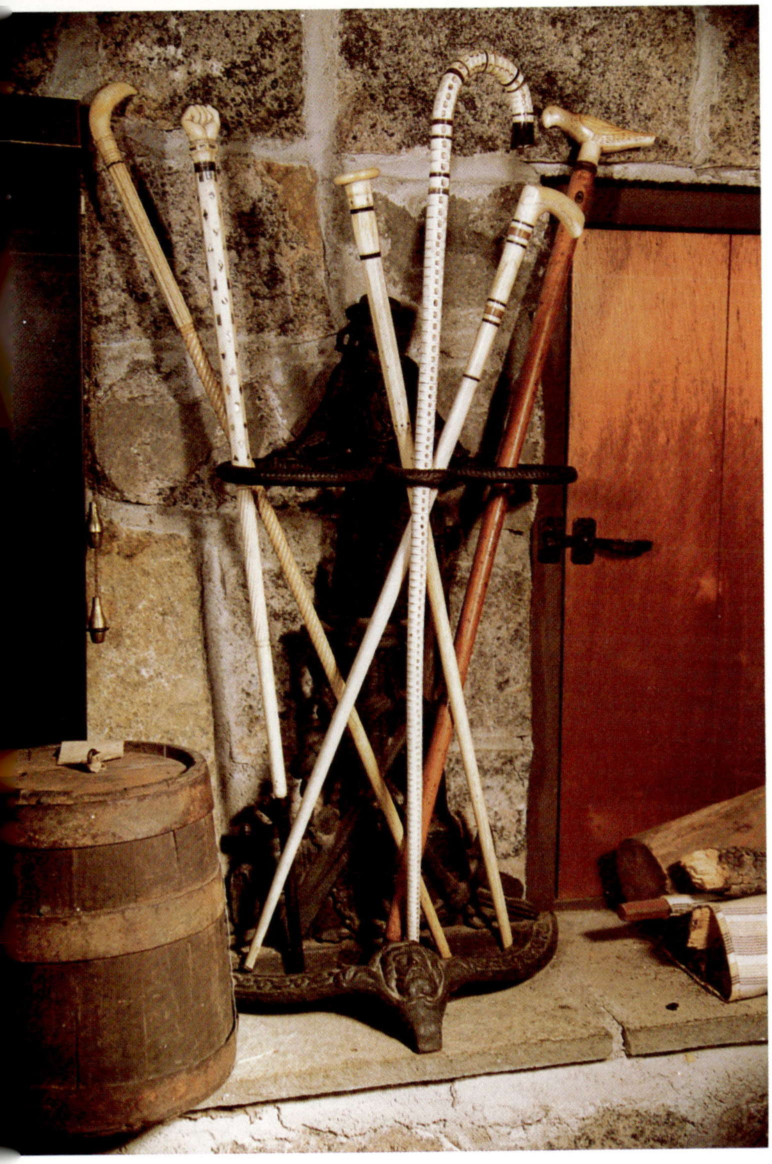

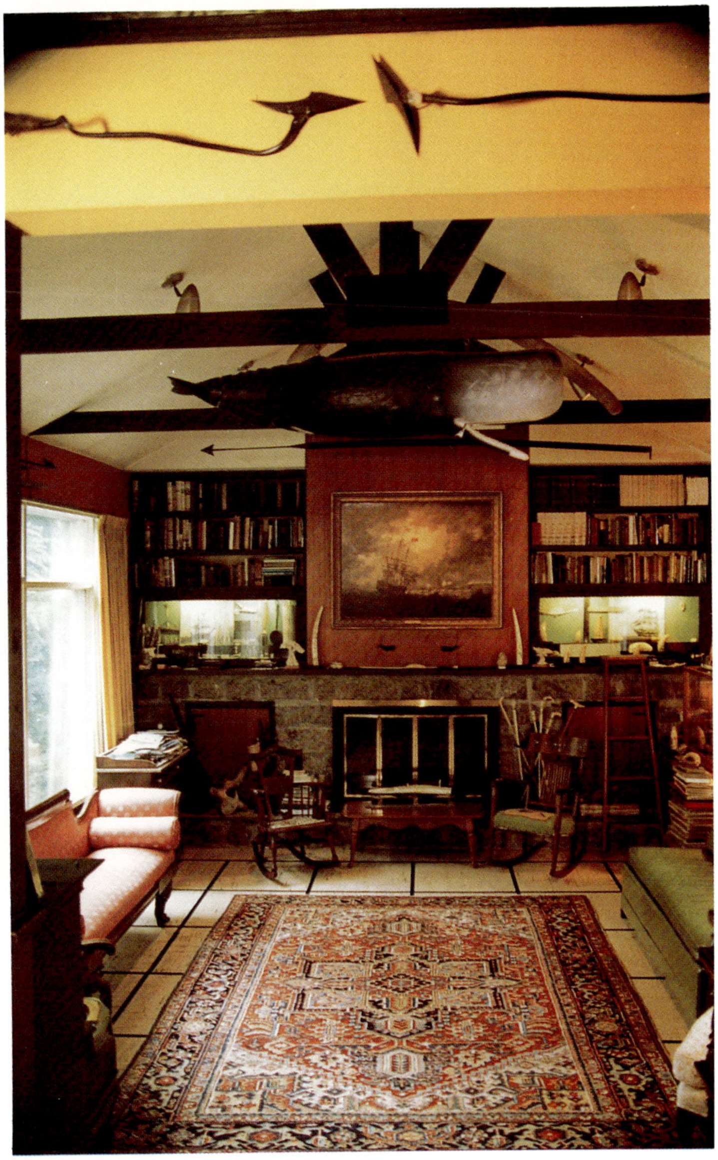

Collection of Raymond and Elizabeth De Lucia

Often contemporary scrimshanders are asked to reproduce a certain piece for collectors. The original might reside in a museum, unavailable to the collector, or simply unattainable for reasons of price. In such a situation, the scrimshander may carefully recreate a famous piece such as a "*Susan*'s Tooth". However, a legitimate reproduction will be clearly marked as such, usually bearing the name of the contemporary artist.

There are techniques which can help collectors differentiate new work from authentic nineteenth century scrimshaw.[1] However, they are mastered only after much familiarization with antique pieces as well as a thorough survey of the existing literature on whaling, scrimshaw and scrimshanders. The new collector is encouraged not only to spend time in research, but also to enlist the aid of a reputable dealer, knowledgeable in the somewhat esoteric field of scrimshaw.

01 Martha Lawrence, "Kendall Hosts Scrimshaw Symposium", *Mass Bay Antiques* (June, 1992), 16.

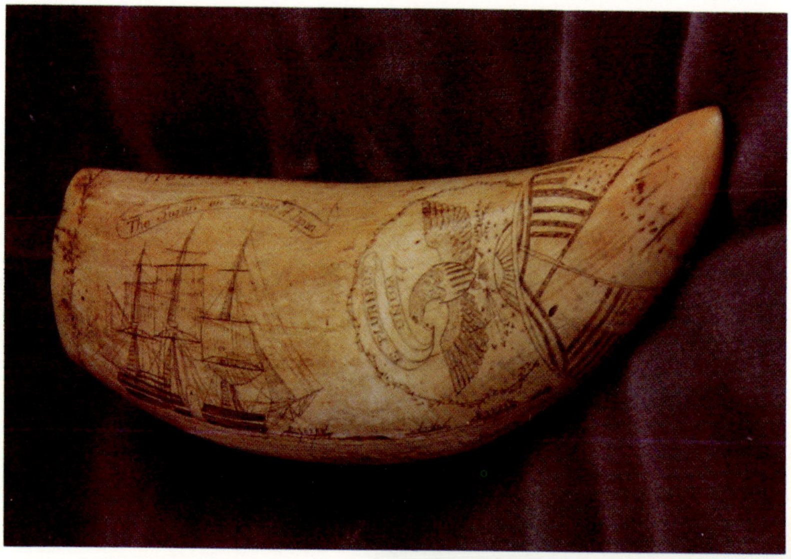

Charles A. Manghis engraved scenes from four original *Susan's* teeth to create these two *"Susan"* composites. The teeth themselves are antique.

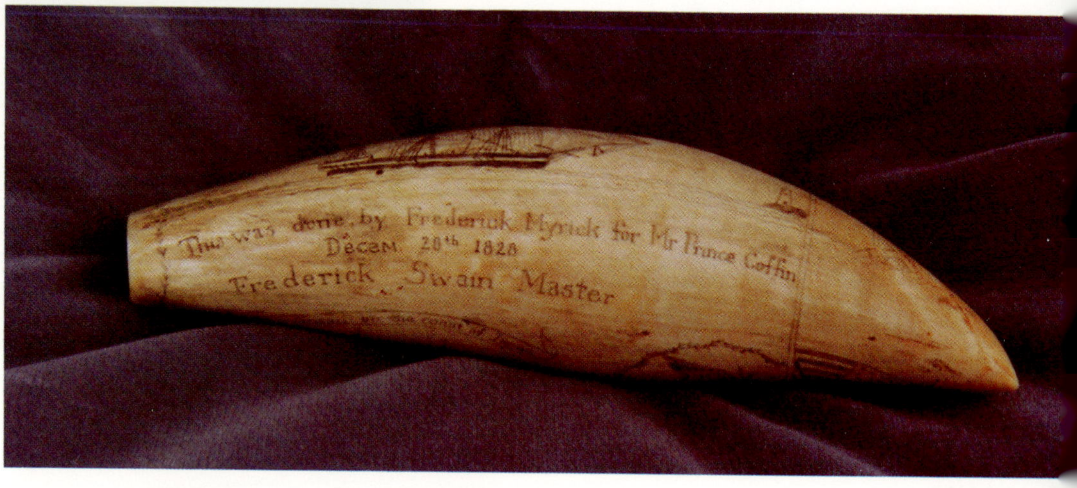

Collection of Charles Granick

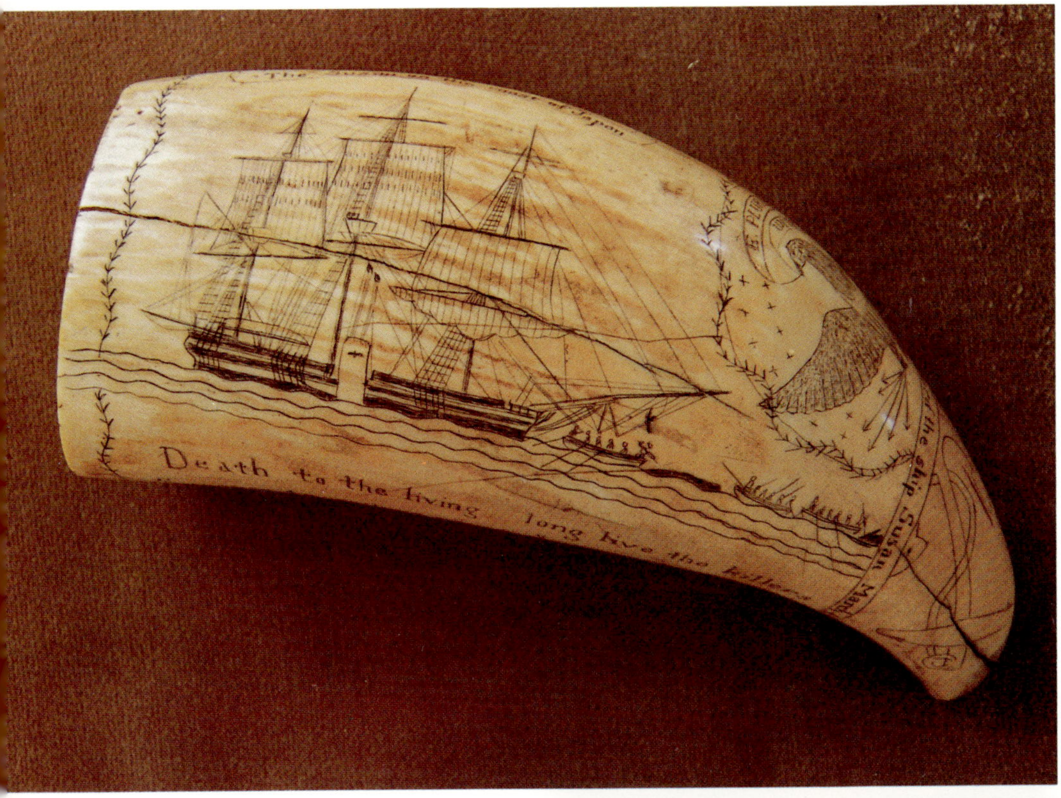

Private Collection

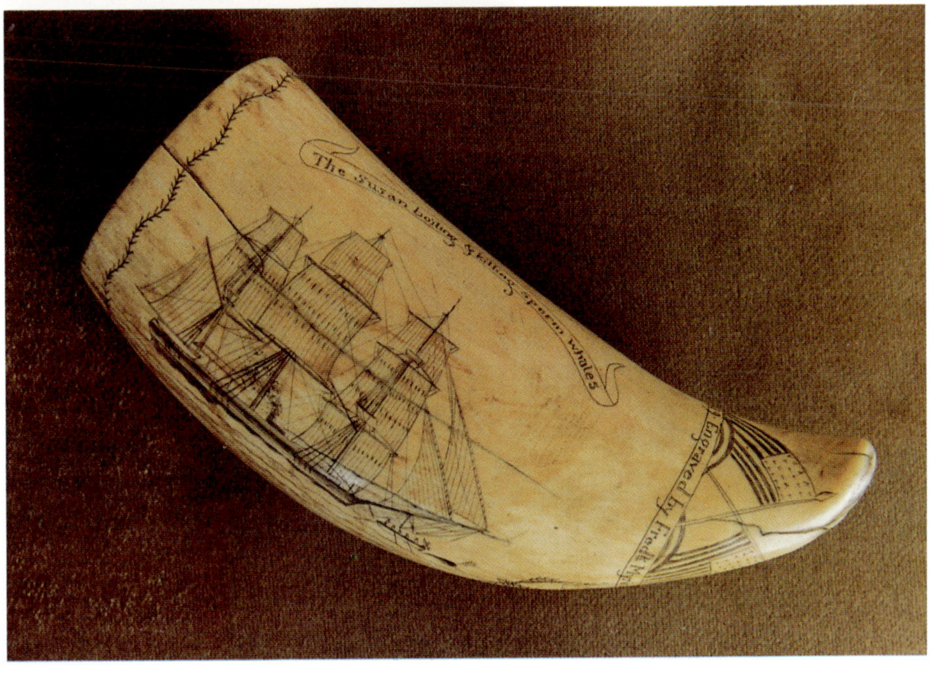

8. The Legacy Continued: Contemporary Scrimshanders

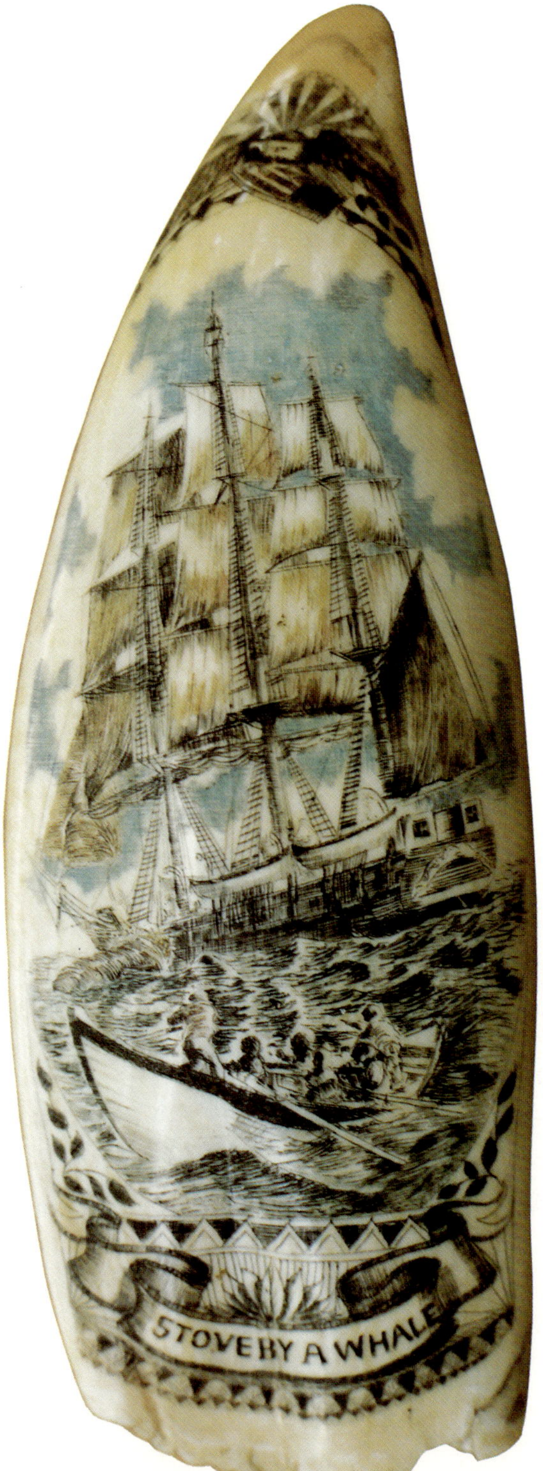

Purely defined as the occupational art of whalers, scrimshaw ended in the early twentieth century along with the Yankee whale fishery itself. However, many artists today continue the legacy of the whaler/scrimshanders, although their practice of scrimshaw is a commercial as well as artistic pursuit.

William Perry is considered to be the transitional artist who links nineteenth century scrimshanders to contemporary practitioners. Born in New Bedford, Massachusetts in 1895, Perry was unable to follow the family tradition of whaling. Artistic from boyhood, he began to practice scrimshaw about the time the last square-rigged whaleship sailed from New Bedford in 1924.[1] Over the next forty years Perry produced a large body of work and provided a continuity between contemporary artists and their whalemen predecessors.

Contemporary scrimshaw is decorative rather than functional. Swifts, bodkins, seam rubbers and fids remain nineteenth century curiosities. Occasionally an ivory basket or pie crimper is crafted, but these are the exception rather than the rule. While the themes of recent scrimshaw often reflect the decorative taste of the day or region in which it is produced, many contemporary artists echo the spirit of nineteenth century work in ship portraits, whaling scenes, and representations of marine mammals.

Instances of angry whales ramming the ships of their predators, as portrayed here by David Lazarus, were rare but did occur.

Presentation pieces such as engraved teeth and ivory carvings comprise much contemporary scrimshaw. Collaboration between Nantucket ivory carver Charles Sayle and the creator of the contemporary Nantucket Lightship Basket pocketbook, José Reyes, resulted in the plethora of scrimshawed adornments which now grace this Nantucket classic. Some contemporary scrimshanders are also involved in restoration for both collectors and museums. Frequently, delicate examples of scrimshaw such as swifts have not survived the years and are candidates for such attention.

The Marine Mammal Protection Act of 1972 and the Endangered Species Act of 1973 prohibit importation and interstate sale of threatened species. Elephant ivory was still legally imported, however, from certified African game reserves where it was obtained by natural death or reserve-organized culling. Monies from these sales were returned to the reserves for maintenance and protection of wildlife.

However, illegal poaching still occurred, fueled by overseas manufacturers churning out mass-produced ivory wares. In response, the trade in elephant ivory was effectively banned by a 1989 enactment of the Convention on International Trade in Endangered Species.

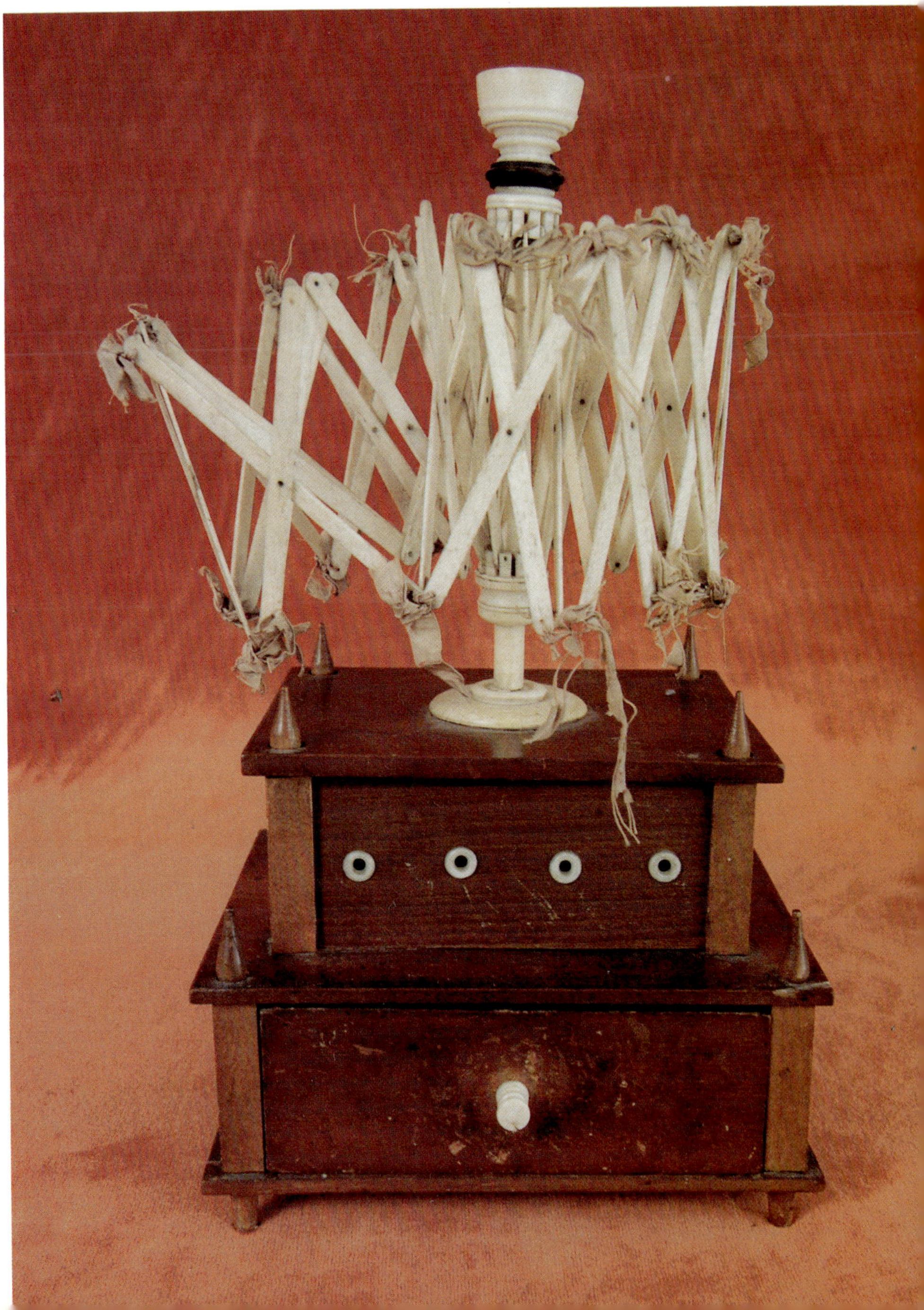

Talented scrimshanders are able to restore pieces even more badly damaged than this antique swift.

Materials employed by scrimshanders today include whalebone and whale ivory imported before 1973, and elephant ivory obtained legally before 1989. Fossilized walrus ivory has become increasingly popular not only because of its impeccable environmental credentials but also because of its remarkable crystalline appearance and unusual color variations.

The contemporary scrimshanders whose work is illustrated on these pages represent only a small fraction of the many fine artists at work today. They are known, however, for the quality of their work, their encouragement of and commitment to legal protection of endangered species, their appreciation of the work of their nineteenth century predecessors and their conscious continuation of that legacy.

[01] William Gilkerson, *The Scrimshander* (San Francisco, Calif.: Troubadour Press, 1975), 23.

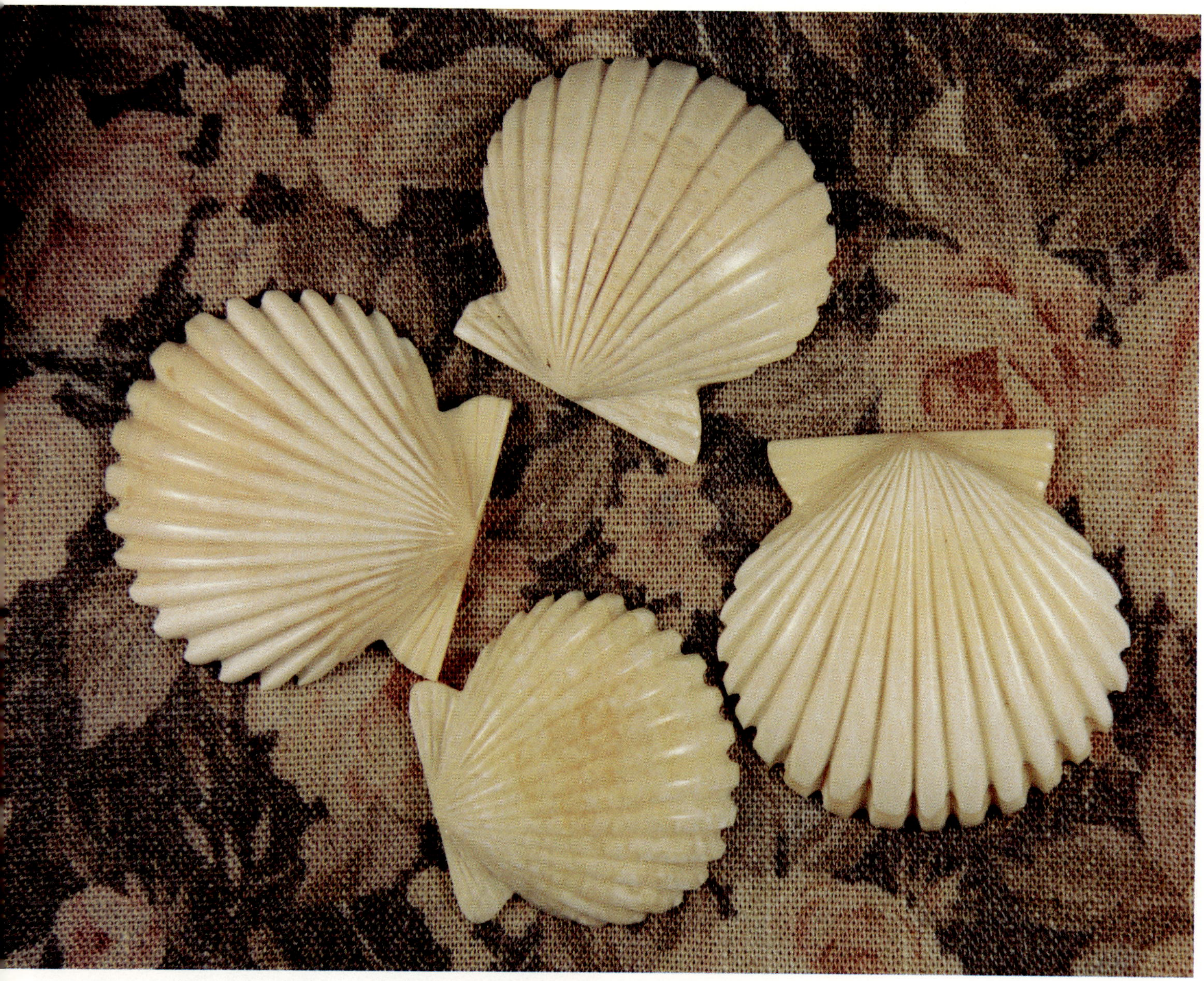

Various materials are used in contemporary scrimshaw. These scallop shells were carved by Charles A. Manghis from (clockwise from top) whalebone, whale ivory, fossilized walrus ivory and whale ivory.

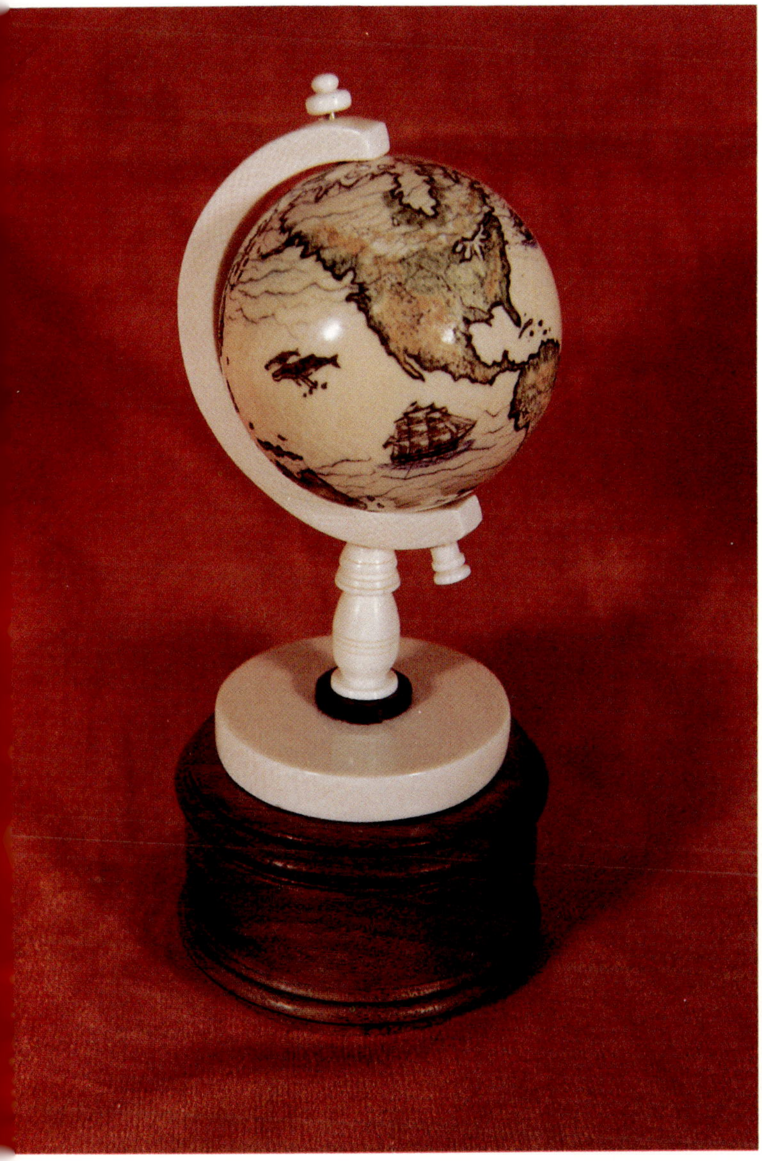

Carved by Charles A. Manghis from an antique elephant ivory billiard ball, the engraving on this unusual globe includes whaling scenes and species of whales located in their respective habitats. *Private Collection*

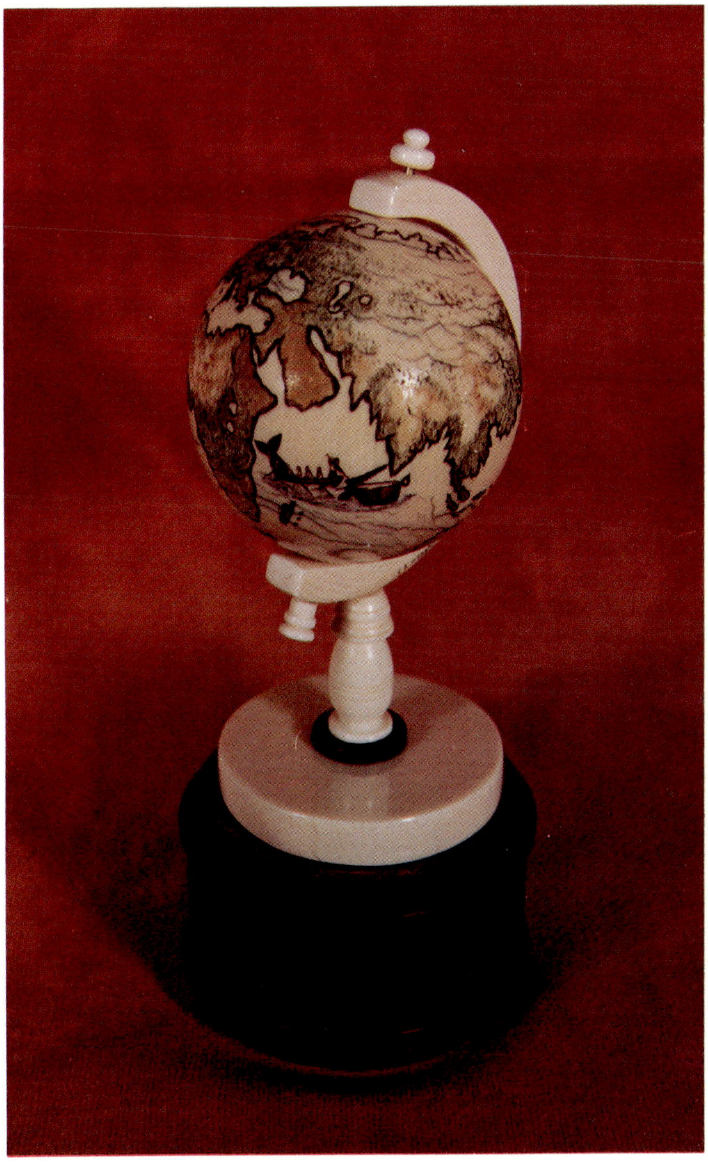

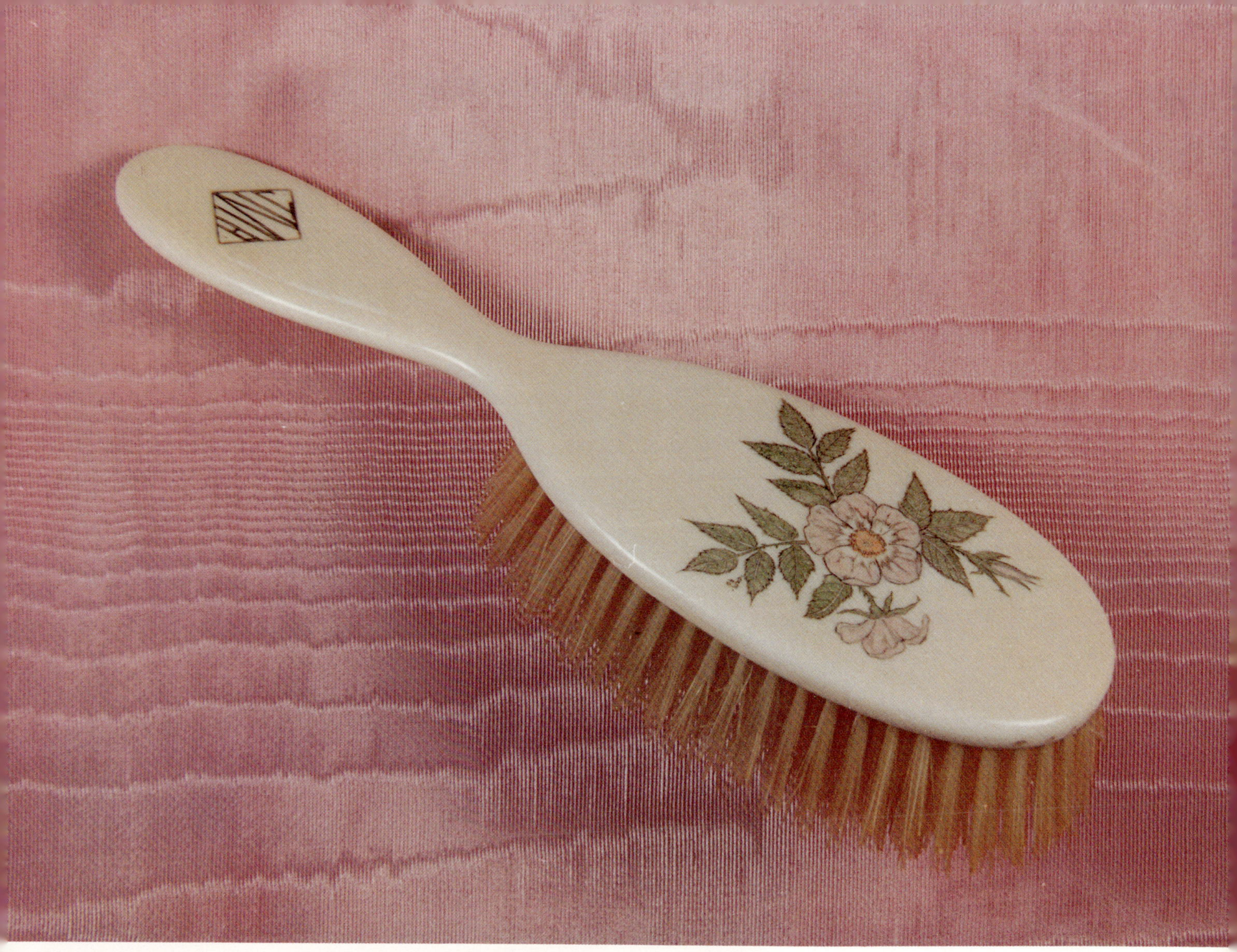

Early twentieth century elephant ivory hairbrush has been engraved with rosa rugosa by Charles A. Manghis.

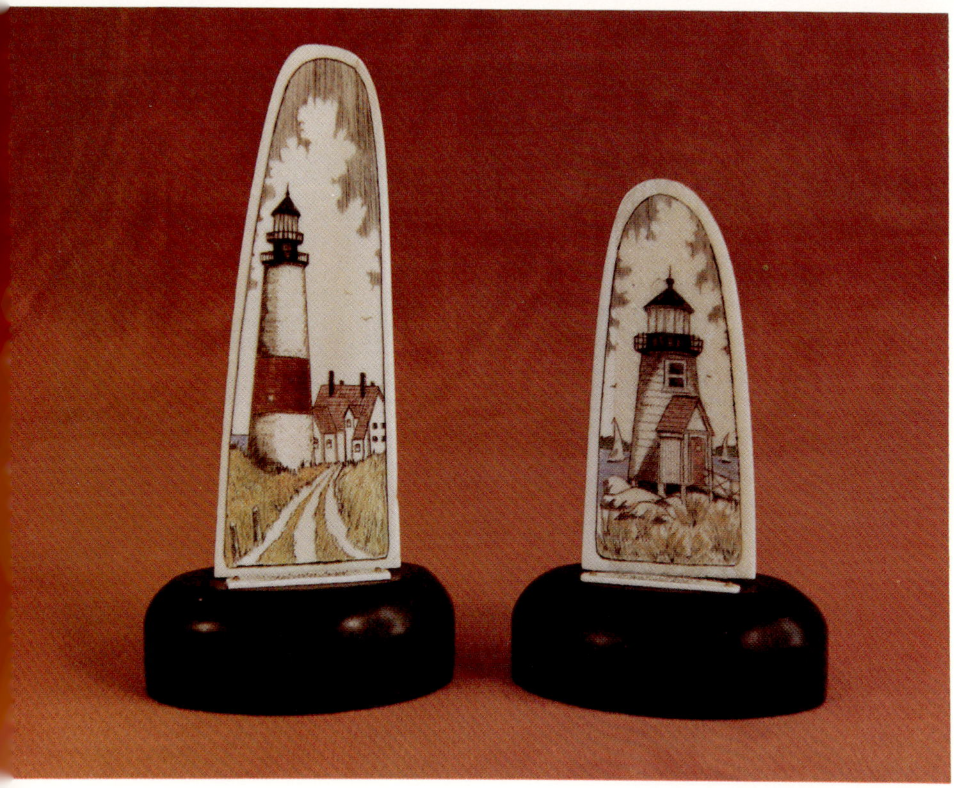

Nantucket's Brant Point and Sankaty Head lighthouses are engraved on fossilized walrus ivory by Charles A. Manghis.

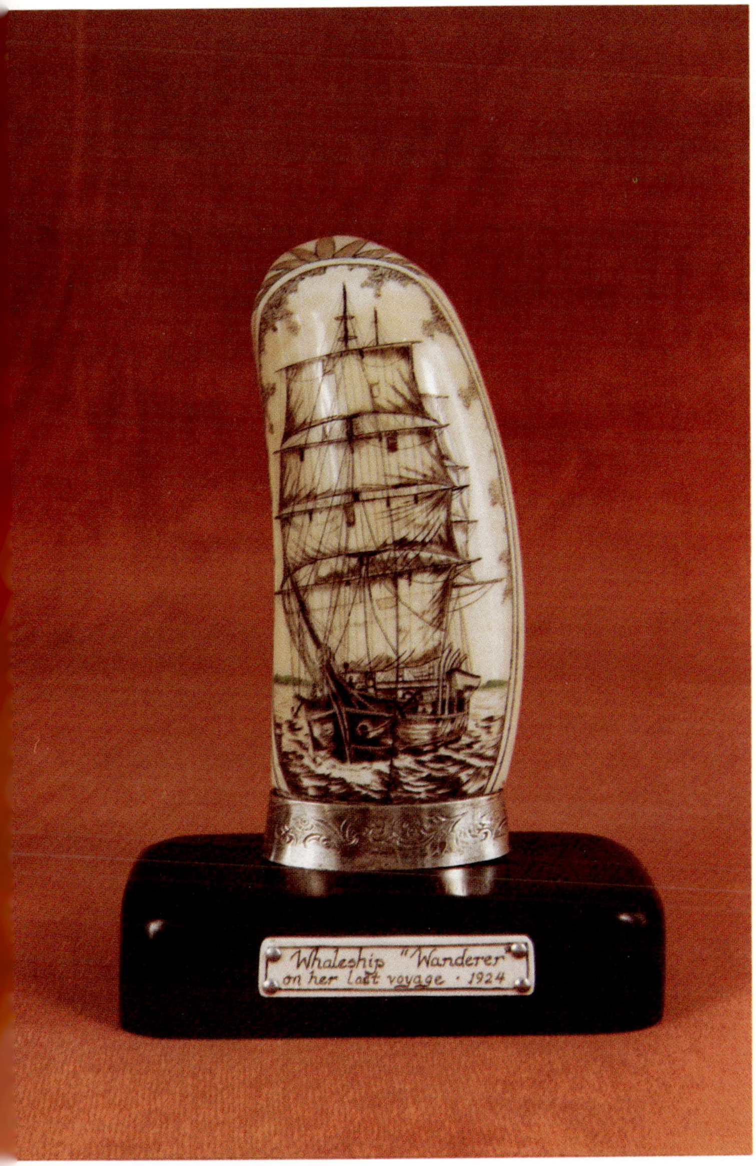

The bark *Wanderer*, the last square-rigged whale ship to sail from New Bedford, is commemorated on this tooth engraved by Charles A. Manghis.

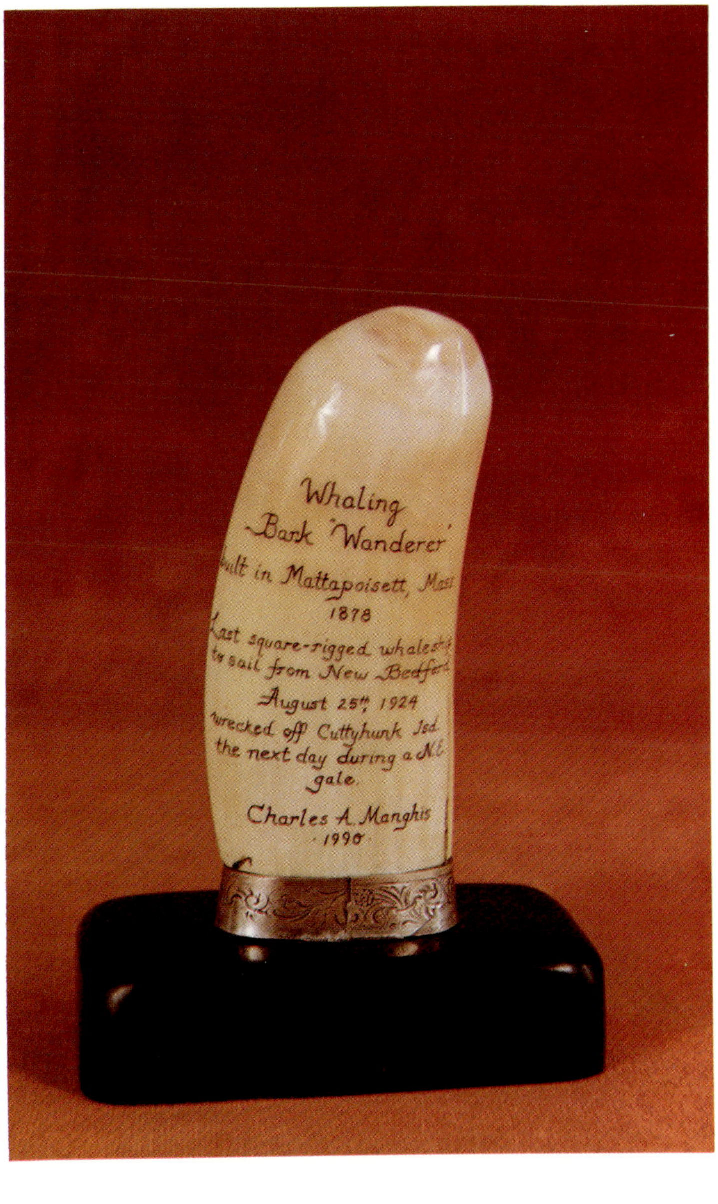

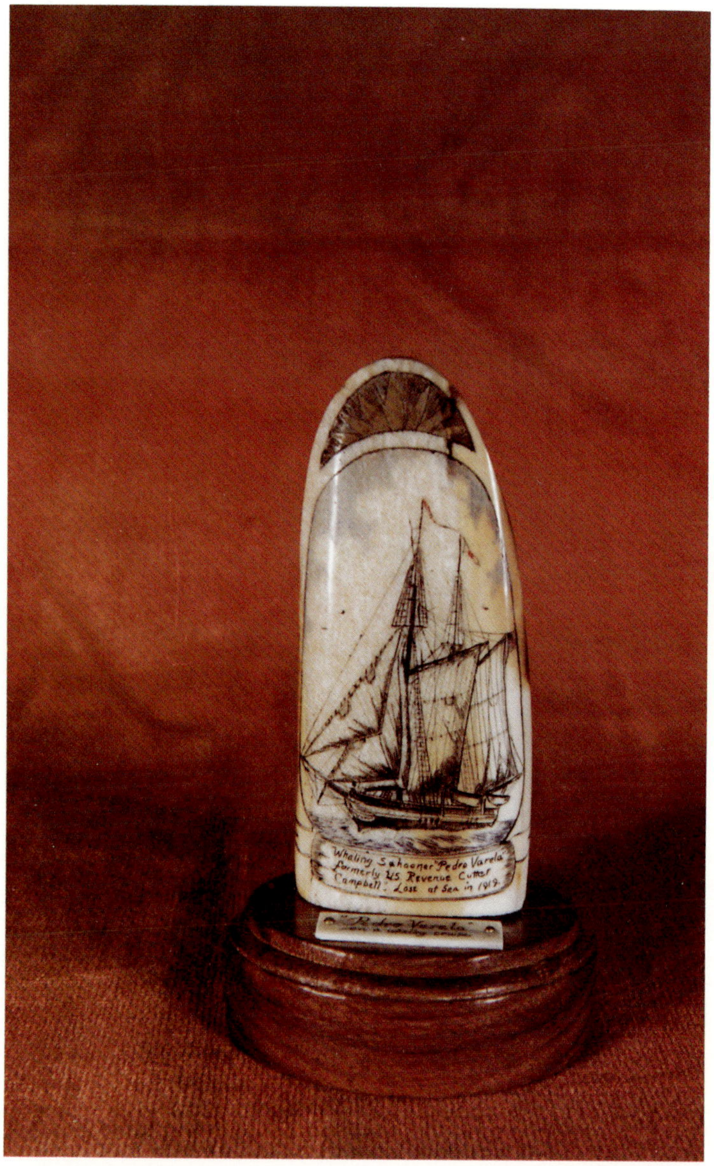

The whaling schooner *Pedro Varela* sails once more on a piece of fossilized walrus ivory. This piece was carved and engraved by Charles A. Manghis.

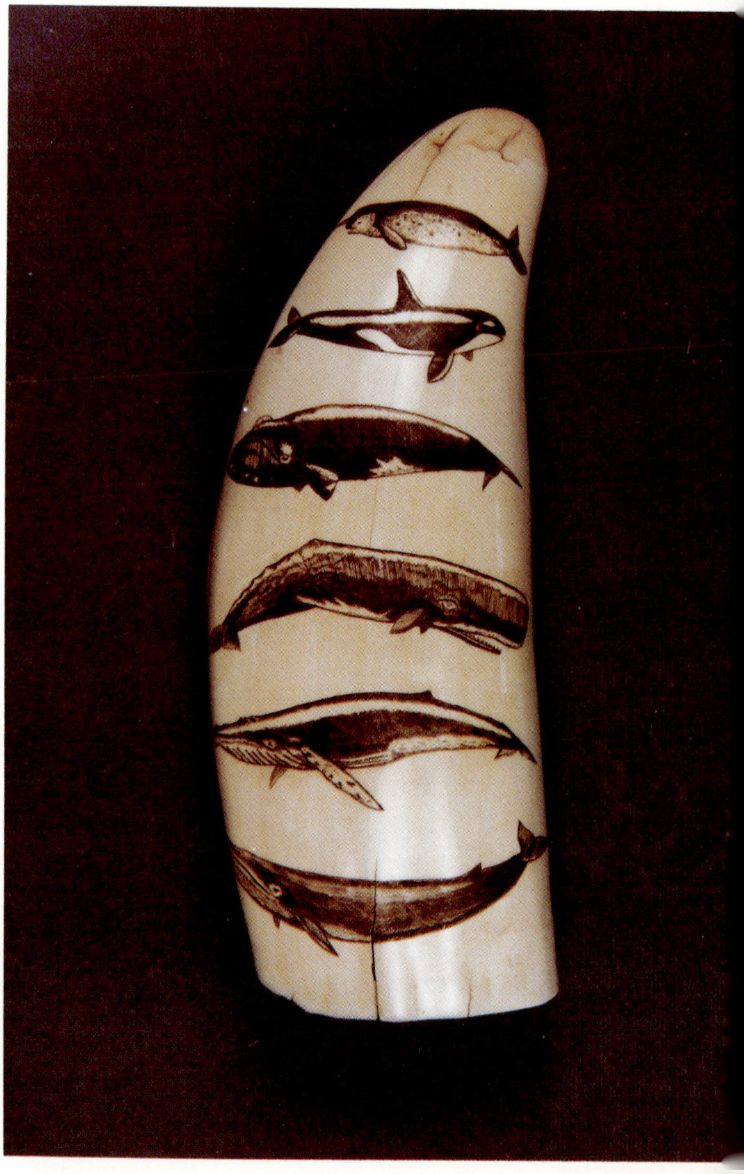

"Whales of the World" adorn this large sperm whale tooth engraved by Charles A. Manghis. From the tip down, the whales depicted are: narwhal, orca, right, sperm, humpback and finback. *Private Collection*

Charles A. Manghis reproduced an 1871 lithograph on a walrus tusk. The scene is set in the Bering Strait; the coast of Siberia's east cape is visible on the left and the Alaskan mainland on the right. *Private Collection*

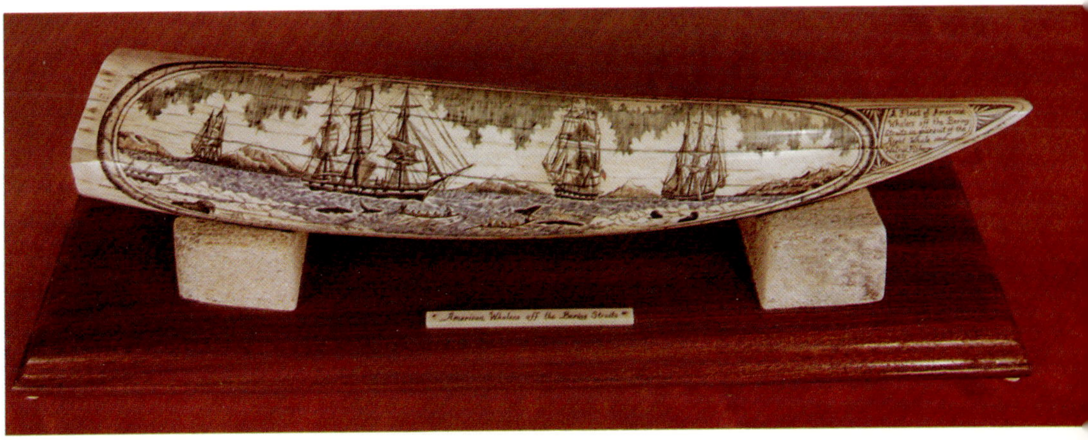

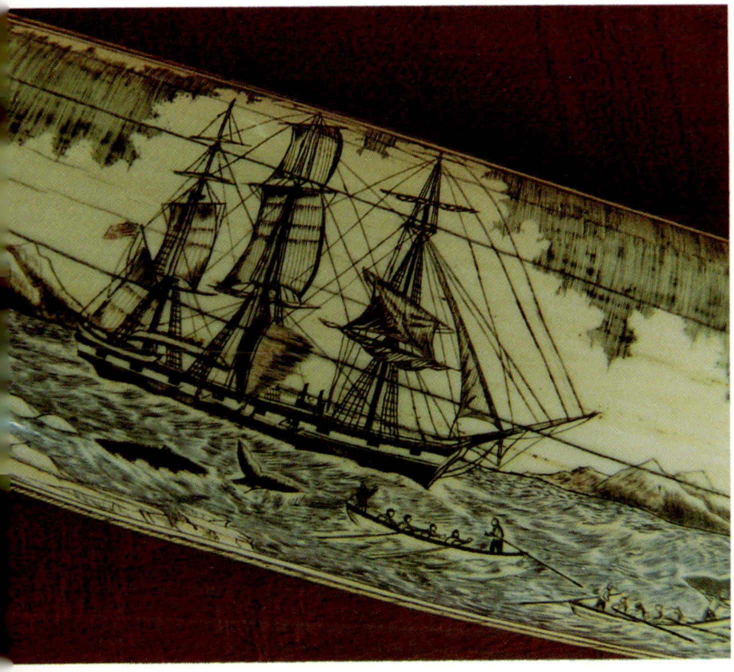

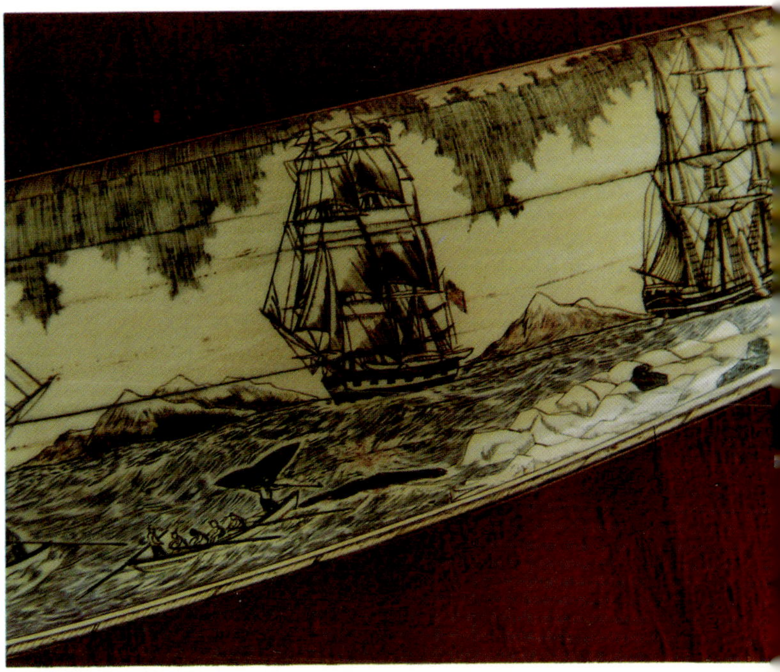

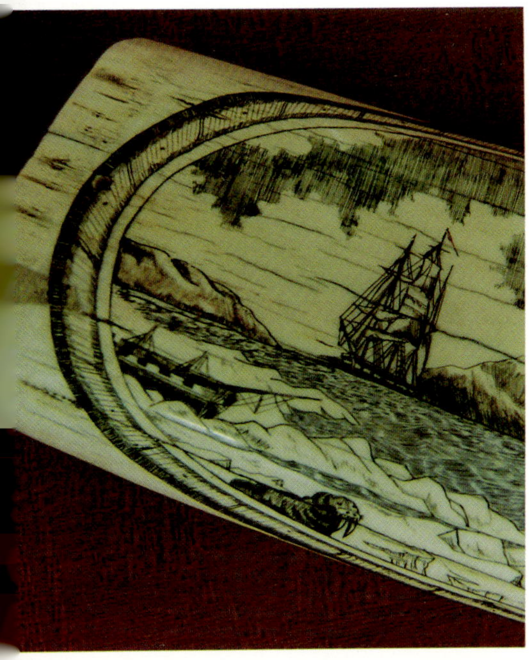

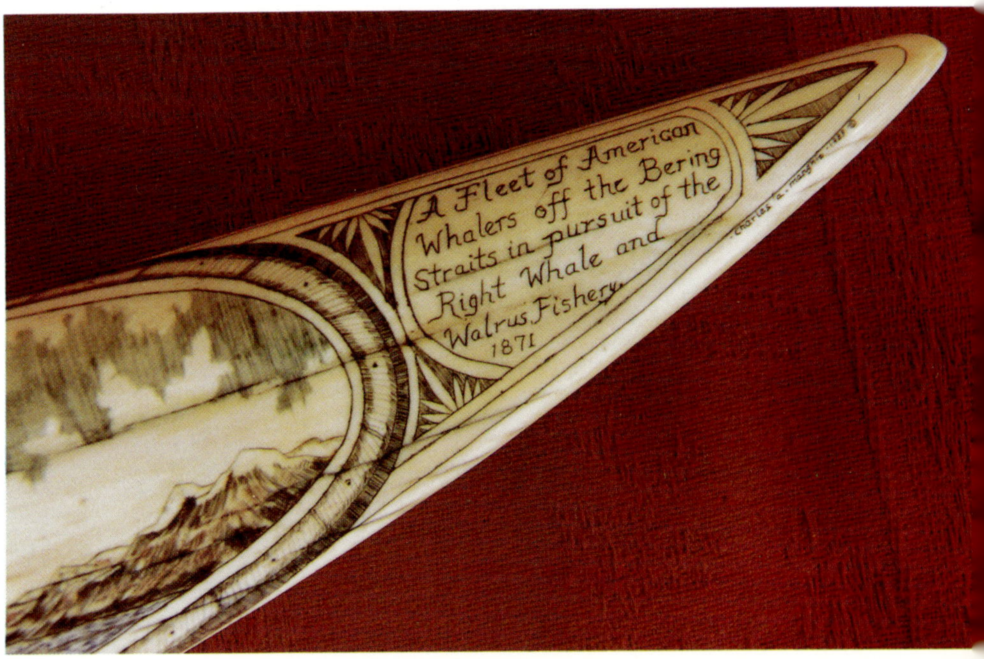

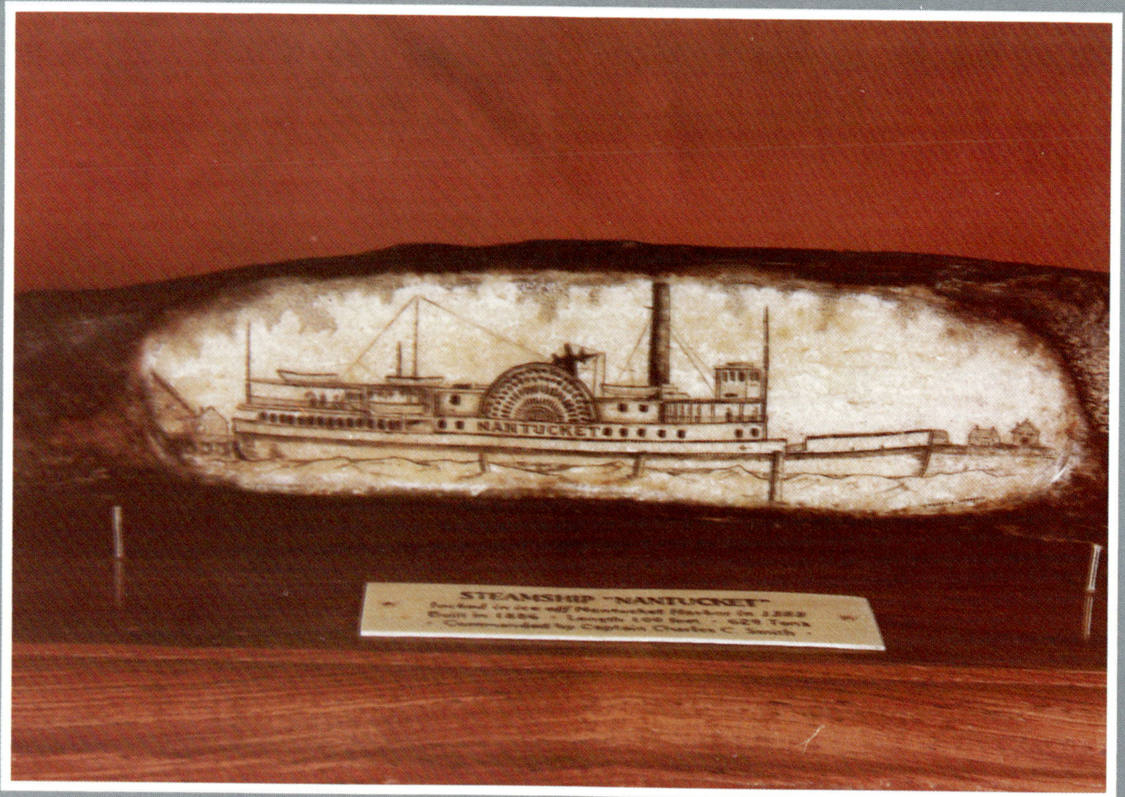

The steamer *Nantucket* locked in ice off Nantucket Harbor in 1888 is the subject of this work by Charles A. Manghis on a fossilized walrus ivory artifact. When cut, the dark exterior reveals the beautifully variegated core. *Private Collection*

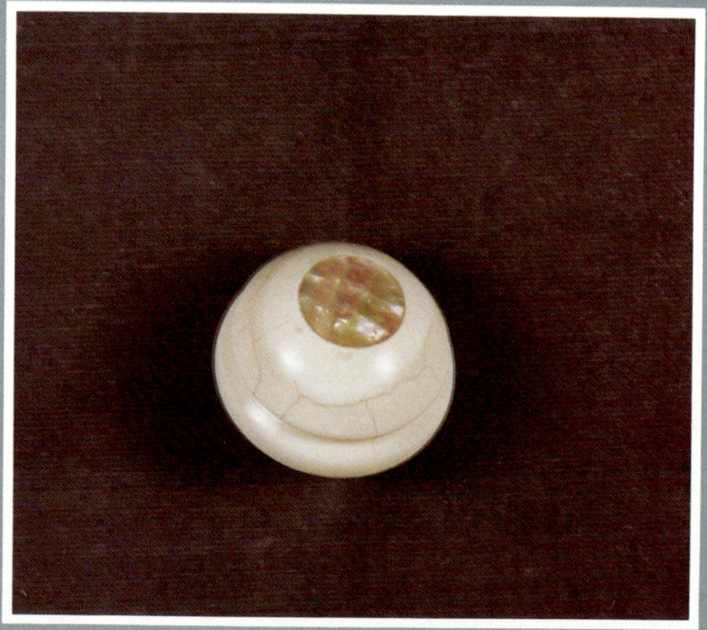

This "mortgage button", carved from antique elephant ivory by Charles A. Manghis, is inlaid with mother of pearl. Historically, when the mortgage was paid off, a celebratory button was set in the newel post of the home's stairway covering the ashes of the burned mortgage papers.

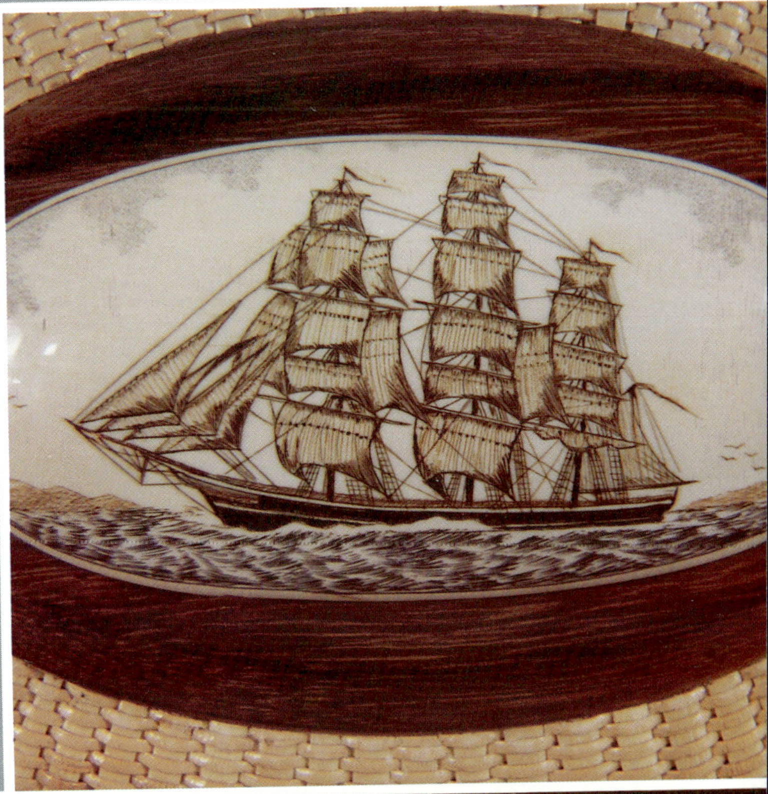

The *Cutty Sark*, engraved by Charles A. Manghis, graces the top of this Nantucket Lightship Basket.

The staves of this Nantucket Lightship Basket, made by the author, are antique baleen collar stays.

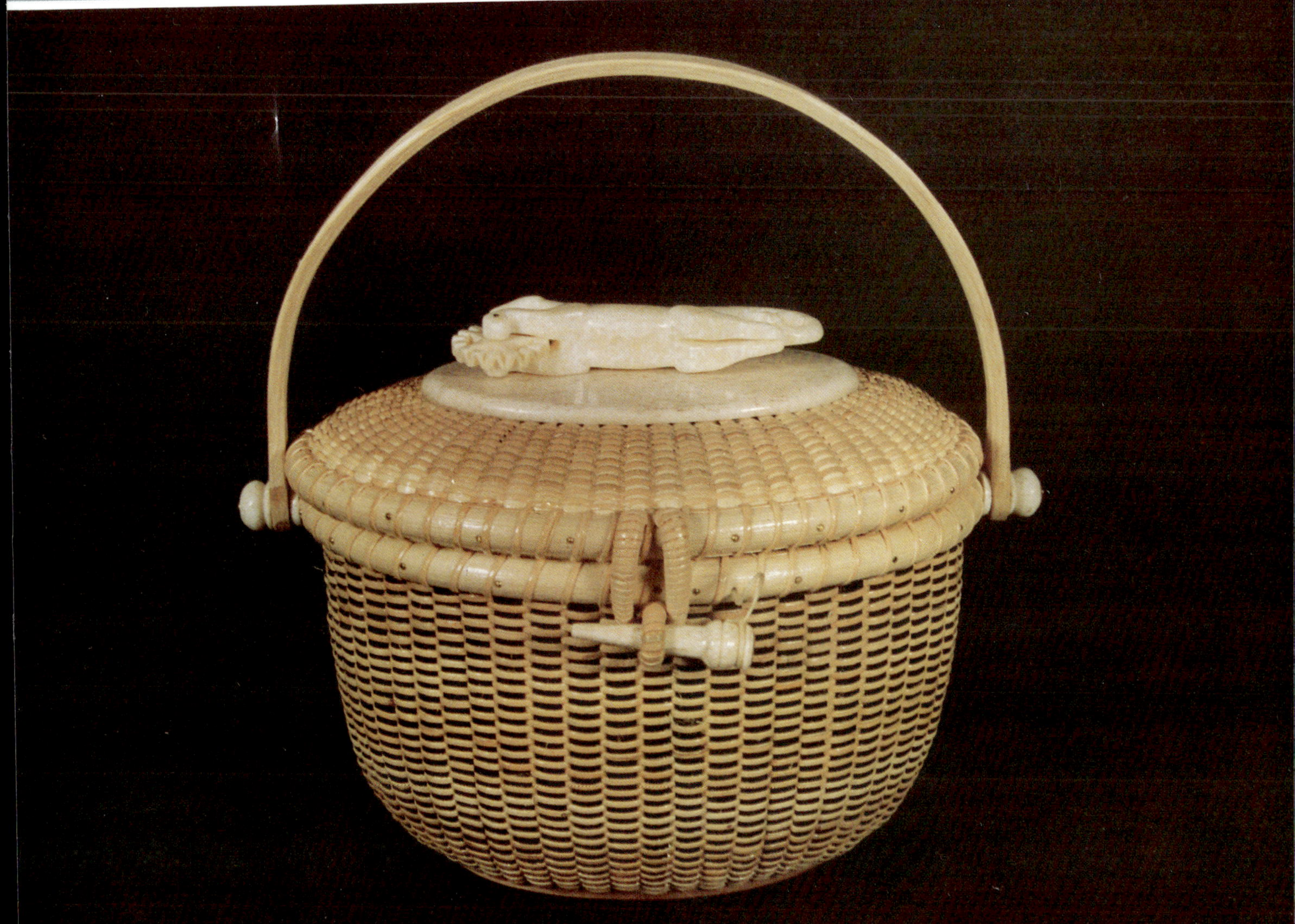

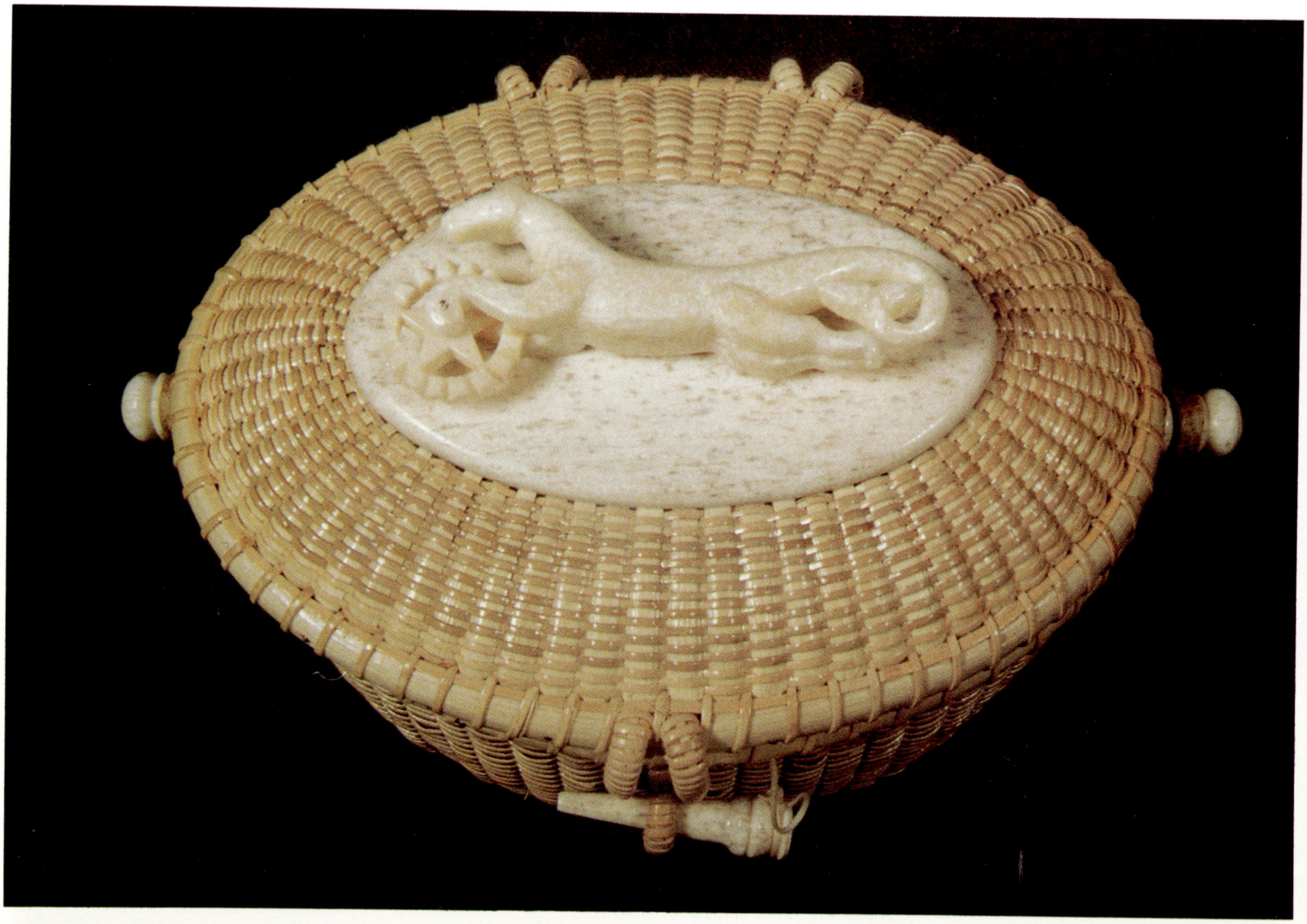

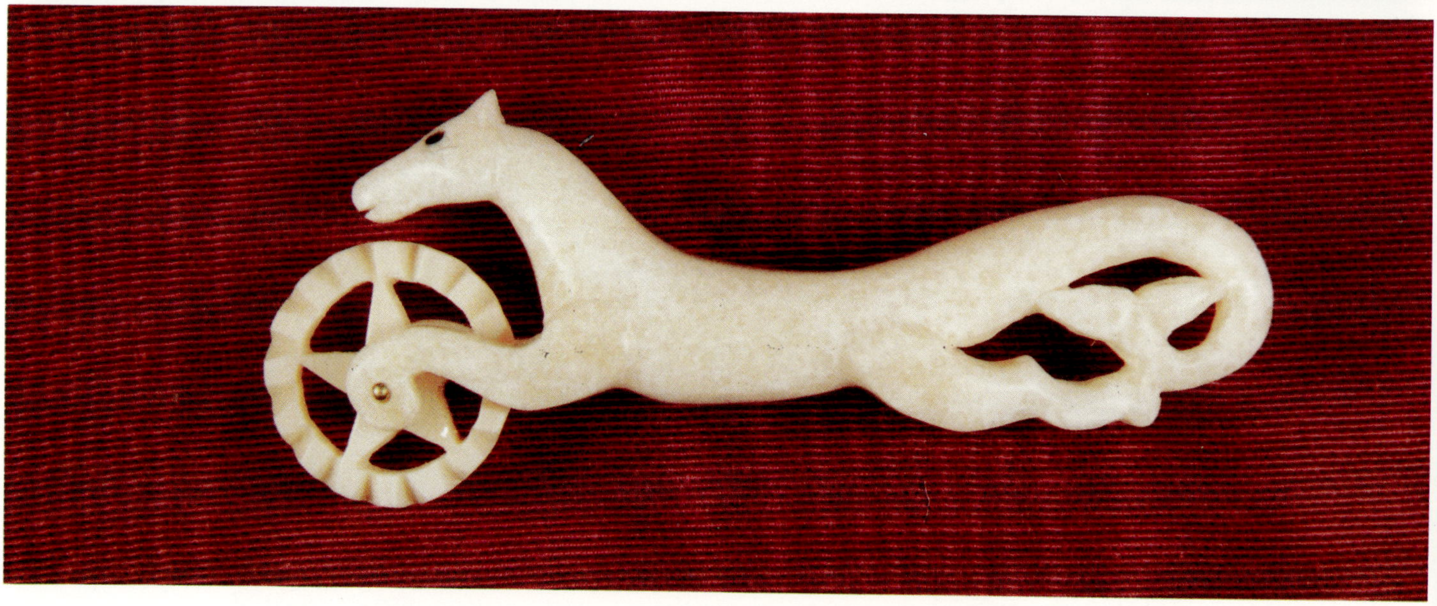

Intended as a gift for his daughter, Charles A. Manghis fashioned the basket's top plate of whalebone and, on the reverse, ebony. He chose fossilized walrus ivory, whose crystalline composition is especially apparent in this piece, to carve a reproduction of an antique pie crimper to top the basket.

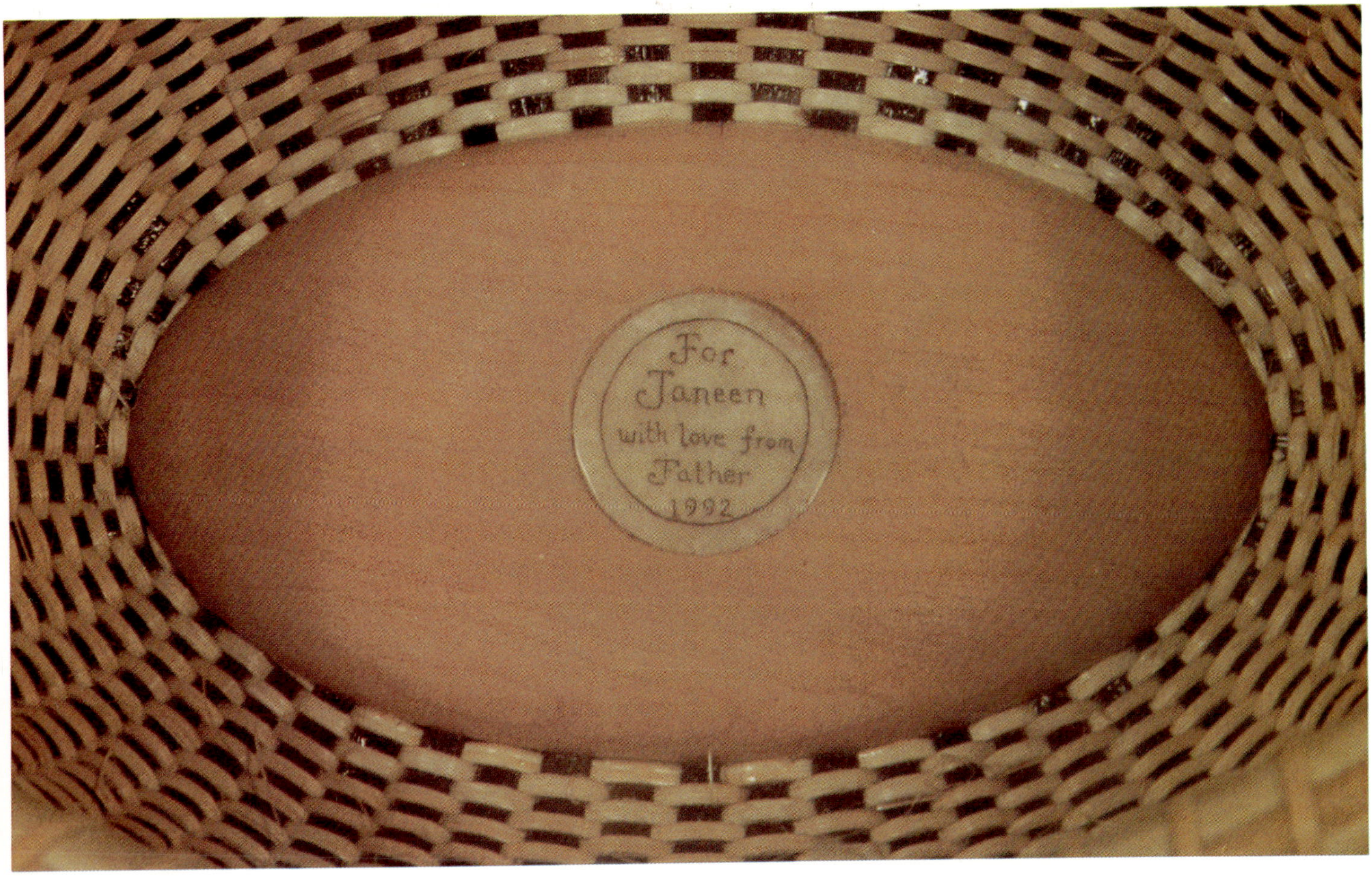

Fossilized walrus ivory was also used for an engraved disc inlaid within the basket to commemorate the gift's presentation.

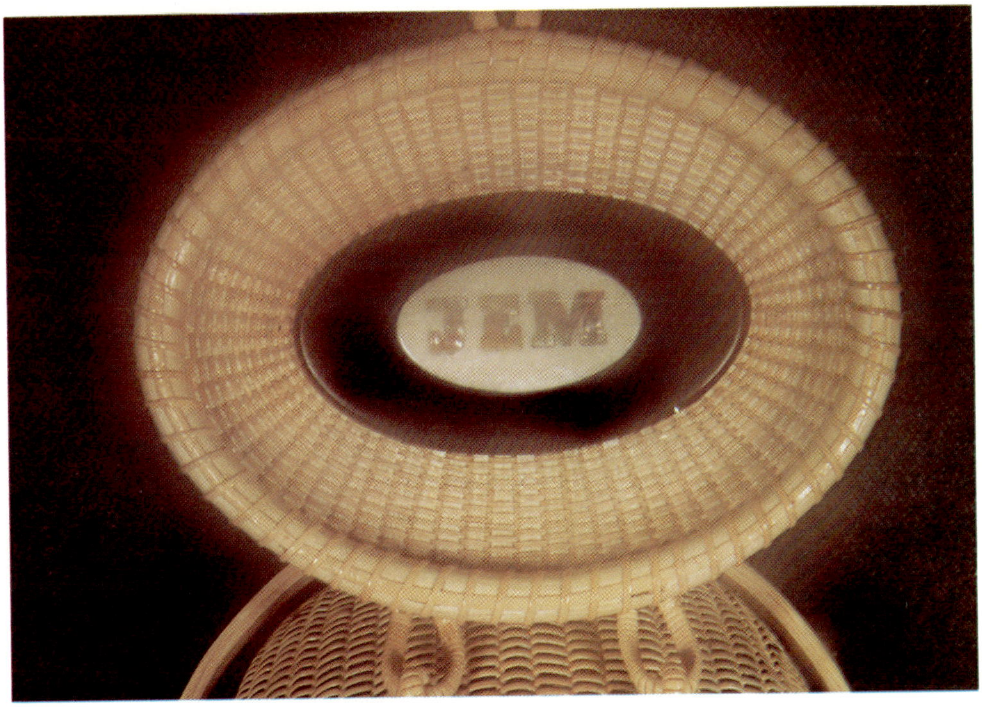

Inside the basket's lid, Manghis inlaid his daughter's initials, carved of mother of pearl, in whalebone.

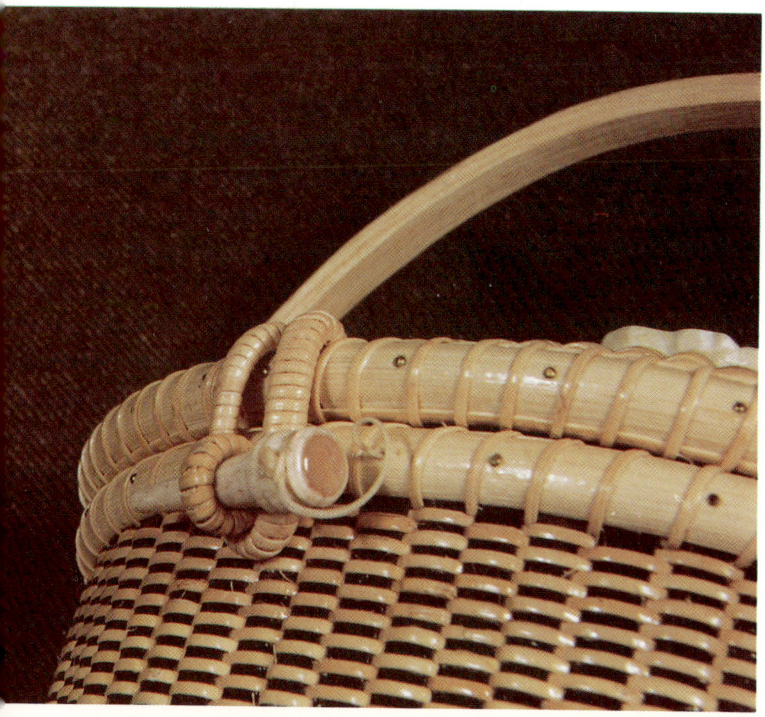

Carrying his theme to the smallest detail, Manghis carved the basket's latching peg and handle knob of whalebone inlaid with mother of pearl.

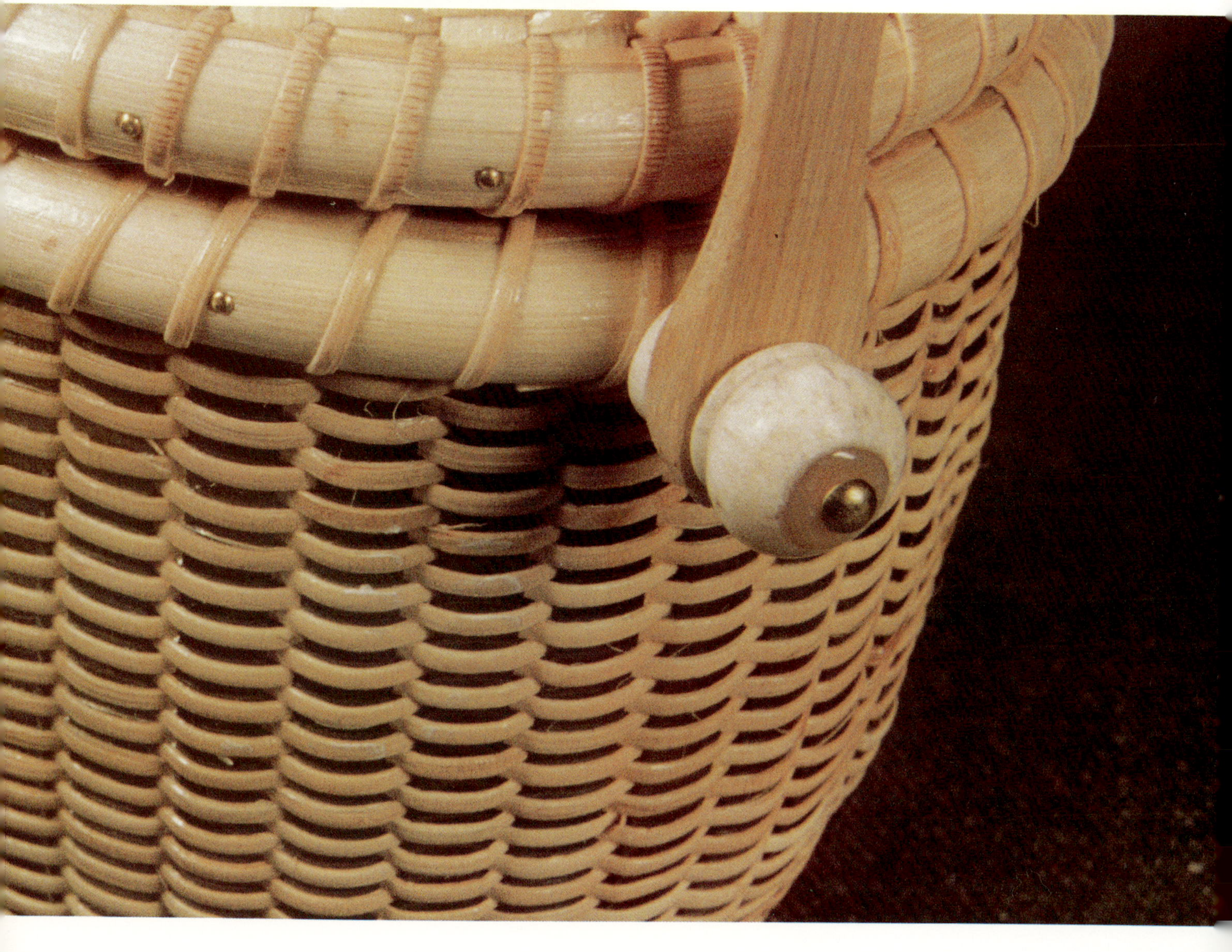

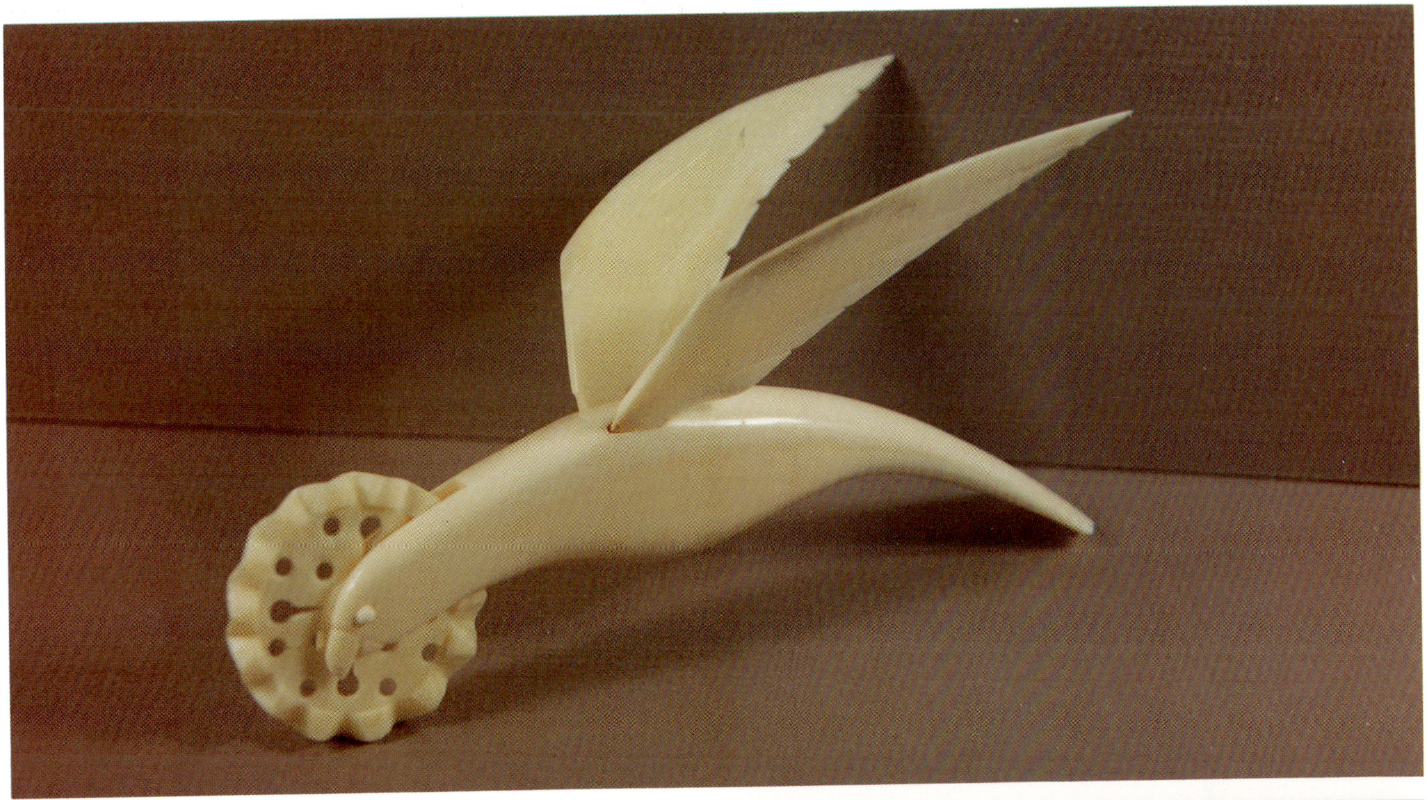

This contemporary version of a nineteenth century classic is carved from whale ivory. *Collection of Jeanne Kitz*

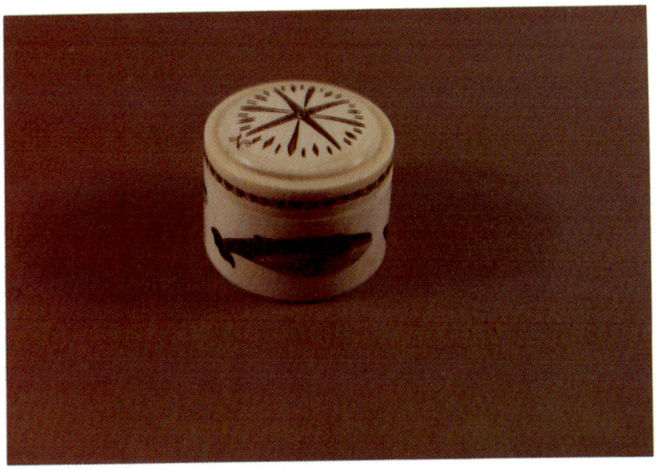

This small box was carved and engraved with a compass rose and various whales by Don Thomas. *Collection of Jeanne Kitz*

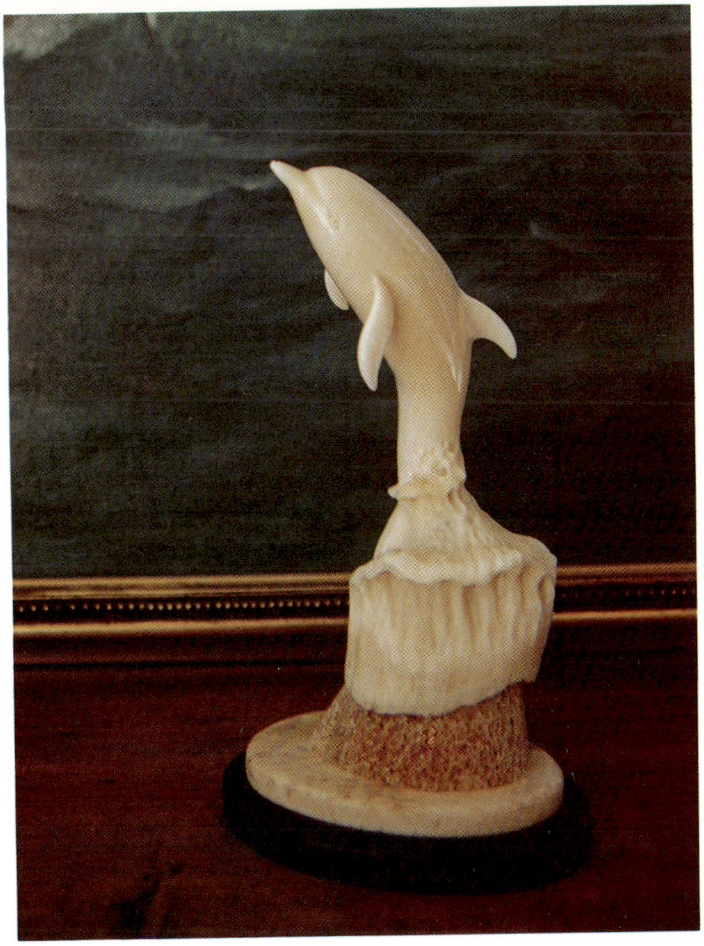

Al Doucette carved this graceful dolphin from a whale's tooth. *Collection of Jeanne Kitz*

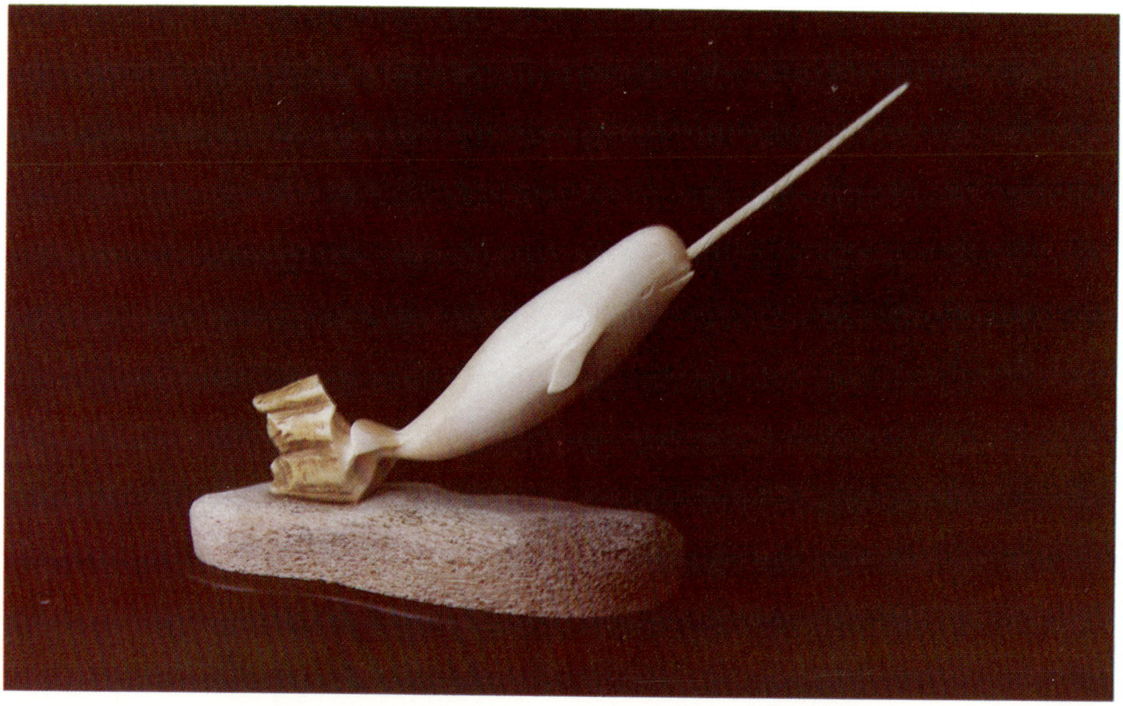

This narwhal carving by Al Doucette was carved from a whale's tooth. *Collection of Jeanne Kitz*

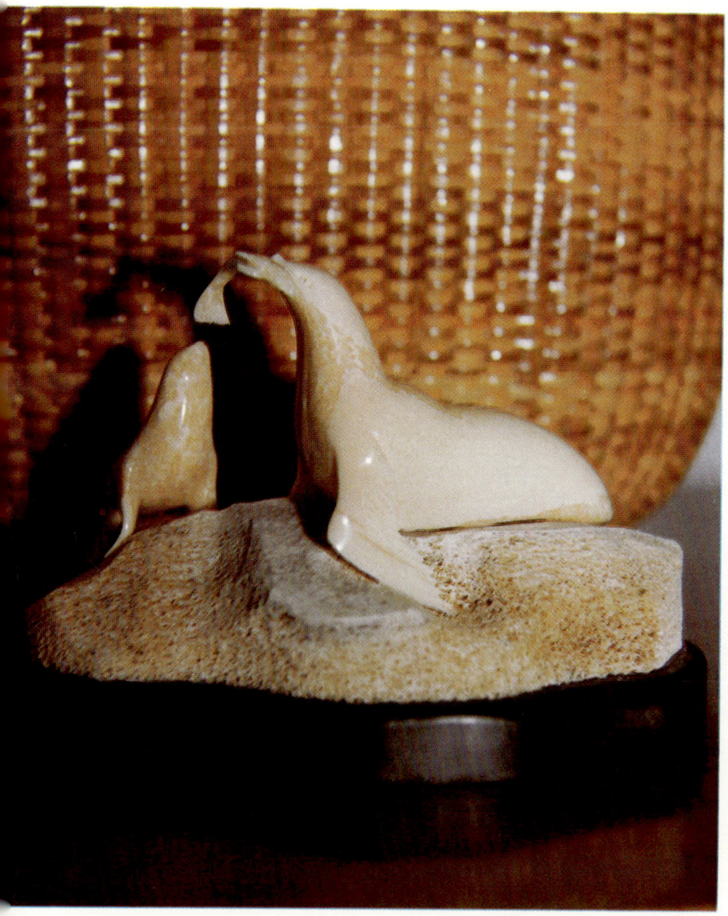

Fossilized walrus ivory was the material chosen by Al Doucette to portray this mother and baby seal. *Collection of Jeanne Kitz*

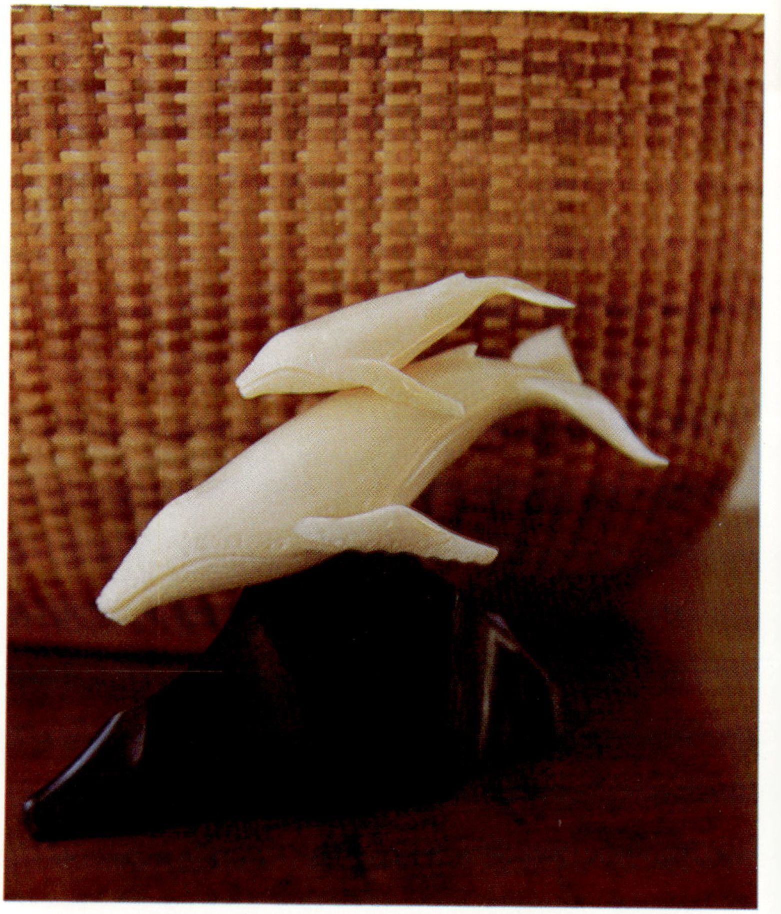

Al Doucette's whale ivory mother and calf humpback whales glide over a sea of ebony. *Collection of Jeanne Kitz*

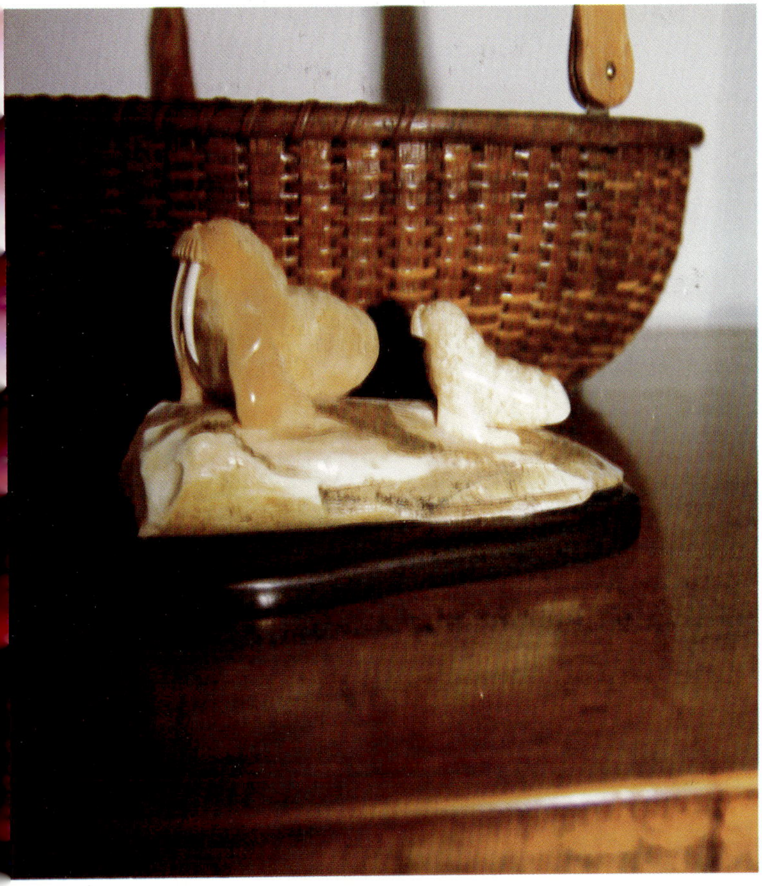

This walrus mother and calf were fittingly carved from fossilized walrus ivory by Al Doucette. *Collection of Jeanne Kitz*

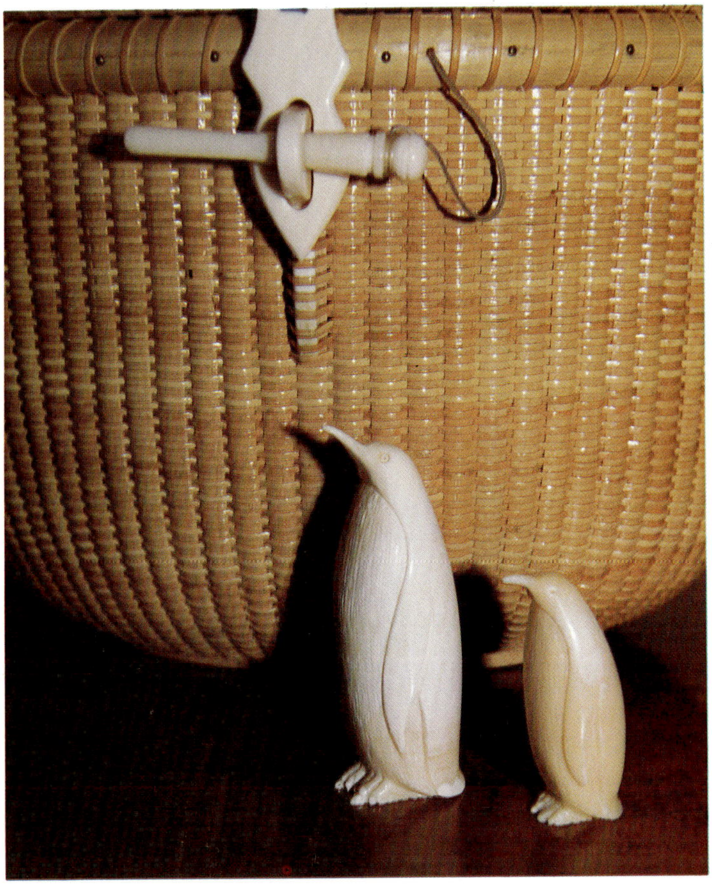

Each penguin was carved from a small whale's tooth by Al Doucette. *Collection of Jeanne Kitz*

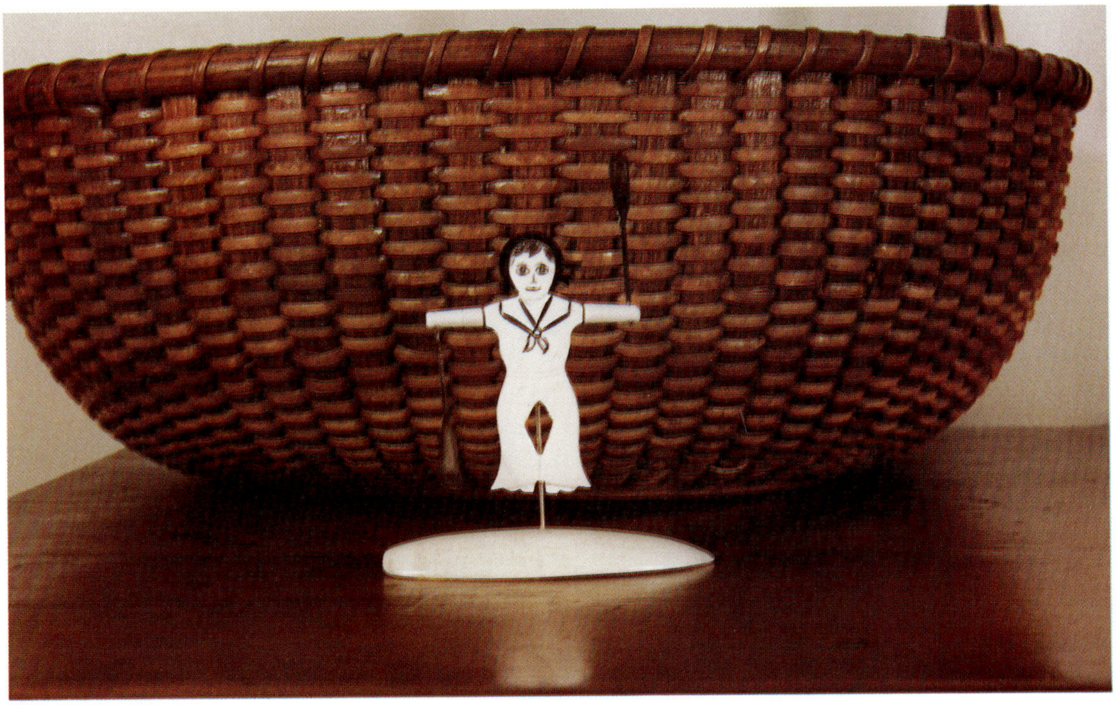

This delightful sailor-boy whirligig was carved by Nancy Chase from whale ivory and baleen. *Private Collection*

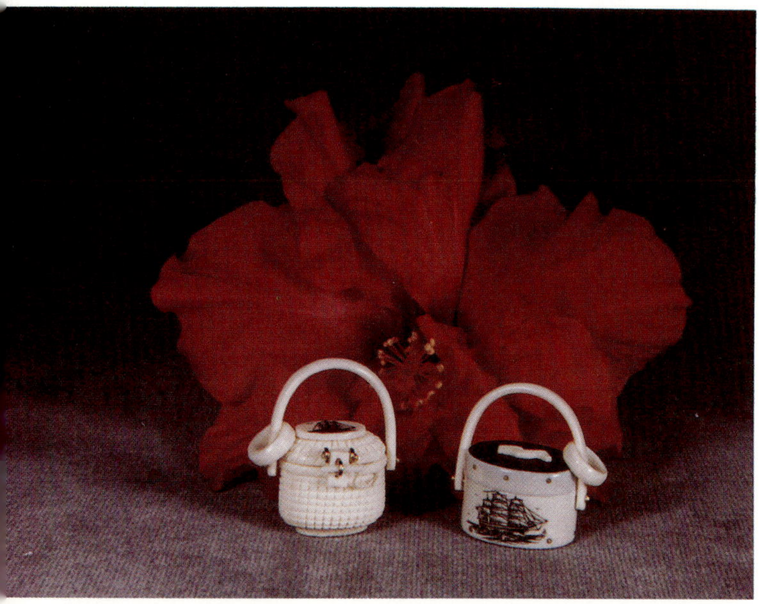

This miniature Nantucket Lightship Basket and engraved ditty box were painstakingly fashioned from antique elephant ivory by Al Doucette.

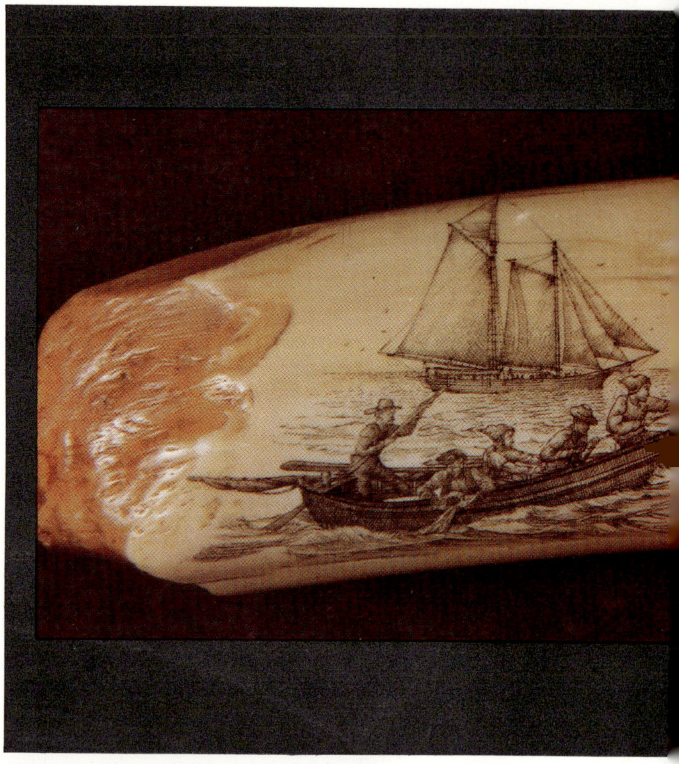

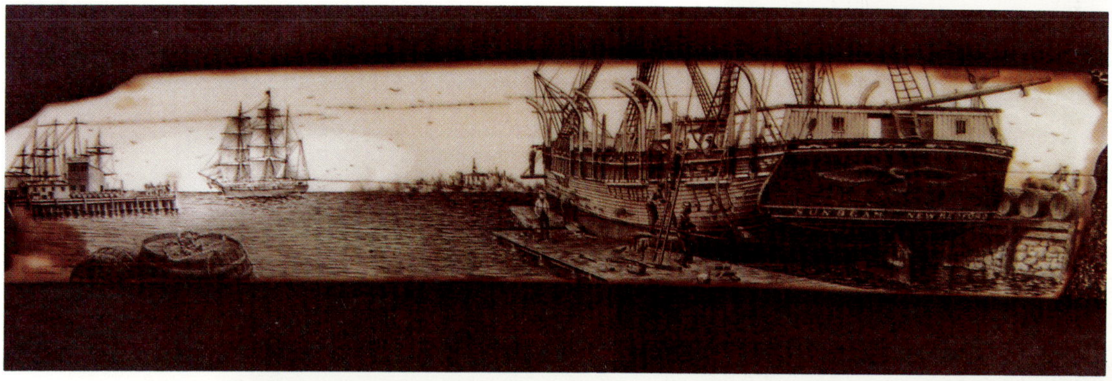

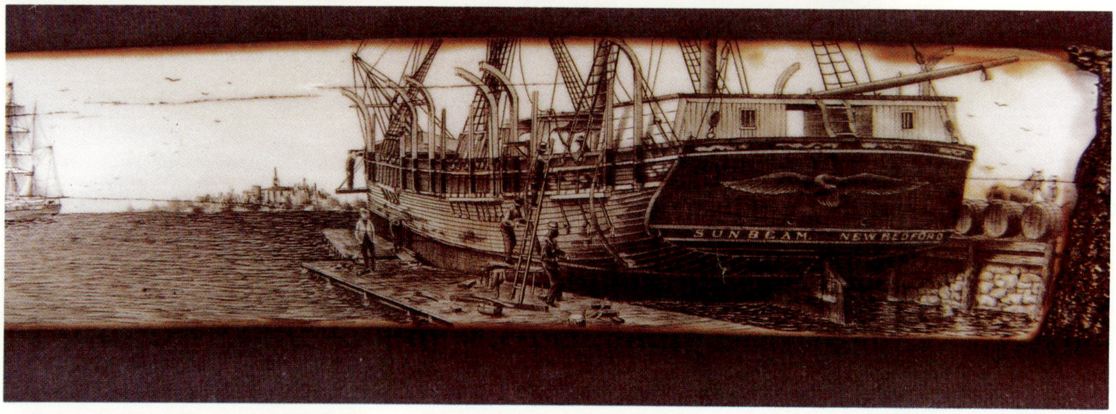

A fossilized walrus ivory sled runner is the background on which Dan Cronan engraved this view of nineteenth century New Bedford and the bark *Sunbeam*. The *Sunbeam* was the whaler on which marine artist Clifford Ashley shipped in 1904. His detailed account of the voyage, *The Yankee Whaler*, became a whaling classic.

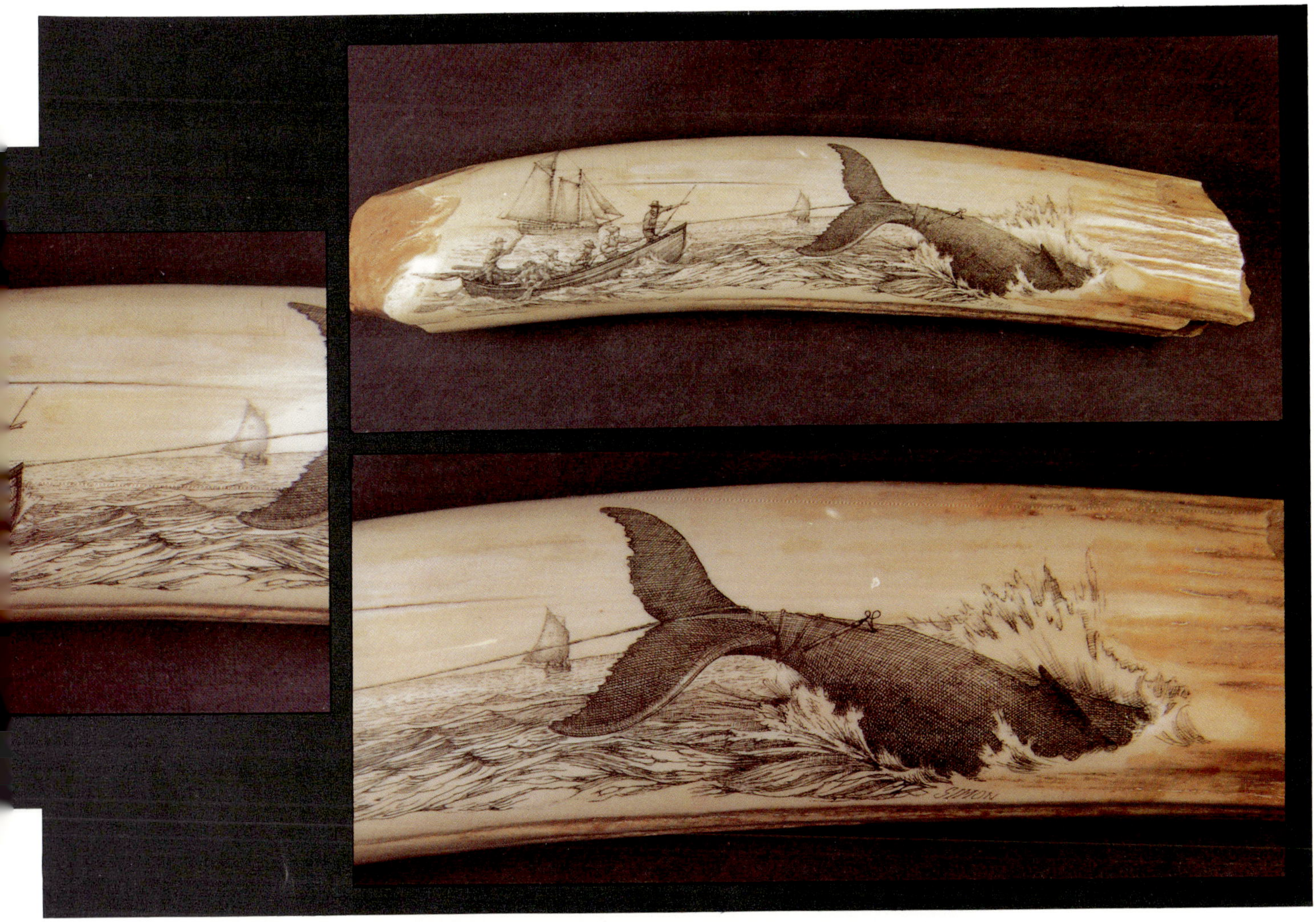

A fossilized walrus tusk ax head was the artifact chosen by Barry Simon for the setting of this classic hunt scene.

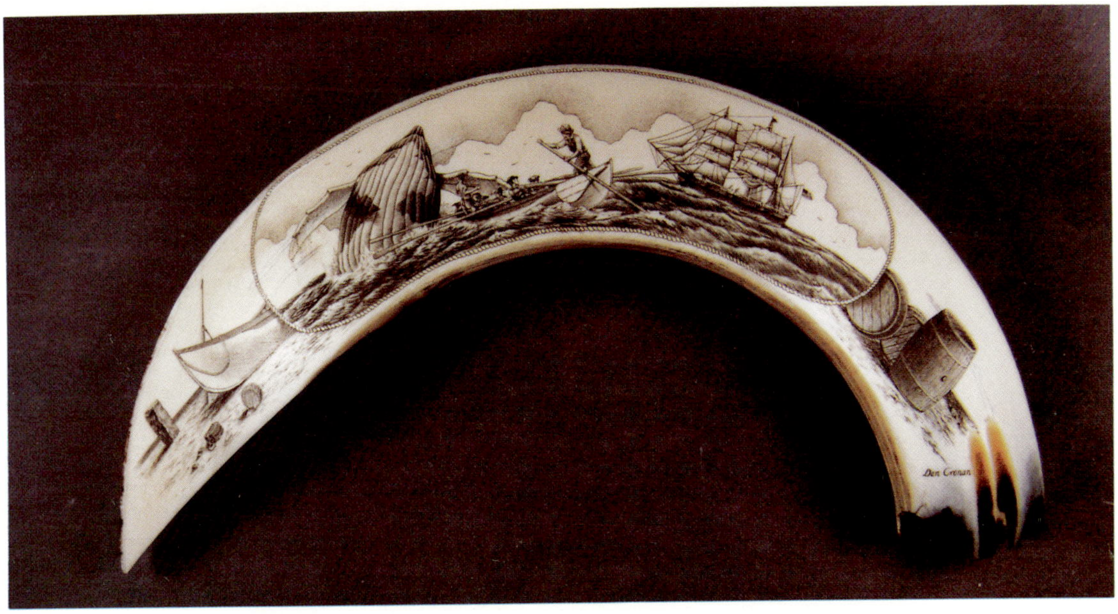

Dan Cronan engraved a hippopotamus tooth with this detailed scene depicting the capture of a humpback whale.

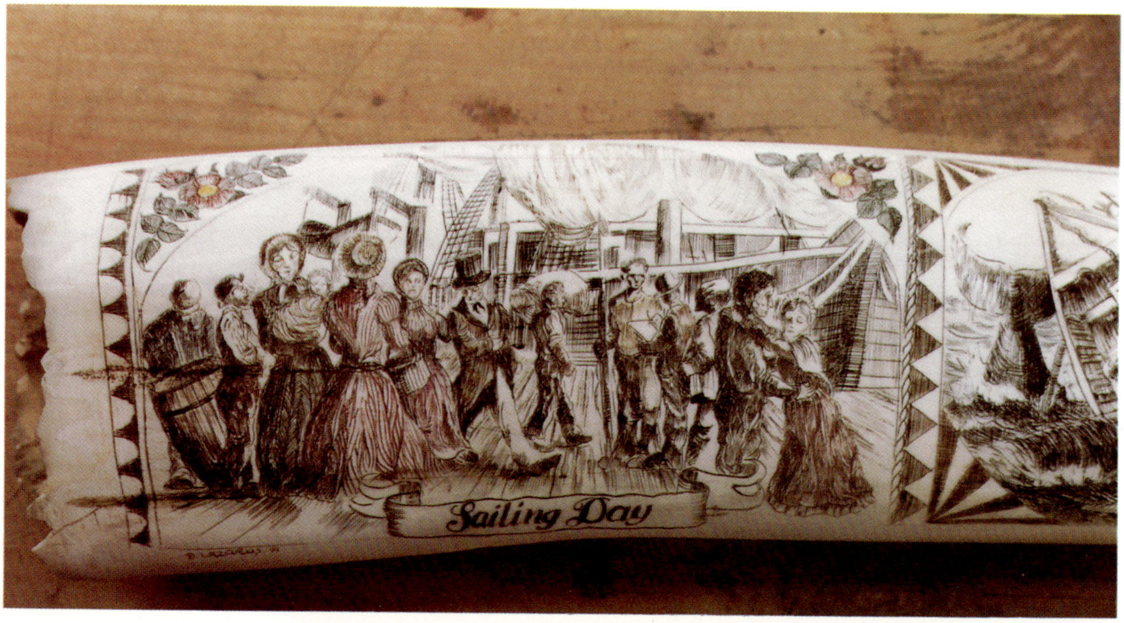
Sailing Day

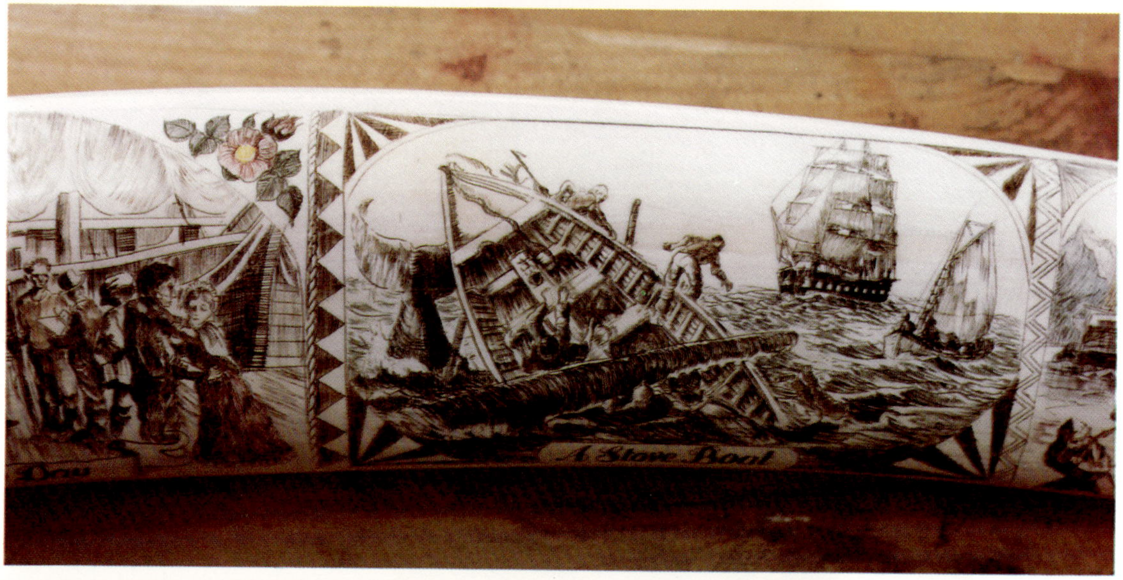
A Stove Boat

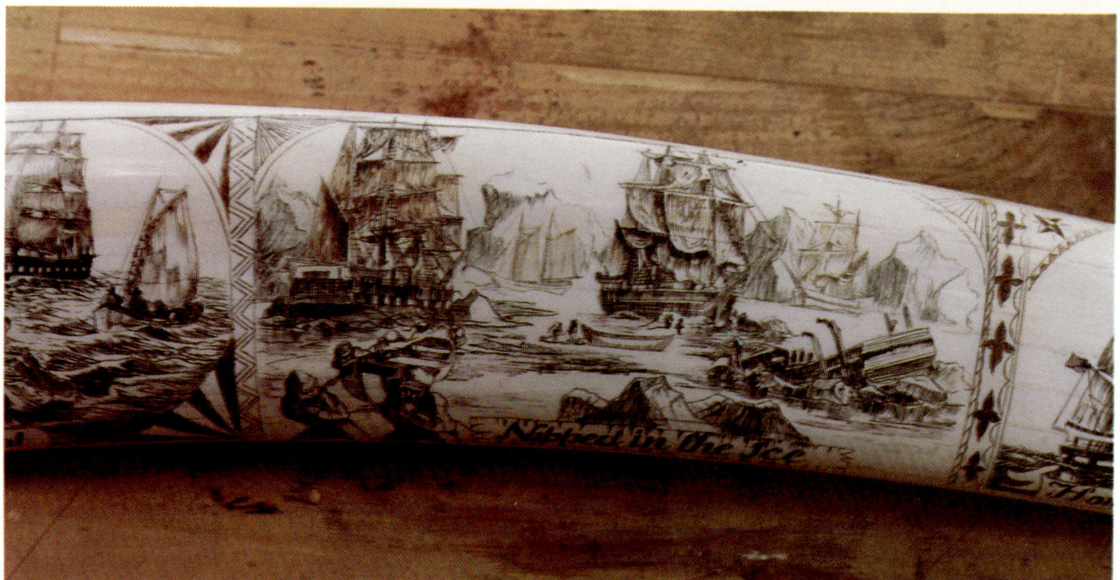
Nipped in the Ice

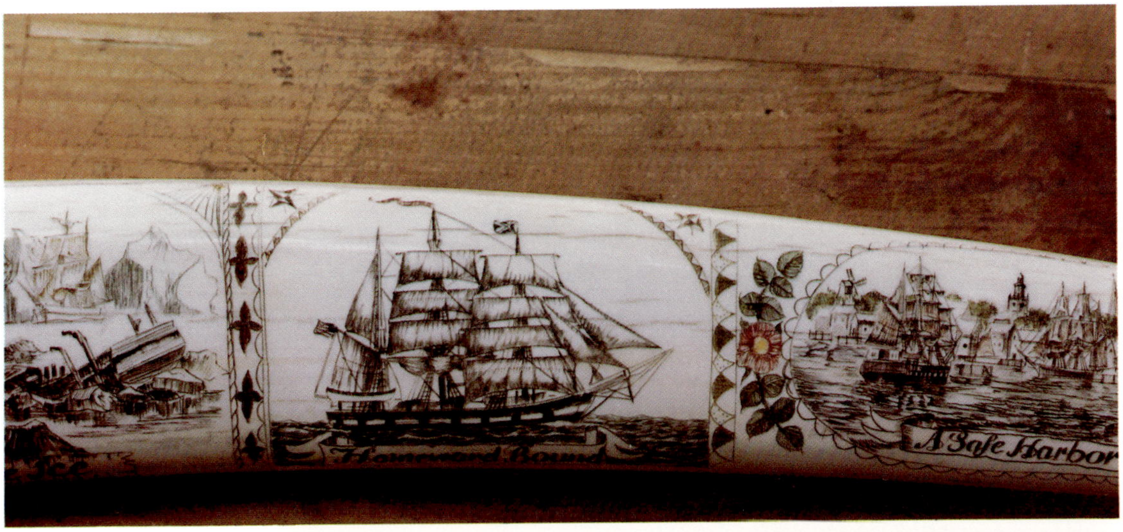

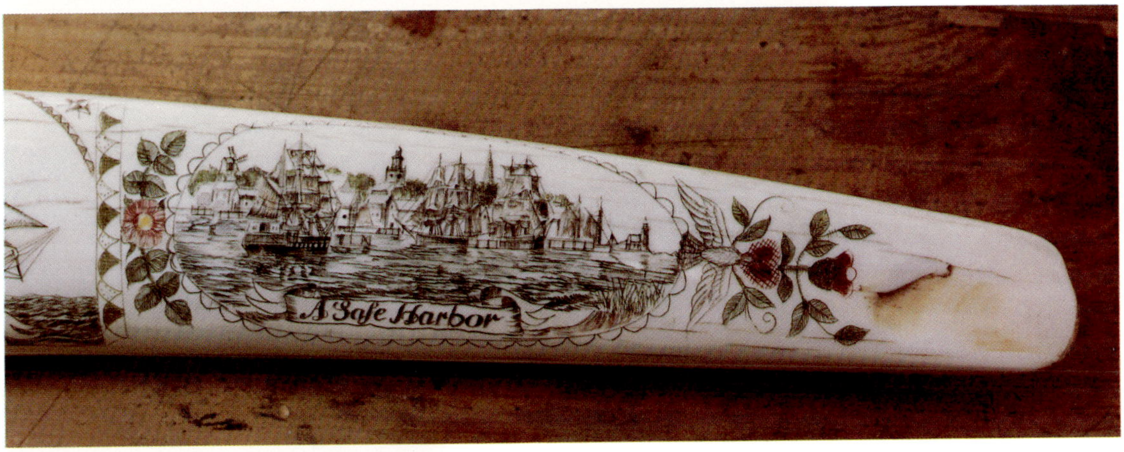

The ample length of a walrus tusk enabled David Lazarus to engrave detailed highlights of a typical Nantucket whaling voyage.

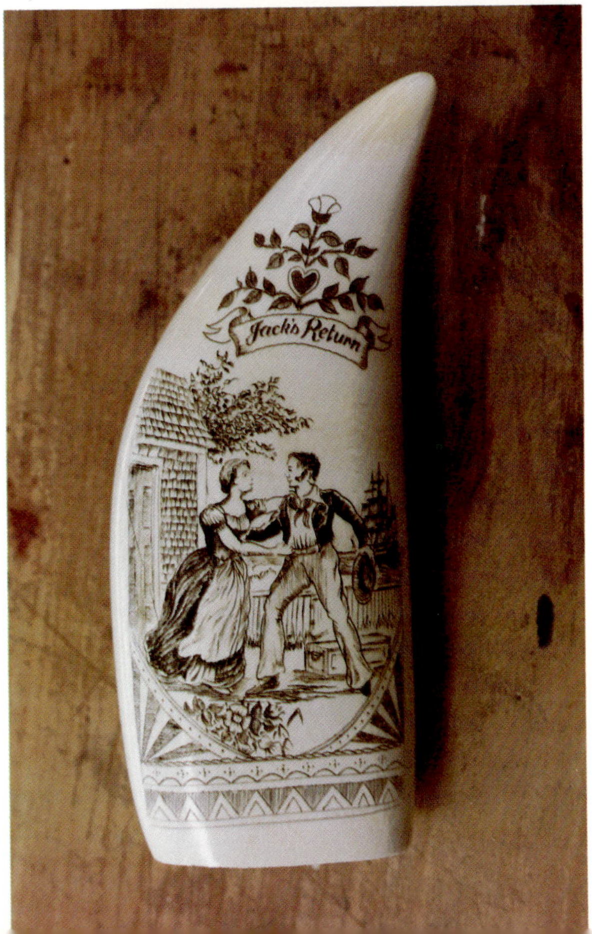

"Jack's Return" by David Lazarus is evocative of the romantic themes of nineteenth century scrimshaw.

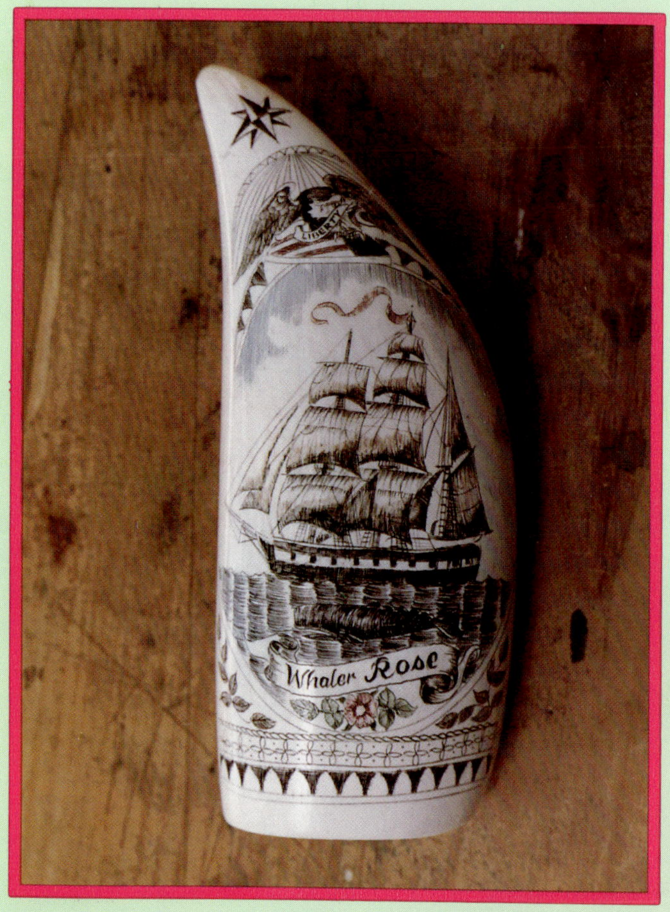

The bark *Rose* is the subject of this piece by David Lazarus.

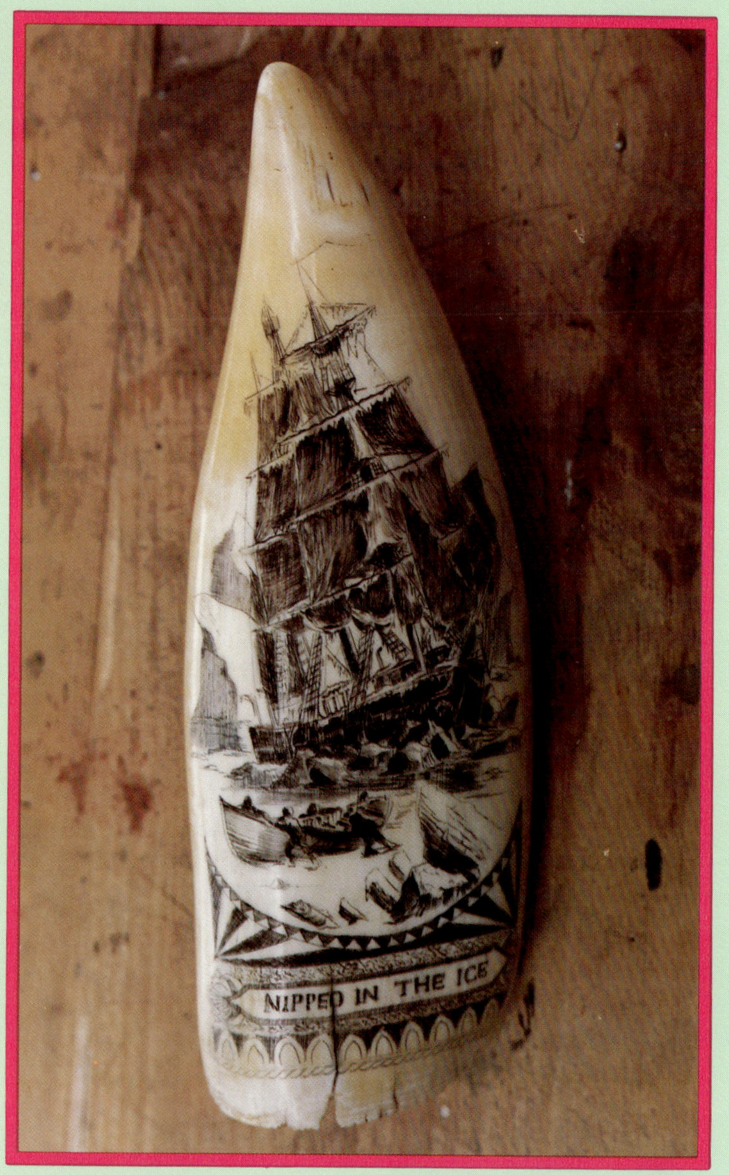

A typical hazard of Arctic whaling is portrayed by David Lazarus.

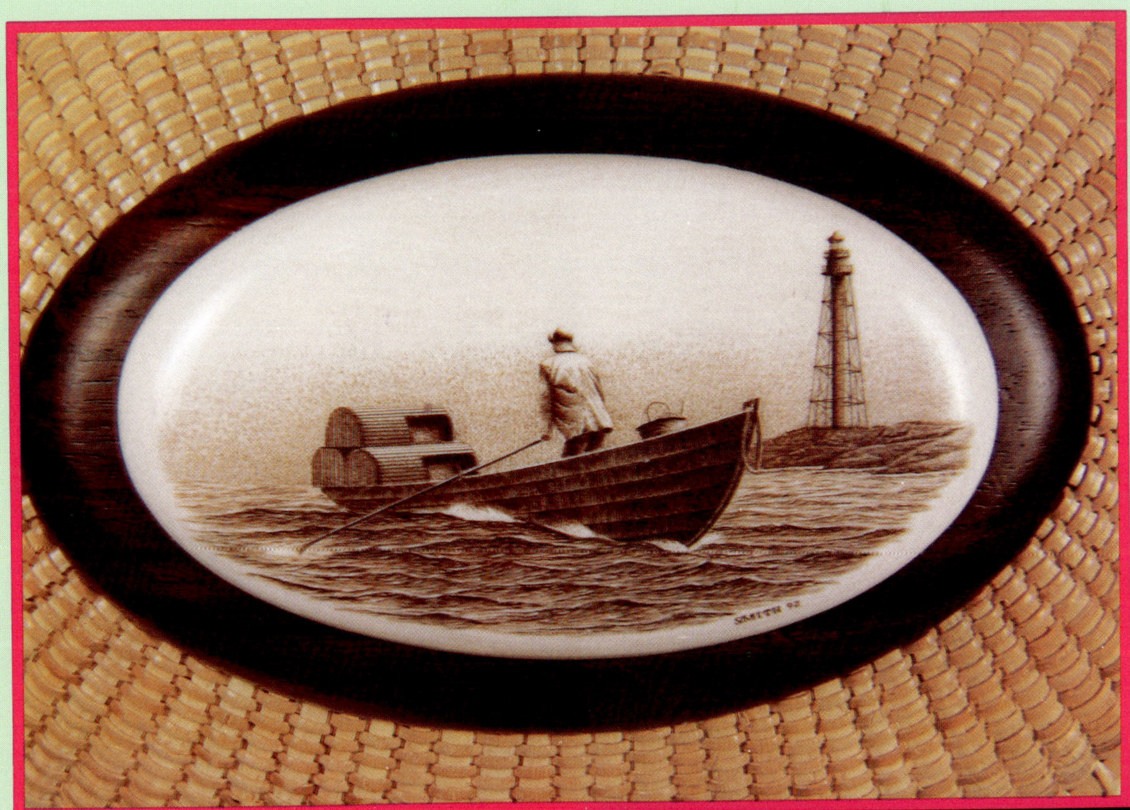

David Smith engraved "Marblehead Light" for a basketmaker who was raised in that seaside town. *Collection of Susan Johnson*

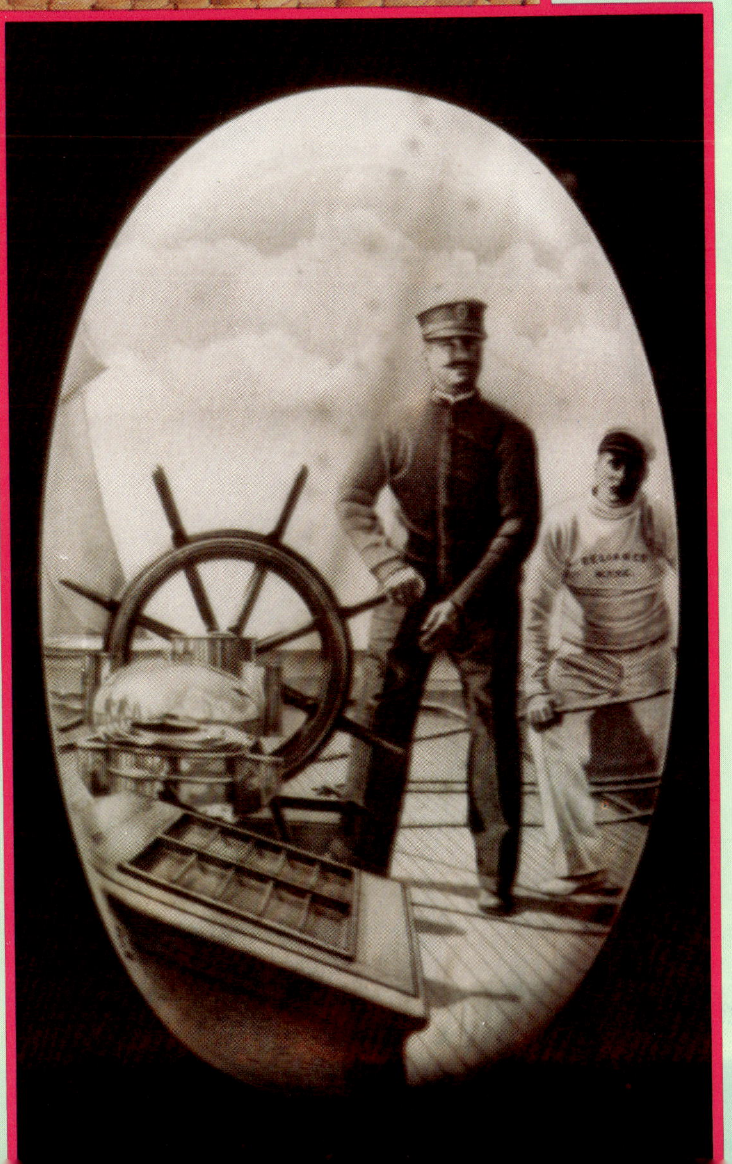

The helm of the yacht *Reliance*, which was racing in the 12th America's Cup, has been rendered on antique elephant ivory by David Smith whose work is characterized by a highly detailed stippling technique.

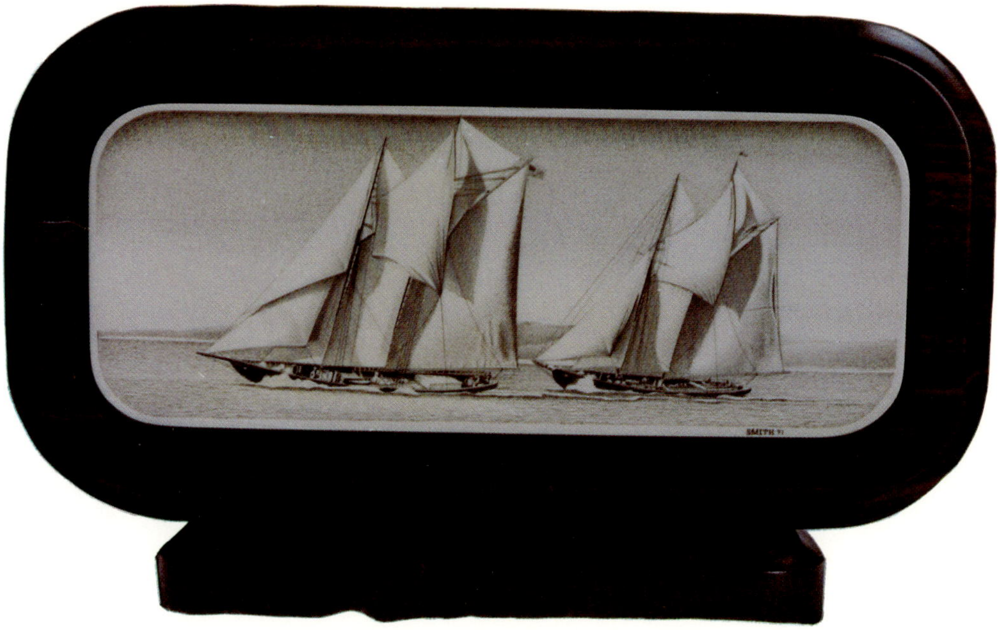

David Smith engraved this scene of the fishing schooners *Bluenose* and *Gertrude L. Thebaud* challenging each other in a race to the day's fishing grounds. The material is antique elephant ivory.

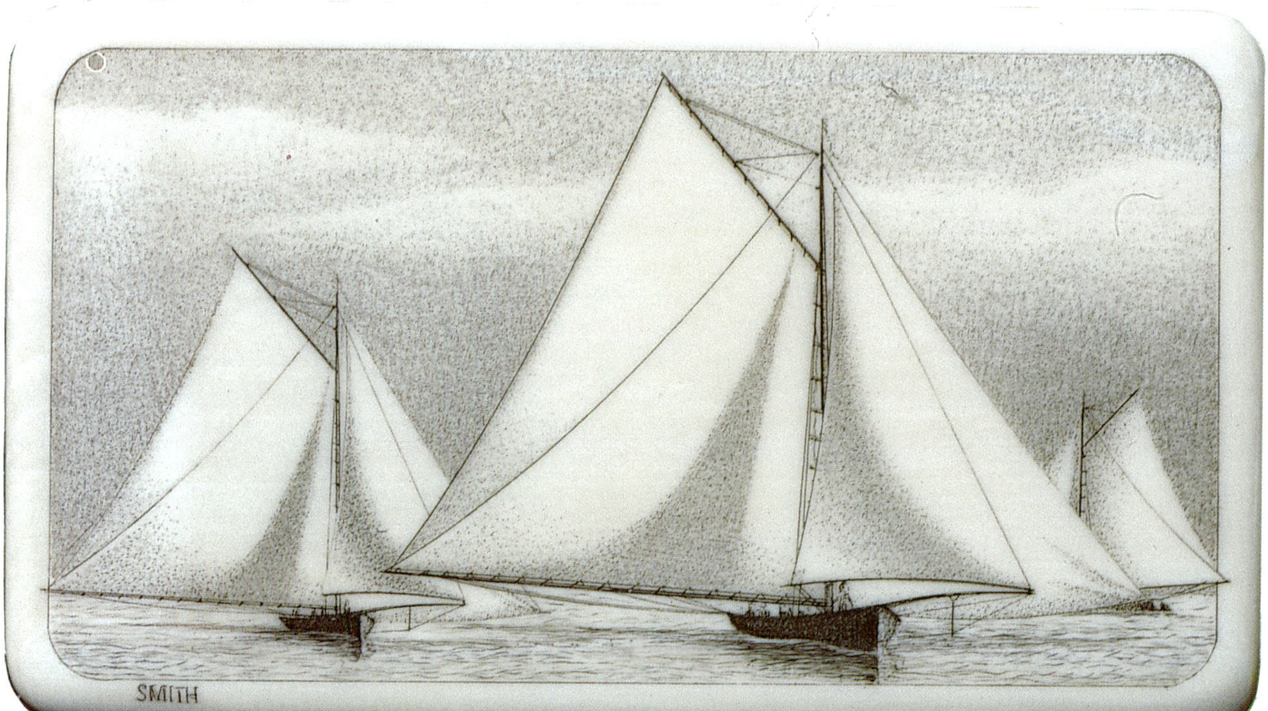

Gaff-rigged "sandbaggers" race before the wind on this antique elephant ivory piece engraved by David Smith.

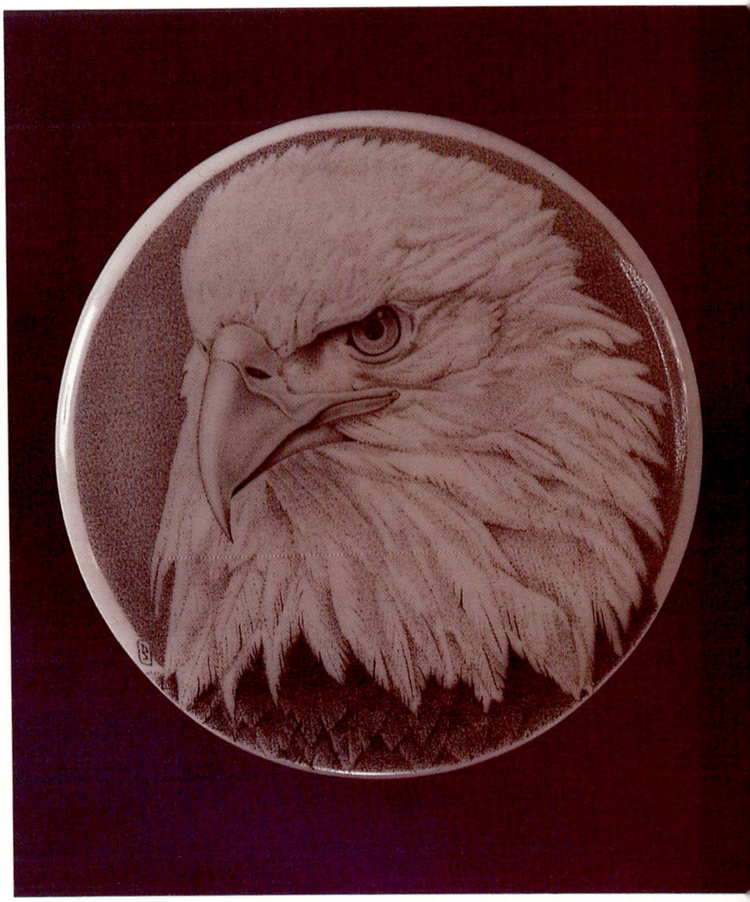

A bald eagle is engraved on antique elephant ivory by David Smith

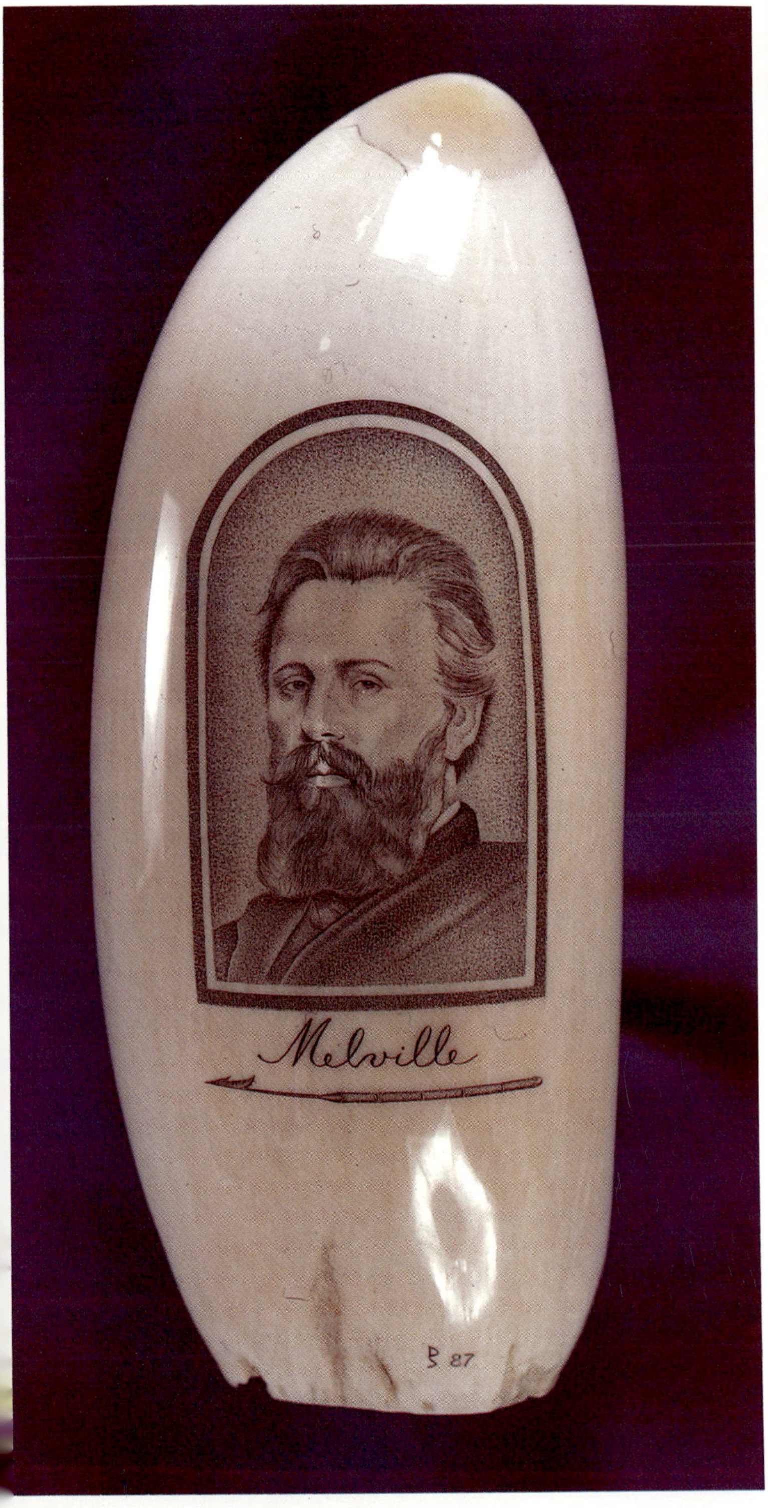

A sperm whale's tooth is an appropriate canvas for this portrait of Herman Melville engraved by David Smith.

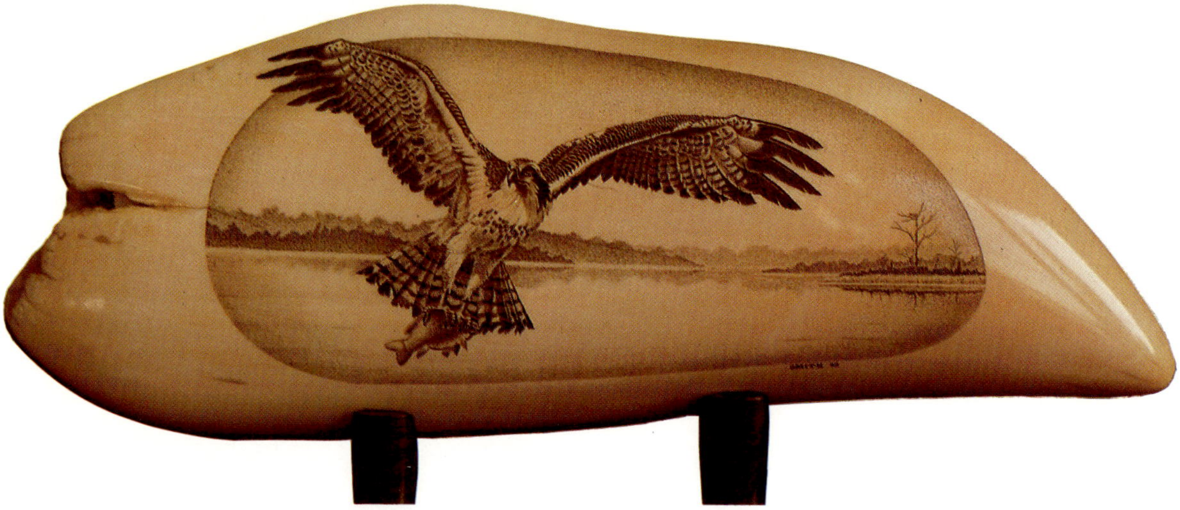

A moment in the life of an osprey was captured on antique elephant ivory by David Smith

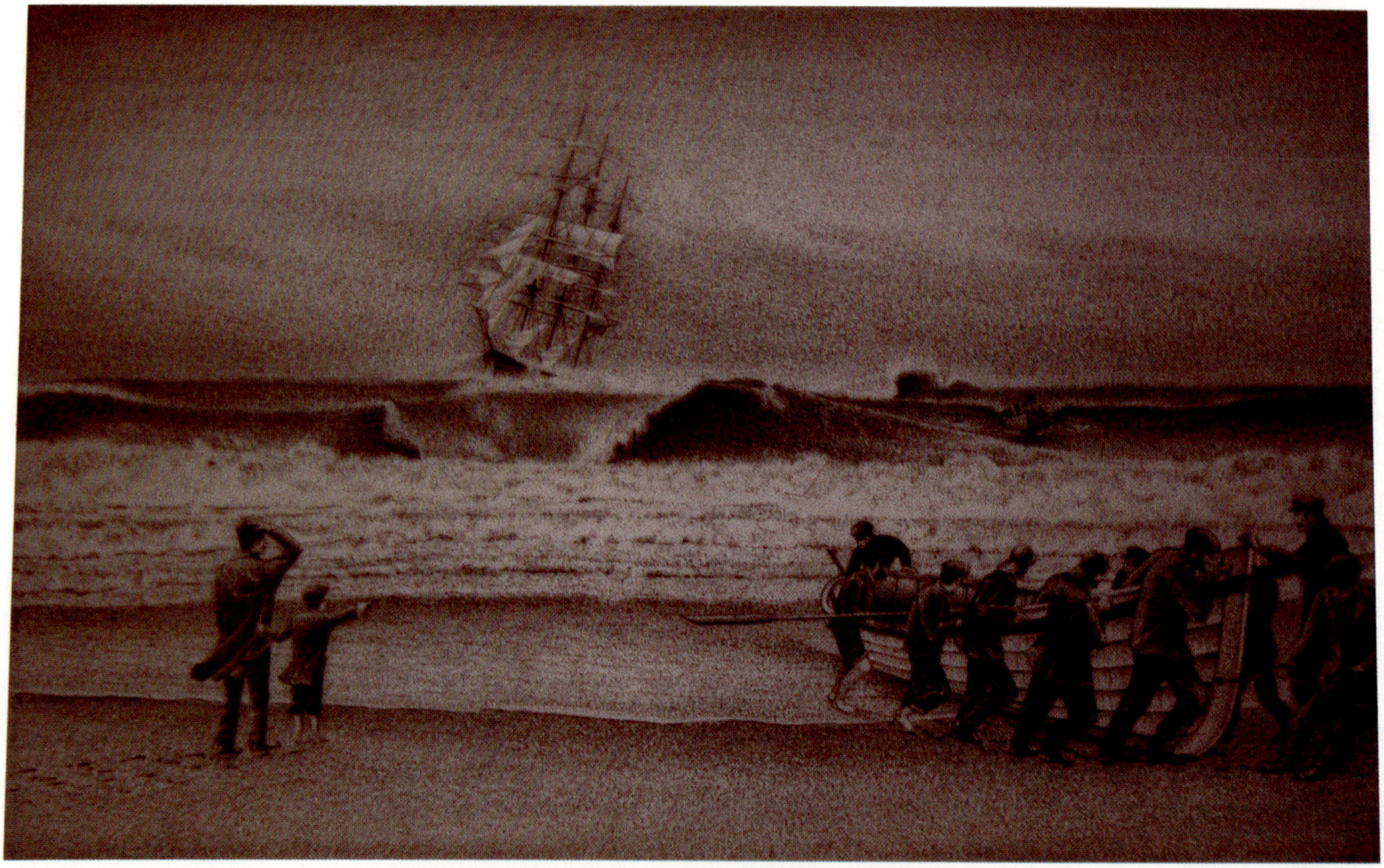

"On the Reef", a beautifully engraved scene by David Smith, depicts the fortunate crew of a wrecked ship who have safely reached the shore. The scene is worked on antique elephant ivory.

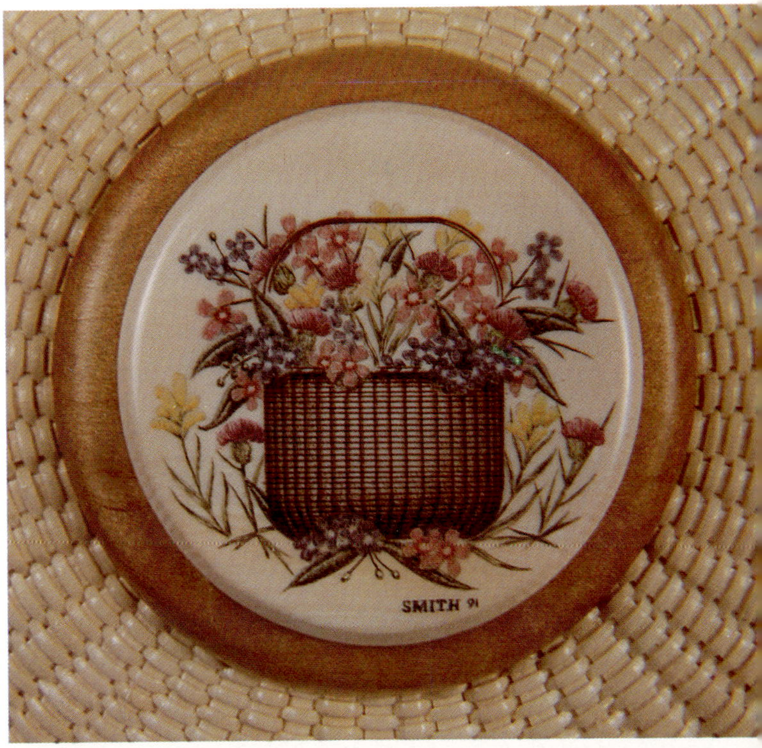

A Nantucket Lightship Basket filled with spring flowers engraved by David Smith graces the top of this delicate Nantucket Lightship Basket. *Collection of Donna Lowell*

Inventive artisan, Gladys Sherman Ellis has incorporated scrimshaw into intricately worked pine-needle baskets and christened the resulting creations "Mattapoisett Baskets" after her home town, located near historic New Bedford.

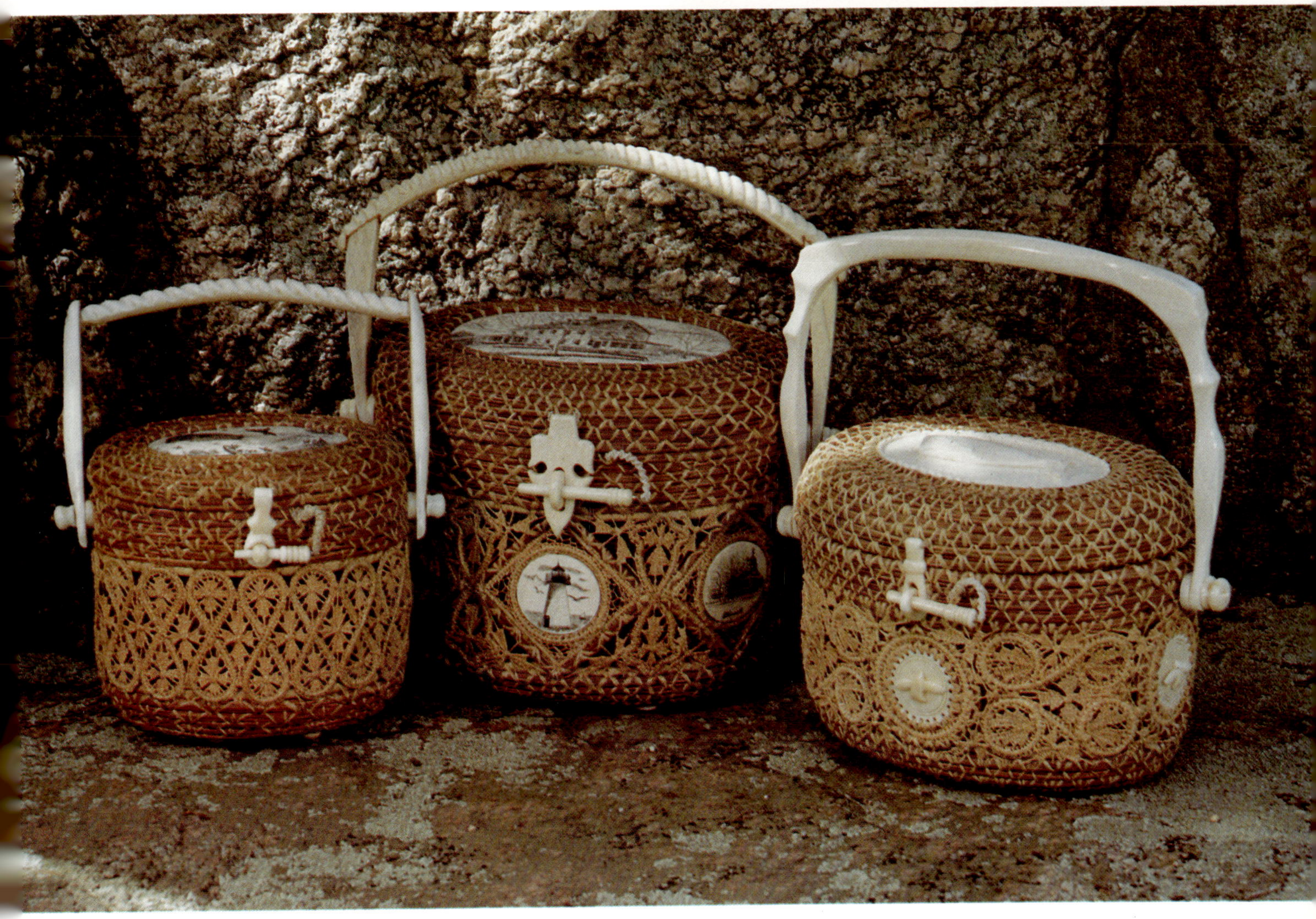

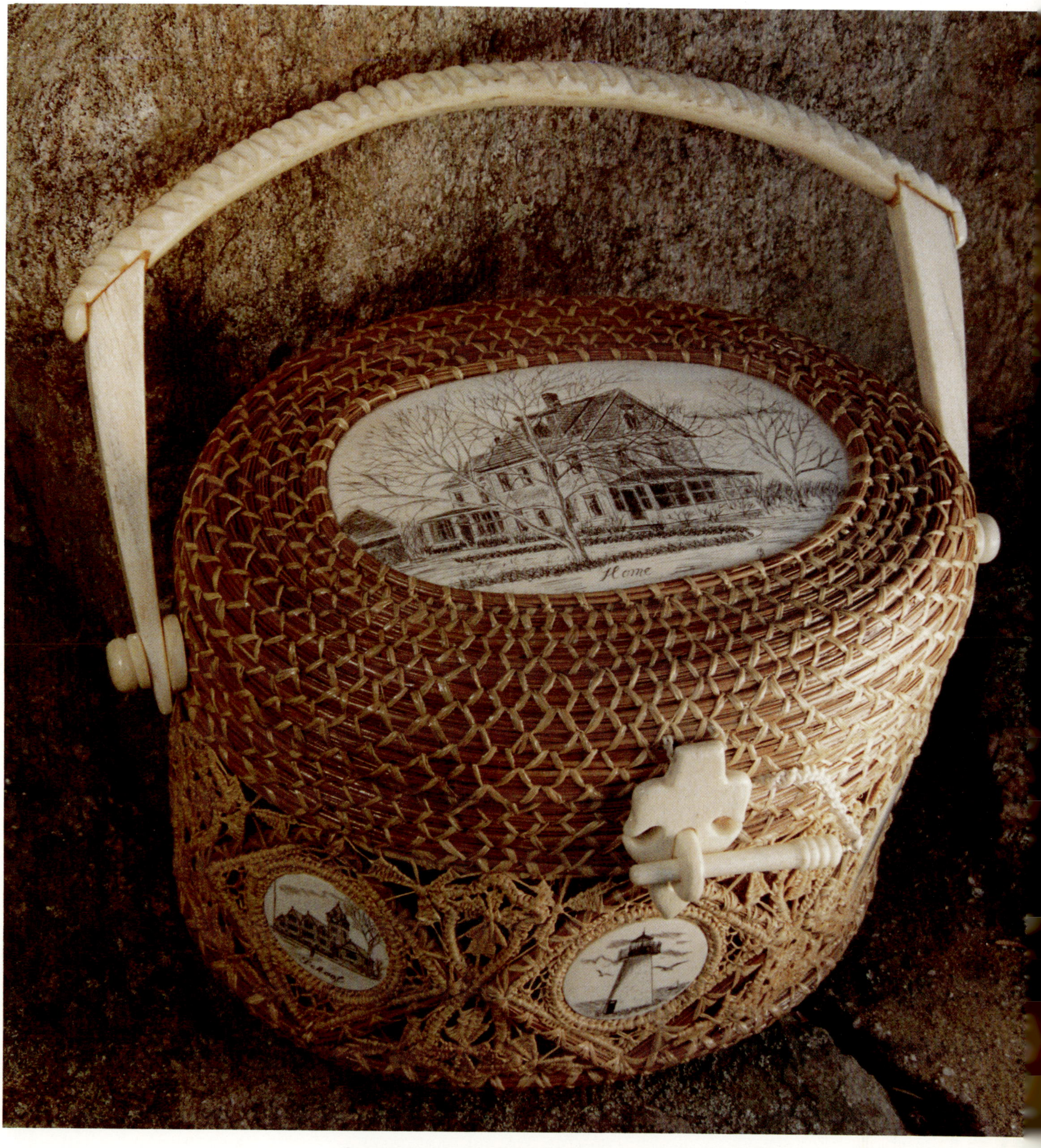

Created for her daughter, this basket captures the spirit of nineteenth century scrimshaw with its frequent references to home and family. Topped with a rendering of the family residence, the other engravings Ellis has executed portray familiar spots in Mattapoisett, designed to remind her daughter of her childhood home.

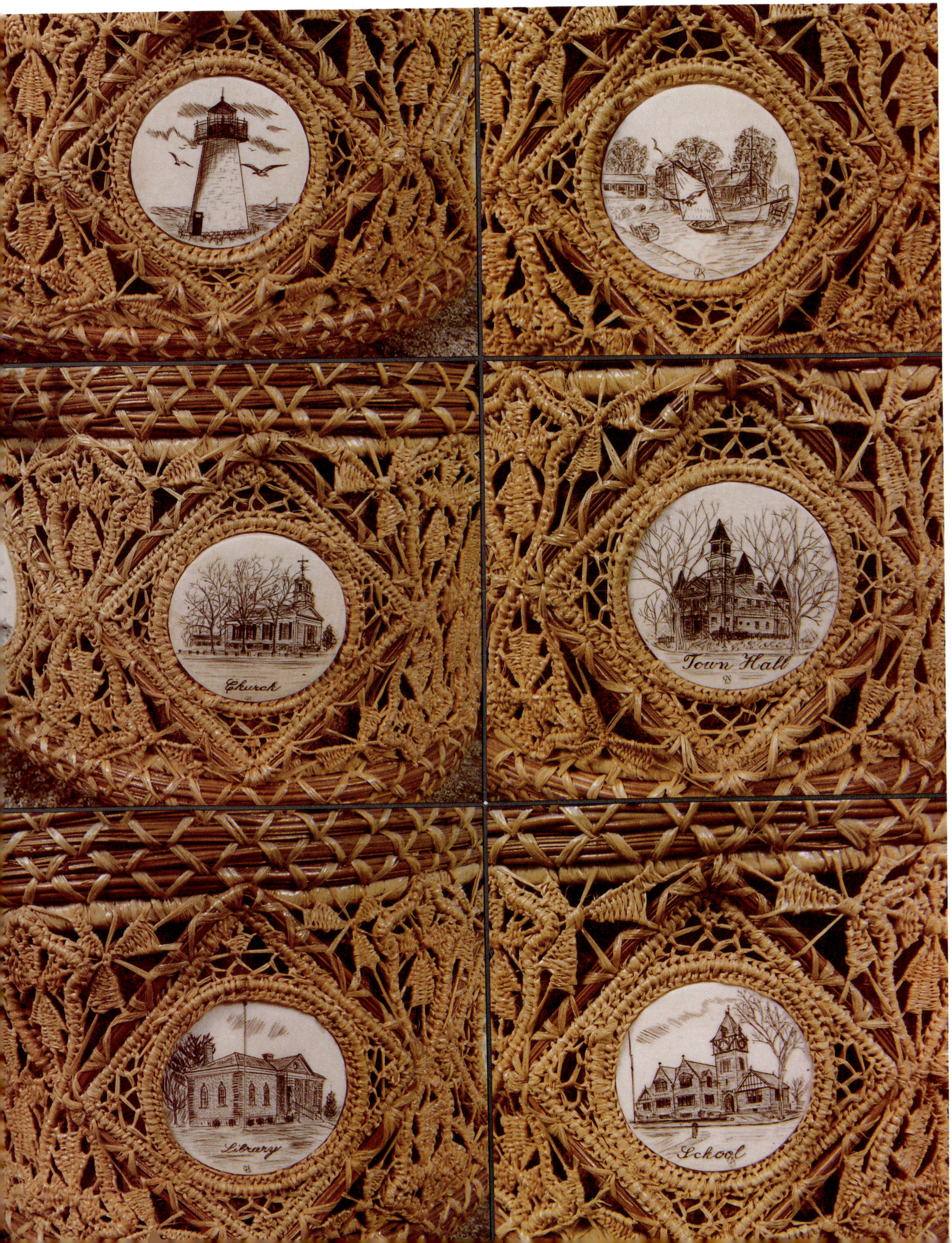
Church
Town Hall
Library
School

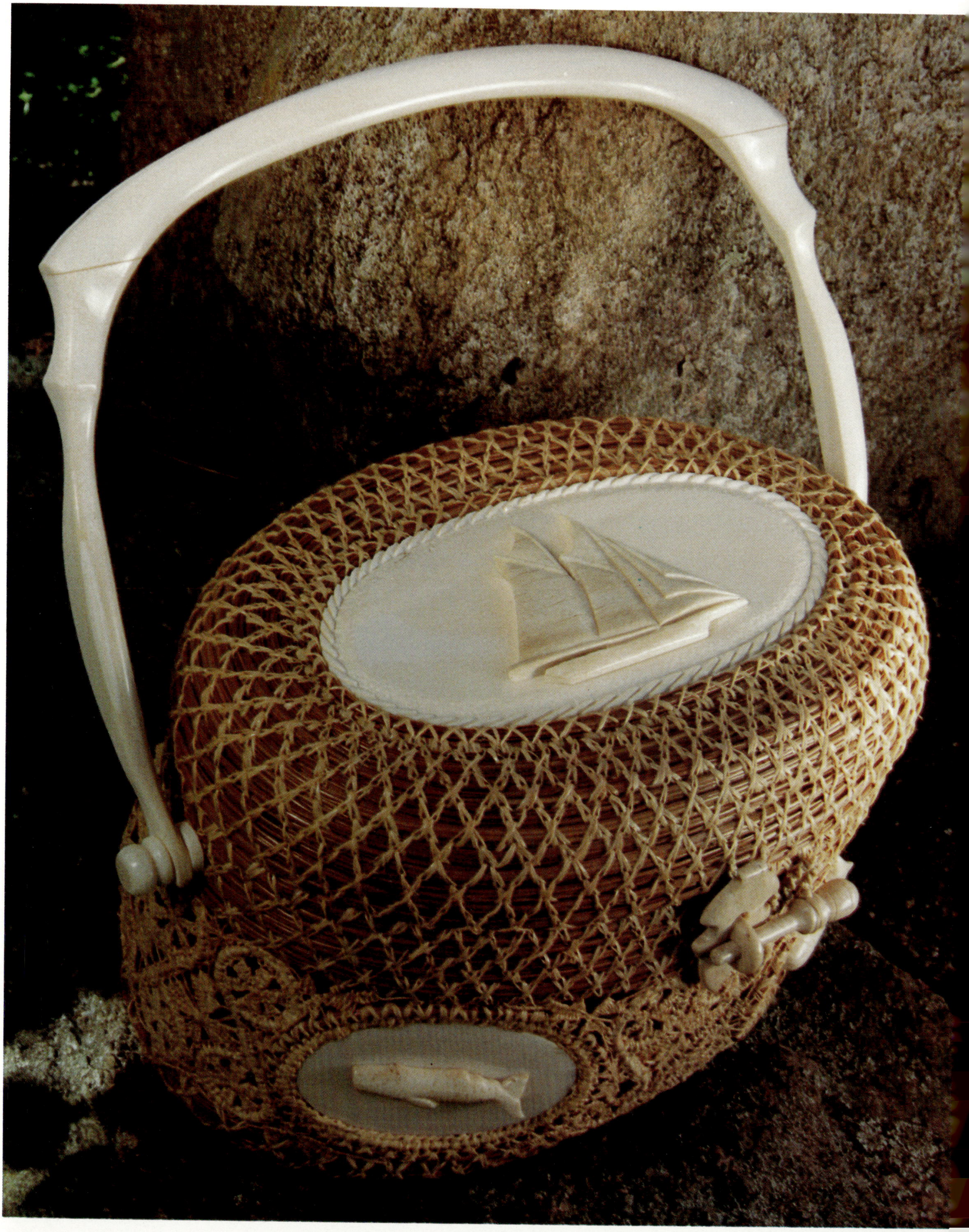

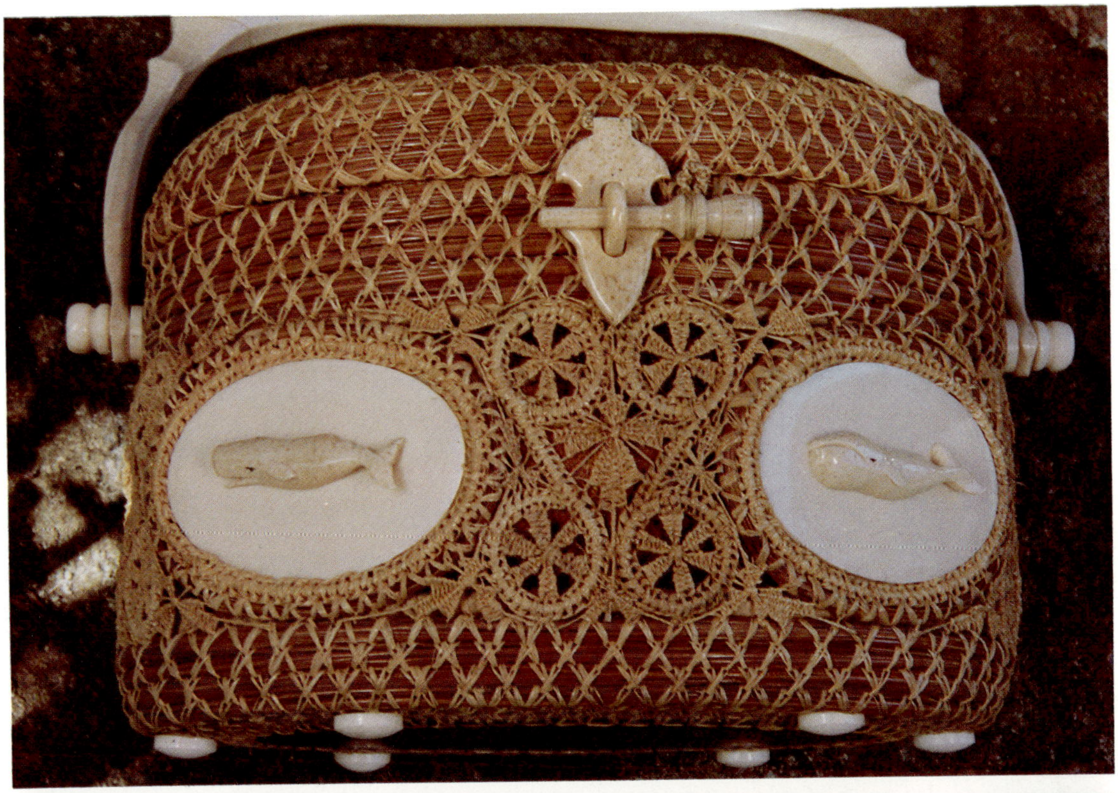

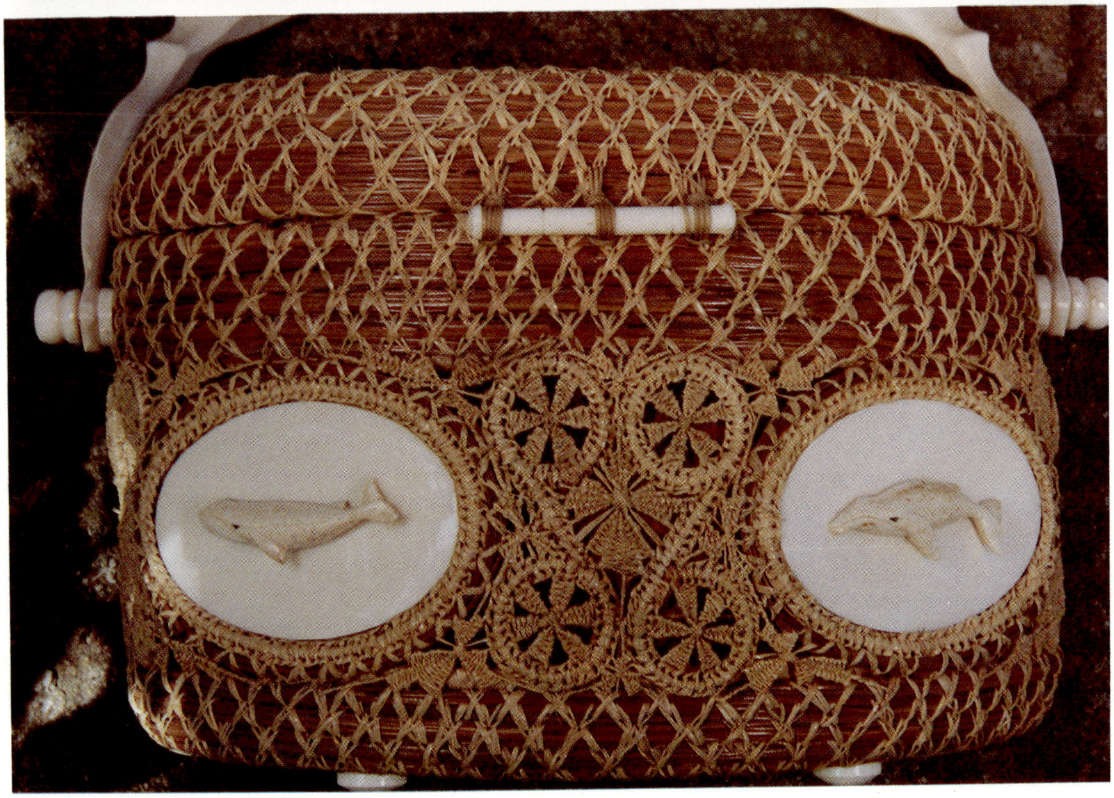

Al Doucette carved this handsome schooner and the accompanying examples of various whale species from whalebone. The carvings are mounted on antique elephant ivory. Ellis chose them to commemorate her daughter's two seafaring great-grandfathers, one of whom was a whaling captain.

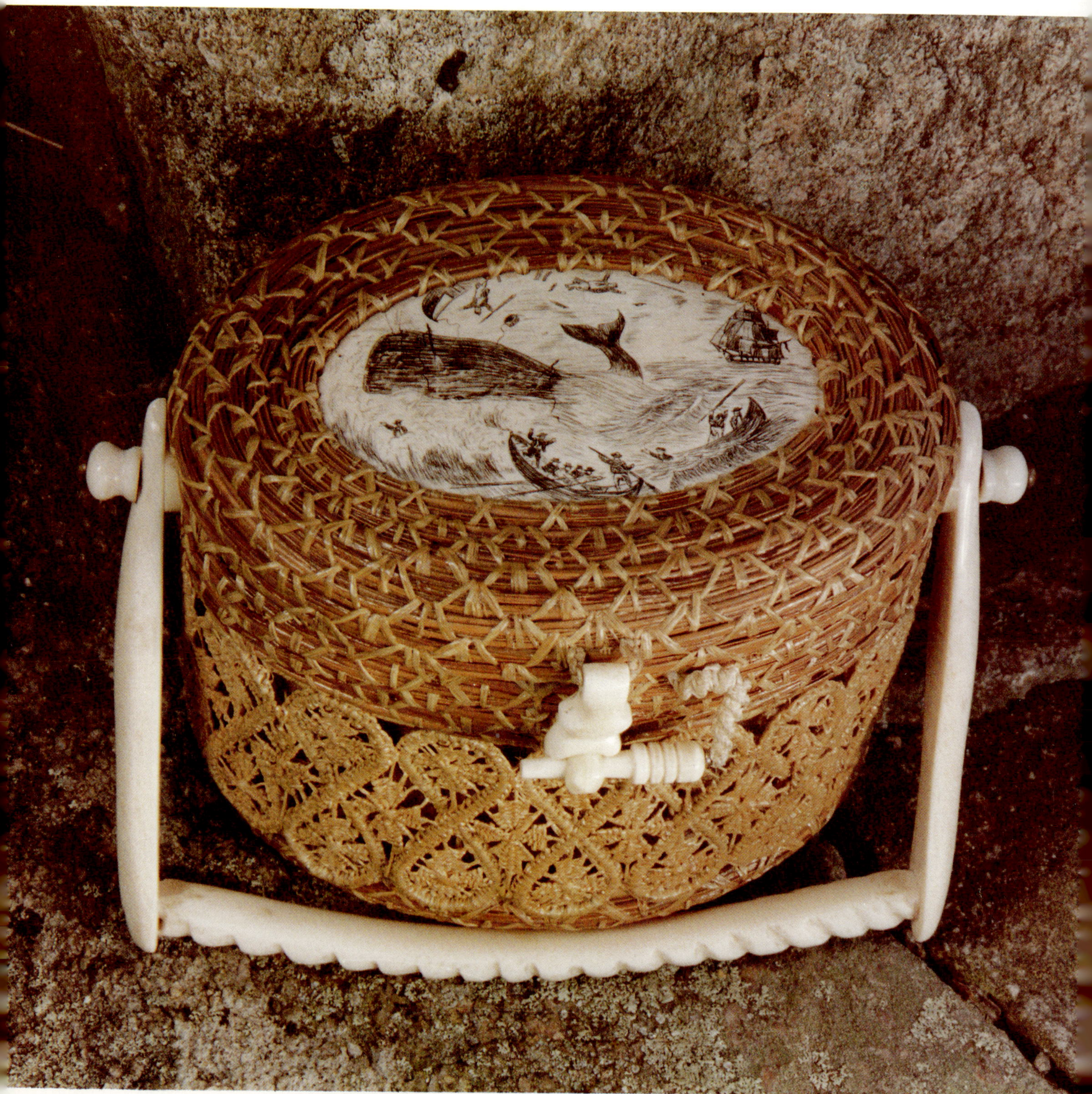

A turbulent whale hunt rendered by Gladys Sherman Ellis tops one of her Mattapoisett Baskets.

This nest of Nantucket Lightship Baskets made by Alan Reed and Nap Plank are trimmed with antique elephant ivory ears and handle overlays engraved by Lee Ann Papale. *Photo by Jack Weinhold*

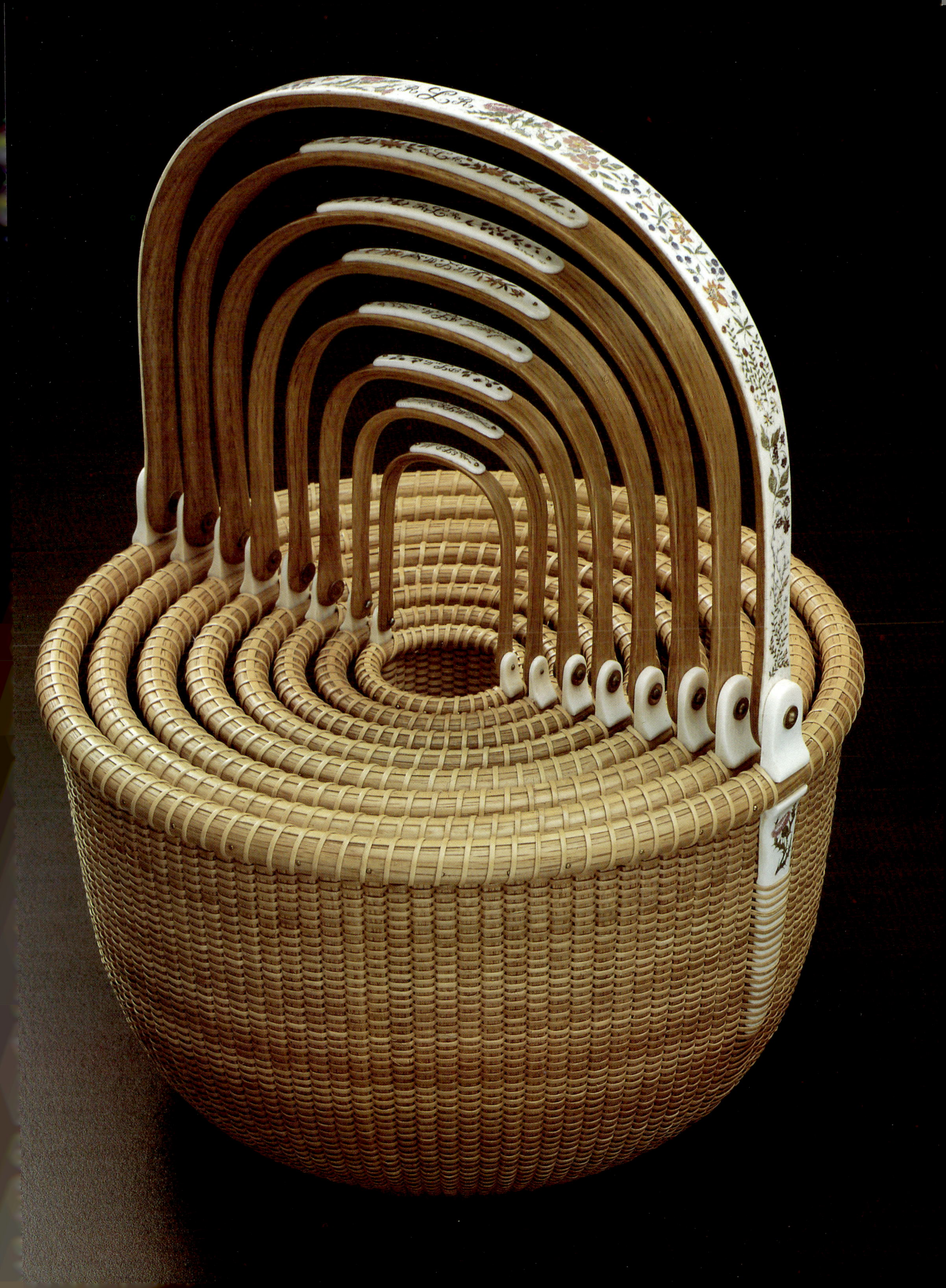

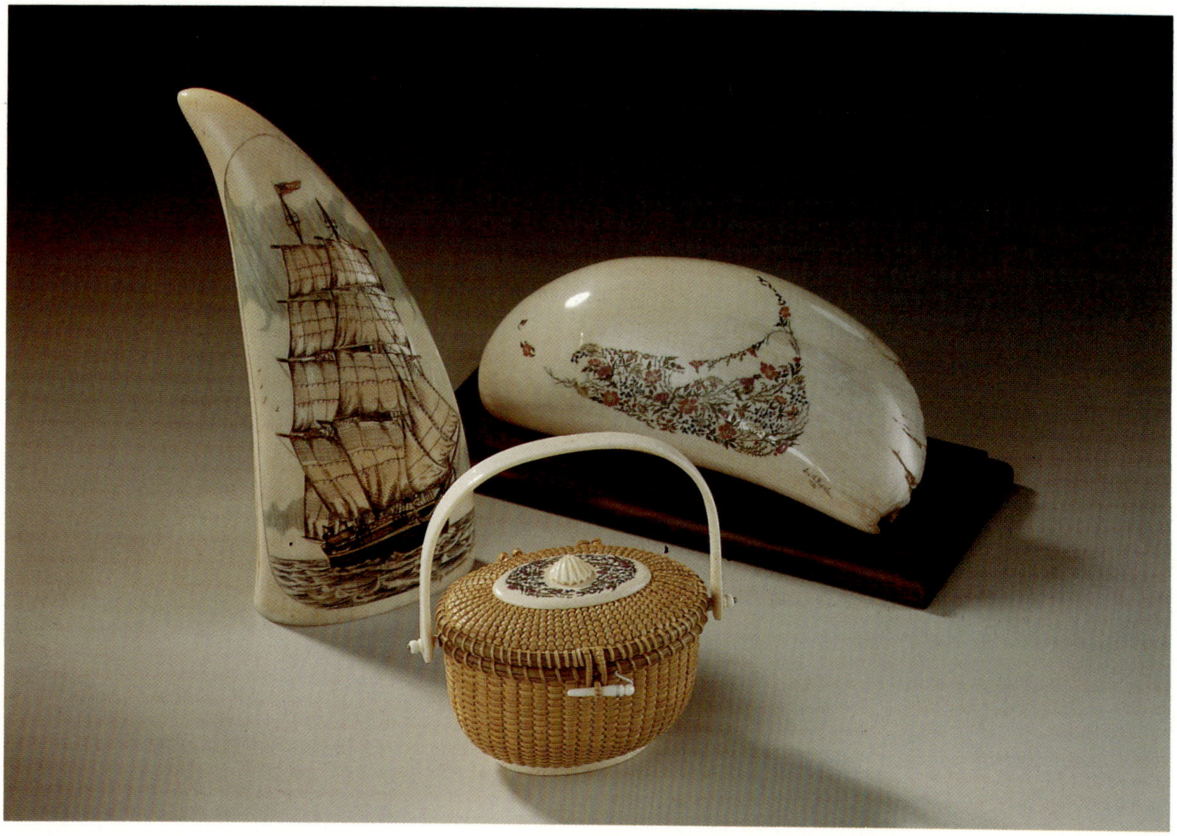

Lee Ann Papale has engraved the sperm whale's tooth featuring a map of Nantucket created from island wildflowers as well as the top of the miniature Nantucket Lightship Basket created by Nap Plank. The other tooth was engraved by Michael J. Vienneau. *Photo by Jack Weinhold*

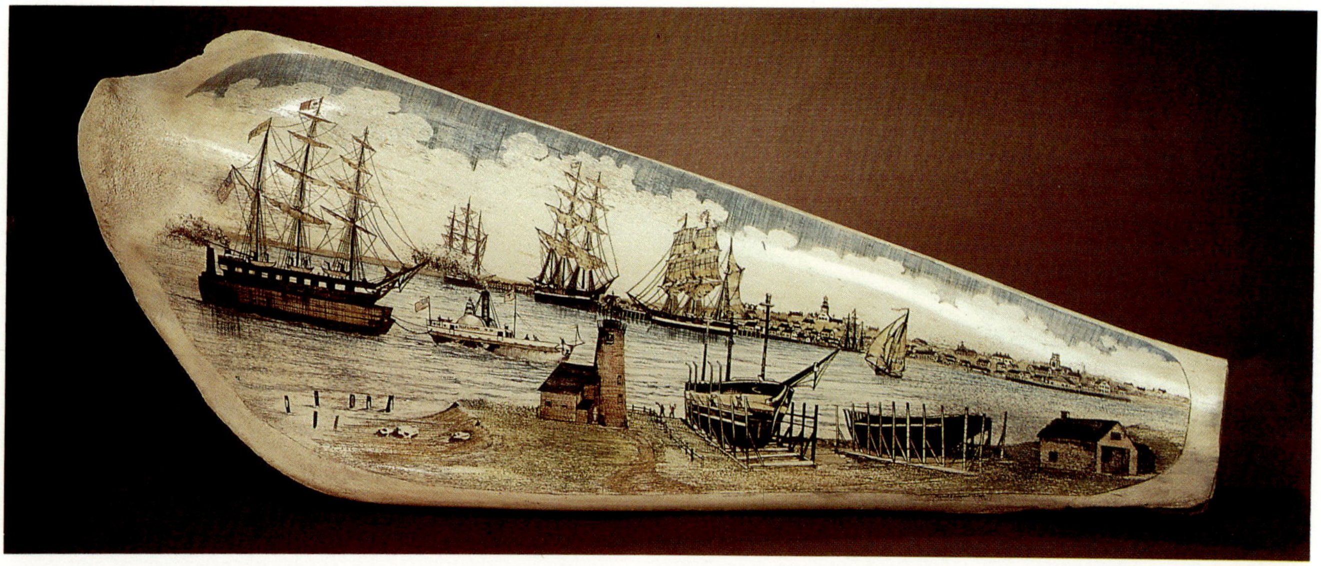

Michael J. Vienneau was inspired by a 1900 James Walter Folger painting when he engraved this dramatic four foot panbone. It depicts the ship *Peru*, Joshua Coffin, master, rounding Nantucket's Brant Point on October 13, 1842, after a three year Pacific voyage. The *Peru* was the first ship to be brought over the bar by Peter Ewer's "camels". Jubilant Nantucketers, believing that Ewer's invention would give large vessels access to the harbor, greeted the arrival of the *Peru* with ringing bells and gunfire. *Photo by Terry Pommett*

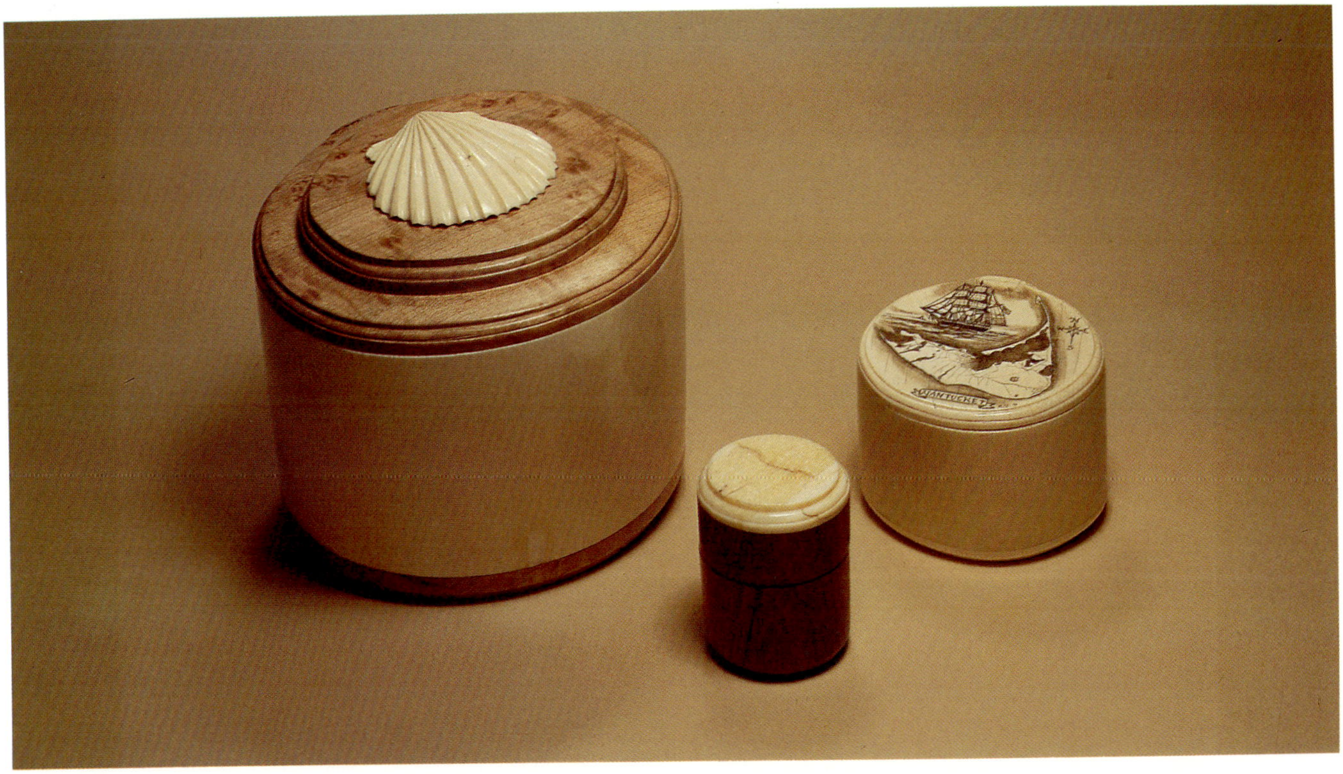

These three boxes were created by Michael J. Vienneau. The largest was made from an antique elephant ivory tusk hollow and is topped with bird's eye maple. The smallest is carved of rosewood and also covered with a lid of antique elephant ivory. An engraved map of Nantucket sets off the other piece, also created from antique elephant ivory. *Photo by Terry Pommett*

The larger tooth in this grouping of work by Michael J. Vienneau is engraved with a portrait of the *Charles W. Morgan*. Both plaques are cover adornments for Nantucket Lightship Baskets. The basket of flowers is worked on antique elephant ivory, while the bark under sail is engraved on a piece of whalebone. *Photo by Terry Pommett*

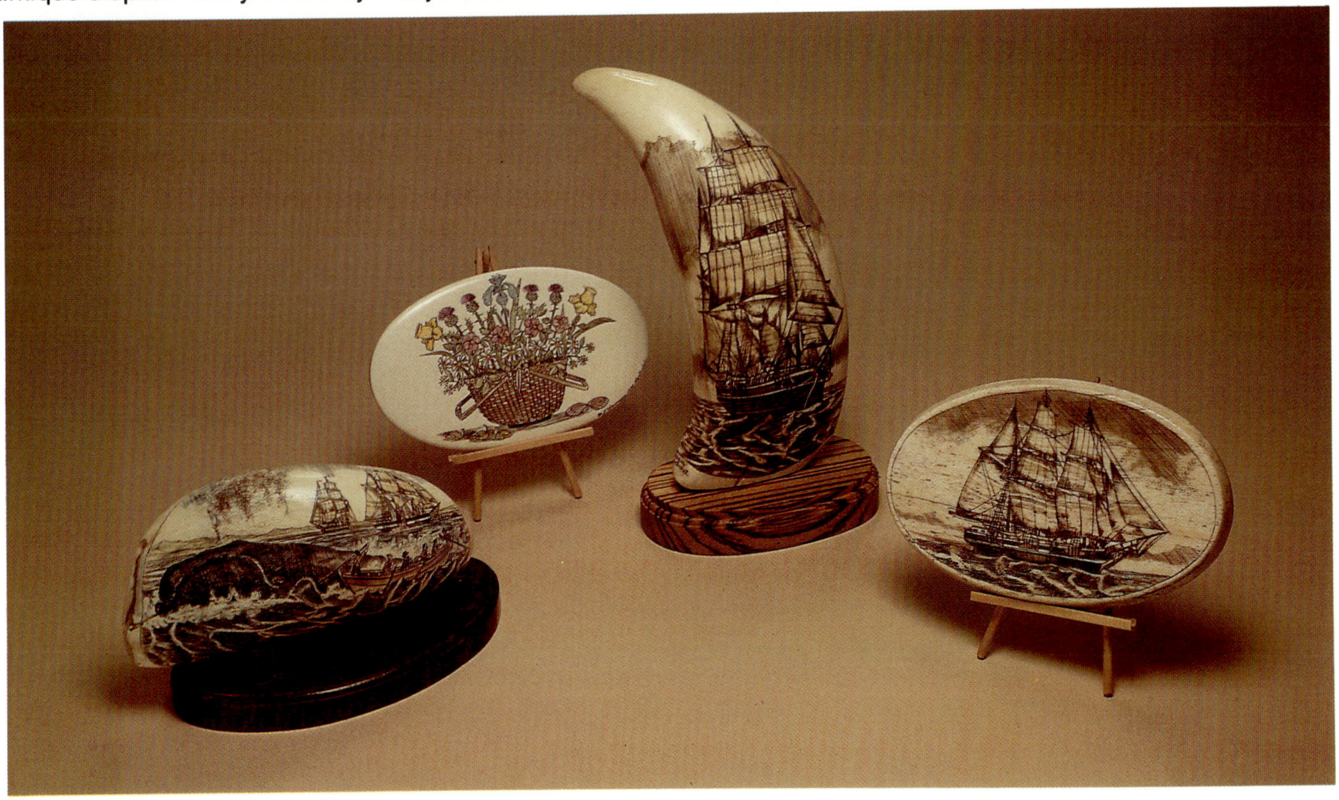

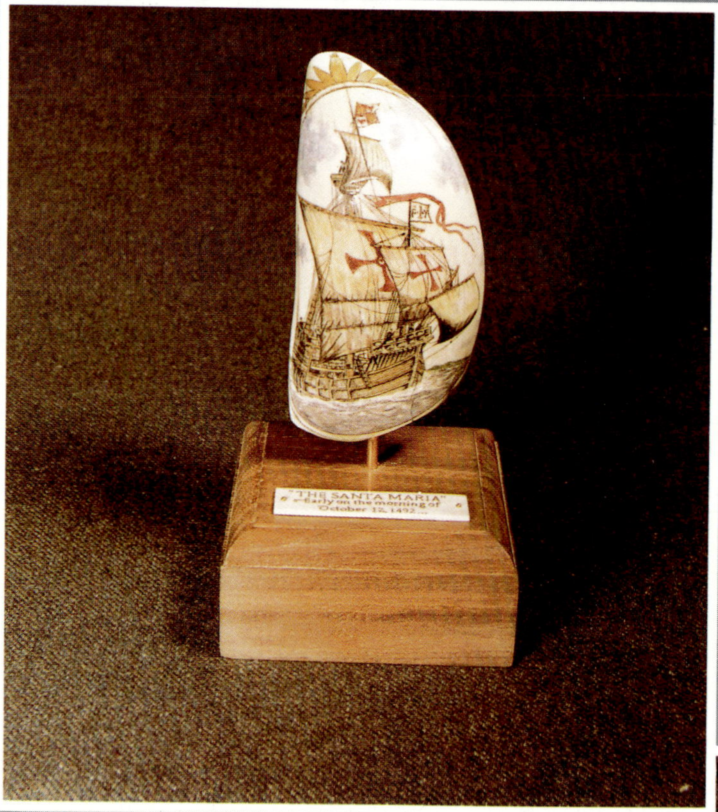

On this tooth, Charles A. Manghis has engraved the *Santa Maria* as she may have looked sailing to the New World.

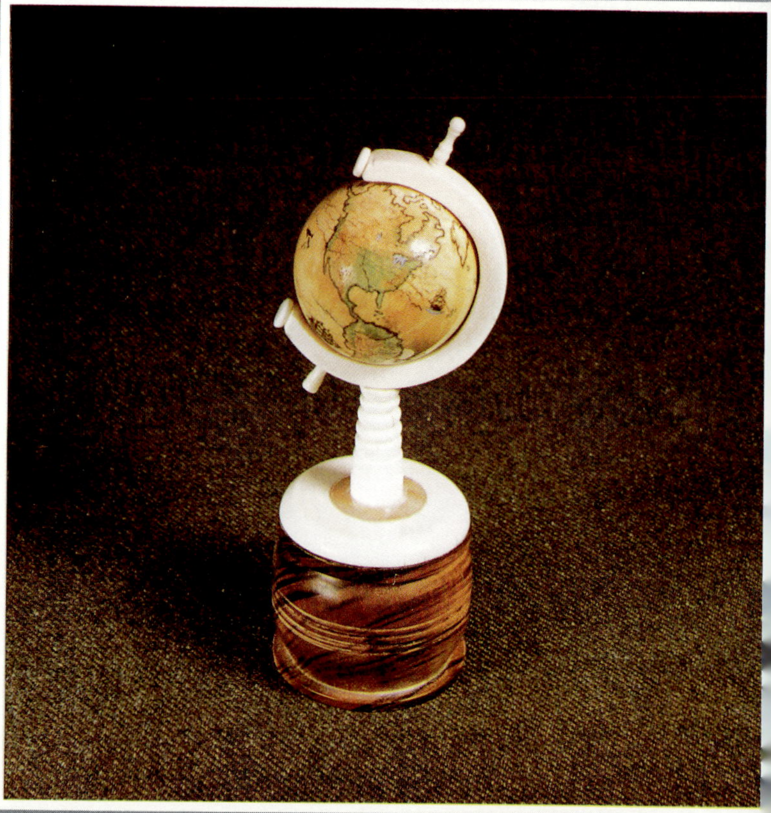

This globe, transformed from an antique elephant ivory billiard ball by Charles A. Manghis, is set on a beautiful rosewood base inlaid with mother of pearl.

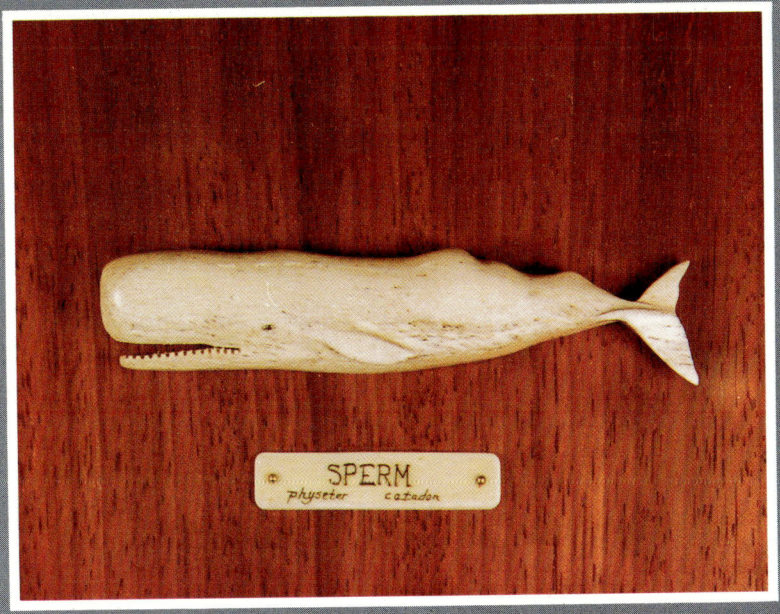

Charles A. Manghis carved examples of various species to create a handsome "whaleboard". The grouping is topped with a sperm whale, and includes a right, pilot, grey and humpback whale. *Private Collection*

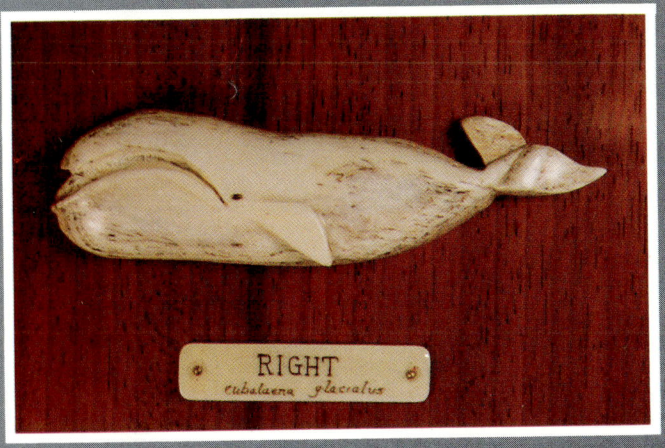

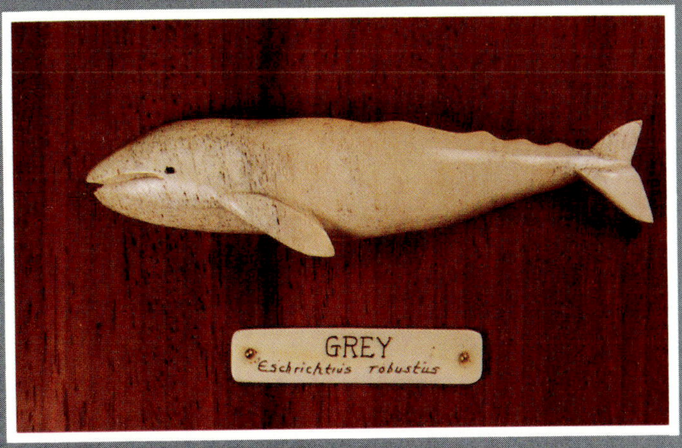

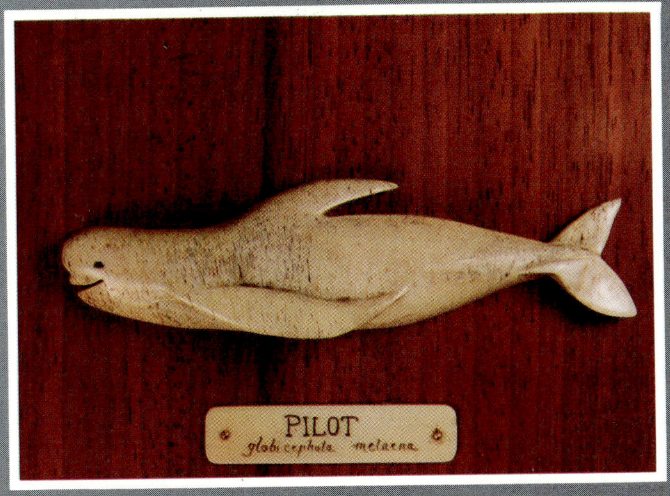

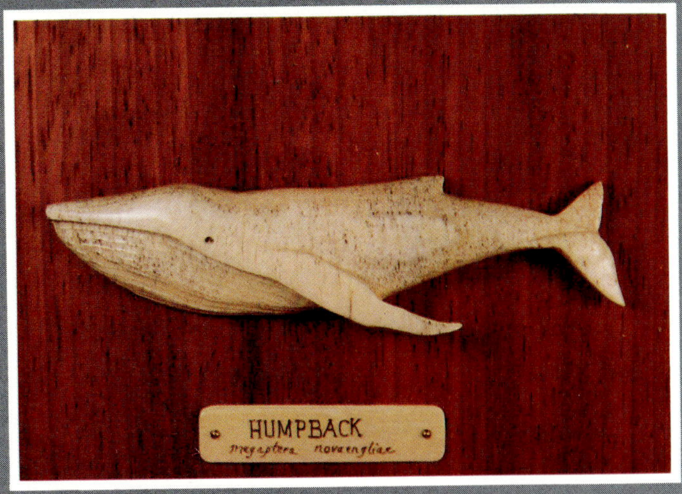

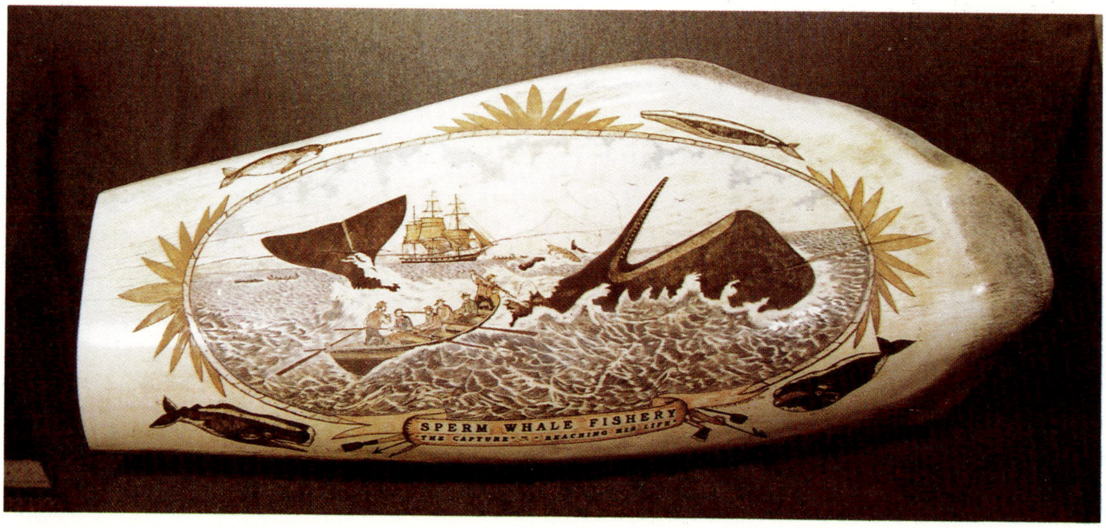

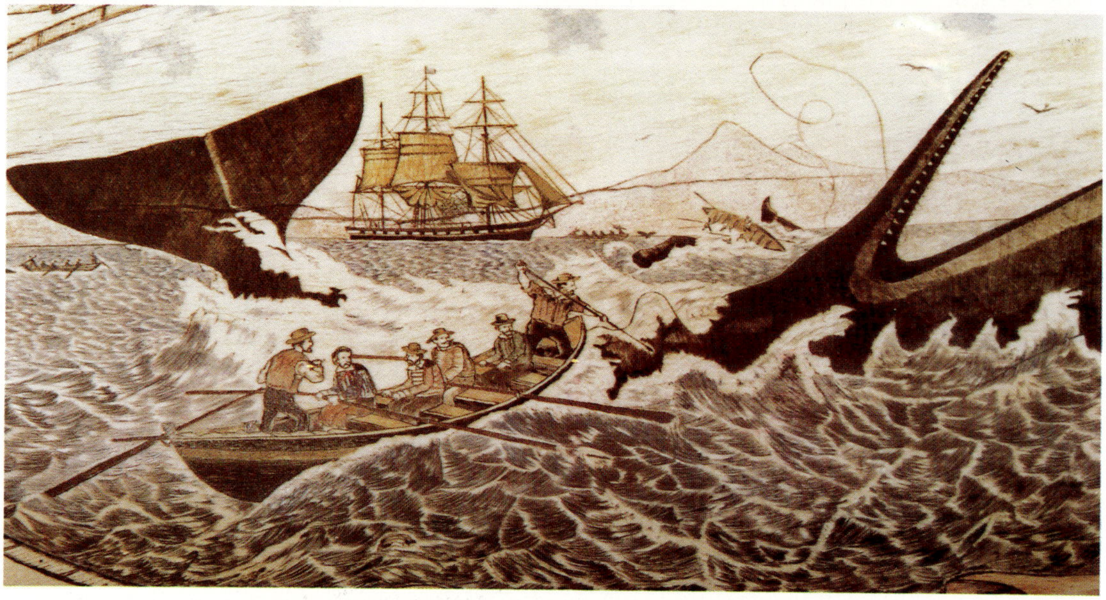

This wonderful two and a half foot panbone was engraved by Charles A. Manghis. Inspired by "The Capture", an 1862 lithograph after drawings by Van Best and Gifford, the central scene is further embellished with renderings of narwhal, finback, right and sperm whales as well as various whaling tools.

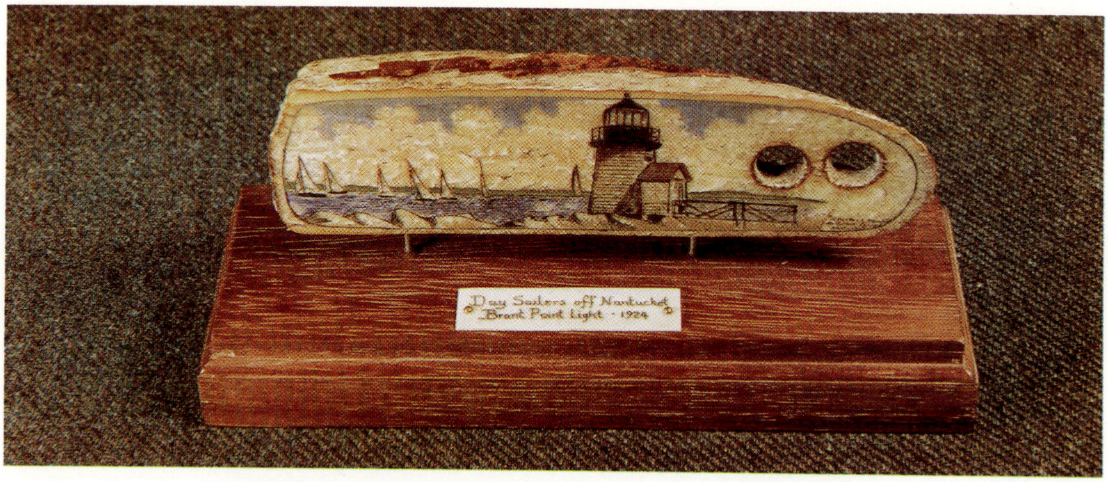

Sailboats race past Brant Point in this 1924 scene recreated by Charles A. Manghis on a fossilized walrus ivory sled runner.

Bibliography

Ashley, Clifford W. *The Yankee Whaler.* Boston: Houghton Mifflin, 1938.

Barbeau, Marius. "All Hands Aboard Scrimshawing." *The American Neptune,* April, 1952.

Barnes, Clare Jr. *John F. Kennedy, Scrimshaw Collector.* Boston: Little Brown and Company, 1964.

Basseches, Joshua and Frank, Stuart M. *Edward Burdett, 1805-1833, America's First Master Scrimshaw Artist.* Sharon, Mass.: The Kendall Whaling Museum, 1991.

Basseches, Joshua T. "Visual Analysis of Scrimshaw: The Challenge of an Anonymous Art". Unpublished manuscript, The Kendall Whaling Museum, Sharon, Mass. 1984.

Blanchard, George. "Logbook of the Ship *America,* 1839-1842". Old Dartmouth Historical Society, New Bedford, Mass.

Bullard, John M., ed. *Captain Edmund Gardner of Nantucket and New Bedford—His Journal and His Family.* Milford, N.H.: The Cabinet Press, 1958.

Bullen, Frank T. *Cruise of the "Cachalot".* Philadelphia: David McKay Publisher, 1899.

Carpenter, Charles H., Jr. and Mary Grace. *The Decorative Arts and Crafts of Nantucket.* New York: Dodd, Mead and Company, 1987.

Cary, William S. *Wrecked on the Feejees.* Nantucket, Mass:The Inquirer and Mirror Press, 1949.

Cheever, Rev. Henry T. *The Whale and His Captors.* London: Thomas Nelson and Sons, 1851.

Coquin, John S. "A Journal of a Voyage in the Atlantic Ocean 1869-1872 on board the Bark *Globe*". Old Dartmouth Historical Society, New Bedford, Mass.

Creighton, Margaret S. *Dogwatch and Liberty Days.* Salem, Mass.: Peabody Museum of Salem, 1982.

Crosby, Everett U. *"Susan's" Teeth and Much Ado About Scrimshaw.* Nantucket, Mass.: Tetaukimmo Press, 1955.

Davis, William M. *Nimrod of the Sea.* North Quincy, Mass.: The Christopher Publishing House, 1972. (originally published, 1874)

de Crèvecoeur, J. Hector St. John. *Letters from an American Farmer.* New York: Fox, Duffield and Company, 1904. (originally published, 1782)

Dias, Joseph. "Logbook of the Ship *Clifford Wayne,* 1841-1844". Old Dartmouth Historical Society, New Bedford, Mass.

Dow, George Francis. *Whale Ships and Whaling—A Pictorial History.* New York: Dover Publications, Inc., 1985.

Earle, Walter K. *Scrimshaw—Folk Art of the Whalers.* Cold Spring Harbor, N.Y.: Whaling Museum Society, Inc., 1957.

Ellis, Richard. *Men and Whales.* New York: Alfred A. Knopf, 1991

Ely, Ben-Ezra Stiles. *There She Blows.* Middletown, Conn.: Wesleyan University Press 1971. (originally published, 1849)

Flayderman, Norman E. *Scrimshaw and Scrimshanders, Whales and Whalemen.* New Milford, Conn.: N. Flayderman and Co.,Inc., 1972.

Forbes, Allan. *Whale Ships and Whaling Scenes as Portrayed by Benjamin Russell.* Boston: The Rand Press, 1955.

Frank, Stuart M. *Biographical Dictionary of Scrimshaw Artists in the Kendall Whaling Museum.* Sharon, Mass.: The Kendall Whaling Museum, 1989.

Frank, Stuart M. *Dictionary of Scrimshaw Artists.* Mystic, Conn.: Mystic Seaport Museum, 1991.

Frank, Stuart M., ed. *Meditations from Steerage: Two Whaling Journal Fragments.* Sharon, Mass.: The Kendall Whaling Museum, 1991.

Gilkerson, William. *The Scrimshander.* San Francisco: Troubadour Press, 1975.

Haley, Nelson C. *Whale Hunt—The Narrative of a Voyage by Nelson Cole Haley, Harpooner in the Ship "Charles W. Morgan", 1849-1853.* Mystic, Conn.: Mystic Seaport Museum, Inc., 1990.

Lawrence, Martha. "Kendall Hosts Scrimshaw Symposium". *Mass Bay Antiques.* June, 1992.

Lawrence, Mary C. *The Captain's Best Mate—The Journal of Mary Chipman Lawrence on the Whaler "Addison", 1856-1860.* Providence: Brown University Press, 1966.

Leavitt, John. *The "Charles W. Morgan".* Mystic, Conn.: The Marine Historical Association, Inc., 1973.

Lipman, Jean. *American Folk Art.* Meridan, Conn.: Meriden Gravure Co., 1948.

Little, Elizabeth A. *The Indian Contribution to Along-Shore Whaling at Nantucket.* Nantucket, Mass.: Nantucket Historical Association, 1981.

Little, Elizabeth A. "Nantucket Whaling in the 18th Century". Ottawa: Papers of the Nineteenth Algonquian Conference, Carleton University, 1988.

Macy, Obed. *The History of Nantucket.* Mansfield, Mass.: Macy and Pratt. 1880.

Malley, Richard C. *Graven by the Fishermen Themselves.* Mystic, Conn.: Mystic Seaport Museum, Inc., 1983.

Malloy, Mary and Frank, Stuart M. *Heroes in the Ships: African Americans in the Whaling Industry.* Sharon, Mass.: The Kendall Whaling Museum, 1990.

Manchester, William M. "Logbook of the Bark *Palmetto,* 1880-1884". Old Dartmouth Historical Society, New Bedford, Mass.

Marchant, Henry M. "Logbook of the Ship *Almira,* 1824-1826". Nantucket Historical Association, Nantucket, Mass.

Murphy, Charles. *A Journal of a Whaling Voyage on Board Ship "Dauphin", of Nantucket.* Mattapoisett, Mass.: Atlantic Publishing Company, 1877.

Olmstead, Francis Allyn. *Incidents of a Whaling Voyage.* Rutland, Vt.: Charles E. Tuttle Co., Inc., 1969. (originally published, 1841)

Pentley-Jones, Evan W. "Scrimshaw—The Decorative Folk Art of the American Whalers". *Antiques,* 98, 1970.

Pinckney, Pauline. *American Figureheads and their Carvers.* New York: W. W. Norton and Co., 1940.

Ray, Joseph E. "Logbook of the Ship *Edward Cary,* 1854-1858". Nantucket Historical Association, Nantucket, Mass.

Ricketson, Annie H. *The Journal of Annie Holmes Ricketson on the Whaleship "A. R. Tucker" 1871-1874.* New Bedford, Mass.: Old Dartmouth Historical Society, 1958.

Sotheby Park Bernet, Inc. *Barbara Johnson Whaling Collection. Parts I—IV.* 1981-1983.

Spear, Laura Jernegan. "A Child's Diary on a Whaling Voyage". *New England Quarterly,* Volume II, Number 1, 1929.

Stackpole, Edouard A. "The *Ann Alexander's* Scrimshaw Set". *Historic Nantucket,* January, 1980.

Stackpole, Edouard A. *The "Charles W. Morgan"—The Last Wooden Whaleship.* New York: Meredith Press, 1967.

Stackpole, Edouard A. "The Romantic Whaleman—Artist Joseph Ray, Log Keeper of the Ship *Edward Cary.*" *Historic Nantucket,* January, 1986.

Stackpole, Edouard A. *Scrimshaw at Mystic Seaport.* Mystic, Conn.: The Marine Historical Association, Inc., 1958.

Stackpole, Edouard A. *The Sea-Hunters.* Philadelphia: J. B. Lippincott Co., 1953.

Starbuck, Alexander. *History of the American Whale Fishery.* Seacaucus, N. J.: Castle Books, 1989. (originally published, 1877)

Starbuck, Mary Eliza. *My House and I.* Boston:Houghton Mifflin, 1929.

Stevens, William O. *Nantucket The Far-Away Island.* New York: Dodd, Mead and Co., 1947.

Tobey, Warren P. *The Cabin Boy's Log.* Boston:Meador Publishing Co., 1932.

Tripp, William H., ed. "Extracts from Whaling Log-Books, New Bedford Whaling Museum". Unpublished manuscript, The Kendall Whaling Museum, Sharon, Mass.

Watson, Arthur C. *The Long Harpoon*. New Bedford, Mass.: George H. Reynolds, 1929.

Watson, Arthur C. "Scrimshaw, the Perfect Hobby". *The Technology Review*, March 1938 (as reprinted in Crosby, Everett U. *"Susan's" Teeth and Much Ado About Scrimshaw.*)

Whiting, Emma M. and Hough, Harry B. *Whaling Wives*. Boston: Houghton Mifflin Co., 1953.

Williams, Harold W., ed. *One Whaling Family*. Boston: Houghton Mifflin Co., 1964.

Index

Values Reference

The potential collector will find that prices of nineteenth century scrimshaw span a broad range. Authenticity, however, is actually a more compelling concern than price when first considering the purchase of certain pieces. As mentioned in chapter seven, thorough study of the field and the help of knowledgeable collectors and dealers is imperative.

Authenticity

The following excerpt from a review of a presentation by Desmond Liddy at the Kendall Whaling Museum's Fourth Annual Scrimshaw Collectors' Weekend, while not addressing all authentication techniques, gives some suggestions for scrimshaw analysis:

> Desmond Liddy, Australia's foremost scrimshaw authority, shared some of the techniques he employs to authenticate 19th century scrimshaw. Primarily discussing sperm whale teeth, Liddy spoke of the need to authenticate the age of not only the tooth itself, but also of its engraving, as an old tooth with contemporary engraving will often be misrepresented as antique. Liddy's criteria for evaluation, which ranged from microscopic analysis to common sense, centered on the nature of the engraving, the condition of the pigment, and the surface appearance of the tooth.
>
> To a connoisseur, the surface of a tooth can reveal volumes. An old tooth will have a lovely translucency that has developed over the years as water-containing collagen fibers dry out and become transparent. Light is then reflected not from the surface of the tooth but from inorganic crystalline structures below. Despite advanced methods of polishing, contemporary scrimshanders cannot reproduce this effect and light from a modern tooth is reflected from its surface.
>
> Before working the tooth, the scrimshander has to smooth out its rough surface. Polishing techniques available to the whalemen could not eliminate many of the lengthwise scratches incurred when sanding the tooth, and with magnification such markings can be seen. Contemporary techniques eliminate such telling "flaws."
>
> During the whaling era, teeth were routinely sawed off at the bases so that they might stand on end. Saw marks are often visible on these examples. Contemporary workers, perhaps loathe to cut a few inches off an expensive tooth, often leave their work uncut, with the bottom edge naturally narrow and jagged.
>
> Teeth received as gifts in the 19th century usually show the effects of over a century of wear and neglect. Used for anything from a mantel decoration to a doorstop, old teeth can reveal microscopic paint specks, wear marks, chips and denting. Liddy discussed the presence of "good dirt" as a testament to a tooth's age. After years of indoor pollution from fires, heaters, kerosene lamps and house dust, magnification will often reveal a wealth of microscopic rubbish in the inscribed lines of a piece of scrimshaw.
>
> The second criterion to consider is the nature of the engraving itself. Only a very few scrimshanders had any background in art. The vast majority were working scrimshaw primarily as a means to pass time, albeit creatively. Furthermore, they worked in very poor light, with uncorrected vision, and primitive tools. Their cuts were often of differing lengths and depths and the details of their work were inconsistent. Of course, contemporary scrimshanders have at their disposal fine tools, good light and magnification which all contribute to work generally more well done and consistent.
>
> Perhaps because scrimshanders were not professional artists and had little "artistic ego," they rarely signed or dated their work. Nor does the majority of scrimshaw carry inscriptions. Thus, a tooth conveniently labeled, "The Bark

Amelia – 1843" is immediately considered suspicious if offered as a 19th century piece.

Teeth worked on a whaleship were fresh and soft. When lines intersected, cracking did not occur on the soft tooth. Such crossover points in new work, however, often show cracks, as the now dried and brittle tooth does not respond as well. Another clue to age found in the lines themselves is the feel of their edges. Lines engraved on a fresh tooth have sometimes almost closed as the tooth has dried over the years. The sharp edges of new work, however, can be felt with the fingers.

Pigment analysis is the final criterion on which to judge the age of a piece. Oil based paints, common aboard ship, were often used to color the engraved work. If such paint is old, it has often cracked and shrunk leaving stress marks along the line of the cut.

The age of water-based paints can also be estimated. Collagen fibers in the tooth have a great affinity for water, so watercolors often soaked into the tooth's cementum to a considerable depth. Today, the watercoloring in an old tooth may appear to lie below the line in which it was once placed.

As teeth crack with age, they provide another basis for authentication. When a line of new engraving crosses an old crack, pigment placed in the line may bleed into the porous walls of the crack. If the work is old, however, the crack would have occured after the pigment had set, and there would be no bleeding.[1]

The question of authenticity having been reasonably satisfied, the scrimshaw purchaser can proceed to the equally complicated analysis of value.

[1] Martha Lawrence, "Kendall Hosts Scrimshaw Symposium," *Mass Bay Antiques*, June, 1992, p. 16

Value

As with any antique, prices for 19th century scrimshaw can vary widely depending on the quality of the piece (size, condition, artistic merit, material and provenance), its rarity, and cyclical fluctuations of the marketplace. The following prices reflect high bids received at recent auctions and should be considered general guidelines rather than literally the highest or lowest price ever paid for a certain piece of scrimshaw.

Antique work

Sperm whale teeth are the most popular genre of scrimshaw and command the widest spectrum of prices. An authentic, engraved antique sperm whale tooth can be found for as little as $300. However, if the piece is large or includes a well-executed or unusual scene, prices can swiftly soar to the $500 to $3,500 range. Well-known teeth of exceptional quality, perhaps dated, signed or attributed will sell from $5,000 to $49,500.

Engraved antique scrimshaw is not limited to the teeth of sperm whales. Large, engraved panbone plaques are commonly valued between $2,000 and $7,500. Walrus tusks, porpoise jaws and blackfish jaws command between $500 and $1,200.

Walking sticks, another category popular among collectors, vary in price from $200 to $2,500, although most are priced below $1,000. Elements that affect their value include the materials from which they are constructed as well as the details of their carving or inlay work.

Considerably less pricey than many forms of scrimshaw, but certainly evocative of a whaler's life at sea, are the wide variety of **shipboard tools and accoutrements** - fids, belaying pins, blocks, seam rubbers and the like. Prices for these range from $200 to $1,000.

Kitchen utensils can be found for comparatively modest prices - simple rolling pins, $350 to $1,000 and coconut shell cups and ladles, $100 to $1,000. The prices of pie crimpers, however, reflect the great variety of their designs. A simple sturdy example can be purchased for $250, whereas an incredibly intricate piece might bring up to $12,000. Most crimpers that appear on the market, however, are priced below $1,000.

Most small **sewing implements** such as tatting shuttles, needle sheathes and bodkins cost between $50 and $650. Knitting needles can command higher prices ($200 to $1,500) depending on the materials, carving and inlay work. Spool holders range from simple wooden devices to elaborately carved and inlaid creations. The range of their costs ($500 to $5,000) reflects this variety. Swifts are the ultimate collectible of this genre and vary in price from $750 to $15,000, with most in the $1,500 to $3,000 range. Condition, complexity, size, inlay or carving details and the presence of an attached or accompanying work box affect the value of a swift.

Baleen or whalebone workboxes and baskets range from sturdy workhorses to extremely detailed, intricately engraved or delicately carved pieces. Their values are commensurately varied, $250 to $7,000. Larger vanity chests and similar pieces can exceed $10,000.

Busks can be the basis of an interesting collection for those attracted to engraved work. Their range of prices from $200 to $3,000 reflects the material used (whalebone is more highly valued than baleen), the execution and rarity of the designs or scenes, and any possible attribution. Most busks are found under $1,000.

Prices of **gentlemen's grooming implements** such as toothpicks are similar to those of small sewing items, $50 to $350. Watch stands, however, are comparatively rare, and, depending on their design and detail, can bring $2,000 to $6,500.

Contemporary work

Contemporary scrimshaw work embraces a wide range of quality which is reflected in its prices. The informed purchaser will want to become familiar with the various materials used in scrimshaw - not only to ascertain the medium preferred aesthetically but also to insure that the work is not polymer "ivory" masquerading as "real." (Polymer "ivory" is a wonderful development and has made possible many fine museum reproductions and "scrimshaw" collectibles. However, it is often unfortunately presented as true whale or elephant ivory.)

Authentic, engraved **contemporary sperm whale teeth** can be purchased at prices from $300 to $4,000. Elements increasing the cost include the size of the tooth, its age (antique teeth in good condition are more costly), the degree of detail in the engraving, the use of color, the employment of more intricate engraving methods such as stippling, and the reputation of the artist.

The prices of **three-dimensional carvings** from sperm whale teeth are affected by the size of the tooth as well as the quality, complexity and detail of the work and range from $400 to $2,000.

"Presentation pieces" - engravings on pieces of panbone, fossilized walrus ivory or elephant ivory and mounted for display - sell for prices from $300 to $4,000 depending on the material, size, engraving qualities already discussed, and the artist.

Much contemporary scrimshaw decorates the lids of **Nantucket Lightship baskets** as either engraved plaques or relief carvings. Size, material and quality of workmanship affect the prices of both carvings, $80 to $250, and engravings, $200 to $500.